THE ELEPHANT ON THE RAFT

Remembering Dad on a Mark Twain Odyssey

THOMAS CURLEY

Wilder Street Press

THE ELEPHANT ON THE RAFT
Remembering Dad on a Mark Twain Odyssey
© 2020 Thomas Curley
All Rights Reserved

ISBN: 978-1-7348211-0-9 (paperback)
First Edition. Published by Wilder Street Press, Kirklyn, PA

Library of Congress Control Number: 2020910610
(Paperback)

Cover and Book Design by

Cover photo by the author. Historical ephemera and archival photographs furnished by sources cited. All other public domain sourced data referenced in Bibliography.

Wilder Street Press LLC
wspressllc@gmail.com

TO MY BROTHERS
JACK, MIKE, and JAMES

TABLE OF CONTENTS

FORWARD: VI
PROLOGUE VII

PART ONE: ROAD TRIPS AND RUMINATIONS

1: MARK TWAIN, MY FATHER, AND ME 19
2: THE TOM SAWYER COLORING CONTEST 27
3: WHEN IN ROME, EAT CATFISH 36
4: THE HOLY SEPULCHER AT HARTFORD 51
5: HAL HOLBROOK & THE ROUGHING IT STRATEGY 74
6: AN IDLE EXCURSION: CHARTING THE NEXT ADVENTURE 90
7: A ROAD TRIP TO ELMIRA & THE MARK TWAIN STUDY 105
8: SQUARING A DEBT 123
9: A PHILLUFFIAN SCRIBBLER IN SAINT MARK'S CHURCH 129
10: THE RESURRECTION OF SAMUEL CLEMENS 138
11: REFLECTIONS ON RACISM 155
12: FROM PURGATORY TO MOOSEWOOD 176

PART TWO: INTO THE AMERICAN SOUL

13: CHILDHOOD ROOTS & CIRCUMSTANCE 197
14: THE RELEVANCE OF HUCKLEBERRY FINN 208
15: AGAINST THE TRAFFICK OF MEN: THE GENESIS OF ABOLITION 218
16: A CAUSE FOR SEVERITY 231
17: TALES OF REMARKABLE COURAGE 242
18: THE GREAT TROUBLE 254
19: THE GRAIL BENEATH THE STRIP MALL 269
20: THE LEGACY OF JERVIS LANGDON 284
21: THE GUIDING HAND OF LIVY & THE INFLUENCE OF WOMEN 300

PART THREE: COMING HOME

22: A STOP AT ~~WILLOUGHBY~~ REDDING 317
23: TWAIN'S VALLEY OF THE SHADOW 327
24: HEADIN' HOME 348
25: 100 YEARS OF GRATITUDE: THE MARK TWAIN CENTENNIAL 358
26: HOLLYWOOD & THE MARK TWAIN DECADE 375
27: A LOST EULOGY 391
28: FINDING HUCK FINN 402
29: REDEMPTION AMONG THE NIGHT HAWKS 414
A PARTING OBSERVATION 440
ACKOWLEDGEMENTS 441
BIBLIOGRAPHY 443

FORWARD

This book was written in real time, as memories and revelations unfolded, spanning the period from January 2017 to completion of the first draft in April 2018 (see 'A Parting Observation'). It began as nostalgic remembrance of my Dad, our shared connection through Mark Twain, and recalling the lessons he taught as learned from the great author.

At some point, the manuscript took on a life of its own, steering me head on into the topic of racism in American life and history. This prompted recollection of events from which I had consciously or unconsciously chosen to distance myself and avoid, and initially avoiding their inclusion herein as well. However, to heal my own old wounds, I had to allow myself to walk right through them again.

As I continued to discover more about Mark Twain and his world, it was clear these stories had to be told. It was then I saw that this story wasn't just about me. It's about all of us, the collective us, and most certainly the American us. I then hoped this work might serve to initiate an overdue dialog on race relations in the United States, and contribute towards the needed healing that will lead us to live in a communal spirit of unity and fellowship.

As I write this Forward, protests calling for an end to systemic racism are occurring throughout the US and abroad. It's clear that dialog has already begun. To that end, I hope this book will be received in the spirit in which it was intended.

Thomas Curley
June 7, 2020

PROLOGUE

News of his death had spread with a religious fervor normally reserved for the high and mighty. From Bombay to Boston, telegraphed reports relayed across the globe mourned the passing of America's most beloved secular diplomat of the age. His robust manner of expression had equally captivated the common man and crowned heads of Europe. His scathing political commentary had swayed legislation and influenced policy. His humorous candor had enhanced an international appreciation for the American character. He had been, simply put, our best representative abroad.

On his return to the United States six years prior, Mark Twain had been welcomed as a conquering hero. Planning to settle down in his own home after an extended stay abroad, of the wandering sage a 1907 news article claimed: "The world is his home. His humor and philosophy have made it a fitter place for human life than it used to be."[1] When Oxford University awarded him an honorary degree in 1908, it only further entrenched his widely embraced fame and literary standing as an unquestioned decree for the ages.

In exaggerated hyperbole that would have made him proud, Twain's one-time employer, *The San Francisco Call*, offered a more devasting account spanning two pages with multiple headlines such as "Mark Twain Galled by Death," and "Samuel Langhorn Clemens is called by the Grim Reaper." The detailed account of his life and final hours noted:

> "Twain was more than humorist and wit – he was a profound philosopher with the vision of a prophet." "Serious appreciation of Mark Twain as an artist and not a mere jokesmith began abroad..."[2]

The *London Daily Times* proclaimed:

> "Mark Twain...was also for outside the United States the most perfect embodiment of the American character and genius... the fine flower of vigourous Western culture...Mark Twain conquered his generation..."[3]

Minnesota's *New Ulm Review* announced:

> "The king is dead – long live the king!...The throne of humor, whose kingdom was the world, is empty...The world was his plaything, and he was not content without remapping for himself the entire surface of the big ball."[4]

In its tribute, the *New York Times* claimed:

> "Mark Twain's death has meant to Americans everywhere and in all walks of life what the death of no other American could have meant. His

personality and his humor have been an integral part of American life for so long that it has seemed almost impossible to realize an America without him."[5]

But America would not forget, for as the years moved forward, the groundswell of tribute in one media or another would go on. The memory of Mark Twain refused to die. Unpublished works continued to debut under the guidance of biographer and literary executor Albert Bigelow Paine and Twain's only surviving daughter, Clara. Reissues of his most beloved works transformed into instant classics as new subscription editions kept the Mark Twain brand in steady business for decades to come, perpetuating his fame for new generations.

The 19 aughts and tens saw the concurrent emergence of silent film as an exciting new entertainment alternative. It wasn't long before film adaptations of Twain's works emerged by 1907, with Twain personally authorizing the Vitograph Company's production of his short story *A Curious Dream*, followed by the first film version of *The Adventures of Tom Sawyer* that same year.

Twain made his own screen debut in Thomas Edison's 1909 short reel production of *The Prince and The Pauper*, which included footage of Twain lounging and walking on the patio of his home at Stormfield, in Redding, Connecticut. Edison's cunning resulted in one of the first cinematic hits, inspiring a feature-length adaptation in 1915.[6] The Mark Twain brand proved to be good business for the new media, and as the industry gelled into an increasingly enhanced and refined artform of its own, the cameras continued to role.

Above: A telegram dated May 18, 1915 addressed to Twain in-law and estate executor Jervis Langdon, Jr. from representatives of film producer Jesse Lansky relaying interest in securing the rights to Pudd'nhead Wilson & Huckleberry Finn for the making of the first silent film adaptations. Courtesy NY Public Library Digital Collection.

Left: The 1915 letter from Jesse Lasky referenced in the Telegram. Right: 1916 newspaper theater ad for the film. Courtesy NY Public Library Digital Collection.

Left: Heralding the first film arrival of Huckleberry Finn. Right: Scene from a 1920 Broadway production of The Prince and the Pauper.

Left: 1916 Lobby Card with movie Huck mimicking the 1884 W.E. Kemble illustration of book Huck. Above: Lobby card showing the set constructed for the first film adaptation of A Connecticut Yankee in King Arthur's Court.

IX

1916 brought about a now lost production of Twain's detective novel *Pudd'nhead Wilson*, another adaptation of *Tom Sawyer* in 1917, a contrivance entitled *Huck and Tom* in 1918, a German production of *The Prince and the Pauper* in 1920, and a 1921 feature presentation of *A Connecticut Yankee in King Arthur's Court*.

In the early days of cinema, actor Jack Pickford was marketed as the "All American boy next door." To that end he was cast as the lead in 1917's Tom Sawyer, *left – which was filmed in Hannibal, Missouri, and its 1918 sequel, right, which was created largely with unused footage from the 1917 film.*

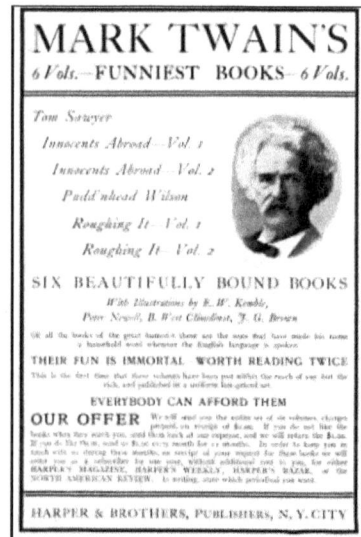

Subscription editions of Mark Twain's books flourished in the 1910s & '20s.

Poster for the first screen adaptation of Twain's A Connecticut Yankee *in 1921.*

Ten years after his death, the *New York Tribune* ran a feature about Twain to capitalize on the expanding interest and seemingly add some fertilizer with a public reminder.[7] While recapping bits of his life, the focus was on the author's final home at Stormfield, underscored by an interview with its architect John Mead Howells, the son of Twain's best friend William Dean Howells, the celebrated playwright and editor of *The Atlantic Monthly*. Until then, Stormfield had sat idly as the inherited property of Twain's daughter. Afterwards, Stormfield would finally sell in 1923.

Coinciding with the evolution of early film was the development of radio. Following its introduction after WWI, by 1920 twelve million American consumers had purchased a radio, and by 1929, the prosperity of the Roaring Twenties more than doubled that total to twenty-eight million. Radio broadcasting became a marvel-inciting new medium, embraced with a level of enthusiasm much like that witnessed with the advent of the world-wide web in the 1990s. Scholars contend that:

> "The power of radio further accelerated the process of creating a shared national culture that had started when railroads and telegraphs widened the distribution of newspapers. Radio was far more effective...Radio created and pumped out American culture onto the airwaves and into the homes of families around the country."[8]

The impact of radio was then unprecedented in global history. By 1926 "Radio was still new and unsure of itself" explains history professor Melvin Patrick Ely...

> "Broadcasting networks did not yet exist. Six hundred local stations throughout the United States haphazardly filled..."the air"...the disembodied sounds of live performances issuing from a piece of furniture in one's living room remained a source of wonder, as did the knowledge that thousands of others might be sharing the experience..."[9]

Within ten years, radio would play a key role in creating a shared national interest in Mark Twain.

A Rodgers and Hart hit Broadway musical adaptation of *A Connecticut Yankee* - which ran for 421 performances in 1927 and '28[10] - set the stage for yet another opportunity to expand Twain's legacy. Though the great author had been dead for almost twenty years, Mark Twain's popularity would become firmly entrenched in both popular culture and public conscience, witnessing an exceptional peak in the decade that followed. It proved to be a now forgotten cultural phenomenon that would mold and influence two generations of fans spanning the next 50 years.

THE ELEPHANT ON THE RAFT

"A man's experiences of life are a book. There was never yet an uninteresting life. Such a thing is an impossibility. Inside of the dullest exterior there is a drama, a comedy, and a tragedy."

Mark Twain,
The Refuge of the Derelicts

OUR MORNING RIDE.

An illustration from Roughing It *by Mark Twain. Attributed to True Williams, the principal illustrator of four.*

PART ONE:

ROAD TRIPS AND RUMINATIONS

1

MARK TWAIN, MY FATHER, AND ME

Watching old movies with Dad was an extraordinary experience. He loved to point out any actor who played other characters in different films, or on a then-current television series.

"That's Bob Steele!" he'd exclaim when Trooper Duffy appeared on *F Troop*. "He was a cowboy star in the 1920s and '30s." And just like that, I got an instant lesson on an entire film genre I might have never known otherwise.

"That's James Gleason," I recall Dad saying while watching *The Last Hurrah*, the 1958 John Ford film. "He played Max Corkle in *Here Comes Mr. Jordan*. Remember that one? He was the guy who always acted goofy when he thought he was talking to the ghost?"

I can still hear him making such announcements with buoyancy, as if it was the biggest surprise of his life, always drawing my attention from building an Aurora model kit on the dining room table, or whatever enterprise then occupied my focus. "That's Allen Jenkins!" "That's George Tobias!" "That's Smiley Burnette!" By the time I was ten years old, I knew the names of all those supporting character actors as well as the principle leads, and I've never forgotten.

Now and then, Dad would pose questions about an actor as if he were giving a pop quiz on a favorite film. He did this so often that it forced me to recollect details of a movie we may have seen months before, and pay sharp attention going forward. Ultimately, I would try to quiz him. He always knew the answers. It became a game we played, and the primary way I came to know my Dad.

His impromptu pop movie culture training cultivated a lifelong appreciation for the art of film and filmmaking. When I was ten-years-old the textbook for our ongoing class was *The New Hollywood and the Academy Awards* by Nathalie Fredrik, a 1971 paperback chronology of all Academy Award winners by year, with lists of other nominees, a forward by Bob Hope, and photos. I poured over every detail of this book, learning about Freddie Bartholomew in *Captain's Courageous*, Jane Darwell in *The Grapes of Wrath*, the great Olivia de Havilland (on whom I developed an early crush), and more obscure Hollywood figures such as Irvin S. Cobb. I studied the book front to back and back again, inhaling all the inconsequential details, which proved invaluable in later years when my family and I would play a few rounds of *Trivial Pursuit*. Now worn, dog-eared and browning, I still have it in my library.

After coming home from work, Dad would put on a V-neck T-shirt and Seersucker slacks, select a channel, adjust the antenna, and settle down in front of the TV with a glass of Schaefer beer and a plate of cheese and crackers. Weekend nights brought out the sliced pepperoni or a trip to Pat's or Geno's for a Philly cheesesteak that was brought home and splayed on a TV tray like a sacred offering presented to the Cathode Ray god.

An unpretentious television blessed our home in those days. Nothing fancy. No exotic wood paneled Magnavox floor console with fabric lined side panel speakers. Not even a medium-sized set in a wooden cabinet with four post legs. Those were "too dear" for our budget. Ours was the in-between model, the "nice" one — a step below the fancier ones and a step above the ones that had given up all hope of even thinking of trying to look fancy.

Dad had a technical affinity that would define his career. He had once taken TV and radio repair correspondence courses with a dream of starting his own business. In our basement he kept a variety of repair tools, a vacuum tube and transistor testing panel, as well as vintage microphones, amps, and other things used in an era before I was born. Knowing the intricacies of television construction empowered him to walk into any appliance store confident that no sales clerk could deceive him. Dad knew he'd stand uncontested, like a consumer warrior with all the muster of a righteous lawman facing a gunslinger at high noon. It was a great source of pride for him to challenge an impatient and aggressive salesman with technical questions that required the aid of a manager.

Long before the days of Best Buy or Crazy Eddie, the place to go for the best deal was Nate Ben's Reliable, an old purveyor of radios, TVs, and related paraphernalia on West Market Street in downtown Philadelphia. After spending a fair amount of time there reviewing the options, Dad settled on a medium-sized, modestly priced, semi-portable TV made of molded plastic. With a fake wood veneer and just one speaker veiled by a plastic grill set beneath the channel and volume dials, it featured a deluxe, flip down, Space-age style control panel hidden along the bottom edge that concealed a row of tuning dials for vertical, horizontal and color control. Dad insisted this was the one to get.

It came with a standard issue, extendable and maneuverable rabbit-eared antenna, and Dad opted to upgrade with the advanced, circular shaped, auxiliary

UHF antenna, which conveniently snapped onto one of the rabbit ears. This miraculous feature replaced the strip of bent and twisted aluminum foil or custom-tailored coat hanger that had served us well until then. The UHF antenna was a singularly important component for our prehistoric television experience because the UHF channels was where all the old films were shown. When not viewing favorites like Jackie Gleason, Johnny Carson's *Tonight Show*, or the sacrosanct, unquestioned airing of a Notre Dame football game, Dad religiously preferred to watch old films.

For kids my age, UHF featured the favorite local cartoon shows. Looney Tunes, Terrytoons, early Fleisher Brothers and Disney shorts, the Trans-Lux incarnation of *Felix the Cat*, and other archaic animation productions were all featured on UHF afterschool programs like *The Wee Willie Webber Show* on Channel 17, *Dickory Doc* on Channel 29, and Channel 48 featured *Captain Philadelphia* hosted by local sportscaster Stu Nahan, who later achieved acting notoriety as a ringside boxing commentator in the Rocky films.

These programs all competed for a market share then dominated by *Popeye Theater*, the longest running local kid's show hosted by the iconic Sally Starr. In addition to being a television pioneer, Starr had so significantly revived a new generation's interest in The Three Stooges on her show that she was given a starring role in the Stooges' 1965 film *The Outlaws is Coming!* with a pre-Batman Adam West in the handsome good guy role.

In our neighborhood, Starr enjoyed added notoriety due to rumors that she had once been the paramour of our high school gym teacher, Mr. Siskel (not his real name). Never acknowledging nor denying it, Siskel would instead maintain a straight poker face while firmly chomping on the ever-present cigar propped in his mouth, directing us curious ballbusters to run laps around the gym. The mystery could be gleaned, however, to those astute enough to detect a revealing, subtle twinkle in his eye, as if our inquiries had ignited a carefully guarded melancholic memory of a true love lost.

Starr's Popeye offerings played a key role in my developing relationship with Dad. He'd remark how he had seen one episode or another while stationed on an aircraft carrier in the Pacific during WWII. Some of those Popeye episodes, created as anti-Japanese propaganda, just as Disney and many studios did at the time, would eventually become banned due to insensitive, racist portrayals of Japanese stereotypes. His conversations and teachings on these now politically incorrect and offensive topics provided an invaluable foundation to the formation of my ethical leanings.

His mention of serving in the Navy instilled remarkable wonder in me, fueling curiosity about his naval exploits while his tales of sailing on the open sea would enthrall me to no end. This manifested then in my assembly of the Revell model kit of his ship, the USS Ticonderoga, around 1970. When finished, Dad was so moved it was given honored placement on the mantel in our living room. These moments formed a deep yearning to someday grasp some sense of what Dad's experience on the open sea had been like, for each time he talked about it, I watched his mind sail off to a different place. Where was that? What was that? Someday, I hoped to find that.

All of those old shorts and films shown on UHF channels had enabled Dad to enjoy a temporary respite from his working class, breadwinner reality and transport him back to a much simpler time. A time before engaging in naval battle, before working in rotating shifts while earning enough to first support his widowed mother and younger siblings, and later a wife and four energetic and mischievous sons in a rough and tumble neighborhood. When I look back now, I see that the man hadn't had a break in decades, continually giving, serving, supporting, always waiting for that day when his ship would come in. All those proclamations of obscure actor names and Hollywood references, designed to draw us into his world, led me to understand that Dad just wanted a buddy with whom he could share those moments of simple joy. They remain among my fondest memories of time spent with Dad. To this day, whenever I watch those old films, there's always something that reminds me of him.

One morning in early 2017, I fixed my ritual cup of Chai, checked my email, and scrolled through Google News to see what happened while I slept. Nothing interested me so I turned on the TV and surfed the channels before settling on *Turner Classic Movies*. I sat on the floor and played with our dogs as a film was just ending, waiting to see what was coming up next. Then, a preview came on and announced that at 10:00 am the next day TCM would feature the 1944 Fredric March film *The Adventures of Mark Twain*.

I looked up from my perch on the floor. Wow, I thought. The last time I saw that film was with Dad more than fifty years ago, when I was maybe seven or eight years old. Through the years I may have caught bits and pieces, but I hadn't seen it in its entirety since that memorable bonding moment with my father.

Of all those old films we watched together, I vividly recalled our specific enamorment with this film and its focus on the iconic author's belief that his life was interconnected with the seventy-five-year cyclical appearance of Halley's Comet. Born when the Comet's perihelion had passed closest to Earth, Mark Twain's commentary on this point remains an important part of his lore.[11]

Fredric March superbly guised in The Adventures of Mark Twain

"I came in with Halley's Comet in 1835" Twain had written in 1909, "It is coming again next year…and I expect to go out with it. It will be the greatest disappointment of my life if I don't…The Almighty has said, no doubt: "Now here are these two unaccountable freaks; they came in together, they must go out together.""[12]

Mark Twain did indeed go out with it at age seventy-five on April 21, 1910, a day after Halley's Comet made its appearance. The last scene of the film featured Fredric March as Twain resting on his pillowed deathbed while a low budget depiction of Halley's Comet is seen through the window. The event is presented as a secular miracle, with those in attendance awed that his prediction came true.

That scene has been etched in my memory since the day I saw it with Dad. It stimulated my tender imagination as something akin to the story of Moses and the burning bush, or the infant Kal-El hurtling through space in his primary colored rocket to escape the doomed planet Krypton. In my young mind Mark Twain became someone special and superhuman, an iconic figure worthy of placement on a pedestal, just like the looming statues of revered Catholic saints that adorned the interior perimeter of my childhood parish church.

From that day on, Mark Twain remained an integral topic that underscored my entire relationship with Dad until his premature passing. I've often since wondered what it was about Twain that so captivated Dad's interest more than any other author, and why that particular film stood apart as his favorite. I had always assumed that Twain's writings were just required reading when Dad was in school, just as they had been in my formative years. Even then, I recognized the way Twain enabled Dad to revisit his youth, and the time we spent sharing this film allowed me a glimpse into that part of him that was once a young boy of eight or ten years old.

Like the river-based characters in Twain's books, my father grew up playing along the banks of the Schuylkill River on the western edge of Philadelphia in a working-class neighborhood with the same name. He often told boyhood stories of swimming in the Schuylkill - a feat we considered gross in our time because by the late 1960s and early 1970s, the river was so polluted by industrial waste that the thought of swimming in it conjured visions of cancerous skin lesions. When he shared how he and his pals used to go fishing there, our nausea knew no bounds. Dad developed a lifelong love of Catfish from having caught and eaten the species as a boy, just like Huck Finn, and talked about it often. Mark Twain once wrote, "Catfish is plenty good enough for anybody."[13] When I was young we never ate it. I wouldn't experience the Mudcat delicacy until many years later.

According to a November, 1969 Philadelphia Sunday Bulletin article about the Schuylkill neighborhood, coal yards set along the banks of the Schuylkill River provided a main stay for employment until they began to go out of business around 1924.[14] Another occupation available to the Irish that settled in Schuylkill was bricklaying, a skill used in a booming industry required for building factories, railroads and homes for the steady influx of arriving immigrants. The primary bricklaying employer in their neighborhood was John B. Kelly Sr., the triple gold-winning Olympic rower and father of Academy Award-winning film actress Grace Kelly and Olympic rowing champ John B. Kelly Jr., to whom I regularly hand-delivered airline tickets for my after-school job when in high school. Several bookbinding factories nearby also offered employment, along with the US Postal Service and the University of Pennsylvania Campus across the river, the railroad industry and the municipal fire and police departments. As such enclaves continued to grow throughout the late Nineteenth Century, politicians recognized the bonanza of eligible voters and elected ward leaders and representatives from their ranks. My great-grandfather became such a ward leader, and his son, my Dad's father, secured work as a policeman in the Fairmount Park mounted unit.

Dad had been accepted to attend La Salle College High School, the prestigious Catholic college preparatory institution in Philadelphia. Dad used to share with pride that his school was once the former mansion of Michael Bouvier, the Great-Great Grandfather of Jacqueline Bouvier Kennedy. However, a few years before Dad attended, in 1935 the school had relocated to Belfield, the former home and estate of famed American painter Charles Willson Peale, cofounder of the Pennsylvania Academy of Fine Arts, which I attended forty-some years later.

It was a big deal for the son of a policeman and working-class Irish-Catholic family emerging from the struggle of the Great Depression to attend a school like La Salle. The generation before his dismissed the need for a high school education, often deciding it was enough to just find a good job. To send Dad to high school spoke volumes about his parent's recognition of Dad's academic ability. Admitting a student from his class status to such a school reflected the broader effort of Catholic Irish-America in their ambitious quest for an enhanced social relevancy in post-Depression and post-Industrial Twentieth Century. To gain the privilege of attending La Salle, Dad's parents must have seen some measure of promise that not only advanced the family's standing but for the pride offered to their clan, and their indigenous, extended Irish community. The effort didn't come to full fruition until 1960 when Catholic Americans of Irish ancestry embraced John F. Kennedy's election as the zenith of their struggle in America.

I also considered that Dad's affinity for Twain might have originated with early film adaptations of the author's most celebrated literary works. Dad would have been ten or eleven years old when his age group was the target market for those types of films. He certainly possessed the defining characteristics of Tom Sawyer, like his relative mischievousness and more reserved qualities, and those of the free-spirited, trouble-prone Huck Finn. Even Dad's nickname - Spike - came from the time he tore the seat of his pants on a fence spike while engaging in some shenanigans along the river side railroad tracks when he was about that age. Wandering the Philadelphia riverfront and adjacent rail yards with an imagination inspired by Mark Twain was a guarantee for harmless mischief.

The banks of the Schuylkill River between Chestnut and South Streets, Philadelphia - my father's childhood playground as it looked in 1924, around the time he was born. The train yards pictured here were once shipping docks teeming with high masted clipper ships and barges towing coal, lumber, stone and other goods to and from ports across the region. My father grew up about a block from here. The similarity to Sam Clemens' childhood environment is evident. Photo courtesy Free Library of Philadelphia.

In his youth, Dad was an avid reader, consuming everything that explored new topics in expanded detail. After once catching pneumonia and losing a year of school, books and reading became his best friends and would remain his most passionate pastime throughout his life. I always imagined that his father might have introduced him to the works of Mark Twain during his convalescence.

In 1944, the same year that the Twain biopic premiered, Dad's father passed away, forcing him to drop out of high school. I couldn't help but note the parallel to Mark Twain, whose father also passed when the author was young, forcing him to drop out of school as well. Perhaps, for this reason, Mark Twain provided a conduit for Dad to connect to the father he barely got to know.

Whenever I asked about the grandfather I never knew, Dad spoke of him with great admiration. He died from what the family called "cancer of the back," a likely reference to spinal lymphoma. Dad must have been crushed by the loss of his father. Work as a policeman on horseback was another source of extraordinary community pride. It undoubtedly inspired some measure of romanticized perspective in Dad, who was growing up in the automobile age as the era of horseback civilization was dying a slow death. I can only imagine times when my grandfather may have hoisted my Dad as a young lad onto the saddle for a short canter or walking gait around the block.

It became easy to understand that all the characteristic traits I knew about my Dad must have surely been inherited from his own father. Dad's whole clan loved to embellish and expand on even the shortest tales, making them sound like the most exciting thing you ever heard, very much in the humorist style of Mark Twain. Very much the way my Dad shared the appearance of an obscure character actor in an old movie. If mannerisms pass down from generation to generation, then my grandfather must have surely been able to spin one hell of a story. The clan of my Dad's generation all responded to any inquiry, comment or conversation on any topic with a smirk and a good-natured teasing retort. My brothers and cousins still do it, and I know it well. It's gotten me into trouble countless times.

The next morning, I turned on TCM to watch the film and seize the chance to revisit a moment of my childhood. After viewing *The Adventures of Mark Twain*, I knew I had to find out once and for all what it was about Mark Twain that so intrigued my Dad. And maybe, just maybe, I might finally understand why it created such a bond between us in my youth, a bond that began to unravel in my teenage years, a bond that we never fully regained. Until now.

2

THE TOM SAWYER COLORING CONTEST

"Always obey your parents, when they are present.
Most parents think they know more than you do; and you can generally make more by humoring that superstition than you can by acting on your own better judgement."

Mark Twain,
Advice to Youth

One day, in the spring of 1973, my father came home from work and presented me with a copy of the *Philadelphia Daily News*. With his familiar, reserved smile, he carefully leafed through the pages, found what he sought, folded the paper over and slapped it on the table before me. He pointed at a black and white coloring book style illustration, firmly tapping the image several times. He explained it was a contest to win a pair of free tickets to see the new, soon to be released musical film version of *The Adventures of Tom Sawyer* with Johnny Whitaker in the title role and Jodie Foster as his sweetheart, Becky Thatcher.

"You color it in, Tommy, and I'll mail it to the newspaper for you. I'm sure you'll win" he asserted.

Coloring came naturally for me. Then twelve years old, I had become a coloring book master. I loved the activity from an early age, and it was how my overall artistic talent was initially developed. My skills had won me a Second-Place award in a city-wide 'Keep Christ in Christmas' poster contest sponsored by the Knights of Columbus, and first prize in a Fire Prevention Week poster contest sponsored by the Philadelphia Fire Department.

Dad's enthusiastic encouragement for the coloring proposal was contagious, and I set upon the task. I reviewed the illustration studiously, considering the proper colors to select from my box of Crayolas. Coloring had taught me how to use chiaroscuro, the technique of lighting and shading effects learned from studying comic books, and which I often used in drawings created for class projects as an extra-credit opportunity.

I recall coloring the Tom Sawyer picture with a blend of orange, brown and red crayon to create a red hair color, and a grey-blue for overalls. The other details escape me, except for its depiction of a cartoon rendering of Johnny Whitaker, the kid from TV's *Family Affair*. When finished, I brought the completed newspaper page to my Dad as he sat in his favorite vinyl recliner in our living room. He took the paper, raised his head to look down through his bifocals, smiled sideways and proudly remarked on what a good job I did, restating his intention to mail it for the contest. I blushed with embarrassment from his praise.

In the weeks following, I went about my routine as a twelve-year-old. That involved being out and about after school with friends until late afternoon, then heading home for dinner when the church bell carillon echoed the Angelus throughout our village promptly at 6:00 p.m. Evenings concluded with homework at our kitchen table, which, if done early enough, served as an incentive for gaining permission to sit in the living room and watch a little TV.

On one such evening, Dad had already come home from work and was eagerly awaiting my return. As soon as I walked in the door, my father lit up, his eyes beaming with excitement, forcing down the recliner foot rest while leaning forward.

"Tommy!" he exclaimed with a broad smile on his face. "You won!"

Having forgotten about the contest, I looked at him with startled confusion.

"The contest! You won the coloring contest!" He grabbed his copy of the Daily News that sat folded on the edge of the textured, laminated vinyl circular table attached to the pole lamp that stood sentry-like aside his recliner. He held the folded paper aloft, waving it briefly in the air before presenting it in my direction.

"Come 'ere," he said. "Look!"

With his free-hand he pointed to a segment in the paper that listed the winners, and right there, in black and white, my name was printed among a relatively long list of winners from throughout the city and suburban regions. It was a moment of shared pride for both of us.

In 1973, getting your name in the local newspaper for any respectable reason was something special, akin then to seeing yourself on TV. Like the time in the mid 1960s when my friend George's dad rigged up a security camera in his home, then invited all the kids on our block to see ourselves on his television. It was magical! Who could see this? Where's the camera? TV was so new we thought the broadcast could be viewed by everyone in the city, maybe even in California! Seeing my name in print that day was like that. It was quite a big deal back then.

Word began to trickle through our neighborhood because everyone read the Daily News in those days. Subtitled "The People's Paper," it was the choice of working-class Philly. Throughout that evening our sole, wall-mounted phone in the kitchen continued to ring with calls from neighbors and relatives asking my Mom if she had seen my name in the Daily News. Aunts and Uncles from both sides of our family phoned. Our neighbor Helen alerted us through our shared back-yard wire fence, a copy of the Daily News in hand. I'm sure Dad had earlier boasted to his work colleagues when he first saw the printed announcement.

The next day my school friends congratulated me too, saying, "I saw your name in the Daily News!" followed by a pat on the back or a thumb-up. Some schoolmates spitefully unfurled an alternate digit from their raised hand in non-verbal acknowledgment, occasionally accentuating their thoughtfulness with carefully chosen expletives. Jealous bullies expressed equally generous sentiments. They celebrated by kindly insisting that I contribute to their coffers, warmly offering the alternate option of a punch in the face, just as they were so thoughtfully prone to do anyway. Any potential for an over-inflated ego was kept in check by schoolmates mentioning another kid in school who also won tickets.

For twenty-four hours, I felt like a minor celebrity in our neighborhood. I had mixed emotions about all the recurring attention. Yet, it gave our neighbors pride to say they knew somebody in the paper. Mom proudly chatted about it with all who paused to smile when I walked down the street. "That's Jack and Betty's kid!" they might say, or "That's my neighbor's kid!"

In working-class Philly, an achievement by anyone was a win for all. My simple accomplishment had brought a moment of pride and celebration into the humdrum, workaday lives of everyone who knew us. It was a tribal thing, a communal achievement. Similar fanfare was lauded on local Mummers' brigade members seen on TV during the annual New Year's parade broadcast. Or when a kid from the street returned from service in Vietnam surrounded by patriotic banners strung across the width of our block, or when someone got accepted into the ranks of firemen or policemen and their family would host a block party. Small moments of pride like these spread far among our tribe. That brief, shining moment just happened to be my turn.

With two tickets won, the conversation evolved into the question of who would go with me to see the film. It was awkward. I had to choose one friend without offending another. Most of my friends thought the film would be corny and expressed passive disinterest. My friend Mike hinted in a phone call that he wanted to go, so he was happy when I asked him. We looked forward to getting the tickets and planned to make a full-on adventure out of the occasion.

When the tickets arrived in the mail, the act of unsealing the envelope was like opening a precious treasure. Free movie tickets! Anything free was a cause for celebration in the working class. Times were always relatively lean in those days, and trips to the movies were an uncommon luxury reserved for a special occasion. Dad was pleased to know the tickets had arrived after I proudly presented them when he got home from work. He smiled, somewhat reserved at first.

"Ooh! There ya go! How 'bout that?" he said, examining the tickets closely.

He handed them back, followed with his simple phrase of approval:

"Atta boy."

Receiving an "Atta boy" from Dad was the clear signal you had done well. We spoke about the tickets, and when it came around to the scheduled time printed on them, I asked Dad if he would give my friend Mike and I a ride to the theater. He turned to me with tightened eyebrows.

"Mike?" my father queried. "Whaddya mean, Mike?"

I explained that I had invited Mike to go with me. Dad's face turned beet red with anger. This profoundly startled me. I recoiled with apprehension as the "Atta boy" moment dissipated.

"You're not taking Mike," he scolded while raising his voice. "You're taking ME!!"

"But I promised Mike I would take him" I tried to reason.

"I don't care who you promised! I told you about that contest, and I mailed it for you! You wouldn't be going at all if it wasn't for me!"

"But Dad...." I began to implore, but was quickly silenced.

"Now I'm goin' and that's final!"

Our shared elation suddenly deflated into a depressing and disheartening showdown. I grew quite despondent. My only ambition had been to declare to Dad my obligation of keeping a promise to a friend. But nothing I said with my naive understanding of integrity mattered. The notion occurred that Dad had used me and my coloring talents to win the tickets for himself. This thought infuriated me. I'd been taught to respect my parents and felt I couldn't protest. It remained one of the most unpleasant memories of my childhood for years, and, frankly, the decades-long process of reconciliation is the catalyst of wanting to share this story. Of course, he didn't *really* want them only for himself. When you live in a lower income household like ours, everything is first shared with the family. That's how he was raised and how he raised my brothers and I. It was just an unwritten and unquestioned rule.

And it wasn't because I didn't want to go to the movies with Dad. My parents always took me to the movies with them up to that point. We saw *The Sound of Music* when I was five years old at the old Broadway Theatre at Broad and Snyder in South Philadelphia. At seven I vividly remember seeing Disney's *The Gnome-Mobile*, and eight when Dad took me to see *Chitty Chitty Bang Bang*. Midway through that one I remember Dad whispering that he wanted to leave. I was loving that film and wanted to stay. Years later I understood why it must have bored him. The film does tend to get a little long-winded, especially early on when the Chitty theme song is sung twice in succession, followed by the saccharine-laced Sally Ann Howe solo scene. Plus, appreciating its European flavored humor required some effort and that just wasn't Dad's thing.

The Broadway Theatre was a grand, old vaudeville and cinema palace serving as the favored cultural hub of South Philadelphia for over 60 years. A true landmark of another era, it was closed and demolished in 1971, then replaced with a McDonald's and later a Walgreens. The demolition of such architectural gems has always elicited melancholy.

Once the Broadway was gone, my Mom and Dad started going to the Yeadon Theater in suburban Philadelphia. There we saw *Cool Hand Luke*, *Viva Max* and *Cold Turkey* with Dick Van Dyke, among other popular films. Going there was always a great adventure. It embodied a temporal reprieve from our concrete, brick and asphalt world of row-homes as we ventured into the land of suburban lawns and tree-lined streets. This was highlighted by a ritual, post-theater stop at a Dunkin' Donuts on the Yeadon/Philadelphia border. It was one of the first Dunkin' Donuts in the Philadelphia area, and among those enterprises that signaled the beginning of the franchise trend in America that brought about the end of the era of patronizing family run, neighborhood bakeries such as the one around the corner from our house.

On one of those Dunkin' stops, we had pulled into the parking lot next to a long, black, stretch limousine, the only other car there. One didn't see too many limos parked outside of downtown, so, naturally we were curious of its occupant. After going into the shop and completing our donut selection, Dad, Mom and I returned to the car and opened the magic waxed cardboard box of glistening, iced and powder-sugared treasures, perfectly arranged in regimented rows, each proudly awaiting its turn to serve our salivating cake-holes. We sat for a short bit as Dad sipped his coffee, with each of us meditatively munching on our chosen sugar-coated indulgence. As we quietly grazed, the limo driver emerged from the Dunkin' with a bag and coffee, which he took to the limo's rear window. The window rolled down, the limo driver handed the bag and coffee to the limo occupant, and then stepped forward to the driver's door.

Dad caught a glance of the recipient passenger in that instant.

"That's Woody Strode!" he exclaimed.

Mom and I urgently turned our heads in unison to look through our opened car windows. The passenger, a Black gentleman with a set of deep, penetrating eyes and distinct, muscular facial features, must have heard my buoyant Dad's identification. He smiled and waved to us before rolling up his limo window.

"That WAS Woody Strode!" my Dad affirmed.

Strode's best-known roles were in *Spartacus*, *The Ten Commandments*, and one of my favorites, John Ford's *The Man Who Shot Liberty Valance*.

"Oh!" Mom exclaimed with musical intonation. "I wonder what *HE's* doing *here*!"

Good question. Why was a Hollywood movie star at a Dunkin' Donuts in the middle of Yeadon, PA? Dad speculated that he must have been in town for a guest stint on *The Mike Douglas Show*, the nationally syndicated talk and variety show then produced in Philadelphia. As the Limo made its way out of the lot and onto Chester Pike, I chimed in too.

"Who's Woody Stode?"

My father pulled the rim of the coffee cup from his lips, turned to me, half grinning with bewilderment from my question. He corrected me.

"STRODE, Tommy! Woody STRODE! S-T-R-O-D-E! STRODE."

"St-Rode," I repeated after him, verbalizing that I understood. I was clear with the name, but the main point still befuddled me.

"Who is he?" I carefully asked, anticipating other aggressive reply.

"He's an actor, Tommy," my Dad tutored. "You know him. He was in Liberty Valance, Spartacus, and some other movies."

Mom interjected. "He was a football player too, wasn't he?"

Mom knew he had been a football player. She intoned such remarks at intervals like these to give her husband the opportunity of empowering Dad as a father, letting him teach his boy the details.

"Yes, he was," Dad gloated, his voice rising with each word. "He played for UCLA, and then the Rams."

Sports, and football in particular, was another arena where Dad and I bonded. That I understood. I played football for my grade school team, and books about the origins of football and biographies of famous players, ordered through the Scholastic Book catalog at school, were my usual reading material. Dad also asked me to pick the winners on the weekly football pool purchased from his brother, my Uncle Bud.

Now I appreciated the celebrity we had seen. "Wow!" I concluded, stuffing another bite of donut in my mouth, trying to envision where I might have seen this guy I was supposed to know.

Dad sipped his coffee, staring past my Mom through the passenger side window where the limousine had been. We continued to graze, until Dad blurted:

"Sergeant Rutledge!"

Mom and I remained silent, a bit perplexed.

"That's the one!" he continued. "I couldn't remember the name of that other film he was in."

Dad looked at each of us, raising his eyebrows above the rim of his glasses, somewhat shocked that we didn't understand what he meant.

"Don't you remember that movie, *Sergeant Rutledge*?"

Mom and I both shook our stuffed, donut chawing faces in the negative, accentuated by a muffled "Nn, Nn."

"You know the one, Betty" Dad huffed. "Remember? With Jeffrey Hunter? And Woody Strode was the cavalry officer on trial?"

Mom lifted a napkin below her bottom lip to catch the donut crumbs and powdered sugar that spurted out with her reply.

"Oh, I think so.... maybe."

Not satisfied with her patronizing answer, Dad craned his neck toward me.

"Tommy? Did you see that one?"

Partially frightened like being quizzed by a nun at school, I was at a loss.

"No, I don't think so."

Dad turned his glance away from both of us, harrumphing with frustration. He took a sip of coffee and gazed out of his open window.

"Woody Strode" he pondered aloud. "How 'bout that. Ain't that somet'in'?"

He paused with humble fascination, turning again to look where the Limo had been parked. He handed his coffee cup to my Mom who set it down in one of the indented circular impressions on the open flap of the glove compartment. No words were exchanged as Mom complied with an established routine. Our 1967 Chevy Impala didn't have cup holders, so Mom's added duty as copilot was to keep the half cup of hot coffee balanced while the car was in motion. Dad started the car and backed out to head home.

When the day came to attend the Tom Sawyer film, I was still embittered by Dad's forced decree and reluctant to go. I would turn thirteen in a month and his demand had been an affront to my burgeoning, rebellious teen spirit. Becoming a teenager meant that I would finally be able to make my own decisions about where and with whom I wanted to go, like my older brothers. Moreover, turning thirteen meant it would be my turn for that honored custom of getting bequeathed with a house-key - a serious rite of passage in blue collar culture.

Dad tried to sugar-coat the strained feelings with enthusiasm, reminding me of the good time always had at the movies. He was excited about it, but I was having none of it. It had not evolved into a happy occasion for me. The whole affair had become mildly traumatic, and I barely recall our ride to the theater let alone much of being there. Our popcorn purchase was a somber moment, followed by an awkward search for seats midway between the rows. I wanted to sit in front, but Dad wisely preferred to avoid the more obnoxious kids who had staked their claim in the front and were already engaged in a popcorn and Jujube battle.

Once settled into our seats, I looked around and noted how many other contest-winning kids were with parents, and how few were with a friend. Gradually, I surrendered to the reality of the situation. So what that I didn't have a friend with me. There was no changing it, so I let it go. Soon afterward the theater lights dimmed as John Williams' scored overture enveloped the room. Captivated in the rising crescendo, I became swept into a feeling we were about to experience something special.

As the opening credits appeared over a sweeping vista of the lazy, lulling Mississippi River on a bright summer day, my mind soon set aside our father and son drama. The panoramic magic of the big screen provided the needed escape. "River Song," the film's opening theme crooned by country singer Charley Pride, captured the essence of why Dad wanted to see the film, of why all things Mark Twain spoke to him back then, just as they had in his own childhood.

"A river's gonna flow..." the song began...
>'Cross the land, Cross the land
>Oh, a river's gonna flow... to the sea
>and a boy is gonna grow
>to a man, to a man...
>Only once in his life, is he free,
>only one golden time in his life
>is he free.
>Then the world turns around,
>and the boy grows tall,
>he hears the song of the river call.
>The river song sings, "Travel on, Travel on!"
>You blink away a tear,
>and the boy is gone."

I'm sure, while sitting in the darkened theater, my Dad was blinking away a few tears of his own. Despite his shortcomings, Dad had a heart of gold. He was a sentimental chap who retained a youthful spirit his entire life. Perhaps at that moment, I grew to understand my father just a little more. Passive things he said or did often gave me pause to appreciate and embrace my boyhood, instilling a nostalgia for youth in real time.

Like the importance of keeping a promise, I had learned to exercise forgiveness, and would eventually forgive Dad for his objectionable demand of going to the film. In hindsight, I'm glad we went together. It was one brief, shining, shared moment between us that I was lucky enough to have experienced with him.

My Dad was forty-four that year and just beginning to endure the throes of a mid-life crisis. I knew that only because of a few books on the topic lying around the house, like Walter Pitkin's *Life Begins at 40*. I also think the time we shared watching the film that day gave Dad a renewed appreciation for the importance of boyhood compacts among friends. As he watched Tom, Huck and Becky conspire activities based on elaborate pacts of secrecy, Dad probably understood the loyalty of my wanting to bring Mike along. Surely, he had exercised the same loyalty with his own friends as a boy. Though he didn't express it to my recollection, I suspect that he, too, forgave me that day, reflecting with a veiled sense of compassion I always knew he had. After all, it is a characteristic I've acquired from him.

In the unspoken silence of the bond between father and son, we left the theater with a better understanding and appreciation for each other. The whole affair must have helped to remind him of just how alike we were when he was my age. As his son, I was pretty much just like him. It could be likened to that familiar quote so often yet inaccurately attributed to Mark Twain:

> "When I was a boy of 14, my father was so ignorant I could hardly stand to have the old man around. But when I got to be 21, I was astonished at how much the old man had learned in seven years."

Regardless of its origins, it's a sensible quote. For Dad and I, it was like that. Through his wordless actions, Dad was trying to teach me to relish my youth while I still had it. I like to think he succeeded.

3

WHEN IN ROME, EAT CATFISH

"If you send a damned fool to St. Louis, and you don't tell them he's a damned fool they'll never find it out."[15]

Mark Twain

Thirty-five years after that awkward day at the theater with Dad and more than two decades after he had passed away, I was transferred to suburban St. Louis, Missouri to oversee my employer's operation there. While focused on the work-related mission at hand from the day I arrived, in the back of my mind I grew preoccupied with the notion that I was in the land of Mark Twain. This was a place I had long wanted to visit since pasting photos of Missouri landmarks in one of the *Know Your America* booklets I enjoyed as a kid. At the time, I wasn't even aware of Twain's birth home in the Missouri town of Florida, and his home in Hartford, Connecticut wasn't even a blip on my radar. My interest on this visit had been conjured during a business trip to St. Louis earlier in the year.

My company had then asked me to escort a client there for a weekend event we were hosting with actor Jane Seymour, one of our celebrity business associates. With some advanced planning, I scheduled a variety of activities for my client and I, which included an afternoon at the Museum of Westward Expansion set beneath the great St. Louis Arch. At the time of this writing, I was sad to learn that after 40 years in existence this wonderful museum had recently closed its doors for replacement with a new and enhanced display. What had most captivated my guest George and I was the charming, vintage kitschiness inherent in the archaic and outdated displays. It added a hometown feeling to St. Louis, making it one of the most memorable stops of our weekend. It had been in that museum when I took multiple tourist brochures referencing Mark Twain as their homeboy and the places to visit.

During the extended work assignment of my second visit, I did some additional research and learned it would take about three hours to drive north from my hotel on the Southwest outskirts of St. Louis to Hannibal, Twain's boyhood hometown. Aside from the TomTom GPS I then owned, reliance on printed directions and an old-school, folded map I'd purchased at a local gas station enabled me to chart my course. I found that taking a more scenic route would allow me to intimately explore this heretofore uncharted territory. After the passing of a few seven-day work weeks, I found a sorely needed window to take a Sunday off and seize the day. With a lifetime of Twain related memories in mind, I counted down the days until I enthusiastically woke on that Sunday, packed a few snacks for the trip, eased into the seat of my rental car, and headed north on Route 79, a straight ride right along the Mississippi River to Hannibal.

Whenever I explore new places, I make it a point to enjoy the drive as much as the destination. With the radio blaring, I took in the surrounding landscape through my open window, thumping the steering wheel and singing aloud. My drive along the Mississippi River marked only the second time I ever saw it. As I neared the Hannibal region, signs and billboards of businesses or landmarks with names associated with the lore of Mark Twain and his writings alerted me that I must be getting closer. Moment by moment my excitement grew, aware that I was driving directly into history, into the very places I had read about so long ago.

When I finally drove into Hannibal proper just before noon, I was surprised to find it virtually traffic free and what seemed to be only a scant handful of tourists, far fewer than expected. I drove around for a bit to study every road and stone and tree and facade, noting the dock area along the river that I planned to visit later. After easily finding a parking space on the street near the primary conglomeration of Twain related tourist spots, I walked just a short distance up the aptly named Hill Street, and made my way to the boyhood home of Mark Twain. As mentioned previously, I wasn't aware then that the child known as Samuel Clemens was born about 36 miles southwest from there in a two-room wooden cabin his family rented alongside a lake in Florida, Missouri. I was visiting the home to which the Clemens family moved around 1839, when Twain was four years old.

Signs directed me through an arched lattice gateway onto a courtyard path that led to a solemn fieldstone structure with a glass doorway. This stone addition was a seminal creation of the Works Project Administration during the Great Depression years. It has significance as one of the very first historical preservation projects assigned to the WPA, designed primarily to safeguard the Clemens/Twain home from risk of fire. The modernity of its entrance contrasted with the whitewashed, clapboard siding of the Twain home seemed oddly juxtaposed. Upon entering I found myself smack in the middle of an all-American prototype tourist gift shop, where admission tickets for a self-guided tour are sold. It's that kind of kitschiness that makes such tourist destinations so endearing. It was the sort of thing I expected and I was not disappointed. With only one other person there when I arrived, I didn't have to wait in a line to get a ticket. That worked for me. After paying the admission, I embarked on my trek into the heart of Mark Twain.

Greeting me as I entered the walkway to the home were floor to ceiling glass partitions that permitted a hand's-off, viewing-only experience. The glass replaced what was once an exterior wall, giving the impression of the structure as a hermetically sealed time capsule. Most striking was the scale of the home's living quarters, with small rooms almost identical to the tight quarters of my own boyhood row-home in South Philadelphia. Twain's living room was the same size as the one where my father and I discussed the Tom Sawyer coloring contest, and sat to watch a UHF channel airing of *The Adventures of Mark Twain* on our Nate Ben's television with the rolling chrome and laminate stand.

A pot-belly stove occupied the central space where one would find a television set in our era. Each room is adorned with period furniture and a life-sized, standing or seated, white plaster effigy of the adult, senior-aged Twain, which lent an eerie vibe, as if Twain's ghost is summoned to join visitors while touring the home. I questioned if the life-sized statuary was necessarily apropos, given it was his boyhood home. After later watching the Ken Burns documentary on Mark Twain, I understood that these effigies were created to immortalize Twain's last visit to the home in 1902.

The small boyhood living room of Sam Clemens with ghostly white effigy of Twain.

Mark Twain during the last visit to his boyhood home in Hannibal, 1902. Photos courtesy Library of Congress.

Next to each effigy was an oversized, framed black panel bearing a famous quote by Twain. Two favorites here touched a nerve in me, such as this one, from Twain's *The Refuge of the Derelicts*, which would ultimately serve to inspire the memoir you're presently reading:

> "A man's experiences of life are a book. There was never yet an uninteresting life. Such a thing is an impossibility. Inside of the dullest exterior there is a drama, a comedy, and a tragedy."

And this, reprinted from a Christian Science publication of *What is Man? and other philosophical Writings*:

> "A person's nature never changes. What it is in childhood, it remains. Under pressure...it can partially or wholly disappear from sight, and for considerable stretches of time, but nothing can ever permanently modify it, nothing can ever impede it."

Reading those quotes made me think of Dad. It was in that instant that memories of watching the Fredric March film, the Daily News Tom Sawyer coloring contest saga, and going to the 1973 Johnny Whitaker film first came flooding back in fuller detail. Something about the size of the living room there transported me back to my own boyhood home. It was as if Dad's spirit was suddenly with me. Considering the looming Mark Twain effigies throughout the rooms and though there were only a few other tourists walking through, it started to feel a little crowded, as if the three of us were there together. Mark Twain, my father, and me. I felt as if I were home. I suspect all three of us did.

Having spent considerable time just absorbing the contents of each room, I returned to the museum gift shop and ventured outside into the adjoining courtyard and back onto Hill Street, where I found myself standing aside a long, white, milk-washed picket fence. An old, cast iron historical marker from the 1920s announced it as "Tom Sawyer's Fence" and further explained:

> "Here stood the board fence which Tom Sawyer persuaded his gang to pay him for the privilege of whitewashing. Tom sat by and saw that it was well done."

In interviews and lectures, Twain had explained that Tom Sawyer was essentially a fictional version of himself with plot elements based on his own childhood adventures. Though I was familiar with the various Hollywood interpretations of these locales, here were the very structures and byways that inspired the stories. Directly across the brick-lined street I noted a modest, two-story clapboard building sporting a simple sign on the roof line that read "J. M. Clemens, Justice of the Peace." Another iron historical marker described it as "Mark Twain's Father's Law Office," with this story:

> "Young Sam Clemens saw a dead man on the floor in here one night. Sam went out at a window, taking the sash along with him. "I didn't need the sash" he recalled, "But it was the handier to take it than it was to leave it. So I took it. I wasn't exactly scared, but I was - ah - considerably agitated!""

Judge Clemens' law office, Hannibal.

An open door enabled one to view the interior through a framed, glass-encased entry way, just large enough to accommodate one or two people at a time. Additional tourists had shown up in town by that point so I had to wait a few minutes for my turn until two folks took leave of the entry. Its contents included a modest assembly of simple, hand-hewn, wooden items of furniture - Judge Clemens' desk topped by a pair of candlesticks, a feather quill pen posed in an inkwell, and a few law books that had seen better days. In front of that was a much smaller desk, no larger than one found in a Nineteenth Century schoolhouse, with a ladder-back chair and a second quill pen and inkwell set, no doubt reserved for the Judge's law clerk. On the opposite end of the room was a medium sized pot belly stove and a long wooden bench.

Straining to see as much as I could by pressing the side of my face against the glass, I stepped back, and, turning to the right of Judge Clemens' office, another historic place marker informed me that the next building was the home of Twain's childhood friend, Laura Hawkins, the young girl on whom he based his Becky Thatcher character. During my visit the home was undergoing restoration, cordoned off with yellow construction tape. A huge metal dumpster sat in the street in front of the house blocking most of the view. By the looks of all three buildings, the Clemens and Hawkins families weren't exactly poor considering the relative economy of the time. The Clemens' modest house was furnished with more than just the essentials, if the display was accurate. The Hawkins/Thatcher house, in contrast, was much larger and wider, fashioned in the classic American Gothic architectural style popular at the time among folks of more substantial means.

On the opposite side of Judge Clemens' office sat Grant's Drug Store, alternately known as the Pilaster House. It's a perfectly preserved and artifact-intact Nineteenth Century Apothecary. Filled with period accoutrements, it gave the impression of a time capsule, as if abruptly abandoned while in use. I assumed this was the store over which the Clemens family had moved and rented when leaner times forced them to move out of the house I'd just visited.

After satiating my curiosity with an extended overview of the Apothecary's contents, I turned and surveyed the street and the homes, and pondered these very places as the physical muse incarnate of Mark Twain's genius. I again reckoned the similarity of these humble environs of Twain's youth to my own. I could picture scores of lively children running about, rolling a wheel hoop with a stick, or just conjuring adventure with the simplest things, long before the advent of modern toys, video games, and television. I was lucky to have been born in an era when my parents, survivors of the Great Depression, taught us how to be imaginative with otherwise nondescript junk, like making a scooter from a wooden crate, a small stretch of flat lumber, a few nails, and a broken roller skate. Or make an afternoon's activity by drawing a Poison Box game board with a piece of chalk on the asphalt street and sliding some jar lids to create a competitive game for my friends and I. Or play stickball with a broom stick. We made many things like that, and the memories serve as the fodder for some really great stories about an era now long gone. Just as Twain said, "There was never yet an uninteresting life. Such a thing is an impossibility."

My tour of the home and adjacent venues complete, I turned my attention downhill to the riverbank of the grand ol' Mississippi. As I walked down the slope of Cardiff Hill, a bronze statue of Tom and Huck loomed to my left, overseeing the entirety of Hannibal like a pair of mid-west American angels.

I continued my descent directly ahead to the river bank toward a large, parchment scroll shaped sign supported by two old-fashioned, crown-topped river boat stacks. With a portrait of an older Mark Twain punctuated with an effigy of his signature, it also featured a quote from Twain's book *Life on the Mississippi*:

"The extensive view up and down the river is…one of the most beautiful on the Mississippi,".

I walked beneath the sign and there I was, perched on the banks of the Mississippi River in Hannibal Missouri. I pinched myself. Let me repeat that: I was on the banks of the Mississippi River in Hannibal Missouri! Though I'm sure the banks had been razed and renovated and made over in decades past, it didn't matter. This was it. This was the same bank, the same river, the same place where young Sam Clemens once played and stood and dreamed of piloting the steamboats from whence he'd tweak his literary identity. It was this very spot romanced so richly in Twain's writings.

Above: The gateway to Hannibal along the Mississippi River waterfront. Photo by the author.

Upon documenting his own return to Hannibal in later years, disembarking right on this dock and looking about from the same vantage from where I now stood, Twain wrote:

"At seven in the morning we reached Hannibal, Missouri, where my boyhood was spent… The things about me and before me made me feel like a boy again—convinced me that I was a boy again, and that I had simply been dreaming an unusually long dream…"[16]

This was his literary muse, the foundation of his best known and most inspired creations. It was in *Life on the Mississippi* that Twain planted the seed which later grew into the Adventures of Huck Finn and Tom Sawyer. The specialness of this very place, the only place exactly like this on planet Earth, did not escape my attention.

What equally impressed me was how time did indeed seem to stand still from this particular spot. All I saw in either direction was lush, green foliage, just as the Twain quote on the sign referenced, which had been extracted from this passage in *Life on the Mississippi*:

"From this vantage ground the extensive view up and down the river, and wide over the wooded expanses of Illinois, is very beautiful—one of the most beautiful on the Mississippi, I think; which is a hazardous remark to make, for the eight hundred miles of river between St. Louis and St. Paul afford an unbroken succession of lovely pictures. It may be that my affection for the one in question biases my judgment in its favor; I cannot say as to that. No matter, it was satisfyingly beautiful to me, and it had this advantage over all the other friends whom I was about to greet again: it had suffered no change; it was as young and fresh and comely and gracious as ever it had been."[17]

No construction, no factories, no tracts of new fab homes with boat docks. Just unspoiled, natural river banks. Was it possible that industry had bypassed sleepy Hannibal, leaving it as intact as the day Sam Clemens had last disembarked here himself? Twain had remarked on this as well:

"I saw the new houses—saw them plainly enough—but they did not affect the older picture in my mind, for through their solid bricks and mortar I saw the vanished houses, which had formerly stood there, with perfect distinctness."[18]

I envisioned how life along the river must have looked in the mid-nineteenth century. I pondered how these docks were once active with merchants and slaves loading and unloading cotton and other goods to and from boats and barges and flat rafts like those described in Huck Finn. I imagined showboats stopping by, and as I looked to the opposite shore, I wondered if these were the same eyots that had inspired the Jackson Island where Twain placed the evasive Huck and Jim in their adventures. I remained sitting on the dock for an extended while, just soaking it in, pondering these thoughts and other memories of Twain's writing, the films I'd seen in my youth, and Dad's enamorment with all things Twain. I considered how Dad had never been here, how it remained just a dream from his own youth and throughout his life, and that I was now there for both of us. I smiled and quietly said aloud "Well Dad, here it is. I made it."

After continuing to sit and ingest this for a considerable while, I stood up, took one last look, then turned and proceeded to explore the town that sat behind me. Back up the hill a short distance away, I found a few open shops. In one high-ceilinged open space showcasing a collective of booths with wares by local artisans and purveyors of touristy merchandise, I managed to find a display of souvenir shot glasses. Getting a Mark Twain/Hannibal shot glass was a must. My Dad had started a shot glass collection representing places he'd visited and gifted by others. When my wife and I purchased our home, my Mom had bequeathed that collection to me, and from time to time, I will add one I think is special. This opportunity posed a priceless prerequisite, a collection-capping gem to add to Dad's ensemble. I chose one that, were Dad still alive, I would have surely purchased as a gift for him. He would have loved it. Cheers, Dad!

Feeling a tad hungry by then I decided to look for a place to grab a bite to eat before heading on the drive back to Saint Louis. In short duration I stumbled upon what I considered the quintessential Hannibal, Missouri tourist mecca - *The Mark Twain Dinette*. I could tell from the exterior that this place must have been there forever. A large, three-dimensional root beer mug towered over the nearby parking lot, and a riverboat's pilot wheel adorned with Twain's profile stood near the entrance. A sign outside explained that the restaurant had been in operation since 1942. It looked it!

Venturing inside, I entered into a nondescript hodgepodge of architectural styles spanning mid-century modern '60s to 1970s Sears living room. But let me be clear - I loved that! This sort of vintage kitchiness is precisely why I selected it. Behind a wood-paneled reception counter, a nice young woman welcomed me and offered her help. I explained that I wanted to first check the menu. Without hesitation she recommended, in a delightfully chipper tone: "Well, whatever you decide to get you just gotta try our faa-mous Root Beer."

"I saw that" I replied. "What makes it different from other Root Beers?"

"Why it's made right here and it's just the best," she snapped, as if it would be an offense to social propriety to not order one.

"Sounds good" I replied, smiling in acknowledgment. I don't typically drink soda, or, now that I was in the Midwest - Pop - but I took her implication to heart nonetheless. Don't want to offend the kindly thoughtfulness of the locals, even if it was a canned sales pitch.

I had encountered this sort of Midwestern graciousness before. It reminded me of the time with my client, George, during that first trip to St. Louis. Our waiter in a local restaurant was insistent that we each order a serving of "St. Louis' world famous, Ooey-Gooey Chocolate Cake" for dessert. Just as I had inquired with the current young Root Beer champion, I had then asked "What makes it 'World-Famous'?" The waiter animatedly explained: "It was first introduced during the St. Louis World's Fair in 1904 and it's considered one of our local specialties. You just can't get it anywhere else," concluding with the same measure of incredulous suggestiveness that I should even consider ordering anything else, just as Root Beer girl had done.

Naturally I deduced from the waiter's averment that the kitchen likely had an abundance of servings they needed to push to avoid spoilage and was probably not an item ordered too frequently by the locals since it was native to the region and readily available. And, after a hundred years, the locals had probably grown sick of it. The restaurant relied on tourist suckers like us to take the bait. So, who was I to argue? I knew George had a sweet tooth anyway, and he was graciously deferring to me as his host.

"Well," I said, humoring the waiter, "I think we should give it a try then. What do you think, George?"

George feigned indifference. "I don't care. Sounds good to me."

I knew George better. Of course it's what he wanted. He was just being polite.

"Sure! Why not?" I said to the waiter. "One for each of us."

The waiter acknowledged our "excellent" choice, reassuring we would not be disappointed as he excitedly added the order onto our bill, cleared our table, and scurried back to the kitchen. After a few minutes passed, an auxiliary server brought coffees we had ordered, followed by our waiter, who proudly set before each of us a small plate embellished with a disheveled glop of moistened dark brown matter, garnished with a generous squirt of canned whipped cream. Our fare had been delivered with all the care of a wedding ring bearer, as if presented with a crown jewel on a pillow.

"Here you are, gentleman" he intoned victoriously. "Two orders of St. Louis' World Famous Ooey-Gooey Chocolate Cake. Enjoy."

After thanking him, the waiter nodded gleefully, moving on to his other tables. George and I both studied the mysterious mass before us.

"So, this is it" George commented, pausing momentarily to marvel at this alleged delight of legend. Having once worked as a baker, I was a bit more critical.

"It looks like an undercooked brownie" I remarked.

"I don't know" George remarked, already plowing in to retrieve his second forkful. "Tastes good to me."

I took a forkful and tasted it. The flavor was all there. How could you go wrong with chocolate, butter and sugar? It tasted great, but, it certainly seemed like an undercooked brownie to me.

I envisioned a baker in 1904, frantically trying to keep up the pace of pleasing throngs of ravenous guests at the World's Fair and forgetting to put baking powder in a chocolate dessert batter, resulting in a gooey hybrid. With no time to spare and start over, a clever, mustachioed, high-collared and pocket-chain vested restaurant manager quells the nervous clamor of his panicked subordinates by instructing them to inform the multitudes that this was a "special" dessert created exclusively for the occasion, and to persuasively present it with all the requisite flair and grandeur ascribed to an eighth wonder of the world. Tens of thousands of thrill-seeking Fair attendees jubilantly bought the pitch wholesale and without resistance, thereafter traveling back to their respective domiciles with tales of the legendary delicacy, of how the consumption of it had left them feeling like they experienced a pleasure otherwise reserved for royalty. I further imagined how this tradition of spin attached to the rich, chocolate semi-elixir - as it is half liquid and half substance - was perpetuated day after day, week after week, year after year and generation after generation through each decade of the entire Twentieth Century, all the way through our era and into that day when George and I became the most recently anointed gullible chumps. Missourians, after all, must have learned a few things from the success such ceremonious hucksterism had brought to Mark Twain. Hell, Missourians probably invented it! Twain may have ridden on to success by just being his natural Missourian self.

Root Beer girl's charming Missourian demeanor had won me over. I mulled over the Mark Twain Dinette menu a few minutes longer. Satisfied that it offered options I might want to eat, I asked to be seated. I expected the food to be mediocre, but I really didn't give a hoot. I was content with the fact that whatever I ate, this was the best place in Hannibal to do it. This would be the culmination of the Mark Twain/Hannibal tourist pilgrimage.

The entire menu offered a festival of pure Americana, from fried pickles to cinnamon apple rings, burgers, pork tenderloin, beef, fried chicken, and a Sloppy Joe called the Maid Rite, touted as the house specialty since 1942. There was even a Philly Cheesesteak. Nah. On that I'll pass. Seeing that reminded me of the time I was in Rome and saw an Irish-American guy opting to dine in an Irish Pub. I'll never forget the defeated look on the sorrowful face of that guy's wife as she stood next to him, half slumped. What was that guy thinking? In one of the most romantic cities on the planet in the home of superior Italian cuisine, he's opting for the apotheosis of bland food. A steak and potato? Really?

As I continued to scour the Dinette menu in my seat, I noted an extensive list of options that featured - Catfish! They offered a hand-breaded Catfish filet sandwich, a Cajun seasoned Catfish taco dish, a breaded Catfish dinner platter with two side veggies, dinner roll and salad. The special of the day was Catfish fingers with creole dipping sauce. Then, an illumination: Of course! What the hell else was I gonna eat in Hannibal, on the banks of the Mississippi? It was like eating a Cheesesteak in Philly, Lobster in Maine, or Crabs in Maryland. When in Rome, eat Catfish!

I opted for the Catfish filet sandwich and a mug of the Faa-mous Root Beer with a side of fries. The fried pickles taunted me, but I thought those could prove unsettling with a three-hour drive ahead of me and opted to pass, fearing the added indulgence might also opt to pass regardless of my will.

When the sandwich arrived, I elected to discard the top portion of the bun. I didn't care about the bread. I wanted to taste the fish. While cutting off a bite size portion, I examined my dissected filet like a lab specimen. The flesh beneath the breading variated in tone from dark brown to white. I inserted the first cutlet into my mouth. The texture was light and flaky, with a rich, moist density. The flavor was mildly earthy with a distinct sweetness. Was this from the oil in which it had been fried? I selected the sandwich specifically because it was the one option that didn't offer the fish seasoned or smothered in a cream sauce. I could tell from first bite that, while not unpleasant at all, the Cajun spiced menu selection might have been the way to go.

Catfish reminded me of trout, or bass, or even flounder. It had no discernible flavor. It was ok. I liked it. Maybe I liked it because I wanted to like it, because I was in Mississippi River country, in Huck Finn country, but I mainly wanted to know what it was that my Dad liked about it so much. I imagined his memory of it had likely been pan-seared. That didn't seem to be an option at the Mark Twain Dinette, where any Catfish selection was deep fried, leaving me to assume it was likely a frozen item. Either way, I relished each portion, aware that I was fulfilling another bucket-list item for myself, and one of Dad's nostalgic yearnings.

So, this was Catfish. Now I understood something additional about my Dad's personal experience. Small and insignificant in one regard, yet things like this can reveal a man's soul to you. Something as simple as eating Catfish enabled me to once again enjoy the company of my father. This is how life works. This is how one's ancestors are honored. There is something ancient and primordial and tribal and sacred about an action as simple as experiencing a joy known only through the passing down of spoken work. Eating Catfish had been a story told in my youth and that I've since imagined for 40 years. Now I was actually experiencing it, grokking it, again communing with my father's spirit. Catfish became the Holy Eucharist on this Sunday afternoon in Hannibal. My soul was redeemed by the blessed Catfish. The home-made Root Beer, I should add, was the Amen. Absolutely as good as the host had described. Certainly, it was just Root Beer. But this was THIS Root Beer, the Hannibal, Missouri Mark Twain Dinette FAA-MOUS Root Beer. This was the chalice of wine to the Holy Eucharist of Catfish. It couldn't have been more perfect.

With my soul cleansed, my belly content, and obligation to my ancestors fulfilled, I exited the cool, air-conditioned, wood-paneled and vinyl-tiled landmark back into a brilliant and blazing summer afternoon and headed for my car. As I walked on Main Street I noted a pub called Kerley's. This, I thought, was surely an Americanized, phonetically spelled version of my own last name, ascribed at Ellis Island a hundred-plus years ago to some forgotten ancestral relative who arrived from Ireland with an inability to spell. Ancestral spirits were all around me now in Hannibal, celebrating my Catfish benediction, a plenary indulgence offered - and enjoyed - in their memory.

The window of Kerley's Pub, Hannibal.

When I got to my car, I looked over the printed directions and map and decided on a more scenic exit before going on the main highway to Saint Louis. As I drove out of town, I noted more signs for additional tourist stops. But one sign in particular intrigued me enough to veer off and pursue its destination - The Mark Twain Cave. No…could it be? I had to investigate.

After following the signs, I made my way to a gravel parking lot with, yes, another souvenir shop that sold admission tickets. I read over the printed description of the place and learned, just as suspected, that this was the very cave referenced in *The Adventures of Tom Sawyer*. There were specified tour times and I selected the next soonest slot.

While waiting, I perused the gift shop filled with Native American crafts made in China, animal antler trinkets, flint arrowheads, and an endless variety of Tom Sawyer and Huck Finn paraphernalia. When the time on my admittance ticket neared, I approached the rendezvous point to meet a guide, along with six or so others. For conservation reasons, only so many people are permitted in the cave at one time. The guide explained that anyone with claustrophobia should exclude themselves at this time because once the cave was entered we would be unable to exit for an hour. I anticipated the excitement of feeling trapped just like Tom and Becky.

As we entered an ancient tourist entrance - the original entrance of Mark Twain's time having been closed due to falling rock danger - our guide explained the geological history and scientific explanation of the cave's formation. Moving along, we were told of specific points referenced by Mark Twain when Tom Sawyer and Becky Thatcher were lost in the labyrinth for a romantic but harrowing three days - a turning point in Tom Sawyer!

Known as McDowell's Cave in young Sam Clemens' time and renamed "McDougal's Cave" in the book, it's been a popular destination for Hannibal residents since its discovery around 1820. As Twain described, community gatherings, picnics and celebrations were traditionally hosted on adjacent land because of its natural coolness during the sweltering months of the Missouri summer. It was only after the publication of *The Adventures of Tom Sawyer* that it became a tourist mecca, and has been since. Really cool was being aware that this very same cave was explored by young Sam Clemens and his friends. At least one close friend, Tom Blankenship, on whom Twain's Huck Finn character is based, had surely tread these same pathways 140 years earlier.

Our tour guide pointed to one area of the cave used around 1840 as a hideout by Missouri's other favorite son, Jesse James. Was this info just another Missourian hoax fabricated for enhanced tourist trade? Whatever. It might as well have been. I was growing fondly accustomed to the Missourian spin cycle. Regardless, the tour was just good fun, and another aspect of bringing all the Twain tales to life. When a favorite fictional story steps off the page with the discovery of its real-life counterpart, it's magical. It was like Robert Ballard's discovery of the real Titanic. Suddenly the legend takes on a different aura. It's not just a story anymore - it's REAL!!!

Vintage postcard images of the Mark Twain Cave on the outskirts of Hannibal. Above, left: the now closed original entrance, circa 1967; Right: An interior view circa 1930. Courtesy the Hannibal Free Public Library.

My pilgrimage to Hannibal completed something dormant within my psyche. This whole trip had been an important culmination of a lifetime of legends and stories shared by my father, satisfying my own curiosity as well! As much as having fulfilled a personal curious yearning harbored for decades, it enabled me to keep alive the memory of my father by completing an ambition of his own. It satisfied some deeply embedded genetic sequencing. It addressed a pent-up longing to spend more time with Dad, a feat of which I had long felt deprived due to his passing when I was just twenty-seven years old. It was a life that had passed quickly, filled with scheduled activities such as sixteen years of school, free time spent with friends, summers spent in the mountains or moving to Los Angeles for a brief time before coming home to help nurse him during the illness that eventually led to his death. I barely had an opportunity to get to know the man well in our years together. So precious now, are those shared moments of watching old films together, of hearing him play the accordion and sing at family parties, of his explosions of laughter while watching a comedian on TV. I remembered a man who slept when I was awake due to his shift work, yet took the time to bring a special toy or treat when returning home, just because he had been thinking of my brothers and I. That was the expression of his love that I knew. This sojourn to the heart of Twain country had enabled me to a get a glimpse, a fathom - the twain, if you will - of the youthful spirit that piloted him on the river of his life, of the young boy who grew up along a Philadelphia river with a dream. Of a boy just like me.

THE HOUSE POINTED OUT AS HUCKLE-
BERRY FINN'S HOME.
MARK TWAIN SAYS THAT THIS IDENTIFICATION SAVES
THE TROUBLE OF BUILDING A HOUSE
FOR THE PURPOSE.

Left: Century Magazine clipping from September, 1902. During his visit in June that year, Twain identified this as the home of Tom Blankenship – aka Huckleberry Finn, in Hannibal, MO. In his Autobiography, Twain wrote of his friend:

"In Huckleberry Finn I have drawn Tom Blankenship exactly as he was. He was ignorant, unwashed, insufficiently fed; but he had as good a heart as ever any boy had. His liberties were totally unrestricted. He was the first boy to go barefoot in spring, smoked a pipe, and could swear wonderfully. He was the only really independent person—boy or man—in the community, and by consequence he was tranquilly and continuously happy and envied by the rest of us."

Left:: The Blankenship/Huck Finn house today, in a 2009 photo taken by the author.

4

THE HOLY SEPULCHER AT HARTFORD

"To us our house was not insentient matter--it had a heart & a soul & eyes to see us with...we...lived in its grace & in the peace of its benediction. We never came home from an absence that its face did not light up & speak out its eloquent welcome..."

Mark Twain

Eight years had passed since my trip to Hannibal when I was planning a business trip with a series of sales calls between West Chester County, New York and Boston. When travelling, I typically search for any points of interest that might be near my planned appointments, and it was then I noticed a particularly attractive place to incorporate into my plans. Mindful of giving priority to sales calls, I charted my course, noting that it would take me right through Hartford, Connecticut. I calculated that I could spare a few hours for leisure and still arrive at my hotel outside of Boston by a reasonable hour on Sunday night, able to begin my next round of appointments on Monday morning. I saw this as a window of opportunity to fulfill another aspiration of visiting the other famed residence of Mark Twain in Hartford, and, serendipitously, I could schedule it on that Sunday morning, just as I had for the trip to Hannibal. It all seemed too perfect.

I learned added details about Twain's life in Hartford in the years since my Missouri pilgrimage, which had reawakened a sleeping giant of interest in Mark Twain's life that I had set aside. In the ensuing years I'd made a variety of other exploratory excursions while on business trips, such as having a profound experience overlooking the expansive vista at The *Lewis and Clark Memorial* in Council Bluffs, Iowa; discovering an unexpected personal connection while visiting *The John Wayne Home* in Winterset, Iowa; a sobering stop at The *Stonewall Jackson House* in Lexington, Virginia; a writing-inspired outing to The *Margaret Mitchell House* in Atlanta, Georgia; a pop culture jaunt just to take a selfie next to a statue of *Chef Boyardee* in Omaha, Nebraska, and a side trip to *Golden Stake Monument*, a fifty-six foot tall, golden colored, phallic-shaped railroad memorial, also in Council Bluffs. I had visited the latter because of its description as a promotional prop erected for Council Bluff's hosting of the 1939 film premier of *Union Pacific* with Joel McCrae and Barbara Stanwyck, another UHF channel standard back in the day. While I enjoyed each of those places for respective reasons, few had left me with the same degree of palpably powerful and personal experience had during the Hannibal trip. Going to The Mark Twain House in Hartford might bring back that feeling, I'd hoped.

My work at that time involved driving a big-assed truck filled-to-capacity with an artwork line I repped, forcing me to lumber along the highways and byways to the disdain of impatient Northeastern commuters with whom I shared the road. Though I had risen early that Sunday, the slowness of the heavy truck along with the need to take truck-only routes made the trip considerably longer than planned. This meant that if I wanted to arrive at my hotel near Boston before the check-in office closed, I might have to skip the Hartford stop and drive straight through. I had to choose. After pulling over at a rest stop to refresh my coffee, I mulled the options. Feck it, I thought. You only live once. When would I again get this chance? I opted to make the stop regardless and called the hotel near Boston to let them know I'd arrive closer to midnight. They were amenable and provided instructions for when I arrived. So, onward I drove.

As in Hannibal, I arrived in Hartford on a day when few visitors were there. When I arrived at the Twain home parking lot, there was only one other car. An abundance of extra-long, specially designated parking spaces normally reserved for tourist busses lined the lot's perimeter, so I jockeyed my behemoth, diesel powered monster into one of those vacant spots, relieved to finally turn off the loud engine.

It was quiet that Sunday save for an occasional toll of nearby church bells. I stood for a short while just examining the environment, drinking in the atmosphere that compelled Mark Twain to choose this location to build his home in the early 1870s. As I walked from the lot toward the entrance, I studied the exterior of the famed house which sat on a hill above me to the left and took some time to first shoot some photos. With its patterned slate roof and brick facade, the home impressed me as a superior example of American Victorian architecture. I marveled at the network of porches and stained-glass windows, the hidden niches, gables, and artfully constructed chimneys, all nestled in a verdure, sylvan canopy of tall trees. What a splendid retreat for a writer!

The Twain/Clemens home in Hartford, CT.

After ascending the extended plank of steps to the visitor's center, I paused for a moment as I entered to survey the surroundings. The immediate impression is like stepping into an underground bomb shelter, which is understandable given that the center is built into the hill beneath the Twain property. It was a strange, barren sort of entrance which seemed to suggest one was entering hallowed ground, a secular cathedral consecrated to Saint Mark, patron saint of The Writer's Guild. To my immediate right was the expected gift shop, which I decided to scope out first. It didn't take me long to eye a few items I would consider purchasing after a fuller exploration. Leaving the book store, I was greeted with an almost life-sized effigy of Twain created with Legos. This was kind of cool and I was already hoping there'd be more.

Moving toward the admission desk, I was completely enamored with a sculptural maquette for a Mark Twain memorial that had never been erected. An adjoining sign explained that it had been commissioned to commemorate the Centennial of Twain's birth in 1935, but the estimated cost of five-hundred thousand dollars required to erect it wasn't realizable during those years of the Great Depression. A sculptor myself, I found this maquette captivating, recognizing the style as being consistent with the Florentine or French Academy tradition.

Another sign explained that its creator had been the late Walter Russell, a celebrated, classically trained sculptor in his day known for creating busts of Thomas Edison, General MacArthur, George Gershwin, and commissioned by

President Franklin D. Roosevelt to create a metaphorical representation of *The Four Freedoms*.[19] I wasn't then familiar with Russell, but have since learned what a remarkable, forgotten genius he had been, a true Renaissance man in the mold of Nikola Tesla or Leonardo Da Vinci. His accomplishments include successful ventures as a composer, painter, author, philosopher, and more.

The marvelous maquette by Walter Russell for the proposed Mark Twain Memorial, displayed at the Mark Twain House & Museum, Hartford, CT.

This Twain Centennial sculpture study, just one of three copies that exist, is aesthetically flawless. It saddened me to learn it hadn't been erected as intended, having been commissioned by Mark Twain's only surviving daughter, Clara Clemens Gabrilowitsch. Even with support of financial backers at the time, raising the required funds just couldn't happen. It was supposed to have measured 110 feet wide, and situated over a reflecting pool in the manner of those grand monuments erected prior to WWII, like the Jefferson and Lincoln memorials. The more I studied this fascinating depiction of Twain surrounded by twenty-seven of his characters created in just four of his books, the more I felt like the world had been unjustly deprived of such a worthy tribute to the man who defined the American ethos in one package perhaps more succinctly than any memorialized statesmen. Instead, we have a statue of Walt Disney and Mickey Mouse at Disney World. Nothing wrong with that, but without Mark Twain's influence, I doubt if Walt Disney would have become the creator he was.

At the time of creating this project, Walter Russell said:

> "Mark Twain has left an indelible impress upon this and future ages. His characters have had as much to do with shaping the thought of our civilization as the real people of flesh and blood who fought in our wars,

or gave us our philosophies. The sculptured characters…will forever help to keep this great author's name hallowed by his fellow man throughout the world."

Right then and there, I understood why the construction of this foyer seemed like a church. Here was the holy sepulcher representing the true spirit of the man. Where he lived was above us. Where I now stood was the catacomb of his embodied memory.

I can't say enough about this maquette except that it leaves me wondering why it still hasn't been built. I invite readers of this work, at any point in the future, to join me in realizing the possibility of finally seeing this remarkable, world-class tribute created in the scale it was intended. While the prevalent thought is that it may cost multiple times the original estimated cost in today's dollars, we now have the technology to more easily replicate this in a wider variety of sustainable and potentially lest costly materials. It must be done. And to the Mark Twain House Museum, I'll add - move this profound artifact away from the wall and give it a centrally located place of prominence. This Russell maquette is the Kabaah, the Ark of the Covenant, the Holy Grail of all things Twain. Don't relegate it to a fate solely as an entryway curiosity. It is much, much too marvelous.

This is the excitement an artist experiences when they encounter a masterfully executed work that just belittles the sense of one's worth, the sort of thing that is just so incredibly excellent it makes an aspirant desire to abandon all intention of becoming a sculptor. It's like seeing the work of Auguste Rodin, or Michelangelo's David in the Galleria dell'Acadamia. You know the next thought is 'game over'.

I stepped forward to the admission desk, noting that tours through the home were conducted in intervals. After paying the amount due I secured my spot for the next time slot. The museum staffer explained that just past the desk and to my right was a small museum exhibit of Twain artifacts. I wasn't sure if I had enough time to peruse an exhibit, but decided to check it out.

As I entered the central corridor and turned to my right, I found myself enveloped by a well of natural light flooding an open area with wall-mounted letters that informed me I was in Hal Holbrook Hall. Hal Holbrook - of course! I forgot about that. He had been performing the landmark, one-man show about Mark Twain since I was a boy. It seemed to be a fitting tribute, lending a heightened appreciation for this place. I began to get the bigger picture that, more than Hannibal, this place pretty much served as the National monument to Mark Twain. To the left of the museum entrance, a small, transparent and eloquently engraved plaque explained that the Hall had been dedicated to Holbrook only two years before, citing his "singular accomplishment in keeping Mark Twain's legacy alive by bringing his wit and brilliant commentary to so many generations," and his contributions to the restoration of the home I was about to tour. The part of this plaque I relished most is the beginning quote from Holbrook himself: "I found in Mark Twain the clear path to the soul of America." Indeed, indeed. It would be several years before I fully grasped the scope of Holbrook's pregnant remark.

Craning my neck upward, I noticed that sandstone walls above had also been engraved with ageless 'Twainisms', such as "Always do right. This will gratify some people and astonish the rest" and "A man cannot be comfortable without his own approval."

Bringing my gaze back to eye level, dead ahead of me was a life-size photograph of the elder, white-haired and mustachioed Twain, clad in white, holding a book, and staring just slightly askew. It reminded me of the ghostly white statues of Twain in each room of the Hannibal house. Now I was beginning to feel like my encounters with these recurring representations of Mark Twain was like

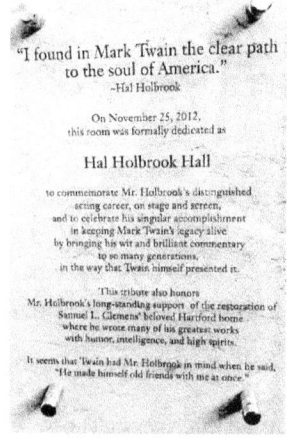

The Dedication plaque in Hal Holbrook Hall, Hartford.

the old Cream of Wheat TV commercial, where the ghostly spirit of a bowl of Cream of Wheat cereal haunts a child while the latter plays in the snow. My brothers and I used to howl laughing at the corniness of the commercial whenever we saw it. "Cream of Wheat, stays with you, to guard you all day through" went the jingle. Now, replace 'Cream of Wheat' with 'Mister Twain' and you'll get the idea.

Cream of Wheat actually did haunt me. When I lived in the Catskill Mountain region in the early 1980s, I worked as a freelance handyman doing painting and assorted chores in the many antiquated bungalow colonies from the 1940s that were then on death's doorstep. I had once been contracted by an Orthodox Rabbi who ran a summer camp for Hasidic Jewish youth from the Williamsburg and Crown Heights sections of Brooklyn in an old, dilapidated, repurposed bungalow colony. On the morning when my small crew and I were to be shown where to start painting, the Rabbi brought us first to the cafeteria kitchen and asked if we would like to join the kids for breakfast. Cream of Wheat was the only thing being served. We had already eaten and wanted to get started, so we politely declined. But none of us could escape the site of the entire length of the pantry wall behind us - 20 to 30-foot-wide and 10-foot-high, with 2-foot-deep shelves jam-stocked with nothing but box after box and row after row of Cream of Wheat. A veritable mountain of Cream of Wheat! None of us had seen so much Cream of Wheat in our lives! Was this all that was fed to these children, we later wondered aloud? Something didn't seem right to us. The Rabbi, a portly fellow with a protrusive jaw and profound under bite, sported a substantially extended mid-waist reminiscent of a Snapping Turtle Turk from the Beatles' *Yellow Submarine*, which contrasted sharply with the conglomerate of lean, seemingly underfed, lanky children, like a scene out of Dickens' Oliver Twist. That wall o' wheat certainly did stay with us all day through. It haunts me to this day!

Upon entering the Aetna Gallery display of Twain artifacts, I feasted on the collection of Twain's personal ephemera. It was here that I first saw photographs of Samuel Clemens' parents and siblings, enabling me to finally put faces to names. I knew the Mary and Sid characters in Tom Sawyer had been based on Twain's brother and sister, and Aunt Polly on his mother. Then there was a photo of Judge Clemens, the struggling father whose law office and frontier courtroom I had visited in Hannibal. A writing desk used by Twain during his early career as a journalist supported a glass covered collection of personal items including a corn-cob pipe, ashtray, a second pipe and tobacco jar, an antique "self-filling" ink pen, his reading glasses, and more. A corner display to the left of this featured some of the steamer trunks used by Twain and his family on transatlantic travels, and just to their left, centrally displayed in the rear of the exhibit, was the mother of all Mark Twain relics - the massive, notorious Paige Compositor.

This was the very cursed invention into which Twain had invested a fortune for more than a decade that caused him to file bankruptcy. I had known about this machine since I was kid, learning first about it, naturally, from the 1944 Fredric March film. I never knew what it looked like, which is markedly different from its ridiculous portrayal in the film.

The Compositor is an automatic typesetting apparatus invented by James Paige, designed as a means to modernize and replace the manual typesetting technique that had dominated the printing trade up to that point for four hundred years since the invention of the Gutenberg press. It was, in effect, an industrial age, Steam-punk computer forged of over 18,000 iron and brass working parts that mimicked human hand motion. Twain, a former manual type compositor himself with in-depth knowledge of the printing industry, had found remarkable promise in its potential. Twain had already become smitten with the earliest prototype typewriting machines developed by Remington, using one of the first "new-fangled machines," as Twain called it, to type a letter to his brother Orion, later using a more refined model to submit *Life on the Mississippi*, which is believed to have been the first typewritten manuscript ever sent to a publisher.[20]

When James Paige came along with his patented concept for the Compositor, Twain was immediately sold and proceeded to uniformly sink into its development all his profits from book sales and his wife's inherited fortune at an initial rate of $3000.00 per month - almost $60,000.00 per month in today's currency. Continuing to regularly pour similar sums into it for years, the ultimate contributed tally came close to $6,000,000.00. Twain and Paige's effort to refine and market the contraption was finally trounced when the introduction of the more easily maintained Linotype Machine prevailed.[21]

Defeated and penniless, James Paige spent his final days in a poorhouse. Twain, bankrupt in pocket and measurably drained in spirit, was forced to leave the beloved family home in Hartford and embark on a decade long speaking tour around the globe to regain his financial footing. It wore heavy on Twain's heart for the remainder of his life that his bankrupting folly had been responsible for added strain to his family's health, contributing to wife Olivia's physical deterioration, and ultimately her death. It is somewhat unsettling to gawk wondrously at it in the museum and simultaneously consider that the very machine responsible for so ruinously undermining the Clemens' family life is now physically situated beneath the home it forced them to abandon.

Clemens' folly: the notorious Paige Compositor.

Noting the time, I exited the Aetna Gallery to take my place at the designated rendezvous point for the scheduled tour of the house. Our guide greeted us en masse, delivered an overview of the home's history along with the rules of the tour, and then led us up a long, ascending set of deep, stone steps to the 2nd level of Holbrook Hall. Along a corridor we passed another exhibition space, continued through The Nook cafeteria, and exited a door to the outside where we all gathered before the Clemens' carriage house. Our tour guide explained that

Clemens family coachman Patrick McAleer lived here for twenty years with his wife and seven children. It was briefly used as a study by Twain after a room so designated in the home was instead co-opted for use as a school and play room for his daughters. It was in this carriage house where the final chapter of Tom Sawyer had been written.

From there we were led along the side of the carriage house to an open area where the magnificent home loomed before us in all its grandeur. It was built in an area known as Nook Farm, a fashionable section of Hartford in its affluent Victorian era heyday, where many important literary types, activists, intellectuals, artists and others resided. One such example stood just across the lawn with the home of the Clemens' next-door neighbor, Harriet Beecher Stowe, author of *Uncle Tom's Cabin*, the abolitionist fueled tome that rang the clarion call for emancipation and set the stage for the American Civil War.

We continued along a slate pathway until stopping on the front porch of the house. The guide explained that in Twain's time, the Park

Being led on the path to the Clemens house.

River ran just below the property, winding around the farm in a way that formed a nook, giving Nook Farm its name. The river has since been covered after being routed through underground pipes constructed in a 1940s municipal project. I spun around and looked down, studying what was left of the terrain, envisioning the river that once regaled there. It made perfect sense that the boy raised on the banks of the Mississippi would choose to build a home along a river. Though veiled now by Twenty-First Century noise pollution, it was evident that one missing, additional meditative quality was the sound of the river, the constant hum and trickle of movement, that Mr. Twain likely relished in tranquil moments of reflective repose. A circumstance like that surely offered some of the fuel for his writing.

I studied the hand-hewn lumber surrounding the open portico of the home. While gleaning each detail of the window exteriors and painted patterns in the deep, burgundy brickwork, I imagined Mark Twain or another family member standing in this very spot at one time. I could barely contain myself. It was the same, breathless experience as I had while standing on the banks of the Mississippi in Hannibal, when I said: Pinch me! Was I really here? I considered my trip to Hannibal a pilgrimage, but this was the ultimate. This was Mecca for me! Just as adherents of any faith make pilgrimages to their respective shrines and holy places, a trip to this Mark Twain house in Hartford is a must for any literary aspirant with even a passive interest in the craft of writing. In fact, our guide explained that it is ranked as one of the top ten most visited tourist sites in the world, in the same league as the Eiffel Tower or Taj Mahal.

From there we were led over to the original carriage stoop, just across from the front door. Our guide pointed out the path where the Clemens' carriage would have carried them up a slight incline to this point from Farmington Avenue below. I envisioned family scenes from 140 years before, of Susy, Clara, Jean, Sam or Olivia stepping down onto this aged and worn brownstone carriage stoop, followed by Patrick McAleer directing the horses to pull the empty vehicle to the carriage house and stable along the path we had just walked.

As the guide told stories about the restoration of Twain's color choice for the painted brick on the exterior, I studied the powerful oak door opposite me. How many great ones had stood here and knocked, paying a call to visit Mark Twain? I recalled the story about a young fan of Twain named Rudyard Kipling who had once visited Twain unannounced, setting the stage for Kipling's career as both journalist and story teller.

Our guide then opened the door and led us into the foyer, where I was immediately awestruck by the level of decorative, detailed accents in places where no one would typically pay any attention. With patterns reminiscent of an M. C. Escher artwork, the intricacy of ornamentally inlaid wood and stenciled wallpaper in even the most insignificant segments of wall and ceiling is breathtaking. The tiled floor is accented with curious triangles juxtaposed in only one corner of each tile. The iridescent wall paper patterns, it was explained, were hand-painted in 1881 by the staff of Louis Comfort Tiffany's Associated Artist Company to mimic a much costlier mother of pearl motif adored by Mrs. Clemens on their foreign travels.

An enthralling, high Victorian bannister system, composed entirely in hand-carved wood, is supported at the onset by a dominating, wide-girthed, octagon-shaped newel base, elegantly adorned by a prodigious, multi-globed etched glass and brass lamppost that took center stage. A second and third newel base of lesser proportion at ascending intervals were capped by swirling, rope motif newel posts that extended to the ceiling, where they were embraced by ornamentally carved pilaster tops. The bannister proper, lower than the standard height for a staircase in our time, had a Gothic look akin to those commonly found in churches and rectories of the era.

The twisting staircase features exquisitely carved wainscoting panels, also custom-finished with hand-applied metallic paint, with the upper portion of the walls enrobed by matching, rich, burgundy and scarlet tones. A Turkish lamp hung in one corner, and a hand-carved, rope-patterned wooden support column stood alone in the center of the room. A doorway, with a decorative motif more likely found in a Rajasthani palace and tucked beneath the staircase, once concealed Hartford's first residential telephone booth. There was no stone of hand-crafted architectural detail left unturned. And this was just the foyer!

The grand foyer and staircase. Photo courtesy Library of Congress

This rivaled the work of other renowned architects and designers of the era such as Frank Furness, whose Victorian masterpieces, like the facade of the Pennsylvania Academy of Fine Arts and its exquisite interior grand staircase, are found throughout the Greater Philadelphia region where I live. I initially wondered if Furness might have been the architect, but the guide informed that credit belonged to Edward Tuckerman Potter. I was amazed to learn that this splendid, exceptional masterpiece of American architecture was almost razed in 1929. It had been spared due to efforts of several Hartford organizations backed by high profile fans such as President Woodrow Wilson, the tenor Enrico Caruso, and most notably Kathryn Seymour Day, the grand-niece of Twain's next-door neighbor, Harriet Beecher Stowe. It was Day who largely championed the cause for preservation and restoration of the home as it is seen today, along with the assistance of Twain's daughter Clara, who, then at age fifty-six, helped to raise funds with a performance and visit to the home for its dedication ceremony in 1930.[22]

The guide elaborated further on the level of involvement by the artisanal design firm headed by Louis Comfort Tiffany. In this one space, Tiffany had combined motifs found in Turkey, China, Morocco, Japan, India, and elsewhere, into one cohesive, elaborate magnum opus. The room was noticeably dark, with light from strategically placed gas lamps reflecting on the iridescent paint to create an added, shimmering ambiance at night. In daytime, sunlight illumined the paint design from an interior window set above a fireplace where one would normally find a chimney stack, here replaced by a cleverly designed split flue that ran along the window's left and right sides. The light came from the adjoining drawing room, which we entered next.

Less ornate, airy and more simply decorated than the foyer, this parlor, used for proper, Victorian era entertaining by Twain's wife Olivia, was brightened by two bays of windows. A much brighter, pink-toned wall paper with a more subdued hand-painted pattern lent a refreshing air. A baby grand piano sat in one corner, where Olivia, her girls and Mr. Twain would gather for an evening of song and recital. Daughters Susy and Clara, both aspiring opera singers, most certainly entertained here for guests. Members in our group noted the assorted conch shells intermixed with decorative statuary and knick-knacks on multiple surfaces. These had been a favorite collectible of the ladies of the house.

I inquired about the authenticity of the wall paper. The guide directed us to look behind one of the Taj Mahal motif doors where the only remaining segment of the original wallpaper is located, serving as the master guide to recreate the room as originally designed. She further explained that much of the home required extensive restoration because, after the Clemens family sold it, the next owners stripped it of many of the Tiffany fixtures and other original features.

By 1929, the home had been used as a private school, a warehouse, divided into apartments, and used as a public library. Our guide reiterated how lucky it was to be standing at all, again mentioning the real estate developer who had wanted to raze it and build a rental complex with the planned name of The Mark Twain Apartments. That rang true. While earlier driving to the parking lot entrance, I noticed the numerous "Clemens Apartments" buildings nearby. What a shameless rip off that was. I'm betting that Twain's daughter Clara prevented use of the copyrighted Mark Twain name for that purpose. Saved by the efforts of Ms. Day, the house was finally purchased with the intent of making it into a museum. The thought of such an amazing, priceless structure being carelessly razed is horrifying.

Through a doorway the drawing room adjoined an opulent dining room. One could easily imagine a casual evening of song around the piano with family or visiting guests while servants set the table behind the closed, sliding pocket doors. At the behest of butler George Griffin, Olivia would then invite everyone through the opened doorway to gather at the table for a sumptuous meal accentuated by home spun, wondrous tales delivered intimately by Mark Twain. A finely crafted white lace table cloth, set with fine china, glassware, and silverware that belonged to the Langdon family, served to brighten this cozy but darker room by reflecting the flicker of candles and the luminance from an overhead gas chandelier. An Asian room screen near a second door opposite concealed the curious George outside of the butler's pantry while he and other servants eavesdropped on Twain's fantastic yarns.

From there we passed through another oak trimmed doorway into the library. Described as the centerpiece of the home, it served as the more relaxed family room. Wooden bookcases with hand-carved ornate trim lined the perimeter of the room,

The Clemens' proper Victorian dining room. Photo courtesy Library of Congress

crowned with an elaborate fireplace featuring stone from India and topped with a hand-carved antique mahogany mantel spanning twelve feet in width, with a traditional family crest centrally featured.

Twain had discovered the hand-carved oak mantel while visiting Ayton Castle in Scotland with Olivia. They purchased it, had it dismantled, shipped, and reassembled here. When attempting to install it, they found the height of the piece in its totality exceeded that of the library's high ceiling. So, the top segment of carved cherubs was cut off and installed over the transom between the dining room and library. The carved mantel served as the backdrop for countless evenings when Twain charmed his daughters with clever stories, bore witness to intellectual chats with visiting friends and luminaries of the literary world, and hosted first draft readings of recently written manuscripts for which Olivia had served as editor throughout their life together. Twain was quite fond of this mantel. When the Hartford house was sold, it was one of the few architectural installations that was removed, stored, and later incorporated into the design of Twain's final home at Stormfield, in Redding, Connecticut.

After Twain's death, the Redding home became the property of his now married, sole-surviving daughter, Clara. She then sorted and sold many of Twain and family's personal possessions and furniture at auction, eventually putting the house up for sale in 1917. As mentioned earlier, Stormfield was finally sold in

1923. While under renovation that year by its new owners, Stormfield caught fire and burned to the ground, any remaining contents transformed to ash. Years after the home in Hartford had been painstakingly refurbished through exhaustive research and opened as a museum, some of the original artifacts sold decades before were gradually returned or graciously offered on loan by their new owners. This is the primary reason photography within the home is not permitted, as many of the home's contents are not owned by the museum foundation. The Ayton Castle mantel, sold with Stormfield, was presumed lost in the fire.

One day, Lawrence Banks of Redding, Connecticut was on a house tour just like mine. When the tour guide brought the guests into the library, they were told of cherished times spent with family as described above, and, while showing old photographs of the room, lamented the loss of the carved oak mantel that had once graced the room as its crowning focus. Studying the photos more closely, Mr. Banks chimed in matter-of-factly, something to the effect of: "I think that mantel is in my father's barn back in Redding."

The astonished tour guide inquired further, bringing it to the attention of the museum director, who shared the story with a museum trustee, who in turn made haste and travelled to Redding to investigate the claim. There, in the barn just as Banks had described, was the long-lost Ayton mantel, disassembled in pieces, but preserved intact from rot by an abundance of straw.[23] Banks further explained how his father had salvaged the mantel from Stormfield while the home was under renovation. Given that it's Mark Twain's house, I think he might have enjoyed this adventurous scenario.

As the guide spun tales of the room's various features, my mind drifted with thoughts of the time Twain must have spent in this very room, researching background material for his writing projects, or reading and critiquing the works of and with his contemporaries. It

The Ayton mantel at the Clemens home in Hartford. Photo courtesy Library of Congress

really touched me to see that Twain had selected to have a quote from Ralph Waldo Emerson inscribed in the brass hood over the fireplace. Among the New England Transcendentalists, Emerson has been a favorite of mine since being first introduced to his work at age fifteen, when a volume of Emerson's essays became one of my constant companions in high school. For this reason, I was pleasantly surprised to find his quote here, which read: "The ornament of a house is the friends who frequent it." It put a smile on my face to discover this previously unknown link between two of my favorite authors.

In a letter dated April 10, 1886, Twain confirms that the quote is indeed by Emerson, "grammar and all," and that the quote had been selected by his wife, Livy, "who has been an Emersonian devotee all her life."[24] Twain added:

> "I do not mean that the grammar is not correct, I merely mean that in one place it all at once arrests the flow of your serenity for a moment, like gravel in the bread."[25]

The quote is extracted from Emerson's essay *Domestic Life*. This one snippet of information is remarkably revealing about Livy's intellectual and aspirational character. It says a few things about the significant literary influence behind Livy's guiding editorial hand during her review of Twain's writing, as well as the personal import she and Twain must have placed on vicariously enjoying Emerson's company.

One of the most famous incidents of Twain's speaking career was the night in 1877 when he bombed – out-right choked - while attempting to humorously tease Emerson and other giants of Nineteenth Century literature. The ultimate who's who of New England enlightenment had assembled together like an English language super group for the 70th birthday celebration of Quaker poet and abolitionist John Greenleaf Whittier. In attendance with Emerson was Henry Wadsworth Longfellow, Oliver Wendell "Boston Brahmin" Holmes and about forty-seven other movers and shakers, with Twain hired to deliver the evening's entertainment.

In his Autobiography,[26] Twain recalled the absolute shame and embarrassment experienced while delivering what he perceived to have been a carefully and cleverly crafted speech that just flopped. Twain misjudged these "littery swells"[27] as a few more good ol' boys, but that wasn't the case. The response had been so chilling and, frankly, nonexistent, that Twain's good friend William Dean Howells had to escort him from the room. Twain explains:

> "the expression of interest in the faces turned to a sort of black frost. I wondered what the trouble was. I didn't know… I struggled along… but with a gradually perishing hope -- that somebody would laugh, or that

somebody would at least smile, but nobody did. I didn't know enough to give it up and sit down...so I went on with this awful performance...in front of a body of people who seemed turned to stone with horror...there is no milder way in which to describe the petrified condition and the ghastly expression of those people. When I sat down it was with a heart which had long ceased to beat. I shall never be as dead again...as miserable again as I was then...Howells, who was near me, tried to say a comforting word, but couldn't get beyond a gasp. There was no use -- he understood the whole size of the disaster..."[28]

Ah, to be a fly on the wall for that one. Twain esteemed those eminent thinkers and felt considerably crushed to have so miscalculated the expected response and fail before them. It took him two years to put it out of his mind. Twenty-eight years later Twain maintained that the speech was a good one.

I, of course, was aware of this speech from the scene in the 1944 Fredric March film. Regardless, the fact that Twain thereafter lived with an inscribed quote by Emerson reveals much about his reverence for the "deity," as Twain had referenced him.

As the Emerson quote suggested, the library was the primary spot where Twain entertained his guests, where holidays were celebrated, and serving as the epicenter of family life to just enjoy each other's company. At its far end was a sunlit, oval-shaped Victorian glass conservatory, where exotic flora and lush greenery grown by Olivia provided escape during the drearier months of long New England winters. A stone fountain and shallow pool adorned the center, later used to house a pet alligator by subsequent owners.

We were then led into 'the Mahogany room' on the first floor just off the foyer, with windows opening onto the porch. Used as a guest room, its name is derived from a grand, Mahogany-framed, canopied bed flanked by two narrower, Mahogany doorways on either side which led to a sitting lounge on one side, and on the other a bathroom complete with indoor running water, a tin tub trimmed with more Mahogany, and a simple, wooden-lidded chamber pot.

From there we returned to the foyer and ascended the grand staircase to the second level. At the top of the stairs to the immediate right was the entrance to a small sitting room, and to its right the bedroom of Twain's eldest daughter, Susy. It was heartwarming to see Susy's room. Following the infant death of his son, Langdon, Susy had grown to become Twain's favorite. Proud of her celebrity Dad, at age thirteen Susy had written a biography simply called "Papa" which Twain so cherished he had it published in 1888 with his own added commentary.

That effort endeared Susy to Twain's heart, becoming more so when, at age twenty-four, Susy passed away from spinal meningitis in 1896, perhaps in this very room. Susy's death proved to be an unbearable tragedy for the Clemenses. In a letter dated January, 1897, Twain described the family's condition as that of 'restless and unsettled derelicts', explaining further:

> "…we cannot look upon that house yet. Eighteen years of our daughter's life were spent in it; & by blessed fortune she was visiting in the town when she was taken ill, & so was privileged to die under the roof that had sheltered her youth, with none but familiar things before her fading eyes, & with the same servants to minister to her that had served her as a child. The house is hallowed now…"[29]

Twain learned of Susy's death while Olivia, Clara and he were in Europe. It had taken him years to get over the loss of their son Langdon, and he still felt responsible for the toll on his family from poor investments and subsequent bankruptcy. And now this. Their shared sadness was palpable. Olivia could not bear the thought of returning to Hartford. After a brief visit once while in town for a funeral, Twain refused to step into the house again. With heavy hearts, their loss of Susy compelled the Clemens family to sell the beloved home in 1903.

Opposite Susy's room, we entered the master bedroom of Twain and his wife, Livy, with its most imposing element being the magnificent bed. Acquired during a trip to Venice, Italy in 1883, it bore elaborately carved, Baroque style walnut head and footboards with cherubs that seemed to float independently. With twisted bedposts reminiscent of Bernini's columns in St. Peter's Basilica, the bed's intricately carved side panels give one the impression that the entire bed could float on air or sail on water.

As shown in numerous photos, Twain used the footboard for propping himself up with pillows while writing, smoking, or reading, preferring this so he could face the intricately, sculpted headboard and footboard to "appreciate what he had paid for." Twain's fondness for the bed is well documented, having once explained that for him it was "the most comfortable bedstead that ever was, with space enough in it for a family, and carved angels enough surmounting its twisted columns and its headboard and footboard to bring peace to the sleepers, and pleasant dreams."[30]

As the tour guide led the others in the group onward, I paused a little longer, contemplating the more solemn aspects of this juncture of our tour. First it was Susy's bedroom and the tragic twists her death had brought to the family, and

The fabulous, Italianate "most comfortable bedstead that ever was." Photo courtesy Library of Congress.

now the Baroque Walnut bed - the very bed in which Mark Twain had died.

After the death of his daughter Jean, Twain had traveled to Bermuda only to cut the trip short and return to Stormfield in January of 1910. His health was so poor that he had to be carried from the carriage to this bed, where he slowly declined until his passing in April, 1910. It was among Twain's most cherished possessions, and wherever the family moved, the bed went with them, ultimately finding its way to Stormfield, in Redding. It was retained by daughter Clara for another thirty years before donating it the Hartford house museum in 1940.

As I studied the Bernini like bedposts, I smiled slyly while imagining a giant-sized Mark Twain, attired in a long white, flannel night shirt, frivolously lying atop an over-scaled, colossal version of this bed atop the actual Bernini columns in St. Peter's basilica. He kind of looks like the stereotypical caricatures of God anyway. Twain himself once remarked on this, stating:

"More than once I have been humiliated by my resemblance to God the father; He is always longing for the love of His children and trying to get it on the cheapest and laziest terms He can invent."[31]

I took leave, noting a closed door next to the master bedroom where the master bath would have been, now replaced by a township-required fire escape. To its left is a charmingly appointed mother-in-law suite with a delicate, regal-looking, canopied bed used by Olivia's mother on occasional visits.

Down the corridor are the bedroom and playroom of youngest daughters, Clara and Jean. Our guide pointed out the animal motif used in the decor throughout the room, highlighting an 1877 'Lil' froggy goes a courtin'" wallpaper design created by Walter Crane. Little details like mentioning the artisan who designed the wallpaper reveal the impressive level of detailed research behind the restoration and ongoing conservation of this property. While on the topic of animal motif, our guide informed us of the numerous cats the Clemens family had, to whom Twain had given names like Famine, Pestilence, Sour mash, and Satan, with a kitten named Sin.

From the bedroom, we were then brought into 'the schoolroom.' Originally designed as Twain's study and office, it was instead used for play and privately tutored lessons given by a hired governess, as well as home schooling by Olivia. An upright piano on which young Clara learned to play marked the roots of her later profession as an internationally respected concert pianist and singer.

From there we were then led upstairs to the third floor. At the top of the landing was a small bedroom used by the Clemens' butler, George Griffin. Born into slavery, Griffin began to work for the Clemens family as a free man from the year they moved into the house in 1874. Remaining in their service for 17 years, George and Sam became close friends. After purchasing his own home in Hartford, George maintained this bedroom in the Clemens house.

Twain described George Griffin as

"handsome, well built, shrewd, wise, polite, always good-natured, cheerful to gaiety, honest, religious, a cautious truth-speaker, devoted friend to the family, champion of its interests.... He was the peace-maker in the kitchen—in fact THE peace-keeper, for by his good sense & right spirit & mollifying tongue he adjusted disputes in that quarter before they reached the quarrel-point."[32]

Some Twain scholars claim that George Griffin may have been one of Twain's inspirations for the Jim character in the *Adventures of Huckleberry Finn*. In fact, George Griffin is the "GG" to whom Huck Finn is dedicated. Curiously, in his essay *My Uncle's Farm*, Twain had written that the "Uncle Dan'l" of his youth was the basis for Jim. Not sure about the consensus.

Across the hall was "the pink room," so-called because of its décor. Alternately called the "artist's friends" room, many had crashed there after being entertained for hours by Twain in the next room we were to visit.

Through a set of double doors at the far end of the floor we were led into the piece de resistance of the whole house - the billiard room. This was the holy of holies, the obscure sanctuary, the master's chamber. This...this was the sole reason I drove to Hartford, to stand in this specific room.

Being here was the culmination of this writer's dream, for it was my understanding - at the time - that in this very room Twain crafted his best-known, best-selling literary masterpieces - *The Adventures of Tom Sawyer, Adventures of Huckleberry Finn, The Gilded Age, The Prince and the Pauper, Life on the Mississippi, A Tramp Abroad,* and *A Connecticut Yankee in King Arthur's Court.* I was excited, thoughtless, breathless, knowing I stood now on sacred ground. I wanted to just be a sponge and absorb the Shakti, the Chi, the conscious, living energy force, the creative mojo of Twain which emanated from every cell of fabric and wood and paper that now surrounded me. Awestruck, I surveyed every nuance; the letters, notes and other artifacts strewn across the green felt of the billiard table; the billiard sticks mounted on the wall, undoubtedly used by Twain while composing with a cigar gripped in his teeth; a bookshelf lined with inspirational publications; glass doors leading to the open-aired, hexagon shaped portico I saw from outside; and Twain's small, informal desk with inkstand and quill, reminiscent of the modest clerk's desk back in Judge Clemens' office in Hannibal. I felt like a Catholic altar boy, standing with sanctioned privilege in the arresting, sacred sanctuary of my boyhood church. I couldn't be here long enough to savor every moment.

It was in this room that a mature Sam Clemens, a young man who had piloted a river boat on the Mississippi, who had traversed the expanse of pioneer America, who had camped rustically and panned for gold in the heart of the West coast gold rush, who created for himself one of the most storied, adventurous lives, had reflected on his youth and his journey with all the wisdom of his experience and recorded it with flair and humor for posterity.

I looked across the room at the small table strewn with handwritten notes, offering an insight into Twain's working habits. I noted the partitioned cubbyhole cabinet along the back wall, where Twain would store incomplete manuscripts while working on another. And then I studied the billiard table proper. Though a few sheets of notepaper spread on the felt might serve to suggest that Twain was a busy guy, I was aware of his fondness for billiards, and it wasn't just about the sport.

Sure, he enjoyed the game while squaring off against friends in a good-natured competition, but then there were those times of solitary reflection, when it was just Twain, a pool stick, a cue ball, and the aim at a side pocket. Billiards had been one of Twain's secrets. It was his focus on the game that held his mind attentive, effectively distracting it from interfering with the creative process. He played billiards for the same reason a Buddhist monk might spin a prayer wheel, or a Hindu might practice Ajapa japa as a technique to still the mind and open themselves to experiencing divine kinship. I assert that Twain had learned this skill early in his life when he was still a cub pilot on a Mississippi River Steamboat. The focus required to correctly navigate the Mississippi certainly trained young Sam Clemens' mind to focus on the task at hand. That was his dharma, his duty, in that moment, and it would enable him to simultaneously posit imaginative thoughts independent of the required attentiveness for the task. We all have this experience. It's one thing to recognize it, but it's another thing to use it. That's what I knew about the billiard room. In my painting studio, I use similar 'distractions' to stoke the creative flames of visual expression. Even the practice of just mixing paint and the process of painting serves in the same way. For writing, I get most of my ideas while walking my dogs or driving my car. It always seems that when one's attention is focused on some lesser important, laid back activity, that's when freedom of spirit prevails. Billiards would qualify as such an activity.

This room, the uppermost, elusive segment of the Hartford House, inaccessible to outsiders unless invited, was like the equivalent of a holy shrine. The same experience could be had by a Hemingway fan when brushing away a feral cat while visiting his home in Key West, or while walking the streets of Dublin and thinking of James Joyce, or sitting in Stratford-on-Avon and watching a Shakespearean play. The life-force of an individual employed in the creative process, where he or she performed alchemy, can still be felt and experienced in a place like this. When I visited the studios of N. C. Wyeth in Brandywine, PA, and Paul Cezanne in Aix en Provence, I've felt this. It's palpable - you can touch it, like a mystic air that you just want to inhale with a straw and make sure it is coursing through your own blood when you take leave.

That's what this billiard room meant for me. As the tour guide invited our group to move along, I lingered, allowing the others to leave the room ahead of me. With only one brief, final, moment alone, I scoured the room with my eyes madly, making sure I hadn't overlooked a single thing. I took a deep breath during my final glance, and murmured in respectful benediction: "Thank you, Mr. Twain. Thank you," believing his spirit had enveloped the atmosphere right then and there.

Our guide then maneuvered us down the obscured rear fire escape steps that led to the kitchen, through a staircase door that had once contained the first private, in-home phone booth in Hartford, across the foyer and onto the front porch, and there we ended our tour. As our group dispersed, I continued to study every nuance of

The sanctum sanctorum - The billiard room in Twain's Hartford Home. Photo courtesy Library of Congress.

the detailed surroundings. Walking further out onto the lawn to get a full view of the home's exterior, I noted the extended, dual chimney stacks from the divided flue inside, reminding me of a description I'd read that the home resembled a Mississippi River Steamboat.

As I strolled the grounds, I thought of Dad and how much he would have liked this. I found it interesting on that day in Hartford that the association of Mark Twain, my father, and I had already completed its cycle on the Hannibal trip. I recognized that the Hannibal trip had allowed me to close that lingering chapter of ill feeling originating from the Tom Sawyer coloring contest ticket fiasco of thirty-five years prior. This trip to Hartford had been about recognizing the story of a man who reflected with fondness on his youth. Hannibal was about a boy growing up along a river, dreaming about becoming a man. Hartford was about the man looking back at the nucleus of that dream. The Hannibal trip had been about completing something for my Dad, while this trip had been to complete something within myself. However, I would soon learn that my journey was far from over.

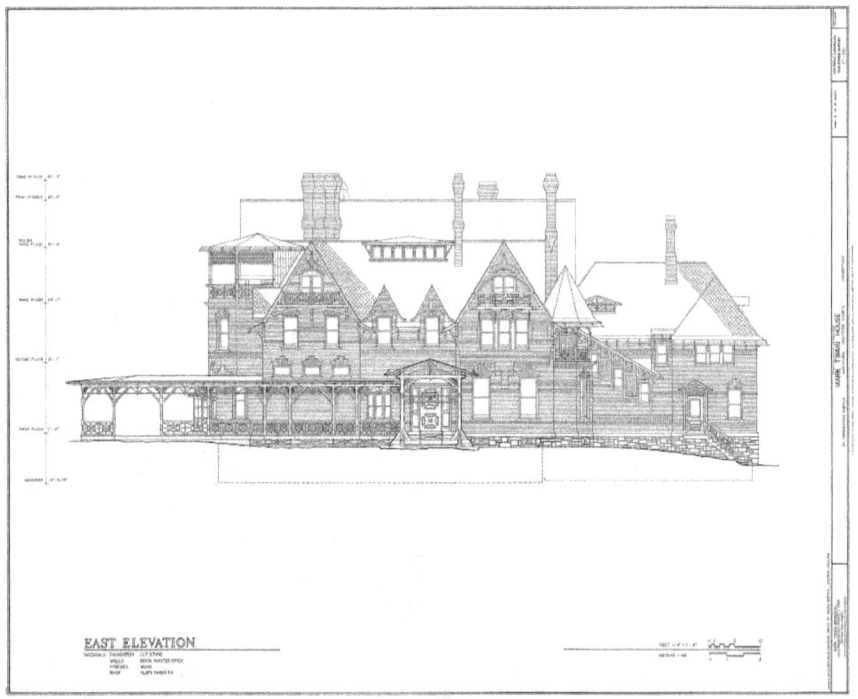

Edward Tuckerman Potter's original 1871 architectural design for the Clemens' home at Nook Farm in Hartford, CT. Photo courtesy Library of Congress.

The Elephant on the Raft · 73

The Clemens family on their porch in Hartford, 1885. Below: Post card from Olivia Clemens in happier times at the Hartford home. Courtesy New York Public Library Digital Archive.

An 1888 Stereograph of the Mark Twain home in Hartford, a favored stop for tourists even in Twain's lifetime. Photo courtesy New York Public Library Digital Archive.

5

HAL HOLBROOK &
THE ROUGHING IT STRATEGY

"It liberates the vandal to travel - you never saw a bigoted, opinionated, stubborn, narrow-minded, self-conceited, almighty mean man in your life but he had stuck in one place since he was born."

Mark Twain

My repeated Google searches for Mark Twain info had established a programmed algorithm, evidenced by the sheer quantity of Twain-themed ads and links appearing of their own volition in my daily news feed. For the most part I routinely ignored them. I was about to scroll past another such ad on my phone when one caught my eye. It was an announcement that Hal Holbrook would be performing his one man play *Mark Twain Tonight* in Philadelphia for one night only. Hal Holbrook as Mark Twain? In my town? Without hesitation, I clicked on the link to learn the details, scoured the seating chart, noted that the performance was about to sell out, and ordered a ticket.

My visit to Holbrook Hall in Hartford had reawakened a dormant appreciation for the actor, who had performed as Twain as long as I could recall. I was aware of the notoriety he'd attained from this role, but not its full extent until I arrived at the theater that evening. While browsing through the Playbill notes before the performance began, Holbrook, I learned, had been performing his portrayal of Mark Twain since 1954. 1954! For sixty-four years, spanning the last half of the Twentieth Century and approaching the first quarter of the Twenty-First, this man was single-handedly responsible for bringing Twain to life for several generations. Playbill also noted his celebrated, first television broadcast performance in 1967, a revelation which jarred me. I had forgotten a vague memory of watching that original broadcast, recalled it being a much-discussed topic at the time, and Dad tuning it in while assembling us all to watch it together as a family.

The Elephant on the Raft · 75

> MAR 12 1967
> **The Twains Shall Meet**
> Hal Holbrook, left, recreates an interesting characterization when he plays Mark Twain at age 70 in a one-man 90-minute special "Mark Twain Tonight," Sunday afternoon at 5:30 on Channel 7.

Press library clipping referencing the 1967 televised broadcast of Mark Twain Tonight.

    The Holbrook television performance was all the buzz at that time, having been advertised as a national event. It was promoted as a family-oriented program and national educational opportunity that could be utilized by teachers across the United States. Given the era, in the midst of civil rights and racial segregation conflicts, Mr. Paley at CBS undoubtedly saw an opportunity for the compassionate wisdom - and humor - of Mr. Twain's words to offer some measure of healing to a nation weary from its own internal strife (and earn some bonus advertising revenue, of course).

    America in the mid 1960s was enduring the growing pains of coming to terms with its identity. Just several years prior, JFK had been assassinated and with him went the secure notion of what had defined America since WWII. On the heels of JFK's death, the Beatles arrival a few months afterward heralded a new day, albeit a resurgence of all things British as well. After the Beatles appearance on The *Ed Sullivan Show*, other British acts soon followed. Parodies of the British Invasion found their way into every popular sitcom and variety show. Any Hollywood film production with a British reference, even badly made films, were overnight crowd pleasers. Every show, on TV or radio, couldn't regurgitate enough British influenced content. An America engaged in a new search for its identity needed to counter this British cultural invasion with an injection of its strongest American-made ammo. What better than Mark Twain?

    I did find it fascinating, as I read the *Playbill* notes, that I was likely discovering the very root of my own father's renewed enthusiasm for the writings of Mark Twain. It had to have been that Hal Holbrook performance of 1967. Surely, I rationalized, that as CBS conquered the television ratings with this broadcast, other networks equally sought to capitalize on the occasion. And what better way to do that than to offer their own Mark Twain related programming by airing a rebroadcast of 1944's *The Adventures of Mark Twain*?

    There it was. I'm sure my initial curiosity with Mark Twain at seven years old spurred me to ask Dad about Twain, and he was only too happy to relay his lifelong fascination with the author, tutoring me through the related movies he'd seen in his youth. Without question, my observation of his enthusiasm on seeing the TV Guide listing for the 1944 film must have ignited a feverish interest in my yearning young cranium to absorb all that I could. That's got to be how it all began.

So here I was now, sitting in a theater fifty years after that televised broadcast, awaiting the same man to appear on stage and deliver the same performance in person before my very eyes. The stage was sparsely decorated: one chair, a small desk topped with a few books, a small pitcher of water, a glass, a cigar and lighter, all set on a simple, aged oriental carpet. To the right was a Victorian style wooden lecture podium, topped with a copious stack of notes. The audience murmured and milled, until the house lights began to dim. From the vantage of my front row balcony seat I looked down at the sea of cell phone lights power off one by one, as those standing took their seats, and a hush came over the room.

After a few moments of near-deafening quiet, from behind the left curtain Hal Holbrook emerged, walking slowly in halting, measured steps onto the illumined carpet. The audience exploded with applause, rising to its feet in sheer, unconstrained adulation for this lion of American theater. Shouts of "Bravo" filled the cavernous hall as Holbrook waved - in character - with acknowledgment. The applause was sustained for an extended length of time. Holbrook could have exited the stage at that moment and I'll bet most may not have minded. Just seeing him dressed and mustachioed as Twain was enough. Here was the man who had become synonymous with Twain, interchangeable with Twain, who's performance as the author is estimated to have been seen by thirty-million people worldwide in nearly three-thousand appearances spanning sixty years. At ninety-one years of age, Holbrook was older than Twain had lived by fifteen years, and had organically transformed into the aged author to the extent that they were almost indistinguishable.

The reticent, mild shrill of Holbrook's style of intonation leaves one with the distinct impression that one is hearing the exact cadence of Twain himself. It's Holbrook's variegated yet restrained inflection during the delivery that breathes life into Twain's words. Holbrook begins the show, set in 1905, by talking about "The President" and American politics in general. From the onset, it was evident that much of Mark Twain's commentary yet remains as relevant today as it was in his time. Though Twain is known to have been openly critical of Theodore Roosevelt during his presidency, one got the distinct impression that Holbrook's delivery was targeting the current state of affairs in American politics. And that was precisely the point of this performance, that commentary uttered by Twain over one-hundred years ago still rings true today, just as it had in every decade before.

1976 press photo of Hal Holbrook as Mark Twain in Mark Twain Tonight.

From his first performance in 1956, Holbrook understood the timelessness of Twain's perspective on the innate humanness of our species. Old habits resurface with each generation, and what was true in 1905, 1956, or 1967 was still spot on in 2017. Mark Twain had an uncanny, organic ability to penetrate every single veil of human pretense on virtually every topic in the span of social behavior. Whether it be politics, domestic affairs, youth and old age, travel, religion, or racial discrimination, the commentary of Mark Twain was honest and direct, unconcerned with vindictive retaliation.

Holbrook delivered Twain's quotes like a concert of greatest hits. Many are familiar, yet audiences remain delighted to hear them uttered anew, cheering in acknowledgement. For example, on religious views, Holbrook quotes Twain as saying: "I don't like to commit myself about heaven and hell. You see, I have friends in both places" or "Go to Heaven for the climate, Hell for the company." On patriotic sentiment - "Patriotism is supporting our country all the time, and your government when it deserves it." On journalism - "Get your facts first, then you can distort them as you please."

But then there were those more biting quotes that weren't necessarily a greatest hits selection. Instead, they enabled a contemporary audience the opportunity to experience a Twain speaking engagement as had audiences in his time, offering a silent awakening of clarity that could compound a personal or collective viewpoint. This was the power of Holbrook's ingeniously composed performance, and such was the case with this quote, for example, which had the effect of forcing the audience to slightly squirm in their seats:

> "These lobbyists are called our invisible government in Washington with headquarters on Wall Street where they understand the virtues of addition, division, and silence. The rich corporations have to be shielded and protected in the Congress and this requires vast sums of money to keep their political party in power."

We hear remarks like this on contemporary news programs all the time. But somehow, the association of it as a quote of Mark Twain's compels one's ears to perk with attention. Unlike other literary and philosophical sages of his era, Twain's down-home manner of communicating in layman's terms allowed the least educated among us to grasp weighty topics in a practical and approachable manner. The average Joe could feel comfortable articulating in his or her own humble way in any manner of social settings. And this was part of that distinctly American character that Sam Clemens as Mark Twain embodied and represented so well in his travels abroad, in the company of crowned heads of Europe, scholars at Oxford, as well as the servants and workmen in his family's employ. Twain was the living essence of egalitarianism. All were equal, and it pained his heart throughout his later life to have witnessed the tragic imbalance of racial discrimination. To that end, Hal Holbrook addressed this very agenda superlatively when reciting passages from the *Adventures of Huckleberry Finn*.

From Twain's perspective, the character of Huck Finn represented the only truly honest person in his community. Through Huck Finn's eyes, readers can see the foibles of human nature. Huck is perpetually happy, thinking, talking and reasoning with common sense in even the most terrible of situations. Such is his relationship with his river raft companion Jim, the runaway slave for whom Huck struggles through the complex quandary and adult responsibility of deciding the fate of Jim's freedom. In Nineteenth Century America, Huck was presented as everyman, and his candor still rings true today.

We identify with Huck, we enjoy him, we admire him. When a generation of civic minded leaders forbid the reading of the book and have it banned from libraries and schools, our inherent, rebellious nature -just like Huck's- cajoles us to seek him out and enjoy him even more. Mark Twain wrote what we thought in a way that made us jealous of not having voiced it first. Deep in our psyche, it is still Twain whom we all aspire to be. Twain is the quintessential American. As the quote by Holbrook displayed in the Hartford hall named for him says: "I found in Mark Twain the clear path to the soul of America." He embodies our national identity like few others in our brief American history. Because of Twain, we can know who we are, and who we are not. In times of social division, Holbrook has reminded us that just turning to the writings of Twain can reawaken a compassionate, balanced, and honest understanding.

In Ken Burns' documentary on Twain, Holbrook hones in on a very important and redolent quote. He explained that once during Twain's travels, when asked if he was American, the author replied "I'm not AN American, I am

THE American." I found this very revealing. It was as if Twain was fully self-aware of what he had become. His self-understanding in this way was not unlike that of an avatar in the Hindu tradition. The definition of an avatar in this context states one as being "a manifestation of a deity or released soul in bodily form on earth; an incarnate divine teacher." The root of the word from Sanskrit references one who has 'crossed down' from heaven, one who has descended. I thought this interesting considering how Twain had once regarded Emerson and Longfellow as "deities," not realizing that he, himself, would eventually become an American deity who surpassed all of their combined greatness in the only way that had relative importance in the new republic - that of being embraced as the voice of everyman. Maybe those who had once been deemed "deity" could only embody and represent a prevailing level of perception and communal soul development to a limited extent, and a next 'avatar' would be the one who could elevate and guide a community to its next level of evolution. That's what Mark Twain is about. Chew on that for a while. Or, more aptly said in a Twainian context - put that in your Missouri Meerschaum and smoke it.

Unlike other world traditions, America doesn't really embrace a culture of 'saints' in the traditional manner or understanding. We erect monuments to selectively sanctioned civic heroes who've contributed to a betterment or uplifting of our society. Some are well known in this regard - Benjamin Franklin, Abraham Lincoln, Susan B. Anthony, Franklin D. Roosevelt, Martin Luther King. We visit their memorials with pause and reflection, hoping to take leave with some spark of that essence that made them stand apart. As far back as archeology has revealed, we have entombed the great ones with exceptional reverence and relative religious protocol. In Italy and Israel, in Medina and Mumbai, in cities throughout the old world, the tombs of those deemed saints for their ability to heal with wisdom, to enlighten with candor, are respected and worshipped. Prayers are offered to the memory of their soul in the presence of their mortal remains, with the hope that the aspirant can thereafter live in a manner worthy of their approval. They ask for blessings. They seek inspiration.

I had travelled to Mark Twain's boyhood home in Hannibal with a similar mindset. I left there having rediscovered a lost connection with my father. I visited the home in Hartford for my own desire to connect with Twain the writer at the billiard room font of his inspiration. I attended the Hal Holbrook performance to hear afresh the spoken recitation of Twain's profound, embraceable wisdom. Mark Twain had given me much. I left Holbrook's performance with a revelation, it had been Twain's own life of varied experiences compiled in his book *Roughing It* that had inspired me as young man to "rough it" myself.

I had then viewed Mark Twain's *Roughing It* as a Nineteenth Century version of Kerouac's *On the Road*. Both books are ultimately about the discovery of independent identity. *Roughing It* might alternately be named 'Zen and the art of Pioneer Maverickism' - the journal of the new American species - engaged in what only can be viewed as the equivalent of an Aboriginal Walkabout. *Roughing It*, as well as *Life on the Mississippi* and similar travelogues of the younger Samuel Clemens, became vitally important guides for curious and confused young folks of the era, right along with similar works by other authors sharing their process of self-discovery, such as Whitman's *Leaves of Grass* or Thoreau's *On Walden Pond*. Twain's works are publicly embraced to a larger extent because they glorify adventurousness in an accessible way void of platitudinous tone: the path to discovering self can be fun!

On Christmas of 1982, I had given my Dad a copy of Mark Twain's *Roughing It* as a gift. I had hoped the book would communicate to my Dad some of my aspirational attitudes where previous attempts with words had failed me. In short, with my Art School graduation a few months away, I was trying to tell Dad of my plan to leave home and move out of state. My parents were still trying to guide me with what they viewed as helpful suggestions for my career path. I knew they meant well, but it just fueled confusion for me and fraught discussions between us. When I voiced my dreams of traveling and other pursuits, it was often negated with a sermon on working class practicality. I understood that, having grown up with that voice talking just over my shoulder. But I just wasn't ready to settle. I wanted adventure. I had difficulty explaining this to my parents, but mostly to Dad, which perplexed me as it had been Dad's own affinity for travel, shared in tales of his wartime adventures in the South Pacific, in Yokohama, Japan, in Hawaii, Seattle, and elsewhere, that served as my seminal inspiration.

Though I had concentrated my academic career on studio art and art history, I was already interested in exploring other things. I remained open to checking out unexpected opportunities with plans to milk as much as possible out of this life I'd been given. As a way of trying to relay these intentions, I bought Dad the copy of Twain's *Roughing It* so he might get the hint, and aid in fostering a more receptive view due to his fondness for Twain. If Dad never read more than the first page of the book, that would be enough to relay my message. On the opening page of Chapter One, Twain wrote:

"I was young and ignorant, and I envied my brother. I coveted…the long, strange journey he was going to make, and the curious new world

The copy of Roughing It given to my Dad on Christmas, 1982.

he was going to explore. He was going to travel! I never had been away from home, and that word "travel" had a seductive charm for me."33

Our house had produced a similar predicament: all three of my older brothers had left home and ventured to exotic places years before. My oldest brother Jack had moved to South Bend, Indiana. My brother Mike had travelled the world as a Merchant Marine, then settled in Houston, Texas. My brother James had travelled to Boulder, Portland, and Houston where he met his bride-to-be and settled in her hometown of Chicago. From my naive vantage, all three of my brothers had lived these extraordinary, adventurous lives. I hadn't ventured much further than my cousin's house in Northeast Philly - which was kind of a huge deal for an inner-city dweller like me. Before I was ten years old, staying with my cousins had been like a retreat to Walden Pond. They had a tree! They had a lawn! They had a patio! They had - a dishwasher!!!

This contrasted sharply to splashing around in the makeshift stream running along the curb from an illegally opened fire hydrant. A couple of our neighbors had a tree in their back yard that we could see over the fence, and seeing a tree on periodic jaunts to the playground was like visiting a museum display. Otherwise, our street had no trees until 1971 or 72. The only grass grew between crevices in the sidewalk, and wildlife consisted of pigeons, rats, and feral alley cats, viewing cockroach colonies with a flashlight through manhole cover air vents or hunting for grasshoppers and caterpillars in weed choked alleyways.

My Aunt Florence and Uncle Paul in Clifton Heights had Peach and Mimosa trees in their backyard. This was a miraculous, awe-inspiring thing. Visiting them was like a trip to Florida. Clifton Heights alone was Xanadu, a fast-food wonderland where we took free-spirited Sunday drives with our dog Barney to the then new McDonald's restaurant, and our post-theater stops at Dunkin' Donuts. Going on vacation to the Jersey Shore? Fuggedaboutit! That was another world! This was the extent of my exotic adventures as a kid. So, like Mark Twain voiced in the beginning of Roughin' It, I was kind of envious of my brother's travels beyond Clifton Heights.

The objective behind giving my Dad the book was my plan on moving to California to study animation at Cal Arts. In 1978, animation wasn't quite on my parent's radar for me. Dad and Mom both thought I was delusional to think I could make a living in an animation career. I explained to Dad that it would be a door into the entertainment business, and animation was an emerging field.

"It's Hollywood, Dad! Hollywood!" I would argue. "You yourself said you wished you had always gone there after the War when you got off your ship in Seattle. Cal Arts is run by Disney, Dad! It's a feeder school to the industry!"

Dad wasn't buying it.

"Tommy, there's no future in animation. Computers are where you want to be! That's the future. I can get you into a training program right now."

Dad had been a career IBM computer programmer and operator since the early 1960s. He had been trained to operate an IBM 7090 series, followed by the System 360 in 1964, and then the System 370 around 1970. It was a big deal for Dad when he was promoted and sent to Chicago in 1970 on an all-expense paid training trip - a first for him and in our family - to learn the latest details of the IBM System 370. It was the furthest he'd travelled since the end of WWII. I remember that time because Dad let his sideburns grow longer, a fashionable thing for Forty-something guys seeking to retain their youth. It was something of a cultural, men's fashion hybrid between the long haired, Beatle-fueled youth movement and the hardline establishment. On his return, Dad assumed a supervisory position as shift manager overseeing the computer payroll tabulations for all Philadelphia municipal employees.

Dad used to bring my brothers and I to his workplace around the holidays to watch the Mummer & Thanksgiving Day parades from his office window in the Municipal Services Building on the North side of City Hall, which overlooked the established parade routes at the time. It was exciting in those days to visit a modern, futuristic, science-fiction type place filled with row after row of towering computer terminals. This was the advent of the computer age and I beamed with pride to be the son of a Dad who worked on the starship Enterprise.

Yet, Dad's workplace had an even greater technological marvel - vending machines! A sugar-laced wonderland filled with mechanically protruding coiled arms that held forth successive rows of *Zagnuts*,

A futuristic, starship-like IBM 7090 series computer office circa 1967 much like the one in which my Dad worked.

Clarke Bars and *Baby Ruth* and *Zero Bars, Fifth Avenues* and bags of potato chips, pretzels and *Dipsy Doodles,* cans of delicious Frank's *Black Cherry Wishniak* or *Cream Soda, Coca Cola,* and instant hot chocolate made by a machine!

Sugar-coated food that could magically drop before me within a robotic automaton was just the best! Mind-blowing! I ate so much sugar and junk in those days that I'd grown boy-boobs and an ass the size of a basketball by the time I was nine. I became a bit of a porker then, a "husky boy" as defined by Goldstein's on Passyunk Ave. and Krass Brothers on South St. - our South Philadelphia haberdashers of choice. My body was a continuous, curved contour line that began below the cowlick on my forehead and continued uninterrupted to my crotch. No neck or chin demarcation. Think of Alfred Hitchcock's TV show graphic profile. Forget the ass side of my body. Stuffing my ass into swimming trunks was an incomprehensible feat, like stuffing two Butterball Turkeys into a sock! My stomach hung over the front waist band of my swim trunks like a pregnant Wallaby.

My routine diet was relatively healthy then, consisting of whatever nutritious stuff my Mom made. But sugar was my crack. It was pure addiction. My skid row was the 'plus' sized sections of the clothing stores. Being fat at the onset of puberty was a joyous but conflicting hell. On the one hand completely delightful in the absolute bliss experienced during consumption of sugar-coated sugar products, yet countered by the antithetical depression arising from being the subject of persistent teasing and bullying. In fact, so addicted to junk food was I, that, each year when Dad brought up the subject of watching the parade from his office, my inner response was "To hell with the parade…take me to THE VENDING MACHINES!!"

The vending room was also the quietest room in Dad's workplace. That computer room was one of the consistently noisiest places I'd ever experienced. Dad had been encouraging me - all my brothers and I - to pursue a career in the computer field from the earliest age. Like my Mom, he had his own connections and could also help me get my foot in the door. But I had seen the toll taken on Dad's health from decades of working shift work in the perpetual cacophony generated by those large, room-sized, early computers. One couldn't converse at a normal decibel. Everything was communicated by shouting. When Dad would consistently remind me that computers were the wave of the future, I only saw visions of those visits to his workplace and the resulting ill-health and stress he experienced. Nuh-uh. Not for me. Not listening to Dad then and his advice for a computer career may have been one of the biggest errors of my life, but at what price? Because of this, I was blindsided and didn't see the future of computers that he knew was on its way. He had used the first IBM Selectronic typewriters - the forerunner of the word processor that would come to dominate word tabulation, and forerunner of the very device I am using to type this memoir. He also toyed around with the earliest commercial personal computers offered to the public. It is curious here to note the comparable affiliation of Dad's life affected by the early IBM computers and Twain's obsession with the Paige Compositor and the very first typewriters. Computers devastated the well-being of both Mark Twain and my father - another thing in common they share.

And so, as I rejected a future with computers, Mom and Dad never quite accepted my earliest college decisions. I was never sure why, except that I think Mom and Dad didn't want me to move too far from home because I was the only one left, my brothers having already moved on and married. Maybe, psychologically, they understood that my exit meant the twilight of their parental life. I know now that postpartum, empty nest feeling when your child leaves home. When my daughter left to attend college in Pittsburgh it left a palpable void in our home. Perhaps this is why I am now able to look back with such a measure of compassion for my parents.

Roughing It could relay my ambition to explore my life perfectly, I thought. Young Sam Clemens had explored so many different gigs and had so many anecdotal experiences that his decisions offered an appealing, romanticized way of growing into adulthood. And then there was that parallel in the lives of Twain and Dad that was the catalyst for both of their varied career paths: how both left school at an early age after their fathers died to work and bring money into the household.

At assorted points in his career, Twain had been: a printer's apprentice and typesetter, a riverboat assistant cub pilot in pursuit of his initial ambition of becoming a riverboat pilot - a goal he ultimately achieved; a gold and silver prospector, and eventually news correspondent. That led to a variety of writing and editing positions in the world of journalism.

The timing of my Roughing It strategy was predicated by an offered opportunity for me to travel to Santa Monica, California and work as a baker. I had been doing that between semesters in the Catskill Mountain foothills and became quite proficient at it. I enjoyed it immensely and did think of baking as a new-found career option at that time. I was completing a four-year stint of Fine Art study and saw the window as a way for me to pursue my ambition for an advanced degree at Cal Arts. The timing felt right, as I had given Dad the copy of *Roughing It* just a few months prior. This time, as sad as he was to see me go, Dad then understood my itching wanderlust, and gave me his blessing.

That trip in September of 1983 across the United States to Santa Monica was my burning travel dream come true. A small group of friends and I took a route west from upstate New York to just south of Chicago, before dipping southwest through Monument Valley and the Grand Canyon, then on to Hoover Dam and Four Corners in the Southwest. The places we visited were like a drive through history, and only previously seen on TV. I recall carousing in an ice-cold Rocky Mountain stream in only a pair of tangerine colored underpants, with my blinding-white Caucasian Irish skin competing with the snowcapped mountains around us, and my melon-sized ass void of melatonin the cause of considerable fright for deer and other wildlife, as well as my travel companions.

Another highlight was the discovery of the Great Sand Dunes National Monument. We spent some extended time there just climbing and rolling down the expanse of dunes at the foot of the Rocky Mountains. The latent geologist (an earlier career ambition!) in me was mesmerized by the distinct smell of oceanic beach! It served as empirical proof that the Great Plains had once been a vast, primordial ocean, and I wondered if perhaps Great Salt Lake in Utah was the last remnant of that.

At some point on that adventure, I recalled Mark Twain's *Roughing It* description of his similar stagecoach trip to Nevada. Our caravan, literally a 1980 Chevy Caravan, contained at least 6 to 8 of us that I can recall. Like Twain's coach, the quantity of luggage we could take along was limited due to weight and the quantity of passengers. One memorable experience from that trip was waking in the middle of the night after sleeping in the back seat of the van with my head propped against the window. My first, dreamy vision was of passing buttes illumined by our headlights. It was the only semblance of a landscape in the vicinity. When I looked up, surrounding those and all around was an endless sea of stars. I had only witnessed such an abundance once in my life before then. Seeing buttes and stars after waking from a deep sleep gave me the impression I had arrived on an interplanetary landscape. I suspect we had been passing through Monument Valley, but I haven't been back since to confirm that. I recall contemplating how ancient Native Americans had witnessed this for ten thousand years and incorporated the experienced wonder into their cultural and spiritual life. I felt I had travelled back in time, reveling in what seemed to be a timeless moment.

Our stop at the Grand Canyon remains one of the most enthralling moments of my life. One can't adequately describe it in words. Ya just gotta go. From there we spent a fun evening in Las Vegas, my first time there. When I finally made a return visit there thirty-three years later for business and my clients Bill and Danielle took me to Fremont Street, I realized that's where I had been in 1983 when it was still uncanopied and filled with low riders and abundant traffic, and was all that existed of the town. I couldn't believe the same place had since become a museum of itself.

Once we arrived in Santa Monica, I resumed my baking position and felt right at home. There I lived in a yoga/meditation center with cool, conscious, positive people, and the 4:00 am to noon shift of my baking gig was perfect. Every day after lunch I walked two blocks to Palisades Park, then down a substantial flight of steps along the bluffs to the beach, and spent my afternoons basking in the sun along the Pacific Ocean. Could it get any better than this? I felt unbelievably blessed. At the time, I recall being aware that I'd finally made it to the ocean where Dad had spent his navel career during WWII, an experience I wouldn't recapture for another 37 years. That story comes later.

I lived this delightful existence for a short while until taking on a second job as a display artist in a mall department store. I began to save money with the intention of getting my own apartment and kick my life into gear. But within a year, Dad had suffered a major heart attack and needed extensive bypass surgery. My Mom asked me to move back home, but I explained that I had already committed myself to my jobs, plans, and career path. Then, one day, Dad got on the phone.

With a frail voice, he meekly asked if I would come home to help. "Your mother is driving me crazy," he half-joked. I knew him well enough, though, to know he was desperate and feeling a bit isolated. He explained that he would now need to retire earlier from his job than planned. I understood. Dad just needed a friend, another guy to buffer the heightened anxiety that often envelopes family health emergencies. My parents had done much for me. How could I say no to Dad's heartfelt request? At least Dad was able to ask for help over the telephone. He hadn't been as lucky when his own father passed away, and at a much younger age than my Dad.

So, I gave notice to my employers, spent a last day on the beach, booked my one-way ticket, packed my bags and headed to Philly. Once settling back at home, I secured employment at a popular Philly bistro known for its baking. Within a year, my experience helped our baked goods win the coveted Best of Philadelphia designation from *Philadelphia Magazine.*

As Dad's health gradually improved, I expanded from there and began working on weekends for the bistro's upscale catering operation. I quickly moved up the ranks to become one of the head servers, and was regularly assigned to the head table for a variety of celebrity and VIP events. One highlight was serving the table of US Speaker of the House Tip O'Neill and local dignitaries at a high-profile function at Philadelphia's Memorial Hall. I was instructed to refrain from serving when O'Neill rose to deliver his scheduled speech. When that commenced, I went outside through the back door and down the steps to the driveway to have a cigarette. After some time had passed, Mr. O'Neill emerged from the same door and began to briskly descend the steps in my direction. I remained where I was, casually exhaling gentle billows of smoke. Tip hadn't noticed me at first, and was mildly startled to see me when we were about ten feet apart. I noted the momentary fear in his eyes. Who was I? What was I doing there? Did I have a gun? I suppose I could have looked like a Hollywood casting call political assassin. In my waist length black waiter's tuxedo, with a crop of long, mullet-cut auburn hair and mustache, my coworkers used to say I then resembled Wild Bill Hickok. Two secret service agents who were trailing behind him suddenly stepped forward. Tip's uncertain eyes never left my gaze, and I could clearly see him flourishing the strong, Irish bravado I knew so well from the neighborhood where I grew up. His body language was essentially saying "Don't fuck with me." I didn't flinch because at least one of us knew there was no need to worry about me. All of us who worked the event had been given security clearance anyway by the Secret Service. When Tip was just a few feet away I simply smiled, exhaled another round of smoke, and nodded a respectful gesture of hello while saying "Mr. Speaker." I think Tip then recognized me as his server and nodded in return with a half-smile and half-pissed sigh of relief before the agent on his right walked between us as they passed, escorting him to a nearby limousine.

As time went on, things back home proceeded relatively well. Dad's health had improved significantly, and I decided to stay and settle into the Philadelphia area. I moved out of my parent's house and lived in a string of apartments. Dad himself had helped me move into my first apartment, with Mom accompanying him to help out with Mom type stuff like sweeping and assessing window treatments. It was the start of new chapter for me, thereafter proceeding to take advantage of unexpected opportunities that continued to come my way. I had nothing to lose by roughing it to learn something new. Mark Twain's *Roughing It* had become my guiding light, as it were, and because of its influence, over time I would try my hand at a truly diverse array of jobs, from restaurants to teaching, from construction trades to the art business, and more. By 1990, Dad's career wisdom finally set in. I saw the light and enrolled in computer classes for desktop publishing.

My elected path by default had been financially challenging at times, but the experience has been priceless. I share these details because it dawned on me as I was writing this segment that I had wholly forgotten how Twain's life had been the seminal inspiration for this arbitrarily accepted series of life choices I'd made. Of course, other factors influenced me as well, like the travel tales shared by Dad, my Uncle Jack's stories of his travels with a circus and serving with the Civilian

Conservation Corps, my Uncle Gyp's tale of being stationed at Pearl Harbor on the morning of December 7, 1941, and the assorted stories my older brothers shared of their respective treks when home on a holiday visit. I relished these stories because they served as a confirmation that what I was doing was ok. My own treks to Hannibal, Hartford and Holbrook resurrected an awareness that the decisions I'd made in my youth had been underscored by a direct link to Mark Twain. I was feeling a deep need to somehow acknowledge the overt influence of this great man, of honoring his profound, multi-generational influence, of completing some unfinished aspect with recognition of what Mark Twain had contributed to the soul-life and ambition of the American family to which I belonged. If there was anything else I could do, I felt it was time to pay a direct visit to the man himself.

Left and Right: Two 1871 promotional advertisements announcing Roughing It as Mark Twain's newest book, marketed as a companion volume and prequel to his best-selling The Innocents Abroad, the latter of which would remain the best-selling of Twain's books in his lifetime. Courtesy of Clifton Waller Barrett Library, Special Collections, Papers of Mark Twain, University of Virginia Library, Charlottesville, Va.

Detail of embossed cover plate on the first edition of Roughing It.

The Elephant on the Raft · 89

Portion of a letter dated April 20, 1872 hand-written by Twain to his lecture manager, James Redpath, in which he requests this info be passed along to newspapers for press coverage about the book. Courtesy of Clifton Waller Barrett Library, Special Collections, Papers of Mark Twain, University of Virginia Library, Charlottesville, Va.

Illustrated depiction of Twain dreaming of his adventures in Roughing It.

Left & Above: Cover and spine of the first edition of Roughing It, 1872.

6

AN IDLE EXCURSION: CHARTING THE NEXT ADVENTURE

"What a robust people, what a nation of thinkers we might be, if we would only lay ourselves on the shelf occasionally and renew our edges!"

Mark Twain,
The Innocents Abroad

Elmira, New York, was the name of a place I'd forgotten. I only knew of it in reference to the location of a Twain background story, as the home of his wife Olivia and her family. I had regarded it as just a footnote and hadn't given the name much thought beyond that. While working on this project in spare time spanning six months, throughout my research on an ever-expanding amount of information about Mark Twain's life, the name Elmira kept popping up.

Watching the Ken Burns documentary stimulated my curiosity about Twain's time spent there. In Elmira the Clemens' family vacationed each summer at the home of his sister-in-law Susan Crane. To help Twain feel more at home and provide adequate seclusion to write, Crane had a study built for him as a gift. When images of Mark Twain's study were presented in the documentary, the shape, design, and airiness of the building grabbed my attention. I had worked on the construction of an exact replica of this unique building when I was in my mid-twenties, and had completely forgotten about it until that moment.

The yoga retreat center in the Catskill Mountains where I had previously lived and worked as a baker years earlier had acquired an old Borscht Belt hotel and needed help with its renovation as part of a sorely needed expansion project due to an increasing influx of yoga students from around the world who came each summer for its popular courses and extended retreats. I had been living back in Philly working as a baker and on the catering staff as described before when I was contacted and asked if I might be available to assist. There was no need for a baker then, but I was offered an opportunity to try my hand as an apprentice plumber on the construction crew instead. Learning a new trade could be cool, I thought. The timing was right and seemed like a good way to keep me out of trouble.

One of the reasons I had spent so many summers in the Catskills during my early twenties was to get away from a drug and alcohol addiction pandemic that had taken over our neighborhood, replacing a prior scourge of racially motivated violence that had established a prevailing communal malaise for years. So many old friends and schoolmates had ruined their lives from addiction to coke, crack, crank, heroin, and booze that I, like many sober-minded friends, felt compelled to remove myself from the environment. When John, one of my best buddies from high school, had OD'd on heroin and was found dead in his apartment after a week had passed, I was particularly motivated to get away. John had one of the most brilliant minds of anyone. He used to constantly break my balls that I had the worst album collection of anyone he knew. The last time I saw John, he gave me a hand-woven God's Eye from the Navajo reservation he had visited on a trip to Arizona. He told me when he saw it he knew he had to get it for me "Because I know you're into God and all that kind o' shit and thought you'd like it," a sentiment which flawlessly personifies South Philly love. Now a weathered and faded dust magnet, that God's Eye remains one of my most cherished possessions. It reminds me of John every day, and the memory of his remark still ignites a fond smile.

This time, I had a new motive for retreating to the mountains again. In the interim since moving home from LA, I had gotten a little wild, spending my free time sowing my oats and partying with friends at local clubs. I took on an extra job doing night security at a jazz club where some friends worked and started developing a habit of routine cocaine use. It was always available everywhere I turned, and increasingly I became uncomfortable with this. I only did it casually with friends, I reasoned. And at work. And when alone. And other times. I didn't think too much of it until I saw how it had drastically changed the personality of another close friend, who began to care less about spending time with us when his coke dealer became his new best friend.

Around the same time, my cool, purple-haired, New Wave band-singing girlfriend broke up with me on Christmas Eve, resulting in the gloomiest holiday ever. I spent most of the next day sequestered in my apartment, depressed and unmotivated. It was Dad who cajoled me out of my despondency on that Christmas Day. He phoned and had a caring, fatherly talk that helped me to rally and join our family for Christmas dinner at home that evening. After that, with my heart broken and a pile of cocaine as the only refuge before me, I refused to allow myself to sink any further, and decided that getting away would help. So, I gave up my apartment, sold a bunch of stuff, shaved my long Wild Bill Hickock hair down to a buzz cut, and retreated to the mountains.

While others in our neighborhood sought counsel in AA meetings at parish church halls, or enlisted into a branch of the armed services, I sought to refresh myself with yoga and meditation as therapy, for self-improvement, and starting over. So, I spent the winter of 1986-87 learning the plumber's craft there while crawling in the belly of this once respected Borscht Belt venue, documenting the schematics of the entire network of water and drainage pipes. This was another manifestation of having used Twain's *Roughing It* as my career counselor.

My guide through this post-kosher netherworld was an older African-American fellow named Matt. I don't recall Matt's last name, but I didn't know it then either. Matt always reminded me that just knowing him as Matt was enough. Matt must have been in his late fifties or early sixties, and had worked for the previous hotel owners for over thirty years. He knew every corner and crawlspace and soffit of that place like it was nobody's business. He was slightly pudgy and walked with a slight limp, requiring him to pause periodically to set down, take off his baseball cap and glasses, and blot the sweat from his face and forehead with a crumpled hanky he produced from his back pocket when needed. Matt would then point blindly over his left or right shoulder, and proceed to explain why this was an important area for me to map on the schematics I was creating.

"Now," Matt might begin, then briefly *grunt* then *spit* before continuing in a heavy, Southern drawl. "This he'e…?" he'd ask, to confirm I was paying attention before explaining details. When finished, he'd look at my notepad and ask "D'ya git all that?" Once I said yes, he'd put on his hat and glasses, stand up and point one way or the other, explain what we'd find either way, and walk in a random, chosen direction. "Come on, now" he'd say. "I'll show yo' that place."

Matt rarely addressed me by name. Occasionally, when I might recount a story that made him laugh, he'd turn to me afterwards and ask "What's your name ag'in?"

"Tom" I'd say.

"Tom" he'd repeat, then say something like "That's a funny story, Tom. Real funny" and then guide us along to next destination in the endless basement. It was only after spending the second or third of five or six months that Matt started to remember my name. He had taken a liking to me and would recount stories of the old days at the hotel. We became good buddies that Winter, and I looked forward to his company each day.

When the warmer weather eventually made its way back around, we emerged from the kitsch underground and all on our plumbing crew then spent more time working on a variety of new outdoor projects, the number of which continually increased in addition to maintenance of the extant property.

One such outdoor project required me to supervise a backhoe dig to unearth some underground electrical conduits. As the backhoe operator carefully scraped away measured levels of topsoil and stone, I stood by with a five-foot spade shovel, periodically jumping into the hoed hole, manually dig a little more, determining how much deeper the backhoe could go. The field in which we were digging was used as a cow pasture by a resident calf named Lakshmi, the most loving, endearing and affectionate non-pet creature with whom I'd ever become acquainted. As a city boy, cows as a species in general had always been an elusive, virtual thing to me, visible only on TV commercials, at a distance through a car window, and maybe on a petting zoo visit when I was a kid. Until then, I had never really known a cow, personally.

I was leaning on my firmly implanted spade shovel while watching the backhoe do its thing, when suddenly the massive head and neck of the young brown and white bovine appeared beneath my extended arm and along my side. I turned, simultaneously surprised and delighted, and stroked Lakshmi's neck as I greeted her. She responded by proceeding to lick my thigh and ribs with the longest tongue I'd seen of any animal. She was giving me dog kisses! I was blown away! I didn't know cows did that. My coworker in the backhoe, wearing an ear-protecting headset, grinned with equal amazement as he turned off its engine. Then from behind me I heard a voice:

"Looks like you made a friend!"

I turned around. It was singer-songwriter John Denver! He was leaning on the rail fence that lined the 'country road' along the pasture just a few feet away. John had been a frequent visitor to the yoga center there for many years, though I'd never met him personally.

This was cool. I thought of my friend Cheryl, a huge fan of John Denver. She played his records all the time when we spent countless hours of our high school years in the mid to late 1970s in her basement - exactly like the one in *That '70s Show*- smoking joints and singing along with Denver tunes like "Country Roads" or "Thank God I'm a Country Boy" as well as songs by the Beatles, Credence Clearwater Revival, CSNY and others. So, here I was now, being introduced to John Denver by a cow. Fa-ar out! I couldn't wait for the chance to tell Cheryl.

"He-ey!" I exclaimed with recognition of John but not wanting to make too much of a fuss about it. I turned toward the cow beneath my arm in acknowledgment of Denver's remark.

"This is Lakshmi, John" I remarked, assuming an instant posture of familiarity. "She's kind o' like a big dog."

"I see that" John replied, smiling widely.

I began to lead Lakshmi over towards Mr. Denver until she continued on her own initiative to the fence's edge. John extended his arm which Lakshmi promptly began to affectionately lick with her big tongue. John had been taking a walk with Eddie, the manager of the yoga center. Eddie and I knew each other from a few years prior, when I was working in the bakery and enlisted his help along with actor Marsha Mason, who regularly visited the yoga retreat as well, to throw a surprise birthday party for our friend Uma, who managed the retreat's on-site cafe.

The surprise party for Uma. I'm holding the cake, Uma is wearing the hat. Photo taken by Marsha Mason.

The surprise had been planned for an afternoon when the cafe was closed. As my fellow staff and I arranged to have Uma join us without arousing suspicion, at one point she mentioned that she had made plans to go shopping in Manhattan with Marsha. We didn't know what to do. Everyone had helped prepare in some way, and I spent hours working on this amazing double-layered sheet cake with an iced caricature of Miss Piggy. Drastic measures were required.

I paid Eddie a visit in the management office, and after brainstorming for a bit, we devised a plan to tell Uma that the Mayor of the town was coming along with local dignitaries which would require a VIP spread of refreshments. In the meantime, on the day of the party, I intercepted Marsha Mason as she arrived in the parking lot to fill her in and assure her that once we presented the cake to Uma and had a slice with some punch, they could still go shopping. Marsha was game and loved the devilish plot. The best part of the whole thing was watching Uma unwittingly direct us to set up her own surprise party.

As Eddie and John Denver continued to chat with Lakshmi, I smiled and turned my attention back to the hole digging project. My work partner had dismounted the machine to inspect the hole. He indicated that we had successfully accessed the electrical conduit needed for the electrician's project, and our work was done. Gathering my tools, I said goodbye to John Denver and Eddie, gave Lakshmi a pat on the head, and headed back early to our plumbing office.

My supervisor Pete was excited to witness my early return, thrilled to have an unexpectedly available man to tackle another delayed project. With Pete, that was every project. Pete then directed me to head back up the same hill where I had been, but a considerable distance beyond the Lakshmi pasture, to a remote, lakeside construction site of a project I had only known of from overheard conversations among the construction crew. Pete and I met with the architect and crew foreman who explained that I needed to do the roughing out and sweating of water and drainage pipes in the crawlspace of a newly erected, octagon-shaped artist studio that overlooked the lake. We chatted briefly about the design aesthetics, focused on the urgency of deadline. All were grateful to have someone qualified available to do the task. At that time, I was much leaner, having evolved considerably from my porkier 'husky boy' days, and was one of the lankier few on the construction crew with the ability to squat fully while resting my knees pressed against my upper chest. I could reach around my legs and work in such a compact manner with relative ease. It was a yoga center, after all.

Once I arrived on site, I set down my tool bag and surveyed the terrain. An elegantly designed, moderately elevated, octagon shaped, Gazebo-styled bungalow with wide and high windows and a single-stack, stone fireplace had been built atop an elevated flat terrain. I reviewed the accessibility of the crawl space beneath, assessing the full scope of the task before me, reached for a tape measure, Sharpie and paper, and got started. This was a pretty cool assignment, I thought, working contentedly in this gorgeous, isolated, serene place in the mountains. There were no other workers around at the time, as the plumbing work I was doing was the next stage needing completion before the other contractors could continue.

Whenever I took the time to emerge from the crawlspace for a break to stretch my limbs and drink some water, I would stand absorbed in absolute stillness, fixated on the harmonious, symphonic cadence of crickets, bullfrogs, Cicadas, and unknown bird species, while surrounded by nothing but still lake water reflecting a lightly speckled, perfect blue sky. Lush, fully pronounced trees swayed ecstatically in complete yield to the direction of the random mountain breeze, and a wonderful array of varied wildflowers humming with honeybees, river plants and foliage served as a playground for enchanting dragonflies, and the occasional chipmunk, rabbit, or other wildlife that might make an appearance now and then.

It was extraordinary, one of the first times in my life when I felt truly alone on the planet, as if my feet were the sole anchor planted on this huge orb that extended from beneath me in all directions. It was one of the most complete moments of my life, and precisely why this city boy so relished those Catskill days.

Since our portion of the project had been lagging and now had an urgent deadline, I pressed myself to complete the job before nightfall that day. As late afternoon approached, I took fewer breaks and kept going. After I completed the task and gave it a passing inspection, I emerged from that crawl space having remained in the same squat position for a considerably extended period of time. When I stood up, something in my back promptly snapped, and a sharp pain seared across my ribs and along my spine. I doubled over in severe pain, contorting my body to any strange position that might bring relief. With no one around - and no cell phones yet invented to call anyone - I mustered myself to the best of my ability, gathered my tools, and began what seemed like an endless trek back along the lake path and down the cow pasture hill then across the road and through the compound to the plumbing office.

That pipe sweating task was my last hand's-on assignment as a journeyman plumber. Thereafter I was permanently assigned the light duty of drawing schematics on a drafting table in the plumbing office. From that day on, I had since associated that lake side studio and my crawl space experience as the beginning of a string of herniated disc and back problems. Until I watched the Ken Burns Twain documentary, I had completely forgotten the conversation I had when I first met with the architect to review the blueprints.

On the first part of that day when I went out with Pete to meet Frank the architect and review the detailed instructions, I had complemented Frank on its aesthetically sensitive design. It was then when he explained it had been modeled as an enhanced, and slightly enlarged modern replica of the Mark Twain study located "upstate near Ithaca." I probably just mindlessly responded "Wow! That's cool," further mumbling about the influence of *Roughing It* before focusing on the blueprint examination and creating a list of needed materials.

I went online to search for details about the Twain study and learned a great deal more. Recurring references to it were made throughout the Albert Paine biography, and most notably it was in that study where the majority of the first draft of Huckleberry Finn had been written. I was also surprised to learn that it was still standing. Though moved from its original location, it has been residing on the campus of Elmira College since the 1950s. It was now a public artifact, with access restricted to the summer months on weekdays until 4:30 pm, and closed after Labor Day. Hmm, I thought. This was something I just had to check out in person, and with Labor Day just around the corner, I had better plan this soon.

Above, left: Twain's study in its original location on East Hill at Quarry Farm, overlooking the town of Elmira. Right: The study being moved in 1952 to its present location on the Elmira College campus. Courtesy The Center for Mark Twain Studies, Elmira, NY.

I checked the route and discovered that Elmira was just under four hours from my home, a virtually straight drive from outside of Philadelphia due north to the Finger Lakes region of upstate New York. As I studied the maps, I realized that I had previously been close to Elmira in my years of traveling on sales calls, and hadn't lived too far away when I resided in the Catskills. Looking at my calendar, I tried to find a window when I could make this work. With another business trip scheduled for a Saturday in late August in West Chester County, New York, I checked the distance from there to Elmira. Curiously, it was the exact same distance and time from my booked hotel in White Plains as it was from my home west of Philadelphia. I began to figure that I could check out of my hotel early on - yes, another Sunday - and arrive in Elmira by early afternoon. After spending a few hours there, I could then drive home in the same time span. I've done appointments at such distances in a day in the past, and though I hoped being in West Chester might lessen the travel time, it would be an extraordinary adventure. It did not escape me that it was in West Chester when I decided to make a similarly timed journey to Hartford several years prior. Mr. Twain surely seems to make me work for my allegiance.

Though the study is closed on Sunday, I reasoned at worst I could just look through the windows. By not going, I risked the chance of missing the opportunity of some miraculous twist of fate that someone, somehow, might show up and let me in. If that didn't happen, that would be ok. Because, in my quest for information, I had stumbled upon an equally and perhaps more meaningful goal for this journey, and that was to visit the site of Mark Twain's final resting place, located there in nearby Woodlawn Cemetery. That was something I had overlooked until then. And that, I learned in a phone call, was open and accessible on a Sunday.

It's a curious thing, I noted, that one doesn't really think of Mark Twain and 'dead' in the same thought too often. One gets so engrossed in the voluminous output of his available written material that he remains an ever-present and fresh entity. Each time I read something by Mark Twain that I hadn't read before is like discovering some new corner of his mind. Like most of us, I hadn't read his most popular works since I was in high school, so re-reading those again has been like enjoying a vacation in a favorite but forgotten place.

This speaks volumes of just how successful a marketing campaign had been set upon the commodity known as 'Mark Twain.' Even seeing Hal Holbrook kept Mark Twain propped up in his coffin, like an animatronic Disneyland figure creating the illusion of a living being. We just don't think of Mark Twain as a dead creature.

In advance of my journey, I took the time to read some of the many glowing, archived obituaries that had been published by every prominent journal of Twain's day: *Harper's Weekly. Century Magazine. Colliers.* All explained the details about Twain's public funeral service, how long lines of fans and the curious assembled outside and made their way through the long-gone Brick Presbyterian Church in New York City to catch a glimpse of the man in white, laying in state like a fallen king. The articles all recounted how he had passed peacefully at his home in Redding, Connecticut, where his mortal remains had been prepared by a local undertaker. From there his coffin was transported by train to New York City for a final public appearance, before again being transferred by train and carriage to the Langdon family home in Elmira for a private family service. Following that was internment in the Langdon family plot in Elmira, where his remains would rest alongside his beloved wife, Livy, his daughters Susy and Jean, his son Langdon, as well as his Langdon family in-laws. How many of you reading these few facts and details about Twain's death and funeral had given them much thought before? See what I mean?

Mark Twain, lying in repose at Brick Presbyterian Church, New York City, as featured in coverage published in Harper's Illustrated Weekly, May 7, 1910. Courtesy Clifton Waller Barrett Library, Special Collections, University of Virginia Library, Charlottesville, VA.

It was late July, and based on information I was finding online, my best option was to schedule a day in the coming month of August when I could visit both study and grave site. I telephoned a number found online for more info. A young lady answered and confirmed the study's hours through Labor Day. I asked if it was just open and accessible, or if a ticket needed to be purchased. She explained that an 'ambassador' was usually on hand to escort or permit entry. I asked if any exceptions could be made for admission on a Saturday or Sunday. She said no, adding that admission was free but donations were always appreciated.

I then called the Woodlawn Cemetery following a link about the Twain gravesite. A young man answered and explained that the office was only open during the week, and wasn't sure about access on the weekends. When I mentioned the Twain gravesite, he interjected that I was phoning the wrong office, emphasizing that I had called the Woodlawn *National* Cemetery, a site maintained by the US Army with the graves of 3000 interred confederate Civil War veterans who had perished from disease while imprisoned in what had been named "Hellmira," as well as those who had died on an 1864 prisoner transport train. What I wanted, the gentleman explained, was 'Woodlawn Cemetery,' a separate entity managed by another administrative firm. He provided a different number to try.

I phoned *The Friends of Woodlawn Cemetery* via the new number and a young woman answered. She said the cemetery is open every day until 4:30, and to be sure to use the Walnut Street entrance. I thanked her and again Googled 'Woodlawn' sans 'National' Cemetery, and read additional info. Apparently, the film producer Hal Roach is buried there also, which I found curious. Reading that reminded me of a sales call I had once made in this region almost twenty years ago. I scratched my head. Had I been to Elmira before and not known it?

During that sales call my client had told me enthusiastically about Hal Roach's local affiliation. He owned some Hal Roach artifacts in his collection of vintage, pre-WWII movie ephemera, the highlight of which were several rare Ub Iwerks film posters that he claimed had been appraised at that time to have an estimated combined worth of more than one million dollars. A fan of early film myself, I well knew of Iwerks as Walt Disney's original partner and co-creator of Mickey Mouse. I was knowledgeable about much of his collection, and certainly who Hal Roach had been, which greatly impressed my client and helped me get the account. I was just surprised to learn he was buried in upstate New York and not in Hollywood. I couldn't figure how I knew about Hal Roach in Elmira all those years ago and not about Twain's grave.

While driving home from work one night, I remembered the client's name and the non-profit organization he represented. It was just like the cartoon light bulb going on over my head, as if some lazy brain cell had awakened from a long slumber like a hibernating bear, suddenly being required by some cortexual commander in chief to reveal its purpose for being. The organization's name contained the name of the County in which it was situated, which I later looked up and found to be nowhere near Elmira. I distinctly remember him saying Hal Roach had lived there and was buried nearby. Wikipedia explains that Hal Roach was born, raised and buried in Elmira, but lived the rest of his long life in Bel Air, California. But, if I am recalling correctly, and I'm fairly certain that I am, Elmira is at least 200 miles west of where my client lived. I suppose I should have detected some modicum of exaggerated malarkey even then. Either the guy was just a wishful, nostalgic fan of Roach or he was bullshitting with the aim of winning me over. Either way, he was a nice guy, and it was a nice enough story that I still remember it. Apparently, he did win me over. Bully for him! For me, it relieves the angst of having thought that I could have been so near Twain country in New York without knowing it. One interesting note in the Wikipedia entry indicates that while in grade school, Hal Roach had attended a lecture given by Mark Twain in person. Was that, perhaps, Roach's inspiration to pursue a career in humor?

Later that evening, I enjoyed a glass of wine with my old friend Google when together we continued to discover a whole variety of previously unknown Twain related things. Though my understanding was that Samuel Clemens' last known descendant passed away in the 1960s, I nonetheless Googled "Relatives of Mark Twain" to learn if there were any accessible members of the Langdon family I could interview. Instead, I stumbled across the fascinating story of one Susan Bailey in a *USA Today* article from 2014.

Susan Bailey is the author of a book called *The Twain Shall Meet,* which focuses on the life of Twain's only grand-daughter, Nina Gabrilowitsch, the daughter of Clara, as the back story to support Bailey's claim that she is Mark Twain's illegitimately conceived great-grand-daughter and that Nina was her mother. I was astonished!

Google and I Googled further, and found numerous transcripts of interviews with the author, some of which concluded with announcements about her scheduled speaking engagement at a conference of 'Twainian' scholars in Hannibal, Missouri. I must confess, it wasn't until I read this article that I learned there was such a species called the Twainian, let alone that they organized annual tribal gatherings.

Intrigued, I continued to investigate further, reading every related interview and article I could find, until I read a gem of an investigation[34] into Bailey's claims by David Carkeet, an established author, professor of linguistics and writing at the University of Missouri-St. Louis, and self-described Twainian. Bailey's story, I thought, opens a whole new bowl of wax. It's a great story. From reading just a few snippets of Bailey's claims, there seemed to be some fascinating evidence to support her story. The main thrust is how she details her memory of repeated visits from a mysterious "Aunt Clara" who takes her to symphony performances and on extravagant shopping sprees. Think of Bette Davis' character Charlotte in *Now Voyager*, when she anonymously looks after Tina, the daughter of Jerry, Charlotte's lover. 'Aunt Clara' would be something very much like the doting Charlotte. Bailey goes into detail about some loopholes in the recorded life of Clara's daughter Nina that suggest an attempt to hide an unwanted pregnancy and putting the baby up for adoption. Susan believes she is that child and that "Aunt Clara" was Clara Clemens Gabrilowitsch, the daughter of Mark Twain, and Susan's grandmother.

As I continued to read on, most intriguing was how much the photos of Susan Bailey show a striking physical semblance to Samuel Clemens. Professor Carkeet, among those initially wanting to earnestly believe that Bailey's claims were true, openly shares his reluctance of deriving at the need to ultimately debunk Bailey's claims. "Though skeptical" Carkeet writes, "I found Susan's tale to be fascinating, entirely plausible, and begging for further investigation."[35] I found myself curious of a potentially whole new avenue of exploration. Is it possible, I wondered, that a descendant of Twain's is out there?

Carkeet begins his essay[36] by explaining how he met Susan Bailey in February, 2015 in the office of Cindy Lovell, then Executive Director of the Mark Twain House and Museum in Hartford. All three had been in town to attend Hal Holbrook's 90th Birthday performance of *Mark Twain Tonight*. Ms. Lovell had invited Bailey to join her for dinner with Mr. Holbrook, who compassionately listened to Bailey's summarized version of her claim. Holbrook countered with a story of how he had met Clara Gabrilowitsch personally in the earliest years of his performance. This was fascinating.

Bailey's book is composed of childhood memories allegedly supported by DNA evidence. Carkeet's detailed segment on the endless DNA connections Bailey had unearthed left me with a burning desire to submit my saliva to ancestry.com and investigate my own family tree. Remember my hypothesis about 'Kerley's' Pub in Hannibal, Missouri? Maybe there's something to that after all.

The thought of wanting to meet and chat with Susan Bailey came to the forefront of my mind. This had to be some of the most exciting news to surface within the extended Twain inner circle in some time. My desire to meet Ms. Bailey stems from a sort of "hem of his cloak" syndrome, that somehow meeting a possible blood descendant of Mark Twain was the closest I might ever get to meeting the man, although having seen Hal Holbrook live in Mark Twain Tonight came pretty damned close. I located contact information and emailed Susan Bailey with hopes to interview her, but had not received any replies. I did manage to contact David Carkeet, who reconfirmed his conclusion that Susan's story was flawed.

Having been impressed with Carkeet's remarkable detective work and his writing style, prior to contacting him I was curious to learn more and paid a visit to his website during my research date with Google that evening. It was then I found news that was simultaneously delightful but saddening: that very next day marked the convening of the Mark Twain Quadrennial Conference of Twainians and Twain scholars at - Elmira College, in Elmira, NY.

"Damn!" I thought with some urgency. "Tomorrow? Really? No way?"

I promptly started to conjure ways that I might play hooky from work and shoot up to Elmira pronto if my schedule permitted. Carkeet mentioned in his dissertation that these conferences are held regularly, alternately hosted in Elmira, Hannibal, or Hartford. How have I never known of these things? Well, for one thing, as said, I'd never even heard of a Twainian until reading Carkeet's piece that very evening, and Elmira wasn't even on my radar until a few weeks prior. It occurred to me that I was now venturing into serious Twain terrain, an unexpected turn of events when I started writing an intended blog piece about a coloring contest when I was twelve years old. Who was this mysterious posse of Pudd'nheads, this Cabal of Calavaritans, this herd of Huckle-bingers? I wondered how this conference of Twainians began their gatherings.

I envisioned a hotel banquet room enveloped with cigar smoke, populated with academically inclined, professorial looking men and women, each dressed in some variation of white or cream linen, chit-chatting about Twain's smoke of choice, the proper mustache thickness required of re-enactors, or the literary merits of Twain's body of philosophically oriented essays versus "the fun stuff," until the conference chair steps up to the podium, bangs the gavel a few times, and calls the assembly to order:

"TOM?" is called out a first time, no answer expected, a signal to those assembled to move to their seats.

Then, when all have gathered and are standing by their seats, the chairperson delivers a second intonation of "TOM?" voiced a little louder. This is followed by a brief, sustained silence, a "no answer" segue, signaling that they are united in mind and cause, willfully surrendered with allegiance, and then, while focused on the stage front and center, they all recite in unison the established responsorial creed:

"WHAT'S GONE WITH THAT BOY, I WONDER?"

With the attention of everyone established, the chairperson bangs the gavel, and sparing no words, leads the final incantation that is enthusiastically shouted by all in a collective, synchronized, thunderous voice:

"YOU TOM!"

Everyone then applauds wildly as they gleefully take their seats to begin the proceedings. The chairperson exits the stage, the lights dim, and a musical overture fills the room from hidden loudspeakers. The curtains part to unveil a large, back-lit river pilot's wheel followed by the entrance from side stage of the sensational Mark Twain Dancers, each dressed in white, vested, sequined suits and river pilot's hat, twirling an oversized corncob pipe while dancing stylistically to *Down South* by Tom Petty and the Heartbreakers. The opening musical song and dance extravaganza produced at each gathering is always a much-anticipated highlight, alternately featuring Jimmy Buffet tunes like *Take another Road* and a different Twain themed dress and set each time.

I jest, of course. The truth is, I hadn't a clue about what went on at such a conclave. I wasn't sure if the whole affair was something like Comicon, where hawkers of Twain ephemera and collectibles set up booths or tables to sell and/or trade with other Twainians, or if it was strictly an academic symposium where specialists fertilized the Twain field with presented papers on some new Twain twist that served to enhance the legend, lore, and legacy. Of course, I assumed it was the latter, which appealed to me even more. Was it open to the public? Or was it an advanced reservation only sort of ordeal? Regardless, I was quite bummed that I would not be able to party crash the Twain Quadrennial this time around due to scheduled appointment conflicts that I could not change. Dang! Maybe I can look into what's required to attend in the future.

For now, my appeasement lay in simply going to Elmira to explore on my own. Over the subsequent few days, I went back and forth looking at my options: should I make it a day trip or should I plan to book an Airbnb and explore the region for a few days? It was looking more and more like I would have to let go of my default tradition of visiting Twain sites on a Sunday, since the Study and related exhibit at the college aren't open on the weekends, and to just make it a one-day trip. There is something adventurous about day trips. That's what had made the treks to Hannibal and Hartford so memorable, not that it had been on a Sunday. And besides, doing it in a day would save the money otherwise needed for lodging to spend on a concert ticket, a dinner with my wife, or something else. The Gilded Age for me it is not.

As the weekend approached, I checked the weather forecasts and compared it to my schedule. The Weather Channel online indicated that rain was in the forecast for the weekend I had planned in West Chester, and the optimum choice would be Wednesday, with a predicted 80-84 degrees and sunny; 10% chance of rain; and 60% humidity. This would be ideal. I juggled my schedule with a coworker which freed me up to make the trip on that promising Wednesday.

In the interim, my wife informed me that our budget was tight that week from having made our daughter's college tuition payment. That confirmed my hunch to nix an overnight stay. I fetched a jar of pocket change I keep on my bureau and drove it to the Coinstar machine at the supermarket. I do this when extra cash is needed maybe once or twice a year. The last time I cashed my coin was for Christmas, when I had saved enough in the jar then to purchase a special gift for my daughter. In the summer prior, it provided an extra $150.00 of pocket money for vacation. This day I netted $49.02 for use on my trip to Elmira. Along with a $50.00 credit I had on my Amex card that I planned to use for gas and $40.00 in cash already in my pocket, I was confident that I had the adequate resources necessary to make this trip.

On my way home from work that Tuesday night, I stopped at a local market to load up on bottled water and snacks to bring along. The pocket cash would enable me to buy a few incidentals or lunch as needed. If time and gas permitted, I'd see if I could squeeze in another hour north to Ithaca to visit the famed Moosewood Restaurant. I gathered a few other things on my check list: my phone charger, laptop, portable voice recorder, my industrial sized, large-screen trucker's GPS, and went to bed. Another great adventure was about to unfold.

7

A ROAD TRIP TO ELMIRA & THE MARK TWAIN STUDY

> "...perched away up here on top of the hill near heaven I have the feeling of being a sort of scrub angel & am more moved to help shove the clouds around, & get the stars on deck promptly, & keep all things trim & ship-shape in the firmament than to bother myself with the humble insect-interests & occupations of the distant earth."
>
> Mark Twain,
> *Letter to Charles E. Perkins, May 8, 1874*

Early the next morning I first took care of my routine chores then made myself a cup of Chai and sat down to review my itinerary. After showering and dressing, I let the dogs out for a final run, made my daily protein shake and along with snacks, a selection of CD's, bottled water and other travel accoutrements, I loaded my car and left home at 9:30 am. I made a quick detour to our local Wawa for a 20-ounce coffee, set my GPS for the address of Elmira College, and noted I should arrive around 1:30 pm. This was perfect timing, I thought. Rush hour traffic had lessened by then so I should have smooth sailing.

I turned on the ignition, buckled my seatbelt, and just as I was about to pull out of the parking lot and get on the road, my employer phoned from Europe about a business matter that I needed to address right away. I didn't fret much. Arriving in Elmira by 2:00 pm or so still left me with two and a half hours to see what I wanted. In the parking lot I made the necessary phone calls to complete the task and texted the results to my employer. I knew it would be several hours before I heard back from him, so, with business done, I was on the road.

I was unusually tired that morning from not having slept well. A neighbor left their dogs outside all night, compelling them to bark and whimper in protest for hours. I couldn't blame the dogs too much as my mind was stirring with anticipation for today's trip anyway, and it probably didn't help that I had finished a cup of coffee around nine PM before leaving work the night before.

I had noted that it's a fairly straight ride from my home to Elmira, going the full distance of 476 North, well past any place I'd been in recent years, then onto I-81 towards Binghamton and a stretch of Route 17 in New York. I knew Route 17 when living in the Catskills near Monticello thirty-seven years prior. Though relatively nearer, I'd never driven as far west as Elmira.

Geographically, Elmira is situated on the northernmost tier of the Appalachian Mountains on the Allegheny Plateau, which stretches from the Finger Lakes region of New York and dipping far south into West Virginia, Kentucky and Tennessee and the Cumberland Gap region made famous by Daniel Boone. On the Western end, it reaches into Ohio and the Mississippi River watershed. Looking earlier at the terrain map, I realized that over the course of my life I had driven along most of this entire stretch of Appalachia. The mountains of West Virginia, through which I had once navigated from North Carolina to Pittsburgh in the aforementioned big-assed truck, offered some of the most impressive vistas I'd ever encountered. Even the rest stops had incredible views.

As my drive to Elmira progressed, I noted how the weather couldn't have been more accommodating. It was gorgeous, like a mild day one would expect in the middle of Spring instead of early August. In the North this indicates that Fall is approaching much sooner than normal, with intermittent hot weather likely for weeks ahead. Man oh man, it was clear: I picked the right day to go.

Though I had brought an ample supply of CD's with me, I was hoping the abundance of country music radio stations in the mountain regions might play some Glen Campbell tunes. Campbell had passed away just the day before, and hearing some of his work would offer a great opportunity to join in on the national tribute. I had another motive as well.

Just as I was about to leave my house that morning, the Philly radio station WXPN was playing *By the Time I get to Phoenix*. I hadn't heard that song in a long time. I remembered Dad liked the song and purchased the Glen Campbell album on which it was featured. It was among the few 33rpm albums he had selectively purchased, which are still sitting in our old stereo cabinet in my mother's basement. Dad wasn't a country music fan per se, but he did like Glen Campbell, watched his TV show, and I remember him playing the record in our house. To this day, whenever I hear "Phoenix" or *Wichita Lineman*, I immediately think of Dad. It had been another instance of serendipitous kismet that something reminded me of Dad while embarking on another Mark Twain trip. I was beginning to feel the planets align.

Within an hour into my ride on 476 N, I was already starting to feel peaked from lack of sleep, and began to think that I should plan a nap before I later hit the road home. That wasn't unusual for me. It had become a routine consideration throughout my years as a road warrior. I distracted myself by enjoying the lush green farmland that now surrounded me, with the lovely, permeating aroma of horse manure and fertilizer keeping me alert. It's an expected component of driving through the country. It was a pretty cool, synchronistic moment of perfection when the radio station then began playing *Mother Nature's Son* by the Beatles, reinforced when the next song was Paul McCartney's *Heart of the Country*.

With my windows rolled down and a modicum of caffeine from my coffee kicking in, I began to sing along. Now the energy of the drive was kicking into gear. With each new song, if I didn't know the words, I just banged my steering wheel in rhythm with the beat. There's nothing quite like driving on the highway at seventy miles per hour with some good Rock n' Roll to see ya through. As I approached the Lehigh Tunnel, music by the Spencer Davis Group came on and everything was just groovin'. I looked at my GPS to determine how far my next exit would be. As perfect and jammin' as it was, with another sixty miles yet to go before picking up I 81 toward Binghamton, I had an urgent need to urinate.

The combination of Chai, coffee, and my liquid breakfast had finally introduced itself to my bladder. Since February of that year I'd been drinking a protein shake each morning and that's all I would consume until dinner time. I had lost 20 pounds since beginning the routine and hadn't felt as consistently healthy in years. But the one side effect was the need to make more frequent pit stops. I scanned each road sign for any indication of a forthcoming rest stop that would aid my predicament. Finally, a sign informed that there was a stop about fifteen miles away. I took a deep breath and held steady.

I was driving through the Mahoning Valley by then, and though every other radio station featured country music, I was disappointed that none of them played anything by Glen Campbell. Other stations offered Christian music and biblical preaching consistent with the abundance of billboards attempting to convert my sinning ways.

I fiddled with the tuner and found a station playing Pink Floyd - a marked contrast from the others. There seemed to be only three stations playing anything I liked, leaving me to wonder if it was time to load up one of my CDs when I saw a sign indicating that the last rest stop on the Northeast extension was just ahead. I had been driving for two hours at that point, halfway to my destination, so this pull over was in order.

By 11:30 I was back in the saddle and Elton John's *Goodbye Yellow Brick*

Road came on the radio. My mind drifted off as I remembered a time when I was thirteen years old, playing pinball and smoking cigarettes with my friends on the second floor of a neighborhood enclave called Bill's Variety Store, which would later be abbreviated to just 'The Store.' Bill's second floor was like a speakeasy of sorts for we recalcitrant youths. There was no alcohol involved, but marijuana smoke was often detectable. The room was filled with pinball machines and it was there where we honed our wizardry of the game. To that end, because of his cover version of The Who's *Pinball Wizard*, Elton John was a communal favorite, and one song on the *Goodbye Yellow Brick Road* album - *Bennie and the Jets* - was *owned* by our friend Jimbo.

Jimbo was one of the older guys one grade up from my age group. He was the most likable fellow among us. Always positive, always cheerful, and almost always animatedly mouthing the words of one popular song or another, there wasn't one person who didn't like Jimbo or whom he could have offended. Though he played air guitar and mouthed the words of a good many popular songs of the time, when it came to *Bennie and the Jets,* Jimbo was the unquestioned master. With his expressive facial gestures and hand movements mimicking Elton's opening keyboard segment, Jimbo forced us all to stand back and weep with envy.

After high school, like other friends desirous to extricate themselves from our neighborhood's troubles, Jimbo enlisted in the Navy. I didn't see him again for many years, until I attended a grade school class reunion, when some old classmates and I stopped into Callahan's bar in the Schuylkill neighborhood where my father had grown up. There were a lot of old faces there I hadn't seen in a while. Franny Doc, whom I've known since high school, was tending bar, and he filled me in on the whereabouts of some of the guys I'd known from his neighborhood. Some were married, some lived elsewhere, and some had passed away in the intervening years.

After chatting with Franny until he moved on to serve other patrons, I grabbed my beer, turned around, and as if no time had passed, there was Jimbo standing right behind me, playing air guitar just as he always had, mouthing the words to whatever song the DJ had been playing. My jaw dropped and my eyes widened.

"Jimbo!" I exclaimed. His mouth stopped and his fingers paused as he looked at me quizzically, not recognizing me at first. I reached out my hand and said my name.

"He-ey - Curley!" he replied in his soft-spoken way, shaking my hand the old school way just as we always had by interlocking our thumbs and fingers wrapping over the upper wrist. "What's up, man?" he asked. "How are you?"

We chatted for a while, filling each other in on what had transpired in our lives. I asked what he'd been up to, and he told me he'd become a Fireman. I smiled. "Oh my God" I said, putting my hand on his shoulder. "That's perfect! That is so perfect for you!" He closed his eyes and smiled, nodding in agreement. Anybody who had known him would agree - Jimbo as a Firefighter was a perfect vocational match.

After chatting a little while longer, Jimbo looked over my shoulder, then excused himself saying "I need to go set this DJ straight." That was par for Jimbo's course. Though a hired DJ spun the records, if Jimbo was in the room, he most assuredly ran the show. I smiled, reassured that he hadn't changed a bit.

That was the last time I ever saw Jimbo. Within a year of that mini-reunion, he was driving home from the Poconos with some friends when their vehicle slid on some ice and hit a tree. His friends in the front seat had been saved by airbags. Jimbo didn't survive. I was later told that shortly before he officially joined the Philadelphia Fire Department, Jimbo just being himself had run into the burning home of a Black family and saved the lives of two children. This old friend was a hero.

When I was told the story of his death, I could only imagine Jimbo in that back seat taking center stage while enthusiastically entertaining his buddies in the front, probably trying to direct them to change the radio station or a CD that had been playing. He died as he had lived - fully and passionately engaged in the moment. To this day, whenever I hear any cut from *Goodbye Yellow Brick Road* I think of Jimbo. Hearing it on my drive that day prompted a melancholic nod to his memory. RIP to a good buddy who made it - beyond the yellow brick road.

Music does that. Certain songs always bring us back to another time and place. The next song on the radio was *Safety Dance* by Men Without Hats, and my mind drifted from Jimbo and the neighborhood bar in Schuylkill to the time I lived in Los Angeles. That song was a huge hit at the time, and I remembered being on the beach in Santa Monica when a bunch of my friends and I formed a small parade around our beach blankets while mimicking Ivan Doroschuk's robotic dance moves from the 1982 MTV video, with the shortest of stature among us playing the part of the jester-dwarf. I sang along in the car, trying my best to reenact a few of Doroschuck's gestures while wriggling my butt cheeks in a noble effort to dance in my seat, limited only to an extent allowable by the restraint of my seatbelt. It's one of the things I love about road trips.

As much as I enjoy rockin' out to good tunes while driving at accelerated speeds, I generally prefer to drive with no music at all for the most part. I like to use the time to think and muse. This is often when I come up with concepts for things to write about, song or lyric ideas, or ideas for paintings that I'll sketch when I pull over. On this trip, I had used a recording app on my phone to take voice notes for a few writing projects. In the past, I hadn't recorded much and so many good ideas were lost.

Though I was still on the Pennsylvania side of my drive as far as I could tell, the scenic landscape all around was bringing me back to what I have always loved about this region of the country. I was beginning to see why it appealed to Mark Twain. As I continued to careen along the rolling hills, *Won't get fooled again* by The Who came on the radio. I cranked it up and was just startin' to rock and sing along at the top of my lungs when all of a sudden I rounded a bend aaannd… traffic came to a virtual standstill for miles ahead. I noticed road work signs and wasn't sure how much of a delay this would cause. My eta to arrive in Elmira at that point was 1:55, so this could create a little setback. Although I wasn't too far off my original schedule, each minute counted now if I wanted to spend some extended time at the sites I wanted to see. With no signs for nearby towns to gauge my status, a matter of greater urgency arose as mild panic set in: I had another and more direful need to piss.

As I inched along in traffic for what seemed like forever, my bladder increasingly recoiled in protest, threatening to form a confederacy of organs demanding justice. I wasn't sure how I would make it to my next scheduled exit. I needed to find a way to get off road ASAP. There was only one solution for situations like this: time to pop in a Grateful Dead CD. The kicked back tempo of the Dead perfectly suited that Do-Dah segment of my drive, and sure enough, before long I got through the road work and resumed a normal highway speed.

I drove for a while in a hunched posture, constricting the muscles beneath my waistline, scouring every bend and turn for any sign of even a decent shrubbery along a shoulder. After another 20 miles or so had passed I saw an unmarked exit approaching. Uncertain if it was a highway crew access road or not, I threw caution to the wind and hightailed off the highway post-haste. As I turned the bend at the bottom of the seemingly unending exit ramp, my eyes beheld the most sublime visage possible - the radiant glory of a Mobile gas station sign. I muttered prayers of gratitude as I drew closer to the parking lot, blessing myself in acknowledgement of the benediction bestowed by the sacred red Pegasus. I barreled my car into an open parking spot with the agility of a seasoned Hollywood stunt driver, stopped the engine, leapt from the car, and lunged toward the resplendent, grime-encrusted exterior rest room. I entered the motorist sanctuary with all the respect due a confessional booth at church while invoking forgiveness from the kidney and bladder deities, willingly conceding to any accorded penance. Then, at last, heavenly hosts sang "Alleluia" as the waters receded. Thank you Jesus!! Holy mother of God and all that is sacred and good in creation. Nothing brought more relief then that moment of actually relieving myself. It was redemption at the river Jordan.

I returned to my car, pausing to drink some water, and noticed my earlier tiredness from lack of steep had abated markedly. That pit stop must have been the one I was waiting for, the mother of all micturition. Feeling revived, light and energetic, I reset my GPS, which indicated that I was about 32 miles from Route 17. I started the car, resumed play of my Grateful Dead CD, took a deep breath and got back on the road.

I was diggin' on the Dead that summer because 2017 marked the fortieth anniversary of the release of their *Terrapin Station* album and their first public performance of it, which I attended with my friend Cheryl and over 125,000 fellow Deadheads on September 3, 1977 at Raceway Park in Englishtown, New Jersey. Now considered one of the greatest Dead concerts ever, the event was like a Woodstock redux, inadvertently providing closure for the missed opportunity at the infamous "Woodstock West" concert of December, 1969 at Altamont Raceway, which had brought the 60's Peace and Love era to a crashing end, and served as the closing chapter of the large-scale rock festival culture that hallmarked the 1970s. Being there remains one of the most memorable experiences of my life. Playing Terrapin Station in the isolation of my ride that day brought me back, as my mind soared into another dimension. It's my favorite Grateful Dead song and album. Listening to the Terrapin title cut is sixteen minutes of life not wasted.

I had attended a Dead and Company performance in Camden, New Jersey only two months prior, where I was lucky enough to meet Bob Weir and Mickey Hart backstage in a Wayne and Garth "We're not worthy" type moment, kicking off a life-affirming summer that made me feel like I was seventeen again. I was hosting clients at that show, one of whom was wheelchair bound. When we went to our seats in a designated handicapped area, there was a mix up and our seats had been assigned to someone else. After a number of folks jumped through hoops to help, they returned to inform us there were no more seats available, and apologetically offered "the only place we can seat you is on stage with the band." Moment of silent numbness. Professionally I replied "That's ok," but inwardly I was like "Are you friggin' kidding me?" Forty years after attending that seminal, life-altering Dead concert in Englishtown, there I was, sitting to the band's left, ten feet from Mickey Hart's percussion ensemble, looking out on the ocean of fellow Dead enthusiasts from the band's vantage. Mind blown. Heart fulfilled. This was the most extraordinary boon of good fortune a guy like me could conceive. My incarnation was complete.

For the final hour of my drive I had such a blast playing and singing along to the Grateful Dead that I found myself entering the outskirts of Elmira before I realized it. I figured I must be in the right place when I turned onto Jerusalem Road and drove past a ball field with a large sign over the entrance that read "Home of Huck Finn Little League."

So, this was Elmira, I thought. I was certain that it didn't look anything like it did in Twain's day. A Holiday Inn and a pre-fab housing development greeted me on my right, and a beautifully landscaped park along the Chemung Canal welcomed me on my left.

My welcome to Elmira.

The Chemung Canal was a segment of the grand Erie Canal project that had been designed to create a direct, overland, navigable water link between the Atlantic coastline at New York City and the Great Lakes region, providing a more accessible means of moving goods from Eastern seaports and manufacturing centers to the doorstep of the Western frontier.

Conceived as early as 1780, the Erie Canal posed the prospect of being the most ambitious and costly project for the economically struggling new republic. President Thomas Jefferson called the project "a little short of madness" and rejected funding appeals from New York Governor Dewitt Clinton. Despite much opposition, construction on "Clinton's Folly" commenced in 1817, having been excavated entirely by hand, mainly by Irish immigrants with the aid of oxen, horses, and mules. It was a massive, laborious effort, requiring the felling of virgin forest and blasting through solid limestone with kegs of gun powder across the then nearly impassable Appalachian Plateau. Thousands lost their lives from accidents and the primary segments of the Erie Canal were completed by 1825 for the equivalent of $140 Billion dollars today - an astronomical sum at any time. The project provided such a significant economic impact that it defined New York City as the financial capital of the Western Hemisphere, leading to its respected designation as The Empire State.

The Chemung connection between Lake Seneca and Elmira was completed in 1833, and became a primary artery for the transport of coal and lumber from Pennsylvania to all accessible ports along the canal system and eventually to points west. This latter fact is a key part of the Elmira story relevant to my Mark Twain quest that I would discover later.

Along with its sister canal Chenango, completed in 1836, the canals linked Utica to Binghamton with the Susquehanna River in Pennsylvania, the longest river on the Eastern Seaboard. The continued expansion of the canal system set the stage for the industrial revolution and established the United States as a formidable economic powerhouse on the world stage. The increased growth of the steam operated railroad system beginning around 1850 gradually replaced reliance on the canal system. The Chemung Canal, instrumental in establishing Elmira as an important manufacturing center, fell into decline and was obsolete by the 1870s.

Among the Elmira entrepreneurs who had made a substantial fortune in its boomtown era was the lumber and coal merchant Jervis Langdon, who would become the future father-in-law of Mark Twain. But riding Twain's coattails wasn't his meal ticket to a place in history. In addition to reliance on the Chemung Canal for the transport of coal from Pennsylvania mines, Jervis Langdon, I would learn later that day, utilized the canal system in service of an even greater purpose that would ultimately contribute to integral change in US law and politics, leaving a legacy of influence that would ripple into the 21st Century.

As I turned right onto Elmira's Main Street, I was disappointed by what seemed more like a highway strip of generic buildings than the Main Street of an iconic Nineteenth Century industrial powerhouse. This town had surely experienced rough times in recent years. Based on some of the older buildings I saw, I gathered that Victorian era homes which may have once stood here had been torn down at some point. One such stretch of strip called Langdon Plaza was situated on the very land where the Langdon family mansion had once stood.

I discovered the home had been offered to the city of Elmira by the Langdon family in the late 1930s specifically with recognition of its historic significance from the town's economic heyday. As the home of such an important citizen as Jervis Langdon and its direct affiliation with Mark Twain, the Langdon family had hopes for its use as a museum. The city council declined the offer, deciding the home would be too costly to maintain. This storied piece of property was torn down by shortsighted developers in 1939.

I was quite bummed to learn of the home's fate this way. It was one of the locales I'd hoped to investigate, but hadn't planned on such an abrupt conclusion. Surely one might expect to find at least some sort of monument or memorial. But a shopping plaza? A sad case of hindsight being 20/20. As Mark Twain once said: "I was seldom able to see an opportunity until it had ceased to be one."[37]

After passing St. Patrick's Roman Catholic Church at the intersection of Main and Clinton Streets, the town grew less generic and increasingly residential, and within a short distance I was driving along the campus of Elmira College. I found my way to a parking lot behind the college proper, located a good spot close to the campus common, turned off my weary engine, unstrapped my seatbelt, got out and stretched my legs, grabbed my backpack, water bottle, and laptop, and made my way up the rear incline toward the campus buildings.

I had no clue where anything was, so I ventured to the building nearest to my car to see if anyone there could direct me. Gillette Hall was a fascinating, ancient, weathered building constructed of brick and stone, and sporting a lovely covered porch that harkened back to days of dismounting from a horse or carriage. Based on the intact, preserved oak doors, windows, and adjoining frames, it had surely been erected prior to the Twentieth Century. As I surveyed the twelve-foot ceilings with louvered glass windows over the doors for air circulation, I couldn't find anyone available in the building to help me, so I stepped outside again. A plaque by the entrance door indicated that it was listed on the National Historic Registry. I looked around the campus grounds before me, and noticed that aside from empty Gillette Hall, there was no one on the campus, which made it kind of really perfect for me. With no corporeal hominid entities to distract, my visit could take on the function of a walking meditation, providing the opportunity to dictate notes with my recording app. As I continued to survey the landscape before me, I detected, directly ahead of me and scarcely visible past a few trees, the left side of an octagonal structure that was surely the study, and I began to walk in that direction.

Outside Gillett Hall, Elmira College.

This was an exciting moment! I had only learned of the study's existence a few months prior, and had already grown enamored by its legend. As magical as I thought the billiard room in Hartford had been, this place had a distinct resonance for me. For one, it was the inspiration behind my lakeside plumbing project, and secondly, it was, as they might call it in India, Mark Twain's meditation cave. I say the latter because when you truly investigate how he employed this smallish retreat, you recognize that something about it created the very foundation that enabled Twain's wellspring to summon the muse that begat his greatest literary legacy.

With eager anticipation, I volleyed forth and passed the great tree that obscured it, and… it was closed. Oh well. I was here. I studied the structure. It was much smaller than I had envisioned. It reminded me of the Fairmount Park Guard hut in Philadelphia's Rittenhouse Square, but only in design, as the Rittenhouse hut is considerably smaller. Compared it to the replica on which I worked, this was a bit smaller.

I walked about, stepped up to the door and peered through the glass. I was getting a good glimpse, but damn! I really wanted to go inside now that I was here. I took a moment to Google more info on my phone. It indicated that I needed to stop first at Hamilton Hall, which I thought was on the other side of the campus, so I walked to find that. After winding my way past a small, man-made pond that divides the central campus, I saw some students emerge from one of the buildings. I asked if they could direct me to Hamilton Hall. They were uncertain, and pointed to some buildings on the opposite side if the Quad suggesting it might be there. So, I ventured in that direction and found not Hamilton but Harris Hall, and discovered a celebrated statue of Mark Twain I'd read about.

Dedicated by the Elmira class of 1934, the height of this statue was designed by Pennsylvania sculptor Gary Weisman to stand exactly two fathoms tall, which is the equivalent of the measurement a riverboat pilot calls "mark twain." Having studied sculpture, I appreciated its overall design. It's a great work, well weathered and nicely situated. I thought it was cool to find the titles of Twain's books chiseled into the base. The statue's planned placement enables Twain to oversee his study across the campus. I paused to take a few photos, including an obligatory selfie for my friend Kevin, the greatest, unknown literary mind of the Twenty-First Century, as the continuation of an ongoing joke between us of me taking selfies with a statue. Any statue. It was for Kevin that I had taken the selfie with Chef Boyardee in Omaha, with Perry Como and Abe Lincoln in Gettysburg, John Wayne in Winterset, Iowa, and some forgotten civic hero during a cruise ship stop in the Bahamas.

The Elmira College class of 1934 Mark Twain statue by sculptor Gary Weisman.

I entered Harris Hall and inquired about admission to the study. A nice young man explained that it was Cowles Hall I sought, not Hamilton. The website must have had old info, he explained. Cowles Hall was located directly opposite Harris on the other side of the Quad. I had been standing right in front of it when I peered into the closed study. That's ok. It was a gorgeous day and I was just surrendering to whatever showed up on my walking meditation. It was a good stretch of the legs.

As I walked back, I noticed an historic marker just outside the wrought iron fence, so I veered in that direction. I checked out its details about the Twain study, which simply stated:

"MARK TWAIN STUDY: Built on East Hill 1874, given to Elmira College in 1952. He wrote "Tom Sawyer" and other novels in the study when summering in Elmira."

State historic marker for the study.

I thought Tom Sawyer had been written in Hartford, and completed there in the carriage house, and started to wonder if this was just tourist blather akin to claims that "George Washington slept here."

As I walked past the fence and back onto the campus, I came across a more detailed display about the study and Twain's life in Elmira that I hadn't seen on the first go around. The sign explained how Sam Clemens first encountered Olivia Langdon via a photograph owned by her brother Charles, whom Twain had befriended on The Quaker City transatlantic steamship. This story I knew, of course, from the Fredric March film. It further explained how Sam and Livy Clemens and family spent every summer in Elmira between 1870 and 1889 at Quarry Farm, the home of Livy's adopted sister Susan Crane and her husband Theodore. It specified the study's original location on nearby Quarry Farm, which I intended to seek later in the day. The sign stated: "By Clemens' own admission, life in Hartford offered many distractions, while the relatively quiet life at Quarry Farm allowed him to "pile up manuscript."[38] This fact spurred my intrigue.

The study had been designed by Alfred Thorpe, an associate of Edward Tuckerman Potter, architect of the home in Hartford. Susan Crane's request was to incorporate decorative features from the Hartford house into the study's design so that Twain would feel at home. It was in this very private retreat space, I learned, where Twain penned the larger portions of Huck, Sawyer, Connecticut Yankee, and Life on the Mississippi. This made sense when it referenced Twain biographer Albert Bigelow Paine's perception that the study was "somewhat suggestive of a pilot house - overlooking the long sweep of grass and the dream-like city below."[39] In an 1886 Chicago Tribune interview, Twain himself said that the study: "may be called the home of Huckleberry Finn and other books of mine, for they were written here."⁴⁰ So, it was here and not the billiard room in Hartford! This was a major awakening for me.

Paine's quoted assertion offered an insight into the type of environment most favored by Twain for inspiration. Between the Hartford billiard room, with its sylvan canopy surround overlooking the Park or "Hog" River, and now the "long sweep of grass" beneath the hilltop precipice on which the study originally stood, one can easily glean that it was stillness and serenity in a reflective, meditative environ that served as the primary fuel behind Twain's genius. I had suspected as much, and it was the reason I had brought my laptop with me, with the hope that I might sit inside the study with church-like reverence, to absorb some remnant of the magic resonance that might yet emanate from its atmosphere.

And there it was, standing serenely to my left. I turned and paused momentarily, somewhat gobsmacked at the largess of this humble cottage. I took a few photos with my phone and was debating where to go next, when a middle-aged guy wearing a groundskeeper's uniform pulled next to me on a golf cart and asked if I would like him to take my photo with the study behind me. "Sure!" I replied. After showing him how to use the camera features and he took the shot and I thanked him. He asked if it was my first visit and where I was from. It was, I explained, adding that I was disappointed to have driven four hours only to find the study closed.

"I can get you in!" the groundskeeper exclaimed.

"Really?" I asked, somewhat surprised, though this is exactly what I envisioned could happen.

"Sure! Lemme get the key from security, and I'll be right back"

"Wow!" I gratefully replied. "That would be great!"

"In fact," he continued, "get in the cart. I'll show you around while I do that."

"That's mighty nice of you, my friend" I said, stepping into the cart. "I can't thank you enough."

As we started the drive up the walkway toward adjacent Cowles Hall, I mentioned to the fellow that I had planned on heading there next to

Posing before the study.

check out the Twain artifact exhibit. He started telling me about the unique chapel within Cowles that I should take time to see, when I noticed a young woman wearing a purple and gold Elmira College tennis shirt descend the steps from Cowles and walk in our direction. We had only driven about forty feet when the groundskeeper slowed down to intercept her.

"This man would like to see the study" he said to the girl. "Are you the ambassador today?"

"I am!" the girl confirmed, then looked at me to continue. "I'm going there now. I can let you in."

The groundskeeper turned to me. "There ya go, buddy. You're all set."

"That was easy!" I remarked, extending my hand to shake. "Thanks much! I really appreciate your help. It was a nice ride, anyway."

The groundskeeper laughed as I stepped off the cart. "No problem. Enjoy your day."

As the kind man drove away, the young lady welcomed me.

"I had just stepped away for a break" she explained as we walked toward the study. "Have you been waiting long?"

"Not really" I replied. "I was reading the marker over there for a bit, though I did get a little lost earlier. Is there another exhibit in Cowles Hall there?"

"Yes!" she acknowledged. "There is an exhibit there, of personal items that belonged to Mark Twain, along with some furnishings from the Langdon Home."

Her mention of the Langdon Home sparked my curiosity.

"Yeah, I was wondering where their home might be. Is that open to the public?"

It was then I learned the sad fate of the Langdon Home. She paused and turned on the step of the study, key in hand, and pointed to the street behind us where the blue and gold historic site marker stood. "That wrought iron fence along the campus walkway" she explained "is all that is left from the Langdon Home. That was their fence. It lined the perimeter of the property."

"What is located on that site now?" I inquired.

"It's a shopping center now. Which way did you drive into town?"

I pointed down Main Street indicating that I had approached from our left.

"Then you probably drove right by it. It's called Langdon Plaza now."

"You mean the strip mall?" I asked, half fearing the answer. Her reply then confirmed the sinking hunch in my stomach.

"Yes, that's it" she replied, unlocking the study doors.

"That's sad" was all I could say. Then, turning to the matter at hand, the study doors opened before me.

"Welcome to the Mark Twain study!" the young lady intoned. I stood transfixed, as if heavenly beams of light bathed me from the study interior while an invisible choir of cherubim chanted exalted tones of celebration. I had arrived at Ozymandias! I ascended to the top step and crossed the sacred threshold into the study, gawking profoundly.

Interior view of Mark Twain's study.

"This was Twain's study from 1874 to 1889, where he wrote some of his most famous works, including *The Adventures of Huckleberry Finn, The Adventures of Tom Sawyer, Life on the Mississippi,* and *A Connecticut Yankee in King Arthur's Court.* Is this your first time visiting?"

It was, I replied. I explained that I knew a fair amount about the study's history but was sure she could enlighten me on points I didn't know that I didn't know, then added: "I really just wanted to come and do exactly this, just stand inside and breathe the air."

"Absolutely" she acknowledged. "Would you prefer to look around first?"

"Sure!" I replied. "That would be great."

"No problem" she said, taking a seat behind an old wooden table. "My name is Jade. I have a lot of information here" she said while lifting a binder stuffed with laminated pages. "Feel free to ask any questions."

I thanked Jade, noting a long wooden bench to my right. "Would it be ok if I just sat here and wrote some notes on my laptop for a few minutes?"

"Absolutely! Help yourself!"

This was all that I had really hoped to accomplish. I sat down, unzipped my backpack and withdrew my laptop. I paused, studying every nuance of the interior. Old, framed black and white photos were hanging all about me. A cordoned-off chair to my right left me to presume it was the very chair Twain used to write. A photo of Twain sitting in it, hung just above the chair to my right, supported my evident hunch which Jade later confirmed.

On my laptop I typed some notes derived from the exterior info panel, about the study's location on Quarry Farm, about the demolition of the Langdon Home and the Langdon Plaza strip mall referenced in the preceding paragraphs. I looked up again. It was utterly cool in that moment to be sitting in Mark Twain's study, writing in real time. Some additional notes I wrote are as follows:

August 9th, 2017, 2:47 pm (writing in real time, in Twain's study):

> I am presently sitting in Twain's study on the Elmira campus. I'm sure thousands of tourists have been in here since it was moved in 1952 from its original location. Before it was moved from Quarry Farm, Jade, an employee ambassador working for the college, explained that it had endured substantial vandalization over the years. Moving it to the campus had been a conscious effort to preserve it. This is good news after learning about the fate of the Langdon home. Evidence of folk's initials can still be found carved into the wood. Were these carved by Elmira students or local Hooligans?
>
> The building is ancient, with a few notable features. Great ornamental detail in the worn, semi-tarnished hardware; high Victorian, top notch stuff. It is one of the small hallmarks that reveal its intended replication of the Hartford house. The windows are unusual too, opening upward into a hidden pocket in the wall space above them. Looking around I can't help but think that Mark Twain's eyes had gazed fondly on these same features and inclusions when he was first gifted with it by Susan Crane. What was it he is quoted as having remarked? That it was the "loveliest study that you ever saw?"
>
>
>
> The most moving aspect, though, is sitting here with the awareness that Mr. Twain himself spent a considerable amount of time in here, ruminating upon correct phrasing, composing a choicely worded sentence, accurately relaying a local dialect (Huck Finn), and brilliant word-crafting in general. This alone is magic enough. This is something special, a timeless moment for me.'

Ornamental Victorian window hardware.

I wrote some additional thoughts before

setting down the laptop to ask Jade some questions, requesting permission to record her with my phone app. I explained my reasons, that I was working on this discourse you're now reading. She wholeheartedly consented, pointing out that I could pretty much account for the accuracy of anything she said because it was all based on typed notes she had before her, all of which had been composed by Twain scholars. Jade graciously offered to make copies if I would like. I thanked her but declined the offer.

Jade then explained details about the folks in the numerous photos of Twain and his family all about us. She honed in on the photos of the study in its original location and mentioned that while Quarry farm is privately owned, visitors were welcome to drive by the property, and take advantage of the view from its vantage on the hill overlooking Elmira. I asked if there was a specific place. Jade said it was called Jerusalem Hill, but wasn't sure how to get there.

This bit of info surprised me. I had the understanding that Quarry Farm was owned by Elmira College. I'd read that Jervis Langdon, Jr., the grand-nephew of Twain and great-grandson of Jervis Langdon, had donated it to the college some time ago, and was used to house visiting scholars and host Twain related conferences in the barn. Had this changed since I had read that online? I didn't have much else to go on, though, as Jade was not a student at Elmira, but just a local gal working during the summer recess. I figured I'd just meander and attempt to find it before I left town.

After going through the photos, Jade explained about some features of the study's structure. She pointed out that though originally built with two chimneys to mimic the split-flue fireplace in the Hartford home - and because Twain smoked up to thirty cigars a day - it was later restored with just one. I did note that singular stack when I was outside as I thought photos I'd seen previously showed two. The fireplace screen and wrought iron tools were original, as was the adjacent, cordoned off chair. Jade pointed along the edge of the floor at what appeared to be drainage holes. I said I had noticed those and was curious, mainly because my wife and I had rented a cottage in West Cape May a few months prior, and it, too, had similar "floor vents." The proprietor in Cape May explained that hers were air conditioning vents, while Jade explained that these were constructed as entryways for Twain's numerous cats to come and go as they pleased.

Jade pointed at one final photo of the study resting on a flatbed truck while being moved downhill from the farm in 1952. I studied that and the other photos a little longer, asking Jade to explain one or another again. A laminated sampling of hand-written note pages displayed on the table served as an example of how Mark

Twain wrote everything on 5" x 7" sheets of paper in pencil or ink. Whether or not they had been originally bound in a journal or not wasn't clear. Some displayed pamphlets offered some additional information.

I looked about again as I took a series of photos, thanked Jade for her generosity and time, then stepped outside, I turned to take one last look, inhaling and exhaling with a tender sigh of melancholy.

Mark Twain's study on the serene campus of Elmira College.

Elmira College campus nearest the study. Cowles Hall is on left, Gillette Hall center-right.

8

SQUARING A DEBT

The sun was blazing brilliantly as if the gates of heaven had opened in expression of approval. Mark Twain had described his experience in Elmira as a "foretaste of heaven"[41] and I was beginning to understand why. I was certain that if anyone earned the privilege to sit at the right hand of God, surely it must be Mark Twain, the only person I could think of that could humor God for an eternity in an agreeable manner. I could imagine Mark Twain and God sitting on rocking chair shaped clouds, swaying to and fro.

God: "Well, now. Lookee yonder, Sam. Seems you have a visitor at your study."

Mark Twain (leaning forward for a better look): "Well, well. So it is. Looks like that feller from Philly ag'in. Wonder what he's a pokin' aroun' fer now."

God: "Now you know that boy's a fan, Sam. He's come to square his debt the same as Kipling. He knows as much about you as anyone."

Mark Twain: "There you go ag'in. Always havin' to remind everybody of your infernal, almighty omniscience."

God: "Well, I Am God, after all. That's kind of my job description, isn't it?"

Mark Twain: "You are most assuredly correct by my account, sir. I have a particular vantage now that enables me to assess that perception rather directly."

God: "You didn't always see it that way. What was it that you once wrote? That I was 'as quaint and naive a spectacle as has yet been imagined?'"[42]

Mark Twain: "Yes, and for which I repudiated all responsibility in the very next sentence, adducing the proper attribution of alleged origin."

God: "True, true."

Mark Twain: "Now that remark only confirms my other assessment that you do tend to behave at times as 'a small God,...fretful about small things.'"[43]

God: "Ohh, but that's my method. You know: 'To everything there is a season, and time to every purpose…'"[44]

Mark Twain: "Mm Hmm. 'And a time to keep silence, and a time to speak,' too."[45]

God: "I make a fuss over small things to keep the wise and learned ones guessing, to make sure their egos don't get too big for them to brag in their britches."[46]

Mark Twain: "Is that why my commentary on these concerns wasn't published until 1962?"

God: (Looking down at his fingernails) "Maybe."

Mark Twain: "Harrumph."

God: (Chuckling) "So, what are you going to do for this fan of yours?"

Mark Twain: "What am *I* gonna do? I've done all I need to do. It seems to me it's been MY house that he visits on Sundays more often than yours."

God: "Well, we do kind of look like each other. It's easy to confuse us."

Mark Twain: "Except for the beard. Don't care much for the beard myself. Fact is, you look more like George Griffin, and you're almost as noble a creature as he."

God: "Now *that* I can take as a compliment."

Mark Twain: "That's what I like about you, your Lordship. You're willin' to meet eye to eye on some matters. Now, about that Philly feller, in my mind I'd say he's already squared his debt. It seems he has been fairly receptive to everything *I've* created. So, from where I sit, the question that arises, my old friend, is what clever new creation can *You* come up with?"

God: "Touche', my friend. He's always been receptive to what my messengers have had to say, so I'd say he's pretty much squared his debt with me as well. Well, let's see…. I gave him life, and a decent sense of humor. He never asks for much, doesn't pester me with persistent prayers over lottery tickets… seems pretty set in my mind. How 'bout if I give him some extra good weather for the day?"

Mark Twain: "*Weather?* Is that the best you can come up with? He's a writer. Why 'fuss up the weather?' You've already given the 'ablest weather that can be had.'[47] You can do better than that, I think."

God: "Hmm. You're right. It should be something unique, something special, something that will show that both of us are conjointly mindful and appreciative of the attention he's paid to us. It's gotta be something miraculous, indicative of divine origin but something also reflective of, well, those special qualities instilled in you that we'll just call…'Missouri morals.'"[48]

God smirks, pleased with his poke in Twain's ribs. Twain raises an eyebrow, glancing sideways at God, feigning mock displeasure, half grinning in response, delighted to receive the sort of tease that has endeared this ancient of days to him. Both ageless entities gaze back toward Elmira, pausing momentarily to reflect. Twain brushes his mustache with his thumb and index finger and then rests his chin between the two.

Twain: "How 'bout a cigar?"

God grins with agreement, beginning His response before Twain had finished uttering his proposition, as if the Lord had been waiting for the anticipated response.

God: "I was thinking the same thing. What type?" he intoned enthusiastically.

Twain: "Give him the sort that I like, one of the 'cheap and devilish ones.'"[49]

God: "'Devilish' isn't my department. And if I did that, he'd think it was just from you."

Twain: "Alright, then give him one of those noble, elegant ones, so he can humor the notion that your hand is behind it. But remove the fancy label an' keep it humble, and that'll let him know it's from me, too."

God: "Fair enough. Done!"

Twain leans forward, looking down toward Elmira in earnest. A few minutes pass.

Twain: "I don't see it. How are you planning to deliver?"

God: "Oh ho, my friend, you're not getting off that easy. You'll just have to trust me - something you've had some difficulty with."

Mark Twain: "Fair enough. I can hardly wait to see what Hocus Pocus you have up your sleeve this time."

God: "Oh, it's a doozy. It's perfect!"

God closes his eyes and smiles, arching back in his rocker.

Satisfied, Mark Twain too, leans back on his cloud rocker, withdrawing a pipe and match from his pocket.

"Nacherly" Twain smugly remarks, eyeing the match flame as it ignites the tobacco with each suck of his pipe stem. He fans out the match, and casually blows out a slow, exhalation of smoke.

"I wouldn't expect anything less."

Resting his head, he takes another relaxed inhale from his pipe, lifts his head slightly more skyward, watching as his smoke expands to form another cloud.

Billowing clouds and extra glorious sunlight.

Meanwhile, back on the Elmira campus, I took some photos of the exterior of the study as the clouds above me billowed playfully and some extra glorious sunlight seemed to flood earthward, bathing all of Elmira and Chemung County with a sun-kissed blessing that afternoon, further accentuating an already perfect day.

I turned to consider my next stop, when I noticed a large stone memorial marker nearby, inscribed to Clara L. Clemens and dated 1874, the year of her birth. Upon closer inspection, I noticed a small bronze marker mounted on the lower right, which read "Mark Twain Watering Trough" and explaining that it was "One of four originally located beside the road to Quarry Farm. Moved to the college campus during the Bicentennial."

The marker confused me at first. Why only one with Clara's name? A quick Google search turned up a reference to "Mark Twain and the Watering Troughs" from a Summer, 1938 article authored by a Judge Dow Beekman for a publication called the *Mark Twain Quarterly*, published in Kirkwood, Missouri.[50] Beekman recounts the tale of how Mark Twain had commissioned the four watering troughs referenced on the bronze plaque as his way of celebrating the births of each of his children, each inscribed with their name and the year they were born. This one, perhaps the only one to have survived intact as far as I knew, was moved here as indicated.

The more I investigated details of Elmira, the more I began to discern that as much as the Clemens family adored their house in Hartford, it served as the primary location where the seeds of Twain's prolific creative output had been sown, Elmira was emerging in my view as Twain's true spiritual home, where those seeds were nourished and brought to fruition. I began to wonder if Hartford, without intending to diminish its significance in Twain lore, served more as a smoke and mirror deflection of sorts, an outward manifestation of Twain's need to protect his family - and himself - from the

The trough dedicated to daughter Clara.

glare and pitfalls of celebrity life. It was here, in Elmira, where Twain could fully explore his inner world and express that journey in earnest. This was an accurate hunch I realized when I later read Rudyard Kipling's account of meeting Mark Twain in 1889, in which he quotes:

> "I spend nine months of the year at Hartford. I have long ago satisfied myself that there is no hope of doing much work during those nine months. People come in and call. They call at all hours, about everything in the world...I do very little work in Hartford. I come here for three months every year, and I work four or five hours a day in a study down the garden of that little house on the hill."[51]

Elmira, I discovered, had been where Kipling, when still a young and unknown British reporter, had travelled fourteen-thousand miles from India for the sole purpose of tracking down and meeting in person his most revered influence - not Hartford as I had earlier thought. Kipling had arrived in Elmira late one night in 1889 and checked into what he described as a cheap "frowzy hotel"[52] Having travelled first to Buffalo the day before, there he was told that Twain was in Portland and by another that he was in Europe. Devastated that he might not have the chance to shake hands with his idol, he was then directed by someone who said "Elmira is the place. Elmira in the State of New York - this State, not two hundred miles away."

Once in Elmira, Kipling met folks who knew "that man Clemens" but unsure where he lived. A policeman said he'd seen a man resembling Twain's description riding in a buggy the day before, adding that the man he sought lived in a house on the "East Hill" just three miles away. Thrilled that his journey had not been in vain after all, Kipling hired a carriage for the ride to Quarry Farm, stopping first at a "small white shanty," where a young lady who was sketching wildflowers directed them further along the road. The annoyed carriage driver continued to the Crane home, where they were greeted by "a lady used to dealing with rampageous outsiders," only to learn that Mr. Clemens had just walked down the hill to his brother-in-law's home in town. The driver, "swearing audibly," turned the carriage around and speedily transported Kipling back down the hill, back to the center of town where his trek had begun. Upon arrival at the Langdon mansion, Kipling paused before knocking, thinking himself mad to call unannounced.

After mustering the courage, Kipling was admitted, where Twain greeted him with: "the slowest, calmest, levelest voice in all the world" saying: "Well, you think you owe me something, and you've come to tell me so. That's what I call squaring a debt handsomely."[53] The two writers proceeded to converse for two hours on a variety of topics, with Kipling enjoying a few of Twain's cheap cigars and relishing the moment when Twain placed his hand on the novice journalist's shoulder.

Kipling's account of his own journey to secure Twain's greeting paralleled the internal feeling I had experienced throughout my ten-year trek across the Eastern half of the United States in effort to tap and distill the essence of Mark Twain's spirit. I suppose we all possess some internal need to square a debt with Mr. Twain. And though, like Icarus, I had soared increasingly closer and closer to the source of that literary wellspring, the few hours I had spent in Elmira seemed to have brought me the closest of all. I was really onto something now. And here it was, hidden in plain sight, the Twain study in Elmira, the true athenaeum El Dorado, the Sangreal of Sawyerdom, the Excalibur of the Innocents, a genuine American Samadhi shrine, the living, breathing, beating heart at the source of all things Mark Twain.

Two interior views of the Langdon home. Twain likely met with Rudyard Kipling in one of these two rooms. Photos courtesy of Distilled History Blog, distilledhistory.com

The Langdon mansion in 1927. Photo courtesy of New York State Archives Digital Collection.

9

A PHILUFFIAN SCRIBBLER IN SAINT MARK'S CHAPEL

I walked the short distance from the study and watering trough toward the impressive all-brick Cowles Hall, ascended the brief flight of steps and beneath the column-arched portico over the entrance. Upon entering I was greeted by a vast octagonal foyer of white marble, dominated by a fine bronze statue of "Dr. Augustus Cowles - First President of Elmira College - 1856-1889," which was set on a superlatively carved Art Nouveau marble pedestal with a swirling pattern suggesting undulating flora, which contrasted stunningly against the flat, barren marble floor. A thoughtfully designed, site-specific monument worthy of mention. It's always a pleasure to see when an artist gets it right, and more so when it exceeds that lofty expectation.

The hall itself posed some confusion for me. Jade the study ambassador had directed me to "an arched doorway" that would lead to the Mark Twain exhibit. I thought it would be easy to find based on that description, but there were arched doorways throughout the hall in each direction like an amusement park maze, each adorned with ancient stained oak Doric columns - as to be expected in a Victorian era college.

Statue of Dr. Cowles and the arched doorways.

From prior photos I recognized this foyer as the site of student assemblies in its early days, and was aware that Cowles Hall was the first, original building erected on the campus. It had once served as the sole venue for the college, having incorporated everything - the Dining Hall, student dorms, faculty offices and classrooms. Elmira was the first all-women's college in the United States, and one of the first of its kind in the world. Olivia Langdon had been a student here, and her father, Jervis, had been a founding trustee in his day. Having learning this, one point that aroused my curiosity was why the Clemens's decided to send their daughter Susy to Bryn Mawr College, outside of Philadelphia, instead of Elmira, which was infinitely closer to their home.

I had been delighted to learn that Susy Clemens attended Bryn Mawr.[54] I knew Bryn Mawr well due to its proximity to my home. My daughter had attended The Baldwin School, the all-girls college prep institution that sits directly across the road from Bryn Mawr College. Bryn Mawr was begun as an ambitious, Quaker affiliated institution when it opened in 1885, and was likely modeled after Elmira College with its own dedication to women's education. Actor Katheryn Hepburn, class of 1928, had honed her craft at Bryn Mawr and remains among its most famous alumni. President Woodrow Wilson served as its first professor of history there from 1885 to 1888,[55] though, ironically, he resigned because he allegedly detested teaching women. Raised in Virginia with a conventional, male-dominant, Southern Presbyterian perspective, Wilson was not in agreement with the notion of cultivating "career women."[56] Curiously, as fate would have it, twenty-one years after his tenure at Bryn Mawr, Woodrow Wilson and Mark Twain shared rounds of miniature golf on Twain's trip to Bermuda in the final year of his life.

Susy Clemens attended Bryn Mawr for a short duration. When enrolled in 1891, the president of the college invited Twain to give a talk. Susy was horrified by the idea, fearing her father would tell a ghost story he had learned as a child from "Uncle Ned," a slave on his uncle's farm. Twain did anyway and Susy was mortified,[57] offering some insight to why Susy did not attend Elmira. Possibly the rock star level of fame enjoyed by her father had a subsequent ripple effect for family members. We see this with celebrity families today. Perhaps the Clemens family had thought this enhanced notoriety might prove a distraction and put Susy at an educational disadvantage.

Susy Clemens at Bryn Mawr College.

That same year, Suzy left Bryn Mawr to join the Clemens family when they relocated to Europe, and remained for several years. She continued her education in Geneva and Berlin before returning to the US in 1895 following a bout of illness and treatments for "nervous complaints." She lived at Quarry Farm with sister Jean and their aunt Susan Crane, while Sam, Olivia, and Clara remained in Europe. The following year, Susy died at the family home in Hartford.[58]

Recently I stumbled across *Papa, An intimate biography of Mark Twain,* which was written by Susy when she was just thirteen-years-old. I found a 1985 edition by the late Twain scholar Charles Neider in The Book Trader, a favorite used book store of mine in Philadelphia which I've frequented for over forty years. I nabbed it because I had only read Twain's references to *Papa* in his biography, never the actual text. Though Susy's bio intrigued me, I found Neider's introduction an even more compelling read, filling in many of blanks about Susy's life. Neider's details about Susy's time at Bryn Mawr were especially revealing, offering additional insight into why Susy's death may have so particularly devastated her father.

Neider reprinted a letter written in 1949 by one of Susy's Bryn Mawr classmates that explained a few things. For one, while at Bryn Mawr Susy had decided use her first name - Olivia, the same as her mother's. Susan was her middle name, having been affectionately called Susy since infancy. Here, in that letter by Mrs. Charles M. Andrews, the reference to Olivia is about Susy:

> "I realized how strong was the tie between [Susy] and her father, how much they minded being separated, and also how eager Mrs. Clemens was that Olivia should be happy in a new environment, leading an independent life of her own as a college student among girls of her own age, free from the influences of home...Mrs. Clemens would come down occasionally for a short stay, I think in order to keep Mr. Clemens from coming, because she told me that he would make anything an excuse, even to bringing down her laundry."[59]

Based on this letter, it's evident that Mrs. Clemens sought to provide for Susy the same independent women's education she experienced at Elmira, and, as suspected, precisely away from the influence of her father and the home environment of Hartford or Elmira. The letter implicates that Susy also wanted to get away from home. Twain must have not been too fond of the idea. In a letter to his sister Pamela dated October 12, 1890, he wrote:

> "The last time I saw [Susy] was a week ago on the platform at Bryn Mawr...[60] Our train was moving away, and she was drifting collegeward afoot...and she was crying."[61]

In February of 1891, to his friend William Dean Howells, Twain wrote:

> "Mrs. Clemens has been in Philadelphia a week at the Continental Hotel with Susy (who to my regret is beginning to love Bryn Mawr)."[62]

Neider then provided answers to the curiosity I held about Susy's brief tenure, followed by some weighty hypotheses, most notably backed with evidence that Susy had developed a love relationship with a classmate named Louise Brownell. Based on Neider's description, one aspect of Twain's fondness for Susy as his favorite daughter may have been that she was as boyish as himself.

Based on the letters written by Susy to Brownell now archived in the *Saunders Papers* [of her husband] at the Hamilton College Library in Clinton, New York, there are found remarks such as this in a letter dated October 2, 1891:

> "We could sleep together tonight - and I would allow you opportunities for those refreshing little naps you always indulged in when we passed a night together."[63]

It's an easy assumption in our era to conclude Susy was gay. However, according to David S. Reynolds, a CUNY graduate professor specializing in Nineteenth Century American culture, "Showing passion and affection was a more common part of the daily experience than it is today."[64] Reynolds was discussing the "omnisexual" poetry of Walt Whitman in an article addressing the ambiguous distinction of sexual mores in late Nineteenth Century America.

> "It's absolutely wrong to impose today's version of homosexuality on Whitman... That's done much too often...It was a much less institutional world than we live in today -- a much more personal world."[65]

Peggy Wishart of the Sarah Orne Jewett House in South Berwick, Maine, added,

> "Women were perceived as being non-sexual to begin with...You have to remember, ever since Freud, we've viewed everything through this very sexualized lens...For a Victorian person, that was not the case. I think it's almost impossible for us to fully understand the way they saw these things back then."[66]

As the child of a progressive, feminist and somewhat bohemian family, Susy was undoubtedly exposed to liberal expressions of love in the abundant volumes of literature and frank discussions at home. Nonetheless, homoerotic tendencies in Victorian America were regarded as a form of mental illness, a stigma not lifted in the United States until 1973, and to some extent, still prevailing today. Charles Neider touches on this point. "Were [Susy's] parents afraid to leave her alone at college?" Neider posits.

> "If so, why?... We know of Clemens' jealousy of Bryn Mawr because the college separated him from her, and of his remark... "Bryn Mawr began it. It was there that her health was undermined." Cryptic enough. No attempt at an explanation as to how her health was undermined. What "health" did he mean? Physical? Mental? Emotional? The letters indicate without question a profound relationship between Olivia [Susy] and Louise Brownell, and one that was passionate, regardless of the extent to which it was or wasn't platonic."[67]

Susy's letters to Brownell in the Hamilton archives are all that survive today. Any letters to Susy from Brownell are gone, presumably destroyed by her sister Clara, who so carefully managed the public identity of their father following his death. Twain, however, did know Brownell, as evidenced by several letters found among the Saunders Papers. Brownell had written to announce that she had named her second daughter Olivia Clemens Saunders after the dear Bryn Mawr companion of her youth. Twain replied with delight, saying: "those hallowed names [Olivia Clemens] thus consecrated, and in reverence I bow my white head before them in their new place."[68]

Records of a strong bond between Twain and Susy in the early years of her life bear a striking contrast between the separation experienced during the Bryn Mawr period. It seems Susy may have been a tad too attached to her father, and that Livy wanted to break that cycle for both her husband and daughter. "If [Twain] felt threatened" Charles Neider posits,

> "as apparently he did, by Susy's growing love for Bryn Mawr, it could not have been reassuring to hear her college friends call her by another name than the one used at home - Olivia…Susy's decision to use her first name on this, her major break from home, probably stimulated his sense of the psychological distance she was putting between herself and home (and him), a distance highlighted by her embarrassment over his telling of the ghost story…"[69]

Susy, the oldest of the three surviving Clemens children, was simply going through the growing pains of young adulthood, endeavoring to establish her independence the way many college-age kids still do. In that late Victorian period, there was something akin to a sexual revolution occurring as Susy was coming of age. The fact that she was surrounded, taught, and influenced by strong, progressive and liberal female role models compounded by exposure to the libertine sexual attitudes likely encountered on extended trips to Europe must have certainly began the process of molding Susy into a what could be considered a modern woman. From her writing ability evidenced in the Bryn Mawr period letters and the earlier biography of her father, Susy Clemens surely had a promising future as a literary heir to her father's legacy. What a tragic loss. Susy would have surely gone on to an independent career that could have exceeded the largess of Mark Twain. One can only wonder what she might have accomplished.

One can also glean from photos and biographical accounts by others that Twain found in Susy the boyish companionship he had lost and yearned for following the death of his son Langdon. Sensitive Susy, too, may have detected this, and found a fulfilling allegiance by providing for Dad the son he never had. In this regard, Susy's personality was the most like her Dads. She had inherited those rough and tumble pioneering qualities that gave Twain his inner strength and resolution. Clara, on the other hand, as the one Clemens child who did ultimately outlast the others, seems to have inherited the organizational and domineering qualities of her mother. Clara went on to have the singing career for which her older sister Susy had desired and trained, and there seems to be enough evidence to suggest that Clara harbored some measure of jealousy for the affection Susy received from their father.

These thoughts about Susy left me curious about the fate and current location of the other watering troughs dedicated to her along with Jean and Langdon Clemens. A brief investigation led me to an account stating that the other three troughs still sat along the Quarry Farm property on Crane Road,[70] a fact I had not known during my visit to Elmira.

Snapping out of my ruminations on Susy, I tool some photos in Cowles Hall, and resumed my intended quest. Along the entire main hallway of Cowles are identical oaken arches which were sealed by wallboard, as well as a row of windows. I wondered if they had each been doorways at one time. Unsure of which open archway to pursue, I picked the one to my immediate left, which led to a corridor of offices. Wrong doorway. I emerged, and looked directly across to an entrance to the Peterson Chapel the groundskeeper in the golf cart had mentioned. He had described it as one of the first all-faith, multi-use, non-denominational chapels of its kind in the country.

I was struck by the imposing height of the chapel's three-story vaulted ceiling as soon as I entered. This wasn't a chapel, this was a cathedral! The entire structure was a simplified Gothic affair constructed of richly stained oak. Lining the perimeter on the first level and a balcony above were a consistent row of brilliant, jewel-toned, non-denominational stained-glass windows. The windows on both sides of the first level featured depictions of some of Elmira's traditions such as an annual "Holiday Banquet," "Mayday" and "Mountain Day" with each window labeled as such. The corresponding windows on each side of the upper balcony level featured depictions of historical events and persons which and whom have had an impact on the college from its inception. The most notable, of course, was a radiant portrait of Mark Twain, standing before his study, clad in white and gazing skyward, holding a manuscript in one hand and a cigar in the other. I like this chapel. If ever there was an analogous portrayal of the playful, Twainian reference of him as "Saint Mark"- this was it!

I exited Peterson Chapel and made my way to the next arched doorway to my right. Nope! Not the one. I reemerged into the rotunda and walked a short distance to the next doorway and - bingo! I was greeted by an enlarged black and white portrait of the white-suited Mark Twain, seated in the same chair I just saw in the study, obligatory cigar in hand, posed beside the study pocket window nearest the fireplace. This must be the place. I navigated down the narrow corridor to a common hallway, then another left into a second corridor, which led me to an oak trimmed doorway that opened into a small room filled with Twain related artifacts. The walls were divided by stained oak wainscoting on the lower portion, with the upper segment of each wall dominated primarily by enlarged photos of Twain in his study, at Quarry Farm, and other locales around Elmira.

Saint Mark - the stained-glass window in Peterson Chapel, Elmira College.

Throughout the room were furnishings salvaged from the Langdon mansion - a chair here, a mantle clock there, a pewter charger, with the highlight of those objects being the frame of Olivia Langdon's bed, which served as a support for a tent-shaped display featuring photos and brief biographies of Langdon and Clemens family members.

The life-sized photo in Cowles Hall

Directly ahead on the wall space between the windows were encased first edition copies of Twain's books. Now that was cool. Some of the Twain related highlights displayed included one of the author's inventions - a Self-Pasting Scrapbook consisting of pages layered with a dried adhesive that only required dampening to affix photos, notes, clippings, etc. An information card pointed out that Twain had sold 25,000 of them netting a profit of $12,000 in 1877.

Directly opposite was an oak and wicker swivel chair cordoned off with rope which supported a crumpled old Panama hat that once belong to Twain. I recognized that hat from photos. Standing next to the chair was a pedestal ashtray on which rested two cheap cigars. On the wall above it was mounted one of Twain's walking sticks. Taking center stage of the room was a medium sized glass case displaying "Mark Twain's Lap Desk." No additional information was provided. I surmised that he likely used this when traveling by train or during his numerous trips abroad. A table near the door displayed laminated copies of his handwritten notes, and a glass enclosure featured one of his actual notebooks. It wasn't a bad exhibit. I didn't stay long as it was now approaching 3:30 in the afternoon and I wanted to venture to other locales and keep myself on schedule.

Left: The exhibit at Cowles hall. Center: Twain in Bermuda, holding the hat seen in photo to right, 1910, a few months before he died. Right: Twain's chair and crumpled Bermuda hat. Left/right photos by the author. Center photo courtesy NY Public Library Digital Archives.

Just outside the door was a steel library book cart and wall mounted display offering books for sale. The cart had some used and antique books with a sign that read "Your choice: $5.00 donation." I fingered through the titles and my eye caught an older, vintage looking hardback. I picked it up and examined the spine: *The American Claimant*, Mark Twain. I opened first to the copyright page, which listed six recurring copyrights, which in and of itself comprised the seed of a whole other story.

At the top of the list were two 1892 copyrights, one by Samuel L. Clemens, the other attributed to Charles L. Webster & Co., Twain's own publishing company that had produced such efforts as the autobiographical *Personal Memoirs of Ulysses S. Grant*, biographies of General Custer and Pope Leo XIII, works by Tolstoy and Walt Whitman, Twain's own *The Adventures of Huckleberry Finn, A Connecticut Yankee in King Arthur's Court*, and others. This was the same Charles L. Webster & Company that brought Twain to bankruptcy a second time in 1894, initiating his world lecture tour. Twain reluctantly embarked on the tour at age sixty-six as a moral - not legal - duty to raise the cash needed to pay off all of his creditors.

Already feeling burnt by his defeat in business, a legal announcement in the September 19, 1894 edition of the *New York Times* with added details surely poured salt on the wounds:

> "BUSINESS TROUBLES - The schedules of Charles L. Webster & Co., book publishers at 67 Fifth Avenue, in which firm Samuel L. Clemens ("Mark Twain") and Frederick J. Hall are the partners, were filed yesterday. They show liabilities of $94,191, nominal assets of $122,657, actual assets of $69,164, less $15,000 hypothecated to the United States National Bank, and net actual assets of $54,164. There are more than 200 creditors scattered all over the United States. Among the creditors are: Mount Morris Bank, $29,500; United States National Bank, $15,000; George Barrow, Skaneateles, N.Y., $15,420; S. D. Warren & Co., Boston, $6,332; Jenkins & McCowan, $5,363; Thomas Russell & Son, $4,623. There is due for royalties: Estate of U. S. Grant, $2,216; Col. F. D. Grant, $727; estate of Gen. P. H. Sheridan, St. Paul, Minn., $374; Mrs. E. B. Custer, London, $1,825."[71]

In today's currency, the total for just the six creditors listed here out of the 200 referenced, plus the listed royalties due, is just over two-million dollars. Despite the challenge, with the financial guidance of his good friend Henry Rogers, then Vice President of John D. Rockefeller's Standard Oil, Twain paid off every penny within four years, and came out ahead of the game with a substantial estate deposited in the bank.

Because of the Webster Company's failure, subsequent editions of the book I was holding thereafter are attributed to Harper and Brothers in 1896 and 1899, followed by a 1917 copyright to Mark Twain Company - the post mortem publishing collaboration between Albert Bigelow Paine and Twain's daughter Clara, with a final copyright in 1924 attributed to just 'Clara Gabrilowitsch.' The story of Clara inheriting the publishing rights to her father's material after his death, while protecting a carefully cultivated public image of Mark Twain and controlling which of his writings were or were not published is another saga.

Fascinated as I was with just reading the copyright page, at that time I was unacquainted with *The American Claimant* and considered this a score. I looked around to pay for the book, but seeing no one, on my way out I stopped at the study and gave my $5.00 to Jade, who was still there assisting visitors. I asked if she knew the directions to Woodlawn Cemetery, which she did and graciously furnished. Thanking her for her helpfulness I bid farewell, and made my way back to my car. Now it was time to truly square my debt with Mark Twain.

10

THE RESURRECTION OF SAMUEL CLEMENS

"Don't part with your illusions. When they are gone you may still exist but you have ceased to live."

Mark Twain,
Following the Equator

With the first focus of my adventure complete, I took a short break at my car to recharge my phone and review information I had printed before leaving home. I took a few minutes to type some notes on my laptop, then put into my GPS the address for Woodlawn Cemetery given by Jade. It seemed fairly straightforward and not far at all. After meandering my way through the streets along the other half of the Elmira College campus, I made a few turns and arrived at the Cemetery in minutes. As I passed through the opening in the wrought iron fence, I wasn't certain which way to go until I noted clearly marked signs offering easy guidance to the Mark Twain grave location. I followed the signs while navigating through a winding series of paths, recognizing why the signs had been put up to begin with. It might not have been so easy to locate without them. After a final turn, ahead to my right I saw the taller memorial marker which I recognized from photos, prompting me to slow down and find a suitable place to park.

Grabbing my backpack, I emerged from my air-conditioned car and was embraced with a noticeably thick blanket of humidity. My pores immediately began to generate sweat as the sun blazed down with formidable heat. I assessed that the humid conditions must originate from proximity to the Chemung River and assumed the cemetery grounds must be situated at a lower elevation. I looked around to see if I could locate how near I might have been to the river and found that my car and the Twain grave were set atop a high ridge that sloped down to a road. I didn't see a river, and began to wonder if endurance of this sweltering climate was routine penance when visitors paid homage to the remains of Mr. Clemens. Ironically, the weather reminded me of a similar level of humidity I had experienced on my visit to Hannibal, situated as it was along the banks of the Mississippi. Was this an added reason why Mark Twain had felt so at home in Elmira, I wondered? Personally, I detest humidity, and couldn't understand how anyone would want to spend an entire summer in such conditions. Had it rained recently? It was that humid that such questions kept leaping up in my mind. Undeterred, I took a sip from my water bottle and began a short trek toward the grave plot.

I was alone at the time, with no other visitors in the cemetery as far as I could see. Except for the sound of an occasional passing car on the road below the incline, the call and response of cicadas dominated the forested atmosphere. Dragonflies darted to and fro in the open area around me, with an unfolding variety of flying insects buzzing my ear now and then in repeated succession. I kept waving my free hand around my head to keep them at bay. The abundance of insects was so great that it bears mention. I was compelled to consciously surrender to their will and endure this momentary fate to proceed with my plan.

As I meandered past the grave markers that align a slate walkway leading up to the tallest of the monuments, I realized then the plot belonged to the Langdon family. That notion hadn't even occurred before, but made total sense. At once I began to view Mark Twain in a differing light.

I approached the tall carved granite monument designed with a simple art Deco motif for closer inspection of the green, weathered and oxidized bronze bas-relief medallion featuring a profile of Twain's bust, beneath which were featured the capitalized letters of "Mark Twain" carved in relief in the granite. Directly beneath Twain's portrait was an equal sized, similarly oxidized bronze medallion of another profile referenced by the capitalized relief name "Gabrilowitsch." An inscription in the marble base at its foundation explained:

"Death is the Starlit Strip between the Companionship of Yesterday
and the Reunion of Tomorrow. To the loving memory of my father
and my husband. 1957."

Aha! This wasn't the grave at all! This was a memorial obelisk erected by Twain's daughter Clara in tribute to the two primary men in her life. The obelisk had been commissioned by Clara in 1937 following the death of her first husband, Ossip Gabrilowitsch, the Russian-born pianist, composer, and conductor of the Munich Philharmonic and the Detroit Symphony Orchestra. I recalled the maquette for the proposed Twain memorial seen in Hartford, the one that wasn't realized due to lack of funds. This, then, I reasoned, must have been a compromised solution Clara had commissioned for a more approachable sum. It was elegant enough, but fell a bit shy to my expectation of the national memorial Twain deserved. I suppose, in those Depression years, it made sense to double up on the budget and incorporate a tribute to her husband as well, though I was confused about the twenty-year span between the commission request and the date on the plaque at the base.

On the one hand, it didn't seem fair to Twain's memory to have him share space with what I then assumed to be the lesser celebrity of his son-in-law. But that was just me, guilty of wanting to isolate my hero apart from any other association. It's a common syndrome of celebrity infatuation. In that moment, admittedly, I wasn't even familiar with the name "Gabrilowitsch," uncertain of whom the medallion portrayed, and was puzzled why it shared the same physical space with a memorial to Mark Twain. On the other hand, it was, after all, a family plot, and they certainly had the right to pay tribute in the way that they deemed fitting. Who was I to criticize?

Ossip Gabrilowitsch in 1935

Left: The Clemens family burial plot and memorial obelisk. Right: Obelisk close up

I later stumbled upon information that Clara had been offered two memorial design options by Enfred Anderson, an Elmira based artist whom she had commissioned. In her book *Hidden Story of His Final Years*, Twain scholar Laura Skandera Trombley explains that initially Clara had asked the artist to design a memorial only for her husband. It was Anderson who conceived of an alternate concept that would incorporate a then non-existent commemorative memorial to her father as well. One design, Trombley explained, "featured a bust of Twain on top with his birth name [Clemens] beneath it" and below it a medallion portrait of her mother and her maiden name, Olivia Langdon, with a kneeling Huckleberry Finn sculpted at the base.72 The second option Anderson offered was the one chosen by Clara, and is the memorial seen today.

From photographs I viewed online prior to my trip, I assumed the obelisk was Twain's headstone. Understanding the distinction, I wondered which marker, then, belonged specifically to Mark Twain. I turned to my immediate right and there before me was the marker dedicated to his beloved daughter Jean. Its inscription read:

"In Memory of Jean Lampton Clemens - A Most Dear Daughter - Her Desolate Father Sets This Stone,"

followed by what I presumed to be a quote from her father –

"After Life's Fitful Fever She Sleeps Well."

July 26, 1880 – Dec. 24, 1909

Two feet to its right was a marker simply inscribed on the top with the name Olivia Susan Clemens - Twain's dear Susy - with the dates beneath - March 19, 1872 - August 18, 1896. The vertical front bore an inscription of poetic verse:

'Warm summer sun, shine friendly here; Warm western wind, blow kindly here; Green sod above, rest light, rest light, Good-night, Dear Heart, good-night!'

The name of its author, Australian poet Robert Richardson, was inscribed beneath. Its slightly modified words had been extracted from his poem "Annette" about a young girl who had died at age twenty-one.

Seeing the graves of the two daughters after having becoming acquainted with the tragic tales of their respective deaths caused me to momentarily pause in solemn tribute. Here they were. God bless them, I thought. I patted my heart with my hand, feeling it a privilege to be standing so near.

To the right, with equal spacing between, was the marker dedicated to the love of Twain's life, his wife Olivia. The top of the stone was inscribed: "In this grave repose the ashes of Olivia Langdon, the beloved and lamented wife of Samuel L. Clemens" continuing as follows on the front:

"Who reverently raises this stone to her memory.
Elmira, November 27, 1845 - Florence, Italy, June 5, 1904."
Beneath that, along the very bottom, was an inscription in German:
"GOTT SEI DIR GNAEDIG, O MEINE WONNE."
I tried to translate this with my scant memory of German language learned in high school. At the time, I came up with the approximated "God bless you, O my woman." I was a bit off. It's actually: "God be gracious to you, oh my bliss" - a sweet sentiment revealing much of the heartbreak Twain endured at the time of her passing.

And then, two feet away at the end of the row, there I was, standing right in front of the stone marker I had sought. It was simply inscribed on the top: Samuel Langhorne Clemens, with larger carved letters in the middle - MARK TWAIN - and a third line with the dates Nov. 30, 1835 - Apr. 21, 1910. There was no poetic epitaph on the front of the stone as seemed customarily inscribed on the rest. It came across as a rip-off at first glance, but, then again, what can you select to inscribe and express in one phrase or sentence for a man who had written so much, who had practically reinvented modern verbal expression? It oddly seemed fitting.

I glanced behind the markers of Olivia and Sam to a second row behind, and there stood two markers of the same scale as the rest, sitting side by side. One belonged to Twain's daughter Clara, which was inscribed: Clara Clemens Gabrilowitsch Samossoud - the final name in that string being that of her second husband - and the dates, June 8, 1874 - Nov. 19, 1962. A simple inscription on the front of the stone read: "Goodnight darling, until we meet again." I was unsure if the quote was attributed to her father or her first or second husband.

To the left was a marker dedicated to her husband, the man featured on the lower medallion of the monument. On top, it read: Ossip Gabrilowitsch, Feb. 8, 1878 - Sep. 14, 1936. An inscription on the front was inscribed:
"Ossip Gabrilowitsch reflected in his art and in his life the noble
beauty of his lofty ideals."
To the right of the pair was an oddly juxtaposed empty space, which left the final marker of the plot sitting forlornly alone. It was the marker of Twain's only granddaughter, Nina. Like her grandfather's stone, it was simply inscribed on the top with her name and dates:
Nina Clemens Gabrilowitsch
Aug. 18, 1910 - Jan. 16, 1966.
The end of Nina's troubled life had found her dead of a drug overdose. I later learned that the odd space between the markers of Nina and her mother was

an unmarked plot where Clara's second husband, the Russian-born composer-conductor Jacques Alexandria Samossoud, had been buried unceremoniously by the Langdon family after his death in June of 1966. Samossoud had allegedly squandered Clara's inherited fortune by gambling, requiring Clara to liquidate what remaining assets and belongings she had just to survive. This had a profound effect on Clara's daughter Nina, further aggravating her addiction to alcohol and drugs. For this reason, the Langdon family did not hold much respect for Samossoud, who had created an emotional wedge between Clara, Nina, and the Langdons. The unmarked grave and the marker for Nina seemed to sadly suggest that this corner of the family plot had been reserved for the black sheep of the Clemens/Langdon families.

I surveyed the markers in their entirety. There were all the familiar names I had heard or read about for so long. I turned and looked down at the marker of Mark Twain before me. A substantial quantity of coins - pennies, nickels, quarters, dimes as well as some of foreign origin - filled the gaps between the raised letters. This was a custom I wasn't familiar with, though I had seen it from time to time. Was this form of tribute a superstitious custom to invite good luck?

Directly before the stone's unmarked front someone had placed a long stemmed, battery operated, plastic white rose. It was not illumined, but I thought it a charming albeit cheap looking gesture. I stood pondering for a moment longer, before looking about for a place to sit. A second, larger obelisk that divided the plot between the Clemens and Langdon halves offered a slightly sloped ledge that would serve the purpose. I removed my backpack, sat down, and withdrew my laptop while swatting mosquitoes that had been taking liberty with my flesh throughout my visit so far. I gazed back at Twain's headstone, and began to write:

3:47 pm - At the grave of Mark Twain

> I am sitting now about six feet from Mark Twain's grave plot, overlooked by the memorial. I shall not linger due to excessive mosquitos. I ask for your blessing, Mr. Clemens, that my writing be fruitful. More importantly, thank you for a life time of all good stuff. I've followed you around, and now I find you, resting in peace.
>
> The grave is adorned with stones and coins, placed by fans. I would like to meditate longer, but the bugs may be getting the best of me. Perhaps the Langdon family keeps them here to shoo away those with lesser ambitions. As I write this, some multi-legged critter just landed on my neck, scampered down the length of my torso inside my shirt, then leapt out from the waist onto the ground, and slithered into a crevice along the slate. Lovely.

A cool breeze just alighted my way, and the mosquitos seemed to have abated...until I started writing that sentence, when one landed on my right wrist and another on my left calf.

Here lies the man. The great American who touched so many. The great soul whose radiance illumined the world. His spirit seems to jest with me, now, as if I can hear him saying: "I may have illumined then, but it's a tad shadier now from my point of view down here."

I leave inspired. Thank you.

The funny thing about my visit to the grave site of Mr. Clemens that differed from my visits to Hannibal or Hartford, was that suddenly the fact of considering Mark Twain as a real man that had lived and died came into a different perspective. In fact, it occurred to me that Mark Twain was a fictional character, created by Sam Clemens of Missouri. We forget that. We have a way of generally forgetting that about those whom we prefer to elevate and sustain with mythical status. Mark Twain the entity had attained immortality. It was the grave of Samuel Clemens I was visiting.

It is interesting to note the headstone design for Twain's grave. The name 'Mark Twain' appears larger than the man's actual name - Samuel Langhorne Clemens. Even in death he is presented as larger than life.

Samuel Clemens was a man not unlike any other who lived through the Nineteenth Century, who endured family tragedy in ways not uncommon for that era. The mortality rate in infancy or childhood prior to advances in modern medicine was always high, and frequently expected. Victorian era families had initiated the somewhat morbid custom of hiring daguerreotype photographers to take photos of their deceased children posed in a manner which created the illusion that their corpse was still living at the time of the photo.

The fact that Olivia and Sam Clemens endured the pain of losing their children is not being desensitized here. But what distinguishes their situation is that the head of the household was a writer who wrote about it, and did so in a very popular, appealing manner that didn't ascend to the lofty literary platitudes of the great English poets and authors whose work until then defined the literary standard. Sam Clemens knew how to talk to common folk, and that's at the core of why he was so adulated.

During the course of this research journey, possibly while watching the Ken Burns documentary, someone referred to Mark Twain as a rock star of his day. Twain was, in fact, THE rock star. He was the Elvis, the Frank Sinatra, the Eminem, and perhaps more accurately, the Ziggy Stardust of his day. Yet, having read his posthumously published *Letters From The Earth*, I wonder if he had been more like a Punk Rock star, closer in spirit to Johnny Lydon, but softened with the elegant swagger of a David Byrne. It's a tough call.

Some of a lesser literary inclination may lump Mark Twain into a category of old, obsolete writers of an era passed, with the level of his perceived celebrity referenced in a contextual category that might enable a younger generation to acquire the capability of comprehending the enormous popularity he enjoyed in his day. But without reading the full scope of his written work, it's just another footnote of designation. I assert that to fully understand Mark Twain and fully comprehend why he is called a rock star, one would be better suited to gradually incorporate the reading of his work into a long term, lifetime curriculum. For it really has, from my experience, taken a literal lifetime to fully appreciate this fictional character, Mark Twain, whom Sam Clemens so perfectly embodied and presented to all. From those boyhood days of watching the Fredric March film as a child with Dad, to visiting the grave of the actual man, a great deal has been learned. I feel as if I had been given the opportunity to live his life along with him.

We're born, we live, we age, we die. The life cycle of our mammalian species is an odd thing. Why is it that it takes an encounter with death for us to fully understand and appreciate the value of a life? When we view the news today, with so many reports of senseless acts of homicidal violence, it seems to serve as an indication that we are evolving into a species that retains little gratitude for this precious gift called life.

Samuel Clemens was a man, born in a shack in the state of Missouri in the Nineteenth Century United States, who, when presented with the prospect of serving in the Confederate army on the eve of the American Civil War and the larger requirement of taking a gun and killing an untold number of fellow citizens for a cause which he half-heartedly endorsed and simultaneously questioned, opted instead to leave his defined Southern State and head West to embrace life, to embark on the task of living. And while he had entertained notions of being a river pilot or print compositor, it wasn't until Samuel Clemens made a conscious decision to take leave and embark on a new adventure in the western territories that his act of living truly began. It was then, right then and there, that Sam Clemens captured a key element of the American ethos that defines us until this day.

There were other young Americans of the same mindset in Twain's time. Walt Whitman, another 19th Century rock star, would be the next best example. Both Whitman and Clemens shared a recognition for an ability to break free from the constraints of conventional thinking. They were both fearless in their pursuit of absolute personal independence.

We talk and write and make films about Mark Twain, but Samuel Clemens is the real unsung hero. Samuel Clemens was the man written about, and the man who did the writing. What was it about his ability to separate himself from the entity presented to the world as Mark Twain? The story of Sam Clemens is the one to be told. We are grateful that he took the time to share his story, and didn't really take credit for it. The adulation went to a fictional character, to an idea named Mark Twain.

From my perch on the obelisk ledge, I looked up from my laptop to gaze again quietly at Twain's grave marker. I fancied the word play before me, how this unpretentious, modest piece of granite served as the plumb for the leadsman's final call of "mark twain" on the broad river that remains a celebrated life for this giant of American literature. As I gazed mindfully at the stone, predisposed in thought, I noticed something resting on the ground at the base of the grave marker I had overlooked before. Is that a cigar? Where did that come from? How did it get there, I wondered? I could swear that wasn't there when I was standing right in front of the stone only minutes before.

I put away my laptop, stood up, and walked over to the grave. I picked up the cigar, fingered it for a minute, then smelled it. Whaat? It was fresh! The rich aroma that wafted through my olfactory glands indicated that it possessed just the right amount of humidity for a fine smoke. How is this possible? There has been no one else in this cemetery since I arrived. How could it be so fresh? Was the swampy weather in the cemetery that humid?

As I studied the specimen, I noted there was no label on it to indicate the brand or quality, whether it was a cheap smoke of the sort which Twain was known to have been fond or if it was a superior brand left in high tribute. I was still obsessed with why I hadn't seen it before. I entertained the thought that it was some sort of miraculous gift from Mr. Twain, delivered from his soul's resting place in the great riverboat in the sky, as some sort of divine nod of thanks for not only showing my appreciation for him and his written canon, but for acknowledging the graves of his daughters and wife with equal sobriety. Nah, it couldn't be. Could it?

I considered pocketing the cigar to enjoy later. Surely, I reasoned, this was left for me in acknowledgment of my appreciation. I held it a little longer. Should I? Shouldn't I? Certainly, it would be justified in the divine scheme of things if I purloined a cigar from Mark Twain's grave and enjoyed it in his memory. He would have offered me a cigar if he were here, I reasoned. And maybe, well, maybe he was now doing just that.

The better angels of my Catholic conscience prevailed, just as they always do, and I set the cigar back where I had found it. This surely had been left by an adoring fan who had visited earlier, I reasoned, though the trident-toting little doppelganger in a red devil costume on my other shoulder was whispering how the cemetery caretakers must routinely scoop up such booty and pocket it themselves or toss it in the trash, with the coins going to some fund reserved

The grave marker of Samuel Langhorne Clemens and the miracle cigar

for preservation needs. After all, I wasn't the first visitor to have paid tribute in some form. More cigars and coins would surely find their way here. Putting it back was the right thing to do. Wasn't it?

I left the cigar where it belonged and picked up my backpack while surveying the rest of the plot and casually walked over to explore the Langdon family markers on the opposite side of the center marker where I had been sitting. I recognized the grave markers inscribed with other names I had come to know: Charles Langdon - Twain's fellow Night Hawk, the brother who had met Sam Clemens on the transatlantic trip which brought about his courtship with sister Olivia. There was Jervis Langdon, Susan Langdon Crane, the owner of Quarry Farm, and the most recently dated marker from 2004 belonging to Jervis Langdon, Jr., Twain's grand-nephew and former president of the B & O, Penn Central, and Amtrak railroad lines, and donor of Quarry Farm and Twain's study to Elmira College. The very end of the plot was marked by a smaller scaled marker inscribed:

Grave marker of Langdon Clemens.

Langdon, son of Samuel L. & Olivia L. Clemens.

Born Nov. 7, 1870, Died June 2, 1872.

This was the toddler who's young death forever antagonized Mark Twain with guilt. It seemed a shame that he was buried at such a distance from the other siblings whom he'd never grow to know.

As I swatted and shoed the prevalent flying bloodsuckers, I headed back to my car to take leave of this profoundly moving pilgrimage site. I might have stayed longer were it not for the infestation of mosquitoes swarming all around. As I opened my trunk to set down my backpack, I glanced to my right at the antique, ornately designed wrought iron gate and railing that surrounded another family plot. An inscription atop the gate, melded into the wrought iron, bore the name John Arnot II, and dated 1869. Arnot was the name on the outside of an art museum in downtown Elmira I had driven past earlier. I could tell by the fence around the plot that it belonged to a family of considerable wealth. Months afterward I learned that the Arnot name was associated with the financing of the Chemung Canal, had served in leadership roles in local politics and eventually as a member of the forty-eighth Congress, by marriage with the construction of the Trans-Pacific Railroad, and the founding of the city of Chicago.[73] I also discovered that the Arnot family today remain one of the largest purveyors of real estate in the Elmira region, with the area's largest shopping mall bearing their name. It revealed that Elmira remained a living community, active with the descendants of those who've populated the town and contributed to its growth and sustenance for hundreds of years.

The Arnot family plot at Woodland Cemetery, Elmira.

But who was John Arnot 2nd, the presumed head of family for whom this plot was dedicated? He had been born in Scotland in 1793 and brought to America in 1801.

> "At the age of forty [John Arnot] was recognized as one the most substantial business men of Elmira and one of its most devoted and patriotic citizens. The list of the commercial and financial enterprises with which he was identified is long and notable."[74]

It's amazing what history one can find by just taking time to look up from where you park. There was a lot of history to be explored in Elmira, I was learning, but not today. I took a photo and then got in my car, slapping dead the remaining mosquitoes that elected to hijack along for the ride. As I paused to locate any marker of Quarry Farm on my GPS, another car of visitors slowly approached in search of a place to pull over and park. The license plate was, of all places, from, Missouri. I smiled and took it as an appropriate queue to start the ignition and move on.

As I neared the exit of the cemetery, I slowed down to take a closer look at a large directory of specified grave sites with a list naming some of the more prominent cemetery residents. I was completely surprised to find the entire marker dedicated to 21 interred in Woodland Cemetery who had been active participants in the Underground Railroad, among them Jervis and Olivia Langdon, the parents of Mark Twain's wife.

The memorial sign at the entrance of Woodland Cemetery, listing Twain's in-laws Jervis & Olivia Langdon among those interred and honored as conductors on the Underground Railroad.

This was the first time I learned of their abolitionist sentiments, leading me to further understand that this unassuming town had once been a primary leader in the cause against slavery in the United States. It spoke volumes on the ethically minded influence of a great deal of Twain's thinking, writing, and manner of living. It unveiled additional insight on the conversations that Charles Langdon and Samuel Clemens might have had when they first met on their transatlantic trip, compelling Clemens to expand his association with the family for reasons beyond the romantic part of the tale, about Clemens' infatuation with the portrait of Olivia that Langdon carried with him. I would also come to learn how Clemens grew to admire Jervis Langdon as a surrogate for the father he had lost in his youth. Now I was beginning to understand why. This was significant information worthy of further research, I thought at the time, prompting me to record a reminder on my phone app to investigate later.

I left the cemetery and drove in the direction of the tall hill that overlooked Elmira based on Jade's reference back at the study. As I drove up a wildflower and weed lined narrow road, I pictured this as the same road Twain had once used for his carriage rides into town, or his walk to the Langdon mansion on the day he met Rudyard Kipling.

As I rounded the top of the hill, I approached an open, deforested area of mowed grass with a convergence of some smaller roads, uncertain if they were actual roads or private driveways. At the edge of this confluence stood a newer bronze historic marker on a post informing me I was in the right place. I pulled over to get out and take a photo. It read:

'Quarry Farm, Home of Susan Langdon Crane and Summer home of Mark Twain. Here he wrote some of his most famous books (1870-1903).'

Below was an indication of its donor: 'Elmira College Center for Mark Twain Studies.

Gift of Jervis Langdon, Jr. 1982.'

I looked about, tempted to drive on the road that looked like a driveway, deciding instead to just continue on the main road. As I drove slowly, I saw a grizzled old mountain man with unkempt, long white hair and equally long white beard poking through the wildflowers along the right side of the road. He had a small sack slung over one shoulder, and his clothes seemed a bit on the tattered side. He seemed to be investigating certain plants, or maybe foraging for wild berries. He would remind you of a John Muir kind of guy, yet reminded me of similar looking mountain guys I used to see when I lived in the Catskill foothills of neighboring Sullivan County. His appearance was so virtually identical that I humored myself with the thought of a conclave of aged mountain men at some sort of meeting place or clubhouse where all members were required to look and dress the same, with the hand-hewn wooden walking stick and weathered canvas knapsack had by this fellow being the required standard issue tools for the purpose stated in their mountain man field manual.

The Quarry Farm marker at the fork in the road.

I drove slowly and saw an older looking, seemingly Victorian-era country house with a nice front porch approaching on my left. Was this it? I slowed down to slight of stopping to study the property, not wanting to linger too long with respect to my understanding of it then as a private residence. Was this the farmhouse referenced on the marker? Was that the front porch where Twain might have sat with his in-laws and family members on lazy summer evenings just like this? I refrained from taking a photo and continued to drive on, looking to see if there was some place where I might get out and explore on foot.

As I approached the end of the drive, a car turned from an intersecting road and drove toward me. I slowed down, hoping I might hail the driver and inquire about the exact location of Quarry Farm. Before I said anything, I noted that the driver was looking directly at me with a concerned, almost angry look on his face, leaving me to immediately assess as being one of the locals. One thing I had learned long ago when living in Sullivan County is that mountain folk were a species fiercely protective of their habitat when outsiders came to call. Suddenly I didn't feel welcome, and instead just nodded to the driver with a smile as we passed each other. I drove to the intersection at the very top of the hill, uncertain which direction to take. I looked at the time on my dashboard. It was nearing 4:30 pm and I noted that I was almost out of gas. My spider senses cajoled me then to abort any further extension of my trip with concern for running out of gas in the middle of country no-mans-land. After seeing the look on the face of that local in the car, I especially thought this might not be the most agreeable place to get stuck. I located the nearest gas station on my GPS, made a U-turn in the intersection and headed back down the hill.

As I neared the old house I passed on my first round, the car that had just passed me was now parked on the road in front, its angry driver hunched over the open trunk. Because of the narrowness of the road, I slowed down to pass, which prompted the fellow to bend upright, turn in my direction and eye me with what seemed to be an even greater measure of consternation than before. Yeah, I definitely wasn't welcome here. I surmised then that this wasn't likely the Quarry Farm house I was looking for, and instead might be the guy who lived in this neighboring house, probably weary of the daily, perpetual influx of lost Twain pilgrims seeking the elusive Holy Grail sequestered deep within the ancient rafters of Quarry Farm. I smiled and nodded again at the guy as I passed, now more humored by the look of unnecessary pain inherent in the expression of his facial muscles. This must have been a well-practiced look he kept in reserve for the likes of unannounced strangers like me.

I continued along the road at a relatively slow pace, studying the environs as a last look at this sacred place, uncertain when Providence might afford me another opportunity to visit. I saw ahead on my left my old mountain man buddy, still engaged with his contemplative foraging among the bushes. He kind of looked like the popular caricature of God the Father. I fancied for a moment that it was Mark Twain's ghost, or the ghost of some long deceased, obsessed fan, an ever present, uninvited entity, self-assigned as Quarry Farm's designated eternal overseer.

When I got to the bottom of the hill, my GPS took me through uncharted sections of Elmira. I got a keen glimpse of a town in economic distress that had seen better days. I noticed a significant number of abandoned factories and shuttered businesses, and scant evidence of a significant population. Certain areas along railroad tracks reminded me of similar small towns I had visited that had also been once thriving examples of small-town USA now struggling to remain relevant. One such town was Reidsville, North Carolina, into which I stumbled only because my GPS took me right through it on a trip to High Point for a trade show.

Reidsville's largest industries had been tobacco and cotton, with the Lucky Strike Cigarette factory being its largest employer until closing in 1994, followed by a thriving textile industry that also petered out. Those two enterprises prospered in conjunction with the railroad that ran straight through the center of town, enabling their wares to be freely exported. Reidsville was similarly void of a noticeable population, and was struggling to live up to the town's motto of "Focused on a Better Tomorrow." Culturally, Elmira reminded me of two other towns I had visited. One was Mount Airy, North Carolina, with its entire economy dependent upon tourism focused on its favorite son, Andy Griffith, and the characters from his television show. Another was Winterset, Iowa, a struggling small Midwestern town on the outskirts of Des Moines which boasted of itself as the birthplace of famed actor John Wayne.

Personally, that's one of the things I like about towns like this in the US, and it's part of the reason I like to drop by and pay a visit. The decline of small-town America is at the root of what could be defined as a vanishing American culture. While many yearn to bring back the good ol' days, accusations for the initial cause of decline are typically slung at one demographic or another, and nothing happens. This is a simplistic way of summarizing it, but the writing is on the wall. One only needs to pay a visit to small towns like this to see the situation first hand.

The more I thought about Elmira, I couldn't help but feel it needed a real shot in the arm to cajole it from its slumber. It's easy for me, as an outsider, to make suggestions, but as I researched data on Elmira, I found that a number of efforts to resurrect it had been made. It has a wonderful college, and at least two significant tourist sites accessible to the public. Were there more? If so, I didn't know about them. As I wrote earlier, Elmira wasn't even on my radar in relation to my interest in Mark Twain. I suspect this to be case for others as well. There is so much untapped potential I was seeing while there. Having been to Hannibal and Hartford, I thought of what distinguished those two locations in the Twainian scope of things. It was more than just the locales to visit. There had been a huge overt effort to sustain their prowess as Twain destinations. Elmira had destinations, too, but I didn't see much evidence that it was overtly supported or marketed, as if Elmira preferred to remain a long-kept secret. Most people, I assumed, fans like myself, come to visit the study and grave and then leave - just as I was doing.

I thought about the Langdon Plaza strip mall, and its location on the former mansion site. Since my visit to Hartford I've kept thinking of that maquette for the large memorial that was never built. I couldn't help but wonder if somehow, with modern technology like 3-D printing, that there wasn't some way that memorial could be realized at a fraction of its original proposed cost. I recalled reading, during the era of its inception, how multiple towns had bid on the chance to be selected as the site for the full-scale version. None were chosen, largely because the funds never materialized.

But now that I've visited these Twain towns, and learning of Twain's preference for writing in Elmira due to lessened distraction and interruption, about that lovely little study on Quarry Farm that had served as the very birthplace of Twain's greatest writing, and with Elmira College as the location of The Center for Mark Twain Studies, it seemed apparent that Elmira was the true spiritual home of the Twain oeuvre, and always was the place that should have had that memorial.

Elmira wasn't all that different from my hometown, I thought. Philadelphia had been the thriving manufacturing hub of America's industrial age, having once produced and distributed everything from umbrellas and buttons and Stetson hats to upscale apparel and locomotives, and has since seen its own share of decline and troubles. I could even see in Elmira a kinship to my very neighborhood of Grays Ferry, which once had its own nucleus of business enterprises offering economic opportunity to the working-class residents in the brick, factory town row-homes surrounding them.

Like Hal Holbrook's remark about Mark Twain, I saw in Elmira the physical manifestation of the soul of America. Once a mighty, economically prosperous industrial engine, Elmira had been a shining example of successfully integrated, interracial cohabitation. It served as an actualized, living example of all that America could and wanted to be. Elmira is America's childhood home, I reasoned. It is that shining city on the hill mentioned by Ronald Reagan, which has since lost a little polish and become a little rough around the edges. Its beacon light hasn't fully extinguished, offering yet a lesson of potential. Perhaps a visit to Elmira and taking a long hard look might provide the needed inspiration to find solutions for healing our national woes. Plus, the bonus Elmira offers is that one is never too far from the influence and guiding wisdom of its most memorable citizen, Mark Twain. After all, it was Elmira which had inspired him!

Before departing town I stopped to fill my gas tank while debating what to do next. It was now approaching 5:00 pm and after a day of munching on just the snacks I'd brought along, I was feeling a tad hungry. When I was originally planning the trip, I had considered spending the night near Ithaca and including a stop at the Moosewood Restaurant. I had been using cookbooks from the place for forty years and wanting to visit just as long. I had never been to Ithaca, and my GPS indicated it was only twenty-nine miles away from Elmira, just a forty-five-minute drive. Being on my tight Coinstar budget, I already decided that I wouldn't spend the night. But being so close to Moosewood after so long, how could I pass up the opportunity? I reckoned how I could get there, eat, get back on the road, and still make it through the mountainous areas of highway before nightfall. Why not? You only live once, and I wasn't sure when I might be in this neck of the woods again. Moosewood it is.

Once I drove out of the more congested areas around Elmira and got on the longer stretches of highway, I reflected on my day so far. I pondered the joy experienced while seeing and writing in Mark Twain's study, on items in the exhibit like Twain's lap desk, on the heartfelt visit to his grave and the miracle of the fragrant cigar. I thought about the hill of Quarry Farm, and how the old mountain man and paranoid car man provided perfect accessories to an otherwise boring segment of this story. As wonderful as all those thoughts were, the one point that kept coming to mind was the significance of learning that day for the first time about the role of Elmira and its citizens as abolitionist activists and participants in the Underground Railroad.

This alone, I thought, would be worth serious investigation when I later got home. It awakened in me a profound interest to learn just how much Mark Twain's life had been intertwined with the abolitionist movement. In Hartford, he had Harriet Beecher Stowe as his next-door neighbor, and in Elmira, Stowe's brother was pastor of the church attended by the Langdon and Clemens families, and now the Underground Railroad reference in Woodlawn Cemetery. The Langdon's designation as participants in the Underground Railroad was a significant discovery for me. There was more to this story than I had been previously aware. Because, really, one can't have a complete conversation about Mark Twain without including more than just a mention of his written sentiments on racial relations in the United States.

11

REFLECTIONS ON RACISM

"If I'm gonna be White, don't make me be Irish. That's the *worst* one."

Titus Andromedon,
Unbreakable Kimmy Schmidt[75]

As much as I had enjoyed Huckleberry Finn as a charged work of literature, I hadn't had a conversation about why Twain wrote it in a long time. It was more than just a nostalgic reflection on the innocence of boyhood set within a complex narrative that incorporated elements of controversial period topics; it was boyhood amid the most overtly racist era of our nation's history. There was more to the mind and soul of Mark Twain, I was learning, than I had allowed myself to perceive. It brought to fore a refreshed notion of Twain as representative of one coming of age just as the nation was brought into an actual war over the issue of adjudicating sanctioned slavery or unmitigated freedom.

Racial discrimination is the defining underscore of American history. Since the publication of the *Adventures of Huckleberry Finn*, Twain had been in the forefront of that conversation for more than one-hundred and thirty years. I contemplated how racism had been a festering boil on the American complexion since its inception, and, incredulously, how it remains a conversation today that still hasn't fully concluded. As I drove on, my mind drifted while reflecting on powerful incidents and circumstances throughout my life where racism had reared its ugly head in my own world. I clearly saw these repressed memories as the elephant on the raft, for racism had been no stranger to me.

In the decade before I was born, my Dad performed as an interlocutor and end man in amateur minstrel shows organized by neighborhood guys and staged as benefit programs in church halls of Catholic parishes throughout Philadelphia. As I took a harder look back, I couldn't deny that Dad was a man who participated in a racist cultural tradition, and, by default, had been racist in a relatively unconscious racist culture in denial. I never saw him perform and he didn't speak of it much when I was young. I only knew this from stories I'd been told or overheard when growing up, along with evident clues like the vintage microphones in our basement from his stage performance days, through program booklets he had saved, and the remaining burnt stubs of cork he would later use to apply a five o'clock shadow to accessorize our hobo costumes on Halloween.

In our house, a few rounds of drinks at family parties were enough to encourage Dad to break out his accordion. After singing some standards like the Ray "Scarecrow" Bolger Broadway show tune *Once Upon a Time*, then popularized by Vic Damone's redux, a little cajoling from friends would entice Dad to break into some of the old minstrel standards. Along with the Al Jolson hit *Waiting for the Robert E. Lee* Dad regularly sung two particularly racy numbers: One was *Shine*, a song recorded and popularized by Bing Crosby and The Mills Brothers in 1932, and a Louis Armstrong rendition in the 1932 short film *A Rhapsody in Black and Blue*. The refrain went like this:

>Oh, Chocolate Drop, tha's me
>'Cause my hair is curly,
>Just because my teeth are pearly,
>Oh just because I always wear a smile,
>I like to dress up in the latest style,
>Just because I'm glad I'm living.
>Ohh.. I takes all my troubles, all with a smile,
>Mmm Just because my color's shady,
>Makes no difference, maybe
>That's why they call me "Shine."

While certainly offensive by today's standards, Shine was lightweight compared to *Mammy's Little Coal Black Rose*, a minstrel standard penned by Raymond Egan and Richard Whiting in 1916. Among the most virulently racist songs ever composed, the lyrics go like this:

>I heard a pickaninny crying down in Tennessee one night,
>his little heart was nearly breaking just because he wasn't white.
>Then his dear Mammy kiss'd him,
>and she said "Chile don' you sigh….
>Weep no more my baby." Then she sang a Dixie lullaby:…..
>You better dry your eyes my little Coal Black Rose, -
>You better go to sleep and let those eyelids close,
>Cause you're dark, don't start a pinin',

You're a cloud with a silver lining.
Tho' ev'ry old crow thinks his babe am white as snow,
Your dear old Mammy knows you're mighty like a rose.
And when the angels gave those kinky curls to you, -
They put a sunbeam in your disposition too, that's true, -
The reason you're so Black I 'spose,
They forgot to give your Mammy- a talcum powder chamois,
So don't you cry, don't you sigh,
'Cause you're Mammy's little Coal Black Rose.

1916 Sheet music for Mammy's Little Coal Black Rose, illustrated with romanticized images of plantation life with lovely fronds of cotton blossoms and the king of Blackface Al Jolson, who made the song popular.

A typical program cover for an amateur minstrel show like those offered in communities throughout the US. I grew up discovering programs like these tucked away in junk drawers in our home.

Dad sang this up to a certain point when I was kid, and then it vanished abruptly from his repertoire. I don't recall him ever singing it again. Something shifted within my Dad in those latter years. My brother Mike often says that I grew up in a different household than he and my older brothers. I believe this may be due to my coming of age while our Dad was coming to terms with the better angels of his moral conscience in the changing, socially integrative climate of America, and I, as the youngest, was around more often and able to witness this inner transformation as it unfolded.

My mother explained that Dad had been performing in a community minstrel act when she met him in 1949. At some point prior he had joined the group of men from his neighborhood that regularly rehearsed and performed in a community venue. I can't explain why other than Blackface performance was then as relatively accepted as it had been for over a hundred years at that point.

Buffooning Black stereotypes had been a popular form of entertainment in the United States since the early 19th Century. The legendary Philadelphia actor Edwin Booth – brother of Lincoln assassin John Wilkes Booth – had launched his stellar career as a minstrel performer. In downtown Philadelphia, a popular venue was Frank Dumont's Minstrel Theater on the edge of present-day Chinatown. In 1899, it was Dumont who had authored the definitive tome on the subject in the *Witmark Amateur Minstrel Guide and Burnt Cork Encyclopedia*, in which he states: "Minstrelsy is the one American form of amusement, purely our own...It has lived and thrived even through the plantation darkey, who first gave it a character..."

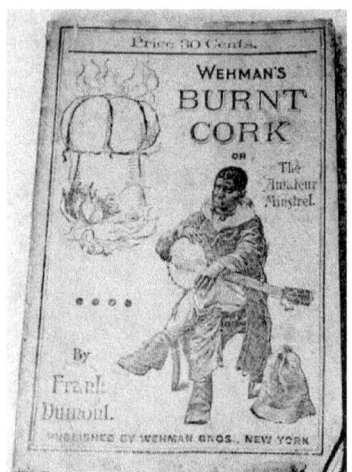

Left: Frank Dumont's 1881 handbook on amateur minstrelsy. Right: Dumont's minstrel theater on the corner of 9th and Arch Streets, Philadelphia, in 1917. The last of Philadelphia's once numerous minstrel theaters, it burned to the ground in a 1929 fire. Photo courtesy Philadelphia Department of Records.

Dumont's statement embodies the prevailing attitude that was extant as my dad was coming of age. I suppose there is a part of me that doesn't like to talk about my Dad's minstrel history. I recall addressing it in one of my pop history courses at University of Pennsylvania that reviewed Black stereotype representation in pop culture. My professor and most of the class weren't inclined to discuss it, which surprised me because we were then reviewing the life and times of controversial boxer Jack Johnson, renaissance man Paul Robeson, and the legacy of Amos and Andy. It seemed as if everyone was too frightened or overly cautious to offer an opinion – except for one fellow student who approached me after class. A young

African American, he was fascinated and wanted to learn more, disappointed by our classmates' reaction. I understood its offensiveness then and now, but I wanted to seriously engage a group discussion and understand other's perspectives. I gather, that, even then, I was trying in some way to reconcile issues with my Dad by trying to understand his world and proclivities. By reviewing his transformation from racist minstrel performer to an adherent of conscious ethics due to Mark Twain's influence, I saw an opened window through which I perceived both a foundation and turning point of this investigation.

As I read about Mark Twain's references to his father's ownership of slaves as just a routine way of life into which young Sam Clemens had been inadvertently indoctrinated, I saw another avenue of kinship to my Dad's circumstance and how I responded to it in years following. Certainly, Blackface minstrelsy isn't the same as slavery, but a denigrating tradition nonetheless. I found it curious when I came across a letter written by Twain in 1873, in which he viewed Blackface minstrel performances as a subpar, cheap imitation of an authentic experience at the heart of the Black community. Twain wrote:

"To Tom Hood, Esq., & Messrs. George Routledge & Sons, London: Gentlemen...

The Jubilee Singers are to appear in London, & I am requested to say in their behalf what I know about them—& I most cheerfully do it. I heard them sing once, & I would walk seven miles to hear them sing again...

I think these gentlemen & ladies make eloquent music—& what is as much to the point, they reproduce the true melody of the plantations, & are the only persons I ever heard accomplish this on the public platform. The so-called "negro minstrels" simply mis-represent the thing; I do not think they ever saw a plantation or ever heard a slave sing.

I was reared in the South, & my father owned slaves, & I do not know when anything has so moved me as did the plaintive melodies of the Jubilee Singers. It was the first time for twenty-five or thirty years that I had heard such songs, or heard them sung in the genuine old way—& it is a way, I think, that white people cannot imitate—& never can, for that matter, for one must have been a slave himself in order to feel what that life was & so convey the pathos of it in the music...

Yours faithfully,
Saml. L. Clemens.
"Mark Twain."[76]

Twain was referencing The Jubilee Singers of Fisk University in Nashville, Tennessee. As contributors to the Mark Twain Project explain:

> "[The troupe] had undertaken an extended singing tour in 1871 to raise money for their school. The third year of their tour took them to Great Britain, where they performed from May 1873 until May 1874, raising nearly ten thousand pounds. According to their agent, Gustavus Pike, the eleven singers—eight of them former slaves—won acclaim for the "spiritual and religious power of the songs of the slaves of the South, and thus touched the hearts of the Christian people everywhere and secured their sympathy and liberal aid."[77]

A review of The Jubilee Singers in the Hartford Courant explained their performance as:

> "a sensation rarely equaled...It is the first time that we at the north have heard the genuine songs of their race, executed with their faith and their feeling. It was like a revelation...One heard in those strange and plaintive melodies the sadness and the hope of a trusting and a really joyous race."[78]

The Jubilee Singers in an 1881 promotional photo.

As popular as minstrelsy had been, it was widely viewed as a lowbrow form of entertainment. In an 1869 review of a lecture delivered by Twain, the Decatur Republican described those in attendance as:

"a large and respectable audience. Broadcloths and silks were in the ascendant, and the rowdy or 'fast' element congenial to negro minstrel exhibitions was but slimly represented. The intelligence of our city was out in full force...and decency and decorum were the marked characteristics of those assembled to hear Mark Twain's discourse."[79]

In a more critical review of a Twain lecture on the topic of then popular humorist Artemus Ward, which had been deemed a "decided failure," the Erie observer described Twain's delivery as a "pitiful attempt to ape the style of Artemus Ward, in which he only succeeded in reaching the standard of a negro minstrel."[80]

Artemus Ward

Despite the lowbrow distinction, by the turn of the 20th Century, Frank Dumont's assertion of Blackface minstrelsy as a distinctly American art form had become gospel, enabling the genre to thrive as an accepted and enormously popular expression of American culture. Mark Twain had included a minstrel scene in *The Adventures of Tom Sawyer*. Broadway legends George M. Cohen and Irving Berlin had produced, performed, or written songs for Blackface minstrel shows. Black performer Bert Williams put on Blackface makeup for the Ziegfeld Follies in 1919. Al Jolson reigned as the king of Blackface performers throughout the Roaring Twenties, capped by his 1927 performance in *The Jazz Singer*, the first motion picture with sound. Laurel and Hardy donned Blackface in the 1930 film *Pardon Us* for a singing performance of *Lazy Moon*, set against disheveled Negro plantation shacks. Shirley Temple performed with the Dixie-Anna Minstrels in the 1936 film *Dimples*, with a narrator explaining the performance as an anniversary celebration of the first publishing of *Uncle Tom's Cabin*. The Three Stooges wore Blackface while lampooning old Southern culture at large. Mickey Rooney and Judy Garland had donned Blackface for a feature number in 1941's *Babes on Broadway*. The inclusion of at least one minstrel tune or performance in the repertoire of many big stars seems to have been a must.

One of the more outrageous affronts of Blackface minstrel culture was offered in the 1939 biopic *Swanee River* about composer Stephen Foster, featuring Al Jolson as Edwin Christy of the famed Christy's Minstrels, the leading minstrel troupe of the Reconstruction Era. Intended as a cinematic tribute to Foster, the film's end (sorry - spoiler alert) features Jolson as Christy dedicating his stage performance in memoriam to the composer on the day he died (which is inaccurate, Hollywood hype). With 30 to 50 minstrel performers seated on a large stage before a packed audience, Jolson leads the Blackface ensemble as they wave their white gloved hands left and right while a back row of similarly attired men wave tambourines. Jolson sings a heart-wrenching rendition of *Swanee* accompanied by nostalgic, romanticized vignettes of the old South: a steamboat sailing slowly down the Mississippi, Negros picking cotton in a field, the columned, grand plantation house, and the contrasting, roughly hewn, ramshackle slave quarters. While lampooning blacks was a widely embraced form of entertainment, many Caucasian folks naively thought they were just celebrating Black culture.[81]

1939's Stephen Foster biopic Swanee River romanticized the old South of "darkey" plantation life and endeavored to justify Blackface minstrel culture - in technicolor! Right: Co-stars Al Jolson & Don Ameche as Foster in a studio promotional lobby card photo. Courtesy NY Public Library.

In South Philadelphia, where I grew up, use of Blackface and Negro culture satire had been, at one time, an assimilated component of the local subculture. The Philadelphia Mummers had maintained the tradition of using Blackface for over 150 years until it was banned in 1963 by Philadelphia's city council under pressure from the NAACP and civic leaders from suburban wards. Parade officials defied the ordinance, citing the tradition as a mainstay for generations, and proceeded to march in the 1964 New Year's Day parade as planned without interruption. One Mummer interviewed at the time by the Associated Press remarked:

> "Minstrelsy is a part of the tradition… No offense ever was meant, and so far as I know, none was ever taken."[82]

The common reasoning was that it was all in good fun, and no harm was intended. This was a city-wide, working class Philadelphia thing. But that didn't make it right. Tension rose to a feverish pitch over the ruling. Word spread of anticipated "blood on the streets" and "rumors that Black people had been recruited from Harlem and Chicago to wreak havoc"[83] keeping many parade attendees away.

Mummery as an annual New Year's Eve/Day celebration has been an unbroken tradition in working class Philadelphia since colonial days. Its roots were founded in European immigrant traditions with revelers dressed up in drag and Blackface, firing shotguns into the air, and playfully challenging wealthier downtown citizens for food or drink or have their property besmirched. Think of it as an adult, drunken interpretation of Trick or Treat. "The history of the Mummers" wrote journalist Emily Guendelsberger, "particularly the comic brigades, is entwined with the Blackface minstrelsy popular in the mid-to late 1800s."[84] By the end of the 19th Century, in effort to quell and control the New Year's Shooters, city officials organized the parade with the enticement of prize money, launching the tradition that prevails today.

Prior to 1847, the southern border of Philadelphia ended at South street. "But the roots go back further" Guendelsberger continues,

> "before South Philadelphia was even officially part of Philadelphia. It was a poor satellite town of immigrant laborers and free Blacks, and its poorest neighborhood was a swampy, near-rural shantytown known for its garbage-fed pig herds. This was the Neck - the birthplace of Mummery."[85]

In other words, the region of the city which now comprises the majority of South Philadelphia was an integrated community very much like Elmira. As I researched more about the 1963 Blackface ban in the Philadelphia Mummer's parade, I found myself vaguely recalling some scant memories of that time, though I wasn't yet four years old. Many South Philadelphians held a consensus of resentment about the decision, and my father was not excluded – that I do remember. Even Black residents of South Philadelphia who had marched in the Mummer's parade alongside their White neighbors in Blackface for generations concurred that the decision was to be blamed on outsiders who misunderstood an entrenched cultural custom. Like Mark Twain's assessment that he didn't know slavery was wrong because he was taught from all angles that it was just a way of life, the use of Blackface in South Philadelphia had just been a similarly accepted norm. Certainly, they were aware that African American stereotypes were being lampooned, but this was South Philadelphia, where everyone and everything is subject to equal opportunity lampooning.

In 2020, a handful of members of one Mummer's comic brigade in that year's parade were again accused of donning Blackface, prompting the mayor to threaten a ban on future parades. The accused brigade members explained they weren't intending to lampoon Blacks but had only painted their face to complement the color of their costume. The matter was sensationalized by television and print media who brought to fore concerns about not only repressed racist sentiment in Philadelphia's working-class neighborhoods, but citing the incident as further evidence of a national trend of resurging racism that had been on the rise since the 2016 presidential election.

Having grown up there, I may be poised more than many to objectively see both sides of the discussion. There are guys I've known since childhood who march every year in the parade, and I well know how a Wench brigade outfit has color-coordinated face makeup. Officers of the brigades know these rules and enforce them responsibly, and wouldn't permit such an offense. In this context, the member's rebuttal held water.

However, it is simultaneously true that many don't even realize the subtle ways racism is innately expressed. Recently a friend of mine nonchalantly shared a story about his retail store interaction "with a cute Black girl." Not a girl, not a store clerk, but specifically a Black girl. There's the subtlety I reference. This is evidence of the prevailing, assimilated racist subculture in which Americans are unconsciously raised. This is how racism persists. While overt racism is increasingly flaunted across the nation, many more don't realize the ways in which their behaviors unconsciously endorse it, and this is what African-American leaders have been trying to convey for decades.

In the case of my Dad, he had undeniably participated in the perpetuation of these attitudes and traditions. Outwardly he was as normal as any neighborhood guy. An honest, decent, church-going working man, not seeming to embody a racist bone in his body. But there were those moments, such as when he may have been angered by a negative interaction with a person of color, when a racial epithet might have been uttered in knee-jerk reaction, and even then, it was with restraint. Yet, afterward, I would witness subtle demonstrations of his remorse for this behavior in calmer moments, such as the hours following Sunday mass, or quiet times at home when his mind was able to focus on something of a more relaxed nature.

Dad harbored a private piety. I had the good chance to see this side of him while growing up, perhaps more so than my brothers. While they were in school and I was too young yet to attend, Dad and I spent afternoons together at a playground in his boyhood neighborhood of Schuylkill. I got to see and know another side of him then, and it was during these times when he opened up with stories of his youth, of insights he'd learned, and how it made him a better person. He was a reflective man and I'm sure the cross hatching of these culturally conditioned views and his deeply religious convictions embodied his inner conflict because they were in many ways diametrically opposed.

Religiously, Dad subscribed to the canon of The Sacred Heart League. Also referred to as The Apostleship of Prayer, the mission of The Sacred Heart League is described in the Catholic Encyclopedia as:

"the practice of prayer…[through] three practices…The first…a daily offering of one's prayers, good works, and sufferings, the second, of daily recitation of a decade of beads for the special intentions of the Holy Father…and the third, reception of Holy Communion with the motive of reparation… members are also urged to observe the practice of the Holy Hour, spent in meditation on the Passion."[86]

Similar to Opus Dei, the hard-line Catholic organization known best from Dan Brown's novels *Angels & Demons* and *The DaVinci Code,* and which translates as "Work of God," Sacred Heart advocated acts of reparation performed as a conscious turning to God, initiating a change of heart and achieving reconciliation with others. Members of the League were encouraged to lead ordinary lives, with traditional families and secular careers, and exhorted to find God in their daily life,

Dad's scapular of the Sacred Heart League.

with the understanding "that everyone is called to holiness and that ordinary life is a path to sanctity."[87] That mundane, secular work should be viewed as a service to God, that one can unite their professional, social, and family life with their inner spiritual life without renouncing the world as traditionally pursued by those inclined to enter a religious order.

The common emphasis behind both Opus Dei and Sacred Heart is spiritual reparation. The dictionary defines reparation as "The making of amends for a wrong one has done, by [expiation]…or helping those who have been wronged." Expiation specifically entails conscious guilt, and a prompted act of atonement. For Dad, this manifested when we left the playground and stopped to drop off clothing, food or other donated items to Saint John's Hospice, a refuge for the homeless, alcoholics and other unfortunate, lost souls who'd fallen on hard times. Misfortune did not discriminate over race, creed or color, and it was here where I most often witnessed Dad's compassionate side in service to his fellow man.

I saw in my Dad that Sacred Heart fueled conscientious side of him who knew minstrel performing and harboring racist sentiment had been morally wrong, and I witnessed his moral transformation as he endeavored to atone and make reparation. I suspect his interest in the works and life of Mark Twain enabled him to find the balanced and practical path through it. Twain is our cultural exemplar of reparation in this context. It was the very practice of Dad's Christian faith which further reinforced this awareness, and I saw Dad's way of grappling with his guilt and remorse was to teach us an alternative, non-racist approach to life, even while dealing with racially motivated conflict on our front door step and within the community around us.

In the end, it was his spiritual outlook that won the battle. In what could be viewed as a complete reverse of the story of The Jazz Singer, in which a would-be Synagogue Cantor breaks away to sing Jazz in Blackface, my Dad performed songs in Blackface and broke away to offer his vocal talents in our church choir. Witnessing this healing manifest before my eyes is among those characteristics of Dad that has had the greatest impact and influence on me.

My Dad, second row, second from left, singing with Saint Gabriel's Church choir circa 1969. Photo courtesy Saint Gabriel Parish archives.

A similar kind of change in Mark Twain's conscience had been influenced by Livi and his Congregationalist in-laws. Dad and Mark Twain were very similar characters in many regards especially when it came to Samuel Clemens' earlier racist inclinations that were just bred organically from the culture around him. Dad was raised in a similar environment, as many of us were.

The influence of my mother and grandmother had an impact too. My grandmother, an Irish immigrant from Newcastle West in County Limerick, liberally respected her Black neighbors without fail, inviting them into her home for lunch and treating them with the same cordiality that was extended to her Irish friends and neighbors. Not so much for the English, though. My grandmother never held a warm place in her heart for the British and would make derisive comments now and then. She knew all too well the history between the British and the Irish, and recollection of that legacy was something she forwarded on to us.

While Irish-Americans and African-Americans have a long and periodically violent history as working-class adversaries, many Irish in Philadelphia retained a soft spot in their heart for the American Negro plight due to their own experience of historically being derailed as "white niggers" from the minute they stepped off the boat following their flight from the Irish potato famine and subjugation at home by the British.

My Dad's ancestors had been among those Potato Famine refugees arriving in

Philadelphia in the mid 1840s to mid 1850s on the heels of the Nativist/Anti-Catholic Riots. As both Irish and Catholic they were greeted with extreme prejudice and further welcomed with the added celebration of employment signs announcing "No Irish need apply." A copy of one such sign hangs in my living room right over our doorway, serving as a reminder of what my ancestors endured, as well as instilling a sense of gratitude when I exit that door on my way to work each day.

The sign over my doorway.

An 1855 ad for domestic help in Washington, DC.. Note the emphasis on "A slave preferred" and "No Irish need apply." Just another day in America.

But this was nothing new. The Irish in Philadelphia had long been scorned and relegated with an almost subhuman status, a prevailing attitude carried over from the English view inaugurated by Oliver Cromwell and King James II. A 2013 article in *The Irish Examiner* discussing the assertion that close to 500,000 Irish were sold into slavery remains a topic of debate by scholars. According to its author, M. Sullivan, "Oliver Cromwell...and his army generals were seriously bad news for the Irish...Many [Irish] were held on Spike island in Cork's lower harbour. They were sold in the slave 'markets' to plantation owners for sugar..." And, citing John Martin of the Center for Research and Globalization in Montreal, Canada, "Charles I also led a continued effort to enslave the Irish."[88]

Frequently transported as indentured or bond servants, they were treated as harshly as slaves, could be resold, and runaways were hunted, as suggested by this colonial era notice printed in Philadelphia's *American Weekly Mercury* dated March 3, 1721:

> 'Run away from James Logan's Plantation near German Town the 28th Instant, an Irish Servant Lad, named Patrick Boyd, aged about 17 or 18 years, with streight [sic] dark hair, a freckled Face and a smooth Tongue...Whoever takes and secures him will be well rewarded for their Trouble'[89]

This ad is cited in a 1901 book segment[90] about Irish servitude in colonial America. Distinct from an indentured servant working off a debt, a bond servant is defined as "a person bound in service without wages."[91] The synonym for bond servant, is slave.

Throughout the Eighteenth Century, "Sheriffs of Irish Counties received five pounds for each person transported" writes historian Dennis Clark,

> "but paid only three pounds for his passage. They and other officials made a steady profit from this trade...The colonial period with its servitude and strict class distinctions cast the Irish in the role of menials of a not-too-trustworthy character."[92]

In the Nineteenth Century, they were regarded as undesirable refugees, labeled as "hordes of wild Irishmen" by politicians who urged Americans to prevent their entry into the country, further described as "the mass of vicious and disorganizing characters who cannot live peaceably at home."[93]

In the wake of the Irish famine, these Irish refugees, often of a rural, clan-based folk culture, struggled to adapt to the urban ways of the industrial/manufacturing giant that had evolved into mid 19th Century Philadelphia. Their increased number unleashed a public outcry.

"The Know-Nothing riots and church burnings in 1844 had placed the Irish vividly before the eyes of the city as a troubling force" writes Dennis Clark.

Thomas Nast's stereotyped depiction of an Irishman and Irish behavior, as my ancestors were viewed on their arrival in America. A sharp contrast from the same artist that defined our concept of Santa Claus.

"...the violent events of the 1840's helped to brand the Irish Catholics as a source of disorder and distress. The antipathy toward them rested...upon their competition for jobs at the lower occupational levels, their menial status, their foreign aspect and clannishness, and their notorious intemperance. No white men in America were so thoroughly stigmatized...This image of social disability...lasted for several generations. Prominent upper-class reformers penned pseudonymous satires of the Irish...and one such effort popularized "Mulhooleyism" as a synonym for ignorance, corruption, and crudity...with "revolting and vicious habits. Being of the lower order of mankind, they were repellant to those who were further advanced in the social scale."[94]

Right: 19th Century engraving depicting the 1844 Philadelphia riots between the Irish "aliens and foreigners" and nativist Americans. Courtesy The Pennsylvania Historical Society.

For protection and safety, Irish families like my Dad's settled within reclusive ethnic enclaves nearest whatever industries provided opportunities for work. Some moved into the Northeastern Philadelphia sections of Kensington and Port Richmond to work on the old Delaware River shipping docks or in the fabric mills. Some settled in Southwark and further south along Second Street in the heart of Mummer country and The Neck to work other river docks and the rail yards. Others settled in Grays Ferry, where I grew up. My Dad's clan made their homestead in the section then called Schuylkill on the western outskirts of the city along the edge of the Schuylkill River.

The west end of Spruce Street along the Schuylkill River in the 18th Century, apparently a hot spot for baptisms. Courtesy Pennsylvania Historical Society.

The same location as above in 1860, lined with Paddlewheel river boats, very much like the Mississippi of Twain's youth. This is how it appeared when my Great-Grandparents arrived from Ireland and settled there. Courtesy Pennsylvania Historical Society.

In neighborhoods like this productions of "The Minstrels" were regarded as bonding, community cultural events. The microcosm of their Irish community simply reflected a national acceptance of lampooning Blacks in this way. Dad just saw himself as a participant in the continuance of an American stage tradition that had prevailed from before the Civil War right up until the early 1960's. His parents and grandparents - my ancestors - likely reveled in such shows as well. My mom certainly remembers them. I knew at least one of my father's siblings, my aunt Cass, had also participated in them. My oldest brother and older cousins remember having attended some of those minstrel shows. This was the Amos and Andy era, when Black stereotypes were routinely exploited on Radio, Film, and during the advent of Television. These were accepted social norms. But, by the time I came along, changes were brewing.

Like Mark Twain's conversion from slave holding southerner to champion of Black civil rights, my father, too, had experienced a change of heart and conscience. Somewhere in the recesses of my formative synapses are the archives of conversations I must have overheard. I was lucky enough to have seen how Dad, in his heart, as guided by learned memory of Irish struggle and the Christian conscience of his Catholic faith, had probably known all along that it was just inherently wrong.

The last time we spoke of his minstrel years, I was about 22 years old. Two years prior to that I had been hired as marquee and set designer and sound and light operator for Philadelphia's Black Theater Festival by director Robert Hubbard. Rob liked my non-prejudiced ethic, empathetic spirit, and willingness to support productions about the Black experience, and for several years Rob and I worked on a variety of plays with scripts and themes addressing related issues.

A favorite on which I worked was Rob's powerful production of South African playwright Athol Fugard's *The Bloodknot*. I can still vividly recall the actors, scenes, the costumes and dialog, largely because my role each night in directing the lighting and sound required keen attention to every line and scene change. For one key scene, Rob had selected 'My Song' by Keith Jarrett. Because of that play, it remains one of my favorite Jazz piano compositions to this day, and, in my opinion, one of the best jazz compositions ever conceived.

In 1982 Rob recruited me to work on a production of Ntozake Shange's *Spell No. 7*. The show had run in New York for three years to great acclaim following its inaugural run in 1979, and I was proud to be involved in what would be the play's second production anywhere in the nation. For this, Rob commissioned me to create a massive, nine-foot by six-foot, base-relief Blackface mask designed as the primary set backdrop that would loom above and behind the all-Black cast, an effigy representing minstrelsy's overshadowing history. Rob asked me to also make six Blackface masks to be worn by each cast member, which I made at home on our dining room table. Dad sat with me then, looking over my shoulder with interest, asking me about their purpose, the play's story, etc. My project reawakened memories of his minstrel days, and for the first time since the late 1960's he shared stories of those times, remarked with fascination about Blacks addressing a painful chapter in their history in this way, and concluding how wrong the practice of Blackface had been, wanting to be certain my purpose wasn't ill-conceived or in opposition to his newfound ethics.

I think the underscoring story for my Dad and I is that, as I looked to him for guidance as a role model, I was able to bear witness during these formative, transformational years when Dad and all who came of age in the WWII era were learning to acquiesce to the changing climate of America, when Blacks were asserting their dignity with charge and courage in a renewed campaign that had been waged since the Roosevelt era. This was the reality of their changing world.

My first direct experience of racial prejudice happened in 1968 when I was just seven years old. I was too young then to have a complete understanding of all that was going on with the Civil Rights movement. As a Caucasian boy from the Quaker City of Philadelphia in the North, I didn't fully understand the key events of years prior that had been occurring in the South and around the nation, and I wasn't directly aware of the circumstances and history that had fueled the movement at large. When I was a child, my parents tried to shield me from watching the more graphic, segments of the evening news broadcasts. At that age, I was more enamored with NASA and the Space Program and my childhood hero, John Glenn.

To my young perception, before 1968 the Civil Rights movement was just another thing that happened on the other side of the TV screen. There had been discussions and comments I may have overheard at family or neighborhood functions, and now and then someone would drop the "N" word. My Mom had forbidden use of the term in our house. If any of my brothers or I heard and repeated it, Mom would instantly correct us, conveying its negative connotations and essentially how un-Christian it was to use the word. Even now, while writing this, my innate reflexes still prevent my ability to type out the word with the same measure of free expression and casual abandon employed by Mr. Twain.

My Mom had been raised in an Irish-Catholic home with intolerance for use of derogatory racial slurs, and as such we'd been taught to use the term 'Colored.' The nuns at school and the priests in their church homilies also used Colored. As an upstanding Irish-Catholic family, we were obliged to adhere to its use as the advocated, morally and politically correct and respectfully descriptive adjective. 'Black' as a reference didn't become a common part of our lexicon until I was a bit older, and then seemed to be more commonly used by the African-American community when referring to themselves. But looking back now, one can clearly see how teaching children to view some people as "different" through the actions and words of parents and adults cultivates a learned behavior.

I didn't pay much attention to it beyond that. At that age, we only viewed our Colored friends at school as Colored because we were taught to distinguish them that way. Otherwise, we just considered them kids like us. We all looked different from each other in our own way. If we talked about our differences it was done so innocently without knowing any better or worse that no one's feelings were hurt. However, in hindsight, I see how it was gradually introduced.

In the Spring of 1968 we were second-grade students at Saint Gabriel Catholic School in the predominantly Irish-Catholic neighborhood of Grays Ferry in South Philadelphia, when the big day had arrived for us to receive our First Holy Communion. This is an important rite of passage in Catholic Communities because it marks the receipt of only the second sanctioned Sacrament permissible after one's baptismal Christening at birth. In the First Holy Communion ceremony, the baptized Catholic child receives his first unleavened wafer of the Holy Eucharist in a ritualistic reenactment of the Gospel story of the Last Supper when Jesus breaks and distributes bread to his Apostles. For us seven-year-olds, it essentially meant that we were now and forevermore invited to breakfast with Jesus, provided we fasted after midnight on Saturday night and didn't eat an actual breakfast until after mass on Sunday morning.

As special as the First Communion ceremony was, what really mattered was what followed: the all-out family party at our house in my honor. It would be like a birthday party but with adults as guests as well as kids. Instead of just cake, ice cream, and a basket each of pretzels and potato chips, this party would feature Aunt Mary's famous homemade potato salad sandwiched between Saltine Crackers. From Ed's Deli around the corner we'd get a large platter of fresh, thinly sliced ham, turkey and sliced American cheese that softened to an addictive, melt in your mouth consistency the longer it warmed at room temperature. These were served with a big basket of just-baked, soft, pillowy Snowflake roles, so called for being kissed with a light dusting of raw white flour, and always from Krause's bakery around another corner. Snowflake rolls were a hallmark of special occasions like this, and served as a community recognized symbol of status.

At Krause's there had been a sweet, caring, but somewhat melancholic older German immigrant woman who worked behind the counter. She was the one who always helped with our order and gave us kids a free, day-old donut whenever we visited, whether we bought something or not. At Halloween time, Krause's set up a large plastic jack-o-lantern with an animatronic black cat that would emerge from the top of the pumpkin at slow intervals. This incited squeals of delight when we were toddlers, making the trip to the bakery feel like a visit to Disneyland. Anna would smile beamingly and playfully say "Boo!" with a German accent each time the cat popped out, the pumpkin top balanced on its head. Anna delighted in seeing the wide-eyed surprise on our faces. Then she would always give us some freshly baked treat and smile with great love. It was apparent that she just enjoyed the company of children. In later years, I learned that Anna never had children of her own. She was widowed at a young age when her husband, Bruno Hauptmann, was put to death as the accused kidnapper and killer of Charles Lindberg's baby in the 1930s.

The grand affair was planned for the evening. A specially ordered, decorated cake also from Krause's would have my name written in colored, edible gel and topped by a ceramic figurine of a boy dressed in a white communion outfit with hands folded in prayer. The cake would be placed center stage on our dining room table, which was pushed up against the buffet to allow milling room for the anticipated crowd and the addition of folding chairs borrowed from the local funeral parlor, VFW post, or Dad's AOH - the Ancient Order of Hibernians men's club that celebrated Irish Catholic heritage. The party also created anticipation for the eagerly awaited receipt of cards and envelopes with cash gifts that would finance the summer supply of new comic books, toys, or a privileged trip to the movies.

As guests arrived, the events began with a brief, solemn interlude of wishing congratulations to the initiate on his or her day, followed by an obligatory need to endure each Aunt and Uncle's recounted story about the day they had received their first Communion. Once that was accomplished, the beer bottles were cracked opened and highballs were mixed while us kids dove liberally into a bottomless cooler of multi-flavored Frank's sodas. Then Dad would break out his accordion to lead everyone in song for hours.

They were magic times, and they marked those rarer occasions when I got to visit with my cousins and the kids of my parent's friends whom I saw less frequently.

On the afternoon following the Communion ceremony at our church, my mother was walking me to visit my grandmother who lived a few blocks away. I was clad in the traditional all white suit composed of white pants and jacket, a white shirt, white tie, polished white shoes and socks, and affixed to our lapel was a shining, polished brass pin of a priest's chalice signifying our official membership into the holy breakfast club. Our faces and fingernails were scrubbed and we boys all got our best crew cuts at Joe's barbershop a week ahead. My proud Catholic Mom had wanted my

At age 7 in my First Communion outfit, with Dad and Mom, 1968.

grandmother to see my Communion outfit before I took it off for the party that evening. She also wanted to do it that day because I had already scuffed and torn my pants from falling on the concrete while running excitedly from the schoolyard after the ceremony.

My Mom held my hand as we walked north on 27th Street in South Philly. From the other side of the street a teenaged boy of color came walking pointedly toward us, staring intently. My Mom and I just looked at him, puzzled at first, until he lifted an empty, clear glass soda bottle over his head and yelled "White Crackers!"

White Crackers? What did that boy mean? I immediately thought of the *Premium Saltine* crackers used for the potato salad sandwiches. Just as he pulled his arm back over his shoulder, my Mom pushed me into a doorway near us and stood in front of me for my protection. I was confused by this sudden action.

"We aren't bothering you!" she angrily yelled to the kid. Suddenly, my Mom curled her face back toward me, arching her back to protect us both. I stretched up on my toes to see what was happening, my eyes barely peering over Mom's shoulder. I saw the kid launch the soda bottle in our direction and felt it smash at our feet, the glass from the bottle shattering all over us. I quickly pressed my face and eyes onto Mom's shoulder to avoid the glass as she embraced me tightly.

Then I heard a man's voice yell "Hey! You leave them alone!" My Mom lifted her head to look as I peered around her arm. An older man across the street who had witnessed the event was rushing with urgency in our direction. My Mom called out a thank you to the man, who had backed off once the kid ran in the opposite direction and saw that we were ok.

"Come on" she said to me, yanking my hand and pulling me in the direction of my grandmother's street. I kept looking back to see if something else might happen, then turned to walk alongside Mom, staring at the ground, completely befuddled. I was puzzled by the whole ordeal and began to ask Mom typical kid styled questions.

"Mom, why did that boy throw that bottle at us?"

My Mom remained quiet at first and kept walking at a quick pace. "I don't know, Tommy" she replied after a moment passed. "Some people just don't like us because we're different."

"Different how?" I asked.

"Because of our color I guess."

"Our color? What color?" I asked, further puzzled.

"Our skin color, Tommy."

"Our skin color?" I looked at both sides of my free hand. "What's wrong with our skin color?"

"There's nothing wrong with it, Tommy. Some people think that just because we look different from them that they need to start trouble."

"Why do they think that?" I asked.

"Oh, I don't know, Tommy," she said with an exasperated tone. "Let's just keep walking."

Mom was still visibly upset from the ordeal and her senses were on high alert as she looked quickly around every corner on our now briskly paced walk. I wasn't sure whether to continue asking questions or not. I always asked an endless string of questions of my Mom and Dad about everything, and it always drove them crazy with frustration. But I was just an inquisitive kid who earnestly wanted to understand everything. This was the first time I had experienced anything like this. I walked quietly for a few minutes in compliance with my Mom's request. I looked down at my scuffed white shoes and the sleeve of my white suit jacket and my white pants with the torn knee, still confused by what the boy had said.

"Mom, what's a 'white cracker'?"

Knowing Mom as I do, she probably rolled her eyes upward, thinking "Jesus, Mary, and Joseph. Will this kid ever stop asking questions?"

I heard her huff before beginning a quickly created reply, seizing the moment to cleverly diffuse the need for further concern.

"They're the Saltine Crackers Aunt Mary uses for her potato salad sandwiches. Maybe that boy was just mad because we had all the crackers and he wanted some. We need a lot of crackers for all the people coming to the party tonight."

And just like that, my Mom miraculously changed the conversation from the experience of being attacked because of the color or our skin to the promise held in the eagerly awaited party by going on to describe all the wonderful foods we would have and all the friends and relatives who would be visiting later. That only led me to bug her with even more questions, like which cousins were coming to the party and how far certain relatives were driving and what time would everyone be there and could I invite my friends and would Dad play his accordion and so on. And then I'd ask the same questions over again, a habit I still have today, only it now drives my wife crazy.

Mom injected answers enough to satisfy me until we arrived at my grandmother's house. Crisis averted. Once we got there I forgot all about it, distracted by playing with the old toys she kept stashed in a brown paper grocery bag behind her sofa. We stayed at my grandmother's house until my Dad later came by in his car to drive us safely back the few short blocks to our home. That was the last time I would ever walk to my grandmother's house. That, along with many other joyful routines of my childhood, were forever shattered with that broken soda bottle.

12

FROM PURGATORY TO MOOSEWOOD

> "Each man is afraid of his neighbor's disapproval--a thing which, to the general run of the human race, is more dreaded than wolves and death."
>
> Mark Twain,
> *The United States of Lyncherdom*

With such a rude awakening having been foisted on me that Communion day, my young eyes began to open wider to the realities of urban life in the second half of the 1960s. 1968 had brought a new series of developments that were even hard for a young person to ignore. In April of that year Martin Luther King, Jr. had been assassinated, followed by Bobby Kennedy's assassination in June. King's assassination marked the onset of somber conversations I vaguely recall. "He was a good man. What a shame" I remember Mom saying one evening when watching the news.

It was at that point that I began to try to understand who Dr. King was and comprehend the civil rights movement with the resources that were readily available - the daily newspapers my father brought from work and the encyclopedia set in our home. As I read about the Civil Rights events - rendered comprehensible due to the encyclopedia's added illustrations and photos - I began to become more keenly aware of an increased foment of racial hatred being expressed by our neighbors. It didn't take long for me to figure out why their behavior was changing this way. Black on White or White on Black altercations started to occur with recurring frequency on our street and throughout the neighborhood.

From that point on, in the years immediately following, the level of racially motivated conflict in our neighborhood rose to an unprecedented, considerably exacerbated measure that began to make national news. Both White and Black kids jumped each other after school. Blacks were chased by Whites, Whites were chased by Blacks. Then completely innocent neighbors of both races began to get stabbed randomly and simultaneously mugged without provocation. Crime increased as the numerous corner variety stores began to get robbed at gunpoint with an alarming frequency, and one by one they closed up shop, ending a hallmark of community lifestyle that had been a mainstay since the turn of the 20th Century. Protesters chanting "We're fired up! Won't take no more!" marched from 31st to 25th Street along Dickenson Street, twenty yards from my back door. What begun as smaller squabbles would break into violent flash riots all around our neighborhood. A White schoolmate's home was firebombed after their windows were smashed. On our street, riots could break out suddenly on any otherwise quiet, normal day. Windows of homes and cars were broken, bottles and bricks were thrown, and anyone who happened to be outside their house might get an abrupt beating. It became routine for my friends and I, the youngest kids on the block, to anticipate having our play aborted abruptly at any given moment and scooted into the home of the closest neighbor during such attacks. The battle would continue until one group chased another back down the street and around the corner where a full-on battle of bottles, stones, sticks, knives, chains and fisticuffs would rage on until police showed up.

One day after school, when I was about twelve years old, my brother Mike asked me to deliver his newspaper route. I was pushing a supermarket shopping cart he kept for the task, when just such a flash riot erupted. A gang came running quickly around Dickenson Street and onto 26th where I was pushing the cart. Stupidly, I didn't run because I was more concerned that my brother would get pissed off if his shopping cart was stolen. That's what happens when you grow up poor - even the stuff you 'borrow' for free is respected.

As the kids threw rocks and bottles all around, I watched as they smashed car windows and attacked workers coming from their jobs at Fleischer's Mill across the street. I crouched behind the back of the cart with my back on the step of the side entrance to Marino's Variety Store. It was the same type of one-step doorway that had served to protect my mother and I just a few years before. Then I watched fearfully as an older boy of about sixteen or seventeen came running directly toward me. As he drew closer, we made eye contact. I can still envision the wide-eyed, angry look on his face while lifting a wooden baseball bat high over his head. I knew instantly that bat was aimed right for my head. I crouched further behind the cart, pulling myself closer to Marino's door. I heard the slap and squeak of his Chuck Converse sneakers on the concrete and I braced myself as he slowed his pace just enough to swing the bat and slam it down on the top of my head. Luckily, the impact to my head was lessened when the bat partially hit the handle of the shopping cart, which hit so hard that the vibration hurt my hands. I slumped slightly forward as the kid lifted the bat and swung a second time to thwack me across the back while running past. All in all, I was lucky. That shopping cart handle may have well saved my head from being split open.

Right after the gang of kids had passed and turned onto the street where I lived, one of the Marino family members opened their door and whisked me inside as I bawled with pain. I said something about not wanting to leave my brother's cart but was urgently told by one of the Marino boys "Fuck that cart! Get the hell in here!" Mrs. Marino sat me down and put an ice pack on my head. She called my Mom to let her know where I was and that I was safe. I stayed at the Marino's for a short while until the riot had abated, and either Mom or one of my older brothers came to bring me home.

A funny thing about those days, I don't recall ever having been taken to an emergency room for things like this. There was another time, while riding my bike, when I had been hit by a car with an impact so forceful I was launched across a parked car and bounced my head a few times on the concrete sidewalk. We didn't wear helmets in those days. Despite such severity, my Mom and Dad just brought me home and made me sit with an ice pack on my head.

As the random wolf pack attacks on our street continued, the level of danger eventually escalated beyond rocks and bottles. Now and then gun shots would be heard, forcing our parents to command us to quickly get down on our living room floor below the level of the bottom window sill. I recall opening the front door of our house after one such incident had quietened down only to find an older kid sitting on our front steps, beaten badly and bleeding from a knife wound. I called my Dad, who came to the door and yanked me back into the house, instructing me to quickly run and grab some water and towels from the kitchen while asking my Mom to call an ambulance. I complied post-haste and brought them to Dad, watching as he administered first aid to the kid until an ambulance came. This is what had become the new norm in our wee village of Grays Ferry.

The assassination of Bobby Kennedy only further inflamed the situation. Like my parents, many Irish families in our neighborhood had been Kennedy Democrats. With my naive understanding at that age, I thought I was as well. I assumed one's political party affiliation was inherited, like being baptized a Catholic. The promise offered by the prospect of Bobby being elected president that year was the continuation of the Camelot dream, and of Irish-Catholic influence at the top level of American government. It was something in which our community held great pride. But after Bobby was shot the ascendancy of the

Irish in America began to crumble, and the old country village life our Irish-American ancestors had replicated in our corner of South Philadelphia, which our families had known for generations, would soon become a thing of the past.

The growing awareness of White-Black relations in my young mind posed a great deal of confusion for me. At age eight, I was already seeking answers to come to grips with this crazy stuff. I grew increasingly mesmerized by the tenets of our Catholic faith and the teachings of Jesus that I learned in my catechism and religion classes in school: everyone was God's child, love one another. Even the Beatles sung about the need for love. Teachings like this initiated my questioning of the injustices I was witnessing in my immediate world. Things like prejudice and racism were just wrong, I postulated. Why were people fighting and hurting each other over this? Why were there wars in places like Vietnam? Why were there wars on our street? I was being taught in school that everything happening in the world was antithetical to its creator's intent for peaceful coexistence. This was serious stuff for an eight-year-old to digest. Moreover, we had been admonished to understand that by not choosing to heed these moral lessons we were guaranteed a one-way ticket to the fires of hell, or, at the very least, to Purgatory - the partially hellish but relatively tolerable waiting room, located somewhere slightly above Hell but not quite at St. Peter's gate. The description of Purgatory didn't really register with us. It just sounded like the everyday reality of the streets where we lived.

1968 was also the year we kids were prepared for the ritual receipt of Confirmation, the formal initiation into the Catholic faith, which we received in the Spring of 1969. It kind of gave us the impression that Baptism had been an initiation of lesser import, like the stamping of a passport, a sort of temporary sacrament to hold us over until this big event – the receipt of our official Visa into the Customs office of heaven. Confirmation was the real deal, the Catholic equivalent of the Jewish Bar or Bat-Mitzvah or the Grihya Sutra initiation of the Hindu Brahmins. The impression the nuns instilled in us was that an unquestioned need for adherence to a moral, ethical and spiritual code of conduct was required to be put into daily practice. This conflicted with the code of the street we were simultaneously learning, where anger, hate and negativity seemed to prevail. Because of the Communion day incident with Mom, and witnessing the riots and stabbings and race related battles on my front step, I was posed with a Kierkegaardian existential dilemma at the age of eight as pangs of racist sentiment concurrently crept their way into my being.

By 1971, these topics would be more openly discussed when our family gathered every Saturday night at my Aunt Mary & Uncle Ken's house to watch TV's then popular *All in the Family* sitcom. At that time, Norman Lear's hit show provided a cathartic outlet for self-reflection and national healing with regard to race relations. The Queens neighborhood depicted in the show mirrored ours in many ways, and all of us knew real folks like Carol O'Connor's bigoted Archie Bunker. That show shifted our - and America's - consciousness into a new era.

With the memories of these early experiences weighing on my mind, I arrived in Ithaca and found my way to the heretofore mythical Moosewood Restaurant. After finding a parking spot nearby, I was surprised to find it situated on the bottom floor of a multi-storied apartment-office complex. For some reason, I had always envisioned it to be a standalone enterprise set in a refurbished old house with a front porch in a more rural setting. My limited concept of Ithaca led me to think the town was more like Woodstock, which I last visited around 1996. I had assumed all upstate towns north of New York City looked like Woodstock.

While awaiting my turn for a table, I took out my laptop and wrote the memories recounted above. After a considerable length of time my name was called, and I allowed my mind to momentarily put aside the heavier thoughts of being cracked over the head with a baseball bat as I sat down and scoured the menu for a unique dish that might be something I couldn't get anywhere else but Moosewood.

They had a few standards that sounded awesome, like a sautéed maple bourbon shrimp entree, coconut-cashew fishcakes, a fresh, homemade ravioli option, and their Ratatouille, a delicious dish I had made many times from the recipe in their cook book. But those were too similar to entrees that could be had anywhere. I opted for their Southwestern Sweet Potato Roll, which included curried sweet potato, corn and pulled chipotle-lime seitan served fajita style on a fresh tortilla with brown rice, watermelon salsa, and cilantro sour cream. It came with a house salad of exceptionally fresh veggies topped by a creamy basil and spinach dressing. Yum! For all of this I was charged just $16.00, and with a $4.00 tip I was able to stay well within my Coinstar budget, with my only other expenses that day being a bottled water for $2.00, metered parking in Ithaca for $1.00, and $5.00 for the 1924 edition Twain book I had picked up in Cowles Hall at Elmira College, which brought my tally to $28.00 out of pocket. Along with a tank of gas I had paid with a credit on my Amex card and estimated tolls, my total trip cost was brought to around $75.00 or $80.00 for the day.

After so congratulating myself while waiting for my meal to arrive, I resumed my laptop notes and continued to ponder the thoughts about the Langdon family and the Underground Railroad, about the Northern states' role and particularly the area of New York I was in as having played a more significant role in the abolitionist campaign for the rights of African Americans than I had ever been taught. There was so much history needing to be learned and understood.

While writing this in the summer of 2017, the leading news was about the torch lit assembly of White supremacists in Charlottesville, followed by the felling of statues of Confederate generals and other post-Civil War era advocates of segregationist policies throughout the South. Elsewhere, other memorials were then being challenged as well: in Chicago, a bust of Abraham Lincoln was defaced; in Philadelphia, a statue of former mayor Frank Rizzo was called upon for removal; and by October the status of a statue of former New York Governor and US President Theodore Roosevelt was challenged with a request for removal from the front of New York's American Museum of Natural History. This ongoing campaign for statue removal seemed to be spreading worldwide and simultaneously becoming the fodder for jokes on social media platforms.

Television news forums and talk shows questioned if the reactionary removal of statues of Confederate generals in Southern states was the right course of action. Were we risking the opportunity to learn from these reminders of the imperfection of a marred union? Or, was it the correct decision as a visible demonstration of taking one step toward righting the injustices of the past? I had learned much on trips to some of those very statues, from visiting a confederate cemetery in Leesburg, Virginia, to seeing slave quarters in the home of Stonewall Jackson, and stopping at Stone Mountain in Georgia on a drive back from Atlanta, where I had viewed a curiously perplexing scene.

Below the massive frieze on the mountain's side sat a strangely utopian, garden-like park punctuated by an elegant fountain. People of all races and creeds had set up camp all about the park, engaged in family reunions and picnics, with Frisbees tossing to and fro while dogs romped playfully. All this was normal enough, I recall thinking, but my understanding was that this was at the foot of the very sight where the Ku Klux Klan had declared its revival in 1915 following the release of D. W. Griffith's *Birth of a Nation*. The palpable incongruity led me then to question - had we come that far? Had the horrible injustices of the past been forgiven, or accepted to a point of our finally ceding the reality of the Declaration of Independence's opening credo of all men being created equal? Or was I just being placated by my naiveté? Personally, visiting these sites only further entrenched my resolve that the horrible truth of our murkier history should never happen again. Would the absence of them have the same impact?

Integrated utopia at the foot of Stone Mountain, Georgia. Photo by the author.

The nascent historian in me always finds a way of gleaning the correct lesson to be learned. All these monuments and sites had given me a direct visual access to issues I had only previously read about or knew of through references on TV and in film. I understood the sentiment behind the decision to fell these memorials as representative tokens of a falsified portrait of White noblesse oblige. Mark Twain's writings, I thought, had begun the process of their dismantlement a hundred years ago. And then I thought about how his works on issues relating to the history of race relations in the United States had so impacted me early in life, and were continuing to do so even today. This brought the relevance of why Mark Twain had become so endeared to me into a much broader context than just being a fan of his style of writing and storytelling.

I tried to remember conversations had with my father on these points. They were some of the added reasons for his fondness of Twain that he had instilled in me. Dad's simplified viewpoint was boiled down into an easy philosophy: Do unto others as you would have them do unto you. Of course, he didn't always word it that away. He'd say something like "If you don't bother people they won't bother you" to which my Mom would add "Let the bee be and the bee will let thee be." Dad maintained a working-class democratic perspective. He had worked with guys of differing ethnic and racial backgrounds his whole life. "Everybody's just trying to get along the best they can" he would say, then adding "But there's always a few troublemakers who have to spoil it for everybody else." He met everyone regardless of difference with friendly candor, a cautious respect and always looking for an opportunity to wriggle in a joke and have a laugh together.

I regularly saw this when Dad stopped at Frank's Esso station on Snyder Avenue. All the mechanics at Franks were Black, and any interchange between Dad and those guys was always a good time. Even when he didn't stop for gas, if he drove by and saw the guys outside he'd honk his horn and wave as he called out their names to say hi. I remember when those guys, whose names I now forget, came to Dad's funeral wake and shared with my brothers and I how much they enjoyed Dad's company, what a good guy he was and how he had always made them laugh.

There were many better memories like this, but it was the more difficult times in those pre-adolescence years that had continued to challenge my idealistic notions back then. By the time I was thirteen I had been jumped, beaten, and cracked over the head with a baseball bat numerous times all because of the color of my skin. Once, when I was about ten years old, I went after school to the home of my schoolmate Frankie. After spending some time doing a homework project and playing a board game for a short duration, Frankie's Mom told me it was time for me to leave, but that I had to exit their house through the back door and down their alley if I wanted to avoid getting jumped. Those were the conditions for just leaving a friend's house! Another time I was sucker-punched and almost pushed in front of an oncoming subway train by a gang of five or six kids for purely unfounded, racially motivated reasons. I fought my way madly out of that one. Once getting to safety, I forgave those fools for their socially conditioned lack of conscience. I was more pissed at the adult commuters standing nearby on the platform who just watched and did nothing – and I loudly vocalized that to them. There was no mistaking it for Saltine crackers then. It had just become the routine way of life.

This was just prior to the days, in 1970 or '71, when the playground just a half a block away from Frankie's house and one block from our school had become a literal police state. Busloads with hundreds of Philadelphia police had been deployed to line the perimeter of the Lanier playground day and night to prevent more bloodshed and rioting. The mayor had declared a state of emergency for our neighborhood and curfews were imposed with two cops stationed on every corner. I hadn't gone to the playground too often specifically because of the fierce rioting taking place there that we had all seen on the local and national TV news. I started going more frequently because Mom used to pack bag lunches she asked me to bring to my Uncle Bud, who was among the Policemen stationed there. The only reason I felt safe enough to venture through the neighborhood was having my dog Barney with me. No one bothered us when we were together.

I was with Barney in the back of Lanier's ball field one day when I witnessed a riot unfold behind the batter's cage where local bar teams played softball on a regular basis. In short order, older guys with bloodied team shirts and bludgeoned faces or stab wounds wrapped in the cloth from a torn shirt sleeve hobbled past to get some first aid. The playground had literally become a battlefield.

With Barney, circa 1972.

As I continued to bring my Uncle his lunch, I kept running into classmates from school who lived in that part of the neighborhood. The playground sponsored a street hockey league, which I joined post haste. After finishing a game one day, my friends Mike, Doc, Bozo, Burnsy and I sat along the edge of the basketball courts to watch some of the older guys shoot hoops. At one point, a group of Black kids came into the park, took one of the open basketball courts and started shooting hoops as well. Initially all was fine but tension started to build and eventually some derogatory remarks were exchanged. When a "fair one" was called out, two guys started a fist fight until it became four guys and then erupted into an all-out gang fight.

The Black kids, clearly outnumbered, began to take flight and ran toward the gate. The scuffle continued all the way through the gate, but one Black kid, the youngest and shortest among them, got cornered in the park's concrete pavilion as the White guys began to deliver a ruthless pummeling. I watched as the kid crouched to protect himself, then drop to the ground to assume a fetal position while covering his face with his forearms as the White kids beat every exposed part of his body. It all happened so fast. I remember being quite distressed by what I was witnessing. Within minutes some police ran through the playground gate along with some adult white men from the neighborhood. The police forced the White kids away to protect and aid the kid on the ground while their fathers grabbed them by the arm and slapped their heads to "drill some sense" into them.

I felt compassion and empathy for that kid and the brutal pain he was feeling. I remember at that very moment thinking "This is wrong. This is just wrong!" And it wasn't just this specific incident I was reacting to. That was just the catalyst.

In five years I'd already witnessed so much racially motivated hostility that this pissed me off. Enough was enough. There had to be another way. It was so antithetical to my moral, ethical and Christian rearing. If this is what racism looked like, I wanted no part of it. There had to be a solution. The Saint Francis prayer we sang in church had taught us: 'Let there be peace on Earth, and let it begin with me.' That incident was a turning point, firmly ingraining the aversion to racial prejudice that I still maintain.

Within a year of witnessing that, during what thereafter had become my 'Preacher' phase, I was cornered by some Black kids one summer night and beaten severely with a three-foot length of half-inch steel construction rebar and an equally long strip of two-inch thick vulcanized rubber. The kids had waited in ambush behind a mailbox, and when I was separated from my friends they pounced and attempted to steal my Sears Spyder bike from beneath me. I was having no part of that. I loved that bike, having gotten it for Christmas just six months prior. With its faux tiger skin banana seat and muted, metallic orange frame, it was one of the coolest bikes on the block. My Dad didn't earn much and my parents always bought Christmas gifts on a Sears credit card which took them months to pay off afterward. Not only did I not want to give up my bike, but it was out of respect for how hard my parents had worked to get it for me. Letting go of the bike would be a win for racism and a loss for my parents and I.

I credit my friend Jimmy for saving me that night. It was that bad. I would have surely incurred much worse injury and possibly getting stabbed in short duration were it not for the imposing specter of Jimmy, a taller, overweight kid whose countenance while running madly toward us and screaming like a banshee at the top of his lungs had surely scared the shit out of my attackers. They urgently aborted their endeavor and ran back to their homes a half block away.

Sure, I was badly hurt from the beating I endured. Sure, I was pissed off that this was racially motivated. But after going home to take care of the bruises, I went to my room and prayed for some understanding in this madness. I eventually reasoned that the beating I got must have been an example of penance or instant karma for not intervening to help that boy who had been beaten at the playground. I had witnessed so much racial hatred in my

A vintage Sears Spyder Bike exactly like mine.

brief life up to that point that I clearly understood if I elected to allow myself to also become consumed with an equal measure of it, then, again, racism wins. I just couldn't allow that. "Let it begin with me." Instead of allowing the incident to instill hatred, I sought forgiveness for not helping that kid. I adopted that anti-hatred view at twelve years old, and it remains my credo even now. At that age I had no clue about Soren Kierkegaard, but that incident provided one reason why in later years I completely grasped his philosophy of ethical choosing. Studying philosophy as a teenager was how I rationalized my way out of the trauma.

By 1974, the racially charged violence began to temper a little, but not before having excelled to the point where more kids close to my age had been beaten, stabbed, or shot, with some not surviving. The recurring and increasing number of these incidents compelled my parents to seek a new home, and we eventually moved off my childhood street that summer to a calmer, relatively safer section of the neighborhood, away from the troubles and nearer to the High School I would attend that fall.

Not long after we moved, I went back to the old house with my buddy Mike. I walked around the now empty home, dolefully sharing my childhood memories which I gleaned from each glance at every wall and crevice. I stood in the kitchen on the heating vent with a turn of the century cast-iron grill in the center of the floor which had been our sole source of warmth during cold winter months. I stood in the living room where my Dad and I had watched *The Adventures of Mark Twain* and other cinema treasures on our Nate Ben's color TV with the faux wood and chrome stand. I stooped before the mantle where we had hung our Christmas stockings over our fake fireplace. I reached behind the fake logs to a small switch beneath that powered the red and yellow light bulbs that had illumined the room. It still worked. The muted amber glow of the bulbs cast a soft, warm haze throughout the vacant space, projecting our shadows against the corner where my Dad had sat next to his book case and lamp table. My eyes moistened while I paused to look there, recalling so many moments with Dad in that very spot, now replaced with illusory silhouettes borne of longing. Just next to that was where Dad and I set up the aquarium he had given me as a twelfth birthday gift, along the wall where we stowed our bikes in the warm weather, and where we set up our Christmas tree each holiday season.

I went into our cellar way and down the steps to the basement where I had spent so many hours playing, with Dad's TV tuning equipment, my brother's dartboard, my chem lab and geology kit, and dreaming up so many fantastic, imaginative adventures with a wide assortment of toys and games.

I made my way back upstairs, to the second floor and into what only months before had been my bedroom, remembering the pop culture posters that had hung on each wall, the crucifix that hung over my bed with an inserted frond of Palm each Easter season, and the little metal cabinet that supported the twelve-inch black and white TV on which I had watched Saturday morning cartoons while lying across my top bunk bed, from which I once fell hard while trying to mischievously annoy my brother James as he slept in the bunk below.

In my bunkbed, the end of First Communion Day, 1968. I remember Dad asking me to pose for this to use the last exposure on a roll of film.

I remembered the time I was watching cartoons there when my teenaged neighbor Patsy rushed in, saying we had to hurry because our house was on fire. She whisked me from my bed, wrapped me in my robe, carried me downstairs, outside, and across the adjoining steps into her rowhome next to ours, where her parents Helen and Joe sat me down in front of their magical and massive color TV console and fed me breakfast. After firemen arrived and inspected, they determined no fire, having sourced the soot and smoke to a backed-up furnace in our basement.

I looked out the bedroom window through which I often tried to scare off wailing alley cats fighting in the middle of the night by making sounds whose source the cats could never determine. From that same window I would listen to the midnight wail of freight train whistles and the sound of their repetitive clunking along tracks in the distance, imagining all the distant towns and exciting places to which they might travel, far away from the bleak, tight-knit rows of brick, concrete and asphalt that we called home. I remembered how I was awakened each morning by the sound of the seven o'clock whistle from the Philadelphia Naval Yard that signaled the time for workers to begin their day, followed promptly by my mom's vigilant, reliable shout from downstairs: "Seven o'clock! Time to get up!"

I walked out of the room - because I could no longer call it 'my' room - and sat on the top step, along the wooden balusters of the upstairs banister through which I used to stretch my head as a toddler to eavesdrop on my parent's conversations downstairs or listen for evidence of Santa's arrival. I began to weep, my heart heavy with the awareness that all those wonderful things I had grown up with in the first fourteen years of my life would be no more. So many happy times that were then beginning to recede into the realm of memory.

Mike sat next to me and patted me on the back. "It's ok, buddy" he consoled, adding some humorous remarks to liven my spirits. He was always good at that. "Everything's gonna be ok. There'll be more good times. You'll see." Of course, he was right. Mike had also been forced to move from his original childhood home for the same reasons. He knew quite well what I was going through.

1974 was also the year I became a freshman at Bishop Neumann High School, an all-boys Catholic Prep in my neighborhood run by the Norbertine order of priests, which offered an excellent curriculum with dedicated teachers who knew the fine art of breaking through the knuckle-headed, adolescent cautiousness of inner city, working class neighborhood boys.

Our teachers generally operated with a remarkable measure of patience and a cool, broad sense of humor. Many knew first-hand the pitfalls and challenges of urban living we all confronted daily, and understood the struggle endured by preceding generations that got all of us to this point in our communal evolution. They understood the importance of pride a sound high school education brought to our families. Many of our parents had not received much education beyond grade school, like my Dad, who had to drop out of high school to help support his mother in the wake of his father's death, and then joined the Navy to answer the national call to service during World War II. That was how it was for men of his generation.

In this regard, the high school education of my brothers and I was endorsed with great fanfare. Just going to high school was an enormous privilege and gift not to be taken lightly. If you went on to college and graduated, you were esteemed beyond compare by older relatives, many of whom hadn't gone to school past the 8th grade. The administrators and teachers at Bishop Neumann were well aware of these family scenarios. Most of them were college educated children of lesser educated, immigrant parents and grandparents.

Parental involvement in support of the school was notable and kept all of us on our toes. It wouldn't be uncommon to see a parent slap his or her son across the face outside of the disciplinary office for even the most minor infraction that required a parent to be called to the school. An angry South Philly parent is the most frightening species you could encounter, and a South Philly mother the most formidable of all.

"Whad'ya mean ya t'rew a piece a papah at th' othe' kid?" one might overhear a South Philly mom yelling at her forlorn and slunken boy outside the disciplinary office.

SLAP "Whut's wrawng wit'jchoo?" *SLAP*

"Heh?" *SLAP*

"What th' hell wuz yu thinkin'?" *SLAP*SLAP* "Heh?"

The mom would then lean in closer, her face an inch away from the terrified son, sporting an intense stare, waiting for an answer, emphasized at this stage with a second and audibly louder "HEH?"

"Heh" is the mandatory punctuation used in South Philly whenever arguing your point of view, typically following a double-edged question that included your assertion within it. It's spoken quickly and pointedly, with a higher intonation than whatever question preceded it. The timing of its utterance within the context of a conversation is not always intended to elicit an answer, and in such instances the appropriate, preferred answer is silence and surrender. In this instance, if a son would begin to answer, the mom would be right back on his case before he could finish a sentence.

Son: "I only….."

SLAP

Mom: "Yoow ownly? Whaddya mean yoow ownly? Yoow ownly whut?"

SLAP

"Whudif I ownly pudda foot up yer ass? Heh? Woodjya think that wuz funny? Heh? Woodjya?"

SLAP

Then issuing forth would come the most fear instilling, terrifying reinforcement of all.

"Waydle you git home an' deal widjour fathah. It won' be so funny then, will it?"

At this point, a South Philly mom, having spoken her piece, usually withdrew with the slightest detection of a modicum of love. This love was typically expressed with a resigned sigh, followed by

"Whadam I gonna do wit'chu? Heh? Whadam I gonna do wit'chu? Aaahh….fix your shirt. I don' pay awl dis money fa youda come he'a an' loowk loiyke a slob an' be stoo-pid. Wennaya gonna get it t'ru dat t'ick head of yools? Heh? Aaahhh…."

Then the hand would be raised, poised to deliver another stinging blow, but now withheld with contempt and compassion for the wearied fruit of her womb, and instead used to clench a handful of hair that allowed a lip-biting, South Philly mom to vigorously shake her yielding boy's head to and fro, and, if the cause of offense was severe enough, proceed to slam the back of his head against the ceramic tiled wall. It should be noted here that South Philly girls were not exonerated from similar displays of wrath and brimstone from their South Philly moms.

The script seldom varied no matter who you were. But then the scolding would conclude with an acquiescent repudiation that differed depending on your ethnic background. If your parents were of Irish ancestry, the summary remark was always intoned with a form of prayerful futility:

"Chaysus, Mary and Joseph!" uttered breathily, almost undetectable should one hear the forbidden sin of taking the Lord's name in vein.

If you were of Black African ancestry, the closing statement was a similarly intoned prayer, spoken firmly and unabashedly with a slight melodic lilt:

"Loorwd, he'p meh!"

If you were Italian, you heard "Ma-donn'!" - with the 'd' pronounced as a rolling 'r' – "Mah-rron!." This was the abbreviated, prayerful invocation of the mother of Jesus, announced audibly and intentionally to ensure it was heard by anyone within earshot. Punishment by public shaming!

The German, Slavic, Polish and other kids of Northern European ancestry were too smart to get detention. They knew from experience that they'd be assured of getting a pure, bonafide and unforgettable ass-whoopin' at home. They probably received preventive ass-whoopin's anyway. If they did get a detention, their parents never came into the school. They didn't need to. You knew when those guys had gotten a detention when they sat in class quiet and sullen, rarely lifting their gaze from the book on their desks. Those guys were left alone to suffer and reflect with the fear of God from anticipation of the wrath they'd most assuredly incur when they got home. Whatever neighborhood you lived in, South Philly was an unshakably tight-knit community. If you tried to hide something from your parents, somebody else's parents would surely spill the beans. News of an infraction learned secondhand in this way would only multiply the severity of any punishment ten times over.

In our community, it wasn't wise to screw up the privilege of attending high school. Doing so would be viewed as a blemish on the efforts made by generations of hard-working family members and relatives that brought you to this point. Although forgiveness would likely be extended in time and usually was, it came only after an undetermined period of prolonged shame and embarrassment: good old Catholic guilt at its finest. In our house, my parents regularly reinforced reminders of an undereducated, alternate fate.

Our teachers had methods that empowered each of us to exercise an innate ability for embracing our youthful, immature foibles and use them as the springboard for educational and personal growth. This, countered by the moral, ethical and spiritual guidance in the religion classes taught by the Norbertines, rounded and molded us into our potential selves.

It was there, after engaging in assigned readings from Mark Twain and William Faulkner - specifically Twain's essay *My Uncle's Farm* and Faulkner's short story *Was* from his *Go Down, Moses* compilation - that we were able to have frank, candid discussions about racism, slavery, Jim Crow, and relevant, associated current events. In South Philly and in our neighborhood, these conversations were essential, the stuff of missionary work. Our teachers had a unique way of keeping the peace and keeping it on task and academic. Once in a while, some wise guy classmate might ask a question with inclusion of the N word purely to get a rise out of everyone instead of purposes of genuine academic inquiry. This would agitate the Black students in the classroom, who justifiably responded with anger. The street-wise teachers managed to navigate us through that with the finesse of a skilled counselor, and by the time the end of class bell rang, most of us had already transubstantiated the negativity into an educational perspective.

Certainly, some of the guys would leave the classroom and challenge one or another to a 'Fair one' - meaning a fair fist fight - after school. But in time these things quelled, and in many instances a White and Black kid who started the semester off as enemies would become fast friends who defended each other among the peers of their respective race or ethnic background. The religious education we simultaneously received only aided in building the positive aspects of those relations further. We were maturing into well rounded but scrappy Catholic gentlemen, which was the primary mission of the school.

Access then to a fresh treasure trove of books and short stories by authors offering a myriad range of thinly veiled, socially relevant concepts and ideologies, such as works by John Steinbeck, J. D. Salinger, George Orwell, Charles Dickens, and, of course, Mark Twain, and the *Adventures of Huckleberry Finn* in particular, underscored an important component of our broader education. Though South Philly had been rife with racial and ethnic conflict throughout the 1960s, this was the '70s now, and cooler heads were generally prevailing with our generation. We had all seen enough racial violence in our brief lives up till then, and the more relaxed mode of interaction for our age group was to cast aside racial and ethnic derision in favor of embracing the variety of cultural colorfulness. In short time, we didn't engage in racial squabbles. Our differences were meted out by posing arguments about the merits of one top 40 band against another. Aside from that, we all just wanted to smoke joints with each other and be introduced to the other's music preferences while engaging in a stimulating discussion of persuasive reasons for our choices. I was introduced to a lot of great music this way.

Our changing taste in music was a minor distraction, however, and provided the fodder for friendly teasing. At our core, we learned to love and respect each other, and acceptance of our cultural differences allowed us to engage in healthy, in-class discussions on topics such as the social impact of Mark Twain's use of derogatory terminology. When I entered high school as a Freshman in 1974, Mel Brook's *Blazing*

Saddles had been an influential hit that tempered some of the civil angst with humor. By January, 1977, viewing the Alex Haley *Roots* miniseries had been assigned homework, and I recall watching it with Mom and Dad. We recognized it's social significance. To my recollection, the series had been the first televised national event with such significance since the Hal Holbrook Twain special ten years prior, and seemed then to serve the overdue national need for dialogue on race relations, putting our troubles to rest in a civil and respectful fashion, and opening the door for the creative era of expression and integrated culture that was the 1980s, culminating with Nelson Mandela's release from prison in 1990 and the end of Apartheid in South Africa.

Back in high school, we discussed Roots. My classmates and I maturely listened to each other's points of view, which only broadened our scope of understanding. This is why I find it so disturbing when I read of one school district or another wanting to ban Huckleberry Finn from their reading curriculum. It proved to be an invaluable aid for adjusting in a social climate of differing ethnicity. My own review of Huck Finn and Mark Twain's entire oeuvre for one year proved to spawn an intense curiosity to research the historical and social background that created the popular entity and identity of Mark Twain. And all of this started with the influence of my Dad simply engaging me with an open mind while we watched a movie.

I was jarred out of my reflective mode by the sound of a glass breaking on the floor nearby. I finished my meal at Moosewood and asked the waiter for a check. I continued to ponder, in hindsight, how many of the reactions to the racially motivated conflicts during my youth had fostered an attempted cultivation of racism.

The street taught us that trust was not to be trusted. It developed into a behavioral attitude that we were just supposed to learn. But my conscience battled with it as I was concurrently learning an enhanced understanding of values, ethics and morals in school. My consideration for religious vocation was founded on my young vision of wanting to find some way that I could help with the healing of what I saw as a very disturbed world filled with people experiencing real emotional pain. I wanted to be part of the solution and not the problem. It got to the point where I began to quote passages from scripture during daily conversation, which effectively nauseated my friends, leading some of them to nickname me "Preacher." I had taken on a "turn the other cheek" and "forgive those who trespass against you" attitude, which was a tough path to walk at that time and place, but I trusted that my parents and some of the more ethically minded friends and adults in our community had my back.

I left Moosewood Restaurant and began my drive home. I didn't turn on the radio while allowing these thoughts and memories to continue. Some of these incidents I hadn't recalled in decades. The long ride provided ample opportunity for me to fully analyze how the intermingling of learned Christian founded ethics and morality in such a challenging environment had provided the foundation of lessons on race relations that I had explored at home and in school. These things hadn't just happened in my neighborhood, they had been happening in communities across the United States. Every citizen was learning anew the ways of growing within a changing society in the post-Civil Rights era.

It occurred to me how those recommended reading choices of Mark Twain's work had so profoundly contributed to the way I thought about these issues. The conversations between my father and I during those difficult years had evolved substantially from a preponderance on Fredric March interpretations and Tom Sawyer coloring contests to a more mature dialog about Huck and Jim and Twain's views on racism.

In my teenage years and thereafter, Dad and I didn't always see eye to eye, which caused some strain between us. Sometimes Dad would threaten a whipping from his folded belt, other times we'd poise to fistfight, yet somehow we always managed to back off and maintain a mutual respect for each other. Dad was passionately opinionated, and whenever our discussions started leaning in the argumentative direction, he would typically shut it down, just too distraught to continue.

It was this separation and disconnect for which I sought closure on my trip to Hannibal so many years after he had passed. I had to go past those mildly rebellious years of teenage disagreement, further back into my past, to the better memories that had been supplanted by troubling ones from those difficult, challenging years of just learning to survive on the streets, to get to the root of those times when Dad and I had been buddies.

Recalling those troubling years hadn't been pleasant, and I was amazed to find the influence of Mark Twain at every turn. The fact that just learning some basic intro about his father-in-law had awakened so much unpleasantness from my past led me to see the therapeutic benefit of taking another hard look. So much I had forgotten, so much beyond the pleasant memory of sharing a film. What Dad learned from Mark Twain had pierced into his very identity, as minstrel performer, as a working-class White man in post war America. The lessons he passed on had been invaluable as I came of age.

Now, I was a bit more curious about the psychology of Twain himself. What had guided his conscience? What had formed him, had contributed to his personal evolution? How had he become, as Hal Holbrook described, a clear path into the soul of America?

OUT OF BONDAGE.

E. W. Kemble's illustration of Tom, Jim and Huck for
Adventures of Huckleberry Finn

PART TWO:

INTO THE AMERICAN SOUL

13

CHILDHOOD ROOTS & CIRCUMSTANCE

> "…an atmosphere like this meant a tropic development for the imagination of a delicate child. All the games and daily talk concerned fanciful semi-African conditions and strange primal possibilities. The children of that day believed in spells and charms and bad-luck signs, all learned of their negro guardians."
>
> Mark Twain,
> from his Biography

In Chapter III of his biography, Albert Paine references a slave girl named Jennie who was owned by Samuel Clemens' parents during their move from Tennessee to Florida, Missouri[95] before Sam was born. After settling in Florida, his father partnered with a businessman there who owned thirty slaves, the same man Twain referred to as his Uncle John Quarles.

In Chapter IV, Paine recounts Twain's memories of his childhood companionship, which included: "the still more potent influences of that day and section, the intimate, enveloping institution of slavery, the daily companionship of the slaves. All the children of that time were fond of the negroes and confided in them. They would, in fact, have been lost without such protection and company."

"It was Jennie, the house-girl, and Uncle Ned…" Paine transcribed,

> "who were in real charge of the children and supplied them with entertainment…But if the negroes were the chief companions and protectors of the children, they were likewise one of their discomforts. The greatest real dread children knew was the fear of meeting runaway slaves. A runaway slave was regarded as worse than a wild beast, and treated worse when caught…bound him with ropes. His groans were loud and frequent. Such things made an

impression that would last a lifetime...Slave punishment, too, was not unknown, even in the household...Jane Clemens...once undertook to punish [Jennie] for insolence, whereupon Jennie snatched the whip from her hand. John Clemens...tied Jennie's wrists together with a bridle rein, and administered chastisement across the shoulders with a cowhide. These were things all calculated to impress a sensitive child."[96]

In his memoir *My Uncle's Farm*, Twain poses another view of his mother's outlook, citing an incident that occurred when he lived later in Hannibal at the age of 11 or 12 years old, and which seems to indicate the root of his own abolitionist sympathies that he would come to cultivate once among the Langdons.

"We had a little slave boy whom we hired from someone," Twain wrote.

"He was from the Eastern Shore of Maryland and had been brought away from his family and his friends, halfway across the American continent, and sold. He was a cheery spirit, innocent and gentle, and the noisiest creature that ever was perhaps. All day long he was singing, whistling, yelling, whooping, laughing - it was maddening, devastating, unendurable. At last, one day, I lost all my temper and went raging to my mother and said Sandy had been singing for an hour without a single break, and I couldn't stand it, and wouldn't she please shut him up. The tears came into her eyes and her lip trembled, and she said something like this:

"Poor thing, when he sings it shows that is not remembering, and that comforts me but when he is still I am afraid he is thinking and I cannot bear it. He will never see his mother again; if he can sing, I must not hinder it but be thankful for it. If you were older, you would understand me; then that friendless child's noise would make you glad."

'It was a simple speech and made up of small words but it went home, and Sandy's noise was not a trouble to me any more. [My mother] never used large words but she had a natural gift for making small ones do effective work.... I used Sandy once...in Tom Sawyer. I tried to get him to whitewash the fence..."[97]

Twain goes on to reveal a greater depth of appreciation:

"All the Negroes were friends of ours and with those of our own age were in effect comrades. I say in effect, using the phrase as modification. We were comrades and yet not comrades; color and condition interposed a subtle line which both parties were conscious of and which rendered complete fusion impossible."[98]

Above: Twain's Uncle John Quarles' farm, Florida, Missouri. Date unknown. Below: The slave quarters at Quarles Farm, where Sam Clemens spent a considerable amount of time in his youth. Source: The Hannibal African American Life & History Project, Huck Finn Freedom Center, Hannibal, MO.

Twain is talking about the unspoken segregation that separated Whites and Blacks. Reading these tales of his boyhood affiliations reminded me of a few times while I was growing up when circumstance imposed a similar "subtle line."

Since toddlerhood I had known our next-door neighbor Bessie, a kind woman who showered great affection on me as a child. I wasn't aware at the time that Bessie was South Philly royalty with serious props since it was in her kitchen where the South Philadelphia String Band Mummer's brigade had been founded by her husband Jim and his brother Sam. By default, we were one stoop removed from the epicenter of South Philly culture. Then, at some point in the mid 1960s, I never saw Bessie again, uncertain if she passed or moved.

Not long afterward, maybe around 1967 or so, an African American family moved into the house. By then this was becoming routine because several other Black families had already lived there for a few years, and to the best of my knowledge ours was one of the first integrated street in the neighborhood.

My Mom and our new neighbor-Mom gradually became acquainted through the wire fence which lined the top of a short row of cinder blocks between our back yards. Mom and she enjoyed nice chats and laughter on sunny days while hanging laundry on the clothes lines in the yard. Mom used to remark what a nice woman and family they were. In short time, I became friends with our new neighbor's son, Junior, when he approached me on my front pavement one afternoon when I was playing with my Captain Action figure. I had all the accessories that could turn Captain Action into Superman, Aquaman, and other heroes, but on that day, Junior brandished Captain Action's nemesis - Dr. Evil. Yes! Dr. Evil - long before Mike Myers conceived of the character for the *Austin Powers* franchise. This was cool, I thought. Someone who liked the same things I did, and we became friends somewhat instantly.

When it snowed, Junior and I built and played in snow forts on our conjoined front sidewalk. Sometimes he'd hang on our front steps to play a board game, and sometimes we'd sit on his steps to play cards. We had great times together, and the slightest thought or feeling of any racist sentiment or racial difference never came up. On our street, despite the troubles in the neighborhood, the real line of demarcation was whether someone was Irish or not Irish, Catholic or not Catholic, parochial or public schooled. Black and White was a present yet unspoken topic. In hindsight, I can clearly see that both Junior and I overtly played together because in our hearts, both of us maintained a youthfully idealistic view that racism and segregation could be overcome by just chilling out together, and sharing a nonjudgmental interactive friendship. At eight or nine years old, we didn't think of it in those words. It was just something we innately understood and wanted to believe.

One summer night in 1969 or '70, my Mom, Dad and I had gone out for the evening, probably on one of our movie nights at the Yeadon Theater followed by the obligatory trip to Dunkin' Donuts, and my brother Mike was asked to mind the house. When we returned home later that night, Mike told us that someone had broken into our house while he played cards on our front steps with his friends. He explained how, at one point in the evening, he went inside the house to get some ice-water from the glass Sealtest Milk jug Mom kept perennially filled in our Kelvinator 'ice box' when he heard our back screen-door slam, followed by the rattle of the chicken wire fence that separated our neighbor's yard from ours. When Mike ran to the back of the house to investigate, he heard only the sound of our next-door neighbor's back door shutting quickly.

My Mom, the vigilant housekeeper, noted that some things seemed to be missing. She first went into the yard and called our neighbor's name - which I'm pretty sure was Blanche - through the fence. After no one answered and their back door remained closed, Mom went to our neighbor's front door and knocked. When Blanche answered the door, my Mom respectfully inquired if she knew if any of her kids had been in our house. Blanche questioned the insinuation and became instantly infuriated. How dare my Mom make such a suggestion, that she didn't raise her kids that way, and that my Mom was just being racist and accusing them because they were Black. My Mom tried to explain the details of what my brother Mike had witnessed, but Blanche wouldn't hear of it and slammed the door in my mother's face. My Dad, needless to say, threw an expletive-laced fit. He was taking medication for high blood pressure at the time and that was the type of thing that would have set him off in a bad way. Nonetheless, Dad stood by my Mom and made even stronger inflammatory remarks, which was likely what had inspired Blanche to slam the door to begin with.

The next day, Blanche called through the back fence to my Mom, whom she called "Miss Betty." My Mom had been busy with something, but hearing Blanche call, went out into our yard. Blanche was crying profusely, apologizing while explaining through her sobs that she had found "the black dress" in her daughter's bedroom, and upon inquiring where she got it, the daughter confessed that she had come into our home through the back door, just as my brother had described, and had stolen the items that were missing.

Me, left, in blissful samadhi at age 1, with Mom and my brother James in our backyard, South Philadelphia, 1961, standing before the fence to Bess and Jim's house into which Blanche, Junior and family moved, as described herein. Note the clotheslines, a working-class fixture of every row home back then.

The black dress was actually my brother's black altar boy cassock, reserved for use at funeral services, which my Mom had hung on the edge of the china closet in our dining room after ironing it, just as she always had. The other missing items included an empty dress purse Mom had borrowed, and a family heirloom, a bronze medallion that had been brought from Ireland by my Mom's grandmother when they immigrated to the United States in 1912. It had been passed on to my grandmother, who passed it along to my Mom, who had set it in a small frame with a strand of dried Heather brought from Ireland by an older relative of her father. It was a cherished family artifact my Mom displayed proudly on the cedar chest that had set along the base of the stairs in our dining room.

The theft incident was the beginning of the end of the life we knew on Wilder Street. After that, I was pretty much discouraged from playing with Junior any more, and was firmly told by Dad that he was not welcome within our house under any circumstances. It was awkward for me; an imposed segregation twelve to fifteen feet from our front door. I recall seeing Junior for brief, passing moments after that from time to time, with little said between us save for a half smile with a nod of the head and a "Hey!" He must have been relatively embarrassed by his sister's action. He had become ostracized by my friends, and he sheepishly avoided us as well. His mother must have been so embarrassed by the incident that Junior's demeanor thereafter became the embodiment of apologetics. We never hung out again. This was an unfortunate turn. I liked Junior and we got along well. I don't recall which of our families moved off the block first - his or ours - but I never saw Junior again. I've often wondered how he's fared in life, and I wish him well.

Like Twain, elder African Americans I came to respect would become mentors. When I was in high school I got job after school and on Saturdays working as a stock boy in the basement of John Wanamaker's department store in downtown Philly. My immediate supervisor was a gentle, middle aged Black fellow named Willie. Willie was a Seventh Day Adventist and by nature was a kind, unprejudiced man. Willie had trained me for the task of loading and unloading racks of costume jewelry displays, and assigned errands that got me out of the small office and repair shop we worked in beneath the slanted underbelly of an escalator.

On my errands and during lunch breaks, I'd periodically stop into Martindale's Health Food Store at 12th and Chestnut to grab a healthy snack alternative to hot dogs or soft pretzels. Once when I was back in the shop eating a "Club Sandwich" bar - the 1970's predecessor of today's Balance or Clif bars - Willie asked where I got it. When I told him, he explained that he shopped there all the time. From that point on, Willie and I became fast friends. As a Seventh Day Adventist, Willie was a vegetarian and would recommend different foods to try that I could find at Martindale's, especially after I had once gotten deathly ill from eating hot dogs at a downtown luncheonette. It was because of Willie that I became a vegetarian, and remain so even today. Hence my enjoyment of Moosewood cuisine and my desire to visit there. Where Willie had failed in his attempts to convert me to his Adventist creed and join his congregation to save my soul, he had succeeded in saving the bag of bones and skin that contained it with his recommendations on healthy eating habits.

When we worked, Willie and I discussed all sorts of topics from religion and health food, and I recall once discussing Huckleberry Finn by Mark Twain.

"I'm familiar with it but can't say that I have read it" he remarked.

After I shared bits and pieces of the main plot, I remarked that, in a curious way, our working friendship reminded me of the friendship between Huck and Jim in the book. Willie knew what I meant and found the topic mesmerizing. In his pleasant, slow manner of speaking, Willie responded, without lifting his gaze or focus from repairing some jewelry.

"Well, Tom, I'll have to check that out. Yes sir, I will definitely have to check that out."

I don't know if he ever did read it. Our working relationship had indeed played out like a Huck and Jim story. Willie had often saved my ass from getting fired many times, such as after I'd accidentally knock over the jewelry cart which required hours of separating rack after rack of tangled necklaces or if I delivered something to the wrong address. Likewise, I made up excuses to cover for Willie whenever our boss Bill questioned why a task wasn't completed.

"Oh, that's my fault, Bill" I might say. "Willie had to help me with the racks."

Bill would nod and say "Ok" and turn his back to us to resume work at his own desk. Willie would just look over at me with a silent, knowing smile that expressed his appreciation. I also felt that the boss of all three of us - we'll call him Mr. Stern - the company owner, treated Willie in a mildly demeaning, traditional attitude of White superiority. Mr. Stern would thrust a few dollars in front of Willie's face and say "Willie, go to Chock full of Nuts and fetch me a cup of coffee. Black with one Sweet and Low."

I could see the mild frustration contained in Willie's face. Mr. Stern spoke just this side of derisive to Willie and it was humiliating for him. If Willie hadn't been such a good-natured Christian it could have easily infuriated him. I didn't like the way Mr. Stern spoke to Willie any more than Willie did, and I would chime in, assuming the role of eager young student employee.

"I'll do that for ya Mr. Stern. I could use a coffee myself."

"Don't you have your own work to do Tom?" Mr. Stern might ask.

"Well, yeah, but Willie needs to finish what's he's doin' first so I can get it out in the mail today. I can be real quick about it."

"Ok, Tom. That'll be fine" Mr. Stern would cede, handing me the money, repeating how he liked his coffee: "Black with one Sweet and Low." He never offered to buy any of us a cup for ourselves.

Mark Twain once wrote: "A wise man does not waste so good a commodity as lying for naught."[99] I didn't see my offer to cover for Willie as lying per se. It was just practice of the learned finesse of good old-fashioned Irish Blarney.

Mr. Stern's thinly veiled contemptuousness for those of us from a lower economic class didn't ruffle me. I seized it as a chance to get out of our cramped, dimly lit hovel beneath the escalator. The result of my speedy purchase and return thereafter delegated me as Mr. Stern's permanent new whipping boy when it came to fetching his coffee. It was a break for Willie, who had played this role for years before me. I still didn't mind, again, because of the frequency it got me out into the sunshine for a stretch of the legs and a brief respite.

Willie was always relieved when I did this, and glanced at me with evident gratitude in his eyes and slight smile. Like Huck and Jim on the raft, Willie and I were up shit's creek as subservient employees and needed to paddle for each other just to get to the promised land of our Goshen pay day. I learned a lot from Willie. We didn't always agree on everything but there was always mutual respect between us.

Like Willie's impressionable influence on me, I recognized a parallel to how such influences had similarly impressed the young Sam Clemens, and providing a similar mentoring role in his own youth.

"We had a faithful and affectionate good friend, ally, and adviser in "Uncle Dan'l"" Twain recounted to Albert Paine for his biography,

> "…a middle-aged slave whose head was the best one in the Negro quarter, whose sympathies were wide and warm, and whose heart was honest and simple and knew no guile…I have not seen him for more than half a century, and yet spiritually I have had his welcome company a good part of that time and have staged him in books under his own name and as Jim and carted him all around, to Hannibal, down the Mississippi on a raft… It was on the farm that I got my strong liking for his race and my appreciation of certain of its fine qualities. This feeling and this estimate have stood the test of sixty years and more, and have suffered no

impairment. The black face is as welcome to me now as it was then.'

'In my school-boy days I had no aversion to slavery. I was not aware that there was anything wrong about it. No one arraigned it in my hearing; the local papers said nothing against it; the local pulpit taught us that God approved it, that it was a holy thing, and that the doubter need only look in the Bible if he wished to settle his mind - and then the texts were read aloud to us to make the matter sure; if the slaves themselves had an aversion to slavery, they were wise and said nothing. In Hannibal we seldom saw a slave misused; on the farm, never."[100]

The important passage here is Twain's recollection of how he was raised to regard slavery: "I was not aware that there was anything wrong with it." Multiply that by hundreds of thousands of unsuspecting Southern State youths of his age being taught this same attitude, who would grow up to defend it in the Confederate Army. Likewise, consider how youth of the North, young lads like Charlie Langdon, had been raised at the same time learning the exact opposite, that not only was slavery morally wrong, but must be eradicated.

Young Sam's naiveté served him, enabling him to imbibe the cultural richness provided by the enslaved African Americans of his youth to such a great extent that they molded his very character into the man he became. But it was another slave of Clemens' acquaintance who would become the downright role model for that character.

While Uncle Dan'l served as a spiritual mentor of sorts who influenced Twain well into old age, it might surely be said that the guru of his storytelling prowess was the slave on John Quarles' farm whom Twain affectionately called Uncle Ned. Twain's own description of the impression left on him by Uncle Ned affirms this, with Twain outright stating that he borrowed at least one of Ned's tales.

"Wonderful entertainment it was." he began.

> "That was a time of visions and dreams, small gossip and superstitions. Old tales were repeated over and over, with adornments and improvements suggested by immediate events. At evening the Clemens children, big and little, gathered about the great open fireplace while Jennie and Uncle Ned told tales and hair-lifting legends…"

The tales always began with "Once 'pon a time," and one of them was the story of the "Golden Arm" which the smallest listener would one day repeat more elaborately to wider audiences in many lands. Briefly it ran as follows:

> "Once 'Pon a time there was a man, and he had a wife, and she had

a' arm of pure gold; and she died, and they buried her in the graveyard; and one night her husband went and dug her up and cut off her golden arm and tuck it home; and one night a ghost all in white come to him; and she was his wife; and she says:

"W-h-a-r-r's my golden arm?

W-h-a-r-r's my golden arm?

W-h-a-r-r's my g-o-l-den arm?"

'As Uncle Ned repeated these blood-curdling questions he would look first one and then another of his listeners in the eyes, with his hands drawn up in front of his breast, his fingers turned out and crooked like claws, while he bent with each question closer to the shrinking forms before him. The tone was sepulchral, with awful pause as if waiting each time for a reply. The culmination came with a pounce on one of the group, a shake of the shoulders, and a shout of:

"YOU'VE got it!' and she tore him all to pieces!"

'And the children would shout "Lordy!" and look furtively over their shoulders, fearing to see a woman in white against the black wall; but, instead, only gloomy, shapeless shadows darted across it as the flickering flames in the fireplace went out on one brand and flared up on another. Then there was a story of a great ball of fire that used to follow lonely travelers along dark roads through the woods.'

"Once 'pon a time there was a man, and he was riding along de road and he come to a ha'nted house, and he heard de chains' a-rattlin' and a-rattlin' and a-rattlin', and a ball of fire come rollin' up and got under his stirrup, and it didn't make no difference if his horse galloped or went slow or stood still, de ball of fire staid under his stirrup till he got plum to de front do', and his wife come out and say: 'My Gord, dat's devil fire!' and she had to work a witch spell to drive it away."

"How big was it, Uncle Ned?"

"Oh, 'bout as big as your head, and I 'spect it's likely to come down dis yere chimney 'most any time."

'Certainly an atmosphere like this meant a tropic development for the imagination of a delicate child. All the games and daily talk concerned fanciful semi-African conditions and strange primal possibilities. The children of that day believed in spells and charms and bad-luck signs, all learned of their negro guardians."[101]

His love for Uncle Ned and those wonderful times had in his earliest, formative years surely softened his heart to the extent that it may have made it easy for him to abandon the Confederate cause, but more importantly, enable him to travel the world with open eyes and ears, receptive to people of all race, color, creed and culture. In the final years of his life, Twain took on the role of a grand uncle of sorts to his "Angelfish," the group of young girls he entertained at his final home in Redding, Connecticut. While some psychologists may suggest his behavior indicative of an old man trying to recapture his fatherhood years, or use of the girls as the surrogate grandchildren he would never know, I believe Twain was reaching back to the earthen floor of Uncle Ned's ramshackle quarters on his Uncle John's farm in effort to burrow ever more acutely into the deepest channels of his heart, groping, grasping, reaching for what semblance of a feeling of love from long ago might be extracted. Uncle Ned was the one he sought through a memory, a sound, a story, to rediscover his raison d'être. It would ultimately manifest in his best known work.

14

THE RELEVANCE OF HUCKLEBERRY FINN

> "…a book of mine where a sound heart and a deformed conscience come into collision and conscience suffers defeat."
>
> Mark Twain,
> *Notebook #35*

On my drive home from Elmira, while contemplating those elephant on the raft memories of what I often describe as our respective 'Troubles' – a play on the Irish reference to their Catholic vs Protestant struggle during the same years - I recalled that the *Adventures of Huckleberry Finn* had been the elephant in our own living room when I was a kid. Dad kept two copies of it: a hardback copy which had the honored designation of being placed on the top shelf of his book case right next to his vinyl recliner, and the other a compact paperback copy that he could stuff in his pocket and take to work. This memory ignited a flurry of questions that I would investigate in the weeks to come.

Further fueling this ambition was an article that popped up in my newsfeed the day after I returned home, which discussed a school board's debate over the banning of Huckleberry Finn from its curriculum. I thought the timing of this uncanny, considering that only the night before I had recalled its prominent stature in my childhood home, second only to our family

Left: Huckleberry Finn as he first appeared to the world, dead cat in hand, in The Adventures of Tom Sawyer, 1876 by illustrator True Williams, and right, as he is more popularly known in 1884's the Adventures of Huckleberry Finn by illustrator E. W. Kemble. Courtesy of Library of Congress.

Bible and the massive, five-inch-thick, unabridged and illustrated Webster's Dictionary that required assistance to lift onto a table. Such prominent placement was a significant thing in our home. Why, again, was this fuss over Huck Finn being raised, I wondered, when the consensus had always recognized its importance? Why had Dad so cherished the *Adventures of Huckleberry Finn*? I felt the need to review and ruminate, as this was an important clue in my fact-finding mission to understand Dad's relationship with Mark Twain.

Dad had once explained why the book was considered one of the most important books in American Literature, and how it served as the root inspiration for many renown authors to follow. I wouldn't understand fully what he meant for decades, which is why Ernest Hemingway's famed comment of 1935 rang a bell:

> "All modern American literature comes from one book by Mark Twain called 'Huckleberry Finn,' It's the best book we've had. All American writing comes from that. There was nothing before. There has been nothing as good since."[102]

Of all the celebrated works that contribute to Mark Twain's rock star status, Huckleberry Finn remains his most popular hit one-hundred-and-forty years after its publication. It is also true that the work has since endured a good deal of controversial backlash. In the 1950s, the NAACP had challenged the book's depiction of Jim the slave character and Twain's repeated use of the 'N' word two-hundred-and-fifteen times,[103] inaugurating requests for its removal in numerous communities across the United States.[104] In 1998, parents in Tempe, Arizona, sued their school district for including Huckleberry Finn and what was only referenced as 'a William Faulkner short story' (probably *Was*) on its list of required reading, citing that use of the derogatory 'N' reference in both works was fueling an increase of racially motivated bullying of their daughter and other African-American classmates.

Only a few months after reading the initial article on my phone, an October, 2017 article in *The Guardian* revealed that the school board in Biloxi, Mississippi had voted to remove *To Kill a Mockingbird* from its junior-high reading list citing their declaration that the language in the book "makes people uncomfortable."[105]

It didn't stop there! A March 2019 article in *Politico New Jersey* reported on yet another resolution for school districts to ban Huck, adding that it had already been banned from curricula in Pennsylvania, Minnesota, Virginia, and the above referenced vote in Mississippi.

The Politico article referenced calls to ban the work as far back as 1996, and quoted Nobel Prize winning author Toni Morrison from her introduction to a

Huck Finn course manual in which she had claimed that campaigns to ban the book represent "a purist yet elementary kind of censorship designed to appease adults rather than educate children..." and hailed the work for

> "its ability to transform its contradictions into fruitful complexities and to seem to be deliberately cooperating in the controversy it has excited...The brilliance of Huckleberry Finn is that it *is* the argument it raises..."[106]

Exactly. Having been a high school educator myself, I understood the duress these works could cause, yet my view was consistent with Toni Morrison's, that this only exposes a failure of some educational professionals to teach the work in an expanded, proper context. I'm sure some do, but to what extent?

Our history wasn't just about tea parties in Boston or George Washington crossing the Delaware River. There is a whole array of related, topical issues that no one likes to talk about. For example, I recently happened upon one of my daughter's old middle school textbooks and was appalled to find that only four paragraphs had been written about the Underground Railroad, and the only name mentioned in context in one paragraph was Harriet Tubman. Granted, it was an introductory level textbook to these topics, but I thought it severely inadequate. Is it any wonder that we still grapple with racial conflict in our time? It serves as evidence that we still don't know how to address these issues. Without gaining a full understanding of something as vital in our history as the Underground Railroad in middle school, how can we expect our children to fully comprehend the impact of Huckleberry Finn or *To Kill a Mockingbird* in high school? Besides, as we'll explore in depth, Mark Twain and the Underground Railroad had been intricately intertwined. Was history trying to erase the memory of our bigoted past?

In the very onset of the book, Twain forewarns readers that the book wasn't designed to be comfortable. He knew the whole issue underscoring his entire narrative was intentionally uncomfortable, and that the change needed to address the circumstances around the topic of race as an active participant was likely the most uncomfortable of all. The *Adventures of Huckleberry Finn* was designed as a path directly through the heart of uncomfortable. So, for a school board or parent to perceive the work as causing discomfort, they are precisely correct.

But that's only where the journey begins. The work is not only an invitation for a school board, parent, and child to venture on that journey, but was written for the entire, interracial American community to discuss and learn together.

In an October 2017 interview with *Entertainment Weekly* about the release of his audio recording of *A Connecticut Yankee in King Arthur's Court*, comedic actor Nick Offerman explains his take on Twain's work:

"It's the same as Shakespeare: It will tickle you every time because it's a sublime piece of writing. Yeah. I think Mark Twain himself would be astonished at how prescient and timeless his writing was. It's because he had a very true lens into the heart of the human being, and great writing is what allows all of us as readers to think, "Oh my God, I can't believe he knows that about me. How did Mark Twain see into my soul?""[107]

Offerman's viewpoint reveals the core appeal of Mark Twain's writing, that the author's work has endured as a mirror of the American conscience, serving as a fundamental moral compass specifically on the issue of race relations and discrimination. In this context, the Adventures of Huckleberry Finn is our national, secular Sunday school lesson, among the most vital literary works of our collective culture.

An 1885 help wanted ad for reps to sell a new book by Mark Twain.

First edition cover for the Adventures of Huckleberry Finn.

In the fourth paragraph of the opening chapter, Twain delivers a delicious clue to his conscience in a brief lingual reference that reveals the intended theme. While describing the reform attempts of the Widow Douglas, Huck explains:

"After supper, she got out her book and learned me about Moses and the Bulrushers, and I was in a sweat to find out all about him; but by and by she let it out that Moses had been dead a considerable long time; so then I didn't care no more about him, because I don't take no stock in dead people."

Why did Twain choose to insert that specific reference at the onset of the work? Right there, cleverly embedded, is the author's subliminal entreaty for readers to heed the lesson of the book of Exodus, and a foretaste of what's coming. He subtly offers this as a disclaimer up front that is his unique way of saying "Oh yeah, I'm goin' there" because Exodus, as the tale of the Israelite's delivery from slavery, provided the perfect avenue to discuss the issue of slavery in the United States.

'Not taking stock in dead people' is a further appeal to readers that the ethical issues to be unveiled require active, living participation, that these issues can't be resolved by solely depending on the words of a mythically revered figure such as Moses who lived long ago. It's an invitation for everyone presently living to take responsibility as agents of change.

There are other allusions to suggest the biblical parallel - the raft, the river, the duo's repeated hiding of their raft in reeds along the river as they seek a path to refuge, and even the references in chapter eleven when the undisguised Huck tries to worm out of his dilemma by telling the unnamed 'Illinois woman' that he needs to get to Goshen. Goshen was the land given by Pharaoh to Joseph and the Hebrews in the book of Genesis, and it is the same land from which Moses led the Hebrews to freedom in Exodus. Huck and Jim represent our national need to first get to Goshen before we can go on to the American promised land. The idea of America is, after all, just a promise. We, the people, as the Constitution begins, are the ones who need to walk the walk to realize that promise.

Chapter thirty-one is the core of the narrative where many academics focus their attention. This is where Huck discards the note that would have Jim returned to slavery after grappling with his conscience in a battle between his learned concepts of what was right versus his willingness to 'go to hell' for embracing what he saw as the correct, genuine and ethical thing to do.

In the final chapter, Huck describes his inquiry to Tom Sawyer about Tom's plan which "managed to set a nigger free that was already free before."[108] That one line, veiled within the Marian County, Missouri vernacular of the time, speaks about the abject ridiculousness of the institution of slavery, essentially chiding readers who may harbor supremacist sentiments. There is Twain the humorist, approaching the topic from left field with a tender, brotherly cajoling, a loving chastisement, and essentially concluding with the suggestion that it is time to move on, time to celebrate our freedom and live together as equals.

A confirmation for this assertion of Twain's philosophy to consciously employ humor is found in the author's journal, where Twain noted:

> "All crimes should be punished with humiliations - public exposure in ridiculous and grotesque situations - and never in any other way. Death makes a hero of the villain, and he is envied by some spectators and by imitators."[109]

Twain, the reasonable diplomat, is demonstrating how humor can offer the best avenue for addressing serious, weighty topics. The same formula has been used since, from popular, critical humorists like Will Rogers at the advent of the Twentieth Century, to Civil Rights era comedians like Dick Gregory. A native of St. Louis, Gregory is one of the more successful comedians who followed in the footsteps of fellow Missourian Twain by addressing the challenges of the Civil Rights movement at its peak, becoming the first Black comedian to work in a non-segregated club.

Gregory revered Mark Twain, citing him in his book *Callus On My Soul* as one of only three geniuses of comedy. "Mark Twain" he wrote,

> "was so far ahead of his time that he shouldn't even be talked about on the same day as other people. Look at what he did with his brilliant satire. For the first time in history of literature a White man talked about a relationship between a Black Man and a White boy. Black men didn't even have names; they were referred to as "nigger." Then he wrote The Adventures of Huckleberry Finn in 1884 and talked about "Nigger Jim."
>
> Today some people are outraged by the book and they have banned it from many school districts. That's really a shame, because the truth is that Twain was the first writer to refer to us as someone other than [N]. He attached a name to [N] and made Jim human. Now, we were always human to each other, but Twain's "Nigger Jim" made us human to White folks. They read about Jim and Huck Finn going down the Mississippi River…Jim was not putting the bait on the hook for Huck - they were fishing together as friends…
>
> I really took the word…public in 1963 when I wrote my first autobiography… a book with hard-core facts about Black life in racist White America. Titling my book *Nigger* meant I was taking it back from the White folks. Mark Twain threw it up in the air and I grabbed it."[110]

Through Huck Finn's humorous use of regional dialect, a less educated, fictional character oddly speaks aloud our conscience. Twain uses Tom Sawyer's reply to Huck as a veiled harkening to the famed quote from the book of Leviticus, when Moses says: "Proclaim Liberty throughout all the land unto all the inhabitants thereof."[111] This also happens to be the same quote inscribed on the Liberty Bell, the national symbol of American equality and independence. In Huck's recount of Tom's answer, Twain worded it a little differently:

"And [Tom] said, what he had planned in his head from the start, if we got Jim out all safe, was for us to run him down the river on the

Jim & Huck: two friends - E.W. Kemble.

raft, and have adventures plumb to the mouth of the river, and then tell him about his being free, and take him back up home on a steamboat, in style... and have them waltz him into town with a torchlight procession and a brass band, and then he would be a hero, and so would we."[112]

And what was Jim's response to all of this fuss? In Jim's own words, used by Twain as an allegorical implication of a Negro's birthright as a US Citizen by simply reminding Huck what he had been saying all along:

"I tole you I ben rich wunst, en gwineter to be rich ag'in; en its come true; en heah she is! Dah, now! doan' talk to me - signs is signs, mine I tell you; an I knowed jis's well 'at I 'uz gwineter be rich again as I's a-stanin' heah dis minute!"[113]

Jim's response poses a prophetic undertone. It's Jim - a rightfully free man who was an enslaved member of the disregarded and subjugated race - who bore the torch of truth, justice, of the American way. Jim was the original Superman, the hidden hero of the story employed as a character much in the manner of a Greek tragedy. Huck, the 'Good Ol' Boy' then takes a step back and becomes the illusory hero of the saga, suddenly thrust into a role similar to Shakespeare's Puck - aka 'Robin Goodfellow' - from *A Midsummer Night's Dream*.

OUT OF BONDAGE.

Tom Sawyer, Jim & Huck Finn, as conceived by E.W. Kemble

With Jim's freedom determined, he, Tom, and Huck immediately put the sorrowful past behind them, begin to plan their next adventure, and get on with business. The very presentation of an equal friendship between races in pre-Civil War America was still an unheard of and unaccepted reality in most of the United States during the post war era when Twain drafted Huck Finn in the early 1880s. Places like Elmira, I was learning, were an exception.

It was a hotly debated issue while segregation laws were simultaneously being adopted. Jim's words were used as Twain's jab in the US Government's ribs, a spirited reminder of the passage of the Civil Rights Act of 1875, which had extended the rights of emancipated slaves with the emphasized posit that any person born in the United States, regardless of race, is recognized as a US citizen, with all the rights and privileges that designation entails. The Act was declared unconstitutional and repealed in 1883, while Twain was still engaged in writing Huck Finn.

Twain offers an added voice of encouragement even in the very last line of the book, an expression of his prevailing optimism that there is still hope yet for reforming the vile tendencies of the creature known as man, the species which "can be awful cruel to one another."[114] Huck, the libertine non-conformist, doesn't want to get stuck in the mold of stuffed shirt politicians and law makers and establishment status quo. Twain, again, is teasing the adopted mores and conventionalism in a society that addressed these matters with such a level of seriousness that it led first to civil unrest then an all-out civil war. When Huck says "I reckon I got to light out for the territory ahead of the rest"[115] it may be Twain's subtle or subconscious reference to the status quo required of a young, reluctant and quasi-prejudiced Sam Clemens who had joined the Missouri militia to fight on the Confederate side of the war. Sam saw the light then, knowing the wrong of slavery since childhood, and lit out himself, exacting his own Exodus to discovering American brand liberty.

The stuffiness of a militia uniform, the expected compliant shallowness of faux social etiquette, and pre-packaged, inauthentic concepts of being 'civilized' were not among Sam Clemens' joys, as expressed through Huck, who remarks:

"because Aunt Sally she's going to adopt me and sivilize [SIC] me, and I can't stand it. I been there before."[116]

Bam! That's Mark Twain's invitation to all to begin anew, to reinvent ourselves, to proclaim liberty throughout all the land. What had been deemed civilized by government with repeal of the 1875 Civil Rights Act was barbarism at its finest. Twain himself is the wizard behind the screen, the burning bush behind the Moses embodied in Huck Finn. It's Sam Clemens expressing himself as the preacher he once wanted to be.

The larger point illustrated here that educators need to understand is that Twain's Huck Finn is a redraft of the lessons drawn from the book of Exodus in non-sectarian, non-denominational, separation of church and state America. For most Americans in his time, and especially on the frontier, aside from the Sears and Roebuck catalog, the Bible was one of the only books available from which everything was taught. Another popular book of the era that addressed the issues in a somber manner was Harriet Beecher Stowe's *Uncle Tom's Cabin*, the publication of which would trigger the Civil War. Huckleberry Finn was humorist Mark Twain's post-war response to Stowe's weightier work while delivering the same message with much broader appeal. Twain is, in effect, just saying, "Ok, people, we can get through this, and make a good time of it while we're at it." If analyzed thoroughly in this context, as a national community the importance of the dialog inherent in Huckleberry Finn would be plainly clear. It is still the source of our national dialog on race relations. Whenever and wherever this book is banned, the conversation stops, we cease to grow, the malice goes on.

After reading about the lynching of a Black man in his home state of Missouri in 1901, an outraged Mark Twain sat down and wrote a scathing diatribe aimed at his fellow Missourians first, and the rest of us second. In his essay entitled *The United States of Lyncherdom*, Twain wrote;

> "The child should also know that by a law of our make, communities, as well as individuals, are imitators; and that a much-talked-of lynching will infallibly produce other lynchings here and there and yonder, and that in time these will breed a mania, a fashion; a fashion which will spread wide and wider, year by year, covering state after state, as with an advancing disease. Lynching has reached Colorado, it has reached California, it has reached Indiana — and now Missouri! I may live to see a negro burned in Union Square, New York, with fifty-thousand people present, and not a sheriff visible, not a governor, not a constable, not a colonel, not a clergyman, not a law-and-order representative of any sort."

Twain wrote that over one-hundred-and-seventeen years ago. It seems tragically prophetic now, when lynching has only become supplanted by shootings. How much has really changed? Now is not the time to scuttle books like the *Adventures of Huckleberry Finn* or *To Kill a Mockingbird*. The message of the Adventures of Huckleberry Finn is that we need to navigate our raft beyond the safe harbors of dying modalities and petty discrimination, and instead foster a new modality of unified inclusiveness. That's why it is so vital to its continued inclusion in the American educational curriculum.

I had a hunch that Dad knew this. He had been educated by the Christian Brothers religious order, and they likely seized on these moral and ethical insights inspired by the book. Moreover, Dad's working-class Irish community had been at odds with Philly's Black community for a few generations, and violently so. The Christian Brothers had an imperative mission on their hands to mold young minds away from the trappings of bigoted attitudes.

Having travelled to different locales associated with Twain, it became increasing clear that there was a much more complex man behind all that we've been generally permitted to see for the past 100 years. While much of that information has since been presented in the realm of Twain academia, I suspect that early public withholding of information about some of the details of Twain's life while being fed a more sanitized, Disneyland version of his story has partially contributed to the confusion. I was compelled to hunker down and investigate.

The Elephant on the Raft · 217

Twain with his good friend and neighbor, John T. Lewis. The two met in 1877 and remained close throughout their lives. It is believed that their friendship inspired the foundation for the relationship between Huck and Jim depicted in the Adventures of Huckleberry Finn. Of Lewis, Twain once said:

"He was my father-in-law's coachman forty years ago; was many years a farmer of Quarry Farm, and is still my neighbor. I have not known an honester man nor a more respect-worthy one. Twenty-seven years ago, by the prompt and intelligent exercise of his courage, presence of mind and extraordinary strength, he saved the lives of three relatives of mine, whom a runaway horse was hurrying to destruction. Naturally I hold him in high and grateful regard."

Below: E. W. Kemble's illustration of Jim and Huck

15

AGAINST THE TRAFFICK OF MEN: THE GENESIS OF ABOLITION

> "But to bring men hither, or to rob and sell them against their will, we stand against..."[117]
>
> Francis Daniel Pastorius,
> *A Minute Against Slavery, 1688*

To fully understand the measure of controversy surrounding Mark Twain's publishing of the *Adventures of Huckleberry Finn*, an overview of the world into which Samuel Clemens and Olivia Langdon had been raised was required. Although "Huck" could be viewed as a latecomer to an abolitionist-fueled game, it nonetheless was as an arrow piercing the heart of the very foundational core of US history, which had been weightily teetering on the backs of African-born slaves and their American born descendants for two centuries prior to its publication.

Author-historian David McCullough once wrote:

> "Each new fragment of information leads to something more, almost always, and the personal satisfaction, the education that comes with the search only increases the farther you go...You are caught up, carried forward by all the elements of surprise and fascination in detective work. You find things you were not looking for and these trigger new ideas that never would have occurred to you otherwise. It is what is called the serendipity of original research. The driving force is the excitement of discovery. You feel a bond with those vanished people. They are not just anybody and nobody anymore and they never will be for you ever again."[118]

I could have clipped that quote and included it as a forward to this work. This precisely had been my experience the further I journeyed into the world of Mark Twain. As I made such discoveries as those implied by McCullough, I inevitably would come across a trove of scholarly work that had been submitted decades before on the same point. In fact, one such example was my recent discovery of a book that addressed the biblical themes tucked beneath the surface in the *Adventures of Huckleberry Finn*. Recognizing the theme of the book of Exodus was a thrilling epiphany several months prior when I reread the entirety of Huck for the first time in forty years. I assumed someone at some point had likely addressed it. In *Mark Twain and the Brazen Serpent: How Biblical Burlesque and Religious Satire Unify Huckleberry Finn* by Doug Aldridge, I was glad to see someone had.

These new and unanticipated avenues of research further awakened an awareness of how important it is to self-educate, take ownership of comprehension, and incorporate that data into one's own being. You can almost feel the new information nestling its way into a brain cell, where it settles in, makes itself at home, and becomes ingrained in your memory, accessible as a footnote in your personal, internal library. This further elucidates my earlier point that reading Huck Finn isn't just about reading a fun adventure story. It could be. But why stop there when there are important lessons on human ethos to be savored that Twain, like any good writer, incorporates as a bonus level for enjoyment and personal revelation.

Such was the case while investigating first the historical details of the Underground Railroad and abolitionism in Elmira, which expanded from there to require me to relearn the history of the formation of the United States, and from there, the evolution of thought and belief in Europe that led to the inauguration of events and laws and wars and the people behind the very evolution of Western Civilization - or, perhaps more accurately, the lack of civilization therein.

The more I engaged myself to research and understand just one kernel of information would require the investigation of two more, then those two sprouted four, then eight, and ad infinitum - but not ad nauseam. I found myself uncovering facts and links and connected tales that could keep me busy writing and referencing for years, while juggling twenty to forty internet links and volumes of books simultaneously at various points, cross referencing one to each other. I would go so far out on a limb that I seriously had doubts where it would end, and at times felt it would be wiser to throw in the towel.

But then, in due time, one surprise reference would bring me back to my original intended search and reinvigorate me. Once that circle was completed, I squeezed it like the ripe fruit it resembled and got to the core nectar of historical data. An academically inclined reader may find much to critique. I can already hear the thinking: "But he didn't mention this" or "he's skipping over a key point." Duly acknowledged.

Elmira itself, I learned, had played a significant role in Twain's personal renaissance. For African Americans, the town must have been something akin to a Utopian dream - a living, breathing embodiment of the promise held in the intended founding principles of the United States, that ALL men were created equal (Women still didn't officially count yet). But that promise didn't mean they benefitted from the rights enjoyed by the White population.

Free Blacks had lived in Elmira and the surrounding region beginning around 1800, with significantly more arriving after 1840.[119] The span of these years is key in how they correspond with the growth and influence of the abolitionist movement. Yet, those years embody what amounted to a meager response following decades of debates and passages of laws that addressed the issue of slavery and abolition versus the rights of property owners that varied from state to state while the battle for national independence from Britain waged on. To paint an accurate picture of what "free" meant to Blacks in 1800, one only need look at the struggle for African American civil rights into the Twentieth Century, and the prejudiced attitudes that still prevail today. However, it should be noted that the above reference to free Blacks in Elmira was a bit more distinct in that Elmira was an abolitionist haven, where Blacks were treated with dignity and equality. Consider just how revolutionary this was.

The practice of, and protest against, the enslavement of humans is ancient. History offers countless references of its practice dating back to the Hindu *Vedas*. The Romans enslaved everyone, as did the Greeks, the Vikings, and so on. The Old Testament offers the more widely known references from its first chapter tales of Noah's son Ham and the Canaanites through the plight of the Hebrews in Exodus. With the advent of Islam in the Seventh century, its earliest emissaries simply sanctified a tribal practice of enslaving enemies that had been extant in the Arabian Peninsula for thousands of years. In Africa and the Americas, the practice was also exploited by conquering warlords of their respective indigenous peoples.

With the arrival of sea voyage, the Portuguese purchased slaves from the African warlords and resold them throughout the Mediterranean and Europe. When Christopher Columbus embarked on his ill-fated journey to India, he brought along his own contingent of slaves on his wrong turn to the Western Hemisphere. Thereafter Columbus wrote to the King and Queen of Spain promising six native "Indians" as his gift to them, and in turn requested fifty men so the natives "can all be subjugated and made to do what is required of them."[120]

That was only the beginning of the western slave trade. In a letter to the financier of his voyage in April of 1493, Columbus wrote: "their Highnesses may see that I shall give them as much gold as they need...and slaves as many as they shall order to be shipped."[121]

In response, the following month Pope Alexander VI issued a papal bull (in all definitions of that term) granting ownership of the new world to Spain, along with all its spoils. Emboldened by their Papally sanctioned Divine mission, in 1514 the Spanish Conquistadors who followed with the blessings of Spain's La Corona and Papal Mitre drafted "the Requirement," an ultimatum requiring native American "Indians" then encountered to convert immediately to Christianity with the recognition of "the Church as the Ruler and Superior of the whole world" or have the alternative, which was:

> "We shall take you and your wives and your children, and shall make slaves of them, and as such shall sell and dispose of them as their Highnesses may command..."[122]

The Requirement was often announced with no translation, shouted from the bows of ships before the crew had even stepped on land.[123] The befuddled natives were taken post haste.

The papal bull was inspired by a few passages in the Old Testament book of Genesis. After Adam and Eve had their picnic under an apple tree and got into some mischief which displeased God, everything began to unravel from there. Genesis goes on to describe Adam and Eve's family and the fruit of their fruit grove for ten generations, until we get to Noah. Noah saves all of God's other invented creatures by building a massive boat, while those descendants of Adam and Eve who continued to perpetuate the mischief of the garden were wiped away. Humanity is rebooted by Noah, his wife, and their offspring.

Pleased with Noah's accomplishment, God encourages Noah to have a good time with His blessing. Noah enjoys some adult beverages, gets a little tipsy and falls asleep in the altogether in his Bedouin tent. At some point, Noah's son Ham enters the tent, discovers his naked father, and instead of compassionately covering him with a blanket, finds the whole affair worthy of gossip, running off to giddily relay his discovery to his brothers, Shem and Japheth. Ham apparently inherited the mischief gene from his proteogenic ancestors in Eden. With maturity and modest discretion, Shem and Japheth respond by covering their father without gawking.

A devout and respectful man who taught his sons with God's guidance, Noah later awakens, is told of Ham's immature, uncaring behavior, and proceeds to berate and scold Ham, decreeing that Ham's descendants will forevermore be servile to the descendants of Shem and Japheth.

The King James version of the Bible offers the story, found in Genesis 9, verses 22 - 27, as follows:

> "22 And Ham, the father of Canaan, saw the nakedness of his father, and told his two brethren without. 23 And Shem and Japheth took a garment, and laid it upon both their shoulders, and went backward, and covered the nakedness of their father; and their faces were backward, and they saw not their father's nakedness. 24 And Noah awoke from his wine, and knew what his younger son had done unto him. 25 And he said, Cursed be Canaan; a servant of servants shall he be unto his brethren. 26 And he said, Blessed be the LORD God of Shem; and Canaan shall be his servant. 27 God shall enlarge Japheth, and he shall dwell in the tents of Shem; and Canaan shall be his servant."[124]

It's this story, and verses 25-27 in particular, that underscores the Judeo-Christian justification for slavery. It seemed apparent that referencing the verses were utilized primarily for economic gain as an excuse to perpetuate the profitability of the slave trade, and as a moral pretext during the antebellum and reconstruction periods in the United States to justify the perpetuation of racial segregation.

After the Spanish dust settled, the New World was poised for further exploitive opportunity. Following the establishment of Jamestown on the banks of the Chesapeake in 1619, the first enslaved Africans arrived and were sold to settlers.[125] In 1620, the Plymouth Council for New England established the Plymouth settlement in the Massachusetts Bay Colony. After the famous first Thanksgiving meal had ended and the Pilgrim settlers extended their gratitude to the indigenous native peoples who had joined them in the first pot luck dinner, word of the native hospitality spread back to England. This encouraged more Pilgrims to make the pilgrimage to Plymouth, and in 1624, Samuel Maverick arrived with two African born slaves.[126] This inspired the Plymouth Council to reunite the Pilgrims with their first Native American Thanksgiving guests, and summarily deploy the latter against their will as unpaid laborers.

As Cliff Odle of the University of Massachusetts explains:

> "The settlers needed an inexpensive form of labor to handle the heavy tasks that came with starting a new colony. At first, they looked to the Native American tribes as a source of labor, as the Spanish did before them. But the Pequot and other tribes proved to be too unreliable and too dangerous to be considered useful slaves. In their place came slaves from Africa and indentured servants from Europe. At first, the African slaves were treated like indentured servants…Indentured servitude soon gave way to "life-long" or "chattel" slavery. Laborers were now considered

property, not people. Additionally, their children became slaves as well."[127]

Some distinctions referenced here are important to bear in mind. Indentured servants of either White European or Black African descent were treated with a relative measure of "Christian compassion" and granted freedom after a duration of service. For African servants, this belies the origin of those later referenced as "Free Blacks" during the colonial era and into the Nineteenth Century, such as those earlier referenced from the 1800 census for Elmira, New York.

After two decades of finding indentured servitude and exploited Native American labor too unreliable, in 1643 the New Plymouth Colony conjoined with the neighboring colonies of New Haven, Massachusetts Bay, and Connecticut to form The New England Confederation. In their charter, the Confederation "established guidelines to legalize the slave trade, placing Massachusetts among the first colonies to do so."[128]

The real incentive behind the formation of the Confederation was The Royal Africa Company, which had already staked their claim in the new world slave trade by way of England to the Massachusetts Bay Colony when they arrived with their first shipment of slaves brought directly from Africa in 1634.[129] Royal Africa sought to monopolize their slave trade within the now confederated colonies, especially in light of the fact that the Dutch East India Company was operating its own slave trade in neighboring New Netherland.

In 1641, the New England Confederation had adopted the Massachusetts Bodies of Liberty, the official set of codes that outlined the rules and rights of the settlers, their property, and, the first law regarding slaves. As more settlers voyaged to the new world with the promise of land and liberty in the decades that followed, the sales pitch for a readily available workforce was required to fill the demand. By 1682, as the number of imported slaves increased, concerns for slave rebellions brought about stricter controls and laws that limited the number of Blacks permitted to meet at one time in one place. Concurrent with the rise in the enslaved population, members of those religious denominations who remained ardently opposed to the practice of slavery began to voice their protest.

One of the earliest recorded protests within the post-reformation period was that of Richard Baxter, the Seventeenth Century English Puritan church leader, who spent time in prison and thirty years in exile due to his non-conformist views. Perpetually persecuted by conformist naysayers, in 1665, he is quoted as having said of slave traders, that those who "catch up poor Negroes...and...make them slaves and sell them...one of the worst kinds of thefts in the world...are to be taken as the common enemies of mankind."[130]

From its inception and throughout the evolution of the US, it was the Quakers who defined themselves as the most persistently outspoken denunciators of slavery, thus establishing themselves early as the literal enemy of those enterprises maintaining capitalization of the trade. Quaker activism itself is founded on a verse found in the New Testament book of James, chapter 2, verse 17, which reads: "So too, faith by itself, if it is not complemented by action, is dead."[131]

It is fascinating to consider that the entire debate over the moral endorsement or the abolishment of slavery boiled down to a battle between two biblical passages: the passage from James in the New Testament, and the passage from Genesis about Noah and Ham. Moreover, the passage from James shines another plausible light on the obscured biblical narrative in the Adventures of Huckleberry Finn, for example, when Huck says at the book's onset "I don't take no stock in dead people." Perhaps this was Twain's veiled applause for the efforts of those who had long waged against the institution of slavery, and prevailed. Given his investment in the moral climate and influence of the abolitionist Langdon family, it's not too far-fetched to consider.

In 1688, Quakers and Mennonites who founded Germantown, a settlement outside of Philadelphia, had called for one of the earliest ends to slavery within the new colony of William Penn's Sylvania. Quakers held their earliest meetings at the home of Thones Kunders on 5109 Germantown Ave in what is now Philadelphia, and it was there that Francis Daniel Pastorius drafted *A Minute Against Slavery*, aka the *1688 Germantown Quaker Petition Against Slavery*. It was signed by Pastorius and three fellow settlers in Kunders' home on a small table that is preserved to this day.

In what could arguably be described as perhaps the most important document of its kind in the new world, the Pastorius' 'Minute' has been hailed as the first public declaration of universal human rights, providing the pretext for a similarly themed Declaration of Independence that would be drafted 88 years later. It is the first written public protest against slavery, with the underlying precept of its core message based on the golden rule of "do unto others…," the same, simple philosophy imparted to me by my father in my youth. Pastorius' document was a forthright entreaty based on this singular premise, yet held so much power as to launch a movement that would ultimately change western civilization.

As I read the original content of *A Minute Against Slavery*, I had begun to transcribe the passages into a more readable, contemporary format. But as I proceeded, I found it losing the regional and verbal nuance of an early German settler with limited English skills. Preferring to leave it transcribed intact, I figured out the best way to suggest it be read. If you've seen the 1985 film *Witness* with Harrison Ford and Kelly McGillis, then you are familiar with the elder, Amish, Eli Lapp character played by actor Jan Rubes. If you read the following text hearing his voice as that character, then you will perfectly comprehend it. Moreover, that cinematic depiction of the Amish - the Anabaptists more commonly referred to as The Pennsylvania Dutch (an Anglicized version of the German 'Deutsch') - offers an approximate insight into the lifestyle of Francis Pastorius and his fellow Germans in colonial Pennsylvania, which hasn't changed all that much in 300 years. An edited sampling of the text is as follows, transcribed as originally written:

> "These are the reasons why we are against the traffick of men-body, as foloweth. Is there any that would be done or handled at this manner? viz., to be sold or made a slave for all the time of his life?...we hear that ye most part of such...are brought hither against their will and consent, and that many of them are stolen. Now, tho they are black, we can not conceive there is more liberty to have them slaves, as it is to have other white ones. There is a saying that we shall doe to all men like as we will be done ourselves; making no difference of what generation, descent or colour they are. And those who steal or robb men, and those who buy or purchase them, are they not all alike? Here is liberty of conscience wch is right and reasonable; here ought to be liberty of ye body... But to bring men hither, or to rob and sell them against their will, we stand against..."[132]

After reminding his fellow Quakers how they had come to Penn's Sylvania to flee persecution for their religious beliefs, Pastorius continued with an entreaty for those unwilling to admit their guilt to reason with their conscience:

> "Pray, what thing in the world can be done worse towards us, than if men should rob or steal us away, and sell us for slaves to strange countries; separating husbands from their wives and children...And such men ought to be delivered out of ye hands of ye robbers, and set free as well as in Europe..."[133]

Finally, he appeals to the hearts of his Quaker brethren, asking what they, as practitioners of pacifism and non-possession of arms, will do if their slaves rebel, and will they lift a weapon in defense and war against them? He concludes with love, respect, and recognition that the decision lies within their own conscience, to speak up, to surrender to the truth in the protected environment of a "safe house" among brethren in their Quaker meetinghouse.

It had been remarkable to come across this information. I knew Germantown well, having lived within a mile or two of these locales in neighboring Mount Airy earlier in my life. I had visited friends who lived on Pastorius Street, and had taken strolls through Pastorius Park. I had known the name for years, knew Pastorius had been a founder of Germantown, but did not know of his passion or importance in the abolitionist movement until now.

Across the street from a branch of my credit union is the Concord School House Cemetery, one of the oldest cemeteries in Philadelphia and possibly the United States, where many of Francis Pastorius' descendants are buried. I'd visited there on photography outings and taken photographs of the graves of Revolutionary War soldiers who had been hand-decorated by President Washington. Most of the headstones are inscribed in old German. The cemetery and the foundations of the Concord school were there when Pastorius' "Minutes" were drafted, read aloud, and signed in Thones Kunders' house just a few blocks away. The document itself is preserved and archived at Haverford College. The table on which the signing occurred is a revered artifact displayed in the 1770 Germantown Mennonite Meetinghouse.

Excitedly, I Google-mapped the address of Thones Kunders' house to determine its location, desiring to pay a visit and bask in the spiritual afterglow of that sacred act performed so long ago. Sadly, one of the most important homes in the history of liberty in the United States suffered the same fate as the Langdon mansion in Elmira: it was replaced with a generic strip mall. This is a disturbing trend in America. I've seen antique structures razed around Philadelphia my whole life. Then I travel to Europe, Britain, or Ireland and thrill over sites that have stood for 500 years or longer. At the rate we're going, America will have nothing but the foundations of strip malls to thrill future tourists.

The Thones Kunders House circa 1900. Courtesy of The Library Company of Philadelphia.

At the time Pastorius and Pennsylvania Quakers and Mennonites inaugurated this protest, there were still relatively few slaves in all the colonies as contrasted to the increased numbers resulting from the British endorsed slave trade of the Royal Africa Company throughout the Eighteenth Century. In 1698 New York alone held an estimated

2000 slaves,[134] with another 1000 counted throughout the entirety of the other New England colonies in 1700. By 1750 that number had grown to more than 13,000.

One of the more colorful Quaker abolitionists in the colonial period was Benjamin Lay. Born in England in 1677, Lay became a sailor, married, and moved to the English colony of Barbados in 1718 to establish himself as a merchant, and unexpectedly thrust into a front row seat at the very epicenter of slave trade hell.

Colonized by the British in 1625, Barbados was one of the principal stops in the North Atlantic Triangle of Trade established by Henry Winthrop that operated between Ghana and Massachusetts.[135] By 1660 the cultivation and annual exporting of 25,000 pounds of sugar, rum, molasses, spice, gold, and, of course, both native American and native African slaves, produced more trade than all of the global English colonies combined.[136] By 1700, Barbados' capital at Bridgeport became second in size to Boston as the largest city in the new world. With a population of 65,000, 50,000 of those were African born slaves - fifty times the estimated number of slaves in Massachusetts at the same time. In fact, Barbados had become the primary outlet for slaves being purchased or kidnapped

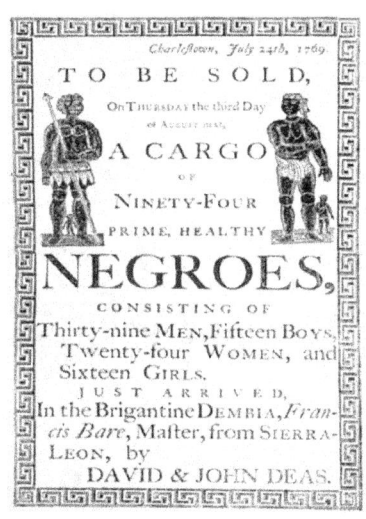

Eighteenth-Century Slave advertisements.

from the African coast, then resold to merchants in Boston. Due to the financial success of slavery deployment in the Barbados colony, the growth of the slave trade in New England was precipitated considerably.

During his tenure in Barbados, Benjamin Lay saw first-hand the abject cruelty and horror of slave treatment, having once witnessed an enslaved African take his own life rather than permit himself be subject to a miserable existence. Lay became an outspoken critic, and was probably not too popular a fellow in the very heart of the trans-Atlantic slave trade. After remaining in Barbados for thirteen years, Lay emigrated to the Pennsylvania colony where he settled in Abington, northwest of Germantown. It didn't take long for him to get noticed. Lay would become renown for an unrestrained and loudly overt manner of voiced protest, repelling everyone with whom he lived and worked with his zealously expressed anti-slavery views. Without fear, Lay spoke with power, courage, and inspired fervor. He was so relentless a force that even his fellow Quakers didn't care for his company.

Above: The Amazing Benjamin Lay as depicted in an 18th Century illustration. Right: Lay's courageous treatise, printed by his friend, Benjamin Franklin.

Benjamin Lay must have been something of a Quaker activist-avatar, characteristically described as something that might resemble a cross between Danny DeVito and John Lennon with a mix of Popeye and Jerry Rubin thrown in.

He might be the sort of outspoken social critic found at any civil protest today. Objecting to slave-made attire and slave-processed cotton he made his own clothes - probably from hemp, which was widely grown in the region at the time, and wore no accessories made of leather. He was a vegetarian who ate only the food he grew himself, and as a believer in temperance drank only milk or water. He authored, published, and distributed over 200 known pamphlets protesting a great number of social injustices.[137] In some neighboring states, and certainly in his native England, such outspokenness would have had Lay imprisoned or executed.

Joe Lockard of Arizona State University and organizer of the Antislavery Literature Project at Iowa State University, writes:

> "Lay attracted great attention during the 1730s in Pennsylvania and New Jersey for his vociferous opposition to slavery and slave-owners within the Quaker community. His physical appearance reinforced this public notice, as he stood only four feet seven inches, had a severely hunched back, and a very large white beard. He was physically ejected from meetinghouses where he vehemently denounced slavery and was disavowed by the Quaker community, although he considered himself a Quaker throughout his life.
>
> Lay had a theatrical talent that accompanied his antislavery rhetoric. On one occasion he threw off his Quaker garb in meetinghouse to reveal a military uniform, denounced slaveholders as men of war, and stabbed his belt with a sword to pierce a bladder containing red fluid"[138] [to mimic blood].

Some versions of this tale claim he plunged the sword and bladder into a bible, splattering fake blood on all nearby. On another occasion, he stood barefoot in the snow in front of a meetinghouse, explaining to the curious that he was dressed as slaves might appear.

Among his pamphlets, the best known was the no-punches-pulled entitled *All Slave-keepers that keep the Innocent in Bondage, Apostates*, printed by his friend Benjamin Franklin in 1737. Lockard continues:

> "*All Slave-keepers* is not only one of the earliest antislavery texts of colonial America, but one of the most vehement ever written. Lay viewed slavery as quintessential moral corruption and condemned it as such. Most of the text argues that slavery constitutes a social evil that offends divine justice...Lay's antislavery writings were frequently viewed as quixotic but had a more pervasive influence on the development of American religious antislavery thought than they have been attributed."[139]

That last sentence alone explains why I considered it vital to offer some detail on Benjamin Lay. Despite his banishment from attending Quaker meetinghouses throughout the greater Philadelphia area, Lay never relented on his stance. After his death in Abington, Pennsylvania in 1759, his likeness became a figurehead and inspiration for abolitionist Quakers who kept a printed copy of his portrait in their homes well into the Nineteenth century.[140] Marcus Rediker of the University of Pittsburgh cites founding father, Continental Congress member and Declaration of Independence signer Benjamin Rush, who had claimed about Lay:

> "The name of this "celebrated Christian philosopher" became familiar to every man, woman and to nearly every child, in Pennsylvania. For or against, everyone told stories about Benjamin Lay."[141]

Benjamin Lay has since become one of those largely forgotten individuals who, in his own unique way, would contribute to the very definition of American character. Certainly, to have included among his friends and admirers the likes of the Benjamins Rush and Franklin, he surely had an influence on the character of those Philadelphia based founding fathers and earliest colonists. In the end, he was revered as a unique brand of hero. Not permitted in meetinghouses during his lifetime, the Quakers buried Benjamin Lay alongside their own in the cemetery of the Abington Friends Meeting, located on the present-day grounds of Abington Friends School in Jenkintown, Pennsylvania.

Grave marker and burial site of Benjamin Lay and his wife, Sarah.

16

A CAUSE FOR SEVERITY

"The dictates of humanity came in opposition to the law of the land, and we ignored the law."

Levi Coffin, Abolitionist

Throughout the first half of the Eighteenth Century, with the young colonies still dependent on trade with Great Britain, the import and export of African born slaves made England the largest and wealthiest such trader, contributing significantly to its resultant growth as a formidable, imperialist force to be reckoned with. These decades marked the largest period of growth in the international slave trade.[142]

The issue became a primary point of contention at the onset of the American Revolution. On the heels of the Boston Tea Party in 1773 and the colonist's response to the Coercive Act passed by the British in 1774, representatives of each colony met in Philadelphia to form their own First Continental Congress and saw the opportunity to use Britain's economic dependence on the slave trade against them by calling for a prohibition on the import of slaves from Africa. The states, whose economic growth had by then become dependent on slave labor, remained divided on this proposal and compromised by passing laws that granted slaves and their descendants limited privileges.

Slave or free, new Americans of African descent were provided few if any rights by law, and were prevented by Congress to join the newly formed Continental army to fight for the colonial cause. In response, the British offered freedom to any slave opting to fight for the Crown.

In the original draft of the Declaration of Independence, Virginia's Thomas Jefferson and his fellow appointed Committee of Five members John Adams of Massachusetts, Benjamin Franklin of Pennsylvania, Roger Sherman of Connecticut, and Robert R. Livingston of New York - specifically assailed England's attempt to sway the Black population against them. With the committee's input, Jefferson had written:

> "He has waged cruel war against human nature itself, violating its most sacred rights of life and liberty in the persons of a distant people who never offended him, captivating & carrying them into slavery in another hemisphere or to incur miserable death in their transportation thither...Determined to keep open a market where Men should be bought & sold, he has prostituted his negative for suppressing every legislative attempt to prohibit or restrain this execrable commerce. And that this assemblage of horrors might want no fact of distinguished die, he is now exciting those very people to rise in arms among us, and to purchase that liberty of which he has deprived them..."[143]

The attack was duly aimed at those Northern Industrialists and Southern Plantation owners (Jefferson & Livingston among them) who held slaves and were equally guilty in perpetuating the trade. It proved to be the most hotly contested and divisive portion of the Declaration. For the sake of maintaining a united front in their battle against the Crown, Jefferson, at the behest of the Congressional Committee of the Whole, reduced the bold statement to a single-line intimation, that read:

> "He has excited domestic Insurrections among us."[144]

On this change, in his autobiography Thomas Jefferson noted:

> "The clause, too, reprobating the enslaving the inhabitants of Africa was struck out in compliance to South Carolina and Georgia, who had never attempted to restrain the importation of slaves, and who, on the contrary, still wished to continue it. Our Northern brethren also, I believe, felt a little tender under these censures, for though their people had very few slaves themselves, yet they had been pretty considerable carriers of them to others."[145]

The 'Northern brethren' remark is most pointedly directed at Massachusetts and New York, then the two principle purveyors of the slave trade in the colonies. The challenge throughout the discussion of forming a new nation lay with each state's demand for autonomous independence. To that end, the final paragraph of the Declaration assertively demands this autonomy as a prerequisite in the formation of the union:

> "we do assert and declare these colonies to be free and independent states, and that as free and independent states they shall hereafter have [full] power to levy war, conclude peace, contract alliances, establish commerce, and to do all other acts and things which independent states may of right do."[146]

In 1775, seventeen Pennsylvania Quakers organized *The Society for the Relief of Free Negroes Unlawfully Held in Bondage,* the first such organization of its kind in the United States. Among the society's founding members were Thomas Paine, Anthony Benezet and John Woolman.

Inspired by Benjamin Lay, Benezet and Woolman had waged an ardent but less theatrical campaign against their fellow Quakers who still held slaves. The new Society successfully persuaded Quakers to take an official stance on slavery in their creed, and threaten banishment to any who refused to free their slaves. Benezet had also formed and taught at the first school for Blacks both free and enslaved in 1773, and organized the first meeting of the society at the Rising Sun Tavern, an important stopover just east of Germantown on the road to Philadelphia.[147] The Rising Sun hosted many such meetings in the early formation of the nation. It was demolished in 1892. A strip mall is not presently located there. In fact, there's nothing there. I took a drive there with hopes of determining some remnant of its foundation, but the location is now just a vacant lot. Whatever precipitated its need to get razed had also been razed.

An 1880 illustration of The Rising Sun Tavern. Courtesy of the Library of Congress.

The Society actively fought for the legal rights of illegally imprisoned Blacks and native Americans. Their efforts resulted in the Pennsylvania government's passing of *An Act for the Gradual Abolition of Slavery* in 1780. The act prohibited the import of slaves into the state, declared that children of slaves born in the state would be free but with the slightly modified status of 'indentured servant,' and, in the interest of appeasing property owners, held onto a clause that any slaves in the state born or living prior to the passing of the act would remain slaves. This portion of the law wouldn't be changed to complete abolition until 1847.

Benezet enlisted the aid of Benjamin Rush, the son of a prominent Philadelphia family who had just returned from studying medicine abroad. With Benezet's influence, Rush became a lifelong activist for the abolitionist cause, and, inspired directly by the storied Benjamin Lay, authored *An Address to the Inhabitants of the British Settlements in America, upon Slave-Keeping*, a work which proved to have a considerable affect given Rush's influential standing in the community. In his address, Rush had written:

> "Slavery is so foreign to the human mind, that the moral faculties, as well as those of the understanding are debased, and rendered torpid by it…The vulgar notion of their being descended from Cain…is too absurd to need a refutation…Future ages, therefore, when they read the accounts of the Slave Trade…will be at a loss which to condemn most, our folly or our Guilt…all this is practiced…by men who call themselves Christians!… But it will be found upon enquiry…from the testimony of historians and travelers, that wars were uncommon among them, until the Christians who began the slave trade, stirred up the different nations to fight against each other…What steps shall we take to remedy this Evil?…The first thing I would recommend to put a stop to slavery in this country, is to leave off importing slaves. For this purpose let our assemblies unite in petitioning the king and parliament to dissolve the African committee of merchants: It is by them that the trade is chiefly carried on to America… Slavery is an Hydra sin, and includes in it every violation of the precepts of the Law and the Gospel."[148]

Rush's plea was a remarkable composition. Powerful, forthright, it was his address, backed by the credentials of status, wealth, and sphere of social influence, which served as the launch, the very foundation of the mission, fueled with righteous zeal and embraced by leaders of religious congregations in the movement to abolish slavery that would persist through to the Civil War.

In short time Benjamin Rush became recognized as the established leader of the abolitionist cause. Yet, had it not been for the influence and camaraderie of his most ardent ally, Anthony Benezet, Rush may not have been so emboldened. When Benezet died in 1784, he, too, had come to be regarded as "the single most prolific antislavery writer and the most influential advocate of the Negro's rights on either side of the Atlantic."[149]

Continuing the cause in Benezet's name, Rush drew up a new constitution for a reorganized *Pennsylvania Abolition Society*, and recruited his old friend,

Benjamin Franklin, to join him in the cause. Franklin, Rush, and the other members initiated a number of lesser known Philadelphia firsts: they offered assistance to Blacks seeking wage-paying employment; formed a Committee of Guardians that placed Blacks in indentured service opportunities; they made personal house calls to Philadelphia's free Black citizens to boost morale and just offer friendship; they helped create the first Black schools; offered legal aid, meals, provision, and general sustenance.[150] The Quaker State of Pennsylvania was setting the standard and leading the way.

1775 seal of The Society for the Relief of Free Negroes Unlawfully Held in Bondage. Note how the illustration, depicting a slave on left stepping free from chains and ankle shackles, provided a sure way to communicate to an uneducated slave seeking freedom. Courtesy of Historical Society of Pennsylvania.

In 1787, the same year as the United States was drafting its constitution, in England a group of British Quakers allied with three Evangelical Protestants met to form *The Society for Abolition of the Slave Trade*. Now, Quakers on both sides of the Atlantic were waging a moral battle to end slavery through every avenue of legal access possible, and through every pulpit that would open its doors to their message. It would take another twenty years for abolition to be achieved in England, demonstrated by the Royal Navy's blockade off the coast of Africa to intercept British slave vessels beginning in 1807. All in all, the efforts of Quaker and like-minded abolitionists were seeing results after one-hundred years of relentless campaigning. This empowered further persistence into the Nineteenth Century.

In the states, the Pennsylvania Abolition Society elected as their president Benjamin Franklin, the man who had published more than 200 pamphlets by Benjamin Lay along with additional entreaties by Anthony Benezet and some of the Quaker's earliest calls for emancipation, who had worked with Jefferson as a member of the appointed Committee of Five on the original draft of the Declaration, and who presided at the convention during the formation of the Constitution. The Society's primary ambition for electing Franklin was to have this broadly revered statesman, philosopher, scientist and first rock star of America bring the issue to Congress with the hope of persuasively abolishing slavery and the colonial slave trade on a national scale - once and for all.

In what would be the final campaign in his long life of public service, Franklin presented his appeal to Congress in February of 1790, which read:

> "From a persuasion that equal liberty was originally the Portion and is still the Birthright of all Men, and influenced by the strong ties of Humanity and the Principles of their Institution, Your Memorialists conceive themselves to use all justifiable endeavors to loosen the bands of Slavery and promote a general Enjoyment of the blessings of Freedom. Under these Impressions they earnestly entreat your serious attention to the subject of Slavery; that you will be pleased to countenance the Restoration of liberty to those unhappy Men, who alone in this land of Freedom are degraded in to perpetual Bondage, and who amidst the general Joy of Surrounding Free men are groaning in servile subjection, that you will devise means for removing this Inconsistency from the character of the American People, that you will promote Mercy and Justice towards this distressed Race, and that you will step to the very verge of the Powers vested in you, for discouraging every Species of Traffick in the person of our fellow Men."[151]

The appeal of the great and esteemed Dr. Franklin was outvoted in the ensuing debates by pro-slavery members of Congress who then held the majority. In appeasement, a special committee was formed and, after a month of discourse, arrived at the consensus that the new Constitution prohibited Congress from passing any laws that interfered with a state's sovereign right to import slaves, or in any way interfere with their decision to postpone emancipation until 1808. The initial effort and opportunity to abolish slavery in the newly formed United States stopped right there. Had the vote swung in favor of Franklin's appeal, the Civil War could have been a fictionalized fantasy that never happened. Two weeks after the decision was rendered, Benjamin Franklin died in Philadelphia at the age of 84.

A 1789 address by Benjamin Franklin as president of the Pennsylvania Society for Abolition of Slavery.

The effort had minimal effect legislatively. Three years after Franklin's appeal, in 1793, the US passed the *Fugitive Slave Law* which legalized the capture and return of fugitive slaves to their masters.[152] The law furthermore made it illegal for anyone in the Northern states to assist Southern runaway slaves seeking freedom offered by Canada. With the latter targeted specifically at abolitionists, the effect of the laws only further ignited their zeal.

For the next decade, campaigns for abolition in increased measure were relentlessly pursued while facing much opposition by those advocating a gradual eradication of slavery or those not wanting to end the practice at all. Yet, these campaigns proved effective, as a growing number of citizens were persuaded to change their views.

30-year-old iron manufacturer Elihu Embree, the son of a Pennsylvania born Quaker minister whose family had moved to Tennessee when it was still a virgin settlement, quickly embraced the Quaker ethics of his youth and by 1816 had joined *The Manumission Society of Tennessee*. In 1819, Embree launched a weekly publication called *The Manumission Intelligencer*, widely regarded as the first regularly published newspaper calling for the emancipation of slaves in the United States. After fifty editions, the name was changed the following year to *The Emancipator*. Embree passionately edited and circulated the work until his death at age thirty-eight.[153]

A year afterward, the publishing rights were purchased by Benjamin Lundy, a fellow Quaker from Baltimore, Maryland, and reissued under the name *The Genius of Universal Emancipation*. In 1824, Lundy moved the operation from Jonesboro, Tennessee to his native Baltimore. During a speaking tour Lundy converted the young journalist William Lloyd Garrison of Boston to the abolitionist cause. Lundy invited Garrison to join him as editor of the paper, despite Garrison's differing opinion that called for a complete and immediate end to slavery versus Lundy's gradualist view. In Lundy's paper, Garrison published "the black list," a column dedicated to listing slavery related atrocities and naming the perpetrators. One so named slave merchant in Newburyport, Massachusetts, sued the paper, and Garrison, unable to pay the resulting fine, spent seven weeks of a six-month jail term before his bail was paid by Arthur Tappan, an anti-slavery businessman and philanthropist from Garrison's home state of Massachusetts.[154]

Upon his release, Garrison returned to Massachusetts and with Tappan began publishing a new abolitionist newspaper called *The Liberator* in 1831 that held the promise of reaching a wider circulation with the added financial backing of Tappan and other like-minded abolitionists in the business community.

Garrison set the tone for a reinvigorated campaign in the first edition of The Liberator, in which he wrote:

> "Assenting to the "self-evident truth" maintained in the American Declaration of Independence, "that all men are created equal, and endowed by their Creator with certain inalienable rights...," I shall strenuously contend for the immediate enfranchisement of our slave population...
>
> 'I am aware, that many object to the severity of my language; but is there not cause for severity? I will be as harsh as truth, and as uncompromising as justice. On this subject, I do not wish to think, or speak, or write, with moderation...I am in earnest — I will not equivocate — I will not excuse — I will not retreat a single inch — AND I WILL BE HEARD."[155]

Masthead for Garrison's anti-slavery publication.

Among newsworthy topics printed in The Liberator that might persuade quaking readers was the 1831 slave rebellion in Virginia led by Nat Turner and more than seventy slaves which had left sixty White slave owners dead.[156] Readership increased and minds were converted. Garrison's Liberator was a hit, inspiring him to form *The American Anti-Slavery Society* in 1833. By 1840, through an aggressive campaign of sending signed petitions to Congress, sponsoring anti-slavery meetings, and the enlistment of more than seventy individual agents and lecturers that traveled to welcoming venues in the Northern states, the society formed nearly two-thousand auxiliary chapters throughout the United States while enrolling an estimated membership of nearly 200,000.[157]

At their national convention held in Philadelphia in 1839, the Society sought alliance and solidarity with their British cousins by declaring:

> "warfare against the soul-destroying system of slavery, till public sentiment shall become so reformed by the pure principles of Christian love and freedom, that Republic and Christian America, following the example of Great Britain, shall drive slavery from her realms and pledge her moral and political influence for the entire extinction of slavery and

the slave trade from the face of the whole earth... the Anti-Slavery cause is a common one...in its success, the whole world is deeply interested and especially England, whose prosperity as a nation will be vastly increased by the extinction of that destructive system, which is cripplying [sic] her commerce and manufactures, as well as our own."[158]

The Society sent representatives to London to attend an International Slavery Convention in 1840, and there formed the expanded, international *American and Foreign Anti-Slavery Society*, whose loftier ambitions still yielded a gradual cessation of slavery.[159] It came down again to the same need of appeasing merchants who would economically lose from complete abolition.

Concurrent with the lecturing, publication, and petitioning work of Garrison's Society, an illegally organized 'underground railroad' was established to aid in bringing slaves to freedom through a network of abolitionists willing to risk imprisonment for them, with even worse repercussions for the assisted fugitive slaves. The abolitionists viewed such activity as an act of morally authorized sedition in direct violation of the *Fugitive Slave Act of 1793*, which gave authority to local governments to aid in the capture of runaway slaves and return them to their owners while imposing penalties on anyone caught harboring or aiding fugitive slaves. "The dictates of humanity came in opposition to the law of the land," wrote Quaker abolitionist Levi Coffin, "and we ignored the law."[160] The act also provided an open door for more scrupulous opportunists to kidnap free Blacks and profit illegally through their sale to equally complicit slave owners in the Southern states.[161] Historian Eric Foner adds:

"There were kidnap gangs on the streets of New York and Philadelphia. Particularly they would grab children, just nabbed off the street, and taken to a boat and shipped off and sold into slavery."[162]

With the aid of the Underground Railroad, in 1838 a twenty-year-old slave named Frederick Bailey escaped from bondage in Maryland. He made his way North first by a train from Baltimore with a falsified ID and a borrowed sailor's uniform, then by steamboat up the Delaware River to Philadelphia. From there, through a series of roundabout, hidden stops at lantern lit Underground Railway stations located in small villages off the beaten track, he eventually made his way to the 'safehouse' of David Ruggles, a

Seal of the British and Foreign Anti-Slavery Society, sister org of their American cousins.

noted abolitionist based in New York City.¹⁶³ "If anyone 'founded' the Underground Railroad" explains Eric Foner, "it was David Ruggles."¹⁶⁴ Referencing the era of the railroad's core years of activity, Foner adds: "This was a moment, where you had black and white Americans working together in the cause of freedom. These are tales of really remarkable courage."¹⁶⁵

Ten days after his arrival in New York, Bailey was married to a free Black woman from Baltimore who had aided in his passage to freedom. To prevent Frederick from being hunted as a fugitive slave, the newlyweds agreed to adopt the surname Johnson. After moving again, he would take on a new surname, and thereafter went by the name Frederick Douglass.

Frederick Douglass might be called the first true American of the new era due to his mixed ancestry of African, European and Native American origin. Many enslaved were just like him - mixed race, mulatto. Of his background, Douglass wrote in his autobiography:

> "My father was a white man...The opinion was also whispered that my master was my father... My mother and I were separated when I was but an infant... It is a common custom, in the part of Maryland from which I ran away, to part children from their mothers at a very early age..."¹⁶⁶

1845 sheet music cover featuring an illustration of Frederick Douglass fleeing in the borrowed sailor's outfit. Courtesy Library of Congress.

Douglass' remark parallels the story of a slave boy from Maryland owned by Mark Twain's parents, likely whisked away and sold in the same manner. As fate would have it, the paths of Douglass and Twain would become directly connected, the story of which has been the driving force of this entire segment so far.

In 1835, the same year Samuel Clemens was born in Florida, Missouri, Frederick Douglass was a fifteen-year-old slave in Cecil County, Maryland. On the one day when slaves did not work, Sunday school classes were led by a Black minister named Father Lawson.¹⁶⁷ Some slave owners permitted such biblical education if only to keep them thinking that their fate was a blessing preordained as the descendants of Ham. Douglass reminisced how those Sunday school sessions had not only formed his better memories but provided an enhanced education (he had been taught to read and write earlier in his youth by the sympathetic wife of his master) and inspired him to become a preacher.

Douglass and his wife, Anna, had settled in New Bedford, Massachusetts, where, in 1839, he became a licensed preacher at the African Methodist Episcopal Zion Church, serving as steward, Sunday school supervisor, and sexton. Frederick and Anna had come a long way. The abolitionists who had assisted Douglass on his journey encouraged him to share his important story with the greater public, confident that it would assist their cause precipitously.

Douglass' preaching delivered a powerful denunciation of slavery that caught attention and created a stir, further pronounced by Douglass' imposing physical stature. Direct accounts of former slaves had been an important feature in abolitionist publications like William Lloyd Garrison's The Liberator. Douglass had become mesmerized by Garrison. Of him, Douglass later wrote: "No face and form ever impressed me with such sentiments [against slavery] as did those of William Lloyd Garrison." Douglass began to regularly attend Garrison's meetings, and became a subscriber to *The Liberator*, which Douglass claimed "took a place in my heart second only to The Bible."[168]

The following year, in 1840, Garrison's abolitionist missionaries arranged for Douglass to give one of his first public lectures in a western New York village that had already established itself as one of the primary connections along the Underground Railroad. It was an invitation he gladly accepted as local abolitionists and Underground Railroad conductors in the village had been among those who aided him two years earlier during his journey to freedom. That village was Elmira, New York.

1872 illustration of the Underground Railroad in action. Courtesy Library of Congress.

17

TALES OF REMARKABLE COURAGE

> "...from the beginning of the world no revolt against a public infamy or oppression has ever been begun but by the one daring man in the 10,000, the rest timidly waiting, and slowly and reluctantly joining, under the influence of that man and his fellows from the other ten thousands. The abolitionists remember."
>
> Mark Twain,
> *The United States of Lyncherdom*

By the time Frederick Douglass began his new journey as a public speaker, abolitionists had become a vilified species. Abolition became a hated word, and its proponent's activism almost facilitated a state's secession countless times. In the political theater of Washington, abolitionists were viewed as annoying, interfering rabble-rousers.

To be an active abolitionist was a dangerous occupation. Historians of Old Sturbridge Village in Massachusetts explain;

> "Abolitionists were the object of a great deal of criticism, ridicule, and even violence. In the 1830s and 40s, anti-abolitionist and anti-black riots were the most common kinds of mob disorder in American cities. But most of the anti-abolitionist mobs were not made up of young rowdies from lower-class neighborhoods. They were well-organized groups of respectable, middle-class citizens who believed that abolitionism threatened their communities and businesses...In the early 1830s, becoming an active abolitionist required courage. Many had to face physical danger at the hands of a mob, but many more had to endure the disapproval of family and friends or the ridicule of neighbors."[169]

The extremes in sentiment formed a wedge that divided communities throughout the nation, and within the movement itself. Moderates advocated the return of enslaved Africans to free colonies established in their native Africa. Among those moderates who supported this vision was a young representative from Illinois named Abraham Lincoln.[170] On the opposite side were radically vocal opponents who viewed this as a shallow effort that only sustained the endorsement of slavery and a consequent failure in the effort to eradicate it completely from American life. They found their voice in John Quincy Adams of Massachusetts.

Old Sturbridge Historians continue:

> "The antislavery ranks grew... Antislavery became a safer and more popular cause, and won the support of many Northern people not originally responsive to its claims. Most Southerners in turn became more entrenched in their support of slavery and resented Northern meddling in their society."[171]

Cover of Minutes for an Abolitionist convention dated 1830. Note the "Twenty-First biennial" reference. The battle to abolish slavery and establish Civil Rights IS the story of the growth of the United States. Courtesy Library of Congress.

As each side sought to elect representatives to persuasively argue on their behalf, the match had gradually boiled down Lincoln and Adams to the two primary contenders. "Adams" explains biographer Fred Kaplan,

> "had become convinced that slavery would destroy the Union... Lincoln, who also abhorred slavery as a moral crime, put all his hopes in the Colonization Society...Both Adams and Lincoln were antislavery moralists...Adams envisioned a multiracial America as inevitable...he became deeply sympathetic to abolitionists and abolitionism. Lincoln detested abolitionism."[172]

While Adams, Lincoln, and politicians perpetuated the debates over the morality of slavery, real people were languishing in the sadistic depravity of an enslaved existence. The growing population of those siding with the abolitionist's "all or nothin'" view increasingly embraced Quaker Levi Coffin's earlier call "in opposition to the law of the land," took matters into their own hand, and "ignored the law."[173]

When school students are taught about the Underground Railroad, it is most often referenced in the biographical context of some of the more outstanding figures of its history, like Harriett Tubman, or with storytelling narrative background images of fugitive slaves being shuttled through darkened woods on moonless nights and finding safe-haven in the damp cellar of a secretively designated stop. To be a conductor on the Underground Railroad was even more dangerous, and potentially life threatening.

In 1837, thirteen years before Tubman's involvement, the 'railroad,' conducted until then in a somewhat informal capacity, saw its crystallization into an organized structure with the founding in Philadelphia of *The Vigilant Association of Philadelphia* by Robert Purvis, who had co-organized The American Anti-Slavery Society with William Lloyd Garrison four years prior. With the railroad's headquarters located in Philadelphia, Elmira, New York was established as "the only regular agency between Philadelphia and St. Catherines, Canada."[174] Among the key conductors in the Elmira agency were a reliable and active abolitionist couple by the name of Jervis and Olivia Langdon.

Jervis Langdon was a coal and lumber merchant who lived with his wife Olivia in the remote, quiet village of Millport, New York, just across the Pennsylvania border. Following construction of the Chemung Canal along the edge of town, tanneries, wool mills, blacksmiths, carriage shops, and merchants and purveyors of all sorts of goods poured into the town as business boomed. Jervis, whose grandparents were farmers in Millport, learned the mercantile trade at age sixteen through his employment in small general stores located in nearby Vernon and Ithaca. By the time he was twenty-three years of age, Jervis was operating several stores of his own, and on July 23, 1832, he married his sweetheart, Olivia Lewis.[175]

The Canal's arrival proved to be a bonanza to Millport, as exports of timber, lumber, shingles and all manner of construction grade wood products were loaded onto boats and shipped east to the larger markets.[176] Bearing witness to growth of the lumber trade and wanting in on the action, the enterprising young Langdon partnered with a lumber dealer and prospered. His ventures enabled him to accumulate considerable wealth, and in the spirit of their religious convictions, the Langdons practiced their gratitude by assisting others. As avowed abolitionists, they liberally opened their home as a station on the underground railroad for the Vigilant Association. With Millport's position along the Chemung Canal, Langdon used his lumber trade connections on road and river to act as conductor for fugitive slaves passing through.

In 1838, the destinies of the abolitionist Langdons and one of the numerous fugitive slaves whom they assisted would thereafter produce a lifelong friendship. The escaped slave was Frederick Douglass, who would become the virtual figurehead of the international abolitionist movement. The kindness shown to him by the Langdons would never be forgotten. Of his arrival in New York, Douglass would later write:

> "I have often been asked, how I felt when first I found myself on free soil. There is scarcely anything in my experience about which I could not give a more satisfactory answer. A new world had opened upon me. If life is more than breath, and the 'quick round of blood,' I lived more in one day than in a year of my slave life. It was a time of joyous excitement which words can but tamely describe. In a letter written to a friend soon after reaching New York, I said: 'I felt as one might feel upon escape from a den of hungry lions.' Anguish and grief, like darkness and rain, may be depicted; but gladness and joy, like the rainbow, defy the skill of pen or pencil."[177]

The heartfelt emotion of Douglass' words surely reflect the measure of gratitude held for Jervis and Olivia Langdon. Jervis Langdon must have been more than a breath of fresh air for Douglass, who had grown so accustomed to a life of degradation and ignominy. Langdon made Douglass feel like a person for the first time in his life.

"A compact man with a square face and mild, quizzical eyes" as described by

Jervis & Olivia Lewis Langdon. Courtesy of The Center for Mark Twain Studies, Elmira, NY.

author Ron Powers, "Jervis liked people, and he liked to laugh, and he liked to sing, and these traits partly tempered an unrelenting reformist zeal."[178]

Douglass had known only a brief semblance of such compassion earlier in his life. At the age of seven or eight he was sold to the Auld family of Baltimore. By age twelve, Mrs. Auld had provided him with a rudimentary education. However, once Mr. Auld learned of this and violently persuaded his wife on the dangers of educating a slave, Douglass witnessed the once-kind woman transform into a demon right before his eyes.

> "My mistress was... a kind and tender-hearted woman; and in the simplicity of her soul she commenced, when I first went to live with her, to treat me as she supposed one human being ought to treat another... she was a pious, warm, and tender-hearted woman...She had bread for the hungry, clothes for the naked, and comfort for every mourner that came within her reach. Slavery soon proved its ability to divest her of these heavenly qualities. Under its influence, the tender heart became stone, and the lamblike disposition gave way to one of tiger-like fierceness...She finally became even more violent..."[179]

Auld had so vocally expressed his view of the danger of giving a slave an education, it caused Douglass to have a personal epiphany; that beyond physical bondage, it was education that truly made a person free. "From that moment" Douglass recalled,

> "I understood the pathway from slavery to freedom. It was just what I wanted, and I got it at a time when I the least expected it...Though conscious of the difficulty of learning without a teacher, I set out with high hope, and a fixed purpose, at whatever cost of trouble, to learn how to read...What he most dreaded, that I most desired...the argument which he so warmly urged, against my learning to read, only served to inspire me with a desire and determination to learn..."[180]

As I read Douglass's own account of his escape and found repeated references to making his way from Philadelphia and winding up in Elmira, I grew curious about the path he had traversed between the two. Most of the initial information I found was vague, without any mention of specific places or stops. Had the Underground Railroad conductors been so secretive that many stops remained so even today? The more I investigated, I learned that the backroads of then rural Pennsylvania had been largely ignored by history, save for the incidental reference here and there of one place or another having been a connecting "station" on the Underground Railroad. Indeed, some historians had claimed that it wasn't all that organized. But that didn't sit well with me. How could risking life and limb in an era when it was illegal to harbor and assist fugitive slaves not have been accomplished outside of some carefully planned network of stops with trusted conductors? I put the question on the back-burner as I resumed my duties at work for the week.

My work as an art dealer based near Philadelphia has required me to travel the mid-Atlantic and Northeast regions of the United States for more than twenty years. For the past ten years, I had accumulated a substantial number of repeat clients in the Lehigh Valley area, including Allentown, Bethlehem, Saucon Valley, Quakertown, and thereabouts. My numerous trips for art consultations and installations had afforded me the opportunity to become acquainted with the region's storied history.

One Sunday afternoon, I had such an appointment scheduled in Bethlehem. The town had become a favorite stop of mine over the years. In that time, I'd made note of many of the historic landmarks throughout, such as Moravian College, founded in 1742, or the Bethlehem Hotel, with its old school, throwback level of hotel service rarely seen in the modern world.

Bethlehem had been established with a wee measure of lore in my mind since childhood. My mother had often made mention of the time when my father and she were first married and desired to see "the lights of Bethlehem" during the holiday season. They had voiced this in front of my grandmother, who decided she also wanted to go. This was probably sometime in 1954 or '55. The three ventured off, but never made it due to car trouble, forcing them to abort the trip and turn around. They never made another effort. The family lore, heard since I was a kid, was enough for me to feel compelled to complete the journey for them, a little at a time, on each of my business ventures to the town. In between appointments, I've enjoyed Bethlehem for Christmas shopping, eating at diners, or listening to live Irish music while dining at McCarthy's.

From the earliest days of European settlement in Pennsylvania, the Lehigh Valley region had been the home of the Lenape nation of Native Americans. Settlers and natives had established trade there along the Lehigh River. A small group of Moravian missionaries founded a mission on Christmas Eve of 1741, and, in turn, named their settlement Bethlehem to commemorate the auspicious date. The Moravian church was one of the oldest Protestant denominations with roots in Fifteenth Century Bohemia in the current day Czech Republic. The designation "Moravian" draws its origin from the old-world section of the Czech Republic where their founders had fled in 1722 to avoid persecution.

Like the neighboring Quakers who are formally known as the 'Society of Friends,' the formal name for the Moravians translated as the 'Unity of Brethren.' The two groups shared common religious values from the onset. Like Martin Luther, the sect's founder, Jacob Hus, objected to many of the same practices of the Catholic Church. Hus advocated marriage for priests, eliminating the selling of indulgences - the middle-aged practice of church-sanctioned blackmail, if you will - and requested that mass be said in their native Czech language instead of Latin, among other dissenting views. For this, Hus was declared a heretic and burned on a stake in 1415. This resulted in the Hussite wars that lasted until 1436. By the Seventeenth Century, the 'Brethren' were forced to practice their faith in secret, with many groups dispersing to new locations throughout old Europe.

By the early Eighteenth Century, they had formed one of the first groups of Protestant lay missionaries and established missions in Asia, Africa, the Caribbean, South America, and ultimately North America, where they settled in the present-day Lehigh Valley to evangelize to the indigenous peoples there. In all these demographics, the Moravians were distinguished as the first Protestant denomination to minister to slaves. Now a curious picture of Bethlehem was starting to emerge.

On a visit just two weeks prior to my Sunday trip to Bethlehem, I had an appointment to meet my client and good friend Judy in nearby Quakertown. After completing our business, Judy and I chatted for a while, and she mentioned her plans for that evening to attend a special dinner at the Sun Inn in Bethlehem to commemorate a frequent guest in its founding years - Benjamin Franklin. I told Judy that I was familiar with the Inn, had a hunch it was historic, but didn't know much beyond that. A native of Bethlehem, Judy proceeded to enthusiastically tell me that the Sun Inn, built in 1758, was the original building still in continual use as a tavern, and where, in 1777, it had hosted a meeting of the Continental Congress when the British occupied Philadelphia. A lover of history, I was enthralled.

The second-floor room of The Sun Inn, Bethlehem, PA, where a delegation of Congress assembled in 1777 during the British occupation of Philadelphia.

Judy then casually mentioned "Well, you know the old Bethlehem Pike was the main route between New York and Philadelphia then, right?"

I had not known that. I knew of numerous such pikes throughout the region named after their destinations, like Baltimore Pike or Lancaster Pike, the road used by Lancaster County farmers who brought produce and dairy to sell at Philadelphia markets. Germantown Pike was the road between Philly and the village of Germantown before the latter was incorporated into the city in 1847. I mentioned that I knew of Bethlehem Pike as synonymous with route 309 from having driven on it, but Judy corrected me.

"No, the OLD Bethlehem Pike" Judy explained. "It parallels route 309. There are only a few miles of the original road still intact."

This intrigued me. When Judy and I finished our appointment, I had another stop to make in the area, and decided, if I had time, I would try to locate those few remaining miles. As I navigated by GPS, I inadvertently passed an intersection with the old Pike while en route to my next appointment.

After making a quick U-turn I cruised along, pondering how this very road had been the carriage path taken by so many notable individuals in our nation's history: George and Martha Washington, Ben Franklin, John Hancock, John Adams, Samuel Adams, and others. I also came across a very old cemetery entrance marked only with a simple, painted, wrought iron entrance sign that read "Our Forefather's Cemetery: 1724." I pulled into a church parking lot across the street, and walked over to the cemetery to explore.

At that time, I was still researching the history of the early Quakers in the region and was curious to check out some of the headstones. I knew Quakertown itself had been named for the Quaker settlers that founded the region hundreds of years prior. When I was researching the role Quakers played in the colonial era abolition movement, I had come across the name of the Quaker Richard Moore, a noted conductor on the Underground Railroad who had assisted with the escape of more than six-hundred fugitive slaves. "Richard Moore's home and pottery studio became known as the northernmost "station" in the Underground Railroad in Bucks County" wrote Dr. Robert Leight of the Quakertown Community School District.

> "The escaped slaves, or "passengers" would come at night from other stations from either Chester County by way of Norristown or from lower Bucks County. When it was safe they would be moved either to a Quaker meeting in Stroudsburg or to Easton for their journey northward."[181]

I was curious to know if, by luck, Richard Moore might be buried in this very plot as I scoured the headstones in search of any clue. My effort was somewhat brief, because if the grave was there, I found it was likely undecipherable. Like the ancient cemetery in Germantown I had visited before, many of the oldest tombstones were simply unreadable, with the rest inscribed in Old German. Some graves showed evidence of still being tended by descendants in the area, while others had sadly weathered to almost nothing from centuries of neglect.

The day I visited was a week before Halloween. I couldn't help but think of the fake cemetery decorations designed to look spooky and scary. But here I was in a real, antiquated cemetery, with some real history, and there was nothing spooky about it. The designation of "spooky" originated from a lack of understanding, I concluded. It made me realize that those who choose not to respectfully explore an old cemetery are missing out on a powerful, spiritual experience. It's one that has not escaped those in some older cultures, such as in Ireland.

When my wife Maureen and I Honeymooned there in 1994, we planned to rendezvous with my cousin Brian and his wife Sandy in Ballycastle, Antrim, where our maternal grandfather had been born,[182] and meet with our Irish relatives. Unbeknownst ahead of time, the day we arrived happened to fall on "Cemetery Sunday," an annual observance when descendants of local families gather in their local churchyard cemeteries to celebrate and honor those who have gone before. It was an unbelievably serendipitous honor to arrive in the village of my forbearers, briefly meet our relatives, who promptly asked us to first join them in the cemetery to honor our ancestors before any official reunion would commence. No celebratory whiskey was poured until the observance was honorably concluded. It was like experiencing an infamous "Irish wake" in reverse, referring to the custom of Irish families hosting a funeral celebration in advance of the departure of loved ones about to embark on their immigratory voyage across the sea, never to be seen again.

I've since felt customs like this are the sort of thing that are missing in the United States, having been lost in the diaspora that was frequently greeted with hostility and an enforced repression or discouragement for continued practice of such traditions. And then, of course, there is the reminder of our own mortality an old cemetery offers, which has an odd way of cajoling one into appreciating everything, and being alive in the present. I suppose that's their purpose. I headed back home that evening having enjoyed this discovery in Quakertown, and giving me one more thing to satisfy my curiosity for history.

In the weeks since my appointment with Judy, I had been engaged with writing the segments here on the Underground Railroad, about the journey of Frederick Douglass from Baltimore, through Wilmington and Philadelphia and ultimately into Elmira and his new life in the North, as well as the founding of his own newspaper, *The North Star*, which he had named after the simple phrase told to slaves in the South who had sought the succor of freedom in the

North. Like Douglass, slaves embarking on the perilous journey were simply advised to "follow the North Star" as their guide to freedom.

On a Sunday afternoon in early November, I had finished with another scheduled appointment on the outskirts of downtown Bethlehem. With some time to spare and ten minutes from downtown, I decided to drive over and check out the Sun Inn based on Judy's suggestion. I had walked by the Sun Inn a dozen times over the years, but had not given it more thought than a passing curiosity. I had assumed it to be a reconstructed historic site, like the rebuilt Graff House in Philadelphia. But, it was original, just as Judy described. The very room where the Continental Congress had met was intact, as was the original colonial era kitchen, the original Innkeeper's desk, and a first floor, period furnished room where Martha Washington had lodged.

While driving toward downtown Bethlehem before our visit, I was in the passenger seat and began to tell my assistant the scant history about the area that I knew. This was inspired by recurring signs and markers we passed indicating one Bethlehem historic landmark or another, each topped with a Moravian "Christmas" Star logo. I'd seen the logo a thousand times before. Bethlehem was, after all, named after the original, "Oh Little town of..." village in Israel where Jesus was born, and had become the greater Philadelphia and Lehigh Valley's regional Christmas village. A mountain that sets high above one end of Bethlehem features a huge illuminated Moravian Star each year during the holiday season that can be seen for miles.

As we passed the succession of blue and white markers topped by the Moravian Star logo, I noticed a few accented with an added slogan evidently adopted by the local historical society advising tourists to "follow the star." And then I had an epiphany: the town of Bethlehem itself WAS the North Star advised for slaves to follow! It had to be! It made complete sense.

The biblical Bethlehem and specifically the nativity story in the New Testament is where the three wise men - representing the three races descended from the Old Testament tribes of Seth, Japheth, and Ham - had visited Jesus, and, in turn, were liberated from their bondage from sin. The beginning lesson in Christianity. Bethlehem in Pennsylvania had certainly been used in an allegorically referential way of alluding to the promise of liberation from bondage. In the nativity story, it was the North Star - the Christmas Star - pointed over Bethlehem which had guided the wise men to the cradle of Jesus. Here, this North Star surely was guiding refuge slaves via Philadelphia along the old Indian trail that became the Bethlehem Pike through Bethlehem and on to New York and freedom.

The Bethlehem, PA road sign that inspired an insight.

When I got home later in the evening, it didn't take me long to find some info to confirm my hunch. I located the website of The Center for Anti-Slavery Studies, which indicates that there were three major escape routes through Pennsylvania. To get to New York from Philadelphia, fugitive slaves were required to follow a series of stations to Germantown, then through Norristown, which was apparently the main departure hub before an escaped slave set off on the longer journey. Contributors to the website explain:

"Quakertown was the major depot...for runaways traveling to upstate New York [en route] to Canada...One of the earliest maps...shows a line, [of] 25 miles between Norristown and Quakertown...runaways & conductors went along...Dekalb Pike until they reached...Old Bethlehem Pike ...

The Old Bethlehem Pike...built in 1763...connected Philadelphia with Bethlehem. It followed the trace of an old Indian trail known as the Minsi Path... [From there] runaways went another eight miles to the basement of Gerhart's Tavern...The tavern is still there today, but is now called the Rising Sun Inn [not the Sun Inn of Bethlehem].[183]...A trip of only seven more miles brought the escapees to Quakertown.

'...after fugitives left Quakertown, some of them continued on Old Bethlehem Pike... about six miles to the northeast, while others went northwest through Milford Township, where they found shelter at the Brick Tavern Inn [which I've driven past countless times over ten years, tempted to stop and explore without cause other than curiosity of its sign indicating it had been in operation since 1818]. Both routes then led to Bingen, five miles south of Bethlehem.

In Bingen, [runaways were sheltered then guided] the final few miles to Bethlehem. Bethlehem... was filled with people who opposed slavery... The fugitive continuing his/her journey from Bethlehem had three options: Easton, Stroudsburg, or Palmerton. Those who chose either of the last two options ended up traveling through, or staying permanently... Fugitives would continue to follow the shores of the Lehigh River northward... into Wilkes-Barre. From Wilkes-Barre, conductors...guided runaways northward...and eventually into upstate New York."[184]

I was convinced. Bethlehem *WAS* the North Star. It was the key stop between Philly and New York. Once a fugitive slave reached there, the town's very name provided hope and motivation to press on. Freedom would soon be in their grasp. From there on to Wilkes Barre, situated a stone's throw from the Pennsylvania-New York border, the next stop afterward would have likely been the home of Jervis and Olivia Langdon in Millport, and, later, their designated stops in Elmira. This was surely the route taken by Frederick Douglass, as well as hundreds or thousands of other runaway slaves seeking passage to freedom.

In 1840, at the invitation of abolitionists in Elmira and remembering the kindness shown to him by the people of the Chemung Valley, Douglass travelled to Elmira to give his first public lecture in a private home to an assembly which included many former slaves who had escaped and found a welcoming home in Elmira. From Douglass's influence, that community of ex-slaves became practicing Methodists, founding the African Methodist Episcopal Zion Church.[185]

1840 was also the year when the Langdons adopted their first daughter, Susan, who had been orphaned by the deaths of friends.[186] The Langdons afterward relocated to the nearby and larger village of Elmira in 1845, where their daughter Olivia was born that same year.

As Laura Skandera-Trombley rightly points out in her book *Mark Twain in the Company of Women*, little has been written or recorded about Olivia and the town of her birth, Elmira. It was vindicating for me to see that I had not been out of the loop due to my own ignorance. Like most of us, I have heretofore only embraced the fanfare surrounding the allure of Mark Twain. And I likely would have maintained the ignorance had I not taken the time to take a drive and explore Elmira on my own. Just going there had awakened a curiosity that led me to understand that one can't fully comprehend the soul of Mark Twain without knowing these important people, places, and components of his background, as well as the cultural climate in the United States during his formative years before, during and after the Civil War.

Above: A PA historic marker commemorating Daniel Hughes, a Susquehanna River lumber raftsman & likely Underground Railroad contact with Jervis Langdon.

Below: A walking route between Philadelphia & Bethlehem, to Hughes location and onto Elmira, a distance of 238 miles with an estimated duration of 81 hours.

18

THE GREAT TROUBLE

> "There was a good deal of confusion in men's minds during the first months of the great trouble...later the secession atmosphere had considerably thickened...and I became a rebel..."
>
> Samuel Clemens[187]

Jervis and Olivia Langdon raised their children Susan, Olivia, and Charles with a balanced, egalitarian set of ethics and values. They were religious, open-minded and life-embracing. Jervis Langdon was something of a jovial fellow and shrewd business tactician, with a standard of ethics that prevented him from being a greedy sort of guy, and it follows that his philanthropy knew no bounds. Not shy about the conviction of his beliefs, when the First Presbyterian Church that he and his wife had joined on their arrival in Elmira maintained the "Bible Defense of Slavery,"[188] they, along with thirty-nine other members, requested to leave the congregation, and with approval financed the founding of the humanistic based First Independent Congregational Church.

By that time, Elmira had grown to become a thriving and substantially influential mercantile hub along the network of canals that had dramatically transformed New York into the economic empire that gave it the nickname 'Empire State.' The town acquired substantial financial pull, and with the arrival of the railroad in 1851, Elmira became the primary hub for all northern railroad lines. When a proposal was put forth to open a new college in the state, the Langdons stepped forward, money in hand, to persuade the overseers to establish the institution in Elmira. "Elmira was a hotbed of social reform during Olivia's childhood" writes Skandera Trombley.

> "Between the years 1852 and 1855, there occurred three events that would determine Elmira's Zeitgeist for the rest of the nineteenth century and well into the first decades of the twentieth. During the decade of the 1850s Elmira was captured, set afire, and ultimately transformed by the winds of reform: the city underwent major changes in health care,

religious and social activism, and women's education."[189]

As I read on, Laura Skandera Trombley continued to lift the veil of Elmira's obscurity. In my mind's eye I witnessed Elmira reemerging as a tour de force metropolis by the end of the Nineteenth Century akin to Pittsburgh, with world class theater venues and performances, the construction of forty-five hotels by 1885, and, as Trombley described, "a thriving cultural scene."[190] What had happened? This was not the woeful Elmira seen when I had visited.

To have been raised in such a social climate, Olivia Lewis Langdon, Trombley explains, "was representative of her generation in her adoption of the tenets of "domestic feminism" via "…her active support of abolition and temperance, her membership in reading groups, and her friendships with women from the suffragist factions of the women's movement…"[191]

Trombley illustrates how Livy had thus been raised in a matriarchal home, after marriage ran her own home in the same way, and passed those same feminist traits onto her daughters. This underscores the earlier assertion of Livy as a driving force behind Twain's body of work. It should also be noted that in lieu of her pioneering feminism, Livy also maintained an atmosphere of respectful equality toward Sam Clemens, a characteristic also learned from her parents.

Pastor Thomas Beecher, the brother of Catherine Beecher, Harriet Beecher Stowe of Uncle Tom's Cabin fame, and Henry Ward Beecher, whom we'll discuss shortly, pointedly noted his observation of Mrs. Langdon during her funeral service that she had been an equal partner in marriage to her husband.[192] This is a significant point to better understand the marital agreement between Sam and Livy. As things would turn out, the Beecher family at large would also have an enormous influence not only on Sam and Livy Clemens, but inadvertently on the minds and conscience of millions as the former played out their roles in history.

Siblings who would all influence American history: Thomas Beecher, Henry Ward Beecher, and Harriett Beecher Stowe. Courtesy The Center for Mark Twain Studies.

Back on the anti-slavery lecture circuit, Frederick Douglass continued to encounter mixed reactions when he spoke. Many viewed him as a sort of side show novelty, voicing surprise that a former slave could be so educated and possess such refined oratory skill, while others tried to discredit him as a liar. It was true that too few Blacks had any education at all nor could they write on their own behalf.

Douglass understood that small-minded, pro-slavery assailants could not fully comprehend a slave's side of the story, and felt it a moral duty to tell his own tale in a larger way. In May of 1845, he published his personal memoirs in *The Narrative of the Life of Frederick Douglass*. The book became an instant best seller, with sales of more than five-thousand copies by Fall of that year. The book mobilized the anti-slavery movement, gave Douglass some measure of respectable accreditation within the White, educated, anti-slavery leaning community, and enabled him to begin speaking more liberally, beyond the constrained limits imposed upon him up until then by the Anti-Slavery Society agents with whom he had been touring.

Against the preferences of The American Anti-Slavery Society, Douglass embraced this enhanced measure of independence and relocated to Rochester, New York in 1846 primarily to launch and publish *The North Star* out of his basement. Though grateful to William Lloyd Garrison for his assistance, Douglass had become disenchanted by Garrison's views which advocated the disbanding of the Union on the pretext that the Constitution was inherently pro-slavery. Their parting was amicable, and Douglass continued to tour independently on the anti-slavery lecture circuit and sell subscriptions to The North Star.

Douglass grew disheartened while traveling as he bore witness to a more conservative climate than expected. "It came to be a not uncommon thing to hear men denouncing South Carolina and Massachusetts in the same breath and in the same measure of disapproval." he wrote.

> "The old pro-slavery spirit which in 1835 mobbed anti-slavery prayer meetings and dragged William Lloyd Garrison through the streets of Boston with a halter about his neck was revived...anti-slavery meetings were ruthlessly assailed and broken up. With others I was roughly handled by a mob... The talk was that the blood of some abolitionists must be shed to appease the wrath of the offended South and to restore peaceful relations between the two sections of the country.."[193]

In Massachusetts, the Sanford Street Free Church in Springfield, founded by African Americans, quickly became one of most prominent organs for proclamation of anti-slavery sentiments through hosted lectures by Frederick Douglass, Sojourner Truth, and other former slaves. Following his lecture there in 1847, Douglass was approached by a parishioner who would later become known as the most ardent, outspoken and probably best remembered abolitionist of all, John Brown.

Brown was convinced that armed insurrection was the only path to ending slavery. He and Douglass spent that evening in a respectful but charged conversation, with Brown seeking to sway Douglass to join him in his vision for an all-out militant effort. The Haitian slave revolt of 1800 and the Nat Turner led rebellion of 1831 were cited by Brown as prime examples of the type of action required but on a much grander and united scale. Brown felt that Douglass, with his persuasive oratory skills and powerful, physical countenance that likened him to a military commander, could provide a key asset in rallying a united cause. Brown believed that evil pro-slavers had been operating from fear, and that the power of God and moral justice were on the abolitionist's side and could not fail. Of the conversation, Douglass would later recall:

> "From this night spent with John Brown in Springfield...while I continued to write and speak against slavery, I became all the same less hopeful for its peaceful abolition. My utterances became more and more tinged by the color of this man's strong impressions."[194]

When Douglass and Brown had met, the nation's westward expansion into new territories began to markedly increase, impacted by talk of the Transcontinental Railroad. Six new states had been admitted to the Union - three as free states and three as slave slates, all in accordance with the Missouri Compromise. California wanted to enter the union as a free state, but protests ensued when the South saw this could upset the balance. The topic dominated the 1848 presidential election campaign, resulting in the formation of a third "Free Soil" party with Martin Van Buren as their candidate. Though Van Buren lost the election to Zachary Taylor, thirteen Free Soil Party candidates won seats in Congress.

Daguerreotype of John Brown taken in 1850. Courtesy Library of Congress.

The debate over whether new territories should be settled as free or slave states continued to dominate the House and Senate. Just a year prior to the Douglass-Brown meeting, the House had passed the *Wilmot Proviso*, which called for a ban on slavery in the any new southwestern territories that might be acquired when the war then waging with Mexico came to an end. The measure was defeated in the Senate and polarized Northern anti-slavery and Southern pro-slavery sentiment as never before. It was then when North and South began to view each other as distinct, practically foreign countries governed by diametrically opposed laws, rights and liberties.

On the national scene, the influx of a new wave of immigrants from Europe in the mid to late 1840s – my paternal great-great grandparents among them - introduced additional jitters over the potential population imbalance between free and slaveholding states. Southern slaveholding states saw the threat of their demise and the end of slave-based prosperity as never before. This was the strain of fear John Brown relied on as he pressed to mount his campaign. Southerners frantically assailed Congress with their long held 'go to' but now aggrandized threat to secede from the union. In a compromised response, Congress passed the *Fugitive Slave Act of 1850*, which historian Philip Foner explains:

> "…supplemented the Fugitive Slave Law of 1793...It provided for the appointment of special federal commissioners to…appoint marshals to arrest fugitives, and these marshals could, in turn, "call to their aid" any bystanders at the scene of an arrest, who were "commanded" to "assist..."A federal marshal or deputy refusing to execute…the arrest of a fugitive slave would be fined up to one thousand dollars. Law officers were liable for the value of any slave escaping their custody."[195]

An added component of the law specifically targeted the abolitionists and Underground Railroad conductors and facilitators. Their activity was now outlawed, punishable with severe measures.

> "Any person obstructing the arrest of a fugitive or attempting his or her rescue, or aiding him or her to escape, or harboring and concealing a fugitive, knowing him to be such, shall be subject to a fine of not exceeding one thousand dollars, and be imprisoned not exceeding six months, and shall also forfeit and pay the sum of one thousand dollars for each fugitive so lost."[196]

To put that into perspective, a $1000 fine in 1850 was the equivalent of just under $30,000 in today's currency. Passage of the bill struck fear into every free Black person throughout the North. In the free cities of Philadelphia, New York, and Boston, nothing could now prevent a free Black from being abruptly whisked away by hired fugitive slave hunters accusing them of being a runaway, whether they were or not. Because the 1850 law gave no trial by jury rights to Blacks, free or slave, they had no defense.

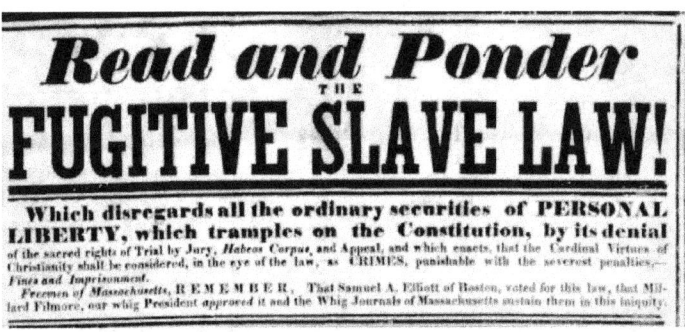

An 1850 abolitionist reaction to the passing of the Fugitive Slave Law.

Alarmed by the law's passage, Black fear transformed into defiance. Free Black citizens in abolitionist Elmira organized to form the collective political voice they had been offered in the town's sympathetic climate, and proclaimed:

"That we, the colored citizens of Elmira, do hereby form ourselves into a society for the purpose of protecting ourselves against those persons, prowling through different parts of this and other States since the passing of that diabolical act of Sept. 18th, 1850, which consigns freemen of other States to that awful state of brutality which the fiendish slaveholders of the Southern States think desirable for their colored brethren, but are not willing to try it themselves."[197]

Erin Doane, curator of the Chemung County Historical Society, explains:

"They resolved to protest against and resist the Fugitive Slave Act though "every one of us be assassinated." They declared that if they discovered anyone working with the slave-catchers, those people would be treated as enemies."[198]

Free Blacks throughout the North furiously echoed the Colored Citizens of Elmira, separating themselves defiantly from the heretofore adopted non-violent approach, and called for flagrant self-defense by any means necessary, until death if need be.

The decision outraged abolitionists. William Lloyd Garrison and his Anti-Slavery Society in Massachusetts advised:

"As citizens, it is your prerogative…to contest it…As moral and religious men, you cannot obey an immoral and irreligious statute…This law is to be denounced, resisted, disobeyed…"[199]

The passage of the law formed the defining wedge between pro and anti-slavery adherents with "two poison pills: the Fugitive Slave Act and the repeal of the Missouri Compromise of 1819" explains author Fred Kaplan. Whereas the former made it illegal to harbor and assist,

"The latter encouraged Southerners to believe they had the right to bring slaves into any territory or state in the country that did not have a specific nonslavery law. The West and Northwest were now potential slave territory."[200]

That very clause would serve to open the gates of hell on the banks of the Mississippi River where the famed St. Louis Arch stands today, marking the entry point of Western Expansion into the new territories. While the debate to end slavery had been waged arduously, the 1850 law now presented the proposition for slavery's proliferation on a scale larger than heretofore imagined. The political rhetoric had fomented to a new height when Senator Foote of Mississippi drew and pointed a revolver at fellow Senator Thomas Hart Benton of Missouri on the floor of the Senate during the debates.

An 1851 abolitionist handbill warning Black citizens of legalized kidnapping resulting from passage of the Fugitive Slave Law.

1851 political cartoon depicting William Lloyd Garrison pointing a gun at a slave catcher sitting on Daniel Webster, who endorsed the 1850 Act. Courtesy of Library of Congress.

The strained emotions on both sides had become a powder keg that could explode violently with the slightest spark. The ripple effect struck fear in the hearts and minds of citizens as discussions on the imminence of secession and war echoed more audibly than ever from the Halls of Congress to newsprint and pulpit across the nation. Emboldened by the law's passage, Southern slaveholders were given the cake walk they had desired for half a century and now sought to exercise this government endorsed strength. Those Northerners who dissented from the more virulent talk spewing forth from the mouth of William Lloyd Garrison felt that alternative and more peaceful approaches to effecting moral suasion should instead be employed to avoid war.

One to dissent from Garrison's view was Harriet Beecher Stowe, who had worked feverishly for the cause, yet viewed her peers Garrison and Brown as too extreme in their fervor. At the suggestion of an in-law, Stowe, a mother of six children struggling to make ends meet, was persuaded to use her talent to write a serial novel that would help draw attention to the plight of slaves. First published in 1851 in the abolitionist publication *National Era*, her work entitled *Uncle Tom's Cabin* instantly caused a national reaction, galvanizing anti-slavery sentiment and serving as a rallying cry for the cause to an unanticipated extent.

Stowe's book became the first comprehensive narrative work of fact-based fiction to unveil the horrors of slavery to the general public. What enabled Uncle Tom's Cabin to stand apart and prove so successful was Stowe's ability to transcend an overtly evangelical tone in her work and present a narrative work in a literary realist style that captured broad appeal. Of her personal inspiration to write Uncle Tom's Cabin, Stowe would later explain: "My heart was bursting with the anguish excited by the cruelty and injustice our nation was showing to the slave, and praying God to let me do a little and to cause my cry for them to be heard."[201]

The published book edition would see three-hundred thousand copies sold in the United States in one year, over one million sold in Great Britain,[202] and would ultimately be translated into sixty-seven foreign language editions.

The combined success of Stowe's Cabin and Douglass' *Narrative* opened the door for other book and periodical publishers to seek out the first-hand

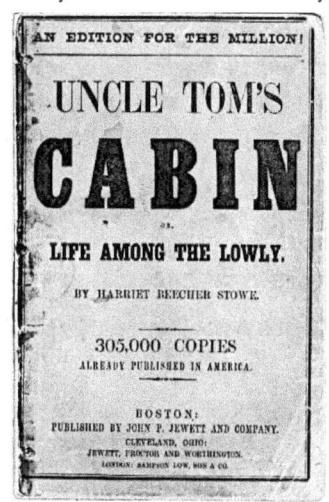

Cover of the first 1852 British edition of Uncle Tom's Cabin. *Courtesy the Collection of the Smithsonian National Museum of African American History and Culture.*

accounts of former slaves. Following this was *Twelve Years a Slave*, which recounted Solomon Northrup's tragic saga of being kidnapped in Washington, DC, and sold "down river" into Southern plantation life, where he languished amidst barbaric horrors before regaining his freedom twelve years later.

When first interviewed after regaining freedom, Northup's story was featured on the front page of the New York Times. "The striking similarities of his story to the recent international sensation "Uncle Tom's Cabin," journalist Michelle Genz explained, "made Northup the hot news of the day."[203] Northrup's book sold 30,000 copies between 1853 and 1856, earning Northrup $3000 in advances in 1853 - the equivalent of just under $100,000 in today's currency. With such publications generating increased national attention, the tide for the abolitionist cause, waged for almost over 150 years at that point, had begun to turn in their favor.

The popularity of these works were threatening to pro-slavery advocates, who became increasingly aggressive. Southern slaveholders decried Stowe's work as underhanded propaganda that painted a dishonorable and unfair picture, claimed the author was a liar, and used any host of other means to denounce it. Stowe's book had fueled the fire, and, indeed, in Southern states, was burned and/or banned outright, proving to be that match for the 1850 powder keg. Southerners considered the sub-title of Stowe's book - "Life among the Lowly" - a slanderous offense, much as Hillary Clinton's "Basket of Deplorables" remark had been received during the 2016 Presidential campaign.

In response, a slew of Southern generated, pro-slavery "Anti-Tom" and "antidote" publications were printed and distributed with titles such as *The Lofty and the Lowly*; *Northwood, or, Life North and South: Showing the true character of both*; *The Parlor and the Cabin or Slaves and Masters*; *Bible Defence* [sic] *of Slavery*, and the best-selling *Aunt Phillis's Cabin or Southern Life as it is*.[204] One big hit from 1853 was a direct assault published in Boston entitled: *Uncle Tom's Cabin in Ruins! Triumphant Defence* [sic] *of Slavery! in A Series of Letters to Harriet Beecher Stowe* By Nicholas Brimblecomb, Esq.[205] Such works tried to paint a picture of slaves being happy with plantation life while, in the background, a wave of militant activity prepared the means to secure that vision and spread it westward.

Conversely, one who had sided with Garrison's view was the more virulent John Brown, who had long viewed the moderate, less militantly inclined advocates for the cause through use of policy and government as weak. In Springfield, Brown had organized *The League of Gileadites*, so named for the Biblical Mount Gilead, referenced in the Book of Judges passage where God offers encouragement to Gideon:

"Now therefore proclaim in the ears of the people, saying, 'Whoever is fearful and trembling, let him return and depart from Mount Gilead.'"[206]

With messianic fervor, Brown had trained and instructed Gileadites to acquire firearms, know their weapons intimately, and act quickly and effectively in their defense of fugitive slaves, forming the nucleus of a ready-made militia prepared to fight to the death for the abolitionist cause. Abolitionism had come a long way from the earliest civil protests of non-violent and unarmed Quakers. In John Brown was found the prophetic incarnation of Benjamin Lay's theatrically demonstrated warning that perpetuating the institution of slavery would result in bloodshed.

Following the passage of the *Nebraska Kansas Act* in 1854, pro-slavery Southerners and abolitionist Northerners sponsored thousands of settlers to move west, acquire land, and sway voting numbers in either's favor. More than 1000 anti-slavery sympathizers, Brown's sons included, had been sponsored by abolitionists to relocate from New England.

Soon after settling, Brown's sons relayed concerns for their safety due to population insurgences by militant pro-slavery "Border Ruffians" from neighboring Missouri, designed to illegally boost the voting count in Kansas elections, establish settlements in the territory, and terrorize anti-slavery 'free-soilers' with threats of violence. One pro-slavery advocate explained their intention...

"to repel this Northern invasion, and make Kansas a Slave State; though our rivers should be covered with the blood of their victims, and the carcasses of the Abolitionists should be so numerous in the territory as to breed disease and sickness, we will not be deterred from our purpose."[207]

In the free state of Illinois, an obscure, Congressional hopeful with political potential named Abraham Lincoln decried the passing of the Act as "conceived in violence, passed in violence, is maintained in violence, and is being executed in violence."[208] Tension over the situation in Kansas reverberated in Washington with fever-pitched quarrels.

In the midst of this, enter nineteen-year-old Samuel Clemens, who just happened to be working in Washington when he wrote to his brother Orion in Iowa to describe his experience of spending time in the Senate gallery during one of the Nebraska Kansas Act debates in February of 1854. "In the House" Clemens wrote,

"nearly every man seemed to have something weighing on his mind on which the salvation of the Republic depended, and which he appeared very anxious to ease himself of; and so there were generally half a dozen of them on the floor, and "Mr. Chairman! Mr. Chairman!" was echoed from every part of the house. Mr. Benton [the Democratic Senator from Missouri] sits silent and gloomy in the midst of the din, like a lion imprisoned in a cage of monkeys, who, feeling his superiority, disdains to notice their chattering."[209]

The anxiety young Clemens witnessed was an understatement, proving to be the quiet before the storm. In May of 1856, Southern congressman Preston Brooks beat Northern Congressman Charles Sumner nearly to death with a cane on the floor of the Senate, leaving him in a pool of blood. The Supreme Court overturned the Missouri Compromise of 1820, which had ruled the land for 34 years. Claimed as a victory by Southerners, slavery was legalized in all territories overnight.

Tensions in Kansas mounted, and after a band of Missouri Border Ruffians burned the abolitionist town of Lawrence, John Brown and six of his men formed a posse, rode into pro-slavery Pottawatomie Creek brandishing swords, and with biblically inspired fervor slayed five pro-slavery settlers dragged from their beds in the middle of the night. A bloody campaign ensued resulting in deaths of numerous settlers, including John Brown's son Frederick at the abolitionist settlement of Osawatomie. Brown returned with forty to fifty militant abolitionist followers along with a shipment of rifles and ammunition packed in wooden crates labeled "Bibles" sent courtesy of Henry Ward Beecher - the brother of Uncle Tom author Harriet, and Thomas, the newly appointed pastor of the Anti-slavery Congregationalist Church in Elmira founded by Jervis Langdon. Hundreds of pro-slavery mercenaries from bordering states retaliated, forcing Brown to withdraw and mark him as a wanted man.

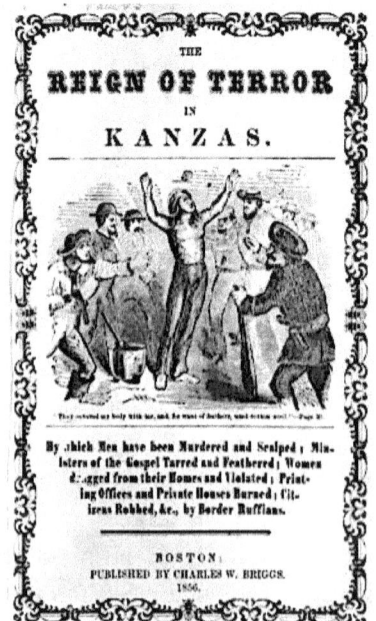
An 1856 abolitionist call to arms handbill about the crisis in Bleeding "Kanzas."

In 1857 Brown returned East to raise funds and rally increased support for his original vision of an armed slave rebellion. With financial aid secured through six prominent and influential New England abolitionists, Brown and his Gileadites headed to Maryland, and on October 16th, 1859, raided the US military arsenal at Harper's Ferry, Virginia, and took hostages. US Marines headed by Colonel Robert E. Lee surrounded the arsenal, overpowered

Brown and regained control. Brown was imprisoned, tried for treason in the State of Virginia, and sentenced to execution by hanging.

Anti-slavers hailed Brown as a martyr. Ralph Waldo Emerson, the chief philosopher of Brahmin New England who famously said "What you do speaks so loudly that I cannot hear what you say" now hailed the especially bellicose Brown as "The Saint whose fate yet hangs in suspense, but whose martyrdom, if it shall be perfected, will make the gallows glorious like the Cross."[210]

1865 illustration of John Brown, as he appeared at the time of the raid and his execution. Courtesy Library of Congress.

An 1859 poster for a protest rally scheduled for the day of John Brown's execution. Courtesy New York Public Library.

In one eyewitness account of Brown's hanging discovered in 1955, reporter David Hunter Struthers had written:

"...a few convulsive struggles & a human soul had gone to judgement. Thus died John Brown...In the manner of his death there was nothing dramatic or sympathetic. There was displayed neither the martial dignity of a chieftain nor the reckless bravado of a highwayman—neither the exalted enthusiasm of a martyr nor the sublime resignation of a Christian...fifteen hundred soldiers stood mute and motionless...The thousand civic spectators looked on in silence. At the end of half an hour the body was taken down... and the day concluded with the calm & quiet of a New England sabbath."[211]

The calm and quiet didn't last long. The abolitionist raid at Harper's Ferry was only a rehearsal for the juggernaut to follow. The issue of slaveholding in the western territories fueled the 1860 Presidential campaign. "When Abraham Lincoln won election in 1860 as the first Republican president on a platform pledging to keep slavery out of the territories" writes Princeton's Dr. James McPherson,

> "seven slave states in the deep South seceded and formed a new nation, the Confederate States of America... By the end of 1861 nearly a million armed men confronted each other along a line stretching 1200 miles from Virginia to Missouri."[212]

During the summer of 1861, young Sam Clemens was back home in Hannibal. Of this time he would later write:

> "there was a good deal of confusion in men's minds during the first months of the great trouble, a good deal of unsettledness, of leaning first this way then that, and then the other way. It was hard for us to get our bearings...I was piloting on the Mississippi when the news came that South Carolina had gone out of the Union...My pilot mate was a New Yorker. He was strong for the Union; so was I. But... my loyalty was smirched, to his eye, because my father had owned slaves. I said in palliation of this dark fact that I had heard my father say, some years before he died, that slavery was a great wrong and he would free the solitary Negro he then owned... My mate retorted... and went on decrying my Unionism and libeling my ancestry. A month later the secession atmosphere had considerably thickened...and I became a rebel; so did he... In the following summer he was piloting a Union gunboat and shouting for the Union again and I was in the Confederate army....

23-year-old Samuel Clemens in 1859, as he might have appeared during his term as a Marion Ranger. Courtesy Smithsonian Institute.

> In that summer of 1861 the first wash of the wave of war broke upon the shores of Missouri. Our state was invaded by the Union forces...The governor, Calib Jackson, issued his proclamation calling out fifty thousand militia to repel the invader. I was visiting in the small town where my boyhood had been spent, Hannibal, Marion County. Several of us got together in a secret place by night and formed ourselves into a military company...we called ourselves the Marion Rangers..."[213]

Sam's commitment to the cause wouldn't last long as his unsettledness compelled him to 'rough it' in another direction. Meanwhile, battle waged,

dividing the nation further.. In a bold effort to restore the Union, President Lincoln presented his *Emancipation Proclamation* in September, 1862 as a direct presidential order.[214] However, "By 1864" Dr. McPherson continues,
> "the original Northern goal of a limited war to restore the Union had given way to a new strategy of "total war" to destroy the Old South and its basic institution of slavery ..."[215]

In February that year, Massachusetts Senator Charles Sumner - the same Charles Sumner almost beaten to death in 1856 - proposed an amendment to the constitution, which stated:
> "All persons are equal before the law, so that no person can hold another as a slave; and the Congress shall have power to make all laws necessary and proper to carry this declaration into effect everywhere in the United States."[216]

A slightly modified version passed the Senate vote on April 8, as follows:
> 'Neither slavery nor involuntary servitude, except as a punishment for crime whereof the party shall have been duly convicted, shall exist within the United States, or any place subject to their jurisdiction.'

Following its affirmation in the House on January 31, 1865, nearly four million slaves in the South were officially declared free. By Spring, Congress was adjourning for Easter recess. Jubilant with their success and the collapse of the few remaining defiant Confederate holdouts, the end of the war was imminent. Abraham Lincoln was jubilant that Providence was steering the nation in the morally correct direction he had envisioned for decades. On Good Friday morning of April 14th, 1865, he conducted business with heightened optimism, desiring to complete tasks quickly to accommodate plans for an early dinner and attend a play that evening with his wife, Mary.

Eyewitnesses would later remark that the two had been mildly flirtatious with one another as they took their seats at Ford Theater.

As Presidential historian Doris Kearns Goodwin explains,
> "During the performance, the White House footman delivered a message to the president. At about 12 minutes after 10, the impeccably dressed John Wilkes Booth presented his calling card to the footman and gained admittance to the box. Once inside, he raised his pistol, pointed it at the back of the president's head and fired."[217]

News of Lincoln's death galvanized Pro-Union sentiment. The perception of John Brown's hanging as a martyr paled in comparison. With Lincoln, the American messiah had been crucified. This only energized the beleaguered Union forces into ending the war at any cost, pressing aggressively into the few remaining pockets of resistance. Within a month, Dr. McPherson explains,

> "all the principal Confederate armies surrendered...on May 10, 1865, resistance collapsed and the war ended...Northern victory in the war preserved the United States as one nation and ended the institution of slavery that had divided the country from its beginning...The long, painful process of rebuilding a united nation free of slavery began."[218]

Nearly four million enslaved Americans were at long last and at immeasurable cost, free. The long cause of the abolitionists had neared its end. It was only after the passage of the Fifteenth Amendment on March 30th, 1870, which gave free Negro men the right to vote, that the likes of William Lloyd Garrison, Henry Ward Beecher, and the countless advocates for abolition could officially declare their mission complete.

1865 commemorative print recognizing the principal leaders of the abolitionist campaign at the end of the Civil War. Courtesy Library of Congress.

19

THE GRAIL BENEATH THE STRIP MALL

"All training is one form or another of outside influence, and association is the largest part of it. A man is never anything but what his outside influences have made him."[219]

Mark Twain,
What is Man?

The back-story of the history of slavery and the abolitionist campaign is vital to fully understand those outside influences that would mold the mind and soul of Mark Twain. Until the Nineteenth Century, only a handful of individuals through two centuries prior were willing to take a risk to stand for universal human rights. The abolitionist campaign defined that time and world into which Samuel Clemens was born, with an impact that rippled across the globe and form the foundation of the century to follow. The fact that the man who would become Mark Twain was raised in the state of Missouri amid this climate seems almost ordained by Providence, hallmarked by his arrival with the return of Halley's Comet. This begins to paint a clearer picture of Mark Twain, who he became, what he wrote, and how that combination would influence a new generation, among whom was a young man who grew up to be my father.

Sam Clemens was a Missouri boy through and through, and by the late 1850s was living his dream as a riverboat pilot on the Mississippi. Yet, prior to that, Sam was just another young man exploring the world around him, seizing opportunity wherever it would take him. In this context, one of the more delightful parallels found between Mark Twain and I was a shared affinity for historic sightseeing. In the same way I was enthralled by all things Twain on my visits to Hannibal, Hartford, and Elmira, Mark Twain, too, from his earliest years, had visited some of the historic sites in my hometown of Philadelphia. In fact, while scouring through the letters posted online by The Mark Twain Project I discovered that Sam Clemens had once lived in Philadelphia and worked at the *Philadelphia Inquirer* when he was eighteen-years old.

During that period, young Sam Clemens wrote to his family expressing: "I like this Phila amazingly, and the people in it." As Ron Powers recounts in his book, some of his friends encouraged him not to get downhearted, to which Sam replied "Downhearted the devil! I have not had a particle of such feeling since I left Hannibal..."[220] During his tenure, young Sam

Young Sam Clemens in 1851, as he likely appeared while living in Philadelphia two years afterward. Courtesy Smithsonian Institute.

had ventured: to 'Fairmount Hill' - the highest elevation point within city limits, and current site of Philadelphia's iconic Museum of Art.; to Independence Hall where the Declaration of Independence had been signed, and the "old cracked Independence" Liberty Bell when it was still displayed inside the main hall before being moved to the foyer and then to its current-day pavilion across the street.

"Philadelphia is one of the healthiest places in the Union" Sam had written in a letter to his brother Orion dated December 4th, 1853...

> "The air is pure and fresh—almost like the country...It was about 1682 that this city was laid out. The first settlers came over the year previously...The city now extends from Southwark to [Port] Richmond—about five miles—and from the Delaware to the Schuylkill [Rivers]—something over two miles...Penn's original [design] was to leave Front Street free, and allow no buildings to be erected upon it. This would have afforded a beautiful promenade, as well as a fine view of the [Delaware River]. But this plan was not carried out. What is now the crooked Dock Street was once a beautiful brook, running through the heart of the city. In old times vessels came up this creek as high as third [street]."[221]

This is a favorite tale told by locals to this day. In years past, whenever out of town friends or family paid a visit, I included in the tour a stop at a depression in the ground behind Carpenter's Hall which is the only visible remnant of this same brook referenced by Twain.

In his letter to Orion, Sam continued:

> "The old State House [Independence Hall] in Chestnut street is an object

of great interest to the stranger. In the east room of the first story the mighty Declaration of Independence was passed by Congress, July 4th, 1776. When a [stranger] enters this room for the first time, an unaccountable feeling of awe and reverence comes over him, and every memento of the past his eye rests upon whispers that he is treading upon sacred ground. Yes, everything in that old hall reminds him that he stands where mighty men have stood; he gazes around him, almost expecting to see a Franklin or an Adams rise before him. In this room is to be seen the old "Independence Bell," which called the people together to hear the Declaration read, and also a rude bench, on which Washington, Franklin and Bishop White once sat...'

'It is hard to get tired of Philadelphia, for amusements are not scarce. We have what is called a "free-and-easy," at the saloons on Saturday nights. At a free-and-easy, a chairman is appointed, who calls on any of the assembled company for a song or a recitation, and as there are plenty of singers and spouters, one may laugh himself to fits at a very small expense."[222]

Left: 1869 Harper's Weekly engraving of the "old Independence" Liberty Bell as it was displayed during the Nineteenth Century. Right: 1856 engraving of Independence Hall interior, as it was when young Sam Clemens visited. Note the "old Independence Bell" on the pedestal. Courtesy Library of Congress.

His "free-and-easy" reference rang a familiar bell. That's an old custom from Britain and Ireland I had known well since my childhood, and there were numerous pubs in my neighborhood that had maintained this tradition, where one could venture in from time to time and catch a second or third generation proprietor offering an earnest vocal rendition of any number of old, traditional Irish songs. Walk into *Dean's Bar* in my neighborhood today and you might catch the proprietor, my friend Phelim, all too ready to offer his rendition of *Galway Bay*. Before his passing, our mutual friend Bill Dunphy sang a version of *Danny Boy* that made proud men weep. Almost everyone had their designated song. My brother, the singer-songwriter James Curley, wrote of the tradition in his song *Tom's Cafe* - the name of a pub our grandfather had frequented - which is immortalized in his lyric "It seems like yesterday when I heard Irish jigs coming from Tom's Cafe."[223] The same custom also prevailed at the parties I knew in my childhood, when Dad held center court with his accordion while he or one of his friends were called out to sing their selected song. Dad's song was an obscure ditty called *Roll The Patrol*, with its memorable refrain "Roll the patrol, closer to the curb, my grandmother can't step that high!" Its recording by The Howington Brothers made the Billboard charts in December, 1948. I thought it way-cool to discover that Twain had been privileged to have encountered and directly experienced this custom. Now the man was nudged a little more deeply into my heart.

There were more Philadelphia landmarks Sam had visited. On December 24th, he wrote again to Orion. After describing shoppers out on Christmas Eve in the fiercely cold weather, Sam wrote:

> "During the week I have visited several places of note near Philadelphia. The first of these places was Germantown, where the Americans made the terrible charge upon the British, quartered in the celebrated "Chew's House"… Germantown is rich in old buildings, some bearing the dates of 1743, 1760…"[224]

At the time Sam Clemens visited, the Thones Kunders house where Francis Pastorius drafted his infamous charge against slavery was still standing. It is likely to have been among those "old buildings" he saw and referenced. Back again in the "Old City" section of Philadelphia, he continues, but with an added, familiar-ringing lamentation about the fate of historic venues. "At the corner of Little Dock and Second streets" he explained,

> "stands the queer looking old house occupied by the heroic Lydia Darrah. It was here, if I remember the story aright, that she left the British officer, and taking her flour bag, set off to inform Gen. Washington of the intended attack of the British upon his camp: and her heroic conduct defeated the plans of the red-coats, and saved the Americans. Well does she deserve a monument; but no such monument is hers. As one might almost guess, her old mansion is now occupied by… a clothing store. The next place of note is the old "Slate-Roof House," …situated in Second street [and Sansom St.], … It was occupied by Wm. Penn, in the year 1700… after years, it was the temporary abode of John Adams, John Hancock, and many other distinguished members of the first Congress, …This noble old relic is also desecrated in the same manner as the Darrah

House. Unless measures are shortly taken for its preservation, it will soon go to decay and be remembered as one of the things that were. Carpenter's Hall, situated in Carpenter's Court, is a pile dear to every American, for within its walls, the first Congress of the United States assembled—a fact which [should] entitle it to a place in the heart of every true lover of his country... The principal entrance leads to the Assembly Room, in which Congress first met. It is now occupied as an auction mart. By an auction mart—the old story. Alas! These old buildings, so intimately connected with the principal scenes in the history of our country, should thus be profaned. Why do not those who make such magnificent donations to our colleges and other institutions, give a mite toward [their] preservation of these monuments of the past? Surely their liberality would be well bestowed. It is painful to look [upon] these [time-honored] edifices, and feel that they will soon fall into decay and be forgotten."[225]

Above, left: 1850 photograph of the Lydia Darragh House, Dock Street at 2nd Street, Philadelphia, exactly as young Sam Clemens would have seen it - as a clothing store. Above, right: 1860 photo of the "Old Slate House" as seen by Clemens. Built in 1685, it was the home of Pennsylvania and Philadelphia's founder William Penn and thereafter referred to as the Governor's mansion. It was razed in 1860. Courtesy Library of Congress.

Twain's remarks blew me away. His visit to Philly in 1853 was identical to my trips to Elmira and Germantown in 2017 - both of us had witnessed historic structures replaced by markets, and we both languished about it as "the old story!"

The Graff House, where Thomas Jefferson had written the Declaration of Independence and was still standing when Clemens lived there, ultimately razed in 1883.

The house where Benjamin Franklin had lived, on Third Street between Market and Chestnut, was sadly long gone before Clemens visited, having been razed in 1812. It languished as nothingness until the land was declared a National Historic Landmark in 1966, followed by the construction of an open air, steel ghost of its framework in 1976 mirroring the contours of the home where it had stood. A fine museum of Franklin related artifacts now situated in its place is worth the visit, highlighted by a marker designating the "privy pit" where, um, well... let's just say where Benjamin Franklin sat.

The first executive mansion - the first White House, if you will - where President Washington resided before the capital was moved in 1800, was razed in 1832. A few party walls remained until the 1950s, but in its construction of Independence Mall, Philadelphia razed those few remaining walls and replaced the site, local legend has it, with a public toilet. In 2000, the foundations were rediscovered, along with the unanticipated surprise of unearthing the foundations of Washington's slave's quarters. The original construction plans were scrapped, and, like the Franklin house, a steel recreation of the home's contour was erected, with a special exhibit addressing the history of slavery in Philadelphia.[226]

Even in Twain's time, so many historic places had already been felled, and many more afterwards. Twain had been awed by his experience in Philly just as I had been awed by those locations relative to him. From a simple marker outside of a cemetery in his summer retreat town of Elmira, I was prompted to revisit a legacy in American history that I had only touched upon maybe for a semester in high school forty years earlier. Revisiting the segments of our history that most prefer to forget or brush under the rug had profoundly restored something that had long been missing. But it only further convinced me that we need to pause, reflect, and discuss before we rashly decide to remove monuments.

Good or bad, right or wrong, ill-conceived or not, they have much to teach current and future generations. If we remove them, we risk reducing our culture to one with nothing to think about, nothing to learn anew, nothing about which to become educated. Once it's gone and replaced by a strip mall, there will be nothing to learn except the pros or cons of putting mustard on a hot dog.

I couldn't help but wonder how young Clemens' time in Philadelphia may have influenced his thinking later in life. Ardently anti-abolitionist but not quite pro-slavery, at the onset of the Civil War Samuel Clemens was a different man than the one history prefers to remember.

"'Missouri was a peninsula of slavery in free territory'" cites Baylor University Professor and Twain scholar Joe B. Fulton.

"Political geography forced Missourians into politics long before the passage of the Fugitive Slave Act of 1850. Suspicions abounded that abolitionists were slipping into the state and ferrying slaves across the river to freedom...For those in Missouri, abolitionists were subversive traitors of the most dangerous sort...[Twain's] father, Judge Clemens, sat on the jury that sent three such "abolitionists" to the state penitentiary for twelve-year sentences... When Sam Clemens recalled..."the infernal abolitionists," he voiced the popular outrage in Missouri that federal law was not protecting their rights...foreshadowing Huck's fear in Adventures of Huckleberry Finn...that he might be labeled "a low-down abolitionist" for not handing over Jim..."227

Discovering Joe Fulton was like reaching the top of the mountain where an elusive High Lama resides, imparting timeless wisdom to only the worthiest of seekers who had successfully scaled a prerequisite precipice. I stumbled across his book *The Reconstruction of Mark Twain: How a Confederate Bushwacker Became the Lincoln of Our Literature* after ten months of research and, as I read through the pages, felt like the curtain had been parted to reveal the Grand Wizard of Twainians. I saw one who had honed in with surgical precision on some of the very information I had sought to deduce. Fulton has a penetrating research mind. Reading segments of *Bushwacker* gave me the impression that I had been handed a Mark Twain microscope that enabled me to pierce the surface more deeply than before. Fulton seemed to dig and dig and dig in the process of finding Twain facts, and was able to zero in on the precise day, hour, and minute of one Twain incident or another.

Fulton explained how the numerous letters Sam Clemens had written to his mother, which were subsequently published by his brother in the *Hannibal Journal*, reveal the embodied confederate leanings of his youth. In the letter I had found previously, where Clemens described Missouri Senator Thomas Hart Benton with sentimental subscription to the states' pro-slavery politics, Fulton cites how Twain also:

"lamented that the Senate Chamber had fallen from its earlier days. "Its glory had departed. Its halls no longer echo the works of a Clay, or Webster, or Calhoun."...The "glory" that vanished with the death of these three senators involved the commitment to secure the Union by guaranteeing the states' rights coveted by the South...The few scholars who have commented on the racist attitudes reflected in the letter from his 1853 visit have dismissed them, suggesting that the writer's attitudes changed rapidly, practically overnight...Clemens' attitudes toward race did not change overnight."228

Fulton was spot on. I had summarized the subtle innuendos suggestive of

Clemens' earlier racist leanings from those same letters, including an occasional overt expression of anti-Semitism. Samuel Clemens as a young man was not the lovable grandfather figure we would collectively come to revere.

"Given his political opinions prior to the Civil War" Fulton continued,

> "his racist views of immigrants, and his belief that "slavery was right, righteous, sacred," there can be no doubt where his sympathies lay in the years leading up to the war… throughout the 1850's, he flirted with nativism and the Know-Nothing Party. When Fort Sumter was fired on, thousands of patriotic southerners enlisted in the Confederate cause. Sam Clemens was one of them… [However] Clemens, like most people living in border states like Missouri, had mixed feelings about secession, slavery, and the Civil War…After Fort Sumter…As many southerners rushed to enlist in the Confederate Army, Sam Clemens vacillated. Events pressured him to decide…In April 1861, Sam was a pilot serving under Captain David De Haven, an ardent secessionist…"[229]

Fulton then referenced a letter recalled decades later by Clemens' childhood friend Will Bowen, Twain's model for the Joe Harper character in *The Adventures of Tom Sawyer*. Sam, Bowen and the latter's brother Sam Bowen had all been river pilots, and the two Sams also enlisted in Missouri's Marion Rangers militia. Fulton cites the letter and Will Bowen's recollection as key to understanding Mark Twain, confirming

> "something long suspected of the future Mark Twain: that he believed in the Union, but not in the North. Before the war, he often chastised those who voiced anti-Union sentiments, yet he sided with the South in the great conflict…according to Will Bowen, Sam had been "swept into the mighty tide of political revolution."[230]

Of his time with the Rangers, in his autobiography, Twain wrote:

> "In June [of 1861] I joined the Confederates in Ralls County, Missouri…and came near having the distinction of being captured by Colonel Ulysses S. Grant. I resigned after two weeks service in the field, explaining that I was "incapacitated by fatigue" through persistent retreating."[231]

As fate would have it, the future President Ulysses S. Grant would one day capture Twain - by the heartstrings. Decades after the war, Twain would edit and publish Grant's memoirs, with the compassionate purpose of saving the latter from destitution in his final years.

John Brown was also six degrees removed from Mark Twain. In his autobiography, Twain discussed the details of crossing paths with one James Redpath, whom, he explained, "was one of Ossawatomie [sic] Brown's right-hand men in the bleeding Kansas days; he was all through that struggle. He carried his life in his hands…He had a small body of daring men under him and they were constantly being hunted by the "jayhawkers," who were pro-slavery Missourians, guerrillas…Ten or twelve years later, Redpath was earning his living in Boston as chief of the lecture business in the United States. Fifteen or sixteen years after his Kansas adventures I became a public lecturer and he was my agent."[232]

Twain recounted one lecture in which Redpath told the story of being hunted and eventually confronted by a jayhawker chief, having escaped only because the fellow mistook him for a less important person. A lecturer scheduled to follow Redpath then took the stage and informed Redpath that he was the jayhawker chief he had encountered.

While Twain jokes about retreating from participation in the Confederacy, he had another motive that made his decision easy; his brother, Orion, had been appointed secretary of the Nevada Territory by the Lincoln Administration. At Orion's invitation, Clemens abandoned the bleak prospect of fighting for a cause that confused him, and headed West to take his chances with other avenues to fortune. After his failed attempt as a silver prospector, Sam capitalized on his previous writing experience and, with the aid of his brother's influence, secured a journalist position for the *Territorial Enterprise* in Virginia City, Nevada. There Sam began to hone his penchant for the humorous expression and style that would define him as a writer. Among his earlier works written at this time was "Lucretia Smith's Soldier." Joe Fulton asserts that in this work can be gleaned the earliest inflections of a shift in Clemens' political leanings. As the war escalated, Fulton reminds us, the daily publishing of battle details followed by the listed names of those soldiers who fell in battle likely appealed to Clemens' sympathy.

"The publication of "Lucretia Smith's Soldier,"" Fulton explains,

> "indicated the importance of Clemens's southern leanings to the development of his reconstructed persona as Mark Twain, for the story was a notable use of literature as a vehicle for political and social polemic. His Nevada writings certainly contained this element from the very beginning…The surrender of Robert E. Lee to Ulysses S. Grant at Appomattox, the subsequent

Twain's oldest brother, Orion Clemens.

collapse of the Confederate Government, and most particularly the assassination of President Abraham Lincoln accelerated the reconstruction of Mark Twain."[233]

Curiously, Mark Twain panned the allure of the Civil War's main figureheads. "Thousands of geniuses" Twain wrote,

> "live and die undiscovered - either by themselves or by others. But for the Civil War, Lincoln and Grant and Sherman and Sheridan would not have been discovered, nor have risen into notice."[234]

It boiled down to Twain's distaste for the resulting capitalization of Lincoln's death for political gain. Twain's answer was humor, sarcasm, and indifference to the wave of mawkish patriotism that swept across the land. Twain called it "waving the bloody shirt" of Lincoln,[235] Fulton explains. "Clemens's criticism of the "bloody shirt" erupted most forcibly in a series of articles he wrote for the Californian."

And here it comes - the nugget of the moment leading to Sam Clemens' renaming of himself with the nom de plume 'Mark Twain'. When writing for the Californian, Clemens admired editor Charles Webb, "but to Radical Republicans" Fulton quotes Twain,

> "the editor was…"loyal to the Southern Conthieveracy, loyal to the Rebellion, and loyal to anything in opposition to our Government." Clemens, having been similarly traduced, had never shied away from accusations of disloyalty…He had dealt with accusations directly when writing such articles as "Another Traitor - Hang Him!"…Scholar Franklin Walker has suggested that Webb "came away with the feeling that it was not safe to walk down the street unless you clothed yourself with the star-spangled banner and slapped its folds in your neighbor's eyes." Shortly thereafter, the name Mark Twain began to appear on the "Answers to Correspondents" column for Webb's paper. Clemens used his column, for which he manufactured both the questions and the answers, to defend Webb, and by extension himself, by tackling all the sacred elements of Unionism: July 4th, war music, and the loyalty oath required of anyone (presumably even Clemens himself) who had borne arms against the Union or uttered disloyal statements. Moreover, in passages that still seem shocking,

Samuel Clemens'/Mark Twain's desk at Nevada Territorial Enterprise, Virginia City, Nevada

Clemens joked about John Wilkes Booth and the assassinated president."²³⁶

So, this, then, is the man who sought to charm young Livy Langdon, and endeavor to win the hearts of her parents, Jervis and Olivia. At first glance, surely a man like Jervis Langdon, the prominent Elmira abolitionist, would have railroaded such a scalawag from his doorstep without hesitation. One can glean that young Sam Clemens was yet harboring some deep-seated resentment and pain from the loss of loved ones: the death of his father had forced him to set aside his boyhood, and, the tragic death of his beloved brother Henry, Sam's idol and motivation for pursuing the river pilot dream, who had died in a riverboat accident. Now in Nevada, with the influence of his brother Orion's new stature in a Lincoln administration appointed role of prominence, Sam likely began to mature out of his boyhood naiveté, and being away from Missouri, was loosening from the effects of having been 'swept into the mighty tide of political revolution.' Nevada was neutral territory, and the neutrality of that climate surely softened Sam's harder edged views.

It would seem evident that Sam's brother Orion likely molded his views as well. In those days, being a Republican meant being a liberal. It's interesting how the roles have reversed today so that we find each party representing each other in sheep's clothing to the point that they've forgotten their respective original identities.

"When grown-up persons" Twain wrote,

> "...have lived narrow, obscure and ignorant lives and at full manhood they still retain and cherish a job of leftover standards and ideals that would have been discarded with their boyhood if they had then moved into the world and broader life."²³⁷

It was evident that the 'exterior influences' which had molded Twain had shifted dramatically in Elmira, and it was there where Jervis Langdon had proven to be the most insurmountable influence on Twain's life for a tenure of just two years. Stanford University's Dr. Shelley Fisher Fishkin writes:

> "Mark Twain well knew" injustice and discrimination had been part and parcel of our democracy from the start. Indeed, some have argued that that awareness is at the center of what makes Twain's greatest works so valuable."²³⁸

In her book *Lighting Out for the Territory: Reflections on Mark Twain and American Culture*, Fishkin addressed the story of Johnson Whittaker, a Black West Point Cadet who had been discharged in 1880 after being savagely attacked by three masked White cadets, left to die, and accused of staging the attack himself. After charges were later dropped following an intervention by President Chester Arthur, Whittaker went on to become a lawyer, teacher, and school principal. Fishkin quotes award-winning author Ralph Ellison, a student of Whittaker's, who once said that Mark Twain

> "grasped the moral situation of the United States and the contrast between our ideals and our activities…One of the functions of comedy is to allow us to deal with the unspeakable. And Twain did this consistently."[239]

"The 'unspeakable'" Fishkin continued,

> "that Twain helped us address was slavery and its legacy - a combustible and unavoidable topic even today…How did Twain come to understand the unspeakable betrayals at the heart of American history? …in 1853…he was rabidly anti-abolitionist… [referring to them in one letter to his mother as] …"infernal abolitionists."[240]

How indeed was the exact question I sought to answer. Like Fisher-Fishkin's own exhortation of never having been to Elmira previously, my flash visit on a Coinstar whim led me into the very portal of understanding that in Elmira was found the holy grail of fully grasping the soul and conscience of Mark Twain. Fishkin had been a scholar of Twain's work whereas I had only been a fan and writer who wanted to know what made the guy tick. Both of us, however, had found the grail buried beneath a strip mall in the ghost and memory of Jervis Langdon.

After Twain had met the family, sought the hand of Olivia in marriage, and endured the Langdon's trials and interviews to review his worthiness, it would be Jervis Langdon who ultimately opened the door, thereupon transforming the socially-conditioned racist Sam Clemens of Missouri into an enlightened man of letters that mirrored the egalitarian ethos of New England Transcendentalism and reflecting the internal struggle of the American conscience.

Fishkin explains:

> "'Haven't you a friend in the world?' Jervis Langdon asked incredulously. "I'll be your friend myself," he said with a generosity that would continue to give Twain ample reason to marvel. This brash young man…had won the heart of the father…and was welcomed into the family… Jervis Langdon was the polar opposite of Mark Twain's own father… John Marshall Clemens was a slaveholder, Langdon an abolitionist… Jervis Langdon did more than allow Twain to marry his daughter. He bought him an elegant, fully furnished house and helped him buy part interest in the Buffalo Express; he also dispensed advice with sagacity and affection. Twain came to refer to him simply as "Father." During the brief period between Twain's first trip to Elmira in 1868 and his father-in-law's death in 1870, Langdon became just that: a new father, a beloved surrogate

father, perhaps the father Twain wished he had had. Both morally and materially, Jervis Langdon was central to the process by which Sam Clemens remade himself into Mark Twain. The heritage of proud antislavery activism Langdon embodied help goad Twain to raise the questions he never asked as a child."[241]

On February 4th, 1870, Samuel Clemens and Olivia Langdon were married. In the grand scheme, the timing couldn't be more serendipitous. Only the day before, February 3, 1870, the Fifteenth Amendment was ratified, guaranteeing all citizens of any "race, color, or previous condition of servitude" the right to vote. The combined events must have surely overjoyed Jervis Langdon, a man who had spent his entire life risking everything for the rights of those unjustly enslaved. Shortly thereafter, Jervis Langdon grew ill, succumbing to death later that year on August 6, 1870.

Like the Halley's Comet syndrome that had colored Mark Twain's arrival and entry in this world, it was as if Langdon's life had been marked similarly. Just two years after ratification of 1807's *Act Prohibiting Importation of Slaves*, Jervis Langdon was born, the same year as Abraham Lincoln, and ended on the morning of the day when all Black men were free and able to vote as fully recognized citizens. One of the many, long unsung heroes of the more peaceful aspect of abolitionist movement and conductors of the Underground Railroad was mourned by many. Twain biographer Ron Powers notes:

"His passing was one of the most-noted events in the history of Elmira. Thomas Beecher offered the memorial tribute at the packed Opera House on August 21."[242]

Elmira mayor John Arnot closed businesses for two hours during the memorial service. This was the same John Arnot along whose grave I'd unknowingly parked when I visited Woodlawn Cemetery months before.

In his tribute, Pastor Beecher remarked:

"At a time when opposition to slavery was costly, when it ruled a man not only out of his political party but out of his church and out of good society, and caused his children to be pointed at with a sneer…and even his personal property be endangered, Mr. Langdon was a pronounced and determined anti-slavery man. Very few fugitives from slavery have passed through this region without receiving a benefit from him…And when at last, by the costly compulsions of civil war, the system of slavery was abolished, Mr. Langdon's redoubled exertions in behalf of the now freed men were sufficient testimony that his previous zeal had not been a cheap destructiveness…but a true and tender-hearted philanthropy."[243]

In a letter written the following day, Twain transcribed his own eulogy for his beloved "Father," which was reprinted in newspapers throughout the North. "Mr. Langdon was a great & noble man" Twain began...

> "He stood always ready to help whoever needed help—wisely with advice, healthfully with cheer & encouragement, & lavishly with money. He spent more than one fortune in aiding struggling unfortunates in various ways... He had so charitable a nature that he could always find some justification for any one who injured him...then his forgiveness freely followed. Instead of sending to prison a man whom he had pecuniarily befriended in time of need, & who...defrauded his benefactor out of a great sum, he forgave him & helped his family... All the impulses of Mr. Langdon's heart were good & generous. He could not comprehend the base or the little. His nature was cast in a majestic mould. Whatever he did, he did with his whole heart. He never was hesitating or lukewarm in anything. In business he worked with all his might; & as fast as his great gains accumulated he toiled to sow them broadcast for the good of the city, the church & the poor. In politics he showed the same decision & energy; he was an Abolitionist from the cradle, & worked openly & valiantly in that cause all through the days when to do such a thing was to ensure to a man disgrace, insult, hatred & bodily peril. Throughout his long illness all grades of the community, from the highest to the lowest, came daily to inquire...touching testimony...to the whole community's respect & strong love for him. He was a very pure, & good, & noble Christian gentleman. All that knew him will grieve for his loss. The friendless & the forsaken will miss him."[244]

Jervis Langdon, I was learning, had become a forgotten hero. Here had been one who embodied and lived - at great peril - the highest ideals of what the soul of America had sought to become. This is the man whose home in Elmira had been razed and replaced with a strip mall.

In a letter written by Quaker abolitionist and suffragette lecturer Anna E. Dickinson to her mother after staying in the Langdon home following a lecture given in Elmira, she recounted the story of Frederick Douglass' visit following Langdon's death.

> "[Mrs. Langdon] was telling me of Frederick Douglass coming into the house -taking her hand, and then the tears so choking & blinding him... "Thirty years ago" said [Douglass], "when it was an invitation to the incendiary, your husband took me home, sick, nursed, & cared for, & tended me as a Mother..."[245]

I marveled with epiphany. The hidden story of Mark Twain's life had been about the influence of fathers, from the death of his own father in 1847 that led him on a journey of self-seeking throughout the country and into a living room in Elmira, New York, where the man he referred to as "Father" continued an enhanced education, only to come to full fruition when Twain became a father himself. This is when I saw that this work was ultimately about Fathers: my father, his father, his father-in-law, his own fatherhood, and my own experience as a father. When I started writing this story about sitting in my childhood living room with my father, I did not anticipate that it would lead me to this conclusion. Like Twain, it had taken my own travels to arrive at a deepened understanding and reinvigorated appreciation for the genius of Mark Twain.

When all of my research of link after link finally brought me to the doorstep of Shelley Fisher Fishkin's book *Lighting out for the Territory: Reflections on Mark Twain and American Culture*, I knew I could stop researching. Fishkin had been on the same trail I was following with regard to the historic influences on Huck Finn that I was discovering, largely from the sign by the entrance of Woodlawn Cemetery in Elmira designating the grave-sites of important abolitionists.

Doug Aldridge, in his book *Mark Twain and the Brazen Serpent* had unearthed the hidden biblical narrative to which I had also awakened when re-reading Huck. Laura Skandera Trombley had already hit the nail on the head about the influential role of Twain's wife Olivia in virtually his entire oeuvre, and that of the Langdon family in his para-abolitionist sentiments. Ron Powers had then woven it all together into one condensed, superior biography that may well be the end all to be all. My investigation into the mind and soul of Samuel Clemens was complete. I had rediscovered his life, and, along the way, the names of all the people with whom he associated were lifted off of page and headstone and had come to life in a very tangible way.

As I journeyed on through countless troves of academic opinion and antiquated memoirs written over a century ago, along with letters by Twain archived by The Mark Twain Project and other resources, I began to see the formation of interlinking connections that took on the form of an intertwined DNA strand. All roads led to Mark Twain.

20

THE LEGACY OF JERVIS LANGDON

> "I find myself regarded and treated at every turn with the kindness and deference paid to white people...I am met by no upturned nose and scornful lip..."
>
> Frederick Douglass,
> In a letter from Dublin, Ireland, 1845

I had a remarkable revelation about what I perceived to have been a shared experience with Benjamin Lay, Abe Lincoln, Frederick Douglass, John Quincy Adams, and Samuel Clemens: all of us experienced an internal epiphany that brought about a life-changing commitment to denounce racial injustice from having witnessed similar manifestations of cruel, physical expressions of hatred for racial difference.

Among these, the one testimony that stood apart was that of Frederick Douglass. His perspective had originated in a life of limited freedom, no basic human rights, and a story offering a profound lesson that indisputably had a direct impact on the molding of Mark Twain. Douglass had fiercely envisioned freedom and the distinguishing avenues that would get him there. He knew without question that education was vitally important not only to the freedom he desired and the right of his fellow enslaved, but for generating hope and moving our society in the right direction. But why it stood apart for me was how his story was akin to what I'd been taught about the struggle of my own immigrant ancestors.

To this end, I found it fascinating to learn that Frederick Douglass' first experience of fully breathing the fresh air of freedom happened when he was on a trip to Ireland. Without judgement, without prejudice, without feeling like an existential other, it had been the Irish people who welcomed him on the content of his character, not on the color of his skin.

"I have crossed three thousand miles of the perilous deep" Douglass wrote of the experience…

"Instead of a democratic government, I am under a monarchical government. Instead of the bright, blue sky of America, I am covered with the soft, grey fog of the Emerald Isle. I breathe, and lo! the chattel [slave] becomes a man. I gaze around in vain for one who will question my equal humanity, claim me as his slave, or offer me an insult. I employ a cab—I am seated beside white people—I reach the hotel—I enter the same door—I am shown into the same parlour—I dine at the same table—and no one is offended... I find myself regarded and treated at every turn with the kindness and deference paid to white people. When I go to church, I am met by no upturned nose and scornful lip to tell me, 'We don't allow niggers in here!'"[246]

Four segments of a letter handwritten in Dublin, Ireland by Frederick Douglass to William Lloyd Garrison, dated September 9, 1845, merged from pages 2 & 3 (of 11 pages). Douglass is here relaying his delight with the respectful, unbiased kindness shown by the Irish people. Courtesy Library of Congress, Frederick Douglass Papers.

Douglass' description resembled the Irish social climate I knew as a child in my neighborhood. This is what vanished after racial strife had engineered a diaspora of the good people I had known growing up to seek a more harmonious and safe life in outlying suburbs and neighboring states.

I have long resented how the racial strife that forever marred our neighborhood had painted a lumped, easily categorized portrait of the people I knew in my youth as White racists. That just wasn't wholly true. That profile had been created by a news media run by outsiders who knew nothing of our ways and sought a more sensational story to spin on television and in newspapers. The expressed anger portrayed in those formats as some sort of myopic, racist isolationism was, in actuality, an expression of cultivated resentment that grew from the disrespect and non-recognition for these same, innately Irish egalitarian values described by Frederick Douglass that were embedded in our genetic makeup.

In the mid 1990s I was contacted by the Norbertine Fathers who ran the high school I had attended twenty years prior, and presented with an opportunity to teach art classes at my old school, which I heartily accepted. Going back home to give something back to the community that weaned me and pay it forward to the children of my peers was a rare honor and blessing. But perhaps the greatest, humble pie scenario that could have happened was having established a desktop publishing and computer aided design curriculum within my weekly class roster. Yes! The very advice offered by my Dad which I had resisted when in the same high school became the foundation of a core curriculum I'd designed with career and collegiate opportunities in mind for the working-class lads in my tutelage. Within a year my efforts had won recognition, awards, and a grant for my department, and I was asked to sit on the Secondary Schools Arts Curriculum Committee of the Catholic Archdiocese of Philadelphia.

I hadn't spent extended time in the neighborhood for many years at that point, and reacquainting myself with countless folks from my past on the school staff and in the surrounding neighborhood was wonderful. Billy "Danny Boy" Dunphy was the custodian and helped me refurbish and update the old art and drafting classrooms. Most of my new colleagues had been my teachers. I'd known some of the cafeteria workers since childhood. And even when I went to deposit my pay check at a branch of my credit union in the neighborhood, I got weekly updates on insider neighborhood news from my friend Annie's husband Pebbles, who worked as a teller. I felt right at home in this gig, and it was great fun to watch students attempt to prank or scam me the same way I had done to my teachers when I was their age. It made for a mutually respectable environment, and I enjoyed getting to know the young men I was privileged to teach, as well as their parents. I reveled in this reconnection to the community of my youth.

During my tenure, in February of 1997 an incident involving some neighborhood guys attending a beef and beer social at my old parish church hall and a Black family that lived next door quickly escalated into a bloody, racially-charged brawl. News of the event provided the next morning's headlines across the city, and before long, coverage of the story was creeping its way into the national news. Having grown up there, I knew what was coming next. Tensions were rumbling, and it didn't take long for the drums of blame to reignite the old passions of anger. It was 1970 all over again, and retaliation would surely rear its ugly face.

It manifested on an afternoon in March, when one of my students - his name was Chris - was shot during a hold-up at the drug store where he worked after school, just one block away from both the school and the home to which my parents had moved in 1974. He didn't survive. This was an awful, heartbreaking tragedy, too similar to memories of the way our friend Skeeter had been gunned down, how I witnessed our friend Danny lay bleeding in Gabber's hands after he had been shot... My emotions roiled in conflict as sentiments I hadn't considered in twenty years returned to the surface. On afternoons when I finished grading papers or prep for the next day, I would go to the school chapel to reflect and pray - for peace. My heart went out to Chris's parents and family. Having endured this before, I did my best to console Chris's fellow classmates.

The press seized on the incident as racially motivated retaliation, and the situation exacerbated to the point of involving the intervention of the mayor and community ecumenical leaders. Within a few weeks, the Nation of Islam called for a 5000 man march of protest through the neighborhood, which only ignited tensions further. Fingers pointed in both directions as tongues lashed and wagged all variations of imaginable rhetoric. The press, of course, had a feast over the developments, making interpretations of the incidents into a sensationalist carnival.

Commenting on the press spin over the 1997 Grays Ferry uprising, the conservative Catholic writer Dr. E. Michael Jones had written:

> "While no one can deny that there is racial tension in Grays Ferry, the meaning of the various incidents is always something that gets manufactured with a particular end in mind...The same could be said about the [A specified Philadelphia media outlet]. It is the mouthpiece of...Philadelphia, and as such it is in the business of manufacturing meanings."[247]

Journalist Howard Altman, then a reporter for the *Philadelphia City Paper*, had also written about the events, but with a distinctly unique perspective. A transplanted resident into Grays Ferry, Altman saw the other side and spirit of the people in the neighborhood I had known and reference here, writing what I consider one of the best independent summaries about the neighborhood of which I knew, as well as a nice tribute to my student, Chris.

"Though Grays Ferry sits on one of the most explosive racial fault lines in the country" Altman wrote,

> "most people there - white and black - are good and decent and want nothing more than to live in peace. A couple of years ago I noticed a crudely painted swastika on the wall of a parking lot near my home...[Altman is Jewish]... I came home to see one of my neighbors... covering up the swastika

with her own paint and brush. It was an act of kindness that is typical of the way my neighbors have treated me, an outsider.

My wife and I...have come to learn a lot about Grays Ferry...And whites and blacks... contrary to most media coverage, actually do live and shop and sometimes even play together... Time and again, in big ways and small, the people in my neighborhood have bent over backwards to make me and my family feel welcome. Chris Brinkman was one of those neighbors.

Chris used to deliver the *Daily News* and had a pretty good sense of humor when I was late paying him. Like pretty much everyone else on the street, he was good to my kids...Chris Brinkman seemed like a son any parent would be proud to have. And now he's gone, gunned down in a robbery cops say had no racial overtones. Some neighbors, who were among the hundreds and hundreds who turned out Monday night to say goodbye to Chris, think otherwise...

There is one line that divides my family and my neighbors and we all know what it is. To us, words like nigger and spook are intolerable, the same as kike and sheeney...Recently, while walking home at night on a "black" street, a young girl, about 12 or so, began to taunt me and call me a cracker.

Nobody I know is happy about the beating suffered by [the] family at the hands of whites. We are all furious about the murder of a great kid like Chris Brinkman. Which is why [the Nation of Islam's] proposed 5,000-man march through Grays Ferry on April 14 is a very bad idea... it sure won't help whites feel any better about blacks, or vice versa...it won't make it any easier for the white kids and black kids on my block - our future - to play together as harmoniously as they have up to now... All it will do is give radicals on both sides of the racial fault line an excuse to buy guns, store up bricks and bottles and vent the fury that comes with constant hurt and anger...But don't come to Grays Ferry. The good people who don't want their loved ones shot and beaten have enough problems." [248]

With the mayor's intervention, the Nation of Islam withdrew, replaced instead with a much smaller, informal assembly of protestors. The Philadelphia Police lined the route as the march proceeded through a four-block radius, followed by a counter protest of Grays Ferry residents hoisting signs with the names of neighbors and friends who had perished from racial violence through the years. Aside from a few charged verbal exchanges and demonstrative acts of peaceful protest on both sides, cooler heads prevailed and the event came and went without incident.

Like the residents of Grays Ferry, the American Irish were a once a proud species because they had struggled for the same rights and liberties as had many ostracized immigrants on their arrival in America. The younger generations have forgotten this, or were never given the opportunity to become acclimated to such an environment. The Irish in America had been scorned, rejected, slandered, and though they had not experienced the measure of sadistic degradation endured by the enslaved ancestors of African Americans, they had sentimental hearts that understood the preciousness of their liberties. The sad tragedy of my childhood neighborhood is that, unlike Howard Altman, many who moved into the neighborhood from elsewhere never gave themselves the opportunity to encounter the hundred-thousand welcomes of the bottomless Irish heart. Even sadder, the violence of our indigenous "troubles" forever scarred some of those Irish hearts, preventing them to know it for themselves, and not cultivating a clear understanding of it for subsequent generations. This is just one of the social tragedies of the broader Irish diaspora experience in America. This is why my father's conversations about Saint Augustine Church and the Irish struggle were so important to impart to my brothers and I, as it had been imparted to him.

Most of the neighborhood folks I knew, even those whose own family members had been murdered simply because they were White and in the wrong place at the wrong time, never wanted revenge in the name of racial retaliation. Instead, they asked for prayers and the desire that no family, Black or White, should ever endure the needless heartbreak and suffering they had experienced, and to live equally and harmoniously. That was the soul and broken heart of the neighborhood I knew. That was a key lesson I'd learned from my father.

It's kind of ironic, from visiting Twain locations and researching the stories of his in-laws, that I was given the opportunity to re-experience one reason why I was grateful to have grown up in a racially divided Philadelphia neighborhood: it had enabled me to expand my awareness not only of the Black experience in America, but of the broader, global and multi-racial propagation of those incendiary practices that have marred our civilization. While outwardly it resembled a race issue, it was more broadly an ethical issue that transcended race. It was about our indigenous, respective, cultural, communal, and personal need to understand and educate ourselves and become aware that we're all in this together. We have much to lose if we continue the course that we are on. "Follow the North Star" as the slaves were advised. If we keep our sights on a nobler vision for ourselves collectively, we can all surely make it to the Jackson Island promised land of Huck and Jim the way they did, by remaining supportive friends regardless of the recognition of our differences.

That's the enhanced message offered by Mark Twain. Though his work had humorously employed a thinly veiled biblical narrative, Twain nonetheless exhorts us to find the same "angels of our better nature" that Abraham Lincoln had espoused in his first inaugural address. The writing and publication of Huck was his underscoring clarion call in post-Civil War, multi-racial America. Twain knew there was no turning back. The Liberia experiment of Colonization had failed, as had the effort of state's secession that led to war. By 1880, when Twain began to pen the first conceptual scribblings of Huck Finn, he must have grown disgusted with the prevalence of racist banter that was forming the foundations of segregationist policies.

As an aspiring writer seeking to use his talents as a means of securing the financial success that had evaded his father, Sam Clemens surely saw the success of Stowe's Uncle Tom, Douglass' Narrative, Northrup's Twelve Years and other works that were popular in the era. The topics of slavery and the battle against it – which pretty much dominated the collective American conscience in Twain's time - provided the means for a booming business. The stories of fugitive slaves and the search for moral and conscientious resolve in the years following the Civil War was the gold he had eagerly sought to strike as a younger man in Nevada and California. With writing, he could finally stake his claim.

Frederick Douglass would revisit Elmira numerous times, each time assured of a place to stay in the Langdon home. He visited in 1873, and again on August 3, 1880. According to an article in the *Elmira Daily Advertiser* of that date, Douglass's arrival was hailed as the return of a conquering hero by Elmira's Black citizens who were celebrating the combined anniversaries of the passing of the British Anti-Slavery Law of 1834 and Lincoln's signing of the Emancipation Proclamation. This was a fitting celebration of Independence for the man who, when asked to deliver the keynote address at an 1852 Independence Day celebration in Rochester, New York, once famously said: "This Fourth of July is yours, not mine…What, to the American slave, is your Fourth of July?"[249]

"His appearance was loudly cheered" the Advertiser described.

"As the venerated and noble colored man stood on the platform, with his head bared, his white

Frederick Douglass in 1870 photo. Courtesy Library of Congress.

and heavy locks, his massive frame and kindly eyes gave him the appearance of a Moses of his race...the foremost colored man in the world."[250]

Former Elmira mayor Jim Hare recounts the day:

"Douglass' visit was a huge event...Delegations from 'almost every considerable place within one hundred miles of Elmira' were at the event...streets were 'thronged with expectant people'...Speeches and ceremonies...were preceded by a grand parade..."[251]

The direct influence of Frederick Douglass on Mark Twain is unquestioned. Through the Langdon family, and specifically Charlie, Twain openly admired the man he came to know simply as "Fred." Following the election of James A. Garfield, Mark Twain wrote an appeal for his brother-in-law on Douglass' behalf to the new President:

"I am writing this as a simple citizen - I am not drawing on my fund of influence at all. A simple citizen may express a desire, with all propriety, in the matter of a recommendation to office; & so I beg permission to hope that you will retain Mr. Douglass in his present office of Marshal of Washington, if such a course will not clash with your own preferences, or with the expediences & interests of your administration. I offer this petition with peculiar pleasure & strong desire, because I so honor this man's high & blemish-less character & so admire his brave long crusade for the liberties & elevation of his race. He is a personal friend of mine, but that is nothing to the point—his history would move me to say these things, without that. And to feel them, too."[252]

When Frederick Douglass had arrived in Elmira in that summer of 1880 and was greeted with great fanfare and public lauding, Mark Twain was in residence at Quarry Farm and surely took note of Douglass' celebrity fifteen years after the Civil War had ended. With hundreds of visitors and dignitaries in town for the occasion, the buzz that weekend must have been about the old times, when assisting fugitive slaves was a dangerous business. The event marked the tenth anniversary of the passing of the *Civil Rights Act of 1870*, which enforced protection of the rights of African-Americans as fully recognized citizens of the United States, their equal right to vote, and enjoy all privileges of American citizenship.

Here was the nucleus of Jim's assertion at the

"Fred" Douglass in 1880.

end of Huck that he had been rich all along, and that he would be rich again. Jim's treasure was freedom, and it was the message the abolitionists had advocated for two hundred years at that point. Surely, in the midst of conversations at the Langdon home where Frederick Douglass had dined and lodged, the seed of an idea compelled Sam Clemens to excuse himself, retreat to the quiet isolation of his study on Quarry Farm away from the fanfare, away from the speeches and celebration, and reflect back on those earliest of memories of Uncle Ned and Uncle Dan and another era along the banks of the Mississippi, and begin scribbling the first pages of notes that would manifest five years later as the *Adventures of Huckleberry Finn*.

When I began this dialog, it was with the assertion that to understand the import of Twain's Huck, one needed to recall the world and social climate that had formed the man who had written it. It took the telling of a two-hundred-year story to reveal that.

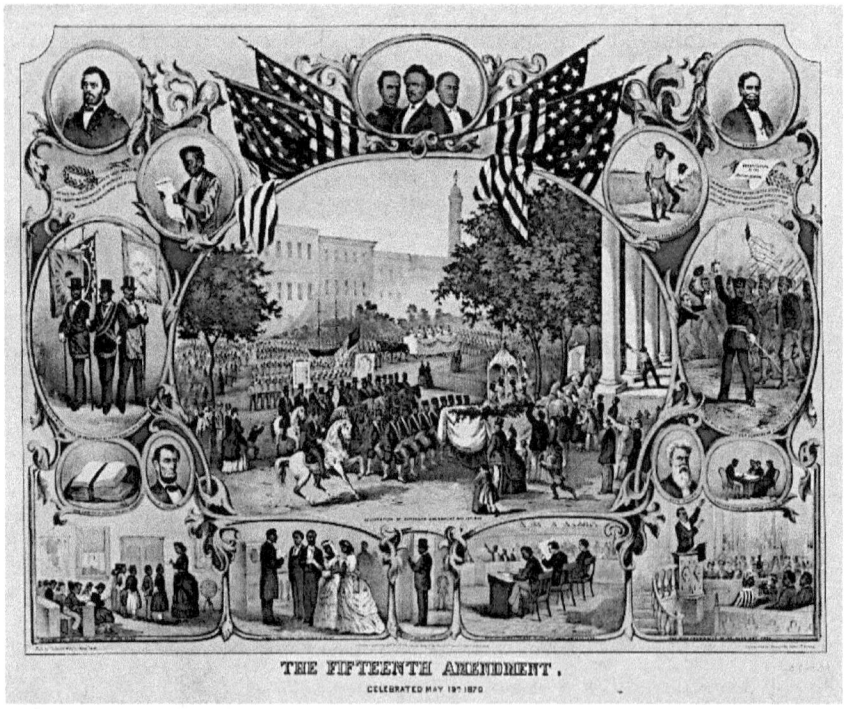

1870 Poster celebrating the passing of the Fifteenth Amendment to the Constitution, which stipulates: Section 1: The right of citizens of the United States to vote shall not be denied or abridged by the United States or by any State on account of race, color, or previous condition of servitude. Section 2: The Congress shall have power to enforce this article by appropriate legislation. Each section depicts 14 newly attained rights for African-Americans. Courtesy Library of Congress.

A little more than a century after Twain delivered his "Plymouth Speech," a letter to the editor written by Jervis Langdon, Jr. was printed in *The New York Times* on April, 7, 1985. "This relates to the wonderful "'From Twain, a Letter on Debt to Blacks'" (page 1, March 14), Langdon, Jr. wrote…

"If Mark Twain had been a racist or had had the slightest inclination in that direction, he never would have been permitted to marry Olivia Langdon. For her father, Jervis Langdon, my great-grandfather, felt so strongly on the issue of slavery that he left his old church, where there was indecision, and established another where there could be none, the Park Church of Elmira, NY.

'Thomas K. Beecher, brother of Harriet Beecher Stowe and of the abolitionist Henry Ward Beecher, presided over Park Church nearly 50 years and always took his naps in my great-grandfather's house across the street. In addition, my great-grandfather ran a secret station on the underground railroad and helped hide countless slaves on their way north to freedom. Mark Twain and his in-laws were very close. In that company, any reflection of racial prejudice would have been cause for real dismay. I am sure there never was any."253

Jervis, Jr. was responding to a March 14th Times story about a then newly discovered letter by Twain "written in the same year that "The Adventures of Huckleberry Finn'" was published in the United States, [and which] describes his offer to provide financial assistance to one of the first Black students at Yale Law School and suggests that Twain was vigorously opposed to racism."254

In the letter referenced, Twain had written:

"I do not believe I would very cheerfully help a white student who would ask a benevolence of a stranger, but I do not feel so about the other color. We have ground the manhood out of them, & the shame is ours, not theirs; & we should pay for it.'"255

The greater part of the unearthing of this letter reveals the full cycle of the influence the abolitionists had on Twain's life. The student, Warner T. McGuinn, had been elected president of the Kent Club at Yale. As one of his duties, McGuinn greeted Twain, then visiting as a guest lecturer, and escorted him from the train station to the home of Yale dean Francis Wayland. In the short duration it took to ride from the train station, Twain became so impressed with the young man, who had been boarding with the college carpenter while working part time to pay his way through college, that Twain drafted the letter to Wayland with an offer to pay McGuinn's board until he graduated in 1887. The influence of Jervis

Langdon, the great-grandfather of the contributor to the April 7th opinion column, on his son-in-law, was quite evident.

Following his graduation, McGuinn went home where he briefly worked as editor for a newspaper before moving to Baltimore to set up a law practice. In time, he was elected twice on the "party of Lincoln" Republican ticket to a seat on the Baltimore City Council, became director of a local chapter of the NAACP, and as early as 1917 was establishing himself as a legal champion for civil rights causes.[256]

Warner T. McGuinn

One African American lawyer who had long ago shared an office with McGuinn at the beginning of his own career, benefitted significantly from his influence and led him to a shining career of his own. After the letter referenced by Langdon, Jr. had been found, he was approached for comment by the New York Times. The now seasoned lawyer recalled McGuinn fondly after the passing of 50 years, saying: "'He was one of the greatest lawyers who ever lived.'"

That young lawyer who shared an office was Thurgood Marshall, the first African American Supreme Court Justice of the United States, and the leading civil rights champion during his fifty-six-year career for ending segregation policies in the United States, setting the stage for the modern Civil Rights movement. Referencing the segregation policies he had spent a lifetime battling, Marshall implies that McGuinn should have been the first Black justice with his simple but loaded remark: "If he had been white, he'd have been a judge."[257]

McGuinn passed in 1937 at the home of his daughter in Philadelphia while recuperating from a stroke. His obituary notes that while in Yale Law School he had been elected president of the Law Club and received the oratory prize at graduation. The obit further notes: "At this time he gained the friendship of Mark Twain, which endured until the latter's death."[258]

As to his political leaning, McGuinn, a lifelong Republican, was remembered for his egalitarian ethos, having been thus praised in a 1927 Sun editorial:

"No member [of the City Council] has been more efficient or more earnest in endeavoring to promote public welfare...He set an example of nonpartisanship in consideration of measures before the Council, and when he spoke upon them showed that he had taken pains to inform himself. His record deserves commendation."259

The torch had been passed, from Jervis Langdon to daughter Olivia, who passed it to Mark Twain who passed it to Warner McGuinn, and from McGuinn to Thurgood Marshall who carried it into our own era, opening the door for the election of the first African American president in US history. At a 2016 commencement speech delivered at Howard University, President Barack Obama said:

> "Change is the effort of committed citizens who hitch their wagons to something bigger than themselves and fight for it every single day. That's what Thurgood Marshall understood - a man who…graduated from Howard Law; went home to Baltimore, started his own law practice…[and] set out to overturn segregation. And after nearly 20 years of effort - 20 years - Thurgood Marshall ultimately succeeded… Marshall, [and his law partner, Charles Hamilton Houston] …knew it would not be easy…. They knew all sorts of obstacles would stand in their way. But they had discipline. They had persistence. They had faith - *and a sense of humor.*"260

The letter written by Twain to Wayland had been authenticated by Dr. Shelley Fisher Fishkin. Fishkin remarked, in a *New York Times* interview recounting the letter's discovery:

> "Twain's brutally succinct comment on racism in the letter is a rare non-ironic statement of the personal anguish Twain felt regarding the destructive legacy of slavery."261

The Times interview also solicited the opinion of Sterling Stuckey, professor of history at Northwestern University, who remarked:

> "It couldn't be a clearer, more categorical indictment of racism in American life, and I'm not at all surprised to find that it came from Twain."262

As an African-American, Stuckey remarked on the controversy surrounding the removal of Huckleberry Finn from school curriculum:

> "My sense of the criticism is that it comes mainly from the non-academic sector of the black community, not from black intellectuals. In my judgment, 'Huck Finn' is one of the most devastating attacks on racism ever written."263

The influence of a small congregation of impassioned individuals in Elmira, New York had come full circle. Another reason why Elmira's role in the Underground Railroad stood out was the reference I found linking it as having being selected for that role due to its proximity to Philadelphia. I got that immediately. Aside from the accessibility provided by the Chemung and Erie

Canals, a simple look at a map will clearly reveal a straight-line South to North from Philly to Elmira. I had had just driven it!

That same summer a friend told me of a home in our neighborhood that had once served as a way station on the Underground Railroad. I had known for many years of numerous homes in the Germantown section of Philly had served as way stations, but this discovery brought the matter that much closer to home.

I went to the Sellers Memorial Library to do some further research on the area's connections to the Railroad. The Sellers' Library is situated in an old home where I had taken my daughter countless times in her youth. My daughter played softball in a neighborhood youth league on the property's adjacent ballpark while my wife and I watched from a shaded patch next to the property's old barn. While inquiring about books or periodicals to aid my research, the librarian on hand that day informed me that the Sellers' family had also harbored fugitive slaves in that same barn. It made complete sense, as the area where I live was once a hotbed of Quaker farms and settlements. To learn that the 'Railroad' passed right through the neighborhood I've called home for the past twenty-three years, possibly right across the land on which my home now sat, proved to be one of those thrilling moments of research referenced earlier by David McCullough.

These revelations accompanied by thoughts about what Mark Twain had called "the great trouble" and its defining role in the creation of the United States inspired another road trip. I had been reading so many details about the Civil War that I was compelled to jump in the Tom-mobile on the spur of the moment that same afternoon and drive to the Gettysburg battlefield. In all the years I'd lived in Philadelphia, I had never been there, despite it being just a two-hour drive away. This seemed to be a necessary excursion if only to provide closure.

I arrived in early evening and after meandering thought the various roads, I found a mid-way point to pull over. From that vantage I could see the vast acres of what had once been farmland, enabling me to envision the fierce battle that had soaked this soil with the blood of thousands. I walked along, pausing now and then to assess

Gettysburg at dusk. Photo by the author.

the monuments to varied regiments from across the Union that had wagered the lives of their favorite sons.

I looked back at the nearby proximity of the town of Gettysburg proper, understanding for the first time just how close the war between the states had encroached into Northern Territory. Though the Mason-Dixon line was a significant distance away, I understood then that this very area had briefly been the dividing line between North and South.

I remembered times when I had asked my Dad to drive me here. He had taken me on so many outings to historic places as a kid, but Gettysburg had always been just far enough away that it never came to pass. Exploring history was something on which we had bonded, and I always remember those special trips. Once again, I felt like I was sharing this moment with him.

I went back to my car with designs to scout the location where Lincoln delivered the Gettysburg Address. A park guard directed me to find the Soldier's National Monument. An iron fence nearby, she explained, marks the approximate location where Lincoln stood. When I arrived, I was moved to find myself in the National Cemetery, surrounded by 3500 grave markers of fallen soldiers, among them nearly 1000 unknowns designated by numbers chiseled into modest stone markers. As I read the details about the monument, I was delighted to note that when dedicated in 1869, the commemorative prayer was delivered by Reverend Henry Ward Beecher of Elmira, the man who presided over the nuptials of Sam Clemens and Olivia Langdon. The serendipity trail continued.

Signs all about requested silence and respect, to which I obliged. As I continued to look about, a uniformed soldier approached the memorial and proceeded to play Taps on his Coronet. This was an unexpected surprise, and I felt honored to be present to share in that tribute on such hallowed ground.

Soldiers National Monument

The sun was just enough above the horizon to amply light my return to the car with plans to leave. I then drove somewhat blindly, not knowing which road led to the exit, when I found myself along signs directing me to the Peace Memorial. I didn't know what that was nor that one existed, but I could clearly see its appealing architecture to my left. I made a quick turn and pulled into the parking area to explore.

As I read the details, I learned it had been dedicated in

1938 by President Franklin D. Roosevelt to commemorate the battle's 50th Anniversary Reunion held in 1913. I was gobsmacked to learn that more than a quarter of a million people had attended to hear FDR's nine-minute speech, and witness the lighting of the eternal flame that adorns the memorial's crown. The only comparisons I could make to grasp the scale were the Grateful Dead concert in Englishtown I had attended, and when I went to see Def Leppard perform at Live Eight in Philadelphia.. The event with FDR must have been something like that generation's patriotic Woodstock at the time.

Spanning the length of its base was a chiseled inscription:
PEACE ETERNAL IN A NATION UNITED.

This was cool. Finding this one expression embedded in this specific edifice provided all the closure I could have wanted. I found this monument infinitely moving, and explored the structure all around, even walking along the soil behind it, contemplating the potential of hand to hand combat having occurred right on the spot.

I noted an unmarked path between the shrubbery that seemed to beckon me, calling me to enter, like some Bizzarro World or parallel universe version of *Field of Dreams* where pain had never fully eased, where baseball games would never be played, where dreams would never come true. I had wandered a short distance into this brush of imaginings, uncertain if I should continue.

I looked back toward the monument to get my bearings, its silhouette serving as a sort of anti-lighthouse, but my eyes were instead drawn to the open field before it, again envisioning the battle but understanding why this structure was a solemn, unsung soldier of hope, standing sentry-like as the light of another day pulled up this vast blanket of horizon, as if I was witnessing nature itself perform an inaudible, visual rendition of Taps. For how many on those days in 1863 had this same vista been their last? How many would never return home? How many had been cut off from that dream of an idea called life in America? I wondered if any long-forgotten or unknown ancestors, conscripted as they stepped off the boat from Ireland, never had the chance to know anything of life in this adopted new

The field of unfulfilled dreams, Gettysburg

home more than a ration of Salt-Pork, a musty, woolen uniform, their rifle and some Hardtack, and the face of their grey-clad adversary as they fell together for a purpose to which neither subscribed nor fully understood.

With heavy heart I stepped out of the sanctuary of uncertainty amidst ancient American brush lined with choking vines and thorny briar and walked back toward the monument and the field of unfulfilled dreams, my emotions compounded further by another inscription on one side of the obelisk, which read:

AN ENDURING LIGHT TO GUIDE US IN UNITY AND FELLOWSHIP.

And there it was. The promise of the ideology behind the very soul of the United States was embodied in those words. This was the result of the struggle of all those patriots and abolitionists and Underground Railroad conductors who unwaveringly followed their conscience to realize a just and equal society. This was a fitting memorial to the efforts of Daniel Pastorius and Thones Kunders, to Benjamins Lay, Rush, and Franklin, to William Lloyd Garrison and Frederick Douglass, to Jervis and Olivia Langdon, and to the many who perished for the dream of humanitarian civility, human dignity, and equal coexistence.

I thought about the polarized climate in present-day United States, and couldn't help consider what a travesty had befallen us as nation. It surely doesn't honor the efforts or memory of those that had waged the noble fight generation after generation. I looked again at the flame atop the memorial, billowing against the dusk-lit sky just as the sun was just about to set. It seemed all too symbolic in the moment. This is what my father had fought for. This was the legacy of exemplary Americans like Jervis Langdon, who had passed the torch to Samuel Clemens, and which has been since passed to us. It's up to us to keep the light burning.

The Eternal Light Peace Memorial at Gettysburg. Photo by the author.

21

THE GUIDING HAND OF LIVY AND THE INFLUENCE OF WOMEN

> "Livy...I thoroughly comprehend your method...& shall practice it, with full faith in it. You are worth a dozen preachers to me, & I love to follow your teachings."
>
> Sam Clemens,
> from a letter to Olivia Langdon, January 12, 1869

So, then, just how did Sam Clemens, this erstwhile Missourian yokel, evolve from a frontier reporter of events in Gold Rush mining camps and globetrotting travel reviewer into the moral gauge of American identity? The unsung credit must go to his association with the Langdons of Elmira, and specifically the influence of Olivia, the woman who won his heart.

From having seen the now famous photo of Olivia that ignited the heart of a thirty-two-year-old Samuel Clemens, I always felt she reminded me of actress Olivia DeHavilland, whom I thought would have been the more appropriate casting choice over Alexis Smith for the role of Olivia in *The Adventures of Mark Twain*. But the more I began to research Olivia, the portrait of an independently minded woman began to emerge, leaving me with the impression that characteristically Olivia may have been more in the mold of a Katherine Hepburn. This made sense, as both, for starters, were the products of progressive women's colleges and feminist-conscious households.

I began to look for biographical info about Olivia online, and many of those sources kept linking me back to the book *Mark Twain In The Company Of Women* by Laura E. Skandera-Trombley. I recalled having leafed through that very book on a more recent visit to the gift shop of the Mark Twain House and Museum in Hartford, but I had instead chosen to purchase Ron Powers' *Mark*

Twain, A Life. As I began to survey Trombley's book again, it occurred to me that she had nailed my very hunch two decades prior. This is an excellent work that I eagerly looked forward to reading in my present expedition to personally discover the essence of Mark Twain for myself. It was one thing to read the views and assessments of others, but it's a whole other level when one takes ownership of revelatory information and imbibe it as fact for one's self. It's the recognition and acknowledgement of that gut instinct that you just need to trust when it's leading you in the right direction. That's half the fun of researching.

Laura Skandera-Trombley possesses a prestigious biography interlaced with superior highlights: As a young scholar accepted to Pepperdine University at age sixteen, she earned her BA in Humanities and English by age twenty. After serving as a professor at numerous colleges she was elected President of Pitzer College in 2003, appointed as the first female president of Huntingdon Library in 2015, and elected as the tenth president of the University of Bridgeport, Connecticut, in July of 2018. She has served on or as an advisor to the boards of numerous organizations, and named by President Barack Obama as one of the twelve overseers of the Fulbright Scholarship Commission. Of the numerous accolades and awards she's received, in 2017 she was given the Lou Budd Award for her contributions in the field of Mark Twain studies, with recognition of her as one of the pre-eminent Twain scholars on today's academic landscape. How she achieved this status is an even more fascinating tale.

In 1994, while engaged in graduate studies at the University of Southern California, Professor Jay Martin asked her to investigate one-hundred old letters which had been presented to him after having been purchased for one dollar apiece at a Los Angeles hobby shop by an area collector. They turned out to be the largest cache of previously unknown letters written by Mark Twain discovered in eighty years. The collector who had purchased them would eventually resell them for a princely sum, the stuff Antiques Roadshow fantasies are made of. But for then twenty-six-year-old Laura Skandera, the discovery changed her life, altering her focused interest on English Romance poets into a lifelong passion for Mark Twain. He does have a way of doing that.

I read with interest how the release of her book *Mark Twain in the Company of Women* was received by some reviewers and Twain purists as "Feminist fantasy,"[264] and how Twain's world, long regaled as one of a man's man, should remain so. But just a casual, insightful and curious visit to sleepy Elmira had led this writer to the same conclusions for which Trombley had been privy via actual source evidence. It was exciting for me to learn that this information had only been a relatively recent addition to the Twain curriculum. I just felt my timing was serendipitous, consistent with how this whole, cross-country investigative adventure had been playing out.

Skandera-Trombley drops her bomb upon the established realm of Twain academia in the closing remarks of her introduction: "What is crucial to note here" she explains,

> "and what cannot be refuted, is that it was only while Olivia was alive that Clemens wrote his greatest works, and only while paired with Olivia that Samuel Clemens achieved the fictional mastery of Mark Twain."[265]

Emphasis on only. I was beginning to sense the same thing, eager to explore Trombley's findings. That one assertion led me to wonder if "Mark Twain" had been a brand name adopted by a husband-wife creative intellectual team in an era when women were still delegated to the side entrance and the back seat, and a man was the socially required mouthpiece. To my delight, Trombley addressed the same point:

> "Clemens insisted from the outset of his relationship with Olivia that theirs was a merging of two persons into one…He believed Olivia was his other self, with which he would finally be united."[266]

I could have stopped reading Trombley's book right there. That's all I had wanted to hear, but I was certain it was much more complex. By page twenty, I was already a fan of Laura Skandera-Trombley, finding her thoughts completely synchronistic with my hunches.

An important component of Trombley's essay is the clear defense of her assertion against that backdrop of earlier critical essays on Twain that either accuse the women in his life as the cause of a perceived artistic failure (Brooks, 1920) or a complete whitewashing and negation of their import (DeVoto, 1942).

"DeVoto creates his own dichotomy" Trombley critiques.

> "He asserts that Brooks was wrong in his critique of the women in Clemens's life, but once he makes the point that they had no ill effect, he concludes that they had no effect at all. They are dropped from further discussion."[267]

With her astute scholarship, Trombley poses that there is so much evidence that even an amateur with a devoted interest in Mark Twain can easily see the surface level of influence he gained from the women in his life.

But my specific focus was on the influence of Olivia and the Langdons of Elmira, because this is where the transitional foment occurs that transforms Sam Clemens into a superstar on the world stage. Clemens aspired to live a refined and wealthy existence surrounded by a stimulating creative and intellectual atmosphere that would fuel his batteries, that resonated with the pulse and manner of perception that had already come to define him as a young journalist. With his dreams of becoming a Riverboat pilot dashed by economic downturn along the river, he eyed a career in publishing. His friendship with Charles Langdon leading to his desired meeting with sister Olivia ultimately brought about the need to prove his worthiness to parents Jervis and Olivia Lewis Langdon. Twain's perception of Mr. Langdon first is that of a highly successful businessman who has achieved the life Sam Clemens had hungered for. In the course of his courting trials, Sam also discovered in father Jervis a kindred iconoclast that surely fostered a mutual respect.

Livy Clemens, the pulse of Mark Twain's life. Photo courtesy the Center for Mark Twain Studies.

"In Olivia's immediate family and in the general ambiance of abolitionist and pro-women's-rights thinking that infused her upbringing and her Elmira surroundings" Trombley explains,

> "Clemens encountered an atmosphere in which his highly traditional attitude toward women gradually but definitively changed. Clemens came to embrace many of the Langdon's beliefs and periodically returned to Olivia's birthplace, Elmira, over the course of more than thirty years."[268]

So, what, then, were those beliefs that so changed the wild Sam Clemens and molded him into the well-dressed and respectable but slight of unconventional rascal that endeared him to all?

Morality was of paramount import for the Langdon family. In a letter written by Olivia's mother during the period of her daughter and Sam's courtship, she voices her concern for what manner of gentleman he is, exactly.

"I have learned from Charlie" wrote Mrs. Langdon,

> "that a great change had taken place in Mr. Clemens, that he seemed to have entered upon a new manner of life, with higher & better purposes actuating his conduct. -- The question, the answer to which, would settle a most wearing anxiety, is, -- from what standard of conduct, -- from what habitual life, did this change, or improvement, or reformation;

commence? Does this change, so desirably commenced make of an immoral man a moral one, as the world looks at men? -- or -- does this change make of one, who has been entirely a man of the world, different in this regard, that he resolutely aims to enter upon a new... Christian life?"[269]

According to Trombley, the important concern for the Langdons was not so much that Clemens adopt a moral code of living, but specifically electing to live a Christian "life of positivity" consistent with the Congregationalist Church interpretation of the designation.[270] In short, it meant Clemens had to ascend to a much higher standard than he had heretofore demonstrated - the very same, refreshing and lively qualities that so endeared him to Charlie Langdon in the first place.

Clemens, left, with Charlie Langdon, right. Photo Courtesy of The Mark Twain Project.

Olivia Langdon had been born into a household of influential progressive thinkers, raised with the understanding uncommon at the time that women were equal to men and deserving of all the privileges and benefits that men enjoyed. Olivia was an avid reader of a wide range of then contemporary progressive thought, a discipline instilled prior to but further nurtured during her enrollment at Elmira College. Among the progressive journals which Olivia enjoyed was *The Independent*, which Trombley describes as "a weekly Congregationalist magazine that advocated abolition, temperance, and equal rights for women; it published stories and essays by such leading women writers and suffragists as Mary Abigail Dodge, Harriet Beecher Stowe, Helen Hunt Jackson, and Elizabeth Stuart Phelps (another of Olivia's favorites)."[271]

During their courtship period, Olivia used to send Sam clipped articles from or full issues of *The Independent*, and in time, Sam became a subscriber. In one letter preserved by The Mark Twain Project at Berkeley, Sam's reply to Livy reveals the response to a strongly worded letter from a forward-thinking, determined woman with unwavering principles. It's clear in Clemens' words that he is committed to demonstrate his worth.

"Why bless your darling heart I do love to hear you scold!" Clemens replies.

> "& rather than have you stop, Livy, I will be distressed when you do it. It does make an impression, Livy—it makes a deep impression, it does indeed—it makes me just as happy as I can be. Now I know you won't stop scolding, since it makes me happy, you precious little philosopher. And besides, whenever it is "something that really troubles you," I will try honestly to listen & behave better, even if I do seem to talk so jestingly about it. But to tell the truth, I love you so well that I am capable of misbehaving, just for the pleasure of hearing you scold."

The letter, dated January 12, 1869, and written from El Paso, Illinois while on a lecture tour, captures the moment of Clemens' first full throngs of new love.

"Forgive me, darling," Sam continued,

> "I could sit there & look into your eyes all the time—it was much better than reading any other book, Livy! I wish I could have a chapter now. But when we are serene & happy old married folk, we will sit together & con other books all the long pleasant evenings, & let the great world toil & struggle & nurse its pet ambitions & glorify its poor vanities beyond the boundaries of our royalty—we will let it lighten & thunder, & blow its gusty wrath about our windows & our doors, but never cross our sacred threshold. Only Love & Peace shall inhabit there, with you & I, their willing vassals…"

Clemens aspires to show Livy that he can share her love of literature, and envisions their days ahead when they can enjoy it together:

> "And I will read: "The splendor falls on castle walls, And snowy summits old in story" - & worship Tennyson, & you will translate Aurora Leigh & be gentle & patient with me & do all you can to help me understand what the mischief it is all about. And we will follow the solemn drumbeat of Milton's stately sentences; & the glittering pageantry of Macaulay's, & the shuddering phantoms that come & go in the grim march of Poe's unearthly verses"

But perhaps most importantly, Clemens reveals his spiritual ascent to a new religious and moral viewpoint. Any moral reservations he may have retained on the back-burner while bandying about as a half-hearted Confederate soldier, as a riverboat captain, or as pioneer journalist, seem to be cast aside with a willingness to surrender to a revised moral perspective that is being presented to him by Livy. Clemens continued:

> "And out of the Book of Life you shall call the wisdom that shall make our lives an anthem void of discord & our deeds a living worship of the God that gave them"

"Livy, I comprehend, I thoroughly comprehend your method of acquiring the religious emotion, & shall practice it, with full faith in it. You are worth a dozen preachers to me, & I love to follow your teachings. Every day in my little Testament I track you by your pencil through your patient search for that wisdom which adorns you so much; & every marked verse calls to mind some remark of yours & shows me how deeply the beautiful precept had sunk into your heart & brain. No unmarked Testament could teach me half as much as this one, & I am so glad you gave it me, & I thank you so much for it, my idolized Livy…Please give my love to the good household. Good-bye, & happy dreams to you, Livy, darling, - & a loving kiss, & all thanks for yours. Always & devotedly Sam$^\ell$. L. C."[272]

The literary based intellectualism harbored between Sam and Livy along with the personal independence advocated by Congregationalist doctrine provided the cruxes for a marital companionship founded on unquestioned mutual respect and recognition of equality. The resultant level of trust and dialogue begat a profoundly successful working relationship. While Olivia refused to be a critic of Clemens' creative style, she did enjoy making editorial suggestions that were underscored by her philosophical and socially critical mode of thinking. With regard to Olivia's influence on the moral context within Twain's work, it becomes increasingly evident that Olivia had assumed the role of something akin to a creative director.

"Olivia's part in co-creating Clemens's texts was not so much in functioning as an editor" Trombley proposes,

> "as in providing an educated audience familiar with transforming and reforming social standards. Olivia was concerned with the scope and treatment of the fictive subject, not with censoring the end product. In effect, she acted as Clemens's "didactic" audience. With Olivia as guide, Clemens could not overindulge in the burlesque; to elicit her approval he had to provide finesse behind the fireworks. Clemens described Olivia's crucial role in a letter to Archibald Henderson:
>
>> 'She would say to me…. "You have a true lesson, a serious meaning to impart here…. Be yourself! Speak out your real thoughts as humorously as you please, but -- without farcical commentary. Don't destroy your purpose with an ill-timed joke." I learned from her that the only right thing was to get in my serious meaning always, to treat my audience fairly, to let them really feel the underlying moral that gave body and essence to my jest. (Henderson183)'"[273]

One of the other women who routinely gave feedback to Clemens at Quarry Farm was the former slave Mary Ann Cord, who was employed as a cook for Susan Langdon Crane and her husband, Theodore. Cord's saga of reuniting with one of her children who'd been sold into slavery was recounted to Clemens, who in turn submitted the story for publication in *The Atlantic Monthly* in November of 1874.

"A True Story Repeated Word for Word as I Heard It," Laura Trombley explains,

> "is of particular importance not only because it marked the beginning of Clemens's contributions to the Atlantic, but also because this oral history of an African-American woman's road to freedom may have served as a prototype for one of Clemens's greatest works [Huck Finn]."[274]

The influence of the Elmira circle of progressive feminine thinkers was already beginning to show itself. Twain was feeling encouraged and engaged in exploration of the most hotly debated issue of his time, a topic he had known his entire life. Who was more qualified to address it? Livy's application of 'finesse editing' brought it to the fore. Twain had already achieved some measure of notoriety and success with the publication of *The Gilded Age, The Innocents Abroad* (which Twain asked Livy to review and edit while they were still courting) and *Life on the Mississippi*. Within two years of the Atlantic publication of 'True Story,' *The Adventures of Tom Sawyer* would be published and received with great acclaim. One can see the gears of Twain's mind as he revisits small memories referenced briefly in earlier works and recycle them into more significant characterizations in the fictional incarnations.

Mary Ann Cord

For example, recall the Duke and Dauphin from *The Adventures of Huckleberry Finn*? Now review this excerpt from *Life on the Mississippi*:

> "When he was an apprentice-blacksmith in our village, and I a school-boy, a couple of young Englishmen came to the town and sojourned awhile; and one day they got themselves up in cheap royal finery and did the Richard III sword-fight with maniac energy and prodigious powwow, in the presence of the village boys."[275]

As for Huck Finn, Twain says early in *Life on the Mississippi*:
> "I will throw in, in this place, a chapter from a book which I have been working at, by fits and starts, during the past five or six years, and may possibly finish in the course of five or six more. The book is a story which details some passages in the life of an ignorant village boy, Huck Finn, son of the town drunkard of my time out West, there."[276]

Therein I also noted the likely root of the character that would become Pudd'nhead Wilson, when Twain describes:
> "How strange it is! We always thought this fellow a fool; yet the moment he comes to a great city, where intelligence and appreciation abound, the talent concealed in this shabby napkin is at once discovered, and promptly welcomed and honored."[277]

It was from Twain's book *Pudd'nhead Wilson* that I was able to glean the moral subtext of Twain's narrative that covertly and cleverly poses abolitionist sentiment toward racial dynamics during the post-reconstruction era in the United States. In short, Twain simultaneously addresses the relatable humanity of the characters while slapping the notion of White patrician supremacy in the face, ultimately represented by having the Tom Driscoll character "sold down river" into a fate of slavery.

Tom Driscoll is described as the child of a Negro slave with skin so Caucasian that he is switched in infancy with the White nephew of a slave-owning, White businessman. While being deceptively raised and educated as the businessman's nephew, the real nephew, the real Tom Driscoll, is raised as a slave by Roxanne, their mutual mammy. Through a series of detective novel intricacies and his inclusion of a variety of colorful characters and plot twists, the truth of the real, enslaved Tom's identity is revealed to the unassuming townsfolk by the title character, Pudd'nhead Wilson, nicknamed as such due to some early social stumbles that led the town folk to view him as a sort of ne'er do well. After the fake Tom Driscoll is found guilty of murder and disclosed as the slave child of the mammy, he is sold back into slavery. The naive, humble, uneducated and real Tom Driscoll who had lived his life as a slave is suddenly set free and inherits a king's ransom while being returned to his rightful, elevated social status into a world in which he is completely clueless and dysfunctional.

In this context, Twain's underscoring theme is about perception of identity and roles in society. Pudd'nhead Wilson is an educated lawyer who can't get a client because of a foolish remark he made when he first arrived in town. In turn, he graciously accepts bookkeeping work extended by compassionate local businessmen who feel sorry for the poor soul, finding him to be an essentially good person at heart, which is the one simple quality that endears him to every other character, whether slave or free, Negro or White, foreign or American.

In a curious way, I suspect Pudd'nhead Wilson is something of a facsimile of Twain himself, inserted into the story in a manner similar to the way Alfred Hitchcock inserted cameo appearances of himself in all of his films. Despite the town's citizen's assessment of him as a good-hearted fool, Pudd'nhead Wilson is a congenial, scientifically minded, progressive individual, with non-prejudicial egalitarian morals. Roxanne, the slave mammy character, is based on Mary Ann Cord of Quarry Farm and her fantastic story Twain had published years earlier. With her clever plan to have her own child raised as a White child of privilege, Roxanne becomes the de facto master of her White slave master, controlling the destiny of her overseer's future in a vein effort to place her own child in a position of power with the aim of securing her own benefit in the future. Her planned fate, too, is upturned after her son is found guilty of murder.

The manner in which Twain predisposes Tom Driscoll's parents as having passed away serves as a cleverly conceived plot twist offering a contrary representation of the reality experienced by Black slave families, who were separated from each other and sold on a routine basis. Twain has so pointedly reversed all the

Above: Opening page of Twain's A True Story, *based on Mary Ann Cord's real-life account, published in the November, 1874 issue of* The Atlantic Monthly.

Below, 1894 sales prospectus for Pudd'nhead Wilson. *Courtesy the Beinecke Rare Book & Manuscript Library, Yale University.*

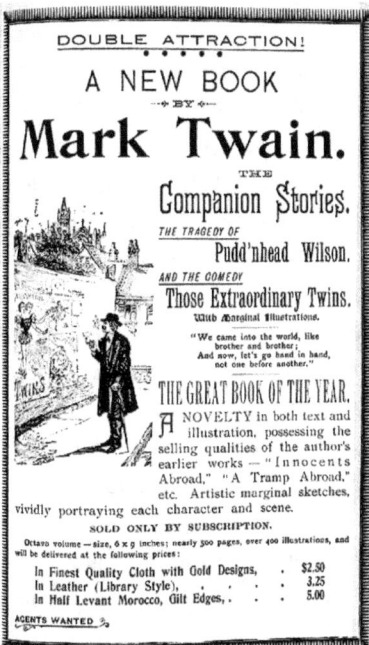

accepted roles of the re-emerging White supremacist society in the post reconstruction era that he is able to play the reader like a fiddle, leaving one with the free will and task of determining for him or her self on the moral, ethical, and humanitarian view of racism. By involving them in deciding the fate of the characters, he has placed the reader in the jury box like a puppet master.

This is precisely how Twain wrote. His work was always subject to review by Olivia, his daughters, Susan Crane and Mary Ann Cord - whoever was around him. Twain clearly does not endorse the prevailing White-favored law of his time, and Tom Driscoll as a character embodies Twain's evident view that reverting to White supremacist legislation and segregation was on the wrong side of history, destined to ultimately enjoy their just desserts in due time. He is blunt about it, with the book's ending presented as swift and exact as an execution.

Pudd'nhead Wilson may be one of Sam Clemens' most important works from the era of its creation and in the canon of works addressing the evolution of racial relations in the United States due to its covert presentation of White/Black role reversal, creatively woven into a work of fiction. Clemens leads the reader on with distracting character elements that could metaphorically represent the way the dominant Anglo-European class that ruled the law turned a blind eye to the intimate details in the lives of the enslaved or subjugated classes. He exercises the "justice is blind" euphemism with all the cunning skill of a riverboat gambling master of poker throughout the narrative, but begins, as he does in so many of his works, to pull his aces from his sleeves and concludes the story with a resounding and merciless swoosh of justice's sword. He is not only blunt but equally unapologetic. I believe this was Clemens' way of asserting the rule of karma, that those who administer unjustly will, in the end, be bitten in the ass by their own insensitivity. Conversely, those who adhere to a righteous path, like the title character, are ultimately redeemed and exalted. In Twain's world, the meek inherit the Earth.

Pudd'nhead Wilson is an American morality tale, a modern lesson presented in then contemporary, regional vernacular, that clearly mimics similar morality tales in the Old Testament, the singular work that so guided the life of early American settlers because it was typically the only book in most households, and which had been the basis for legislation in the highest courts in the land. It is again written by Samuel Clemens as the preacher of sermons, the alternate vocational option he had once considered. It's an acknowledged work in the Mark Twain library, but is often overshadowed by the extensive, aggrandizing focus on Huckleberry Finn as Twain's primary work on the topic of race relations in late Nineteenth Century America, and in his home state of Missouri in particular.

In his essay *What is Man?* Twain wrote:

> "Whatever a man is, is due to his make, and the influences brought to bear upon it by his heredities, his habitat, his associations. He is moved, directed, COMMANDED, by exterior influences - solely. He originates nothing, not even a thought."[278]

I found much revelation in learning of the evident influence of Livy on the emergence of Mark Twain from the cocoon of Samuel Clemens. Laura Skandera-Trombley's assertion that Twain may not have become the writer we know without that influence is well founded. Twain himself summarizes this in the above quote.

However, his association with Livy didn't begin until Twain was thirty-two or thirty-three years old. We've referenced Twain's journeys and activities prior to his life with Livy and the Langdons as an unquestionable component in the formation of the individual we came to know. What is clear is that the voice expressed in Twain's later works shifts dramatically from the pioneer Twain of Jumping Frog and Roughing It. It is evident that Livy played a key role in helping Clemens issue forth his tales with social and intellectual relevance, and may have well served as coconspirator in the invention of the marketable entity known as Mark Twain. Yet, it is important to remember just that - that Livy tapped the wellspring of something she saw dormant in Sam Clemens, and coaxed it to the surface. What she saw were those other heredities, habitats, associations and exterior influences of Twain's that so commanded and compelled his need to express it. Livy clearly saw Sam's unique, formative background and the opportunity it provided for him as an author, setting the stage for him to become regarded as the embodiment of the American soul.

In 1901, Twain wrote, "One of my theories is that the hearts of men are about alike, all over the world, no matter what their skin complexion may be."[279] In an

Commemorative statue of Olivia Clemens by sculptor Gary Weisman on the campus of Elmira College.

address Twain delivered in Philadelphia in 1881 at the First Annual Dinner of The New England Society, Twain presented a blunt, scathing criticism of prevailing White Anglican attitudes of superiority directly to descendants of the Mayflower in attendance. His speech incorporates a plea for them to abandon their self-lauding and braggart manner. The Club's president, in his introductory remarks, denotes Twain's lack of authentic credentials as a New Englander, identifying him as not one of them, and concludes with an attempt to appease him, as well as the self-postulating guests, by declaring Twain to be a member of a nouveau, New England ascendancy. Twain responded in his opening remarks by declaring "I stand in protest!" then proceeds to offer a summary of his own ancestry, which, to the surprise of all, includes Native American, Quakers, Salem witches, and this curious bombshell of an admonition:

"The first slave brought into New England out of Africa by your progenitors was an ancestor of mine - for I am of a mixed breed, an infinitely shaded and exquisite Mongrel. I'm not one of your sham meerschaums that you can color in a week. No, my complexion is the patient art of eight generations. Well, in my own time, I had acquired a lot of my kin - by purchase, and swapping around, and one way and one way and another - and was getting along very well. Then, with the inborn perversity of your lineage, you got up a war, and took them all away from me."[280]

Say what? There were two ways to review this speech. On the one hand, Mark Twain - the humorist - could be exercising his skill by implying to the assembled "Puritans" - the Brahmins of New England - that any motive to distinguish any of ourselves as a separate, removed and more worthy representation of our species is a futile and backward effort in which we all lose. It would also suggest his assertion that, in America specifically, as arbiters of a new and all-encompassing form of democracy, we are all in this together, that we are all mongrels, that the sum total of all the nation's inhabitants compose one corporate species.

On the other hand, as the old adage attributed to Chaucer[281] says, "Many a truth is meant in jest." Did Twain just disclose his genetic heritage? It would substantiate Twain's oft attributed and repeated claim of himself as "*THE* American."

The Puritan speech also seems to summarize the measure by which a fully incorporated influence of the Congregationalist's "living Christian" ideal had prevailed. Mark Twain, not a moralist in the average sense, but Mark Twain the social critic had fully arrived. It was Twain, the unintentional Congregationalist reformer by proxy, who had engaged in seizing a prescient opportunity to reform the very arbiters of established White orthodoxy. There is an evident confidence and clarity in the swagger of his delivery, colored by a sense of duty that surely is the result of the support he has enjoyed after eleven years of marriage and companionship with Olivia.

His speech reveals that he has denounced his identification with Sam Clemens, the westernized ruffian journalist, and pretty much unveils himself as a champion of a new way of thinking. *Life on the Mississippi* would be published two years after this, and *The Adventures of Huckleberry Finn* was in the works at that stage, published shortly thereafter. The Sam and Olivia joint enterprise known as Mark Twain was a force to be reckoned with. They were truthfully the John and Yoko of their day. This was "the man ahead of his times" that comedian Dick Gregory celebrated and revered. Clemens was challenging the White establishment orthodoxy in the same way Gregory would do 80 years later.

Sweethearts Sam and Livy, 1903. Photo courtesy The Mark Twain Home and Museum, Hartford, CT.

Courtesy New York Public Library Digital Collection

PART THREE:

COMING HOME

22

A STOP AT ~~WILLOUGHBY~~ REDDING

"There are no accidents, all things have a deep and calculated purpose; sometimes the methods employed by Providence seem strange and incongruous."

Mark Twain[282]

In late August of 2017, I was scheduled for another business trip in West Chester County, New York, with an overnight hotel stay in White Plains. By this point I was acquainted enough with the region to know that I would be a stone's throw from Mark Twain country. This time, I Googled the distance to Redding, Connecticut and learned that I would be less than an hour away.

Earlier that week I had phoned the Mark Twain Library in Redding to inquire about any displays or artifacts related to Twain that might be on exhibit. The Library Director, Beth Dominianni, was very gracious and helpful in answering my questions and providing the information I sought. Beth explained that while the Library does feature some exhibits, it would, unfortunately, be closed on the Sunday I would be driving through, further explaining that they are open on Sundays after Labor Day. I was mainly curious to see the initial 200 books Mr. Twain had donated to the library to get it jump-started in addition to the check for $6000 he donated for its founding. The tales of Twain's passion for this library are part of his lore. Most notably, whenever distinguished guests wanted to travel to visit him at his home in Redding, Twain required a $1.00 donation of all gentlemen as an admission fee.

I inquired with Beth about the accessibility to Stormfield, Twain's last residence in Redding. As I already knew, Beth explained that the rebuilt home - the original having been consumed by fire in 1923 - was privately owned and secluded in the heart of a wooded area, not accessible nor visible from the road. I attempted to fish out any possible connections to the current owners of

Stormfield to see if there was any way I might secure an introduction with them and just spend 5 minutes or so on the estate's terrace and perimeter stone wall, the only extant remnants of Twain's original home. Alas, it was not to be. But I would be content with just exploring the region and soak up the atmosphere, to intimately grasp what so compelled Twain to be persuaded to purchase the expansive quantity of acreage as the site of a new home in his twilight years.

On the morning of Sunday, August 27th, with my business duties behind me, I hastily scarfed down a quick breakfast, showered, dressed, checked out of my hotel, and set off on yet another Sunday excursion to explore the Twain sites in Redding.

The weather was perfect for such an excursion; mild, breezy, and with full sunshine. I elected not to play any music as I usually do on my road adventures. Instead, I just enjoyed the beautiful Connecticut countryside, practicing mindfulness as I commandeered along the Hutchinson Parkway, taking in the scenery, solitude, and stillness. It was a nice, even-paced fifty mile an hour drive that seemed to enforce an unwritten rule for the need to psychologically as well as physically slow oneself down upon entering this ancient New England region.

As I entered Wilton, Connecticut, time seemed to oddly begin to turn backwards to a comfortable speed. The area grew increasingly more rural, the style of homes almost uniformly of an original New England colonial style, the landscape dotted by older barns and homey farm stands offering locally grown, seasonal produce. I had the distinct feeling that I was stepping back in time. The presence of older, clapboard homes dating back to the era of the Revolutionary War were evident along the drive. I was beginning to understand in that moment what so captivated Mark Twain's desire to settle here. In an uncanny way, this area of Connecticut was very reminiscent of the small towns and ruralness around Hannibal, Missouri. If it still feels this way in 2017, imagine how much more so it must have felt in 1908 when Twain first stepped into the region at the behest of his biographer, Albert Bigelow Paine. Twain had purchased his property here sight-unseen solely from Paine's enthusiastic description.

My first planned stop was the Bouton Funeral Home in the Historic Georgetown neighborhood of Wilton. As I came upon the building, I pulled into the adjacent parking lot. With a hand-carved sign outside the home indicating its founding in 1889, it has been in continuous use since then. Situated just seven minutes from Twain's home in Redding, it is most notably the very location where the bodies of Mark Twain and his daughter Jean were prepared for their respective funerals, and, more recently, Mary Traverse of the Folk singing trio Peter Paul and Mary.

As I walked along the road past the funeral home to an intersection, I was struck by the pervasive quietude and placidity of this sleepy hamlet, nestled away in the heart of Connecticut. Not a sound was to be heard save for the brushing of tree leaves swayed by an occasional gentle breeze. As I studied the details of the Bouton home, a church bell began to softly chime from behind me.

Turning around, I noted two church spires across the street from one another. One, a United Methodist Church, and the other a Roman Catholic church. It surprised me to see two distinct congregations with almost nothing else here in this wee village. The tolling of the bells added an eerie punctuation to what became, in that instant, a sacred moment. For whom were those bells tolling? I like to think they were tolling for me, as if the soul of Mr. Twain was thanking me, an acknowledgment for the revelation of recognition of him as a person, a family man, a man with a heart that endured great personal hardship whose weary mortal form was brought to this very spot in preparation for the eternal life. Moreover, it was the remembrance in that moment of his beloved daughter Jean, while here, that seemed to further accentuate this emotional perception.

In my continued practice of mindfulness that day, I relished the relative quiet enveloping me. It reminded me at once of what I had so enjoyed about living in the foothills of the Catskill Mountains decades ago. I walked briefly, taking some photographs of an old red barn and extraordinary Victorian home on an adjacent property. I could easily envision the barn as the livery stable for either of those properties in a simpler, carriage-drawn, pre-automobile era. It compels one to yearn nostalgically for a return to that time.

As I walked back to my car, looking about, I couldn't help but thinking that I was living a moment in *A stop at Willoughby*, a favorite episode of the old *Twilight Zone* TV series. Written by Rod Serling, the episode was inspired while the author lived in nearby Westport, Connecticut. The story focuses on the workaday existence of Gart Williams, a stressed-out, mid-Twentieth Century New York executive during his daily train ride to and from work. In those scenes of Gart on the train, an older, genteel conductor calls out the upcoming stops of Stamford and Westport/Saugatuck - real stops on Connecticut's old New Haven Railroad line - and ultimately a stop at a fictional town called "Willoughby," each time startling Gart from his commuter snooze.

Whenever the train stopped at Willoughby, a place found between dreaming and waking, through the window drowsy Gart perceives a throwback town from another era, of livery stables and horse drawn carriages, children playing with wheel rims, women dressed in hoop skirts accompanied by well-dressed gentlemen sporting bowler hats and button-down high shirt collars. A uniformed band plays old pleasant standards from a centrally located Gazebo. Gart is fascinated with this incredibly appealing scene which reminds him of the simplicity and innocence of his boyhood. After returning daily to the relentless stress of his routine existence, Gart Williams plans to step off his train the next time it stops at Willoughby, to leave behind the life that is slowly destroying him, and enter into that slower, simpler world from an earlier era. The show concludes with the unveiling of 'Willoughby' as the name of an old, established funeral parlor.

Hmm. Having seemingly stepped back in time on this small corner in the Georgetown area, standing before a funeral parlor established in another era, the notion arose that I had just discovered the real Willoughby. The closing narration of the episode, voiced over with the distinguishable resonance of Rod Serling, suggests:

"Willoughby? Maybe it's wishful thinking nestled in a hidden part of a man's mind, or maybe it's the last stop in the vast design of things—or perhaps, for a man like Mr. Gart Williams, who climbed on a world that went by too fast, it's a place around the bend where he could jump off. Willoughby? Whatever it is, it comes with sunlight and serenity...."[283]

Yeah. For me, on that day, this little corner of the world was just like that.

I had returned to my car in the Bouton parking lot, and set my GPS for the address listed as that of Stormfield, recalling that the street view in Google Maps showed nothing but woods along a road. To some extent, I knew I would be driving somewhat blindly, aware that this whole area was Twain country, and to just content myself with soaking it in on wheels. From the parking lot I made a right at the corner where I had been standing, and found myself driving between the two churches whose steeples were visible from my previous vantage. I noted the road I was on aligned with the town line of Redding, with a sign informing me of its incorporation in 1767. Almost immediately upon making a left turn onto the Redding Road, that feeling of traveling back in time was perpetuated. With the exception of weathered asphalt, the grass-bordered road is lined with one antique Eighteenth or Nineteenth Century home or barn after another.

I read with interest a summarized history of Redding within a documented

The Bouton Funeral Home in ~~Willoughby~~ Wilton, Connecticut, on the day of my visit.

overview posted online by the Redding Planning Commission in its *2008 Plan of Conservation and Development*,[284] which explained a great deal why photographs of Stormfield in Twain's time show a virtually barren, tree-less open space. Once a richly wooded area around the time of its founding, the land had been extensively deforested for the lumber trade while being developed into farmland in the early to mid-Nineteenth Century. Redding and its environs became a major agricultural supplier of corn, oats, potatoes, cheese and butter for most of New England and beyond. By the 1870s, the introduction of less costly produce arriving from newly settled farms in the western states precipitated a decline in Redding's economy, forcing residents to gradually abandon old family homesteads and pioneer westward to "light out for the territory."[285]

Beginning around 1890, the Redding region became an increasingly popular destination for prominent New Yorkers seeking respite from the smog choked and increasingly overcrowded city streets. Smitten by the region's enchantment, farm acreage and properties were scooped up at bargain prices by successful business professionals for use as vacation homes, as well as creative types like the famed photographer Edward Steichen and, of course, Mr. Twain, at the urging of Mr. Paine.

It was still quite rural in Twain's time. Telephones and paved roads were still a few years away, automobiles were new and few, and the local post office was found in a country store. Think of Sam Drucker's store and the town of Hooterville in the *Green Acres* TV program, and you can envision it perfectly.

In the Gilded Age of the non-stop industrial machine that was late Nineteenth Century America, when Mark Twain, the nation's and the era's primary globe-trotting and internationally popular superstar, had grown weary of touring and repeated requests for speaking engagements, the appeal of Redding offered him a long-sought opportunity to retreat and heal after Livy's passing. In June of 1908, Mark Twain departed his New York residence and boarded a train for Redding. Accompanying him was Albert Bigelow Paine, Mr. Paine's daughter Louise, a photographer and several reporters.

Mr. Twain, being chauffeured through rural Connecticut around 1909. Courtesy NY Public Library Digital Collection.

In a *New York Times* interview, Mr. Twain described his new home as "The most out of the world and peaceful and tranquil and in every way satisfactory home I have had experience of in my life."[286] In a letter dated June 19, 1908 to Dorothy Quick, a young girl who befriended the author on a Trans-Atlantic crossing, Twain wrote:

> "I was never in this beautiful region until yesterday evening...It is charmingly quiet here. The house stands alone, with nothing in sight but woodsy hills and rolling country."[287]

STORMFIELD, MARK TWAIN'S REDDING HOME

Century Magazine photo of Stormfield, shortly after Twain moved in. Courtesy NY Public Library Digital Collection.

As the region began to steadily repopulate with new property owners interested in preserving the inherently bucolic nature of the area, formal bylaws were set in place that restricted development and preserved green space. Since many of the new land owners weren't farmers, the area returned to its dense, forested origins, which is maintained even today. This explained why each road around Stormfield and adjacent properties are primarily surrounded with trees reaching forty, fifty, and sixty or more feet in height.

As I drove around, I looked for anything with any semblance of an entrance gate. I saw one set of older, stone pilasters with the space between blocked by several upright posts to prevent vehicles from entering. Was that it? I was disappointed that there wasn't even an historic marker indicating where the property boundary once stood. Yes, as said earlier, this is pretty much what I expected to visually find. What was palpable, however, was the pristinely preserved feeling of unspoiled beauty, a rapidly vanishing commodity in a Twenty-First America filled with eager speculators and ravenous land developers. The Redding Council has done a good and wise thing by taking strains, likely at an economic loss for the township overall, but with a keen awareness of the very characteristic that makes it one of the most precious gems remaining in rural Northeastern United States.

Driving further, I saw to my right a set of old, semi-weathered, forged iron gates bearing the hammered metal name of 'Hill Cemetery'. The gates were open to a long single narrow path straight down the middle. I turned in to allow myself time to explore. The headstones around me dated primarily from the early to mid-Nineteenth Century. One of the better-preserved ones indicated it was the grave of a Civil War soldier who had died in 1862. The stones older than that were indecipherable, but I was aware that this town had roots in the Revolutionary War, that Redding was a primary thoroughfare for invading British troops, and that Washington and his troops had camped somewhere nearby.

Of all the headstones that captured my attention, the most curious surprise was the number of graves bearing the surname of Lyon. Were these the family of Isabel Lyon, the woman who tended to Twain's needs in his waning years after Livy's death? The same Isabel Lyon who had directed the completion and interior design of the estate, and who had ultimately been discharged by Twain for breach of trust born on allegations of theft and intimate impropriety proposed by Twain's daughter, Clara?

The intricate and complete story of the final years of Twain's life here in Stormfield has only recently become unwoven by Twain scholars. Once firmly accepted truths about the author's private life are now viewed as an extension of the carefully crafted persona of the entity and enterprise known as "Mark Twain." This enterprise, planted by Twain himself, was further entrenched through the strong hand of his daughter Clara and Twain's secretary, biographer, and eventual literary executor Albert Bigelow Paine, whom author Ron Powers has perhaps pinpointed with accuracy as a star struck Twain acolyte who maintained the conceptual portrait of Twain with "fawning deification."[288]

Twain scholar Laura Skandera-Trombley addresses some of these complexities specifically in her book *Mark Twain's Other Woman: The Hidden Story of His Final Years*, and in her edited compilation *Constructing Mark Twain: New Directions in Scholarship (Mark Twain and His Circle)*. In the latter, Skandera-Trombley offers a selection of thirteen essays that address views of Clemens/Twain outside of the scholarly box that have been the accepted norm for thirty years, and ventures anew into the study of extended complexities of the man veiled by the white suit. Though I have found myself scratching at this very door, I will leave the profusion of that investigation into Twain's life to the Twain scholars, and I invite readers to explore in a similar vein. Let's suffice it to say, that, for me, my bubble has been burst. The man whom I learned to revere while watching Fredric March's portrayal, who was hailed as the celebrated author behind the 1973 Johnny Whitaker movie, is quite a bit distinct from the man whose grave I had visited in Elmira, New York. Am I disappointed? On the contrary, I am reinvigorated, hungry to know more. For I find myself moving away from the complacency of accepting the pre-packaged and consumer friendly Mark Twain, and relishing the profoundly richer story of possibly an even larger and more significant entity named Samuel Clemens.

Happy days in Mark Twain's heaven - Stormfield, 1909. Pictured, left to right: Twain - sporting his regalia received from Oxford the year before, Jervis Langdon, Jr., daughter Jean, son-in-law Ossip Gabrilowitsch, daughter Clara and Reverend Joseph Twitchell, on the occasion of Ossip and Clara's wedding. Courtesy The Center for Mark Twain Studies, Elmira, NY.

It is a curious coincidence that Samuel Clemens agreed to change the estate's name from his original, Twain-selected "Innocents at home" to "Stormfield" at the suggestion of his daughter Clara. Some have stated that the home had been so named due to Twain's observance of a lightning storm rumbling across the vast acreage surrounding the home, while others suggest it had been in tribute to the success of his 1907 publication of *Captain Stormfield's Visit to Heaven*, the sales of which helped to finance an addition on the Redding home.

"I begin to see that a man's got to be in his own Heaven to be happy" Twain wrote in Captain Stormfield. He envisioned Stormfield as his heaven, which he was happily enjoying with the return of his daughter Jean, and perhaps finally getting beyond the death of his beloved Olivia, until Jean herself had died. He tried again by adopting his "Angelfish" as surrogate grandchildren, until becoming embroiled in the stormy turbulence of the fiasco with Clara, governess Isabel Lyon, and business manager Ralph Ashcroft. Far from the heaven he had hoped for, Redding became something of a purgatory for Samuel Clemens, providing the setting that resurrected the hell in his life, and ultimately killed him.

"Oh, hold on" Captain Stormfield explained. "There's plenty of pain here—but it don't kill. There's plenty of suffering here, but it don't last. You see, happiness ain't a thing in itself—it's only a contrast with something that ain't pleasant. That's all it is."

I hadn't planned on including an extended segment about Twain's Stormfield saga, but now that I had driven there, I could almost sense a resonant somberness yet prevailing in the very fibers of the estate's wooded surroundings. Certainly, the region has become world-known as the locale of Mr. Twain's death. As I contemplated the added details while driving, I felt that I was navigating directly into the immense heartbreak of Mark Twain's final years.

When the Clemens family returned to America in October of 1900 after spending a decade living abroad, Mark Twain was greeted with a hero's welcome.

Biographer Ron Powers explains,

> "The newspapers heralded his return as a prophet, or something larger than a prophet; the soul of the nation personified...America had missed him. America had found something missing in itself when he was away...His round-the-world tour and repayment of his debts had established him as a national hero and moral exemplar..."[289]

Emboldened by this newfound, untarnishable status, Twain held back nothing when openly voicing his criticism of the imperialist, expansionist direction of American government in the wake of the Spanish-American and Philippine-American wars then prevailing. This was not the "polite National Uncle"[290] as heretofore embraced by most Americans. His ardent dissent contrasted sharply with pro-war sentiment espoused by "Congress, the clergy, [and] the captains of industry"[291] just as he had similarly railed against the failings of segregationism following reconstruction. Twain's word became gospel. Unlike the Nixon Administration's legally founded ambition to deport John Lennon for his open protests of the Vietnam War, this American born voice of the American people was virtually untouchable.

While Twain's defiant, unrestrained bravado elevated him to a status of prophet-like idolatry in the public eye, friends and family squirmed uncomfortably. Publishers were hesitant to print some of Twain's commentaries on politics, church, and other hot topics, concerned that he was "jeopardizing the genial goodwill he'd built up with America for more than thirty years."[292] During a Yale University Bicentennial celebration in October of 1901, President

Theodore Roosevelt, in attendance on the dais with Twain for the occasion, grumbled loudly that he "would like to see the likes of Mark Twain skinned alive."[293] Undaunted by the remarks of Presidents or social leaders, it would take a succession of personal tragedies looming on the horizon to bring Twain's revived mercurial rise to a stall.

On their return to the US, the Clemenses took up temporary residence at 14 West 10th Street in New York, just off tony Fifth Avenue, a short walking distance from the home of his dear friend William Dean Howells. Twain had his heart set on moving back into their beloved home in Hartford, but after returning for a funeral, Twain took the opportunity to revisit the old homestead. It was then when he knew instantly that the heartbreak associated with Suzy's death would prevent his family from ever living there again. Livy and Sam instead now sought a residence with some of the grandeur of the Hartford home, and in November of 1901 they found some semblance of it in a temporal residence at Wave Hill, a fine Greek Revival estate in Riverdale, New York, set above the Hudson River with a grand vista overlooking New Jersey's Palisades.

1902 for the Clemens clan began with optimism and promise. With his bankruptcy debts behind them and books sales and speaking fees now providing ample means for comfort, life resumed some normal consistency. Between engagements Twain enjoyed excursions to the Caribbean on the yacht of his financial savior and good friend Henry Rogers of Standard Oil. It was while on a trip to receive an honorary degree from the University of Missouri in May of that year when Twain paid that final visit to his boyhood home in Hannibal, Missouri which would be forever commemorated in the life-size, ghost-like effigies I saw during my own visit there. It proved to be an emotional experience for Twain, when the Lion of literature broke down in tears while delivering a farewell speech to 500 guests of the Labinnah Club of Hannibal, fully aware it would be the last time he would see the town of his youth, and the inspirational wellspring for his most enduring works. As he boarded the train to take leave on the following bright sunny morning, darker clouds were gathering.

23

TWAIN'S VALLEY OF THE SHADOW

While enjoying a family vacation in Maine in August of 1902, Livy experienced a powerful inability to breath, giving Sam and his girls the impression that she was dying. Rushing her back to Riverdale, doctors diagnosed Livy with heart disease. Their prescription required bedrest in an isolated room at Wave Hill, insisting that family members, Sam included, have as little contact with Livy as possible during her convalescence. Daughter Clara set aside her singing career ambitions to care for her ailing mother, while long time housekeeper Katy Leary held down the fort.

With Livy now bedridden and unable to draft letters and tend to her routine functions, that December Twain recruited known acquaintance Isabel Van Kleek Lyon to take away some of the added burden for Katy Leary and his daughters, and serve primarily as Livy's personal secretary. Lyon had been the governess for some of Twain's friends, and the author had taken a liking to her moxie. Twain's timing of hiring Lyon proved to be fortuitous when, in December, daughter Jean, already diagnosed with Epilepsy, succumbed to pneumonia.

Ron Powers explains how, at the onset of 1903, "Sam's efforts to hide that bad news from Livy, increased tensions in the Riverdale household"[294] as Livy's condition deteriorated for the first six months of that year. From August through this time, Twain's only sanctioned means to interact with Livy was by writing notes affectionately slipped beneath the door, signed simply 'Y' for 'Youth,' Livy's pet name for Twain. Periodically he would break the doctor's orders. He had restricted Twain specifically fearing the ostentatiousness of his personality would cause further strain to her condition. With his access so limited, Twain curtailed his public appearances to spend more time near his beloved.

In May their home in Hartford was sold and the history of that storied venue began its series of varied incarnations before and after facing demolition in the late 1920s, its salvation from that fate in 1927, until it became declared as a National Historic Landmark in 1963 and remains today the restored shrine to those happiest of the Clemens' family years.

By June, with Livy feeling a little better, doctors granted permission for her to join the family at their summer retreat at Quarry Farm in Elmira. While there, Sam and Livy enjoyed long, sweet hours together, chatting about their earliest, romantic aspirations, relishing these precious times together. Livy yearned to return to Florence, Italy, to relive some of her fondest memories of their time there a decade before. Eager to please her, Twain made plans, and in October they set sail from New York. Traveling with them were Clara, Jean, Katy Leary, a nurse, and Isabel Lyon, who brought along her mother.

Quarry Farm, circa 1900. Courtesy The Center for Mark Twain Studies, Elmira, NY.

Their arrival at the Villa di Quarto proved disastrous from the onset, a far cry from the bucolic respite Livy had envisioned and Sam had sought to provide. According to Ron Powers, their landlady...

> "seemed spitefully interested in creating obstacles for her tenants: shutting off all water...terminating the telephone service, insisting that the gates be kept locked despite the problems this presented for Livy's doctors.... even the weather was inhospitable - a chilly, overcast winter soon set in, deepening the cheerless mood."[295]

The situation only worsened. In February of 1904, Livy's health began to deteriorate. From April on she had difficulty breathing, and on June 5th, she passed away.

Twain's own, tender account of the time leading up to Livy's death, as recounted by Charles Neider in his 1959 compilation of Twain's dictated autobiography, is as wonderfully composed as anything Twain had ever written, revealing much about his love. "I stood a minute in the door" Twain began,

> "bending inward and throwing kisses, she throwing kisses in response, and her face all bright with that new-found smile...Then...I did a thing which I have hardly done since we lost our incomparable Susy eight years ago, whose death made a wound in her mother's heart which never healed - I went to the piano and sang the old songs, the quaint negro hymns which no one cared for when I sang them, except Susy and her mother. When I sang them Susy always came and listened; when she died, my interest in them passed away...But now...it was if eight years had fallen from me...After a little...it was now getting time to go downstairs

and say good-night...Livy was sitting up in bed...I went around and bent over and looked into Livy's face, and I think I spoke to her...but she did not speak to me, and that seemed strange, I could not understand it. I kept looking at her and wondering - and never dreaming of what had happened! Then Clara said, "But is it true? Katy, is it true? It can't be true!" Katy burst into sobbings, and then for the first time I knew... Only five minutes before, she had been speaking. She had heard me and said to the nurse, "He is singing a good-night carol for me."...She was happy and speaking - and in that instant she was gone from this life."[296]

In Ron Powers' account, Mark Twain concluded with a comment that seemed to capture the flailing spirit that would color his own remaining years. Livy's death had sucked away something intrinsically essential to the character of the man America had come to love. "I am tired & old" Twain said. "I wish I were with Livy."[297]

In December of 1905, Albert Bigelow Paine, who would become responsible for perpetuating the conceptual Mark Twain well into the Twentieth Century, first met Twain during a 70th birthday celebration in the author's honor at Delmonico's. Restaurant in New York. In January of 1906, Paine was hired as Twain's biographer. For the next three years, Paine was with Twain almost daily, recording his dictations, and indulging in the situation for his own devoted satisfaction. The conception for the planning and building of Stormfield began that year when Paine persuaded Twain to invest in 248 acres of land in Redding. Paine had already acquired a considerable tract of his own on which he planned to build his retirement home, and wanted his dear Mr. Twain ever near.

In the same period, Isabel Lyon had assumed greater responsibility in the wake of Livy's passing, practically taking on the role of surrogate mother, and endeavoring, according to her version of the tale, to fill the large shoes of Livy in Twain's life. She fielded Twain's newest outpouring of manuscript when Twain was entering what some

Cover of Delmonico's dinner menu for Mark Twain's 70th birthday, 1905. Courtesy the New York Public Library Digital Collection.

refer to as his darker, Nihilist philosophical stage, trying to coax him back into his lovable storyteller mode, and offer feedback as had Livy for so many years. In the brilliant dissertation *Mark Twain, Isabel Lyon and the "Talking Cure,"* Twain scholar Jennifer L. Zaccara illustrates that the timing of Twain's interest in the then emerging new field of psychoanalysis was what had compelled him to initially explore the act of dictation as a new approach to writing an autobiography, and specifically use as a form of therapy. This was a marked contrast to the hand-writing he'd used his entire career until then.

"Inasmuch as the autobiographical dictations provided Twain with a form of therapy and a means of regenerating himself through confrontation with the past," Zaccara writes,

> "Isabel's listening ear helped to free Mark Twain from the "Valley of the Shadow" that permeated his life during Livy's illness and after her death. Talk [as in, dictation] was important to Mark Twain not only as a way of rehearsing and tuning his voice, but also as a method of self-construction and self-renewal. Isabel Lyon was a supportive, nonintrusive auditor who, like a therapist, would allow Mark Twain to tell the stories he needed to tell and wanted to hear."[298]

The implication of Lyon's 'Nonintrusive' patronization of Twain, contrasted sharply with Livy's open chiding and critique of Twain while simultaneously extracting and hailing the gold nestled within Twain's works. "Lyon could make her suggestions and express her undying enthusiasm and praise" Zaccara continued,

> "but she did not have the authority to correct manuscripts or alter authorial intentions. Mark Twain perceived Lyon's role in Florence and during the second wave of dictations in 1906 as that of a silent auditor, diligent scribe, and enthusiastic coach. Lyon's presence did not cause delays in Mark Twain's work or censor his ideas in any way. But in the interim period from 1906 to 1909, gradual transformations in Lyon's role took place, and these changes began to disrupt the flow of Mark Twain's discourse."[299]

With Albert Paine now taking on those transcription responsibilities, it proved to be a primary source of consternation for Lyon, despite the abundant list of additional duties she had already taken on. "Paine" Ron Powers explains "was waging an internal power struggle with the fiercely protective, and perhaps emotionally involved, Isabel Lyon for possession of Mark Twain's legacy."

Twain had come to rely on Lyon's precision manner of governing the household, and eventually signed over power of attorney to her and husband Ralph Ashcroft, Twain's business manager. This enabled Lyon to freely take care of all routine household expenses, which included control of dispensing allowances to daughters Clara and Jean.

The personal bitterness Twain endured from the loss of Livy and Suzy initiated a cloudy season of mourning prompting emotional removal from his environment. Everything was dumped into the hands of Isabel Lyon or daughter Clara, who had her fill of it and continued pursuit of her singing career and a courtship with Ossip Gabrilowitsch. By surrounding himself with acolytes and angelfish in those waning days, Twain was able to provide himself with some self-assuring succor.

In a letter to his dear friend William Dean Howells, Twain had indicated his desire for moving to Redding as a means "to escape Mark Twain." This is a powerful revelation which clearly suggests that by this point, Sam Clemens had begun to grow weary of the business risks, personal investment and celebrity trappings associated with the Mark Twain brand label. But perhaps more importantly, Sam Clemens had entered a new chapter of life fraught with a deeper, internal psychological trauma that had arisen specifically after the death of the strong-willed, feminist influence of Livy. This is among those areas of study that enthrall scholars in pursuit of a comprehensive understanding of the man.

In her book *Mark Twain in the Company of Women*, Laura Skandera-Trombley critiques the omissions from earlier biographies of Twain that fail to address what appears to be evidence of Twain's psychological dependency on the influence of women, a predisposition that may be rooted in his childhood. Skandera-Trombley paints a distinct picture of Twain that differs from the image of a fiercely independent masculine role model.

> "The new scholarship having to do with women" writes Skandera-Trombley "is directed toward the psychological difficulties Clemens suffered due in part to his sense of familial responsibility, and, as a by-product of that duty, the fragmentation of his personality."[300]

Citing Twain biographer Hamlin Hill, Skandera-Trombley explores this point in depth.

> "With Olivia's death, Hill asserts, the last pacifying influence on Clemens was removed. His moodiness proceeded to rage unchecked, and Clemens grew increasingly estranged from his two remaining daughters…Immediately after her mother's death, [daughter Jean's] epileptic seizures recurred, and her worsened condition culminated in a violent attack on Katy Leary…Clemens was unable to deal with the enormity of Jean's affliction and, inappropriately, thrust the responsibility on Isabel Lyon."[301]

Lyon's response to this newly designated authority was to remove Jean and have her committed to a sanatorium in December of 1906, where she would remain for the next three years. Taking such extreme measures to protect "the King," as she referred to Twain, serves as evidence of Lyon's willingness to fulfill that duty at all costs, even if it meant extricating the very people with whom Twain needed to surround him most, more than he knew himself.

Detailed accounts in letters and biographical notes reveal that Twain yearned nostalgically for the comfort of the family years in Hartford that he would never know again. His psychological trauma began with the irresponsibly caused death of son Langdon in infancy, followed by the heartbreak instilled by Susy's death. Livy's death, it seems, put Twain over the edge, and Jean's death would literally serve as the nail in his coffin.

This suffering must have been evident to all who were intimately acquainted with Twain. Lyon's removal of Jean was one attempt to isolate Twain. Albert Paine's suggestion to have a new home built in Redding to allow for a fresh start seems to have been an agreed effort to remove Twain from the environment associated with the source of pain. The overseeing of this latter effort, like "the problem" of Jean, was thrust into the hands of Isabel Lyon as well.

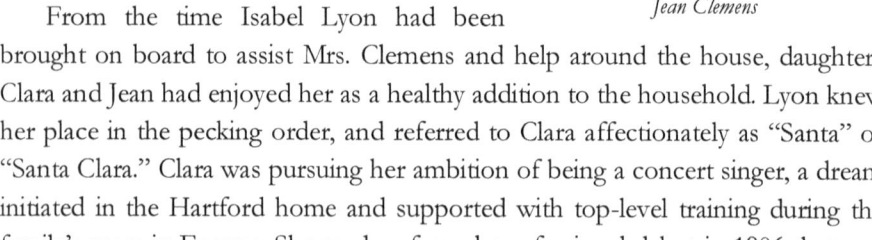

Jean Clemens

From the time Isabel Lyon had been brought on board to assist Mrs. Clemens and help around the house, daughters Clara and Jean had enjoyed her as a healthy addition to the household. Lyon knew her place in the pecking order, and referred to Clara affectionately as "Santa" or "Santa Clara." Clara was pursuing her ambition of being a concert singer, a dream initiated in the Hartford home and supported with top-level training during the family's years in Europe. She made a formal, professional debut in 1906 that was relatively successful, encouraging her to continue rehearsing and prepare for a more extensive performance tour in 1907.

Clara had issues from having grown up in the shadow of Twain's enormous celebrity and harbored some resentment for only being known as Mark Twain's daughter. She desperately wanted to break away, establish an independent identity, and secure recognition for her own accomplishments. This desire was further deepened following the dependency that had been thrust on her during her mother's illness. When Jean was diagnosed with epilepsy, as much as she loved her younger sister, Clara was overwhelmed. Clara's gradual withdrawal caused Jean to feel increasingly isolated. A relatively athletic free spirit, Jean enjoyed horseback riding and long walks with her German Shepherd that only understood commands in the German language. Fluent in three languages, Jean was an ardent reader, who was described by a family friend as being "in face and mind the replica of her father, who adored her and was fond of repeating good stories about her."

"William Dean Howells" explains biographer Michael Shelden,

"was struck by the close understanding between Twain and his youngest daughter, whom he alone knew in the singular force of her mind."302

Jean somberly remarked on the evolving separation between she and Clara.

"I am afraid we have grown apart. I know she cannot understand or sympathize with, my curious nature [a reference to her Epilepsy], and while my love for her has not diminished, I cannot help feeling that lack of sympathy in her."303

Because of Jean's condition and Clara's indifference, Lyon was required to spend a considerable amount of time with Jean, accompanying her on shopping excursions and such, and assisting her whenever a seizure came on. According to Michael Shelden, Lyon was not fond of this duty, found it completely overwhelming, and because of Jean's height and athletic build, Lyon feared her and was relieved when Twain succumbed to her argumentative insistence to have Jean committed to a sanitarium in Katonah, New York.

Jean accepted this opportunity as the frequency of her seizures increased, and this new facility in Katonah, opened only in 1904 with a trained medical staff, was touted as a progressive "country club" of sorts for wellness, consistent with the trend of the period initiated by the likes of Harvey Kellogg.

When I was driving around this hallowed region of Redding, fits and starts of information issued forth in my memory as I tried to recall how I knew certain facts. The story of Twain's years at Stormfield, albeit brief, is a loaded tale populated by a cast of intriguing characters and equally fascinating plot twists. It was months later when I awakened to a pleasant realization: All that I knew of these details came from one book I had purchased and read eight years ago. I looked around my house in the multiple places where I have books stashed away, and found it - the hardback first edition of Michael Shelden's *Mark Twain: Man in White; The Grand Adventure of His Final Years*.

As I leafed through my bibliographic treasure, I recalled having seen a televised interview with Michael Shelden when I lived and worked near Saint Louis, which coincided with the time of the book's release. That's what inspired my original yearning to visit Hannibal, and it was during my visit to Twain's boyhood home that I had purchased the book at the gift shop specifically because I knew nothing about the latter years of Twain's life, or anything beyond my limited concept of him. This was the source, the fountainhead of my neo-infatuation with Mark Twain, the catalyst that facilitated the opening of old, dusty memory synapses containing the recollection of my boyhood interactions with Dad about Twain. Michael Shelden, it would seem, is equally complicit for inspiring this book.

My hesitation for wanting to write too much about Stormfield is that there is just SO much detail. It's so complicated a story that, well, it took a good book by a scholar with an accessible writing style like Shelden's to explain it. And what is frighteningly eerie is when I noticed that I happen to be writing about some of these events that happened 109 years ago to the month! As I leafed through Shelden's book again after eight years, it occurred to me that, while the feuding between Clara and Lyon and Ralph and Paine and Twain had taken center stage, the real story of Stormfield was about Jean.

"In large measure" writes Shelden,

> "Twain's reason for building the house was to provide a country place where Jean would be able to live with him in comfort and safety. He made this clear not only to her, but to many others, including his friends and even to the New York Times."[304]

Twain was obsessed in a tender, fatherly manner for Jean's wellbeing. The building of a country retreat for her, just twenty miles from Katonah, eased his conscience and gave him hope of regaining some essence of that familial warmth they had known in Hartford.

"What he wanted Lyon to do" Shelden explains

> "was the same thing Livy had done long ago - build a bright, fanciful home where he could relax and entertain…During the many months of planning, he was content to leave the details to Lyon."[305]

His hired architect for the project was the son of his dearest friend, William Dean Howells. The combination of entrusting two loyal entities with the matter freed Twain to do his own thing.

Stormfield was indeed a dream home "with a tiled roof and a spacious loggia at one end," Shelden writes.

> "it was the kind of architecture that Twain and his daughters knew well from their past visits to Italy, especially during the eight months they had spent at the very large villa near Florence were Livy died."[306]

It is these details that start to unveil much about the psychological influence of Stormfield's construction. It is clearly evident that Twain wanted to transport himself back to the place and moment just prior to Livy's death, to recapture something lost, and somehow begin anew. Clara and Jean were important, comforting components of that, and it was up to Isabel Lyon to ensure that it all happened as planned. After moving into the new home, the initial experience was everything desired. But little by little, the emotional dismantling of Stormfield began.

Where Lyon had been generally accepted as a reliable secretary, governess, and social companion, evidence of an evolving, contentious rivalry between Clara, Jean and Lyon has been increasingly more available for scholarly investigation. Clara began to resent the authority her father instilled in Lyon as a surrogate replacement for her mother, while Lyon saw Clara as an interfering threat to her total control. Jean grew to find little merit of Lyon being around. "Father came" Jean had once written, "& we had a real visit this time without Miss Lyon & over an hour in length." Though Lyon tried to disguise it, Jean knew the secretary wasn't comfortable visiting Katonah and was often quick to find fault with her. "When Miss Lyon is about," she wrote, "I am always more painfully conscious of my ignorance and stupidities."

Lyon had overseen the entire process for the construction and interior design of Stormfield to an extent that would indicate an intent to build a home she hoped to inherit herself through marriage to Twain. Such inferences would surface in some of Lyon's later biographical notes not published until after Clara's death in 1962, and more overtly from Twain's own detailed account which was only published in 2010. Twain spent five of the final nine months of his life writing about Lyon, not wanting his scathing views released publicly until one-hundred years after he died.[307]

"Lyon's greatest period of control came when Stormfield was being built" writes Laura Skandera-Trombley.

> "At the time she was in charge of large sums of money and was also involved in deciding which personal family papers [Paine] would be allowed to view. Yet her power proved ephemeral, and, ultimately, Lyon's possessiveness of Clemens contributed to her downfall."[308]

As Twain's social secretary, Lyon began to determine who would and would not be permitted to visit or correspond with Twain. The whole scenario at Stormfield became increasingly weird, providing ample material for a good, Hitchcockian psycho thriller.

In Paine's original 1924 biography, a collaborative effort overseen by Clara,

Lyon's role, presence, and influence is completely omitted. In short, both wanted to remove the other. Paine had come to detest Lyon's intrusive control and interference, and plotted a plan of revenge. Clara Clemens, whom Lyon privately began to derisively refer to as 'Santissima,' took to delivering biting warnings to Lyon. Around the same time, the press began to inquire about the nature of the relationship between Lyon and Twain. When Twain was asked to travel to Oxford for receipt of his honorary degree, Clara advised Lyon not to travel with him due to the inquiring gossip and rumors that were beginning to circulate. Jean, as proud of this moment for her father as Livy would have been, was heartbroken that her condition prevented her from accompanying him.

Instead, Twain brought along Ralph Ashcroft, who was then just a business relation affiliated with a health food company in which Twain had invested heavily. Michael Shelden pointed out that the date on which Twain sailed for England was forty years to the day after the Quaker City voyage that had launched his career. Moreover, it was in Shelden's book where I read one of my favorite anecdotes about Twain during his stay in London following the Oxford ceremony. It is a short, quick reference that seems to embody everything about the man that I love in one neat little package. The sort of thing that made Twain a rock star decades ahead of his time.

> "One of Twain's daily habits caused a minor sensation at his hotel" Shelden recounts. "Each morning he went down to the [Brown Hotel] lobby dressed only in a bathrobe and slippers. He then strolled [outside and across the street to the Bath Club] and enjoyed a Turkish bath. Accompanying him at a discreet distance was Ralph Ashcroft…"[309]

Ashcroft, who was born in Liverpool and knew his way around London, was quite familiar with Edwardian era English etiquette. Yet, this was Mark Twain, whose very scoundrelous nature was being celebrated not as an American fault, but rather as an added attribute while Twain was embraced as a hero of the English-speaking world. Just as he had returned to America with an untouchable status, the trip to Oxford must have instilled an awareness within him that he had conquered the world.

"The proper ladies and gentlemen of Mayfair who caught a glimpse of Twain's bare legs as he walked out of the hotel were shocked" Shelden continued.

> "Some stared in disbelief, others laughed. Soon these daily outings were being reported in both British and American papers. The hotel manager was apologetic, explaining to the press that "a great man like Mark Twain must be allowed to do as he pleases.""[310]

The occasion of being invited and recognized by Oxford would mark one of the proudest moments of Twain's life, and one of the most reinvigorating chapters of his latter years.

It was while staying in England that an incident involving Clara and Isabel Lyon made the news, prompting an English reporter to ask Twain if he intended to marry Miss Lyon. Twain's reply was curt and to the point:

"I have not known, and shall never know, anyone who could fill the place of the wife I have lost. I shall not marry again."[311]

His return to the states bore witness to more adventures. With the home in Stormfield still under construction, Twain resumed residing at his townhome at 21 Fifth Avenue in New York. Clara had moved to her own apartment while Jean's health had improved considerably. After being permitted by her doctor to go home for a brief visit to attend a performance by Clara, Jean grew homesick and wrote very clearly of her strong desire to leave the sanitarium. Twain was torn, deferring to her doctor's guidance, but by Christmas of 1907, Jean's doctor gave her permission to leave Katonah for good. Her doctor wanted her to go to a half-way house, of sorts, to live with another patient, but the question arises, why wasn't she permitted to go home?

"The answer" Shelden explains

"is that Isabel Lyon had led [Jean's doctor, Peterson] to believe that neither she nor Twain were prepared to care for Jean at home…Writing in her journal…Lyon had declared decisively, "Jean must never live with her father again, because her affection might easily turn into a violent and insane hatred and she could slay, just by the sudden and terrible and ungovernable revulsion of feeling." Dreading the possibility of having to supervise Jean at home, Lyon had now convinced herself that the young woman…was homicidal…she was firmly set against Jean's return under any circumstances…by confiding her fear to Dr. Peterson, she was making it almost impossible for Jean to return…"[312]

Meanwhile, Lyon began to become increasingly manipulative of Twain as well, stringing him along for the responses she wanted. Albert Paine had lashed out at the woman for lingering a little too long following one his routine evenings of whiskey and billiards with Twain. Lyon had once had a romantic interest for Paine, but when it became evident that Paine had no similar corresponding interest, Lyon became indifferent towards him. Offended by Paine's outburst of anger, she exacted revenge by puppeteering Twain into believing that Paine was taking advantage of him and needed to control the biographer's access to manuscript portions. In his defense, Paine would eventually enlist the alliance of

Clara, and as an ultimate manifestation of revenge, in Paine's Mark Twain Company publication of the official biography in 1924, Lyon's role, presence, and influence would be completely omitted.

The home was completed and ready for occupation in June of 1908. Based on surviving photographs, documents and references, Stormfield seemed to have incorporated the best of all the most loved places the Clemens's had called home. It was Italianate in style yet retained elements of the home in Hartford, with an elevated setting and isolation reminiscent of Quarry Farm.

Press photo of Paine and Twain, circa 1909. Courtesy NY Public Library Digital Collection.

After the move into the new house in June of 1908, Lyon began to take added liberties that would come back to haunt her, and the setup of another situation seemed to be in the making. Twain had purchased and gave to Lyon an adjacent cottage on the property, with the intention of utilizing her services during the day with a place of her own to retire at night. Instead, Lyon set herself up in a guest room in the main house and let her mother live in the cottage. With control over Twain's checkbook, she started to pay related renovation expenses for the cottage without informing Twain, and would purchase items for herself when on shopping errands for the household, assuming they wouldn't be noticed.

The turning point of events unfolded after a burglary attempt in September. Two thieves had planned their entry by studying photos of the home's windows in a *New York Times* article celebrating the grand new home of Mark Twain. During the act after midnight, the pair made off with Livy's engraved silverware made by Tiffany and Company, but only after hauling the entire oak sideboard out of the home to a less conspicuous place down the hill in order to break open the locked drawers. They returned for a second go-round, but their kicking of a brass bowl awakened Isabel Lyon. Spotting the fleeing thieves from a window, Lyon's shouts awakened the entire household, and the local sheriff was contacted. The event made headlines, and Twain's response was to strike a pose for photographers while holding a pointed pistol, demonstrating what he would do if they came back again.

The thieves were caught and incarcerated for trial. On the morning of the arraignment, to everyone's surprise, Mark Twain arrived to confront them directly. "So" Twain began, "you're the two young men who called at my house last night and forgot to put your names in my guest-book?"[313] Michael Shelden explains:

> "Taken aback, they stared at him in silence. They had misjudged the old man. He was not a pushover…Then, as [one thief] recalled, Twain "turned upon me and delivered a scathing verbal castigation and lecture on morality, ending it by denouncing me as a 'disgrace to the human race.;'…After administering his tongue-lashing…his sense of humor returned. "Don't you see where you're drifting to?" [Twain] asked. "They'll send you from here down to Bridgeport jail, and the next thing you know, you'll be in the United States Senate. There's no other future left open to you.""[314]

The rest of the household didn't find it so funny. Clara, along with Katy Leary, as Twain explained to William Dean Howells, "never wants to sleep in the house again,"[315] and vacated at once to an apartment in New York. Following that, all the hired servants resigned. The burglary had disrupted the peaceful solitude for the country retreat that had heretofore been first named "Autobiography House," then to "Innocents at home." But seeing how the fear generated by the event had created an uphill battle to reclaim a feeling of home, and how the home's physical position "is set so high, that all the storms that come will beat upon it, there being no obstruction,"[316] as Twain had written in a letter to Jean - then in Berlin, Germany receiving treatment from a specialist - that the home was rechristened "Stormfield."

With Clara gone, Jean away, and a new team of servants hired, Isabel Lyon took an even greater measure of control than before. Now and then, Clara would return for a visit accompanied by Katy Leary. Lyon harbored resentment toward Clara for moving away, perceiving it as a selfish act of abandonment. According to Shelden, Clara assumed an attitude that she, not Lyon, was the mistress of the house. Lyon felt isolated, but found support in Ralph Ashcroft, who had also incurred Clara's wrath. Ashcroft had been living nearby in Redding on an embezzled dole provided secretly by Lyon, waiting for an opportunity to seize what he viewed as entitled compensation for the many years he'd assisted Twain for no pay.

"Now he saw a chance" Shelden explained,

> "to gain control over not just some of the author's wealth, but all of it - from the copyrights to Stormfield itself…Ashcroft prepared a breathtakingly comprehensive document allowing him the power to manage every penny of Clara's inheritance. The trick was to get Twain

to sign the document without giving him the chance to understand its significance…Ashcroft knew how imprudent and confused he could be in business matters…On November 14, Ashcroft took advantage of Twain's carelessness to get him to sign a document extending the power of attorney granted earlier to Isabel Lyon…The new arrangement included…every possible way that Twain's wealth could be used, and making sure that Ralph Ashcroft and Isabel Lyon possessed the authority to control all of it."[317]

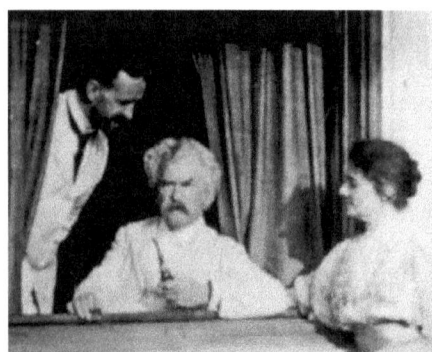

Ralph Ashcroft and Isabel Lyon, with Twain at Stormfield. Photos courtesy of Smithsonian Institute.

The arrangement was the cunning establishment of incorporating Mark Twain and his holdings, with Ashcroft as executor, into the entity known as The Mark Twain Company. "With stunning speed" Shelden explains,

"Ashcroft was able to turn the tables on Clara, leaving behind his humble position as the author's unofficial business manager to become an officer in a corporation in which he controlled the purse strings, and to which he could begin quietly transferring Twain's money and property… Lyon's mistake was to allow herself to be drawn into [Ashcroft's plans]. He couldn't have done much at Stormfield without her cooperation, and he knew it. So, he found her weak spot and exploited it…Because she was hungry for affection, it was easy for him to go from being a confidant to her lover. While he was busy winning Twain's trust, he was also seducing Isabel, and she fell completely under his spell."[318]

Twain was too preoccupied with his own designs of bringing life back to Stormfield in the wake of sensationalist accounts of the burglary to notice the depth of the real burglary occurring right beneath his nose. He dismissed the continued quarrels between Clara, Lyon, Ashcroft and Paine as incessant grumbling that he wanted no part of. In the midst of the tumult, Twain invited friends and guests for leisurely visits or overnight stays.

Among those who paid a call were Archibald Henderson - the biographer of George Bernard Shaw whom Twain had met while en route to Oxford; the photographer Alvin Coburn; the deaf-blind author, lecturer and activist Helen Keller, and the celebrated inventor Thomas Edison, who brought along a movie camera and filmed the only known motion picture footage of Mark Twain.

One very special visit brought about a reunion with the seventy-year-old Laura Hawkins Frazer of Hannibal, MO, Twain's childhood neighbor, sweetheart and the inspiration for Becky Thatcher in *The Adventures of Tom Sawyer*.

Twain with childhood friend Laura Hawkins Frazer, his inspiration for the Becky Thatcher character in The Adventures of Tom Sawyer. *Photo courtesy of Smithsonian Institute.*

"Mr. Clemens" Laura would later recall, "had that rare faculty of loyalty to his friends which made the lapse of fifty years merely an interim. It was as if the half century had rolled away and we were there looking on the boy and girl we had been."[319]

Another visitor, it was announced, would arrive soon as well. It was Jean, returning home after her lengthy treatment abroad. To again keep her away, Lyon arranged for her to stay at a boarding house on Long Island. Jean disliked the new lodgings immensely, which she relayed to Clara, who in turn appealed to Lyon about making a change. Lyon stood her ground, as did Clara's insistence, "and the ongoing feud between the two women became even worse" Shelden explains.

> "For the first time, Clara made a serious and sustained effort to find out why her sister wasn't being allowed to live at Stormfield...Lyon did her best to keep Clara in the dark...using illness as an excuse to avoid any more confrontations. She had a lot to hide and...Lyon...did the unthinkable - she deserted her King and left Stormfield."[320]

Lyon couldn't take the heat any longer and to get a break went to stay in Hartford. Jean, meanwhile, was moved to another home which she found more agreeable. Clara's suspicions grew, and while Lyon was away, Clara used the opportunity to reason with her father, urging him to have his finances audited, bypass Lyon's involvement in Jean's health arrangements, and have her brought home. Despite Twain's attempts to assuage the situation, Clara refused to back down. "Faced with Clara's implacable opposition" Shelden writes, "Lyon and

Ashcroft had raised the stakes to fight her together as husband and wife."[321]

In a 1950 interview, Lyon maintained that this move angered Twain.[322] Forty years after Twain's death, despite adding how she never loved Ashcroft, her words seem to suggest that she still wished to create the illusion that Twain and she had been romantically involved.

"Lyon and Ashcroft..." Skandera-Trombley explains,

> "were married on March 18, 1909 in New York City with Clemens in attendance. Shortly thereafter, Clemens gave Lyon this cryptic warning: "remember, whatever I do is because of a promise I have made to Clara" [citing the...interview of Jan. 5, 1950] "Evidently Clemens's promise meant destroying Lyon."[323]

Though the admittedly loveless marriage proposed as a chivalrous act on behalf of Ashcroft baffled Twain, he thought it a strange but wise move. Clara grew more convinced that they were up to something, and beleaguered her father with a variety of accusations, enlisting the aid of a lawyer and family friend Henry Rogers to support her claims. Despite Clara's protest, Twain still saw no reasonable explanation for not trusting them, and continued to comply with Ashcroft's requests for signatures on legal documents that were, essentially, slowly burying the man. He humored Clara by listening to her, but ultimately ignored it. "Stormfield was a home" Twain wrote to Clara, "it is a tavern now, & I am the landlord...Jesus, what a week!"[324]

Twain accepted an invitation from his old friend Henry Rogers to join him in Virginia. Ralph Ashcroft accompanied him. On his return, Twain paid Clara a solo visit in her New York apartment. Clara again brought up her distrust of the Ashcrofts, and was surprised that this time, her father didn't argue. He explained to his daughter that while in Virginia, Ashcroft had slung an evening's worth of accusations about Clara that left him suspicious. Having heard so much of Clara's argument for so long, he decided to first give Clara the benefit of the doubt and hear her side of the story. Clara was exonerated, and Twain's suspicions abruptly became quite real for the first time. Twain devised a coy strategy of his own, beginning with the announcement that Jean would be returning home. As expected, "the more Isabel protested, the more convinced Twain became that...she had been misleading him for years."[325]

Within days, Twain fired Isabel Lyon Ashcroft. The whole affair had been utterly wearying for him. His only focus and redeeming effort now, was to bring Jean home at long last. But the matter continued to linger.

News of Lyon's dismissal made the headlines, and it was through such press that Lyon learned of a lawsuit placed against her by Twain while on her honeymoon in London. When she hastily returned on the Cunard ship Carmania, reporters were waiting on the dock to hear her version of the story. In a *New York Times* article dated July 15, 1909, Lyon was quoted:

> "I believe the whole trouble is caused by his daughter. Miss Clemens is of the artistic temperament, but in this affair I believe that she has been wrongly advised into taking a step she would never have taken had she the right understanding of the case."

Lyon sought to save face, enacting revenge on Santissima by presenting a charmed and eloquent front. "I cannot think that Mr. Clemens is responsible for what has happened" the Times article continued...

> "He and I were the best of friends, and he has treated me almost as would a father. For seven years I was closely associated with him. I relieved him of every care I could, and he gave me the house, and later lent me the money with which to furnish it. This money, both understood, was to be paid back when I could do so. Knowing him as I do, I cannot believe that he attached the property... If Miss Clemens knows all about the case, and I notice that she says she is fully informed as to her father's affairs, she must know that every step in the restoration of the house was done not only with her father's knowledge but with his approval," continued Mrs. Ashcroft. "She does not exhibit a surprising knowledge of affairs when she presented her case, for in spite of what is said to the contrary, every cent that was expended for renovation I incurred a liability to pay...Mr. Clemens has notes amounting to nearly $1,000, which were signed by my husband when the first rough estimate was made of the cost of fitting up the place. Mr. Clemens made a written agreement with Mr. Ashcroft to accept his notes for the balance of the indebtedness outstanding upon the completion of repairs...The whole case will be settled, but the shame of it is that I should have been placed in an improper and false light."[326]

1909 press photo of Lyons on the Cunard Pier, as featured with the Times' interview. NY Public Library Digital Collection.

Mark Twain had a less dignified take on matters in his September, 1909 autobiographical dictation which he called a "shabby and pitiful tale." Dubbed *The Ashcroft-Lyon Manuscript* by scholars, his mildest reference of them was being "a pair of degraded & sufficiently clumsy sharpers."327 On the envelope of a letter Twain had received containing Ashcroft's most well-mannered, gentlemanly plea on behalf of Lyon in which he, too, cast blame on Clara, Twain had written:

> "Letter from a sniveling hypocrite - who is also a skunk, & a professional liar. It is precious, it has no mate in polecat literature - don't let it get lost. SLC."328

The Ashcroft-Lyon Manuscript was composed by Twain in the form of a letter to his dear friend William Dean Howells, stating in a forward at the onset that it wasn't intended to actually be mailed. Twain explained that writing for an intended audience had respective restrictions, and for this release, Twain wanted to withhold nothing, and elected to write it to Howells...

> "to give me freedom, utter freedom, limitless freedom, liberty to talk right out of my heart, without reserve. I could not talk like that to the general public, I could not strip myself naked before company.
>
> 'Howells is all refinement, by nature & training. Now & then, when I have been obliged to be robust & indelicate in my speech, Howells was an embarrassment to me; I found I could not say things to him which I could not say to a lady...He is as robust as I am myself."329

William Dean Howells in 1910. Courtesy NY Public Library Digital Collection.

As I began to read the opening sentence of the Ashcroft-Lyon Manuscript, which Twain had simply entitled "To the Unborn Reader," I had an eerie feeling that Twain was speaking directly to me. He begins "In your day, a hundred years hence, this Manuscript will have a distinct value."330

It did indeed have a distinct value. After spending over a year recapping and tracing and hunting down Twain related sources, places, and things, ordering great books and bookmarking fantastic websites and driving to various destinations, and then after editing and reediting, the one omission, the one missing link that I needed to call this manuscript finished was to address the Ashcroft-Lyon chapter in connection to Stormfield.

I began this sequence by saying that I had intended to leave out too much of a mention of Lyon, et al, just as Albert Paine had. But to talk about Twain's life in Stormfield, along with my experience of visiting it, it can't be overlooked. As Twain had written; "it will furnish an intimate inside view of our domestic life of to-day not to be found in naked & comprehensive detail outside of its pages."[331]

Unlike his own unsuccessful effort at Silver mining, I've panned through the Lyon Ashcroft Manuscript for only the most premium nuggets of pure Twain. Among them are heart wrenching references to Jean's plight, which shed a more tragic a light on her death that would follow only a few months after Twain had written this. So here, then, are presented some of Mark Twain's choice assessments of the players and events of Stormfield:

> "[Ashcroft] blandly puts himself on an equality with me, & insults me as freely & as frankly as if I were his fellow-bastard & born in the same sewer....And all the while—unsuspected by me, & by me alone—this pair of ~~sneak thieves~~ vermin were pillaging me & conspiring together to rid the house of Clara & of the suspicious servants, & make the pillaging a permanent industry! ...even the cleverest people can lose their heads & degenerate into idiots when they get scared ...She had never had any money; now she had my check-book, & was using it with a free & lavish & unwatched hand. Put a pauper in a motor-car, etc., etc., etc. She was on her way. It was Clara that punched her tyre [SIC]...And dear, dear, what a luxurious mendicant she was! She would get herself up in sensuous oriental silken flimseys of dainty dyes, ...Howells, it is like one old prostitute praising another's chastity...She even persuaded me not to read Jean's letters, but to let her read them & tell me such of their contents as I needed to know...I am aware, now, that in...nearly all these instances Miss Lyon was ~~lying~~ feeding me with falsehoods...
>
> [About Ashcroft] Isn't it interesting? And isn't it just like the-cheap villain in a seventh-rate play?...Ashcroft gives wings to his imagination, & lies freely, briskly, glibly...Things had happened—which revealed Ashcroft as a very very small liar, sneak & swindler ...We know that Miss Lyon had been stealing money from me for two years, & that Ashcroft had been living on it & was guiltily accessory to it. Without a doubt it was Ashcroft who turned Miss Lyon into a thief...Ashcroft had conceived the idea of robbing me on a comprehensive & exhaustive scale, & he did not feel safe to carry out his plan without first closing Miss Lyon's mouth...If I had died while my transfer-signature was still attached to the stocks, bonds, & Mark Twain Company stock...The

Ashcrofts…could have removed them & conveyed the ownership to themselves. It would have been difficult for a court to find an objection to it…The children would have been paupers. However, I didn't die…They were scared. They were in flight, to save Miss Lyon from arrest…I am aware now, just lately, by the testimony of a trustworthy witness, that in one of their indiscreet outbursts they said Jean wouldn't be allowed to ever cross my threshold again. I know Miss Lyon has a cruel nature & is unforgiving & unrelenting—but Ashcroft? Yes, I think he is just about her match in these particulars… …I tell you a body needs to be well fortified with witnesses when he deals with the Ashcroft firm of professional liars…They could not have been a colder pair if they had been on the ice a week…When it comes to lying, Ashcroft seems to have no reserves, no modesties…Ashcroft is even shabby enough to drag the dead out of the grave to give false evidence… To nearly everybody but me she was a transparent fraud…And look at Ashcroft! A sneaky little creature, with beady, furtive, treacherous little eyes, & all the ways of a lackey—obsequious, watchful, attentive, and looking as if he wanted to lick somebody's boots. I was never able to get to my room in time to take my clothes off unassisted…I despised him…moi?—I was hypnotised, & it never occurred to me."[332]

That's just a snippet. The full text of the Lyon Ashcroft Manuscript is an endless string of pages of similar comments. To give you an idea, in my first draft of this work, my attempt to boil down just a fragment of the choicest nuggets to feature here had produced more than three pages. It was difficult to edit it down to what is offered here, and I invite readers to further explore the full text in Volume 3 of Twain's *Autobiography*.

As I continued to drive around this storied place, my mind was then preoccupied with limited recollection of most of these sordid details. It was a shame, I thought, that this idyllic dream home became such a nightmare for the weathered but sensitive old Missouri boy who just yearned to heal from the throes of his life's successive series of heartbreaks. After all the above had transpired, after beginning a new day with Jean back at home with hope for a brighter tomorrow, Jean passed away. It proved to be the death knell for Mark Twain. His spirit evaporated, and his will succumbed. He had endured some of the worst situations a person of his stature possibly could, yet remained strong and determined throughout the ordeal. But when Jean passed, his heart resigned. His dictation about her death would be what he called 'The Closing Words of My Autobiography.'

"Why did I build this house, two years ago?" Twain wrote.

"To shelter this vast emptiness? How foolish I was. But I shall stay in it. The spirits of the dead hallow a house, for me…It is dearer to me to-night than ever it was before. Jean's spirit will make it beautiful for me always."[333]

I glanced now and then through sunlight-dappled clearings in the forested landscape, just wishing I could have even a glimpse of this hallowed ground. And yet, somehow, I didn't need to see it. Just sensing, feeling it, was enough. It was beautiful for me as well.

A valley of shadows - my roadside view of Stormfield

24

HEADIN' HOME

"What the hell do *YOU* want?"
Horace Greeley

I drove past some of the nearby properties that I thought might be associated with Twain. One, I thought, might have been the farm where Jean kept her horses and did her riding. Another plot, I suspected, may have been the site of The Lobster Pot, the home Twain bought and refurbished for Isabel Lyon. Curious about the location of Albert Bigelow Paine's home, I later learned it had been lost to fire decades ago.

After continuing blindly in the secluded, sylvan environs around what I presumed to have been Stormfield, I eventually found myself approaching a sign that read 'Mark Twain Library.' I pulled into the adjacent lot, parked, and stretched my legs while scouring the environs. So, here, now, was the Library funded by Twain's clever fundraising campaign. As I knew ahead of time, it was closed, but that didn't prevent me from exploring the wooded property along the parking lot edge, and taking time to photograph a selfie with the statue of Mark Twain that stood near the entrance.

While there a car pulled up, and a sweet, elderly woman, who had come to return some library books in the book drop, offered to take my photo for me. Delighted, I accepted the offer. She introduced herself as Ginny Coyne, and we chatted for a short bit. I told her why I was visiting, mentioned my stop at the cemetery, the drive past the presumed Jean's farm, and my stop in Wilton. She told me that Jean's farm was up for sale, and that if I was lucky, I might want to drive back to see if they were having an open house. I thanked her for her assistance, and said I might do that.

The historic marker outside the library was the only one I'd seen anywhere around Stormfield. Sad that I was unable to go inside, and with no place I knew of to enter the Stormfield property for a gander (I'd read there were bike trails open

The Mark Twain Library in West Redding, CT, founded largely with donations accumulated $1.00 at a time by Twain himself.

to the public), I noted that it was early in the day, just after 1:00 pm, and pondered my options. After entering a few choices into my Waze app, I decided to go a little further and pay another visit to the Twain house in Hartford. It had been five years since my last visit, and with a healthy measure of research on Twain now under my belt, I decided it would be worth a renewed perspective, and to investigate what might be involved with gaining access to their archives for further research.

While pulling out of the library lot, I again considered the evident remoteness of the region. I could fully grasp what it was that so attracted Albert Paine and other giants of New York industry to want to build their retreats here. I had remarked on this palpable serenity to Ginny Coyne. She voiced how residents recognized that and how it so markedly contrasted with what she termed "the bitter times" endured here by Mark Twain and family due to the tragedy of Jean, the ugliness of the Lyon-Ashcroft fiasco, and finally, Twain's own death. This bitterness set in paradise, I gleaned from Ginny, had remained at the heart of folklore among the locals 107 years hence.

As I neared Bethel, New York, the speed limit was 45 mph, yet it became instantly apparent that this was one of the few places I'd been in America where no one seemed to mind driving a little bit slower than the speed limit instead of the opposite. I think that's what must keep a place like this so precious, and, if anything, it feeds that ease of just chillin' out a little.

While crossing the Danbury town line, I tried to recall why it was this town that I had always associated with Connecticut, long before any awareness of Hartford, Redding, or elsewhere. There was something from my youth, a poem, a short story, something that I just couldn't put my finger on. I wondered if I was confusing it with "Banbury Cross," a nursery rhyme my mother used to sing to me when I was a toddler.

I pictured my Mom, with her youthful, cherubic smile and rosy complexion, her jet-black hair and matching Gary Larson type eyeglasses while holding my hands as I sat on her knee, slowly bouncing my torso up and down to mimic horseback riding, a memory brought to life when I then blindly rode over a pothole. I had not thought of those moments in more than fifty-five years. Maybe there was something to this area of Connecticut that Rod Serling had so delicately captured in *A Stop at Willoughby* that enables one to slow down, step back in time, and recall their youth. Maybe this was the Zeitgeist of Mark Twain still permeating the molecules of the air, stirred up in the dust. Maybe this same effect was precisely why he had elected to settle here, enabling him to again seek his boyhood as he had in Elmira.

As if that weren't cool enough, my GPS, by default, seemed to consciously guide me through smaller towns and backroads instead of primary highways, allowing me an added glimpse into the real Connecticut. I stopped at a gas station in a small suburb of Danbury to grab a cup of coffee. Of course, every cup of coffee from a gas station isn't necessarily a good cup of coffee, and I was not disappointed. Typically I cut my coffee with half decaf, but this place had no decaf. So, I took a tip borrowed from the artist Peter Max, with whom I've worked for the past ten years. During his visits to the gallery I manage, Peter would always ask for a little bit of coffee topped with mostly hot water, so that's what I did to make my burnt black bean water somewhat palatable.

My serene drive experience ended abruptly as my GPS guided me from small town antediluvian Connecticut onto I 84 heading toward Hartford. I was back in civilization and the Twenty-First Century. People were driving as crazy as always, rushing and swerving past me at breakneck speed, just as is expected in the Northeast corridor. I had learned my driving temperament when I worked as an art mover during my art school days from Bill Gannotta, a gifted painter who had won the Mayor's award for his exceptional oil depictions of blue-collar workers on the Philadelphia shipping docks along with sensitive depictions of sunlit Dogwood blossoms in his backyard.

To earn a living, Bill used his customized bread truck to move important, historic works for all the major museums on the East coast. With me along as his assistant, we transported everything from Renaissance masterworks to early Picassos to The Metropolitan in New York, The National Museum in Washington, the Philadelphia Museum of Art, and so on. Whenever crazy drivers like the ones I was now encountering would zip past and around us, honking their horns in anger, Bill would just calmly maintain his speed, laugh like a Thomas

Nast Santa Clause and chime "Me first! Me first!" mimicking their attitude, and continue to laugh with a hearty, belly-born chuckle.

Shortly ahead of me an accident stalled traffic for a considerable distance, setting back my original eta. By 2:38 I crossed the Hartford City line, and made my way to Sisson Avenue through the town's historic district lined with a variety of lovely Victorian homes that reignited that old timey feeling. I didn't recall seeing these on my trip here five years before, probably because I was paying too much attention to controlling the mammoth truck I had then been driving.

In short time, I found myself at the intersection of Farmington Avenue. As I made my way into the Twain house parking lot, I noted that it was more crowded this time, remembering that mine had previously been the only vehicle in the parking lot. Getting out of my car, I studied the adjacent ball field of the school on the neighboring property. I wondered if this had once been the farm portion of Nook Farm, the land on which the homes of Twain and his neighbors had been built, and if it had been one of the attracting features in his time.

With it being just after 3:00 pm, I was aware that I didn't have much time now. My primary interest on this visit was to concentrate on the artifacts in the Aetna Museum. I hadn't recalled much from before, and as I approached the Aetna, a sign requesting no photography explained why. From my previous visit I had no photos, on which I usually rely to jog my memory. Noting the small scale of the Aetna collection, I went back to the admission desk to ask about the duration of the guided house tour, and understood that if I went on the very next one that started in about ten minutes, I would still have ample time to check out the artifacts and end my day at the bookstore before leaving.

I opted to take the house tour, figuring that a recap of the information could be helpful in editing the earlier chapter details of my first visit. No sooner had I purchased my ticket when our guide arrived at the disembarking point for our journey through what Twain biographer Justin Kaplan described as "part steamboat, part medieval fortress and part cuckoo clock."334 Following the guide's obligatory overview, we proceeded up the long incline, across the upper level that spanned over the Hal Holbrook Hall and Aetna Museum entrance foyer, and out into the rear portion of the carriage house, where coachman Patrick McAleer and his family resided from 1874 until 1903, when the property was sold.

Before entering the home proper, we were reminded of the no photography rule. I asked our guide, Kaitlyn Oberndorfer, for permission to audio record her presentation with my phone app, to which she enthusiastically consented. Kaitlyn gave a very fine, well-articulated tour jam packed with an abundance of detail about every nuance of the home and its contents, while interlaced with anecdotes of the Clemens family, butler George Griffin, housekeeper Katy Leary, right down to the names Twain gave to the Clemens family cats, such as Jumbo and Satan. There were some added details Kaitlyn provided that I had overlooked or forgotten that proved helpful, and I was grateful to have the recorded audio for later reference.

After the tour ended around 4:20, I was left with an hour before the museum closed, and proceeded to the Aetna gallery. Knowing I couldn't take photos, on this visit I allowed my eyes to focus and consume the visual details of the artifacts on Twain's desk, the pile of transatlantic steamer trunks and luggage, and the massive, formidable Paige Compositor.

I then went to the gift shop and spent a considerable time debating over which book or books I might acquire. I had my heart set then on getting a copy of Twain's posthumous publication *Letters from the Earth*. I was disappointed and surprised that the museum shop didn't have one. I felt they should have everything, the whole Twain and nothing but the Twain. I wondered if the lack of this controversial work was indicative of the user-friendly marketing concept that was begun with Albert Paine and perpetuated by daughter Clara, or if it's not just in publication now.

I looked about at other titles by Shelley Fisher Fishkin, Laura Skandera Trombley, and others. I lustily fingered the mammoth volumes of the long-awaited Autobiography of Mark Twain, the completed set of volumes that Twain himself had requested not be published until 100 years after his death. This was the same autobiography that Twain had dictated to Albert Paine in a stream of consciousness style versus the traditional timeline approach, the editing of which was only completed less than ten years before and published on schedule as Twain directed in November of 2010. At $75.00 a pop per book, I forlornly set them aside, opting instead to drop a more comfortable twenty bucks for the paperback edition of Ron Powers' biography.

Alleged to have been Twain's favorite photo of himself, seated on the grounds of Stormfield.

Content with a new addition for my library, I walked back outside and took a long look back at the home on the hill above me. I had driven backward in time that day, from the funeral home in Wilton, to the dream-filled and troubled Stormfield, and back to here, the place where the seeds of Stormfield had been planted. A place where an author, his wife, and three lovely young daughters had enjoyed many happy family times together. What a robust life had this man, Mr. Twain. I was grateful to now have become an adventitious part of it.

As I headed home from Hartford that Sunday evening, I 84 was frightfully backed up with traffic. It took me quite a while to meander through this peril until I eventually ended up on the Saw Mill Parkway as the sun was setting. I noticed my gas gauge dipping half way below a quarter tank, and had hoped to stop at one of the easily accessible gas stations I had passed earlier while en route from White Plains. But this time, I wasn't seeing any. I monitored my GPS and its settings that show a gas station icon whenever one was near an exit.

While plentiful throughout most of my earlier drive, none had shown up in quite a distance, and I grew concerned as the gauge steadily inched closer to empty. I decided to take my chances and just get off at the next exit, figuring there surely had to be at least one gas station on the closer side. I pulled off into a somewhat rural, secluded residential area. I drove a half a mile down a road of homes before seeing a live person. A man ahead was standing by his SUV, with his wife and children getting in or out. I couldn't tell. I slowed down and rolled down my window.

As I drew closer, the man turned toward me, and I could tell he had grown frightened. Before I could speak, he was already waving his arm for me to continue going by, shaking his head "No," that I wasn't welcome. I was desperate.

"Hello!" I said cheerfully. "Can you tell me if there is a gas station near here?"

"No" he replied sharply. "No gas station."

I could tell from the brief interaction that he was foreign, and maybe only spoke partial English. I thanked him and drove on, only to find myself in a cul de sac. I turned around, drove back down the road past the same SUV and man who ignored me this time, and continued until I saw a roundabout ahead.

I wasn't sure where to go, so I sought a place where I could pull over and do a quick Google search. Slowing down, I made note of a clearing in the middle of the roundabout next to a tall, life-size bronze statue of a standing figure mounted on a pale granite pedestal. I pulled up next to the statue and put on my blinkers. Unsure of which road to take, I, unlike Robert Frost, had no intention of taking the road less traveled by, as such a decision could, being so low on gas, significantly make all the difference. I Googled "gas stations near me" on my phone. A few selections popped up, with one indicating that a station was about four miles away. Satisfied, I sighed with some relief.

I paused to take a few swigs of water and turned to examine the statue. Dusk was settling in deeply now, and the shaded base made the inscription difficult to read. I leaned closer. "Greeley" it read. Greeley? Horace "Go West, young man" Greeley? Where the hell was I, I wondered? A quick Google search informed me that I was in Chappaqua. Apparently, this is where Horace Greeley had settled on a farm, and from where he could easily commute to New York City for work at *The New York Tribune*.

A further search led me to information about some controversy surrounding this very statue. Sculpted by artist William Ordway Partridge for a sum of $30,000, it had been erected in 1914 following considerable debate about where it would be located. It was decided that the statue would be placed here, overlooking an esplanade that then led to the train station, which locals still find fitting since Greeley is regarded as the first commuter.[335] Discussion over its placement continues today, and talk of moving it again resurfaced in a 1994 *New York Times* article entitled *Greeley Statue has People Heading in All Directions*. In 1934, the construction of the Saw Mill Parkway cut right through the middle of the road to the train station, separating the statue from its intended, site-specific location.

Since then, as Times journalist Kate Stone Lombardi described, "For almost the last 60 years, Mr. Greeley's imposing image has overlooked an entrance into southbound traffic." For at least two of the suggested, alternate locations for the statue, one point of contention in the debate was whether it was desirable to have Mr. Greeley's backside face commuters approaching from the rear of the train parking lot, or have his backside face his own property. The town council must have feared it would become the butt of jokes, because, apparently, they decided to turn the other cheek and leave the statue seated where it was. Ironically, the statue of the man who sounded the clarion call for western expansion faces east.

The East facing Greeley statue at dusk in Chappaqua, NY that I parked beside in my hour of need.

It was a curious twist of fate to find myself situated beneath this statue. I was pondering strategies of where I could go to avoid running out of gas. Was Providence providing the answer by suggesting I go west? Who needs a GPS when you have Horace Greeley? It was an interesting coincidence, though. Hailed as perhaps the most formidable voice for the cause of western expansion in mid Nineteenth century America, Greeley had served as a congressman, once campaigned for President of the United States against Ulysses S. Grant, and with his most notable achievement as founder, editor, and journalist for *The New York Tribune*, he had also been one of Mark Twain's earliest employers. In a 1905 *Harper's Weekly* contribution, Twain described his first encounter of meeting Greeley in 1870. On a visit to New York, Twain decided to pay a visit to journalist friend John Hay who was then working for Greeley's Tribune. Of Greeley, Twain explained:

> "It was difficult to get an interview with him, for he was a busy man, he was irascible, & he had an aversion to strangers; but I not only had the good fortune to meet him, but also had the great privilege of hearing him talk. The Tribune was in its early home, at that time, & Hay was a lead-writer on its staff. I had an appointment with [Hay], & went there to look him up. I did not know my way, & entered Mr. Greeley's room by mistake. I recognized his back, & stood mute & rejoicing. After a little, he swung slowly around in his chair, with his head slightly tilted backward & the great moons of his spectacles glaring with intercepted light; after about a year—though it may have been less, perhaps—he arranged his firm mouth with care & said with virile interest— "Well? What the hell do you want!""[336]

Maybe the imaginative reason I had for the tolling of those church bells in Georgetown earlier in the day wasn't so preposterous after all. Maybe I was being goaded by the playful spirit of Mr. Twain. Indeed, the notion to "Go West" had been simmering in my mind for several weeks at that point. With a planned business trip to Las Vegas scheduled just two and a half months away, I had already been researching some excursion possibilities, such as taking an extended drive to revisit my old home in Santa Monica, take a longer trek to visit John Ford country in Monument Valley, or travel the distance required and see Mark Twain's journalist desk and chamber pot in Virginia City.

As it turned out, I didn't venture further than my hotel. Save for listening to some Irish music in a pub attached to the Mandalay Bay resort one night and a fun business retreat with clients at the home of artist Michael Godard the next, I really didn't have enough time to squeeze in a trip anywhere. Having experienced the carnival atmosphere of the Vegas Strip on prior business trips, I generally enjoyed the quiet of my Vegas hotel courtyard, and the unobstructed view from my room on the 36th floor overlooking McCarran airport and the McCullough Mountains. From that vantage, I distilled the essence of the pioneer days when

Orion Clemens had served as the first and only secretary of the Nevada Territory, and spent the majority of my spare time working on this book.

Samuel Clemens had ventured on and into a young United States still in the ongoing process of expanding, discovering, and defining itself. More than just seeking land on which to settle, westward bound pioneers exposed their vulnerability to any host of encounters - differing weather, hostile Native Americans, outlaws, bandits, narcissistically compelled, greedy politicians and lawmakers, and rascally ruffians of all sorts, - that would mold their naiveté and innocence into hardened, reinvented entities. As a journalist in the field, Sam Clemens witnessed this process of redefinition first hand. Emboldened enough to take a leap into the spirit of the times, Sam allowed himself to jump in head or feet first with all the unabashedness of skinny dipping in a Missouri creek from his youth.

It was in Nevada when the alias 'Mark Twain' first manifested. Sam Clemens knew a river boat pilot who used the name to sign reports earlier in his youth. After learning of the death of his old river compatriot, Clemens would recall:

> "At the time that the telegraph brought the news of his death…I was a fresh new journalist, and needed a nom de guerre; so I confiscated the ancient mariner's discarded one, and have done my best to make it remain what it was in his hands—a sign and symbol and warrant that whatever is found in its company may be gambled on as being the petrified truth…"

'Why not me?' he must have imagined. And so, in February of 1863, Sam Clemens first employed use of 'Mark Twain' as his signature was beneath a report submitted for publication in the Virginia City *Nevada Territorial Enterprise*.[337]

Though I was 420 miles from Virginia City and 150 years late, I was still able to detect the spirit of Sam Clemens and the lingering residue of pioneer era atmosphere from the ancient Nevada dust filtering through the hotel ventilation shaft. Or maybe that was just the scent of some marvelous dish being prepared by room service.

Nevertheless, the West was on my mind during my search for gas, and here was Mr. Greeley himself, hovering above me, his eyes gazing intently forward, though I wasn't sure at the time whether the monument was facing West or East. Here was an effigy of the man whose famed quote, though said by some to have been hijacked for his own editorial use from the original author while others claim it he hadn't said it at all, was printed as advice to wayward Civil War veterans searching for direction. Nonetheless, despite Greeley's denial of his authorship, the association of the phrase with him had inspired a young Sam Clemens to venture boldly into the untamed Nevada Territory and begin the adventure of a reinvented life and identity. The full quote, said to have been attributed to, or at least made popular thorough publication by, Greeley, reads: 'Go West, young man, go West and grow up with the country.'

Samuel Clemens did just that. Not only did he grow up with the country, he would become the nation's identifying character, the summation and definition of a forward-thinking, free-spirited American, the primary identifiable voice as America entered its second century. Meanwhile, like the continuously expanding republic in search of itself, Clemens kept yielding, bending, expanding and growing with new perceptions and modes of expression until his final day. This is the American character; uncertain, but courageously willing to venture into uncharted waters and discover itself anew, despite hardship and travail, failure and setback, obstacles and tribulations.

Of course, there is the perspective that, like Twain's first encounter, the statue of Horace Greeley may have been more aptly asking me "Well? What the hell do you want?" What did I want? At the moment, just a tank of gas, sir.

Or, I could posit the question philosophically and come up with an evening's worth of answers. Isn't "what do we want" the driving modus operandi of our genetic makeup? I'll stick with going west, which ominously seemed like good advice at the time. I bid farewell to the statue of Mr. Greeley, and headed west - to the gas station - before dipping south to head home.

Two Thomas Nast Illustrations of Horace Greeley and "the great moons of his spectacles." Left, from 1866, and right, created during the 1872 Presidential campaign between Greeley and Ulysses S. Grant. The one on the right was later published in the 1904 compilation Thomas Nast: His Period and His Pictures *authored by Twain biographer Albert Bigelow Paine.*

25

100 YEARS OF GRATITUDE: THE MARK TWAIN CENTENNIAL

> "No American youth has knowingly or willingly escaped the lessons, the philosophy and the spirit which beloved Mark Twain wove out of the true life of which he was a part …Mark Twain and his tales still live, though the years have passed and time has wrought its changes…"
>
> President Franklin Delano Roosevelt,
> September 4, 1936

At the onset of this book, I recapped the trend of cultural interest in Mark Twain in the subsequent two decades after his death. I had a hunch that I might find therein a more direct correlation of my father's interest in Twain if I plowed through some archives. I went year by year, through news and journal archives, until I found a significant, consistent sequence of events that painted a picture of a long forgotten and concentrated period of overt cultural Twain mania. Despite unearthing socially significant reasons for my Dad's Twain fandom, with all those remarkable details of Twain's life taken into account, intuitively I knew I had now found the impetus of Dad's interest. The 1930s, when Dad was coming of age, had been the defining Mark Twain decade which would leave an impress on our culture that persists to this day.

By 1930, talking pictures had become the competitive rage among Hollywood film studios, and it was Paramount's talkie production of *Tom Sawyer* with the silent era's popular child star Jackie Coogan that proved to be that year's top box office draw, netting $11 Million dollars despite the sting of the Great Depression on movie goer's pockets. *The New York Times* hailed the work as "an extraordinarily faithful conception of the book."[338] The film's success would fuel a watered-down adaptation of *The Adventures of Huckleberry Finn* released in August of 1931. The popular cast of Tom Sawyer was retained, yet, as stated by Wikipedia contributors, the film omitted -

> "the entire issue of whether or not Huck ought to turn the slave Jim back in after Jim escapes his owners, [and instead] it concentrated mostly on the comedy in the novel, and turned Jim into the typical comic "darkie" stereotype of that era."339

I found that point particularly interesting in light of Dick Gregory's voiced sentiments on what had made the book so important to Black identity during the reconstruction era. What followed instead, as earlier discussed in the rise of minstrelsy, was a cultural attempt to sweep the whole topic of equality under the rug. Films like this not only perpetuated Black stereotypes, but were an insult to Twain's moral intent.

In 1931, America's favorite child actor was Jackie Coogan, recast here after the success of his lead in 1930's Tom Sawyer.

Earlier that year, in April, Fox Films released a modernized adaptation of *A Connecticut Yankee* as a parody of the 1921 silent adaptation created primarily as a vehicle for the comedy of the enormously popular Will Rogers, the Oklahoman folk humorist, journalist, and top grossing performer in Hollywood at the time, who was by then the culturally accepted national successor-humorist to Mark Twain. Rogers was cast as Twain's protagonist Hank Morgan with the modified name of Hank Martin. Instead of portraying him as an inventive tinkerer and mechanic skilled in machinery and firearms manufacturing as characterized in the book, Hank's character in this production is a small-town radio station and retail radio shop proprietor, capitalizing on the popularity of the exciting new medium and technological wonder of the day.

By 1931 when cast in A Connecticut Yankee, Will Rogers had been enormously popular. Groomed as the second coming of Mark Twain, he was cast in other relatively thematic Hollywood contrivances such as 1934's Judge Priest set in post-reconstruction era Kentucky, and, naturally, filling in the shoes of Samuel Clemens as a Mississippi Riverboat pilot in 1935's Steamboat Round the Bend. Released a month after Rogers was tragically killed in a plane crash, "Steamboat," directed by John Ford, served double-duty as a tribute to Twain's inspired legacy then seeing a revival, and as an unintentional memorial to Will Rogers himself.

Shortly after the film begins, Martin is telephoned during a radio broadcast from his shop to deliver a replacement radio battery to the mysterious home of a top customer, a wealthy eccentric cast in the mold of Dr. Frankenstein, who is experimenting with capturing sound waves from the past with an impressive array of radio paraphernalia. When the customer succeeds in capturing the ancient voice of a town crier announcing King Arthur and voices his jubilation, the simpler minded and perturbed Rogers as everyman Hank replies: "I don't care about listenin' to King Arthur an' his Court. I'm going home to get *Amos 'n' Andy*." Referenced was the nation's then most popular radio program which debuted in 1926 as *Sam 'n' Henry*, a ten-minute vaudeville style parody of Black stereotypes played by two White men. Renamed *Amos and Andy* in 1928, the show aired nightly until 1943, remaining on radio as a weekly program until 1960, and further popularized with the advent of television in 1950 with the characters portrayed for the first time by Black actors.

A scene from 1931's A Connecticut Yankee, with silent screen star William Farnum, left, as the eccentric inventor; and center, Will Rogers, as radio pioneer and entrepreneur Hank Martin.

Twain's name was brought to the public's attention when early 1932 theater newsreels cited the January 25th christening of the S.S. Mark Twain by Mrs. PJ Hurley, wife of the US Secretary of War. It was the first of three such vessels commissioned by the Inland Waterways Corporation, a department of the US Army Corp of Engineers, to service the Missouri River, citing the paddlewheel as "one of the largest inland tug boats ever built" with "equipment modern to the last detail."340

1932 also saw the publication of *Mark Twain's America* by Pulitzer Prize winning historian, author, editor and essayist Bernard DeVoto. Recognizing the sanitized interpretations of Twain offered until then, DeVoto drafted this work as a compilation of overlooked aesthetic perspectives and important influences on Twain's oeuvre that he felt hadn't been addressed nor included in Albert Paine's authorized biography. With Paine having been publicly accepted as Twain's hand-appointed sacred cow until then, the work drew simultaneous praise and scorn. Moreover, DeVoto asserted that most of the extant scholarship at the time was woefully malnourished and misinformed. A review by *Scribner's Magazine* in November of that year explained:

> "Mr. DeVoto is profoundly furious...He takes America away from the clinicians...He thinks that various esteemed critics of Mark Twain have a pitiful notion of what he's about. He is through with the Thin-blooded Criticism of America. His book should start a much-needed and extensive row.
>
> It is as a patriot in the 1932 manner that Mr. DeVoto writes...It may very well be that a new period in the history of United States thought will have some sort of ascertainable beginning in "Mark Twain's America..." For plainly, America is looking at itself newly these days; and more effectively than anywhere else... Mr. DeVoto's book contains the makeup of its new attitude. And, therefore, Mr. DeVoto's scoldings... are not just scoldings: they are inevitable declarations of intellectual war..."341

Above, left: Historian Bernard DeVoto, and right, the 1935 Centenary edition of Mark Twain's America.

The arrival of DeVoto's book is the watershed moment, serving as the floodgate that exhumed Twain from the dead, stuffy arenas of exclusive academic study, dusted him off, and released him back fully into the expanded public fold. DeVoto's specific criticism of Paine ignited a polite barrage of literary barbs. "Access of any kind [to view Twain's papers entrusted to Paine and Clara] was consistently denied to all applicants" explain the editors of *The Mark Twain Encyclopedia*,

> "a policy that drew the fire of...DeVoto, who said in his preface...that because only Paine had seen the manuscripts, "they must some day be accounted for. Public benevolence constrains me to offer the Estate [of Mark Twain] my services"...Paine called this offer "the only humor in [the] entire book."342

The DeVoto-Paine feud served to draw public attention to bigger plans that were already in the works. In its edition of February 11, 1934, *The Evening Star* of Washington, D.C. announced:

"A monument will be erected in Washington next year to commemorate Mark Twain, it was learned yesterday, through the donations of admirers at home and abroad...The Fine Arts Commission has received a communication from the International Mark Twain Society stating it is the purpose to erect a suitable memorial to the author in 1935, which year will be celebrated through the United States as the Mark Twain Centennial. The honorary presidents of the society are Premier H. Benito Mussolini for Italy [Yes-*That* Mussolini!], Premier Ramsay H. MacDonald for Great Britain and Chief Justice Charles Evan Hughes for the United States. With this formidable backing, Cyril Clemens of Webster Gove, Mo., president of the society, informed the Fine Arts Commission it is proposed to erect the monument through an international subscription..."343

The international Mark Twain Centennial celebration of 1935 truly put Twain firmly on the map. To be immortalized on a proposed scale akin to monuments of Lincoln, Jefferson, and Washington was unprecedented. But to dedicate an entire year of celebrations to a humble man of letters (well, perhaps not so humble) was a nod of fanfare to the common man in Roosevelt's New Deal America. The celebration began without haste on January 15th when reporters from around the world converged on Hannibal, Missouri to cover the opening ceremonies broadcast on national radio.

Late 1930's postcard of the Mark Twain Memorial Lighthouse, Cardiff Hill, Hannibal.

Presented as a national event, a four-location radio hookup between Hannibal, Detroit, Washington, and New York was set up. Honorary chairperson President Franklin Roosevelt was scheduled to deliver a live address from the White House, where he would then flip a switch to illumine a commemorative lighthouse completed in 1934 for the occasion on Cardiff Hill, just yards below the boyhood home of Samuel Clemens.344 Twain's daughter Clara delivered remarks from her home in Detroit, where her husband, Ossip Gabrilowitsch, served as conductor of the Detroit Symphony, and NBC host Gene Rouse covered events live from Hannibal.

The Mark Twain Society hosted a series of planned centenary dinners across the country. Albert Paine released a new edition of his biography of Twain, and Hannibal announced its own commemorative plans for the entire year. In April, in what would mark her final visit to her father's boyhood home,[345] daughter Clara arrived by private railroad car to a hero's welcome accompanied by Walter Russell, a hailed New York sculptor whom Clara had commissioned to design the proposed national Mark Twain Memorial.

Featuring a seated Mark Twain flanked by characters from his books, the core of Russell's memorial design is embodied in the same maquette now displayed in the Mark Twain Home and Museum in Hartford, Connecticut, with copies in the Redding Library and the Mark Twain Museum in Hannibal. Plans for Russell's proposed memorial, sponsored by Clara, had been initiated several years prior.

To investigate further details, I contacted directors of the Twain museums in Hartford and Hannibal, but neither source could confirm when the plan was initiated. I was referred to the estate of Walter Russell, but no specific timeline information was found there either, and at that time I was unable to contact anyone directly. Henry Sweets, Executive Director of the Mark Twain Museum in Hannibal, informed me in an email that the life sized, completed figures of this sculpture were still sitting dormant somewhere in an undisclosed warehouse on the east coast.

In May of 1934, *The Hartford Times* published the first detailed article about it with photos of Russell's complete architectural model, announcing that the trustees of the Mark Twain Memorial Commission, along with Hartford city officials and directors of the chamber of commerce, had unveiled plans to raise a proposed $500,000 to realize the project as a national shrine to Mark Twain. It continued to explain that Hartford was in competition with Hannibal and Washington, DC for selection as the chosen site for what was described as "an ambitious design of a circular masonry structure 110 feet in diameter with a central shallow pool surrounded by tessellated pavement with characters and scenes from Mr. Clemens' books."[346]

The article further explained that a location in Central Park in New York had been proposed, while beer magnate Anheuser-Busch had already pledged the required $25,000 minimum amount to secure St. Louis as the considered choice, whereas the other cities understood the amount would be raised by subscription. A national fund drive was announced by Allen Zoll of the New York marketing firm Ingersoll, Collier, Zoll and Novell, who would oversee the effort under an organized Mark Twain Foundation, Incorporated. Anheuser-Busch promised an additional $100,000 to secure their bid unchallenged, but, Zoll explained, "the offer has been rejected, the sponsors holding that St. Louis has no reasonable claim as a site."[347]

The sponsors were daughter Clara, Walter Russell, an undefined Mr. Lewis, and prominent New York industrialist Thomas J. Watson, who had been the primary financier and patron to Russell. Russell, it was explained, had been chosen for his status as "ranked among the five leading sculptors if the country" then known best for his bust of Thomas Edison. At the meeting, Russell explained how the proposal had been given the green light by the overseers of Twain's estate, literary executor Albert Bigelow Paine, and long-time Twain publisher Harper and Brothers of New York.

At the time, Hartford seemed to have secured the emotional lead as the preferred potential site, bolstered in the meeting by a telegraphed endorsement from Clara, which read:

> "Am delighted to hear of the wonderful plan for making Hartford the memorial center, thus paying tribute to my father's memory in the most appropriate way and at the same time easing the burden of faithful Hartford friends."[348]

Zoll explained that his firm would oversee a direct mail campaign to secure the funds "in which the cost of the memorial will be raised by the contribution of small sums…directed by the Mark Twain Foundation…with Albert Bigelow Paine as president."[349] Mystery official Mr. Lewis, the article explained, "had been given assurance that [President Roosevelt] will probably attend the unveiling of the memorial" which they envisioned "can be cast and erected in time for the unveiling on the humorist's 100th birthday anniversary, November 30, 1935."[350]

But, these were the years when the Great Depression had exacted its toll on the discretionary spending of most Americans, who were more preoccupied with getting their next meal or keep a better roof over their heads than the dismal accommodations offered by Hooverville encampments. By reading between the lines of news articles of the time, it seems evident that the mail order donation campaign on which Hartford had relied to secure their selection as the memorial site just didn't pan out.

It also seemed that the gracious, telegraphed wire message from Clara failed to provide sufficient inspiration for the cause, which likely underscored her rationale for planning to visit Hannibal in person. On the day she arrived, the *Hannibal Courier-Post* of April 25th quoted her companion, Walter Russell, who explained:

> "I am especially pleased that the decision has been arrived at to erect this monument in the delightful town of Hannibal where I believe it will be of greater sentimental value than though placed in any other portion of the country…Mark Twain…wrote of the middlewest, and I believe it most appropriate that the monument should be placed in Hannibal…"[351]

The article also stated that the finished size of the memorial would be 300 feet in diameter as opposed to the earlier projected 110.

In March of 1935, Russell had been interviewed by the Courier-Post during his visit to Hannibal for the unveiling of a large bust of Twain commissioned by the Mark Twain Centennial Commission of Hannibal earlier that year, along with statues of Tom Sawyer and a reclining Huckleberry Finn. Despite the fanfare about the town of Hartford published the year before in *The Hartford Times*, historians at the Mark Twain Boyhood Home and Museum document that Russell had designed the memorial with Hannibal's Cardiff Hill in mind. He had visited Hannibal on numerous occasions that year, in which he

> "was frequently honored, spoke at meetings, and…was in Hannibal when final preparations were being made for the opening of the first Mark Twain museum in the Trust Building."352

The *Daily Banner* of Greencastle, Indiana detailed specific events across the nation that were planned throughout the year in its May 21st, 1935 issue:

> "Extensive plans are now underway for a nation-wide celebration this summer and fall commemorating the 100th anniversary of the birth of Mark Twain, America's foremost humorist. President Roosevelt is honorary chairman and Dr. Nicholas Murray Rutler of Columbia University, active chairman of the centennial committee. Schools throughout United States will observe the event Nov. 1 while Nov. 30 has been fixed as the date for memorial programs in most cities."353

On November 14th, *The New York Herald* announced that an exhibit of Russell's "working plaster model twenty-one feet in length, a design model seven feet in length, and twenty-two bronzes of individual characters and groups…[and] five busts of Mark Twain" were part of a planned Mark Twain Memorial to be erected in Hannibal at a scale of - now - "sixty feet long, with twenty-eight figures, all more than life size."354 The article goes on to explain about the national fund raising campaign, and that Nina Gabrilowitsch, Twain's granddaughter, will be present for the opening of the exhibition, and that endorsements for the memorial had already been represented in receipt of "over 200 letters from all over the world…[which included] Dr. Albert Einstein, Rockwell Kent, Eugene O'Neill, [and others]."355

It seems evident that the anticipated response to erection of the memorial was much less than expected. With the originally proposed completion and dedication planned for two weeks from this implied date, the exhibit can be viewed as an act of desperation.

366 · Thomas Curley

Press photo of the full-scale model of the proposed memorial as envisioned by Walter Russell, incorporating his maquette found in the photo at end of chapter three, with central reflecting pool and walkway. Published in the Hartford Times, May, 1934. Photo courtesy of Tracy Brindle, Beatrice Fox Auerbach Chief Curator, The Mark Twain House & Museum, Hartford, CT.

1934 news article depicting the completed maquette for the feature segment of the proposed Mark Twain memorial. Photo courtesy of Tracy Brindle, Beatrice Fox Auerbach Chief Curator, The Mark Twain House & Museum, Hartford, CT.

The Elephant on the Raft · 367

"MARK TWAIN WITH HUCKLEBERRY FINN" By WALTER RUSSELL

Above: Sculptor Walter Russell with his bust of Mark Twain.

Left: Photo of the completed centerpiece of the Twain Memorial. Many of these original sculptures had remained in storage for decades, and may now be viewed at The Russell Museum in Waynesboro, VA, that opened in 2019. Photo courtesy Library of Congress.

April, 1935, outside Twain's boyhood home in Hannibal, Missouri. Sculptor Walter Russell is 3rd from right, and Twain's granddaughter Nina is next to him on far right. My source claims Twain's daughter, Clara Clemens Gabrilowitsch, is pictured third from left holding bouquet of flowers, but was uncertain. Courtesy Hannibal Free Public Library, Hannibal, MO.

A grand affair was planned in Hannibal on October 25, 1935 for the christening of the Mark Twain Zephyr, a state-of-the-art, streamlined passenger train manufactured in Philadelphia by the Budd Corporation. Twain's granddaughter Nina Gabrilowitsch was on hand to break the champagne bottle. An eleven-city competition had been held prior to select three children to dress as Huckleberry Finn, Tom Sawyer, and Becky Thatcher for the event. The entire occasion was broadcast coast to coast on CBS radio as railroad officials, dignitaries and guests dined on catfish and apple pie.

However, the grandest celebration planned for that year was the gala held at New York's Waldorf Astoria Hotel on November 19th, 1935. Promoted as a major event, the program was highlighted by an international radio broadcast, with coverage "to Great Britain, to Mexico, South America, Philippines, West Indies, and Bermuda, as well as every city and town in the United States."[356]

A performance of Negro spiritual "songs of the Mississippi" by the Donald-Heywood Negro Chorus offered a reflective homage to Twain's birth in the Antebellum South, followed by a jazzier rendition of *Just keep on a smilin'* by the Dixie Nightingales, invoking the humorist's influence on the broader culture. Toastmaster William Lyon Phelps of Yale University voiced the dismay of all present that Twain's daughter Clara was not in attendance, then relaying remarks she had written for the event:

> "My dear friends, I wish I might be with you tonight on this great occasion. I should like to thank you in person for the wonderful things I know you'll say about my father. But I wonder if many of you appreciate the greatest of his qualities: the breadth and depth of his courage. Courage! Yes, that God-like gift which consumes the pitiful caution and selfish fears of the weak. Father was courageous in big events and small. He was never cautious, at little of his self-protective instincts either physical or moral. For example, his opinions of people or things were crystal clear, and spouted from his lips like cascades on a rainy day. No one's frowns or other fathoms of disapproval could stop the flow from his expressive tongue.
>
> My father never tip-toed in life. He strode into his entrance, hob-nailed boots on, and he kept them on right through the fray. In spite of a somewhat flashy temper, he was able to control himself in other ways. In fact, I should say that his temptations were mainly toward strength. Physical fights were not frequent in Mark Twain's line, and he even liked to call himself morally lazy and a shirker. Quite the opposite was true,

however. He met tribulations and tragedies with sturdy spirit. He labored also to eradicated fault, fully appreciating the measureless vitality of the will and majestic strength of the determined resolution. Even though he did not engage in physical combat he frequently went into moral ones. I sometimes wonder if he spleened the memory to all these years, might not be more as a spiritual patriot than a humorist. Patriotism is surely the dispensation of loving, courageous protection of our people against an intruding enemy. Since we are not obliged to leave the country to find enemies, but discover them well-nourished and active in every corner of our land, it behooves us to bring a powerful offensive against ourselves. This I consider the highest type of patriotism. I hope you will agree with me when I say that my father, Mark Twain, was in the spiritual sense, a true patriot."357

The broadcast was presented as the pinnacle climax of the year-long celebration. In attendance were friends of the author who had celebrated with him personally thirty years earlier at his 70th birthday party at Delmonico's Restaurant in 1905. Toastmaster Phelps read remarks sent by playwrights Eugene O'Neill and Luigi Pirandello, *Peter Pan* author Sir James M. Barrie, author Booth Tarkington and Twain biographer Albert Bigelow Paine, and perhaps his most devoted acolyte, Rudyard Kipling, serving that year as chairman of the Mark Twain Centennial Committee in England, who had written:

"I regard Mark Twain as the foremost recorder and revealer of the American spirit of his time…To my mind he was beyond question the largest man of his time, both in the direct outcome of his work, and more important still, if possible in his indirect indolence as a protecting force in an age of iron Philistinism. He never seemed to me to have said one tenth of what was in his mind in this direction. Even in the implications of Pudd'nhead Wilson. But it was there for later generations to take and use. They don't know their debt, of course. I would be quite surprised if they were told."358

When FCC broadcast regulations were introduced in the mid 1930s, 1935 saw a spike in the popularity of radio. To broadcast a radio program internationally at that time was akin to the first global satellite television broadcast of June 25, 1967, when an international audience of 350 million people watched the Beatles perform "All You Need is Love" live from Abbey Road Studios in London.359

1935 was a pivotal year in general in the United States as some of the most pronounced efforts of President Roosevelt's New Deal plan were put into action.

In April of that year, Congress passed the Emergency Relief Appropriation Act to fund Roosevelt's ambitious vision of ending the woes of the Great Depression in one fell swoop. Among the first projects for which funding was allocated was the renovation of Mark Twain's boyhood home in Hannibal. Included in Federally funded Art, Writing, Theater, and Music programs was the Radio Education Project, designed "to employ relief workers in organizing a radio production unit and experimenting with the use of radio for educational purposes."[360]

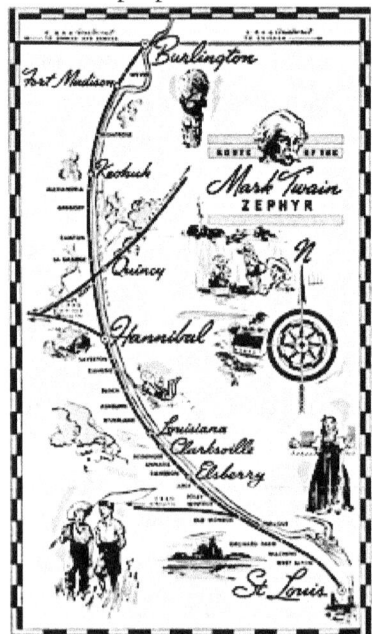

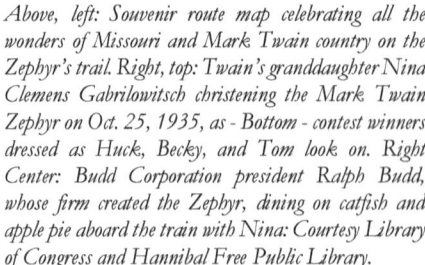

Above, left: Souvenir route map celebrating all the wonders of Missouri and Mark Twain country on the Zephyr's trail. Right, top: Twain's granddaughter Nina Clemens Gabrilowitsch christening the Mark Twain Zephyr on Oct. 25, 1935, as - Bottom - contest winners dressed as Huck, Becky, and Tom look on. Right Center: Budd Corporation president Ralph Budd, whose firm created the Zephyr, dining on catfish and apple pie aboard the train with Nina: Courtesy Library of Congress and Hannibal Free Public Library.

The Elephant on the Raft · 371

 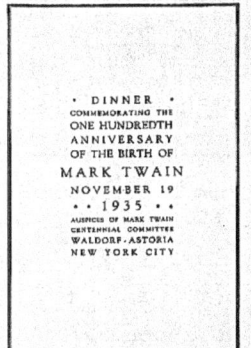 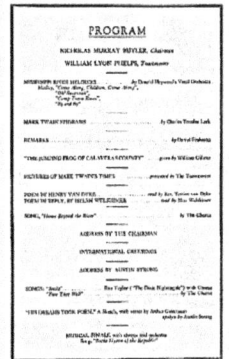

Program booklet with illustrated menu for The Twain Centennial Celebration at the Waldorf Astoria Hotel, NY, 1935. The cover featured an embossed recreation of a base relief sculpture commissioned especially for the event by the renowned sculptor John B. Flanagan. Courtesy NY Public Library Digital Archive.

 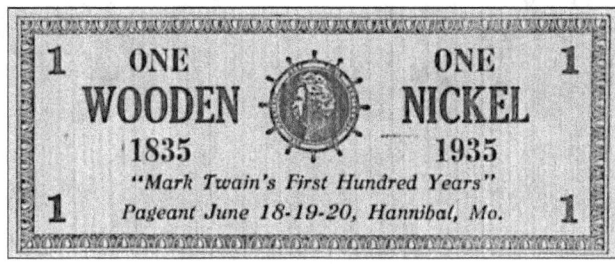

Just two examples of the many commemorative Centennial souvenirs to be had.

On that evening of November 19, 1935, radio had literally made Mark Twain a household name, effectively rebooting his legacy for a new generation. With the November 30th birthdate close at hand, and no memorial yet realized, the Centennial Commission of Hannibal invited Russell to attend their own grand banquet planned for that date to close out the year-long celebration. The gala's highlights included the unveiling of sixteen paintings depicting Twain's work by celebrated illustrator Norman Rockwell, and the cutting of an enormous birthday cake by the granddaughter of Laura Hawkins Frazer – Twain's boyhood neighbor and real-life model for the fictitious Becky Thatcher. Russell did not attend.

Instead, he RSVP'd his regrets by adding that he would send "a representative." On the day of the banquet, "a large crate was wheeled into the room. The program stopped and the crate was opened. It was a statue of Huck Finn..."361 sent as Russell's representative. Having arrived damaged, it was returned to Russell for repair, arriving again in Hannibal in January, 1936.

Clara Frazer, granddaughter of Twain childhood friend and Becky Thatcher model Laura Hawkins Frazer, lights 100 candles on a grand birthday cake during the official Mark Twain Centennial celebration in Hannibal, November 30, 1935. Photo courtesy Hannibal Free Public Library.

But the celebration didn't end there. Though Russell's grand memorial hadn't materialized due to lack of funding, the promise for President Roosevelt's delivery of a memorial speech honoring Mark Twain was fulfilled. On September 4, 1936, the President arrived in Hannibal for the dedication of the federally funded Mark Twain Memorial Bridge that connected Hannibal just north of the Centennial lighthouse area on Cardiff Hill with neighboring Pike County, Illinois, across the Mississippi. In his address delivered to an estimated crowd exceeding twenty-thousand, Roosevelt proclaimed:

> "It is with earnest American pride and with a glory in American tradition that I enjoy this happy privilege today, joining in this tribute to one who impressed himself upon the lives of youth everywhere in the last fourscore years and ten.
>
> To look out across the pleasant vista where the life of Mississippi River boyhood was captured and recorded for posterity and to have a part in its commemoration is a privilege I am happy to experience.
>
> No American youth has knowingly or willingly escaped the lessons, the philosophy and the spirit which beloved Mark Twain wove out of the true life of which he was a part along this majestic river. Abroad, too, this peaceful valley is known around the world as the cradle of the chronicles of buoyant boyhood.
>
> Mark Twain and his tales still live, though the years have passed and time has wrought its changes on the Mississippi. The little white town drowsing in the sunshine of the days of Huckleberry Finn and Tom Sawyer has become a metropolis of Northwestern Missouri.
>
> It was my privilege last year to have a part in the opening of the centennial commemoration of Mark Twain's birthplace. On that occasion from the White House I pressed a key which caused a light to shine from the tall tower on Cardiff Hill - the Mark Twain Memorial Lighthouse.
>
> The perpetuation of Mark Twain's name, birthplace and the haunts of his youth are very dear to me, especially because I myself, as a boy, had the happy privilege of shaking hands with him. That was a day I shall never forget. With every American who has ever been a boy, I thrill today at this great structure joining two great States in the commemoration of youth immortal...the older folks of the tiny river settlement in Hannibal had little thought that Sam Clemens, playing about the steamboat landing, would live through the ages."[362]

By then, for all intents and purpose, Roosevelt had become a national hero. When FDR spoke, the nation listened. By so hailing the name of Mark Twain, the spirit of the planned memorial had been realized.

374 · Thomas Curley

Above: Admission ticket to the 1936 Mark Twain Bridge dedication in Hannibal, Mo.
Below, left: FDR delivering the dedication speech featured herein.
Below, Center: Readying the scissors to...Below, right - cut the ribbon & open the bridge.

THE WHITE HOUSE
WASHINGTON

February 13, 1935

I shall have no fear for the future of America so long as we are able to laugh at ourselves as we learned to do with Mark Twain; he was the embodiment of that sense of humor without which the essential qualities of American human nature could not have been the ones insured. Mark Twain did not bring humor to the American people; he brought it out. He enabled us to focus our minds upon our extravagances, our shortcomings, and our idiosyncracies. Such humor as his is the solvent in which the ore of our Americanism becomes purified and is made to yield the metal of which American character has been built; and we were taught by him to know ourselves; to despise the shame, and to cherish the genuine, to retain a sense of proportion in work and at play. This has been his contribution to our national life, and for this we shall always owe a debt of gratitude to Mark Twain.

Left: Typed press statement hand-edited by President Franklin D. Roosevelt, likely composed for print or radio in conjunction with the many events and announcements occurring throughout the Mark Twain Centennial year of 1935. Here, FDR remarks on the importance of a sense of humor learned by Mark Twain as an indelible trait of the American character.

FDR also remarked that year that the term "New Deal" had been borrowed directly from the writings of Mark Twain. Courtesy of Lion Heart Autographs, NY.

26

HOLLYWOOD & THE MARK TWAIN DECADE

"If all the World Must Have Mark Twain, how can you, an American, do without him?"

Copy from a 1937 magazine ad for a
Commemorative volume of the works of Mark Twain

Mark Twain's name proved to be good business in those Depression years. While not hurting print media, it helped boost the radio audience resulting in added advertising dollars. The simple mention of his name at that time lifted morale and spirit, and Hollywood took note.

Desirous to cash in on the continuing Twain wave, in 1935 MGM purchased rights to *The Prince and The Pauper from* the Twain Estate for $100,000 with intentions of casting then popular child star Freddie Bartholomew in the dual role, but the project never materialized. Warner Brothers then acquired the rights and, wasting no time, planned a 1936 release of their adaptation.

The premier was delayed, which turned out to be a benefit for Warner Brothers. Following the death of England's King George V in December, the coronation of Prince Edward VIII was planned for May of 1937. Warner Brothers decided to release the film that same month, which coincidentally included scenes of a dying king and coronation of an heir. When the scandal of Edward's marriage to American divorcee Wallis Simpson forced him to abdicate and relinquish the throne to his brother Albert, the news was the biggest story of the year, serving to only further enhance mass public interest in all things royal. The timing for Warner Brothers couldn't have been better. At a time when New Deal policy was about reinventing a democratic America that served all from the poorest to the well-heeled, the Prince and the Pauper tale provided great medicine in an ailing era of American life.

With an enchanting musical score composed by the great Erich Korngold, the ambitious production featured a starring cast of Errol Flynn, Claude Raines,

Alan Hale, and Barton MacLane. But, as the opening credits rolled, before their luminous names ever appeared, a larger than life portrait of Mark Twain dominated the screen. Along with his name with credit as author, Twain was bestowed the unprecedented top billing, ahead of Flynn or Raines. Mark Twain was presented as the real star here. In countless literary based films that had hailed their authors in some way, I had never seen an author so honored.

There were elements of the film that seemed discordant with the actual book, and those factors soon became clear. Warner Brothers had taken the time-honored Hollywood liberty to rewrite the saga for the screen, manifesting the change largely by combining multiple characters into one. They preserved key scenarios from Twain's version and maintained the primary story line.

With a distinctly Americanized and hence bastardized script – far from the period linguistics so elegantly employed by Twain in the book - the Prince and the Pauper film depicted Tudor era English peasants struggling to live in a manner that wasn't too far removed from the reality of life separating the haves and have nots during the lean years of the Great Depression. That contrast is evident from the onset by depicting peasants in a miserable pub followed by the splendid grandeur of Windsor Castle.

Despite their hardship, the rag-enrobed, ten-year old pauper Tom Canty and his group of equally disheveled friends entertain themselves by engaging in imaginative play in a downtrodden section of London tagged Offal Court. An immediate reference to Tom's comprehension of Latin offers a passive suggestion about the merits of reading and education. This is further bolstered in a later scene, when less than ten minutes into the film and following a beating by his father, Tom Canty visits Father Andrew, desiring to read the cleric's books. The benevolent, compassionate priest encourages the request, by adding "The more you read the greater opportunity you'll have of escaping Offal Court when you grow up."

A political jab from Father Andrew in the same scene reinforces the Democratic policies that supplanted those of the prior Republican administration which had led to the Great Depression, and specifically the criticisms against Herbert Hoover. "I'm afraid nowadays the king knows very little about his subjects – except those in his court. It'll take great pains he shouldn't learn the plight of others less fortunate than themselves."

Seven minutes later, when young Prince Edward is introduced in the film, what is he doing? Reading. References to reading and learning are mentioned throughout Twain's book, such as when the Prince, in Pauper's clothes, after being bullied and besmirched by the orphans at Christ Church, declares:

"When I am king, they shall not have bread and shelter only, but also teachings out of books; for a full belly is little worth where the mind is starved, and the heart. I will keep this diligently in my remembrance, that this day's lesson be not lost upon me, and my people suffer thereby; for learning softeneth the heart and breedeth gentleness and charity."[363]

Or when poor Tom Canty, after switching clothes with the prince, is brought before King Henry VIII to assess what has been deemed the onset of his son's mental illness. After questioning the lad, Henry asserts:

"List ye all! This my son is mad; but it is not permanent. Over-study hath done this, and somewhat too much of confinement. Away with his books and teachers! See ye to it."[364]

In the film, while assembled courtesans gossip over reasons for the lad's fate, one suggests that his condition was due to "Too much study!" Again, when Tom tries in earnest to explain the truth to Claude Raines as the Earl of Hertford, Raines replies "I believe that you've been studying too hard, your majesty."

The film version offers Twain's story as a social morality tale aligned with the philosophy behind Roosevelt's New Deal, which was just beginning to sway aging industrial-age Americans who came of age before the advent of child labor laws toward embracing the advantages of public education. The character of Tom Canty's father embodies a stereotyped working-class ignorance and lack of appreciation for education, beating the boy to remind him of his duty to beg for pennies to earn his keep. In both book and film, Father Andrew the educator is murdered by Canty's father. Evocative of Huck Finn's brutal Pap, the character sheds light on Twain's revisited suggestion about child abuse in the working class. In short, the film is a mirror of Roosevelt's America.

Inclusion of these elements were not arbitrary. The Warner Bothers studio had been under direct pressure for having pushed the line of the newly adopted Hays Motion Picture Production Code which had begun to be enforced in 1934. The studio had been master of numerous films which glamorized criminal life and ennobled gangsters and underworld characters in films like *White Heat* and *Little Caesar*. Their enormous popularity was viewed as a corrupting influence on America's youth. The Hays Code guidelines prohibited productions that might contribute to "lowering the moral standards" of audiences – and children in particular, requiring the studios to instead focus on creating films that depicted "correct standards of life" which promoted traditional values – better known as 'family values' in our era. The standards were defined by the Code's overseers – the Jesuit priest Father Daniel Lord and Catholic layman Martin Quigley.

Warner Brothers was also struggling financially at the time and couldn't afford the challenge. Yielding to the Code, it was around 1935 when Warner turned to focusing on historic biopics and classic literature. Their adaptation of the swashbuckling adventure *Captain Blood* with Errol Flynn netted the studio a $1.4 Million box office return in December of 1935 with rave reviews. Audiences clamored for more. What project could be more suitable to Code requirements and shareholder's pockets than a mix of Errol Flynn and Mark Twain? The storyline, of working class versus privileged class, was right up Warner Brother's traditional alley of creating films for the common man. Warner's hot collared fear of the Hays Code also explains why the film adaptation of Prince and the Pauper included a heart-filled, emotional scene of Billy Mauch as Prince Edward reciting the entirety of the Our Father, a scene not included in Twain's book.

In book and film, The Prince and the Pauper had also addressed the topic of slavery. Warner Brothers didn't shy away from inclusion of the topic in an era when addressing civil rights issues in America was gaining ascent in public discussion. It simultaneously addressed early rumors of slave labor then coming out of Nazi Germany. In the Robber's Roost tavern scene two thirds of the way in, a farmer explains how his mother had been burned as a witch, resulting in his branding and sale into slavery. "An English slave!" the farmer attests. "The most contemptuous title any Englishman can bear!" The imprisoned Edward, now King after the death of his father, overhears the testimony, prompting him to decree a law ending the practice of slavery at once. The ridicule to which Edward is then subjected is curiously - and probably consciously - similar to the scorn endured by Jesus when he is mocked during his trial and crucifixion, and, might also be Twain's nod to the scorn endured by "infernal abolitionist" leaders.

Twain's historical references to a slave tradition in England and related cruel manner of punishment surely had cast a caustic and time-sensitive light on the similarly barbaric American treatment of slaves, and the justice for freed slaves then playing out during reconstruction. Twain had written: "The King sought out the farmer who had been branded and sold as a slave....and put him in the way of a comfortable livelihood."[365] This is clearly a commentary on ratification of the 13th, 14th, and 15th Amendments to the US Constitution. Twain had also inserted veiled references with pro-feminist leaning in an era when women had yet attained the right to vote in the United States. In the book's concluding chapter, Twain had written: "the wife and brother would not testify against him – and the former would not have been allowed to, even if she had wanted to."[366]

After watching the 1937 film and then reading *The Prince and the Pauper* for the first time in 40 or more years, it was quite difficult to see anyone other than Errol Flynn as Miles Hendon. Though Flynn hadn't been Jack Warner's first choice for the role, it was easy to see why Warner succumbed to Flynn's inflated salary request due to their success with Captain Blood a year prior.

The Prince and the Pauper is certainly one of Twain's finest compositions. It is, quite simply, a marvelously drafted work of modern literature. His prose therein lilts and dances as lyrics with poetic tenderness. Designated as a story for children, it is clearly much more a work written for reading adults of Twain's era. The book is used to cleverly inject his criticism of the body politic, of imperialist policy and unjust law.

Twain's cunning use of Elizabethan era English is at once evocative of Chaucer and Shakespeare, clearly revealing Samuel Clemens as a man of letters so richly deserving of the honor he would receive at Oxford twenty-six years after. It could be argued that it was likely *The Prince and The Pauper* that so engaged a young Rudyard Kipling – sixteen years of age when the book was published - to Twain's literary magic, though Kipling himself once stated that he wished he had authored Tom Sawyer more than any other work in literature. The film may have contributed to the softening of the British Government's prevailing notions of empire, opening the door for their exit from colonial governance of India after 80 years. Twain had jabbed the ribs of colonial imperialism when the book was released by playfully desecrating the royal seal through use as a nutcracker. By utilizing the focus of this plot element, Warner Brothers extended the poke just a few months after the coronation of King George of England had been a highlight of international news. This uniquely American slant was further embodied when, just two years later, President Roosevelt served hot dogs to King George and Queen Mary during their stay at Hyde Park.

The film was a sensational hit. Released in 275 U.S. cities on the same weekend, the film grossed $1.7M at the box office and received rave reviews. *The New York Times* claimed

> "here is a costume picture that is infinitely superior in every way to the average photo drama...the atmosphere of the whole picture is sustained with a considerable degree of realism..."[367]

The noteworthy acting skills of twins Billy and Bobby Mauch are evident from the onset. Their excellent employment of interactive timing, subtle facial gestures and demonstrated ability to hold their own caught the attention of critics. The New York Times continued:

> "Bobby and Billy justify their twinship completely, not merely by investing the Twain legend of mistaken royal identity with a pleasing degree of credibility, but by playing their roles with such straightforwardness and naturalness that the picture becomes one of the most likable entertainments of the year ..."[368]

Left: Theater poster for 1937's The Prince and the Pauper. Reprinted with permission by Time Warner. Right: Film goers thronged in line for hours to see the film, as reported here in the May 5, 1937 issue of Film Daily.

Above, left: Bill Mauch as the pauperized prince clearly upstages Errol Flynn as Miles Hendon in this scene when commanding him not to sit while he eats. Above, right: Promotional still of Errol Flynn with Bob and Bill Mauch, a winning combination for audiences in 1937.

The Mauch brothers made such an impression that on May 3rd 1937, their photo was selected to adorn the coveted cover of *Time* Magazine, holding their own with other newsworthy figures featured on Time's cover that year, which included Leon Trotsky, Clyde Beatty, Virginia Wolfe, Paul Muni, President Roosevelt, Ernest Hemingway, Joseph Stalin, and Walt Disney.

Time declared them "two amiable young actors from Peoria, ILL, who, among Hollywood's currently swollen quota of remarkable children, are perhaps the most remarkable," topped by "more extraordinary than Shirley Temple" who, at that time, had been one of the leading box office draws in the world. The feature article offered a biographical glimpse of their home life as mischievous, unspoiled "pugilists, speculators, sportsmen, collectors and litterateurs" with their professional assets being "energy, lack of precocity and a wholesome distaste for showing off, which prevents them from trying to steal scenes like most of their contemporaries."³⁶⁹ The combination of the Mauch's appealing All-American boyhood characteristics and impressive acting chops all wrapped up in a package stamped with the Mark Twain brand secured their place as perhaps the most influential role models for American youth that year.

To be a Catholic youth in 1937 America meant adherence to strict guidelines for Church approved entertainment. The Catholic News Service reviewed all films, which were categorized as approved, objectional, or condemned. Approved with a Class A, Section 1 rating was the equivalent of G or PG today, Objectional meant an R rating and recitation of three Hail Marys for penance, and Condemned meant you would go straight to Hell for even considering it. This held true even in my home as a kid, when referring to *The Catholic Standard and Times* film section made the final decision if we were permitted to see one film or another. Warner's 1937 *Prince and the Pauper* had made the Catholic Church's National Legion of Decency approval list in April³⁷⁰ of that year, certainly enabling my grandparents to give the green light to Dad and his siblings.

Above: The Mauch Twins, Bill & Bob, holding their own on the cover of Time Magazine for 1937's The Prince and The Pauper.

1937 Catholic News Service Legion of Decency newsletter with Class A blessing of approval for Warner Brothers The Prince and the Pauper. Courtesy of The Catholic News Archive & Catholic Research Resources Alliance.

In April of 1937, Twain's name made the news again when biographer and literary executor Albert Bigelow Paine passed away. Harper and Brothers – Twain's longtime publisher – persuaded daughter Clara and executors of Twain's estate to permit one-time rival Bernard DeVoto access to Twain's papers which resulted in DeVoto's appointment as "literary editor" in 1938, a position he would hold until 1946.

A full-page newspaper ad in November, 1937 offers evidence that the business end of Mark Twain was netting a few bucks, but perhaps not all that it was cracked up to be. Moreover, with New Deal policies influencing the perceptions of economic class, Harpers may have thought DeVoto could sell a few books. The ad offered the opportunity to acquire an entire library of Mark Twain volumes "Almost given away by the Mark Twain Commemoration Committee."371 Moreover, the ad seems to indicate the public response to the proposed national memorial. "Two years ago" a segment explained,

> "at centennial ceremonies all over the world, Mark Twain societies paid tribute to America's greatest author. At that time, in every civilized country, memorial exercises were conducted...and literally hundreds of statues were unveiled in his honor...Also at that time something that means much more to the happiness of your family took place...A few far-sighted men conceived the idea of creating – NOT ONE Mark Twain monument – but thousands of them...NOT cold monuments of stone and bronze – but living monuments that would create happiness, that could be brought right into hundreds of thousands of American homes – into your own home – the one place where Mark Twain himself wanted be remembered."372

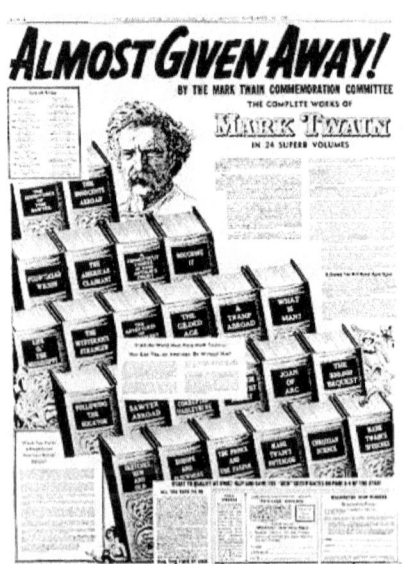

Cashing in on the decade long Twain Goldrush: The 1937 magazine ad for the entire Twain book collection criticizing the Twain memorial plans of 1934-35.

Of course, the ad went on to explain that the alternate "Glorious monuments" was the 24-volume set of books being offered "Practically for the asking" for Fifty-nine cents a copy, "almost as a gift." It also suggested that acquisition of this literary monument was a courageous act of patriotism.

"If all the World Must Have Mark Twain, How can you, an American, do without him?...In Australia, China, Japan – throughout

Europe – in the farthest corners of the earth - If the Spanish people, the Russian, the Chinese, the French must have him – why should you, an American, do without him?"

And, to answer the question, one final volley was offered that seemed to subscribe to the populist viewpoint of Bernard DeVoto:

"Until now you were compelled to because complete sets of Mark Twain's works are so precious and so costly, so rigidly copyrighted throughout and so closely held that only a few wealthy families could afford them. Now, however, you need no longer be without Mark Twain..."373

Hollywood, too, made sure the public wasn't without Mark Twain by carrying the standard forward when David O. Selznick jumped onto the Twain chuckwagon with 1938's ambitious technicolor release of *The Adventures of Tom Sawyer*, featuring Walter Brennan as Muff Potter and, following the success trail used by Warner Brothers with their casting of the unknown Mauch twins for the Prince and the Pauper roles, cast in the lead of Tom was then unknown Tommy Kelly, selected after a nationwide search and a claimed audition of 25,000 boys for the part.

Above, left and right: Hollywood banked on a massive success with 1938's big-budget production of The Adventures of Tom Sawyer. *Right: Tom Kelly and Jackie Moran as Tom and Huck, dead cat in a bag in tow, in a graveyard at midnight.*

Cast as Huck Finn was Jackie Moran, a newcomer to Hollywood who received rave reviews for his role, opening the door for a steady string of parts for the next 7 years, with his most popular casting as Olympiad Buster Crabbe's sidekick, Buddy, in the twelve-episode Flash Gordon matinee series.

As the fourth film adaptation of Sawyer and the first in Technicolor, Selznick's production received primarily positive reviews yet failed to net a profit. Technicolor films were still somewhat rare in that era, offering a magic experience to audiences. The Selznick adaptation succeeded, in my view, with a combination of bringing mid-19th Century Missouri to life, and the casting of unknown Tom Kelly, the son of a Bronx Fireman. Kelly seemed to uncannily capture the boyhood appearance of Sam Clemens himself from photographs I'd seen, while manifesting a real-life match to artist True Williams' illustrative interpretations right off the pages of the 1876 book.

The Sawyer film would have certainly brought Dad back to the innocent shenanigans of his boyhood. Twain had, after all, encapsulated youth in Sawyer, which Selznick and director Norman Taurog faithfully captured so vividly. It also didn't hurt, for Dad and his friends, that a lad of Irish descent – just like them - had been cast in the lead. The part where Tom and Joe Harper play hooky and run away to enact pirate adventures with Huck on the shores of the Mississippi would have translated well to Dad and his friends. Their neighborhood, Schuylkill, was to Philadelphia what Hannibal was to Missouri, and could essentially be considered Philly's own Hannibal due to its adjacency to the river. As mentioned earlier, Dad told stories of playing out scenes very much like those portrayed in 1938's Tom Sawyer, like swinging from a rope into the Schuylkill River to swim, etc. Dad would have been in 8th grade and 13 years old when this film came out, so even those scenes of Tom's innocent flirtations with romance were right in line with Dad's then burgeoning adolescence.

On top of that, the Catholic News Service proudly released word of Tommy Kelly's assignment to the role with such headlines as "Catholic Boy Chosen for Picture Role," as found in the June 10, 1937 edition of *The Catholic Transcript* of Hartford, Connecticut.[374] The Catholic News Service had issued the full press release three days prior, which included this added info: "Tommy...is fond of basketball, football, baseball and boxing. Like his parents, he was born in this country. His ancestors came from Counties Mayo and Galway, Ireland. In recent years of the depression...the family had at times been on relief."[375]

Nuff said. Tom Kelly was a hero to Depression-lean, Irish-American Catholic boys of my dad's era. Like 1937's Prince and the Pauper, the National Legion of Decency gave Selznick's Tom Sawyer the coveted Class A rating, placing it on the top of their list.[376]

Catholic Boy Chosen For Picture Role

(N. C. W. C. News Service.)
Los Angeles, June 10.—Tommy Kelly, 12-year-old student of St. Raymond's Parochial School, The Bronx, New York, has been selected to enact the role of Tom Sawyer, typical American boy immortalized by Mark Twain, in motion pictures. Tommy was selected from among 25,000 boys from all sections of the country considered for the part over a period of nine months.
Totally inexperienced when selected by David O. Selznick, he has been under instruction for three months at the Culver City studios of Selznick International Pictures. He was one of hundreds who received screen tests.

Left: Press clipping from The Catholic Transcript, June 10, 1937, hailing young Tommy Kelly for his selection to portray Tom Sawyer in David O Selznick's 1938 release.

Right: Press announcement of The National Legion of Decency's Class A rating for the film, Feb. 24, 1938.

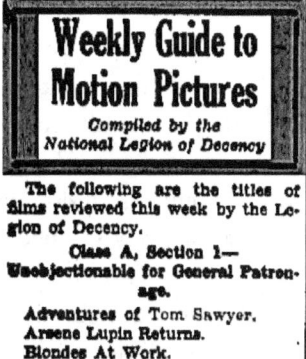

Weekly Guide to Motion Pictures

Compiled by the
National Legion of Decency

The following are the titles of films reviewed this week by the Legion of Decency.
Class A, Section 1—
Unobjectionable for General Patronage.
Adventures of Tom Sawyer.
Arsene Lupin Returns.
Blondes At Work.
Border Wolves.
Bringing Up Baby.

While researching I learned that it was this 1938 adaptation on which the 1973 Johnny Whitaker musical version had been based. Having read that after the passing of 47 years, I finally understood some aspect of the appeal that 1973 version had for my dad, and why he was so passionate about the tickets I'd won. While given the stamp of family entertainment approval in 1973 by the Catholic News Service and praising the transformation of Twain's tale into a musical, the reviewer wasn't as kind to this version of the film:

> "Mark Twain's boyhood world, if it ever really existed, has now been distanced into romantic legend. As an Irish Catholic kid in New York City, I never quite believed in Hannibal, Mo., steamboats, barefoot fishin', and the world of Huck Finn, Becky Thatcher, Aunt Polly, et al. The sentimental ideal of the mischievous all-boy who is good at heart didn't square with my experience, and since most Americans now have urban roots, it probably no longer fits theirs, either."[377]

The review continued to decry some aspects of the film while praising others, including a comparison of 1931's Jackie Coogan and 1938's Tommy Kelly versions, and remarking how the film preserves "a myth of the innocence of the virgin American heartland, as a memory of how it at least ought to have been."[378]

I understood what the reviewer was saying, but I didn't agree. Just as Twain had written "My mother never used large words but she had a natural gift for making small ones do effective work," the simple response among my friends had been to just say it was corny. As for the reasoning behind his review, there wasn't much difference between growing up New York or Philly so it really didn't justifiably hold water. At least to me. As an urban Irish Catholic boy of the 1970's myself who also didn't have the Hannibal experience, I think the reviewer missed the whole point of both the film and Mark Twain's original muse.

Riding the coattails of Selznick's Sawyer, a 1938 Saturday matinee serial version of *Tom Sawyer, Detective*, with a young Donald O'Connor cast as Huckleberry Finn, also kept the kids enrolled in the Twain hoopla that year. Capitalizing on the PR it provided amid a decade's worth of Mark Twain themed events, and because the bigger budget Sawyer film produced less than anticipated box office returns, MGM pulled out the big guns by casting Mickey Rooney, the world's latest top box-office draw, as the lead in a spirited 1939 adaptation of *The Adventures of Huckleberry Finn*. Critics railed. Among other oversights, the topic of slavery was glossed over despite its key relevance to Twain's book, and Tom Sawyer is written out of the script entirely. The New York Times claimed the film featured "more Mickey than Huckleberry"[379] and was generally panned as "cinematic hokum," having failed to capture the humor and spirit of Twain's original work. The effort rendered Hollywood a bit gun shy and Twain's material was shelved for a while, effectively steering the Mark Twain decade to its close.

The final note was sounded when, on September 11, 1939, over 1.5 million acres of rural land in the Southern Missouri Ozark Mountain region was established as the Mark Twain National Forest through proclamation by President Roosevelt.[380] Plans for this designation began as early as 1935 when administrative sites within the area were constructed by the Civilian Conservation Corps as part of the Emergency Work Program.[381]

All-American boy wonder/actor Mickey Rooney cast as America's favorite fictional son in 1939.

With a decade of fanfare around the name, inevitably one question remained in the mind of young audiences: Who exactly is Mark Twain? An answer was already in the works, but not quite yet to be.

In the July 13th, 1940 edition of the Hollywood trade publication *Boxoffice* an announcement listed just below two new Disney releases entitled *Fantasia* and *Bambi*, scheduled for theater distribution in 1940 and '41, was news of a planned production by Clara Clemens Gabrilowitsch called *The Good Life*. It simply states that the Producers Corp of America had added it to their production schedule, and "will follow "Kingdom Come," starring John Charles Thomas…No release has been set."382 Whether this was a short, a documentary or full-length feature isn't clear. I could find no additional information, but having become aware of Clara's affinity for Mary Baker Eddy's Christian Science and her suggestion to Hal Holbrook that he act in a biopic of Jesus, one might deduce it was a religious themed film.

Clara's production, however, never seemed to pan out. In his scathing essay *I Am Your Loving Daughter, Clara Clemens*, author Thomas Larson offers some revelation about what was going on behind the scenes that may have interfered:

> "Clara had grown distrustful of Charles Lark and her uncle Jervis Langdon [Jr], who were running the Mark Twain estate. By the late 1930s Clara felt neither man was providing her enough income [her husband, Ossip, had passed away in 1936] nor upholding her father's public image. Too much personal was coming out about him, and, by extension, her. Lark thought Clara was greedy. He wrote a friend that she felt slighted about movie deals in Hollywood that proceeded without her negotiating royalties and censoring intimacies. Lark wanted scholars and film makers to have access to Clemens's papers, including every letter, but she refused. Clara got wind of Lark's dissatisfaction with her and complained volubly. In 1943, Lark and Langdon resigned, and Clara asked the court to appoint as trustees Manufacturers Hanover Bank of New York and a lawyer, Thomas Chamberlain, who would do her bidding. Clara chose Chamberlain, in part, because he knew nothing about her father."383

As the decade came to a close, Warner Brothers would hold the torch aloft, not with another adaptation of a Mark Twain classic, but instead with a biography of the man himself. According to Frank Miller of *Turner Classic Movies*, producer Jesse Laske had lobbied Warner Brothers persistently for over a year to back him on creating *The Adventures of Mark Twain*. It was only after securing the blessings of Twain's daughter Clara and her hand-picked recommendation of Fredric March to portray her father that Laske was able to get the ball rolling. March agreed to take on the role, and proceeded to painstakingly research Twain's life. The film wasn't completed until 1942, but was then put on the shelf due to America's entry into WWII. It took Fredric March himself to persuade Warner Brothers to release the film for the patriotic purpose of entertaining deployed servicemen in March of 1944, followed by a theatrical release two months afterward.384

Based on Thomas Larson's article, it would seem that Mark Twain had become a bit of hot potato due to the infighting between Clara, Lark, and Langdon, which may have played a role in all of the publicized red tape referenced above. The Twain biopic's eventual release coincided with the dust settling following Lark and Langdon's resignation and replacement.

As WWII and its aftermath occupied the nation's focus, Mark Twain wouldn't be represented on screen again until 1949, when Paramount cast mega star Bing Crosby as Hank Martin in a technicolor, musical rendition of *A Connecticut Yankee in King Arthur's Court*. With a supporting cast led by William Bendix, the film proved to be an immensely popular hit with wide critical praise. Curiously, though, reviewer John McCarten of *The New Yorker* harkened back to the Twain decade that was, when he claimed that the film "lacked the wit of the 1931 Will Rogers version."[385]

In the decades that followed, assorted adaptations of Mark Twain's books would continue to be presented in film and television, with Twain himself making an appearance as characters scripted in TV shows like Bonanza, which featured him as his pioneer reporter self of the Nevada Territorial Enterprise in Virginia City – a neighboring town near the Cartwright family's fictional Ponderosa[386,] and even as daughter Clara and biographer Paine's idealized man in white on board the Starship Enterprise in Star Trek: The Next Generation. All these incarnations would serve to keep Mark Twain in the collective, popular conscience for subsequent generations, but never quite to the extent his memory enjoyed on the focused, international scale of the Mark Twain decade of the 1930s.

All the events of this decade-long celebration of Twain had certainly played a key part in that influence. With all the public fanfare about Mark Twain through these years in every media outlet, my dad had literally come of age in the Mark Twain decade. I was confident that Dad's recollection of his exposure to it and the emotional impress it left upon him was recalled by viewing many of these period films in his later years, and primarily it narrowed down to three key films: *The Prince and The Pauper, The Adventures of Tom Sawyer, and The Adventures of Mark Twain*.

I found it fascinating to consider what Dad and his young friends in Schuylkill may have thought of certain elements of 1937's Prince and the Pauper. The scene when Edward is forced by his kidnappers to steal from a guest at the Running Fox Inn was evocative of Philadelphia's notorious Schuylkill Rangers gang who were known for doing the same sort of thing. In neighborhoods like Dad's, everyone would have known who the Rangers were, yet old clannish codes of the Irish still in practice would protect their identities from outsiders.

The residents of Twain's Offal Court weren't that different from the rough and tumble Schuylkillites of Philadelphia. There are some fun injections throughout the film that reflect Twain's wit, such as when the Inn's guest announces "I've been murdered! They Killed me!" while joining the others in pursuit of the invaders. The scene also provided Errol Flynn with a chance to celebrate his success in Warner Brother's popular 1936 hit The Charge of the Light Brigade. After being accused as "the one with the musket," Flynn replies "Oh no, sir. I was the one that led the cavalry charge. Don't you remember?" The theft scene is also evocative of Twain's real-life scenario when his home at Stormfield was burgled by local Hooligans.

For a young Catholic boy of my Dad's neighborhood, the scene of Billy Mauch's sensitive recitation of The Lord's Prayer won accolades while setting a better example to youth in a desperate economic era. The film's sets also mimicked Philadelphia's fringe neighborhoods at that time. Schuylkill was a working-class hovel compared to the swell estates along Philadelphia's Main Line. Plus, the contrasting scenario of haves and have nots was very real to working class Philadelphians. For Dad and his friends, that scenario was closer to home, based on his stories of seeing classic limousines routinely coming and going along swellegant Delancey Street – Philadelphia's inner-city millionaire's row – while walking to his boyhood school located just a few blocks away.

After recently watching 1938's Tom Sawyer, I now see that for which Dad was reaching back when we saw the 1973 version together. Dad was then in the midst of a mid-life crisis, suffering from high blood pressure and recovering from a nervous breakdown. My brother Jack recently expressed his belief that Dad suffered from an undiagnosed case of post-traumatic stress disorder. It quickly became evident that Dad had experienced all the classic symptoms, borne from his service in WWII. None of us had ever conceived this in earlier years.

Once I found the details of the withheld release of The Adventures of Mark Twain until 1944 for entertaining deployed servicemen during WWII, it became crystal clear: Dad most certainly saw this film while serving his time aboard the USS Ticonderoga, and the turning point scenes of river pilot Sam Clemens boldly navigating a dangerous stretch of water was suitably tailored for Naval entertainment. Amidst the camaraderie of his fellow sailors, the film would have been a cause for bonding, a topic of conversation, an opportunity to share mutual Twain inspired tales of youthful hooliganism, and create a bond among his brother veterans that would last a lifetime.

By the time my brothers and I came along, Dad was able to revisit these moments of his youth, enabling him to transmit to his boys a positive influence and mold our character in our own troubled time, just as it had molded him. It was a conscious and inspired fatherly decision, and it was one that worked, I think, quite well.

In the years that followed, there would be other films and special moments with Dad that would color our time together in his remaining years. Yet, oddly, none would have such an impact as that one film about Mark Twain. How one life that touched so many would reach across time, and, because of a moment of Dad's astuteness in his youth, take root in me and sprout fifty years hence. It's curious, that, while Dad has been gone over thirty years, I still find him teaching me even now.

2007 magazine ad with details about the Mark Twain statue created for unveiling during the premier of The Adventures of Mark Twain *in 1944.*

27

A LOST EULOGY

"The reporters said there were tears in my eyes. True – but they were for me, not him. He had suffered no loss."

Mark Twain,
The Death of Jean

As the summer of 2017 drew to an end, Labor Day weekend was upon us, and the cool weather of the Fall season was beginning to tip its hat to announce its arrival. With my excursions to Elmira, Redding, and Hartford behind me, my mind was engaged with assembling all the information and discoveries I'd acquired. I kept running into road blocks that seemed to stall me until I found some researched bit of information to move it along. Sometimes, that information appeared involuntarily out of thin air.

"Where did this Mark Twain book come from?" my wife asked. "Did you order this on Amazon?" She was referring to the 1924 copy of *The American Claimant* I had purchased at Elmira College.

"No. I got that on my trip to Elmira, at the Twain exhibit."

"Did you forget about all those Twain books that I got for you last year?"

I had. My wife had picked up a collection of six vintage Mark Twain books at an estate sale some time last year and given them to me as a 2016 Christmas gift. I asked where they were.

"I put them in the living room cabinet."

I entered the living room and crouched to see the books again, pulling them from the cabinet. All published by Harper and Brothers, the collection included a copy of *Mark Twain's Notebook* from 1935, *Europe and Elsewhere* and *Mark Twain's Speeches* both from 1923, and a copy of *A Tramp Abroad* from 1921. There was also was a copy of *Pudd'nhead Wilson* from 1935, which I had finished reading via an online download just two nights before. One other, bearing the same, ivory toned cover with a relief-stamped profile of Mark Twain as the 1924 copy of *The American Claimant* from The American Artists Edition series I had picked up in Elmira, was a copy of his philosophical tome *What is Man?* with a copyright from 1917.

"What does Mark Twain have to do with India?" my wife asked. She was referring to another manuscript, a novel set in India, that I'd been working on for five years at that point.

"This is a different project" I replied, explaining how the Twain story had begun with the intention of being a relatively short blog post that had continued to grow into something else. That something being what you've just read.

It was sort of ominous to me, in that moment, that my wife should mention the presence of these books. Just the night before, I had desired to read more of Twain's direct thinking and commentary on assorted topics, and had planned in the coming week to seek out copies of Twain's correspondence, notes, and more philosophically oriented works. It was a weird and cosmic kismet to have been reminded just then that I already had some of those sources currently extant in my own library.

Through trial and tribulation young Sam Clemens expanded his ethical consciousness through the associations he made on the journeys. In his essay *The Turning Point of My Life,* Twain points out how just basic Circumstance - with a capital C - had provided all the fodder he ever needed for the entirety of his literary accomplishments.

"A person may PLAN as much as he wants to" he had written,
> "but nothing of consequence is likely to come of it until the magician CIRCUMSTANCE steps in and takes the matter off his hands."[387]

Curiously, how he began his adventure may not be as what one might expect. He clarifies that as well in this essay, when he states:
> "I can say with truth that the reason I am in the literary profession is because I had the measles when I was twelve years old."[388]

Twain described this sickness in youth as the turning point of his life. It was also when his father passed away, and when young Sam Clemens left school and became a printer's apprentice at the behest of his mother. That trade took him, by the time he was seventeen-years-old, to New York, and then to my own home town of Philadelphia where he worked as a top speed, crackerjack manual page compositor for *The Philadelphia Inquirer*. This was just the stepping off point that ultimately led to his journey of self-discovery as he seized opportunities across the United States, in South America, Hawaii, and back "for ten years, under the guidance and dictatorship of Circumstance..."[389] Then his meeting with Livy broadened and gelled his democratic viewpoint, serving to accentuate a treasure trove of stories he could tell for the remainder of his days.

As I leafed through the volumes, pausing to read a complete essay here and there, my eyes were peeled for any pertinent material that would be relative to topics discussed herein. In the midst of this, I experienced a jarring, spiritual chill when I turned the page to find the original, excerpted publication of Twain's closing Autobiographical segment *The Death of Jean*.

I had not previously read this, and was not aware that it had been published so loosely and liberally intermingled with his other writings. As I read along, I found myself quite aligned with the poetic release of shock that Clemens recorded over the span of Christmas Eve and Day, 1909. This wasn't Mark Twain writing. This was the writing of a loving father about a beloved daughter. This was the family man who was buried in the grave in Elmira, alongside the marked stone graves of the expanded Clemens and Langdon families. That is what struck me most about visiting Mark Twain's grave, that he was just one of many. That I was brought there to have Twain himself remove himself from the pedestal on which I had placed him five decades earlier. Bearing witness to the mortality of Samuel Clemens as just another gravestone in a family plot awakened me to the revelation that Mark Twain, too, was a fictional thing. And like any great fictional character, it's Mark Twain that lives on.

I entertained myself with the notion that I had been invited to his grave by the spirit of Sam Clemens, a regular guy with an extraordinary gift and talent. In this regard, the visit became precisely like visiting the Samadhi shrine of a Hindu or Sufi saint. My experience was akin to Mark Twain's description of his visit to the Church of the Holy Sepulchre during his Holy Land excursion, about which he wrote:

> "With all its clap-trap side-shows and unseemly impostures of every kind, it is still grand, revered, venerable - for a god died there."[390]

I could have only perceived this through direct personal experience by visiting Clemens's grave, and reflect on this observation as it occurred solely within myself in that moment. There was a pedestal, yes, if you will, embodied in the monument erected by daughter Clara. That was the illusion created and sustained with loving appreciation for the legion of fans who regularly overlooked the fact that there was a man who once lived named Samuel Langhorne Clemens. And just like them, I, too, took a selfie of myself next to that same monument. But my perception of Twain shifted dramatically that day at his grave, as Twain receded and Sam Clemens came to the fore.

It was the man named Samuel Clemens who penned, in the opening paragraph of his eulogy for his beloved daughter, Jean:

> "Has any one ever tried to put upon paper all the little happenings connected with a dear one - happenings...preceding the sudden and unexpected death of that dear one? Would a book contain them? Would two....? I think not...They are little things that have been always happening every day, and were always so unimportant and easily forgettable before - but not now! Now, how different! How precious they are, how dear, how unforgettable, how pathetic, how sacred, how clothed with dignity!"[391]

Jean Clemens

A shared moment of precious little happenings: Jean Clemens with her father. Courtesy The Center for Mark Twain Studies.

As I read Mr. Clemens' account of his then recent memories, about Jean's despondent German Shepherd pawing at her casket, of now incompletable plans made by a father and daughter, about how he studied the sweet demeanor of her face throughout the quiet dark of night, it was then when I was first drawn to investigate the home in Stormfield, Connecticut, where Jean had passed, and where, just four months afterward, Mr. Clemens had also taken leave of our world. I hadn't paid much mind to Stormfield before, and was saddened to read that Stormfield had burned to the ground in 1923 and replaced with a reduced scale replica. Yet, undaunted, I was still compelled to investigate the region as described previously herein.

But even more remarkable, having just read Twain's account of Jean's liveliness and death, as I Googled for more info, it was also then when I stumbled across the

Thomas Edison film footage of Mark Twain, which included Clara and Jean. It was another odd "Circumstance" as Twain would put it. I had just read about Jean's death, and now, via this unexpected film, I was seeing her animated and alive. I recalled this same footage from the first airing of the Ken Burns documentary about Twain, but now it was resonating so much more personally.

Clemens' emotionally charged discourse on his daughter's death reveals a lot about this man, evidently in shock and experiencing profound grief, and yet somewhat neutral, from a man who had endured family tragedy from the onset. The death of his only son, Langdon, in 1872 at the age of just 19 months was a profound shock on Clemens, leaving him remorseful with guilt for the rest of his life. Twenty-five years later, his second born, Susy, died of meningitis at the tender age of 24 in 1896. Eight years afterward, Clemens' wife Olivia died of heart failure while abroad in Florence, Italy, in 1904. His daughter Jean, who previously had not spent much time with her father due to her prolonged stays in sanitariums, had greeted her father upon his return from a trip abroad only four days prior, until Jean was found dead in her tub, having succumbed to an epileptic seizure while bathing on Christmas Eve, 1909. Clemens wrote:

> "I lost Susy thirteen years ago; I lost her mother - her incomparable mother - five and a half years ago; Clara has gone away to live in Europe; and now I have lost Jean. How poor I am, who was once so rich!... Jean lies yonder, ...and I sit here - writing, busying myself, to keep my heart from breaking."[392]

The emotional pressure Clemens endured during the 24 hours when he wrote this tribute to Jean must have been immeasurable. He was incredibly distraught.

"I saw her mother buried" he continued.

> "I said I would never endure that horror again; that I would never again look into the grave of any one dear to me. I have kept to that. They will take Jean from this house to-morrow, and bear her to Elmira, New York, where lie those of us that have been released, but I shall not follow."[393]

Jean's death was, for Clemens, the final stroke. Historians have noted how the impact took the light out of his life, that he lost his spark and his will to go on. "In her loss" he went on,

> "I am almost bankrupt, and my life is a bitterness...[394] Jean's coffin stands where her mother and I stood, forty years ago, and were married; and where Susy's coffin stood five years and a half ago; and where mine will stand after a little time."[395]

The heart of Samuel Clemens, the man immortalized as Mark Twain, had

One of the last known photos taken of Mark Twain in public, January, 1910, while carried from a ship on his return from Bermuda. He would pass four months after this photo was taken. Courtesy NY Public Library.

endured its most powerful adversary, and was broken after all, causing his own passing just four months after Jean on April 21, 1910.

Just as my wife's very mention of these books seemed to ominously serve me at precisely the right time, it was serendipitous that I found and read Twain's tribute to Jean on the same day I had paid a visit to my Dad's grave just hours before. Then, I remembered: I had written a similar memorial after Dad had passed away. I have often written many such tributes after the passing of friends, my grandmother, and even my first three dogs. I knew I had something dedicated to Dad, so I set about to find it.

I went upstairs to my library and paused before two shelves filled with several dozen hand-written journals I'd created since I was fourteen years old. Between then and the late 1990s, I recorded everything in writing or sketches. After that, with the purchase of my first laptop around 1996, I began typing almost everything as digital media in my 'cyber journal'. Not sure where to start, I pulled them off the shelf one by one, leafing through a half-dozen or so before finding one with entries spanning October of 1987 through August of 1989. This particular volume is a snapshot of my life at the time. It includes watercolor studies for paintings, life drawings in pen and ink, poems, song lyrics, half-written film scripts, short stories, and more. I also stumbled upon a record of this being the time when I shared an apartment with a girlfriend named Teri. I paused there because it was only within the past year that I learned Teri had taken her own life about ten years ago. Teri had been a passionate, creative woman reminiscent of Stevie Nicks, right down to the fingerless, lace gloves she wore while performing. Yet, she had a fragile nature that often conflicted with this bolder, independent aspect of her spirit. Teri's zest for life, in the end, proved to be too much for her to contain.

Reading the pages about Teri brought recollection of my Dad's reaction when I told my parents that she and I would be moving in together; "So, you're shackin' up" he protested, expressing his displeasure. Ever the conventional Catholic moralists, my parents didn't agree with consensual cohabitation before marriage. I was twenty-seven years old, not immorally minded in the least, and I was dating a woman with whom I was particularly fond at the time. My parents didn't care for her, not so much that I had signed a joint lease with a girl, but for the added Catholic faux pas that Teri had been previously married – to Rob Buck, guitarist of the band *10,000 Maniacs*. Teri, who sang and played keyboard in her own band, had grown up with those guys. She used to tell me that by hangin' out with her friends and she, I had by default become one of the official, anointed 10,000 implied in the band's name. This mattered little to my parents. As far as they were concerned, Teri was leading me into sin.

Shortly after Dad had passed away, I began to spend an increasing number of nights sleeping over at my parent's house as my Mom adjusted to being a widow. It was a difficult time for her as she had never lived a day alone in her life. My brothers and their wives, all of whom lived in other states, returned to their respective homes after the funeral. My Mom was alone, frightened, uncertain, and depended on the occasional visit from family, friends, and some of the priests and nuns from the community.

Before Dad passed, Teri had difficulty adjusting to the amount of time I was spending at my parent's house when Dad was ill, and then afterward was equally troubled by the amount of time I spent with my Mom to support her transition into life as a widow. My attempts to reason with Teri about the need for practicing compassion pretty much fell on deaf ears. As a result, we agreed to end our relationship, and I moved out of our apartment and back home with Mom.

There were some entries Teri had written, which had been her way of passively engaging in an argument with me when I was off caring for my parents. I read her words with tender remembrance of the better times we had shared together, and quietly uttered a short prayer in her memory, wishing her to rest in peace.

In the same span of journal entries, I had made some notes now and then of the unfolding developments associated with my Dad's declining health.

On October 10, 1988, in the middle of one such journal entry I wrote:

> "My father, late at night, dreams of Brigadoon. He wants to hear it [the song]. A story about a love so strong that rules are broken and time stands still. Love is still the genuine force behind it all."

Dad loved *Brigadoon*, the 1954 film with Gene Kelly, Van Johnson and Cyd Charisse. I recall searching unsuccessfully for a soundtrack of Brigadoon on Cassette Tape to fulfill that request. One can glean from this the sentimental side of my father. Here, in the final weeks of his life, his subconscious was grasping for some healing, comforting thing he had experienced while watching that film.

After that, Dad's health began to fail more precipitously. On a page from an un-mailed letter to a friend I had written:

> "I had to take my Dad to the Emergency Room again on Tuesday, so he's back in the hospital for a while again. Poor guy - it's been a lot for him. It's been a strange time. Many changes…"

I had been tending to my Dad's health needs more and more from that point on. Sleeping little, working when I could, spending more time with Mom while Dad was in the hospital. My father died just 19 days later on October 29th, which was also my mother's birthday.

My journal then went silent for a few months, and is not resumed until March 20th, 1989, when I penned:

> "Well, it seems as though the long winter of emotional pain is over. The mourning time waning, and the new cycle, the new day beginning. Much has happened since I last wrote in this journal. Teri is gone from my life in the romantic/lover sense; my father has passed away leaving an unfamiliar void in my mother's house that still spooks us in an unsettling sort of way."

I then go on to describe a new job, meeting another girl who rapidly stole my heart… and broke it within a month. From that point on, I record a period of pure, independent celebration, when I frequented bars and other venues to see live music shows of local bands like *The Dead Milkmen, The Fabulous Fondas, Dr. A-Tree, Crossharp Sharp Blues Review* and others, hanging out with "new friends from a new job" - Marci, Kevin, Rob, and Shirl - and I was able to look back at some earlier heartbreaks with renewed vigor. I was just beginning the process of healing my devastation over Dad's death, and attempting to resolve my incomplete relationship with him.

My journal entry of April 10th, 1989, reads:

> "I ran into Brenda and Will tonight…after seeing *'The Adventures of Baron von Münchhausen'* with Marci. What an outrageously uplifting film! Terry Gilliam is an artistic genius! A brilliant script, uncontrived and hilarious. A movie Dad would have loved!"

Reading that entry was also somber because not long ago I learned that Brenda, too, had passed away from Cancer some years before. I continue the entry with a segment about how I met Will and Brenda several years prior through another girlfriend - a purple-haired, New Wave, quasi-punk rock band singer and fellow yoga student. I continued writing 'of a time' we did this, 'of a time' we did that, until I wrote "of a time when she met my parents, and my Dad hugged her and kissed her sweetly on the cheek…" Dad had liked that girlfriend very much.

That entry, followed by my soliloquy about letting go of an unrequited love, marks the time when I am thinking more openly about my relationship with my father and am finally able to express it. On June 25, 1989, a few days after Father's Day, I was able to sit down and write this poetic testimonial to Dad.

"Father, no longer can I inquire of the tales of the last great war. In your youth, the dapper stud, timid yet proud, went to war and sailed the seas. How, in so many ways, I yearn for your life. Post mortem, I meet your childhood friends, who tell me proudly, their tales of youth spent with you. You, who made the girls swoon, but picked young Elizabeth [my Mom] for your bride. And through the years you kept people smiling and in song, a noble and treasured gift by which all remember you.

'As I drive your car, inherited, I think how my [own, future] family will not have the chance to know you, much as your [own] family not [getting the chance of] knowing your Dad. Ah, great soul - to have seen your frail but well-lived body, crumble and cease before me - I see my own life before me, I see my own fate. So what to do in the intervening time?

'I wish I had the chance to have been a friend - I never sat in a bar with you, because some insecure, shy bullshit kept me from that. I wish I'd been a better son, so I hope to make it up to you by some day being a good father. Your sons try to justify the loss of your presence, but we flounder...

'I smelled the fragrance of death a week before you died, a scent somewhat familiar, but never so close or so clear. Grace was present at the moment of your death, and in the days that followed.

'I miss you Dad, wanting to spend lost time with you, wanting to speak to you, to fish with you, to drink with you, to sing with you.

'You did fight and you did not go gently into that dark night, but your body drained its last drop of warrior blood and essence.

'An hour before you left, you were pleased that the 'Fightin' Irish' [of Notre Dame] were winning, and somehow that satisfied you. In a similar way, perhaps, you, too, knew you had been winning in some way.

'Now the wanderlust that consumed your soul grows larger inside [of me], desiring to be satiated. Have I inherited this from you? I will make your name proud in some noble way, and I too won't give up. I do wear your shoes.

'Your own brother [My Uncle Bud] says "Your father was my idol.

If he had gone to Hollywood, he would have been a star."

'Spike [my father's nickname]. The beloved entertainer. You have gone, and the world you knew is fading rapidly. Your childhood friends are passing on. What's it all about?"

My father's death in 1988 marked the conclusion of a devastating time for our family. Like Twain, our family saw the deaths of four pivotal figureheads in a very brief four-year period, beginning with the passing of my grandmother, the much beloved matriarch and spiritual nucleus of our family, just before Christmas of 1984. Two years later, 1986 saw the death of my Aunt Marie, my Mom's brother Jack's wife, followed in 1987 with Uncle Ken, who married my Mom's sister Mary, and then my own Dad in 1988. Their successive passing swiftly tore the very foundation from beneath us all. We were - and are - a very close, tight knit, typical Irish-Catholic family clan. That period brought us closer.

On a regular basis, our families had joined and mingled at every family event or just for the hell of it on Friday nights at Uncle Ken and Aunt Mary's house. These were the reliable stalwarts, the guiding lights of our respective families. Their humor, loving candor, and crowd pleasing, impromptu house concerts of music and song were the very social fabric on which my generation of cousins had been weaned. We took pride in the celebratory nature of our family, and our friends both envied and conjoined in non-purpose celebrations of the simple joy of family, camaraderie, and heritage. In four quick years, that was taken away. My father, the accordion player, provided the soundtrack of the most delightful years of our youth. It took all of us, the spouses, children, and grandchildren, as well as countless nieces, nephew, grandnieces and grandnephews, and an endless parade of a lifetime of friends, years to rebound from the awful shock of our tragedy. We all recovered in our own respective ways to some extent, but our lives took new direction as we piloted on through the gaping void in our hearts from their absence.

The recollections of my father poised herein reflect the duration it took me to come to terms from this period, and specifically to heal from the loss of Dad. Not the three months of radio silence in my journal of that time, but still evident on a trip to Hannibal twenty years afterward. As this initial blog post grew and expanded, I found it fascinating to discover that a review of the life of Mark Twain ultimately brought me to this moment, thirty years after my Dad's death, to at last administer the final application of emotional salve to heal the wound. I suppose it will never fully heal, but there is an unanticipated sense of resolution prevailing, leading me to think that my smiling Dad is cajoling me for taking so long to fully get it.

My brothers have said that of the four of us I have grown to become a lot like our Dad as they remember him, save for his musical skills. That gene passed on to them. All three are profoundly excellent musicians and song crafters. Like him, though the youngest of us, I am the brother whose hair, just like Dad's, turned prematurely gray and ultimately full-on white by my mid-fifties. I understand that boy who played along and fished and swam in the Schuylkill River. I understand the courage he needed to plow forward in lean times. I understand the battle-wearying depression that could take over his conscience until a hearty laugh or a night of song with family and friends bounced him out of it, fresh and renewed to take on the challenge of another day. I understand his dreams left unfulfilled. I understand the vision he had for his boys. I understand because I've been a Dad myself now for twenty-four years.

My Dad, as we knew and remember him best - always poised with a witty, good-humored pun or a loving, cajoling quip.

I began to think more about Dad in light of my prevalent perceptions of mortality since having visited and written about the grave site of Samuel Clemens. It occurred to me that I had driven four hours to visit the grave of Mr. Clemens and was left with renewed lessons about the importance of family, of cherishing loved ones who are both among the living and those who have passed on. I thought the trip to the study and grave in Elmira had completed my Mark Twain journey triumvirate, and yet something remained missing to complete the story. Then one evening I became aware of the notion that I hadn't visited my own father's grave in some time.

In the past, I had typically paid a visit a few times a year. I had taken my daughter there several times to instill in her an awareness of family, and to know her legacy. I had brought my Mom there when her health enabled. But having driven four hours to the Twain grave, I became acutely aware that it had been a while since my last visit, and Dad was interred just ten minutes from my house. So, I planned to pay a visit on my next day off, which just happened to be on a Sunday.

28

FINDING HUCK FINN

"May He give us a safe lodging and a holy rest and peace at the last."

Cardinal John Henry Newman

Like my Sunday trips to Hannibal and Hartford, I had hoped to make the trip to Twain's grave on a Sunday to complete that consistency for the sake of telling a story. But, as you've read, that didn't work out for logistical reasons. However, while en route to visit my Dad's grave that day, I had the thought that somehow the spirit of Mark Twain, or the hand of divine Providence - Circumstance, had somehow guided destiny to remind me that the completion of the Sunday triduum, and the real story here, was not about Mark Twain. This story was about my relationship with my father. So, how fitting it was that I could make time to visit on this sunny, cloud free Sunday afternoon in August.

After finishing my tea and liquid breakfast, I prepared some items to bring along based on past experience. I packed a nylon shopping tote with two thermoses of warm water, some spray cleaning solution, a bunch of rags, an assortment of varied-width spackle knives, a brush, dustpan, nylon scrubber, and scissors. I stopped for a take-out coffee and made my way to the cemetery near my home.

When I arrived, I first stopped at the cemetery family center to get Dad's lot number, but the office was closed. I had been there often enough to know the approximate location, so I parked my car in a shaded area in the very back edge of the cemetery, retrieved my bag of cleaning supplies from the trunk, and began walking up and down the rows of ground level grave markers looking for Dad. I couldn't help noting how so many of the markers had been neglected or forgotten, covered and indecipherable from layers of dry mud and overgrown crab grass. I stopped periodically in the area where I thought Dad's marker could be to scrape away the soil with my sneaker in order to see the family name. I did this a number of times, occasionally lifting my head to review the adjacent landmarks nearby to get my bearing.

I knew that Dad's stone was in between a row of three tall evergreens and a contemporary sculpture of 'Our Lady of the Rosary,' whose watchful eye and raised hand overlooked and blessed the graves before her. I set down my heavy bag of supplies at the base of the statue and continued looking, row after row, somehow feeling that this was the penance, the mitzvah required to purify the soul and make one worthy enough to approach a sacred site. Eventually I found Dad's marker. It was not too badly soiled as some of the others, yet needed some tending. I took off my baseball cap and left it on the stone to mark my place while I walked back to the statue of Our Lady to fetch my bag, which was now about thirty yards away.

Returning to the marker after sighting my hat, I assessed the condition, pulled one of the largest and firmest of the spackle knives from my bag, and proceeded to edge the grass along the perimeter of the stone. I then chiseled away the tough crabgrass and soil, discarding it to the left or right, grabbing the dust brush to sweep away the loose soil. I got one of the thermoses and poured the warm water all along the sides and in the crevices of the carved granite. I wiped it with a rag, and repeated this step several times until all the mud and soil were gone. Then I sprayed the stone with household cleaner, wiped it multiple times, washed away the soapy residue with water and wiped it again. I took out the scissors and trimmed a few blades of grass that obstructed the view. I set the tools down and watched as the sun quickly evaporated the remaining water.

While preparing for the trip, I recalled the story of meeting Woody Strode at the Dunkin' Donuts, so while en route I took a detour to get a small cup of Dunkin' coffee for Dad. I had carried it with me from the car, and placed it upper left on the now cleaned grave marker. I had also planned, having seen the cigar placed at Twain's grave, to bring a cigarette for Dad. I placed it next to the coffee. In his final years, Dad had hidden his cigarettes from my mother, preventing her from knowing he smoked. He had pretty much quit after a triple coronary bypass operation that brought me back from living in Los Angeles in 1984. But, once when I was driving him somewhere, I dropped something on the floor of the car that bounced beneath the seat. Reaching blindly beneath me, I instead pulled out a small hand towel that unfurled to reveal a pack of Kent cigarettes Dad had hidden there. I remember holding them up and looking at Dad with a facial expression that simply asked "Really?"

Embarrassed I had discovered his secret, Dad took the cigarettes and towel from me, rewrapped them and put them in the glove compartment.

"I have one once in a while, when I'm havin' a beer or somethin'" he explained. As if that wasn't enough, he went on to justify it. "You know, when

I'm at Killeen's with the guys or whatever. I only go there on Fridays once in a while to get out of the house."

After the bypass surgery, Dad had retired from his municipal job, and didn't do too much save for going to a diner for breakfast a few mornings a week with a newspaper. Going occasionally to Killeen's, a small bar in his boyhood neighborhood, was one of the few real respites he enjoyed. He had been on their bowling team throughout the 1970s, and each weekend with his teammates and friends was another way he could blow off the stress of his routine workaday life. How could I deny him the simple happiness of having a few cigarettes once a week, despite his doctor's advice to the contrary? The fact that a half pack of cigarettes hidden under the car seat was evidence enough that he didn't smoke much. What could I say? What could he say? He ended the episode by simply requesting "Don't tell your mother."

But it wasn't solely the smoking habit that contributed to Dad's demise. When I was living in LA in the summer of 1984, I got a phone call from my Mom who explained to me that my father had strained his heart while lifting and carrying our television set to the trunk of his car to take along with them to Wildwood, New Jersey for their summer vacation. They had been told that the place they had rented had no television. Television was Dad's other stress outlet. The terms vacation and television were indistinguishable to Dad. Even though they were going to a quieter haven away from the city, where he would bring along his woven green nylon and aluminum beach chair to rest on a sun-soaked beach along the edge of the Atlantic Ocean, or find release in favorite entertainment spots like the banjo fueled sing-a-long venue The Red Garter, or Cozy "On the way to Cape May" Morley's Club "Ain't this place a shit-hole?" Avalon, Dad couldn't imagine spending two weeks without a damned television.

And it was a damned television. It had been the same Nate Ben's acquired, faux wood paneled television set with the hidden panel of tuning knobs, deluxe rabbit ears and optional UHF ring antenna that had caused Dad to strain his heart, triggering the series of health problems that would ultimately cut his life short within four years. It was, ironically, Dad's addiction to television that killed him. Even more ironic is the fact that when Mom and Dad arrived at the vacation rental place, they had been misinformed by the realtor. There had been a television set in the place all along.

After setting down the coffee and cigarette on the grave marker, I knelt for a considerable amount of time. I compared the year of his birth with the year of his death, recalling that he was just 61 years of age when he passed - only one year older than I am now. My mind drifted, remembering the day he was buried. After the grave service and invitation to the luncheon was imparted, I recalled how I had lingered at the grave while everyone went to their cars. At the time, I was still in shock that Dad was gone. I had moved back home a second time in late 1987 to help my Mom care for him when a second surgical procedure had left his kidneys inoperable, requiring him to get dialysis several times a week. The dialysis is what ultimately did him in. I watched my young Dad, this once lively, jesting, musically endowed man that I had known, wither away to a paltry seventy-something pounds. The memories while I knelt there on his grave were like a post-traumatic stress episode of a particularly devastating time in my early life. The memories continued, like reliving the scene of a battle that had happened within me after the funeral.

 I recalled how I found it hard to walk away once the grave side services were done. My cousin Maryann came back and put her arm around my shoulder to comfort me. I knew she understood. Her Dad, my Uncle Kenny, had passed just a few years prior. "I know how it feels, Tommy" I recall her saying. "You'll get through this." She tugged on my arm, gently pulling me away from the graveside and memories of my living Dad that I didn't want to leave.

 On this visit, I knelt a short while longer, voicing a few remarks and prayers to Dad, until becoming aware of my surroundings. I looked around the cemetery, noticing my relative seclusion save for a few other people at two other graves about thirty and fifty yards away, respectively. The sound of summer cicadas and crickets neutralized the still, stagnant air, effectively removing any awareness of the blazing heat in the moment. I stood up and surveyed the grave again, not wanting to take leave. I studied the now dry, clean marker, satisfied with its pristine state for the time being. I picked up my bag of tools, looked at the marker one more time, and said goodbye to Dad.

 As I walked back to my car, I flashed back to the time when I was about eleven years old and had become an altar boy and was scheduled to serve the much dreaded 5:00 am weekday mass. Getting assigned the 5:00 am masses as an altar boy was like losing the lottery. All of us had to be scheduled to do them at some point, and most of us loathed it. It meant getting up between 3:30 or 4:00 am, showering, grooming, getting dressed in your Sunday best in order to arrive by 4:30 and change into your cassock and white surplus. We also had to affix a hard, plastic collar, button it with a brass tux shirt stud, and strap on an adjustable bowtie. Then we had to make sure the tools needed for the priest were set on the altar.

 Frankly, I didn't mind doing those masses at that time. I felt there was something especially sacred about them. It was always sparsely attended by a handful of nuns from the convent across the street, a regular troupe of exceptionally devout senior aged parishioners, and maybe one or two men or women who just wanted to attend mass before going to work. The senior citizens prayed fervently, with some reciting their rosary throughout. But the best highlight was that the 5:00 am mass was a time when I got to see my saintly grandmother. By then she had moved closer to the church and attended this mass daily. My observation of her in those moments when she displayed her most devout demeanor provided a life-lesson for me, implanting a strong desire to want to understand the nature of God. That's the story of another book.[396]

Assisting the priest with serving communion required us to hold the brass paten beneath the chin of the recipients who knelt on the cushioned marble ledge along the front of the altar railing. When it came to my grandmother's turn, as holy and solemn as I tried to remain, she typically would make me crack a smile and then give me a wink immediately after uttering "Amen" to the priest, who then placed the communion wafer on her tongue.

As all those memories flooded back while I walked to the car, I specifically recalled how Dad used to walk me to the church in those years because our neighborhood had grown so dangerous as described earlier, and it was still dark at that time of the morning.

Once, a light layer of snow had fallen overnight, and the neighborhood seemed to be veiled in a delicate blanket of peace. Not a sound was heard as we walked down Wilder Street save for that barely perceptible ringing that is only audible when it snows, our own footsteps muffled as well by the soft overlay. We spoke quietly about one thing or another, and then Dad started telling me that our walk that morning had stirred up some memories of his own boyhood, of his Dad walking him to his own parish church of Saint Patrick's near Rittenhouse Square in Philadelphia, on mornings just like this. Dad walked quietly for a short bit and I thought he looked sad. He was just introspective. I quietly asked him questions about his Dad and his boyhood. He recounted some stories that I wish I recall now. But what came of it was a mutual knowing that he had arrived at that point in his life when he was filling his father's shoes, and I was cast in the role of son. I only began to understand that sentiment after watching my own daughter grow up. That morning remains one of the fondest memories of my Dad.

My father was just another neighborhood guy in many regards, but in issues of faith he was a fervently devout, deeply dedicated and faithful Catholic. These were traits he greatly impressed upon me. Dad had been quite proud on the day I had become an altar boy, just as he had when I had received my first communion and confirmation, as he had been for my brothers too. Confirmation was also when you were given your second, middle "spiritual" name, distinct from your birth name. I recall that conversation between Mom, Dad and I when I was about eight years old, and I can still picture exactly where we standing by the foot of our stairs. I had come up with a variety of names I had wanted to choose, but Mom and Dad explained our family tradition of picking the name of someone in our family. My oldest brother Jack had been given the middle name of my mother's father; my brother Mike was given the name of my Dad's father; my brother James got Dad's father's middle name, so I agreed on taking my Dad's name.

Just as Mom proudly took me to visit my grandmother and show off my white Communion outfit, Dad made a bigger fuss and took multiple polaroid shots of me in my altar boy cassock and surplus on the day of my investiture. He was so proud that it initiated my thoughts of becoming a priest. But, in time, I recognized that my ship of Circumstance was navigating in a different direction. I learned to trust that a higher wisdom was steering me along, and instead cultivate gratitude for the surprises that came up along the way. Some of those surprises were difficult, challenging, even deadly, exhausting me to a point of standing on the brink of hopelessness, not wanting to continue. But after a while I saw the pattern, that after every season of darkness there was always a season of great joy.

My experience was like walking with one foot in God and the other on earth. The God foot is about letting go, about trusting, about gratitude, about just experiencing whatever comes up in the moment. The earth foot can be anything you like relative to circumstance. My earth foot just happened to somehow get tethered to the leg of Mark Twain. It's as if Providence put us in a three-legged race, and my Dad was the one who tied the string around our ankles when he sat me down to watch a movie with him fifty years ago. For Mark Twain, being tied to me must have surely been his hell, but for me it's been one hell of an incredible journey.

On the Saturday of Labor Day weekend, I attended a family party with my wife and my in-laws. Despite the intention of having been planned as a holiday cookout, a relentless rain kept us sequestered indoors for the most part, but that didn't lend one sour note to the day. In the evening, after most of the guests had left, my sister-in-law Jean turned on her large screen TV to queue up a digital slide show of old family photos that had belonged to their deceased mother. She and my wife had spent some time together sorting and digitally scanning some of them months before.

It was a somewhat bittersweet presentation, as many of those from my wife's family who appeared in the photos, some spanning back 100 years, had long since passed away: My wife's oldest brother, who had passed when she and I were still dating; their Mom and Dad; their Aunts, Uncles and cousins whom I had acquired through marriage, many having been guests at our wedding and with whom I'd reunited on assorted family occasions in years past. Though I was familiar with these folks and had seen some of the photos before, now and then family shots that included myself and my infant daughter would pop up, proving to be wistfully jarring for me to view in this context. As remarks were made by my in-laws who were there, I recalled the occasions when some of the photos had been taken, now 20 to 25 years earlier. I became keenly aware in that moment that I had been accepted into an extended family. As much as I remained a member of my own family, I was also one of theirs. They had welcomed me with love, and do so to this day.

The next day, while driving, I reflected on the experience I had while viewing those photos and recalled my experience in Elmira a few weeks before, when, at the grave of Mark Twain, I saw the graves of the family of Samuel and Olivia Langdon Clemens, and the extended graves of the Langdon family themselves. Like myself, Clemens had been embraced and welcomed into a second, extended family, and it was among them where he had flourished, and among them where the great man would be interred, his own family interred a thousand miles away in Missouri. It's a funny thing about marriage, how it does that. It's part of the deal.

I had been driving to Philadelphia that day to pay a visit to my Mom and drop off some items my wife had purchased for her. I had plans to cajole Mom, who had been ailing for a few months, into taking a drive somewhere just to get her out of the house for a while. She declined the offer, so I instead did a few chores for her. I changed a couple of lightbulbs, took some bags of recyclable items out to her yard, and she asked me to take the things I'd brought and put them in a second-floor closet. Having completed that, I was about to descend the stairs when I paused outside of the spare bedroom which my Dad had used as a den and peered inside. With my mind having been on memories of Dad for the previous eight months, I went in the room to just reminisce.

As I looked about, I opened the closet door to see if my collection of *Know your America* program binders were still stored there. As a young boy, I had enjoyed the subscription to that program given to me by Mom and Dad probably when I was about six years old. This is largely how I had learned about fascinating towns and monuments and historical places in the United States, and was among the visual catalysts for my lifelong yearning to travel. The booklets in each binder featured information about each state in the union, and it was an interactive program that required one to lick and paste postage-stamp media photos of the famous locales. Not only did I see, visualize, and remember each of these places, I had literally tasted them. They all tasted the same, incidentally. I think the main reason I've saved them all these years is that they serve as a physical, visual reminder of those good childhood times in our house on Wilder Street. The binders have been on my mental list of things to move from Mom's house since my wife and I bought our home 23 years ago.

I closed the closet door and looked about. In the corner was a two level, molded plastic étagère that Dad had absconded from my bedroom after one of the many times I had moved away from home. On it he had his own collection of books that filled both of the bottom levels, with a few stacked on top. Except for my own pilfering of a few books to take home for myself previously, the bookshelf had been pretty much left intact as it was when Dad last used it.

I crouched down, turned my head sideways and fingered along the titles. Most of the books were titles about World War II and naval exploits of that era, a two-volume set of printed, spiritual guidance lectures from a Catholic radio program popular in the 1950s, a few works by Jim Bishop, James Michener, and others. And then, to my amazement, nestled between a few larger hard cover editions – was a previously undetected, dust-laden paperback copy of *The Adventures of Huckleberry Finn*.

I pulled the book out, blew off the light layer of dust that had settled along the top, and just held it with some measure of mild incredulity. It was as if Dad was giving some sort of affirmation from the great beyond, an acknowledgment of the tale I was recalling, recording, and intending to share. This very book had been one of the final books my Dad had selected to read in his final years. It revealed without question that this sole book had long been his favorite among Twain's works. As I had known all along, something about Twain's tale of Finn brought him back to his youth again and again.

In the days before Dad released his last breath, he had started shouting in his sleep, calling out "Billy, Billy, watch out!!" When Dad awoke the next day, confined to the hospital bed we had placed in our living room, Dad didn't recall the episode, but said it might have something to do with his childhood friend, Bill Bourke. After Dad passed, I greeted Bill in the funeral parlor reception line at Dad's viewing. I thanked Bill for his condolences, and seized the moment to relay Dad's dream incident to him, inquiring if he could shed any light on it. Without hesitation, Bill Bourke replied "Your Dad saved my life when we were kids. We were playing along the tracks by the river, and there was a train coming and I didn't hear it for some reason. Your Dad shouted my name, alerting me just in the nick of time. I never forgot that." It was amazing to hear that in that moment. In the midst of the sorrow and tribulation of grappling with my Dad's death, his old boyhood friend revealed this amazing story. My heart just melted. Dad had been a hero.

Maybe it was as simple as that. Maybe reading the shenanigans of Huck, Jim and Tom reminded Dad of his boyhood friends, enabling him to briefly escape into its pages and reexperience his boyhood times. Perhaps reading the work in his youth had been the source of inspiration for his play. Perhaps Livy Clemens knew that when she critiqued Sam while he composed the work, affectionately assigning him the nickname of 'Youth.'

I fingered the copy of Huckleberry Finn, noting the fine print along the bottom that this fifty cent Airmont Books Classics Series edition had been published complete and unabridged. This differed from other copies I knew growing up, which had been abridged, sanitized and made family-friendly for a younger audience. The timing of finding this book on Dad's old bookshelf was magical. Just a few days before, I had begun to reread *The Adventures of Tom Sawyer*. I hadn't read it entirely in decades, and wanted to return myself to the fascination I'd held with it in my own youth. I had been reading it earlier that day, just prior to dressing and going to visit Mom. I had set the book down in the middle of Chapter 6, where the character of Huckleberry Finn is first introduced to the world. I left off where Tom told the truth about stopping to talk to Huck as his cause for being late to school, with the motivation of fully knowing the schoolmaster would thrash him and make him sit with the girls, which provided him the opportunity to at last get a tad closer to Becky Thatcher, the object of his adoration. It's a key chapter in the book, when both secondary characters are brought to the forefront of the Tom Sawyer story.

This copy of Dad's had been published in 1962, leaving me to deduce that Dad had probably purchased this copy in old Leary's bookstore, which he had frequented during lunch breaks when working in downtown Philly. Leary's had operated without interruption from 1836 until it closed in 1968. Had young Sam Clemens browsed their shelves when working at the Inquirer? When Leary's doors were locked and its contents were assessed for auction, among the items discovered that had been tucked away in an old book for at least 136 years was a folded, original first printing of the Declaration of Independence dated 1776. It fetched nearly $400,000 at auction and is now on display in the Dallas Public Library. Alas, Leary's was yet another landmark razed and replaced.

Old Leary's bookstore, a Philadelphia institution for generations, now sadly gone.

The pages of Dad's copy of Huck were browned but not quite brittle, possessing that addictively sweet aroma of aged, decaying book pages. Judging by a book mark that presented itself when it stopped me from leafing further, I gathered that Dad had set the book down when he had finished reading chapter 7, where Huck catches five catfish with his disgruntled pap, hightails out of his pap's shanty, kills a wild pig and uses the blood to feign his own tragic death, then scoots off to hide on Jackson Island by way of the canoe he had found earlier.

It was a curious stopping point given the text on the bookmark Dad had placed there. It was a funeral parlor prayer card given in memory of a friend who had passed away a year or two before, and I noted an uncanny parallel of its inscription to the ending of Huck Finn. On it was a quote from Cardinal John Henry Newman, which read:

> "May He support us all the day long, till the shades lengthen & the evening comes, and the busy world is hushed & the fever of life is over & our work is done then in His mercy: May He give us a safe lodging and a holy rest and peace at the last."

At the time Dad had been reading this chapter, the light of his life was just beginning to dim. He did not want to die. He had so much he had wanted to do. With the awareness of such a fate coming sooner than anticipated, Dad had embraced his faith for solace and ease of mind, steadying the helm in the course of surrender. Dad knew more than he let on. It required great courage of him to navigate this part of his river that he knew he'd one day encounter. That day was at hand.

Chapter Seven of Huck Finn was the last writing by Mark Twain that Dad had read. It's a fitting read, one that likely comforted Dad's mind and eased his spirit in the difficult final chapter of his own life.

"I got out amongst the driftwood" Huck Finn explained,

"and then laid down in the bottom of the canoe and let her float. I laid there, and had a good rest and a smoke out of my pipe, looking away to the sky; not a cloud in it."[397]

As Dad's health worsened, it was decided that his dialysis treatments should cease. We knew, then, what was imminent. My brothers and their wives travelled their respective distances to join my mother and I in our home to be together. Dad was happy to see us all again. He rested comfortably, partially upright in the rented hospital bed, drifting in and out of sleep. All of us chatted with mild joviality, periodically interrupting the conversation with glances over our shoulder toward Dad, monitoring his condition with unbroken vigilance. At one point, Dad roused from his sleep, looked about meekly, somewhat confused, as would be normal from someone just waking. My brother Mike addressed him.

"Hey Dad…What do you need?"

Dad opened his eyes and looked at the blank television screen.

"What's the score of the Notre Dame game?" he asked.

We told him they were winning, which was true. This pleased him, and with a faint smile, he closed his eyes again and drifted back to sleep. We waited for him to rouse again, but instead, the pace of his breathing began to slow down to singular, deep inhalations and exhalations. Then, the breaths became softer and softer to the point of being barely audible, only detectable by the slight inward and outward heave of his chest. I was standing next to Dad at this point on one side of the bed, my brother James on the side opposite me. The soft wisp of a breath grew slower, and his chest took one soft heave inward, followed by a sustained outward breath. My brother and I watched intently.

"Is he breathing?" my brother asked.

I leaned over and placed my ear on his chest, listening for a heartbeat. I placed my hand beneath his nose, hoping to feel his breath. We were silent.

"Is he gone?" my brother asked.

I paused before answering. "Yeah…I think so."

My mom had been upstairs and somehow she just knew, descending the stairs as if on cue, stopping midway on the steps to ask "Is he gone?" After confirming, my brother embraced Mom, who was now weeping profoundly, as were we all. I hugged Dad first and then clenched his hand. I wasn't as immediately moved as my brothers, mainly because I had been home, assisting with changing his bedpan and clothes, and had witnessed the day to day progress that led to this moment. I was just numb. What took me completely by surprise, however, was that witnessing my Dad's death was instantly one of the most moving and beautiful experiences of my life. I fully understood, in that moment, the literal meaning of the phrase "pass away."

Dad's pain was gone, his suffering had ceased. With great courage, he had tried his best to challenge this foe, but had gracefully acknowledged defeat and willingly entrusted his soul to his maker.

"Huckleberry Finn had made it safely to Jackson Island. He was certain his troubles were behind him, if only for the time being. He shrouded his traveling canoe beneath the willows, veiling any further sight of him. He felt easier now, confident that he could set back and let go of the troubling circumstances of his world."[398]

"True Comfort" by E. W. Kemble

29

REDEMPTION AMONG THE NIGHT-HAWKS

"Everybody there...was in his way famous"
Mark Twain[399]

As 2017 drew to a close, I was quite busy at work with a fair amount of travel, planning, curating and managing a number of special events, and routine day to day business in between. Creative projects like this manuscript were put on the back burner for several months, and with more business, shows and travel expected after the New Year, I wasn't sure when I'd get back to it. Throughout the year I had been sharing highlights of my research and road trips with family and friends who graciously lent their cheerleading and support all along. So, when Christmas arrived, it served as a nice capping touch for my year-long Mark Twain odyssey when I was presented with a number of Twain-themed gifts.

My friend Nalini gave me a cool Mark Twain coffee mug from the Unemployed Philosopher's Guild line of products. My work colleague Kim gave me a copy of the book *Great Writers on the Art of Fiction: From Mark Twain to Joyce Carol Oates*, edited by James Daley. My wife found a mint-condition set of vintage, linen-bound, 1901 Harper's Library Editions of Twain titles which included *Connecticut Yankee*, *Life on the Mississippi*, *The Prince and The Pauper*, and *The Man That Corrupted Hadleyburg and other Stories and Essays*. The first three retained the copyright of S.L. Clemens from varying years, but the Hadleyburg compilation was copyrighted 1900 by Olivia L. Clemens. *That* was a score!

Seeing Olivia's name as holder of copyright for the first time was a bonus of this new Christmas collection. I hadn't yet seen that anywhere. There was no mark of Albert Paine's editing, no post-Roger Ashcroft reference to "The Mark Twain Company," and no reference to daughter Clara, who controlled what material was released for publication thereafter. Almost every other vintage edition of Twain's works that I own are posthumous editions from the 1920s copyrighted by The Mark Twain Company. I enthusiastically remarked upon realization that these volumes had been published when both Sam and Livy were still alive. It was as if I was receiving the books from them as well, like an empyrean nod of acknowledgement.

My daughter, too, had given me a few books about Twain by assorted authors, including *The Illustrated Mark Twain* by Roy Gasson from 1978, a 1999 Dover Thrift Edition copy of *The Wit and Wisdom of Mark Twain* edited by Paul Negri, and a pocket-sized publication of *The Celebrated Jumping Frog of Calaveras County*. After thanking her, she then handed me a larger, heavier package. Unwrapping it with eager curiosity, I was astonished to have before me a beautiful, pristine hardback copy of *The Autobiography of Mark Twain*, Volume 1, edited by Harriet L. Smith and other's affiliated with The Mark Twain Project. This was the very same book I had so coveted in the Twain Museum gift shop in Hartford. This volume was truly a Christmas wish come true, a capping gem to what had turned into a Mark Twain Christmas.

My own splendid Christmas aside, a gift I had given to my mother really added to the magic of the season. Weeks before, I was in an Apple computer repair store near my home and noted a sign advertising a transfer to DVD service. The lightbulb went off right there. I remembered mom voicing for decades her wish to have a 16 mm color film of her wedding transferred to DVD. I visualized the school bus yellow Kodak box in which it was stored in the precise corner of her cedar chest drawer where the it had been kept since 1953. It was there when we moved the chest - drawer contents intact - into our new home in 1974, where it has stayed in the same spot for forty years since.

When Mom opened the gift and we played it in her DVR, she was stunned. Tearfully she smiled, watching the beautiful, youthful bride that she was, walking and chatting alongside the handsome young man who would become my father. It is the only known film footage of Dad, and this was the first time I ever saw it. It was also the first time we had seen our dad animated and moving about since he passed. As I studied his mannerisms, facial gestures, and the middle finger he flashed to the friend who had filmed it on the steps of the church, I was able to peer into another side of this man whom I had only known in later years. As much as it had for Mom, the film momentarily brought my father back to life for all of us.

One other gift from my daughter and wife was a TiVo recording of the documentary *Mark Twain's Journey to Jerusalem: Dreamland*, which had been advertised for weeks. I had been too busy with work to watch when it aired, so I was grateful to have it to view at my leisure after the holiday frenzy subsided. In early January of 2018, I finally had some time after work one evening to watch it, but in the interim it had accidentally been deleted during a cable outage. Disappointed, I scrolled through our TiVo list and noticed my recording of *The*

Adventures of Mark Twain was still there. I hadn't watched the film since that morning ten months earlier when it inspired the writing of this tome, so I opted to watch it again. Having spent almost a solid year since delving into the nuances of Mark Twain's life, I was curious for a fresh view. This time, instead of experiencing nostalgic recollections, I found myself critiquing the film to such an extent that I had to ask 'Had I become a Twainian?'

Among the film's errors was its depiction of Sam Clemens meeting Charles Langdon on a Mississippi riverboat - not on The Quaker City steamship that carried both on the Holy Land excursion that resulted in Twain's creation of *The Innocents Abroad*. Charlie Langdon was represented as a bit too polished. Granted, he was the son of a highly successful business man, but getting to know the character of the Langdon family in recent months left me with another impression. Charlie was probably an earnest, spiritually-minded man, yet, I gathered that Charlie had a looser side to him that allowed for a few rounds of spirits with the rougher hewn Sam Clemens. I suspect Clemens helped Charlie become a more rounded man on that journey, and that is what opened the door for him to become so trusting of Clemens and bring him into the family.

The character depiction of Jervis Langdon offered a glimmer of the real man's softer side with reference to his purchase of the home in Buffalo for newlyweds Sam and Livy. Otherwise, Walter Hampden's casting portrayed him as tall, lanky and pious, a stuffier, more aloof and calculating person than the "compact" jovial man who liked to laugh and sing as described by Ron Power.

In the Oxford procession scene, I couldn't help but think that Fredric March's excessively coiffed hair made his Twain look like *The Golden Girls*' Bea Arthur with a mustache, or Gene Hackman in drag while escaping through the nightclub in *The Bird Cage*.

Having seen the actual Paige Compositor on my trips to Hartford, a fresh look at the film's interpretation of it resembling a mechanical assembly of bird beaks, each with a mind of their own, is now laughable.

Twain's bad hair day in the Oxford scene of The Adventures of Mark Twain, with Paul Scardon, left, as Rudyard Kipling and, right, Fredric March as Twain.

The Elephant on the Raft · 417

A 1940's newspaper advertisement for The Adventures of Mark Twain. Here Warner Brothers' publicity dept. attempt to pander Mark Twain as a rugged, romantic figure. It's a film for the ladies...

...and for the guys! In this 1944 magazine ad the film is hawked as a western, which it is not. Resembling nothing like Mark Twain, Fredric March looks more like, a rootin' tootin' Fredric March, and the character of Twain's refined, real life Victorian wife Livy is here inaccurately depicted by Alexis Smith as a bit of a loose floozy in the style of Jane Russell from Howard Hughes' 1943 film The Outlaw.

And I wasn't sold on Donald Crisp's casting as Twain's lecture tour manager J.B. Pond. Crisp's steady, recurring presence on the screen does lend a supportive balance to Fredric March's animated portrayal of Twain. J.B. Pond had been an enormous, imposing figure, towering over Mark Twain's 5' 9" height by about a foot. Based on photos, Pond must have stood about 6' 9" with an expansive chest and shoulders, much taller than Donald Crisp. Given his stature, Pond, a Union Army officer in the Civil War and Medal of Honor recipient, served as an apt bodyguard for Twain and his wife as well. A better casting choice could have been made, and frankly, Alan Hale would have been ideal!

Promotional still featuring The Jumping Frog of Calaveras County *scene with March as young Sam Clemens and the great Alan Hale as Steve Gillis.*

On the other hand, March's Twain did effectively embody descriptions of the author based on J. B. Pond's journal reflections of their time together, in which Pond had written:

James B. Pond

"I think I know him better than he is known to most men. Tenderness and sensitiveness are his two strongest traits. He has one of the best hearts that ever beat. One must know him well fully to discern all of his best traits. He keeps them entrenched, so to speak. I rather imagine that he fights shy of having it generally suspected that he is kind and tenderhearted, but many of his friends do know it. He possesses some of the frontier traits -- a fierce spirit of retaliation and the absolute confidence that life-long "partners," in the Western sense, develop. Injure him, and he is merciless, especially if you betray his confidence."[400]

Pond's memoir seemed to have captured the essence of Mark Twain most of all. The photographs he took throughout the lecture tour reveal more about the man than any I've seen. Numerous photos feature Twain wearing a peaked Riverboat Pilot's hat, a precursor to the current popular trend of sporting a baseball cap. An 1895 photo Pond took of Twain lying in bed while giving a press interview in a Vancouver hotel predates the uproar journalists made of John Lennon and Yoko Ono's Bed In for Peace interviews by seventy-four years.

There were other, minor critical observations I had of the film, but it was mostly like visiting an old friend, and by the end, it had been nice to drop by and spend some time together.

Pond, left, seated, with Twain in cap, standing.

The "Dreamland" documentary, I had been keen to watch is an in-depth study on Twain's fabled cruise of 1867. I knew enough about Twain's inner workings by that point to glean that the experience had been life transforming for him, and wanted to find out what underscored that. But, having to wait until it would next air, the next best thing was to instead plunge into rereading it's muse - *The Innocents Abroad.*

Reading 'Innocents' again reawakened memories of a cruise I'd taken two years prior, leaving me to again ponder what Twain's cruise experience must have been like. I recognized its narrative tone as that of the same young man who had voiced his yearning to travel overland at the onset of *Roughing It*. In that saga he had shared his delight to just travel west, to discover opportunity on his stage coach trip to Nevada, then on to California. From there he had travelled to the Sandwich Islands – Hawaii - and then made his way to Washington and New York as a respected journalist. But his cruise adventure was something altogether different. This was beyond a dream. The boy from Hannibal saw an opportunity to catch a grander riverboat and seized it.

Mark Twain's cruise and trip to the Holy Land had indeed impacted him in many ways. For one, his correspondence dispatches had made him a journalistic rock star and household name. The compilation of those reports in book form brought to life the storied lands of Bible lore while providing a contemporary insight for the first time in Western history, or at least since the Crusades. It had produced the best-selling book of the author's career in his lifetime, and rapidly became the second most popular book occupying an honored place in people's homes after the Bible, with the Sears and Roebuck Catalog coming in a close third. Historians regard the chartered Quaker City excursion as America's first ever large-scale cruise.[401] Conjoined with the widespread popularity of Twain's reports and subsequent success of *The Innocents Abroad*, it essentially launched the modern cruise industry. And, as discussed above, Twain's chance rendezvous with Charley Langdon on that cruise altered his course of navigation resulting in his meeting, courting, and marrying Livy, who would redefine his literary career.

Twain scholar Shelley Fisher Fishkin offered one of the best assessments I'd read anywhere of *The Innocents Abroad's* significance and far-reaching impact on American culture. "Mark Twain helped his readers extricate themselves" Fishkin begins,

> "from the sensibilities of the Victorian era and begin the march toward modernity...the journey would mark a milestone in American cultural navigation. The great explorers of the past had planted European flags on the soil of the New World. Twain sailed back the other way and figuratively planted an American flag on the European continent, marking as his own an imaginative terrain that the native inhabitants had for centuries assumed was theirs...Europe was rich with everything America had none of...But time and again, Twain refused to genuflect on command...Mark Twain and his fellow travelers have limited

patience for celebrating dead heroes of European manifest destiny. They are more concerned with capturing new territory across the Atlantic as a province of the American imagination."[402]

Twain's journey of 1867 took place just two years after the horrific Civil War had left the American population reeling for a redefinition of identity. When Innocents Abroad made its debut in 1869, right out of the gate Mark Twain captured and uplifted the spirit of a nation weary of itself, leading the way forward while bearing the standard of humor. What is most remarkable in light of Fishkin's assessment is how, toward the end of his life, Mark Twain had demonstrated his cultural crusade by singlehandedly conquering the world. In those final years, Twain was invited to dine with US Presidents and European heads of state, as well as movers and shakers from all facets of life. He was celebrated in India, because of his anti-Imperialist political viewpoint, which contrasted notably with that of his acolyte, Rudyard Kipling. His coup de gras was being awarded the honorary degree by Oxford University, his most cherished achievement.

As I read on, I considered how Twain acquired inspiration from being around water. From the influence of the Mississippi River to the meditative sound of the Park River that ran along his house in Hartford, and the serenity enjoyed on a plateau above the Chemung Canal in Elmira, New York to his frequent voyages to Bermuda on the yacht of his friend Henry Rogers. What was it that drew Twain to water again and again? After gaining a deepened understanding on my trips to landlocked places associated with Twain, another opportunity for a glimpse of this Quaker City experience might provide the answer. As it turned out, I wouldn't need to view the Jerusalem Journey documentary. By a stroke of serendipitous good fortune, I was given the chance to walk right into Mr. Twain's Top-siders.

When I returned to work that Monday already in great spirits following the Philadelphia Eagles 2018 NFC victory the day before, I received an unexpected phone call from my employer asking if I would be available to work for a week on a cruise ship. My jaw dropped. Are you kidding me? The timing couldn't be better. I saw this as heaven-sent, a most providential opportunity to rediscover what it was about the cruise experience that so engaged Mark Twain in 1867, and reconnect with my Dad's WWII naval experience. The task at hand was to help set up and run an on-board art gallery featuring the art of Def Leppard drummer Rick Allen, with whom I'd worked previously. The only caveat was that I would have to catch an early flight to Miami on the morning following another show at the gallery I managed that was scheduled the night before. It was a no brainer. I certainly said yes and began to prepare in my downtime.

After a week of celebrating a once in a lifetime Philadelphia Eagles Super Bowl victory and an evening art show and reception that ended around 10:00 pm the night before, with almost no sleep I got out of bed at 4:00 am that morning, showered, zipped and locked my luggage and called a Lyft ride to the airport. Anticipating a long line through the security checkpoint because my destination was Miami in the middle of one of the worst and coldest Winters in Philadelphia history, I was pleasantly surprised to enjoy my first ever TSA Pre-Check experience in seventeen years of air travel. Without having to empty pockets, take off shoes, jacket or belt, or wait, things seemed to be off to a good start.

My plane touched down in Miami around 9:30 am. After getting my luggage and taking a brief Lyft ride I arrived at the Port of Miami by 10:30. Cruise guests from around the globe milled excitedly about the outdoor promenade as we handed off our respective bags to a porter in exchange for a claim check. We were then directed into the cruise ship terminal for another round of security screening at an NSA checkpoint. Before long, the line began to move, then up a series of escalators and glass corridors to the embarkation ramp.

Once on board, I first ventured to find my cabin and drop off my carry-on bag. I hadn't yet heard from any of my company colleagues, so I proceeded to explore the ship. I was amazed at the superior scale of this vessel, the fourteen-story tall Royal Caribbean Navigator of the Seas. I'd never been on any vessel this large. The fifth deck interior promenade of shops, pubs, and cafes spanned the length of two city blocks. With cabin windows and terraces towering above for another five or six stories, it gave me the impression of a roofed and enclosed small village. And that's essentially what this cruise would be like - a floating and moving small hamlet populated with more than 3000 refugees from civilization desirous to just kick back and let their hair down, have a few drinks - or none at all for those in recovery - with no need for worry about driving or where they parked their car, and revel in a week long, non-stop Rock n' Roll festival at sea.

This was the 2018 Monsters of Rock Cruise, with forty of the world's best metal bands and solo acts headlined by Tesla, Lita Ford, Thunder, Queensryche, Winger, with special appearances by Steve Harris of Iron Maiden, Michael Sweet of Stryper, other great acts like LA Guns, Beasto Blanco, Autograph, Great White, and more, as well as a few surprises that came up throughout the week.

The remainder of that Sunday into the wee hours of Monday was spent setting up our gallery, and after no sleep the night prior I made it a point to sleep in late that morning. When I did rise and freshen up, I grabbed a bite to eat and headed to the poolside stage deck to check out a scheduled 12:30 question and answer session with members of the band Tesla. One reply that struck a chord was Frank Hannon's explanation of why they named their band after the inventor, Nikola Tesla. The band had celebrated their name-sake for years in their song *Edison's Medicine*, wherein Thomas Edison is decried as the rip off artist of the age, while praising "Man Outta Time" Nikola Tesla with a great, well-lyricized tribute ("He was electro-magnetic, completely kin-etic" - Love that line!) that didn't overlook the fact that "Steinmetz and Twain were friends that remained." The discussion rekindled my awareness of Mark Twain's friendship with the inventor, reminding me of one my favorite photos - the 1894 image of Twain playing with a luminous ball of electricity in Tesla's laboratory while the inventor looks on from behind.

Nikola Tesla, left, with Mark Twain playing with a luminous ball of electricity in Tesla's Lab.

In a letter to Livy dated February, 1894, Twain had written:

"Livy dear, last night I played billiards with Mr. Rogers until 11... and had a most delightful time until 4 this morning...Among the people present were... [fourteen prominent figures of the era including painter William Merritt Chase, the Philly-born actor John Drew - uncle of the famous Barrymore clan of Lionel, Ethel, and John, and great-great uncle of Drew Barrymore, and] Nikola Tesla, the world-wide illustrious electrician; see article about him in Jan. or Feb. Century...Everybody there had done something and was in his way famous."[403]

In his autobiography, Tesla claimed that reading Twain's books had saved his life. "I was prostrated with a dangerous illness or rather, a score of them" Tesla had written...

> "and my condition became so desperate that I was given up by physicians. During this period I was permitted to read constantly...One day I was handed a few volumes of new literature unlike anything I had ever read before and so captivating as to make me utterly forget my hopeless state. They were the earlier works of Mark Twain and to them might have been due the miraculous recovery which followed. Twenty-five years later, when I met Mr. Clemens and we formed a friendship between us, I told him of the experience and was amazed to see that great man of laughter burst into tears."[404]

Mr. Tesla had the opportunity to return the favor by inviting Twain to stand on his invented "healing plate" to help with a bout of constipation, which is said to have effectively sent Twain running to the toilet.

The cruise connection between Tesla the band and Tesla the inventor and Mark Twain added to the serendipitous cycle that seemed to keep coming my way. That evening, Tesla performed an acoustic set with a song list plucked from their renowned 1990 album *Five Man Acoustical Jam*, which had been recorded in my hometown of Philly at the Trocadero, a surviving Burlesque and Vaudeville venue built in 1870. When they began playing *'Comin' Atcha Live'*, I was stoked as that is always the lead-in for their excellent cover of The Grateful Dead's *Truckin'*.

The next morning I went to the poolside deck to enjoy a cup of Chai and was surprised to find that sometime in the wee hours we had docked at the Port of Labadee, Haiti. As I surveyed the island's mountainous terrain from a perch on the railing, its high, sharp mountain peaks and tropically forested slopes that plunged gracefully to the pristine beaches gave the impression of a fictitious, prehistoric world. I didn't know a stop at Jurassic Park was on the itinerary.

After lunch, I disembarked onto a long pier that spanned the length of our massive ship all the way to the island, enabling me to fully grasp the massive scale of our vessel for the first time while relishing this tropical vista that spanned before me. Crystal clear, luminescent blue-green waters lapped gently along isolated stretches of beach dappled with remnants of ancient coral beds. Once on the island, to my left was a longer, gorgeous beach, and to my right were foothills lush with palm trees and other tropical flora. Opting for a Zen moment I chose the middle path for a casual stroll along a wide sandy esplanade also used by rough terrain transportation shuttles.

At one point a jeep zipped past, and suddenly I felt transported to another time and place as the whole scene conjured up a reflective notion of what my Dad's experience might have been on similar terrain of a South Pacific Naval base where he was stationed during WWII. In my youth he'd told many a tale of those days, with my only reference having been scenes from films like *South Pacific* or other WWII naval sagas. Here I could glean how easily Ezio Pinza and Mitzi Gaynor could enjoy *Some Enchanted Evening*, or 'Lieutelin' Joe from Philadelphia becoming enraptured by Bloody Mary's enchanting siren call of Bali Hai. I found myself walking in Dad's shoes, capitalizing on his memories imbedded in my DNA. What a wondrous, elated time it must have been for him for the memory to remain throughout his life, just as the wonder gleaned from this present trip awakened a similar sense of youthful hope and satisfaction.

From that busier path I made my way to a surprisingly less populated coral strewn beach. While strolling along the surf, I couldn't help but reflect on my earlier research findings about this very island, which had once been the French-ruled slave capital of Saint-Domingue. It did not escape me that this lovely tropical cruise tourist mecca I was presently enjoying was once the ocean bound prison of 500,000 enslaved Africans, perhaps with thousands more carted off from Ireland under the direction of Oliver Cromwell, and the very island where Napoleon's army was so decimated by disease that he was forced to sell the Louisiana Territory to Thomas Jefferson and trigger America's western expansion. How surreal to consider Haiti's unique role in world history, now veiled by Pina Colada bars and native trinket shops.

A quiet, traffic-free moment on the path in Haiti

My directionless stroll led me to an outdoor stage where fellow cruisers had gathered for a beach front performance by the LA band Atomic Punk. I hung out and enjoyed the show for a little while before continuing to explore the jungle's edge along the nearby base of a towering cliff and do some photography. Gradually the music volume was overtaken by the crash of surf as I found myself on an empty beach about fifty yards away. With no one about, walking along this tropical retreat proved to be the best medicine for my weary physical self.

Stopping intermittently to take photos, I walked quietly, reflectively along the delicately lapping waves and surf, exercising the moment as a walking meditation to revive and recharge myself. Ruminating further on thoughts of Saint-Domingue history, I envisioned vessels of slaves and cargo, and pirates who may have long ago sailed past or disembarked on these very shores. Now and then I'd pause to explore some cool seashells with unusual colors,

Isolated surf in Haiti

reminding me of the small collection of Livy Clemens and daughters displayed at their home in Hartford. I pondered whether they would have liked the unique shell specimens I was holding, which made me self-aware that I had assumed a familial connection to them, not only from having read so much about the details of their lives, but from the revelation of corporeality had while visiting their graves. I found it fascinating that I had gone so far into the mind and life of Mark Twain that he and his loved ones had practically become family. They were more than just remote research topics: I felt a deep kinship and connection to them. I remembered what David McCullough had written in the passage cited earlier: "You feel a bond with those vanished people. They are not just anybody and nobody anymore and they never will be for you ever again."[405] Now I intimately understood what he meant.

As the time approached 4:00 pm, I decided to make my way back to the ship at a leisurely pace. I returned to my cabin around 4:30, rinsed my feet, changed, and went to get a light dinner. Getting to the cafeteria required a jaunt through the pool deck, where I stopped and took some dramatic final photos of Haiti as the ship lifted anchor around 5:30 pm and slowly headed out to sea.

After dinner, I returned to the pool deck just as Frank Hannon's solo band was beginning their set as a remarkable tropical sunset formed a psychedelic backdrop behind them. Hannon's masterful guitar prowess seemed to serve as the paintbrush for this amazingly surreal tropical evening. Earlier I had met his drummer, Kelly Smith, so it was great to catch him in action. Kelly's percussion lent an air of something ancient, like the synchronistic pulse of indigenous man in harmony with the environment, like the primal rhythms captured so well by the Dead's Mickey Hart on his Planet Drum CD, which probably was no accident given Frank's known affinity for the Dead. Frank and his cohorts didn't miss a beat. The continued heavy rhythm of Kelly's drumming audacity set against the aggressive wailing of Frank's crescent moon shaped guitar punctuated a sense of perfect cohesion, as if the musicians and the rest of us by default had become unified with the movement of the watery foundation beneath us.

I went to the upper deck which overlooked the stage two levels above to fetch myself another Corona. The wind was whipping a little stronger by then. Few people elected to brave it up there, giving the semblance of a private performance. I took my place along the railing as Hannon's band began the opening chords of a familiar song. Could it be? With its deep, soulful bass and Kelly hammering the song's signature drum beat, Frank deftly hit every high, wailing note as this ecstatic epiphany of my generation's music catalog enveloped the atmosphere. They were playing Edgar Winter's *Frankenstein*!

From my vantage high above the stage with sky above and the wind tossing my hair, I was vindicated! I was redeemed! I had not heard anyone play a live version of this in decades, possibly not since an earnest attempt by an area cover band playing one of the long-demolished clubs on Pacific Avenue in Wildwood, New Jersey in the late 1970s. I was blown away! The familiar music chorus interludes brought me back to the first time I heard the song while hanging with my teenage homies in a piss and glass strewn school yard in South Philly. I was transported back to my fifteen-year-old self as I moved my body and bounced my head to the beat. Before the song ended, I already knew this would remain a highlight of this cruise, probably for all of us witnessing this wonderful phenomenon. When Kelly pounded out the final beats, I was beyond ecstatic. All of us burst into a spontaneous, powerful chorus of grateful cheers and applause. This was potentially my most perfect moment of the cruise.

When the band finished I grabbed a light snack and coffee then went to work at our evening gallery reception where I was greeted by Rick Allen and his security detail, Big John Murray. We saw each earlier on the pool deck and so chatted in praise of Frank's band, how the cruise experience was going, and about the shared fun had while working together with Rick throughout the week. Big John was a legend in Rock and Roll circles in his own right, having worked with high-profile talent for many years, and perhaps best known as Brett Michael's security detail on the VH1 program "Rock of Love." Larger than life, John was a bonafide American military hero who had saved the lives of a team of fellow Marines from a burning helicopter while on a detail in Somalia, among whom was John Roberts, who would become National Service Director of the Wounded Warrior Project. Working with Big John was a genuine privilege.

As the week progressed, working with the perennially affable Thundergod[406] evolved into what could be likened to a floating Rock n' Roll summer art camp with Rick Allen as a tirelessly exuberant cabin mate. I couldn't help but compare my situation to Twain's description of his experience in Innocents Abroad. "Sam isolated himself from the pilgrims" Twain biographer Ron Powers explained,

With fellow Night-Hawk Big John Murray.

> "inside a small group of younger bloods whom he called the "Quaker City night-hawks," and, much later in his book, the "sinners."...Dan Slote, Sam's roommate, paid his dues with constant, inspired wisecracking...Then there was...a youth suspended in that magical interlude between callow wonderment and heavy drinking. His name was Charles Jervis Langdon."[407]

Though both heavier drinking and callow wonderment were long in our respective pasts, the parallel was humoring. Throughout the week Rick never missed an opportunity to interject an inspired wisecrack that would send us all reeling in laughter. The merriment he generated in our gallery work evenings formed the foundation of our own circle of Night-Hawks, with Rick as a Dan Slote/Charlie Langdon hybrid, and Big John filling J. B. Pond's large shoes for our present adventure, though Pond wasn't among the original Night-Hawks.

Twain had written of Slote:

> "I have got a splendid, immoral, tobacco-smoking, wine-drinking, godless roommate who is as good and true and right-minded a man as ever lived - a man whose blameless conduct and example will always be an eloquent sermon to all who shall come within their influence."[408]

Dan Slote was a stationary manufacturer from New York whose firm, in the decades following the Quaker City cruise adventures, would produce and distribute the self-pasting scrapbook invented and patented by Mark Twain, which I saw among the Twain artifacts displayed at Elmira College the summer before. I liked Twain's affectionate, playful derision of Slote. It's the sort of teasing good friends will sling at each other. It reveals just how much Mark Twain had embodied a Rock n' Roll spirit in his time.

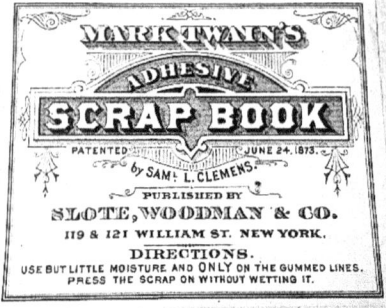 

Left, Dan Slote's 1873 promotional ad for Twain's patented Scrapbook, and, Right, Mark Twain's personal copy of his scrapbook as displayed at Elmira College.

There's something about the Rock n Roll culture that fosters that kind of environment, yet, also seems symptomatic of an unseen yet recognizably detected zeitgeist that manifests in each generation. Mark Twain and Charlie Langdon had found it. Gertrude Stein, Picasso, Hemingway, and their Paris Salon circle had found it. Jack Kerouac, Neal Cassady and the Beat poets had found it. I've rediscovered it on regular intervals since my youth, having an eager predilection for always sniffing out the active, expressive pulse of our culture. Kerouac may have described it best in *On The Road*, when he wrote:

> "The only people for me are the mad ones, the ones who are mad to live, mad to talk, mad to be saved, desirous of everything at the same time, the ones who never yawn or say a commonplace thing, but burn, burn, burn like fabulous yellow roman candles exploding like spiders across the stars..."[409]

That's what Twain's Night-Hawk ethos was all about. It's that spirit which defiantly compels one to extract the *rasa* - the nectar - out of the life we're given. That's what rock and rollers understand, and what is often so misunderstood about them.

Then, as if on cue, Tesla bandmates Brian Wheat and Troy Luccketta dropped by, joining Rick, Big John, my pals Carol and Lyle and my colleagues who were holding court around our work counter, which was a repurposed lounge bar also used to serve Champagne during the evening receptions.

The ship's Cigar Lounge where our gallery display was set up had a bar and paneled walls that were reminiscent of my parent's basement where I'd spent so many times hanging with friends in the 1970s. Like the space-age, flip down tuning knobs on the Nate-Ben's TV, that finished basement with knotty Pine paneling was what had sold Dad on buying the house into which we moved in 1974. He envisioned not so much a man-cave but a family room with a bar for family parties. He decorated it with our family's sports trophies, posters of classic films like *Casablanca* and *The Maltese Falcon*, an enlarged photo of one of the last reunions of his brothers and cousins, and photos and paraphernalia of his tour of duty on the USS Ticonderoga.

Left: Dad - seated furthest to right in his reunion photo with brothers and relatives; Right: Dad's cherished 1945 photo of "The Big T"- the USS Ticonderoga - that he displayed behind his bar in the basement.

Though I was working while the others chatted, at one point I was compelled to pause and stand back for a moment to witness this. Like a movie scene filmed while zooming back on a dolly, I felt like I was having an out of the body experience, removed from the situation while I was in it and yet simultaneously able to observe it, as if I were being transported back in time. Something psychologically fulfilling happened, as if I was completing some unfinished internal business, healing some conditioned residue from earlier in my life. I felt right at home, as if I was a teenager again, hanging with friends at my father's similarly sized bar. It was as if the cruise ship had become my own 1970s Twilight Zone episode.

The last time the basement bar had been used socially was for a surprise 60th birthday party for Dad which I had organized. After that, Dad had grown too sick to enjoy something as simple having a good time with friends in his basement bar. He never entertained there again, having passed away less than two years later. With gratitude, love, and fatherly ribbing, Dad promised one day he would get me back for throwing that surprise party. Little did I know that Circumstance would enable his spirit to pull it off on a rock and roll cruise with a guest list that included rock stars and Marine heroes. As I looked on, it occurred to me that I had found my Night-Hawks in this group of kindred spirits. Just as Twain had described his own night with the original Tesla, "Everyone was in some way famous." I accepted this as Dad's promise fulfilled, a debt squared handsomely, indeed.

After about an hour, Brian and Troy left and my colleagues ventured on to their cabins or catch one of the shows scheduled for that night, with Rick, John, Carol and Lyle staying behind. I seized the chance and jockeyed myself into a spot behind our office counter to review the day's paperwork, make some corrections and take a few minutes to organize things for the next day. Rick proceeded to share stories about wild times he, his Def Leppard bandmates and the Tesla guys spent together in the old days, leaving us laughing as he recounted the sort of details one might expect of a wild, young, touring rock and roll band in the late eighties. For an extended time afterward, we conversed about families and our respective working-class upbringing, about religious backgrounds, about the distinctions between Anglicanism and Catholicism. I joked that in order to be a really good Catholic, it was essential to learn a crusade anthem I had sung as a child in church. So, I proceeded to belt out my most earnest recollection of "*An Army of Youth*."

We discussed raising children, how being a parent offers one the opportunity to revisit one's own childhood, about how watching and supporting a child as they grow enables us to grow anew into a maturity of wisdom that retains some of the playfulness of childhood. Actively engaging as a parent is one of the things that breathes a new life into an aging soul. Our children remind us of this vitally important aspect of aging. It's the lesson Mr. Banks learned in *Mary Poppins*, that Ebenezer Scrooge learned in Dicken's *A Christmas Carol*.

Someone had pointed out that the age of seven seems to be the magic number when a child takes their first steps as a somewhat independent thinking being, when all the learning from birth begins to congeal. I paused for moment, recalling that it was at that same age when my own vivid memories of my father began to become their strongest and comprise the most formative years of influence on the person I've become. Not only was he a provider, but he was my guide, teaching me the skills necessary to navigate this crazy world. The manner in which he behaved and interacted with life had showed me the way.

Shortly afterward, everyone agreed to call it a night. While Carol and Lyle went to their cabin and the mighty Big John escorted our resident Thundergod to his upper level Valhalla, I stayed behind to finish some work before locking up, and just enjoy a moment of quiet reflection, continuing to reminisce about forgotten good times in my parent's basement.

I completed the paperwork then cleaned and straightened up a bit, finishing up shortly after midnight. I had rested well that day and felt overdue for some R & R from having worked non-stop for weeks. One deck below in the Metropolis Theatre the LA band Faster Pussycat was performing, so I headed there and ordered an Irish Mule, made just right with muddled Lime, a generous shot of Jameson Whiskey and Ginger Beer. The band was incredible and I was having such a great time I ordered another round. After the show ended, I ordered another round for the road and headed up to the pool deck around 2:00 am and stumbled into an informal jam with Patrick Kennison of Lita Ford's band holding court while playing KISS tunes on an acoustic guitar, surrounded by maybe fifteen or so other night-hawks who were singing along and dancing.

From where I stood I could see activity through the windows of the Karaoke Lounge above us on the fourteenth level. On the Lebrewski Cruise two years before I had then assumed the Karaoke Bar was a reserved, private party lounge for the onboard talent. This erroneous assumption was corrected the night before when I was having some late-night pizza with my friend Jodi from Pittsburgh. So, being only one or two sheets to the wind at that point, I ventured up to the Karaoke Lounge to check it out.

When I entered it was quite crowded, and as I waded through the thick crowd I was greeted by people I'd met or helped in some way in the days prior. We'd briefly chat as best as we could amid the clamoring din and blaring music, as members of one band or another took the stage to sing favorite songs that influenced them, or in tribute to another band in the room. Each friend I encountered would ask what I was drinking. The next thing I knew, a continuous supply of Irish Mules continued to appear before me, with the server pointing to the friend who provided it. We'd hoist our glasses to each other with acknowledgement. After some time had passed, my buddy Scott from Dallas wanted to buy me a round but I was a bit cozy by then, feeling the proverbial third sheet beginning to envelope me. I call it the point of no return. I thanked him and politely declined, deciding it was time to call it a night and head back to my cabin.

As I emerged from the dimmer light of the lounge, I found myself just barely able to walk a straight line. Oh boy, I thought. Lord help me make it to the other end of the ship and nine decks down to my bed. I began to take deep inhalations of sea breeze while continuing in measured, cautious steps along the exposed, outdoor pool deck to the maze-like interior Solarium. From there I managed to make it to the first bank of elevators and descend to deck five. I could barely see straight now as I made my way across the cavernous promenade, drawing on every ounce of focus in my reserve to just lift one leg and move it in front of the other. To avoid seeing double, I continued the entirety of my trek with only one eye open. This was another episode of what my wife calls 'Popeye Theater' (a nod to Sally Starr, of course), because of my recurring tendency after a few extra drinks to keep one eye closed and one eye opened just to see straight.

Now and then the swaying of the ship caused me to walk more like Charlie Chaplin as I struggled to keep my balance, which I though quite humorous at the time. One great bonus of practicing witness-consciousness meditation for thirty years is that I can experience myself as my own entertainment, like a miniature, perennially sober version of myself sitting inside my body, just observing everything that's going on. So, whenever I've gotten sloshed, I'm mindful that it's only my body that's drunk. It was my non-drunk, inner self that was having a challenging time steering this flesh machine in the right direction. I couldn't wait to get to my cabin and fling myself across that bed soon enough. I had officially arrived at shit-faced, and, remarkably, throughout this entire trek, I was still holding onto my half-filled glass of what I figured the next day must have been my 6th or 7th Irish Mule. As hammered as I was, an Irish-Catholic never abandons a precious shot of Jameson - not to mention the cruise ship cost for such a concoction. Besides, discarding it would be a dishonor to the friend who purchased it, I reasoned, and Ginger Beer is a good cure for motion sickness, which would aid in keeping the contents of my stomach intact - for now.

I made my way at long last to the staircase at the far end of the ship. I held tight to the railing with one hand, balancing my glass of Celtic nectar in the other. When I got to the fourth deck, I saw the sliding glass doors that led to the outside promenade and decided I could use some fresh air before bed, as well as a break to muster the remaining energy required to make it the rest of the way to my cabin. I went out and implanted myself along the railing. A lone guy to my left was scrolling on his phone. We casually said hi to each other, then chatted about seeing Faster Pussycat. He introduced himself as Patrick. I, of course, immediately renamed him 'Dude.' "Where are you from, Dude?" I asked. "New York" he replied. After meeting folks from cities in Europe, Australia, Brazil and elsewhere from around the States, Patrick was the first person I'd met on the cruise who lived relatively close to me. "Oh, cool!" I remarked. "I'm from Philly!"

"Philly?" he questioned. "I should hate you right now. I'm originally from Boston. I only moved to New York last year." Oh boy, I thought. Here we go. Another post-Super Bowl, Boston vs Philly showdown. Just what I needed in my inebriated condition. With my compassionate best I just shrugged my shoulders and said "You can't win 'em all, Dude…although you guys almost did." Patrick chilled and ceded to the victory, extending his hand to officially congratulate me as an inadvertent representative of the entire City of Philadelphia and Eagles organization. "That's cool" I replied. I imagine I must have been the first Philadelphian to whom he'd relayed that. I was happy to have been seminal to his healing.

Just then my buddy Dave from Las Vegas came around the corner. Dave was a roadie with the logistics team that ran Monsters of Rock, and had hooked me all week up with ice and other supplies for our gallery receptions. Patrick asked if we wanted a drink. While swaying in unison with the lolling ship. I held up my fingers before him in the sign of the cross to relay that I had my fill. I said I needed some water and would get one for each of us. I managed to make my way somewhere to get three cups of water and ice, but when I returned Pat and Dave were gone. I set down two of the waters and drank the third, looking out over the vast blackness of ocean before me, mesmerized by patterns of luminescent algae atop sea foam generated by the ship's wake.

When I finished my water I picked up the remaining two and headed inside, descending the stairway to my deck. Every remaining ounce of energy was mustered just to make it to my cabin door. I was spent and sighed audibly on arrival. I set down the waters, concentrating to retrieve my key card and unlock the door. I turned the handle with relief, opening it as if I were accessing Tolkien's long sealed Doors of Durin. There before me, at long last, adorned with an animal effigy made out of a towel, was my glorious bed, beaming with radiant, hallowed light, or so it seemed through my smudged eyeglasses. I felt like I had just scaled Everest or the Matterhorn, ready to implant my victorious flag in the name of soused Bacchanalian revelers everywhere.

I set the waters on the desk, seemingly unable to undress fast enough to make it to that mattress. I went into the cramped bathroom, splashed some cool water on my face and brushed my teeth. While toweling myself dry, my stomach decided the time had arrived to protest. I knelt down on the floor to regain composure, wrapping my arms around the proverbial porcelain bus like a ship's helmsman grabbing the wheel, bracing myself with a foreboding sense I was about to navigate through an unplanned bout of my own stormy weather for the next several hours. My inner mix/meteorologist forecast was right. Like Gilligan's *Minnow*, the weather started getting rough and my tiny ship was tossed. At each pause between interval bouts of expulsion, I would meekly turn and look forlornly at that luxurious, perfectly made bed, beckoning me from just three feet away. The cherubic-faced, terry cloth -what is that? An Aardvark? - stared defiantly while all seven Irish Mules were now kicking this Irish ass relentlessly like a malady from Mordor, as if the Aardvark had united with the mules in a planned mutiny to join forces and teach me a lesson I'd never forget.

After a while I managed to lift myself from the floor, relinquish control of my ceramic ship's wheel back to the helmsman, wash and wipe my face, rinse my mouth and drink some water, and at long last, flung myself in a face-up, cruciform position onto the down and cotton promised land of Valinor. I uttered an exasperated "Thank you Jesus!" and didn't even bother to pull up the covers.

I awoke that morning about 10:30 or 11:00 am, feeling frayed around the edges but relatively ok. Surely a thousand dormant demons from a dozen past lives had been purged in those hours before. I got out of bed and finished the two waters sitting on the desk. The whiskey Gods must have known I'd need them more than my two deck companions. I did some yoga stretches and jumped in the shower. I took the used bath towels to clean up as best I could from my live, solo performance of *The Exorcist*, and left a twenty-dollar bill with a note of apology for the housekeeper who would arrive shortly to make this sanctuary holy again. Before leaving the cabin, I turned back to check if I forgot anything and noticed the Aardvark, still staring at me. "This stays between you and me. Deal?" The Aardvark seemed amenable.

My MOR Cruise cabin mate

I made my way to the fourth deck promenade and settled into a lounge chair to spend some quiet time on our last day at sea. With my laptop resting, well, on the top of my lap, I wrote some of the ruminations above then spent some time reading my old, weathered paperback copy of *The Innocents Abroad*, with loose pages I held tightly for fear of blowing away. As the ship lumbered along at a pace consistent with the word cruise, I overlooked a vast expanse of ocean, noting an additional comparison between Mark Twain and my Dad: both loved to sail and both loved the sea.

"A vast expanse of ocean" - the view from where I sat.

The present vessel was a large one, and I assumed that the basic architectural design and construction materials hadn't differed much from the WWII era USS Ticonderoga on which Dad had served in the South Pacific in that both were like floating cities. I pictured Dad on that ship and imagined what he must have experienced as an eighteen-year-old kid from working-class Schuylkill at a time when the far stretches of the globe were just places with names mentioned on radio broadcasts or read about in the newspapers. Looking out at the vast expanse of endless ocean instilled a contemplative, serene and expansive state of mind that paralleled the endless horizon before me. What imaginative inspirations it conjured even then for me, as it must have for my Dad as well more than seventy years before.

There is a photo of Mark Twain sitting along the promenade of a cruise ship, probably taken by J. B. Pond on one their many voyages. Whenever I view it, I imagine how similar contemplative moments while drafting the accounts that became *The Innocents Abroad* must have enabled him to reflect on his Mississippi River days, both as a youth and later as a pilot. Mark Twain had a kinship with the river and sea that ran through his veins. Surely there was something he sought to recapture following the tragic death of his daughter, Jean, when he embarked on the voyage to the Caribbean that would be his last. It was that trip, abruptly aborted, that brought him back to his home at Stormfield where he needed to be carried to his deathbed. What was that something he sought and so embraced while at sea? I felt I had understood it while sitting on the deck that day, and then I found Twain's own confirmation, written as a young, ambitious journalist at the inception of his career, just as the SS Quaker City embarked on its journey, as if the great vessel and cruise itself served as the prophetic embodiment of the author's grand life to follow:

"The next morning we weighed anchor and went to sea. It was a great happiness…I thought there was never such gladness in the air before, such brightness in the sun, such beauty in the sea. I was satisfied with the picnic then and all its belongings. All my malicious instincts were dead within me and as America faded out of sight, I think a spirit of charity rose up in their place that was as boundless, for the time being, as the broad ocean that was heaving its billows about us. I wished to express my feelings- I wished to lift up my voice and sing…"[410]

Twain on deck in his Pilot's cap.

What had compelled Twain's soul to so soar? Water. It was the primary background for Huckleberry Finn, whose adventures were river dependent. Water gave life, and, as a river pilot well knew, could take life away. The river was the artery of community, commerce and sustenance in the 19th Century. It provided transport and entertainment. For a slave, the Mississippi in particular posed the difference between languishing in oppression or enjoying the fruits of liberty. Frederick Douglass relied on the river to begin his journey to freedom. Jervis Langdon employed the river to amass a fortune, and as a vehicle of humanitarian service to aid those seeking freedom. Without the river, there was no freedom. In Twain's world, the river was God.

The essence of this observation had been captured in Hammerstein and Kern's lyrics for *Ol' Man River* for their Broadway show *Showboat*. I became a fan of the song via the Jim Croce version around 1972 or '73, but there is no comparison to the original version by the great Paul Robeson, one of my personal heroes, whom I would later learn had lived his final years in West Philadelphia, just about a mile from my boyhood home in a house we drove past often when I was a kid.

Nestled within the song's narrative of the oppressed slave, or any toiling laborer, the heart of it suggests the river's hidden message of hope and continuity:

> Show me that stream called the River Jordan
> That's the old stream that I long to cross
> Old Man River, that Old Man River
> He must know something, but he don't say nothing
> He just keeps rolling, he keeps on rolling along

For my dad, water delivered the same revelation. In his youth and for his South Philadelphia community, the river offered respite. It provided a visual diversion from the soot laden, working class world of gritty brick and mortar, glass and steel, and escape from a repetitious, grinding existence. On the cruise ship that day I understood what so compelled Dad to select the Navy as his preferred branch of armed forces in which to enlist. Water had been his constant companion. He knew its secrets and knew it could be trusted. Joining the Navy provided the opportunity to serve the national and moral cause against the Axis threat, fulfilling a sense of duty and an opportunity to escape and breathe free. Water, from river to ocean, would guide and teach, unveiling its ancient secrets along the way.

My cruise view from the stern, somewhere in the South Atlantic.

This was it. Here was the commonality I sought. Just like that moment in Hannibal when I felt the triune presence. Like the biblical reunion of Jesus, Elijah and Moses on the mountain, Mark Twain, my father and I reunited in spirit right then and there on that ship deck in the middle of the South Atlantic. I felt that this is what to which they had been guiding me throughout this entire, year-long journey. The lesson of water articulated by Twain at the onset of his career was its awesome power as the great corporeal equalizer. On water there is no skin color, no petty distinctions or reason to squabble. It is bound by no laws or social convention. It might be harnessed but ultimately prevails. To those who will listen, the river or ocean will reveal its secrets. Once you've heard it, your life is never the same. It's the same lesson imparted in Psalm 23: "He leadeth me beside the still waters. He restoreth my soul..."

It was the same lesson conveyed to my and all our respective ancestors who sailed across the ocean to seek liberty, relief from oppression and starvation, and find new opportunity in a promised land. And there it was. This is what my Dad saw in his adolescence while reflecting on the journey of his immigrant ancestors. I had sailed on the very river in Donegal from where our impoverished forebears had left Ireland to cross the sea, and arrive to struggle after a seemingly unattainable promise along the banks of another river in America. This is why the *Adventures of Huckleberry Finn* was his favorite book. As valued as the lessons and captivating escapades of its principal characters, it was the river, winding its way along every page and paragraph, that spoke so clearly to my young Dad.

This is what the spirits of these two river brothers wanted me to know. It's the message they, and I, wished to relay. And then, like a beacon of light cast upon my deck chair, there it was: I immediately saw the connection to the 1973 Tom Sawyer musical, as if Dad and 12-year-old me were once again buddies, sitting together in that darkened theater as we watched the panoramic Mississippi unfold before our eyes as it had 50 years earlier.

Being at sea seems to cleanse the mind and soul like the waters of redemption. It forgives all sins and allows an independent sense of being to emerge. It gives a person an opportunity to reflect and begin anew. It puts the past in perspective and poses the future as an accessible horizon of potential. It simultaneously reminds man of his mortality and the infinite source of his soul. The scriptures say from dust we came and dust we shall return. And yet, our corporeal forms are composed of what, like 80, 90% water? And salt. Dust is just a small portion of our makeup. It's water from whence we came.

Deep on a cellular level, our DNA recalls this. It recalls our universal connectedness, the kinship that binds us all as one organism. I believe this is the essence of that something that both my Dad and Mark Twain knew. On some level of the greater interconnecting consciousness, even if not consciously understood, the sea gives us the rare opportunity to perceive this. It's something you can never forget, and prompts the desire to recall and experience it again. Some are blessed with the opportunity to cruise on ships like this often. Naval enlistees choose it. Boat owners surely know it. But for a landlubber like me, it's a gift I won't forget, and I found myself on that final day of voyage already wishing it would last a little longer, instilling a desire to come back again.

The next day I bid farewell to the new friends I had made, hailed a Lyft to the airport, boarded my flight and before I knew it was on my way home. As I stared out the plane window, I thought back at the fun and pleasant memories from the week. It occurred to me that all of us on that cruise were, like those on the Quaker City, pilgrims in search of some manner of respective reconciliation. No one had cared about any differences, and all were approachable, friendly, and accepting. I felt lucky to have spent the week among 3000 of the coolest people on the planet, with representatives from every race, creed, country and continent. We could have started our own government and served as an ideal, global role model for social cohesion. Everyone on that amazing rock n roll cruise were enjoyers of living in a way that sustains a good time a little longer. It's something we had all learned at some point in our lives, and there was on that cruise an unspoken, internal recognition that all of us were essentially from the same tribe. Everyone on that voyage had been the Night hawks I sought, and probably for each other as well. We all liked to have a good time, and prolong it with sympathetic compadres and kindred spirits who become trusted not to trample on our mutually exposed, vulnerable hearts. And we all like a good beat that we can dance to.

With that, I realized that I had managed to capture Mark Twain's cruise experience after all. In the conclusion of *The Innocents Abroad*, Twain wrote:

> "The grand pilgrimage is over. Good-bye to it, and a pleasant memory to it, I am able to say in all kindness. I bear no malice, no ill will toward any individual that was connected with it, either as passenger or officer…When we stepped on board, our cares vanished, our troubles were at an end - for the ship was home to us…Travel is fatal to prejudice, bigotry, and narrow-mindedness, and many of our people need it sorely on these accounts. Broad, wholesome, charitable views of men and things cannot be acquired by vegetating in one little corner of the earth all one's lifetime. 'The excursion is ended, and has passed to its place among the things that were. But its varied scenes and its manifold incidents will linger pleasantly in our memories for many a year to come."[411]

So it was. I don't believe I could have worded it much better myself. My cruise experience served as the culminating highlight of my own grand pilgrimage into the heart of Mark Twain, completing an extended internal revival, rebirth, and cycle of personal renewal that began a year before. It was like a long dormant part of myself had awakened from an extended slumber. It took more than a year of travelling the country, poring through volumes of Twain's written legacy, researching the author's psychological formation and transcendence of a racist

America, investigating the pathos of his family life, all to understand why my Dad had been such a fan of Mark Twain.

As my adventure came to an end, it was clear that my one, underlying driving purpose was to simply express gratitude to a man who dedicated his life first to serving his parents and siblings, then to his God, his country, and finally to his wife and family, ultimately passing along his life's best learned lessons as his leadsman's call of "mark twain!" for my brothers and I to navigate through the murky river of our respective lives in safe waters.

An impulsive trip to Hannibal, Missouri on a Sunday afternoon had inspired an extended trek spanning twelve years and thousands of miles that brought me right here, to this moment, to give me the chance to say the one thing his death had taken from me: Thank you, Dad, for giving me my life. I can picture his cocked smile of compassion, reserved for use when he saw that some lesson he'd been trying to impart finally managed to break through my youthful wall of stupidity. I can hear his cajoling affirmation even now, vocalized in a simple, familiar phrase: "Atta boy!"

Dad - Jack Curley - age 18, circa 1944.

A PARTING OBSERVATION

I've mentioned the serendipitous interconnectedness repeatedly experienced throughout this journey recounted herein. Without pre-meditated intention, I find myself completing the first draft of this work on the 108th anniversary of Mark Twain's death.

Throughout Asia, among the Hindus, Buddhists, Jains, Taoists and adherents of Zen, 108 is regarded as a sacred number, believed to represent divine order, symbolic of a means to finding our connection to a greater whole. Zen Buddhist temples are built with 108 steps to symbolize the 108 steps to enlightenment, and at the end of each year their temple bells are rung 108 times heralding the completion of a cycle and marking a time to begin anew.

Now that's what I call squaring a debt handsomely.

Tom Curley,
April 21, 2018

ACKNOWLEDGEMENTS

With sincerest gratitude for the assistance provided by the following:

To my literary cheerleader Kim Trate McCall, who suggested I start a blog and witnessed this work unfolding from page one while offering support, encouragement, and good jokes along the way; To Kelly McVeigh and Phil Polillo, Professor Kelly Smith, Kenna Lynn, Patty Mengers, Dr. Kent Corso, James Curley, Jason Kampf, Joel Spivak, Diane Keller, & Sheldon Jackson for their willingness to support, review the early drafts and offer vital editing suggestions; To S.A.B, for clarity, guidance, and endless support; To Nalini Kersey, my good friend (and highly recommended life coach) who encouraged me to just write; To Prof. Matt Seybold at the Center for Mark Twain Studies, Elmira, NY for his support, suggestions, encouragement and cheerleading; To Dr. Laura Skandera-Trombley for graciously and compassionately offering to read the first draft; To Nathanial Ball, archivist at The Center for Mark Twain Studies, with thanks; To J. Kelsey Jones, Chemung County Historian, and Joyce M. Tice of Chemung County Historical Society, for selflessly offering wonderful links and research sources; To Beth Dominianni, The Library Director at The Mark Twain Library in Redding, CT, for her informative guidance; To Jade Philipi, volunteer Ambassador at The Mark Twain Study, Elmira, NY, for her enlightening and informative tour and directions; To Kaitlyn Oberndorfer, my knowledgeable guide at The Mark Twain Home and Museum, Hartford, Connecticut; To Ginny Coyne, my gracious friend in Stormfield and commendable ambassador for Redding, Connecticut; To Ben Grange of Writer's Clearinghouse (and his mystery editor) who cheered this work onward when it was sorely needed; To Turner Classic Movies, for returning me to many wonderful moments with my father; To my mom for just being Mom and helping to clarify some of the facts of my memories; To my wife Maureen, for her loving support and talent for finding great vintage books; To my daughter Aileen, who inspires me every day and gives my life purpose; To Conan and Queenie, my constant companions and best critics, laying at my feet or sitting by my side, snorting and pawing remarks throughout; To all those friends, family members, coworkers and strangers who contributed so richly to the texture of my life and inspiring so many wonderful stories and memories like those shared herein; And, of course, to Samuel Clemens, for inventing such a marvelous character with a great nom de guerre which embodies a high standard that continues to inspire.

The author would like to extend
A VERY SPECIAL ACKNOWLEDGEMENT
to the following sources, authors, and scholars of Mark Twain, his works, life and legacy, without whose own published volumes and resources, this work would not have been possible:
Matt Seybold & The Center for Mark Twain Studies, Elmira, NY.
Contributors to The Mark Twain Project
Mr. Henry Sweets, Executive Director, The Mark Twain Boyhood Home & Museum, Hannibal, MO.
David Carkeet, Joe E. Fulton, Laura E. Skandera-Trombley, Ron Powers, Shelley Fisher-Fishkin, Michael Shelden, Jennifer Zaccara, Philip Foner, Fred Kaplan , Doris Kearns Goodwin,
Clifton Waller Barrett Library, Special Collections, University of Virginia Library, Charlottesville, VA.

Other books by Tom Curley

MASTERS AMONG US:
An Exploration of Supernal Encounters and Miraculous Phenomena

True accounts of miracles, Saints, & spiritual masters from all traditions

- Amazon.com #1 rank in Transpersonal Psychology titles
- Barnes and Noble Book of the Month Selection

MY STREET LOOKS LIKE AMERICA
A compilation of the author's original poetry and photography

Visit the author's blog @ www.curleyworld.com

BIBLIOGRAPHY

[1] Bismarck daily tribune. (Bismarck, Dakota [N.D.]), 11 April 1907. Chronicling America: Historic American Newspapers. Lib. of Congress .<http://chroniclingamerica.loc.gov/lccn/sn85042242/1907-04-11/ed-1/seq-7/>(Accessed 10/25/2018)

[2] The San Francisco Call, April 22, 1910. Source: Library of Congress: The San Francisco call. (San Francisco [Calif.]), 22 April 1910. Chronicling America: Historic American Newspapers. Lib. of Congress. <http://chroniclingamerica.loc.gov/lccn/sn85066387/1910-04-22/ed-1/seq-1/> (Accessed 10/25/2018)

[3] The London Daily News, Saturday, 23 April, 1910. British newspaper archive. https://www.britishnewspaperarchive.co.uk/viewer/bl/0000051/19100423/066/0003

[4] The New Ulm Review, New Ulm, Minnesota. "Mark Twain, King of Humor" by Robertus Love. April 27, 1910. Source: Library of Congress: New Ulm review. (New Ulm, Brown County, Minn.), 27 April 1910. Chronicling America: Historic American Newspapers. Lib. of Congress. <http://chroniclingamerica.loc.gov/lccn/sn89081128/1910-04-27/ed-1/seq-6/> (Accessed 10/25/2018)

[5] New York Times, "Mark Twain is Dead at 74: His Countrymen's Tributes Express Deep Sense of What Mark Twain Means to Americans. April 21, 1910. © 2010 The New York Times Company. https://archive.nytimes.com/www.nytimes.com/learning/general/onthisday/big/0421.html?mcubz=3 (Accessed 10/29/2018)

[6] Wikipedia contributors. "The Prince and the Pauper (1937 film)." Wikipedia, The Free Encyclopedia. Wikipedia, The Free Encyclopedia, 4 Aug. 2018. Web. 19 Sep. 2018.

[7] New-York tribune. (New York [N.Y.]), 20 Nov. 1921. Chronicling America: Historic American Newspapers. Lib. of Congress. <http://chroniclingamerica.loc.gov/lccn/sn83030214/1921-11-20/ed-1/seq-59/> (Accessed 10/25/2018)

[8] Contributors, Khan Academy Website; https://www.khanacademy.org/humanities/us-history/rise-to-world-power/1920s-america/a/movies-cinema-sports-1920s © 2018 Khan Academy. All Khan Academy content is available for free at www.khanacademy.org

[9] Melvin Patrick Ely, The Adventures of Amos 'n' Andy: Tenth Anniversary Edition. © 1991, © 2001 The University of Virginia Press. Pg 1.

[10] Wikipedia contributors. "A Connecticut Yankee (musical)." Wikipedia, The Free Encyclopedia. Wikipedia, The Free Encyclopedia, 28 Jun. 2018. Web. 22 Sep. 2018.

[11] Paine, Albert Bigelow. Mark Twain: A Biography: The Personal and Literary Life of Samuel Langhorne Clemens. The Writings of Mark Twain. Definitive ed. 4 vols. New York: Gabriel Wells, 1923. Chapter CCLXXXII, 'Personal Memoranda.' https://ebooks.adelaide.edu.au/t/twain/mark/paine/complete.html (Accessed 2/17/2017)

[12] IBID

[13] Twain, Mark Life on the Mississippi, Extracted from The Writings of Mark Twain, Volume 9, Chap. 27, p. 216. Harper & Brothers. 1911

[14] "Schuykill: A Little Irish Village Tucked Into Center City" by Rem Rieder. Sunday Bulletin, November 23, 1969.

[15] Twain, Mark, Life on the Mississippi: With over 300 Illustrations. London: Chatto & Windus, 1883. Chapter 53, My Boyhood Home. http://www.telelib.com/authors/T/TwainMark/prose/lifeonmississippi/lifeonmississippi53.html. Accessed 3/11/2018

[16] Twain, Mark, Life on the Mississippi: With over 300 Illustrations. London: Chatto & Windus, 1883. Chapter 53, My Boyhood Home. http://www.telelib.com/authors/T/TwainMark/prose/lifeonmississippi/lifeonmississippi53.html. Accessed 3/11/2018

[17] IBID

[18] IBID

[19] Wikipedia contributors, "Walter Russell," Wikipedia, The Free Encyclopedia, https://en.wikipedia.org/w/index.php?title=Walter_Russell&oldid=837254833 (accessed April 25, 2017)

[20] SLC to Orion Clemens December 9, 1874. Hartford, CT. http://www.lettersofnote.com/2015/10/new-fangled-writing-machine.html Accessed 3/22/2018

[21] Lienhard, John H. The Engines of Our Ingenuity: No. 50, The Paige Compositor. Copyright 1988-2018 by John H. Liehnard https://www.uh.edu/engines/epi50.htm. Accessed 3/22/2017

[22] Courtney, Steve Saving Mark Twain's House. C. February 21, 2013, Connecticut Explored. https://www.ctexplored.org/sample-article-saving-mark-twains-house/ Accessed 4/13/2018

[23] Morris, Edmund, Twain: Pajamas on the Landing. The New York Times Archives. October 26, 1975, p. 362 http://www.nytimes.com/1975/10/26/archives/twain-pajamas-on-the-landing-twain-a-house-ofgadgets.html?mcubz=1

[24] Twain, Mark. "SLC to Lou W. Benjamin, 10 April 1886 · Hartford, Conn." Source: Mark Twain on Ralph Waldo Emerson: Painful Grammer. Shapell Manuscript Foundation. http://www.shapell.org/manuscript/mark-twain-on-ralph-waldo-emerson. See also: Mark Twain Project Online, Catalog entry UCCL 03382. Berkeley, Los Angeles, London: University of California Press. 2016. Accessed 2018-04-24.

[25] IBID

[26] Twain, Mark Whittier Dinner Speech, From Mark Twain's Speeches New York: Harper & Brothers, 1910: 1-16 http://twain.lib.virginia.edu/onstage/whittier.html (Accessed 4/25/2018)

[27] IBID

[28] IBID

[29] Twain, Mark. SLC to Francis H. Skrine, January 19, 1897. London, UK. The Shapell Manuscript Collection. http://www.shapell.org/manuscript/mark-twains-mourns-the-loss-of-his-daughter Accessed 3/27/2017

[30] For more info, visit: http://www.marktwainhouse.org/house/room_in_the_house.php - Also - http://www.marktwainhouse.org/assets/images/photos_house/master_bedroom.jpg

[31] Mark Twain, from a letter to Clara Clemens, quoted in My Husband Gabrilowitsch. http://www.twainquotes.com/God.html Accessed 4/13/2018

[32] Wikipedia contributors, "George Griffin (butler)," Wikipedia, The Free Encyclopedia, https://en.wikipedia.org/w/index.php?title=George_Griffin_(butler)&oldid=717209622 (accessed April 26, 2017).

[33] Twain, Mark Roughing It, 1980 by The New American Library, Inc. Signet Classic Edition. p. 29

[34] Carkeet, David Special Feature: A Report on Susan Bailey's Ancestry; February, 2016 www.twainquotes.com; http://www.twainquotes.com/Carkeet/AncestryReport.html - Accessed 08/14/2017

[35] IBID

[36] Carkeet's essay is found at: http://www.twainquotes.com/Carkeet/AncestryReport.html

[37] Twain, Mark. Source undetermined. ThinkExist.com Quotations. ©1999-2016 ThinkExist. http://thinkexist.com/quotations/capitalism/ Accessed 05/20/2017

[38] Contributors at Hearthstone Legacy Publications. 2012-2017. My Genealogy Hound http://www.mygenealogyhound.com/vintage-photographs/new-york-photographs/Mark-Twain-Study-Elmira-New-York-photos.html# Accessed 5/12/2017

[39] Paine, Albert Bigelow. Mark Twain: A Biography: The Personal and Literary Life of Samuel Langhorne Clemens. The Writings of Mark Twain. Definitive ed. 4 vols. New York: Gabriel Wells, 1923. Chapter 1, p 507-508 https://ebooks.adelaide.edu.au/t/twain/mark/paine/complete.html (Accessed 2/17/2017)

[40] Contributors at Hearthstone Legacy Publications. 2012-2017. My Genealogy Hound http://www.mygenealogyhound.com/vintage-photographs/new-york-photographs/Mark-Twain-Study-Elmira-New-York-photos.html# Accessed 5/12/2017

[41] Dobbin, Ben, Twain's Words Flowed From Elmira April 4, 2010 St. Louis Post Dispatch © 2017 Lee Enterprises http://www.stltoday.com/travel/twain-s-words-flowed-from-elmira/article_f316441c-46ea-5467-96e1-b2a8069f4dbc.html

[42] Twain, Mark Letters from the Earth © 1991 Harper Perennial edition. Letter II, p 11.

[43] IBID, p 27.

[44] Ecclesiastes 3: vs 1

[45] Ecclesiastes 3: vs 7

[46] Corinthians 1: vs 27-29

⁴⁷ Twain, Mark, From the forward The Weather in this book, in The American Claimant, American Artists Edition, The Complete Works of Mark Twain, Harper & Brothers, NY, C. 1924, p v

⁴⁸ Twain, Mark Plymouth Rock and the Pilgrims, Mark Twain's Speeches, Harper and Brothers, NY, C. 1923 The Mark Twain Company, p. 88

⁴⁹ Twain, Mark Concerning Tobacco, Published in What is Man? (and other essays), Harper & Brothers, NY, C. 1917 The Mark Twain Company, p. 276

⁵⁰ Beekman, Dow. Mark Twain and the Watering Troughs, Mark Twain Quarterly; Kirkwood, Mo.Vol. 2, Iss. 4, (Summer 1938): 5. © 2018 ProQuest LLChttps://search.proquest.com/openview /d4fbe7f79bae4debc47d7e8f87bfaa3a/1?pq-origsite=gscholar&cbl=1818765

⁵¹ From "An Interview with Mark Twain" by Rudyard Kipling. Reprinted from 'The Mark Twain Anthology: Great Writers on His Life and Works' (The Library of America, 2010), pages 66–77. © 2010 Literary Classics of the U.S., Inc. Originally published in The Pioneer (Allahabad), March 18, 1890. Reprinted in From Sea to Sea (1913). https://www.scribd.com/doc/30250943/Rudyard-Kipling-s-Mark-Twain-Interview

⁵² IBID

⁵³ Collins, Cameron, The Langdon Mansion; Drinking Elmira, New York. January 5, 2013. ©2018 Distilled History: A Drinking Blog with a History Problem. https://www.distilledhistory.com/langdonhouse/ accessed 5/2/2017

⁵⁴ Contributors, The Mark Twain Project. © 2007-2017 The Regents of the University of California http://www.marktwainproject.org/biographies/bio_clemens_susy.html Accessed 5/18/2018

⁵⁵ Wikipedia contributors, "Woodrow Wilson," Wikipedia, The Free Encyclopedia, https://en.wikipedia.org/w/index.php?title=Woodrow_Wilson&oldid=837461143. accessed April 27, 2017

⁵⁶ Dixon, Mark E. Scut Work: Like many job-hunting new graduates, Woodrow Wilson took what he could get; June, 2010 Main Line Today. © 2018 Today Media. http://www.mainlinetoday.com/Main-Line-Today/June-2010/Scut-Work/ Accessed 5/14/2017

⁵⁷ Skandera-Trombley, Laura E., Mark Twain in the Company of Women C. 1994, The University of Pennsylvania Press, Philadelphia, P.12

⁵⁸ Contributors, The Mark Twain Project. © 2007-2017 The Regents of the University of California http://www.marktwainproject.org/biographies/bio_clemens_susy.html Accessed 5/18/2018

⁵⁹ Letter from Mrs. Charles M. Andrews to Dixon Wecter, February, 1949; From: Papa, An intimate biography of Mark Twain by his thirteen-year old daughter Susy, edited by Charles Neider. © 1985, Charles Neider. Doubleday & Company, NY. pp. 12-13.

⁶⁰ Of note to readers - that same platform and the old, original Bryn Mawr train station still stands. It presently houses a thrift shop for the adjacent Bryn Mawr Hospital.

⁶¹ Neider, Charles, Papa, An intimate biography of Mark Twain by his thirteen-year old daughter Susy, edited by Charles Neider. © 1985, Charles Neider. Doubleday & Company, NY. p. 12

⁶² Letter from Mrs. Charles M. Andrews to Dixon Wecter, February, 1949; From: Papa, An intimate biography of Mark Twain by his thirteen-year old daughter Susy, edited by Charles Neider. © 1985, Charles Neider. Doubleday & Company, NY. p. 12

⁶³ Letter from Susy Clemens to Louse Brownell, Oct. 2, 1891; From: Papa, An intimate biography of Mark Twain by his thirteen-year old daughter Susy, edited by Charles Neider. © 1985, Charles Neider. Doubleday & Company, NY. pp. 14-15

⁶⁴ Rothenberg Gritz, Jennie, But Were They Gay? The Mystery of Same-Sex Love in the Nineteenth Century. Published September 7, 2012, The Atlantic. https://www.theatlantic.com/national/archive/2012/09/but-were-they-gay-the-mystery-of-same-sex-love-in-the-19th-century/262117/. Accessed November 28, 2017

⁶⁵ IBID

⁶⁶ IBID

⁶⁷ Neider, Charles Papa, An intimate biography of Mark Twain by his thirteen-year old daughter Susy, edited by Charles Neider. © 1985, Charles Neider. Doubleday & Company, NY. p. 14

⁶⁸ Letter from S. L. Clemens to Louise Brownell Saunders, September 3, 1904. Charles Neider, Papa, An intimate biography of Mark Twain by his thirteen-year old daughter Susy, edited by Charles Neider. © 1985, Charles Neider. Doubleday & Company, NY. p. 14

⁶⁹ Neider, Charles Papa, An intimate biography of Mark Twain by his thirteen-year old daughter Susy, edited by Charles Neider. © 1985, Charles Neider. Doubleday & Company, NY. p. 37

70 Bloom, Donna Marked Territory June 18, 2001 Ithaca.com © 2018 The Ithaca Times, Ithaca, NY. http://www.ithaca.com/visit_ithaca/marked-territory/article_4525ce14-781c-5753-9d89-7ffc091c77c6.html Accessed June 7, 2017

71 Bayer, Leon D. Mark Twain Has Filed Bankruptcy! December 8, 2012, ConsiderChapter13.org. ©2018 The NACTT For Consumer Bankruptcy Education. http://considerchapter13.org/2012/12/08/mark-twain-has-filed-bankruptcy/ Accessed June 14, 2017

72 Skandera Trombley, Laura, Mark Twain's other woman: the hidden story of his final years; © 2010 Laura Skandera Trombley. Publ. First Vintage Books, Random House, NY. Pg. 250

73 Americana: (American Historical Magazine). Volume 7; © 1912, The National American Society, NY. "History of Arnot and Allied Families." pp. 346-347

74 Americana: (American Historical Magazine). Volume 7; © 1912, The National American Society, NY. "History of Arnot and Allied Families." p. 338

75 Tina Fey, Robert Carlock, ""Unbreakable Kimmy Schmidt [Television Series] Season 3, Episode 5, "Kimmy Steps on a Crack." Jerry Kupfer, Dara Schnapper, Producers. Produced by Little Stranger, Inc., Bevel Gears, 3 Arts Entertainment, Universal Television. Distributed by NBCUniversal Television Distribution. Netflix.

76 SLC to Tom Hood and George Routledge and Sons, 10 March 1873, Hartford, Conn. (*UCCL 00886*), n. 1. <http://www.marktwainproject.org/xtf/view?docId=letters/UCCL00886.xml;style=letter;brand=mtp#an1> Accessed 9/4/2018 10:05 AM

77 Mark Twain Project, Pike, Gustavus D. 1875. The Singing Campaign for Ten Thousand Pounds; or, The Jubilee Singers in Great Britain. Rev. ed. New York: American Missionary Association, vi–viii, 31, 38, 193. Accessed 9/ 9/2018.

78 Hartford Courant, "The Jubilee Singers," 29 Jan 1872

79 SLC to Olivia L. Langdon ... , 12 Jan 1869, El Paso, Ill. (*UCCL 00227*), n. 3. <http://www.marktwainproject.org/xtf/view?docId=letters/UCCL00227.xml;style=letter;brand=mtp#an3> Accessed 9/12/2018 9:35 am

80 SLC to Mary Mason Fairbanks, 10 Dec 1871, Erie, Pa. (*UCCL 00688*), n. 1. <http://www.marktwainproject.org/xtf/view?docId=letters/UCCL00688.xml;style=letter;brand=mtp#an1> Accessed 9/4/2018 10:00 AM

81 For more information about Blackface minstrelsy, check out: https://en.wikipedia.org/wiki/Blackface

82 Emily Guendelsberger, *Why Blackface still dogs the Mummers 50 years after it was banned*, Philadelphia City Paper, Published 12/19/2013. Archived by My City Paper

83 IBID

84 IBID

85 IBID

86 Wynne, J. (1907). The Apostleship of Prayer. In The Catholic Encyclopedia. New York: Robert Appleton Company. From New Advent: http://www.newadvent.org/cathen/01633a.htm. Accessed April 20, 2019

87 Wikipedia contributors, "Opus Dei," Wikipedia, The Free Encyclopedia, https://en.wikipedia.org/w/index.php?title=Opus_Dei&oldid=858390501 (accessed September 7, 2018).

88 Sullivan, M., Cromwell and the Irish slave trade, February 4, 2013 © Irish Examiner Ltd. (Accessed 06/14/19)

89 Myers, Alber Cook, Immigration of the Irish Quakers into Pennsylvania, 1682-1750, With Their Early History in Ireland, P. 102 © 1901 Albert Cook Myers. Press of The New Era Printing Company, Lancaster, PA

90 IBID

91 https://www.lexico.com/en/definition/bondservant (Definitions from Oxford Languages)

92 Dennis Clark, The Irish in Philadelphia: Ten Generations of Urban Experience. © 1973 Temple University Press, Philadelphia. Pp: 6-7

93 IBID, Pp: 14-15

94 Dennis Clark, The Irish in Philadelphia: Ten Generations of Urban Experience. © 1973 Temple University Press, Philadelphia. Pp: 34-35

95 Paine, Albert Bigelow. Mark Twain: A Biography: The Personal and Literary Life of Samuel Langhorne Clemens. The Writings of Mark Twain. Definitive ed. 4 vols. New York: Gabriel Wells, 1923. Chapter 3, https://ebooks.adelaide.edu.au/t/twain/mark/paine/complete.html (Accessed 2/17/2017)

96 IBID, Chapter 4

[97] Twain, Mark, My Uncle's Farm, Part I; The American Experience: Nonfiction. C 1968 The Macmillan Company, New York. Pg. 208. Reprinted from Mark Twain's Autobiography, © 1924 by Clara Gabrilowitsch; renewed 1952 by Clara Clemens Samossoud. Reprinted by permission of Harper & Row, Publishers.

[98] IBID, Pg. 207-208..

[99] Twain, Mark, The Prince and The Pauper, pg. 147

[100] Twain, Mark, My Uncle's Farm, Part I; The American Experience: Nonfiction. C 1968 The Macmillan Company, New York. Pg. 207-208. Reprinted from Mark Twain's Autobiography, © 1924 by Clara Gabrilowitsch; renewed 1952 by Clara Clemens Samossoud. Reprinted by permission of Harper & Row, Publishers.

[101] Paine, Albert Bigelow. Mark Twain: A Biography: The Personal and Literary Life of Samuel Langhorne Clemens. The Writings of Mark Twain. Definitive ed. 4 vols. New York: Gabriel Wells, 1923. Chapter 4, https://ebooks.adelaide.edu.au/t/twain/mark/paine/complete.html (Accessed 5/17/2017)

[102] Ulin, David L. Celebrating the genius of 'Huckleberry Finn'; November 14, 2010 The Los Angeles Times. http://articles.latimes.com/2010/nov/14/entertainment/la-ca-mark-twain-20101114 Accessed June 22, 2017

[103] Walsh, Mark Schools Can't Ban Books Because of Complaints, Court Says October 28, 1998 Education Week. © 2018 Editorial Projects in Education. http://www.edweek.org/ew/articles/1998/10/28/09huck.h18.html?qs=Kathy+Monteiro Accessed July 11, 2017

[104] Culture Shock Contributors Mark Twain's Adventures of Huckleberry Finn, 1885, © 1999 PBS/WGBH, ©1999 WGBH Education Foundation. https://www.pbs.org/wgbh/cultureshock/flashpoints/literature/huck_a.html Accessed July 23, 2017

[105] Guardian Staff and Agencies, To Kill a Mockingbird by Harper Lee taken off Mississippi school reading list. October 14, 2017 The Guardian Weekly; US Edition; https://www.theguardian.com/books/2017/oct14/to-kill-a-mockingbird-harper-lee-mississippi-school-reading-list Accessed 10/14/2017

[106] Friedman, Matt, New Jersey lawmakers want schools to stop teaching 'Huckleberry Finn' March 21, 2019. © 2019 Politico LLC

[107] Biedenharn, Isabella How Mark Twain helped Nick Offerman become a weirdo; October 6, 2017 Entertainment Weekly, © 2018 Time Inc. Books. http://ew.com/books/2017/10/06/mark-twain-nick-offerman-audiobook-interview/ Accessed 10/17/2017

[108] Twain, Mark, The Adventures of Huckleberry Finn, Airmont Classic Edition, NY. C. 1962; pg. 253

[109] Twain, Mark, Mark Twain's Notebook, © 1935 The Mark Twain Company. Harper and Brothers, NY, publishers. Pg. 193

[110] Gregory, Dick Callus on My Soul: A Memoir, written with Shelia P. Moses, © 2000 Longstreet Press, Atlanta, GA. Chapter 29, On Broadway, P 255 - 258

[111] Leviticus 25:10

[112] Twain, Mark The Adventures of Huckleberry Finn, Airmont Classic Edition, NY. C. 1962; pg. 253-254

[113] IBID, pg. 254

[114] IBID, pg. 203

[115] IBID, pg. 255

[116] IBID, pg. 255

[117] Pastorius, Francis Daniel, A Minute Against Slavery, Addressed to Germantown Monthly Meeting, 1688, 2017Germantown Mennonite Historic Trust, http://www.meetinghouse.info/uploads/1/9/4/1/19410913/a_minute_against_slavery.pdf Accessed 11/22/2017

[118] McCullough David, from the introduction to 'The National Archives of The United States' by Herman J. Viola. ©. 1986 Harry Abrams, Inc., NY, publishers. p 13-14.

[119] Skandera-Trombley, Laura E., Mark Twain in the Company of Women; © 1994 University of Pennsylvania Press, Philadelphia, Pa p 68,

[120] Bourne, E. G. The Northmen, Columbus and Cabot, 985-1503: The voyages of the Northmen, The voyages of Columbus and of John Cabot. New York: © 1906 Charles Scribner's Sons. p114

[121] IBID, Bourne, p 270.

[122] Hanke, L. The Spanish struggle for justice in the conquest of America. © 1949 University of Pennsylvania Press, Philadelphia, PA. p.33

123 Ibid, Hanke, p. 34

124 King James Bible Online Contributors, Genesis 9:25 Context King James Bible Online © 2018 https://www.kingjamesbibleonline.org/Genesis-9-25/

125 Horn, James, 1619: Jamestown and the Forging of American Democracy, © 2018 Basic Books

126 Odle, Cliff, The Rise and Fall of The Slave Trade in Massachusetts, Part 1, Edited by Marisa Calleja © 2017 The Freedom Trail Institute, http://www.thefreedomtrail.org/educational-resources/article-rise-and-fall-of-slave-trade-part1.shtml Accessed 07/02/2017

127 IBID

128 IBID

129 Brooks, Rebecca Beatrice, Slavery in Massachusetts, December 20, 2012, History of Massachusetts Blog http://historyofmassachusetts.org/slavery-in-massachusetts/ Accessed 07/17/2017

130 Robinson, B. A., Christianity and Slavery: Movements toward Abolition, Religious Tolerance © 1999-2007, Ontario Consultants on Religious Tolerance., http://www.religioustolerance.org/chr_slav3.htm Accessed 07/22/2017

131 Source: Berean Study Bible http://bereanbible.com Accessed 07/23/2017

132 Pastorius, Francis Daniel, A Minute Against Slavery, Addressed to Germantown Monthly Meeting, 1688, 2017Germantown Mennonite Historic Trust, http://www.meetinghouse.info/uploads/1/9/4/1/19410913/a_minute_against_slavery.pdf Accessed 11/22/2017

133 IBID

134 Harper, Douglas Slavery in New York, 2003 Slavery in the North http://slavenorth.com/newyork.htm Accessed 07/18/2017, cited quotation from: Edgar J. McManus, A History of Negro Slavery in New York, Syracuse University Press, 1966, p.7.

135 Brooks, Rebecca Beatrice, Slavery in Massachusetts, December 20, 2012, History of Massachusetts Blog http://historyofmassachusetts.org/slavery-in-massachusetts/ Accessed 07/17/2017

136 Sheridan, Richard B. Sugar and Slavery: An Economic History of the British West Indies, 1623-1775, John Hopkins University Press, Baltimore, 1974 p. 144.

137 Archbold, William Arthur Jobson (1892). "Lay, Benjamin." In Lee, Sidney. Dictionary of National Biography. 32. London: Smith, Elder & Co.

138 Lockard, Joe, All Slave-Keepers That Keep the Innocent in Bondage, Apostates; Antislavery Teaching Guides, Antislavery Literature Project eserver_antislavery https://antislavery.eserver.org/religious/allslavekeepersfinal accessed 11/14/2017

139 IBID

140 Rediker, Marcus, You'll Never Be as Radical as This 18th Century Quaker Dwarf; The New York Times Online, August 12, 2017. Published in NYT under the title History's Forgotten Ultraradical August 13, 2017. © 2017 The New York Times Company. https://www.nytimes.com/2017/08/12/opinion/sunday/youll-never-be-as-radical-as-this-18th-century-quaker-dwarf.html?_r=0 Accessed 11/18/2017

141 IBID

142 Harper, Douglas Slavery in New York, 2003 Slavery in the North http://slavenorth.com/newyork.htm Accessed 07/18/2017, cited quotation from: Edgar J. McManus, A History of Negro Slavery in New York, Syracuse University Press, 1966, p.7.

143 Contributors Blackpast.org, The Deleted Passage of The Declaration of Independence (1776),© 2017 Blackpast.org, CA http://www.blackpast.org/primary/declaration-independence-and-debate-over-slavery Accessed 11/22/2017

144 Contributors PBS.org/WHYY Resource Bank, African's in America, Revolution: Part 2: 1750-1805, Rough Draft of the Declaration of Independence, © 1998, 1999 WGBH Educational Foundation https://www.pbs.org/wgbh/aia/part2/2h33.html Accessed 11/18/2017

145 Jefferson, Thomas Autobiography; 1740-1790; With the Declaration of Independence; January 8, 1821, © 2008 Lillian Goldman Law Library, New Haven, CT. http://avalon.law.yale.edu/19th_century/jeffauto.asp Accessed 11/28/2017

146 Contributors PBS.org/WHYY Resource Bank, African's in America, Revolution: Part 2: 1750-1805, Rough Draft of the Declaration of Independence, © 1998, 1999 WGBH Educational Foundation https://www.pbs.org/wgbh/aia/part2/2h33.html Accessed 11/18/2017

147 IBID

[148] Rush, Benjamin 1773 - An Address to the Inhabitants of the British Settlements in America Upon Slave-Keeping - Benjamin Rush, Read the Constitution, Stupid. © 2012-2017 http://readtheconstitutionstupid.com/en/2012-01-27-19-34-40/2012-01-27-19-37-04/miscellaneous/2342-1773-an-address-to-the-inhabitants-of-the-bristish-settlements-in-america-upon-slave-keeping-benjamin-rush Accessed 11/14/2017

[149] Contributors PBS.org/WHYY Resource Bank, African's in America, Revolution: Part 3: 1791-1831, Brotherly Love: Founding of Pennsylvania Abolition Society 1775, © 1998, 1999 WGBH Educational Foundation https://www.pbs.org/wgbh/aia/ part3/3p248.html Accessed 11/18/2017

[150] IBID

[151] Contributors, Benjamin Franklin Petitions Congress, National Archives Online, 2017 The U.S. National Archives and Records Administration https://www.archives.gov/legislative/features/franklin Accessed 11/24/2017

[152] Contributors, Finding Franklin: The Question of Slavery, National Archives Online, 2017 The U.S. National Archives and Records Administration franklin https://www.archives.gov/philadelphia/exhibits/franklin/slavery.html Accessed 11/24/2017

[153] Hoss, Elijah E. (1897). Elihu Embree, Abolitionist. Nashville: Vanderbilt Southern Historical Society. p. 6–7. https://en.wikipedia.org/wiki/Elihu_Embree#cite_note-hoss1-4 Accessed 11/27/2017

[154] Wikipedia contributors, "Genius of Universal Emancipation," Wikipedia, The Free Encyclopedia, https://en.wikipedia.org/w/index.php?title=Genius_of_Universal_Emancipation&oldid=801128919. Accessed 11/28/2017

[155] Contributors PBS.org/WHYY Resource Bank, African's in America, Revolution: Part 4: 1831-1865, The Liberator. "To The Public," © 1998, 1999 WGBH Educational Foundation http://www.pbs.org/wgbh/aia/part4/4h2928t.html Accessed 11/18/2017

[156] Ruchames, Louis (1963). The Abolitionists: A Collection of Their Writings New York, G.P. Putnam's Sons © 2017 Questia, Cengage Learning, https://www.questia.com/library/1385101/the-abolitionists-a-collection-of-their-writings Accessed 11/14/2017

[157] The Editors of Encyclopedia Britannica, American Anti-Slavery Society, Encyclopedia Britannica, Inc. Published July 28, 2016 https://www.britannica.com/topic/American-Anti-Slavery-Society Accessed 11/15/2017

[158] Frederick Douglass in Britain and Ireland, Antislavery in Britain. © 2017 Hannah Murray, http://frederickdouglassinbritain.com/journey/AntislaveryinBritain/ Accessed 11/15/2017

[159] IBID

[160] Greenspan, Jesse, History Stories: 8 Key Contributors to the Underground Railroad, history.com, 2016, http://www.history.com/news/history-lists/8-key-contributors-to-the-underground-railroad; Access Date November 02, 2017. Publisher A+E Networks

[161] History.com Staff, History.com 2009 Fugitive Slave Acts, http://www.history.com/topics/black-history/fugitive-slave-acts Access Date November 02/2017. Publisher: A+E Networks.

[162] Foner, Eric, from a video interview on History Stories: 8 Key Contributors to the Underground Railroad, Jesse Greenspan, history.com, 2016, http://www.history.com/news/history-lists/8-key-contributors-to-the-underground-railroad; Access Date November 02, 2017. Publisher A+E Networks

[163] Wikipedia contributors, "Frederick Douglass," Wikipedia, The Free Encyclopedia, https://en.wikipedia.org/w/index.php?title=Frederick_Douglass&oldid=837947638(accessed 11/05/2017 https://en.wikipedia.org/wiki/Frederick_Douglass

[164] Foner, Eric, from a video interview on History Stories: 8 Key Contributors to the Underground Railroad, Jesse Greenspan, history.com, 2016, http://www.history.com/news/history-lists/8-key-contributors-to-the-underground-railroad; Access Date November 02, 2017. Publisher A+E Networks

[165] IBID

[166] Douglass, Frederick (1851). Narrative of the life of Frederick Douglass, an American slave. Written by himself. (6 ed.). London: H.G. Collins. p. 10.

[167] Stauffer, John, What Every American Should Know About Frederick Douglass, Abolitionist Prophet, Huffington Post: The Blog, 01/08/2013 2017 Oath Inc. https://www.huffingtonpost.com/john-stauffer/frederick-douglass-the-prophet_b_2425712.html Accessed 12/06/2017

[168] Douglass, Frederick (2008). The Life and Times of Frederick Douglass. Cosimo, Inc. p. 149

[169] Author: Old Sturbridge, Inc. Historical Background on Antislavery 2017 Teach US History.org, http://www.teachushistory.org/second-great-awakening-age-reform/articles/historical-background-antislavery, Accessed 12/06/2017

[170] Wikipedia contributors, "American Colonization Society," Wikipedia, The Free Encyclopedia, "American Colonization Society membership certificate, 1833 | The Gilder Lehrman Institute of American History." https://en.wikipedia.org/w/index.php?title=American_Colonization_Society&oldid=836072205. Accessed 12/07/2017

[171] Author: Old Sturbridge, Inc. Historical Background on Antislavery 2017 Teach US History.org, http://www.teachushistory.org/second-great-awakening-age-reform/articles/historical-background-antislavery, Accessed 12/06/2017

[172] Kaplan, Fred, Lincoln and the Abolitionists: John Quincy Adams, Slavery, and the Civil War; © 2017 Fred Kaplan. Harper Collins Publishers, NY. pp. x-xi

[173] History Stories: 8 Key Contributors to the Underground Railroad, Jesse Greenspan, history.com, 2016, http://www.history.com/news/history-lists/8-key-contributors-to-the-underground-railroad; Access Date November 02, 2017. Publisher A+E Networks

[174] Holmes, Clayton Wood, The Elmira Prison Camp: A History of the Military Prison at Elmira, N.Y. C. 1912, G.P. Putnam p.144

[175] Powers, Ron, "Mark Twain: A life", © 2005 Ron Powers, First Free Press trade paperback edition 2006, Simon and Schuster, NY. p. 242

[176] Tice, Joyce M., 2017 Tri-Counties Genealogy & History by Joyce M. Tice: History of Chemung County 1892-Towner, Part V. The Townships, Chapter IX: Veteran. http://www.joycetice.com/books/veterato.htm Accessed 11/14/2017

[177] Douglass, Frederick (1882). Life and Times of Frederick Douglass. p. 170.

[178] Powers, Ron, "Mark Twain: A life", C. 2005 Ron Powers, First Free Press trade paperback edition 2006, Simon and Shuster, NY. p. 243

[179] Douglass, Frederick, The Narrative of the Life of Frederick Douglass, from The Project Gutenberg EBook, Chapter VII. http://www.gutenberg.org/files/23/23-h/23-h.htm Accessed 11/27/2017

[180] IBID, Chapter V

[181] Leight, Dr. Robert, 'Richard Moore and Underground Railroad', Berks-Mont Free Press. 11/08/2007 © 2017 The Berks-Mont News. http://www.berksmontnews.com/article/BM/20071108/TMP01/311089873 Accessed 11/27/2017

[182] Twenty-five years afterward I would learn that Mark Twain's ancestors had also lived and emigrated from County Antrim, very near the village of my maternal grandfather. Who knows? Perhaps Twain and I are ancestrally related.

[183] About Rising Sun Inn, © Rising Sun Inn, https://www.risingsuninn.net/about/ Accessed 12/13/2017

[184] Contributors – 2007 The Center for Anti-Slavery Studies, Underground Railroad Escape Routes, http://cass-montrose.org/local/escape.html Accessed 12/13/2017

[185] Contributors – Chemung County Historical Society, The Frederick Douglass Memorial A.M.E. Zion Church, 2017 Chemung County Historical Society http://chemungcountyhistoricalsociety.blogspot.com/2013/02/the-frederick-douglas-memorial-ame-zion.html Accessed 12/13/2017

[186] Mark Twain's Letters, Volume 3: 1869, C. 1992, University of California Press, p. 49

[187] Twain, Mark, A Private History of A Campaign That Failed. http://www.classicshorts.com/stories/phctf.html. Accessed 7/6/2018

[188] Powers, Ron, "Mark Twain: A life", ©. 2005 Ron Powers, First Free Press trade paperback edition 2006, Simon and Shuster, NY. p. 243

[189] Skandera-Trombley, Laura E. Mark Twain in the Company of Women (Philadelphia: University of Pennsylvania Press, 1994), p 65

[190] IBID, p 68

[191] IBID, p 71

[192] IBID, p 71

[193] Douglass, Frederick, The Life and Times of Frederick Douglass: From 1817-1882. 1882 London edition, p.289

[194] Joseph Carvalho III. "Abolitionist John Brown's years in Springfield Ma. transform his anti-slavery thoughts and actions". MassLive.com. http://www.masslive.com/history/index.ssf/2010/04/abolitionist_john_browns_transformation_years_in_springfield_ma.. Retrieved 11/6/2017.

[195] Foner, Philip S., History of Black Americans: From the Compromise of 1850 to the End of the Civil War (Westport, CT: Greenwood Press, 1983), 8, http://www.questia.com/read/15649785/history-of-black-americans-from-the-compromise-of. Accessed 11/02/2017

[196] IBID, Accessed 11/06/2017

[197] Doane, Erin, Curator, 2017 Chemung County Historical Society, "Colored Citizens of Elmira", http://chemungcountyhistoricalsociety.blogspot.com/2017/02/colored-citizens-of-elmira.html Accessed 11/06/2017

[198] IBID

[199] Foner, Philip S., History of Black Americans: From the Compromise of 1850 to the End of the Civil War (Westport, CT: Greenwood Press, 1983), 19, http://www.questia.com/read/15649796/history-of-black-americans-from-the-compromise-of. Accessed 11/06/2017

[200] Kaplan, Fred, Lincoln and the Abolitionists: John Quincy Adams, Slavery, and the Civil War; C. 2017 Fred Kaplan. Harper Collins Publishers, NY. p. 194

[201] Philip S. Foner, History of Black Americans: From the Compromise of 1850 to the End of the Civil War (Westport, CT: Greenwood Press, 1983), 109, http://www.questia.com/read/15649886/history-of-black-americans-from-the-compromise-of. Accessed 11/05/2017

[202] The Columbia Encyclopedia, 6th ed. (Columbia University Press, 2017), s.v. "Stowe, Harriet Beecher," http://www.questia.com/read/1E1-Stowe-Ha/stowe-harriet-beecher.

[203] Genz Michelle, Solomon's Wisdom, Special to The Washington Post, Sunday, March 7, 1999; Page F01. © 1996 The Washington Post Company https://web.archive.org/web/20051016085440/http://innercity.org/columbiaheights/newspaper/kidnap.html Accessed 11/03/2017

[204] Anika Rede and Maryum Ali, Uncle Tom's Cabin: Generating a Rising Tide of Responsibility to End the Institution of Slavery: Anti-Uncle Tom Novels. Transcribed from a photocopy of an original advertisement. Photo available at: http://66753557.weebly.com/anti-uncle-tom-novels.html Accessed 11/06/2017

[205] Cornell University Library, "I Will Be Heard!" ©2002 Cornel University Library Division of Rare and Manuscript Collection. http://rmc.library.cornell.edu/abolitionism/uncle_tom/Ruins.htm Accessed 11/04/2017

[206] Judges 7:3, New American Standard Bible

[207] Reynolds, David S., John Brown, Abolitionist: The Man Who Killed Slavery, Sparked the Civil War, and Seeded Civil Rights (2005), New York, Vintage Booksp.162

[208] History.com Staff, Lincoln Speaks Out Against Slavery, C. 2009, history.com. Publ. A&E Networks. http://www.history.com/this-day-in-history/lincoln-speaks-out-against-slavery. Access Date: November 14, 2017

[209] "SLC to the Muscatine Journal, 17 and 18 Feb 1854, Washington, D.C. (UCCL 00007)." In <i>Mark Twain's Letters, 1853–1866.</i> Edited by Edgar Marquess Branch, Michael B. Frank, Kenneth M. Sanderson, Harriet Elinor Smith, Lin Salamo, and Richard Bucci. Mark Twain Project Online. Berkeley, Los Angeles, London: University of California Press. 1988, 2007.<http://www.marktwainproject.org/xtf/view?docId=letters/UCCL00007.xml;style=letter;brand=mtp>, accessed 2017-11-15.

[210] Cornell University Library, "I Will Be Heard!" ©2002 Cornel University Library Division of Rare and Manuscript Collection. http://rmc.library.cornell.edu/abolitionism/strategies/Brown.htm Accessed 11/04/2017

[211] Sutler, Boyd B., An Eyewitness Describes the Hanging of John Brown. © February, 1955, American Heritage Magazine. Volume 6, Issue 2.

[212] McPherson, Dr. James, A Defining Time in Our Nation's History. A Brief Overview of the American Civil War | Civil War Trust https://www.civilwar.org/learn/articles/brief-overview-american-civil-war. Accessed November 14, 2017.

[213] Twain, Mark, A Private History of A Campaign That Failed. http://www.classicshorts.com/stories/phctf.html. Accessed 7/6/2018

[214] Abraham Lincoln's Draft of the Emancipation Proclamation | Civil War Trust; https://www.civilwar.org/learn/primary-sources/abraham-lincolns-draft-emancipation-proclamation; Accessed Nov. 14, 2017.

[215] McPherson, Dr. James, A Defining Time in Our Nation's History. A Brief Overview of the American Civil War | Civil War Trust https://www.civilwar.org/learn/articles/brief-overview-american-civil-war. Accessed November 14, 2017.

[216] Stanley, Amy Dru, "Instead of Waiting for the Thirteenth Amendment: The War Power, Slave Marriage, and Inviolate Human Rights"; The American Historical Review, Volume 115, Issue 3, 1 June 2010, Pages 732–765. (2010), pp. 741–742

[217] Goodwin, Doris Kearns, The Night Abraham Lincoln was Assassinated. ©.April 8, 2015. Smithsonian Magazine. https://www.smithsonianmag.com/history/abraham-lincoln-team-of-rivals-180954850/. Accessed November 15, 2017. Reprinted from: From Team of Rivals: The Political Genius of Abraham Lincoln, by Doris Kearns Goodwin. Copyright (c) 2005 by Blithedale Productions, Inc. Reprinted by permission of Simon & Schuster.

[218] McPherson, Dr. James, A Defining Time in Our Nation's History. A Brief Overview of the American Civil War | Civil War Trust https://www.civilwar.org/learn/articles/brief-overview-american-civil-war. Accessed November 14, 2017.

[219] Twain, Mark, What Is Man? And Other Essays. Mark Twain Company, New York: Harper & Bros., 1917. Chapter IV, p. 45.

[220] Powers, Ron, Mark Twain, a Life, p65-66. © 2005 Ron Powers. First Free Press trade paperback edition 2006. Simon and Schuster, New York, Publisher.

[221] Samuel Clemens, To the Muscatine Journal, 4 December, 1853. Philadelphia, Pa.; The Mark Twain Papers, California Digital Library, Mark Twain Project. http://www.marktwainproject.org Accessed 11/27/2017

[222] IBID

[223] The song can be heard here: http://www.broadjam.com/songs/jfcurley/toms-cafe/Play The cover photo used for the CD of the same title was taken by yours truly on a photography jaunt in 1977 with the 35 mm camera my father had given to me for Christmas.

[224] Samuel Clemens, To the Muscatine Journal, 24 December, 1853. Philadelphia, Pa.; The Mark Twain Papers, California Digital Library, Mark Twain Project. http://www.marktwainproject.org Accessed 11/27/2017

[225] IBID

[226] Wikipedia contributors, "President's House (Philadelphia)," Wikipedia, The Free Encyclopedia, https://en.wikipedia.org/w/index.php?title=President%27s_House_(Philadelphia)&oldid=805859617 (accessed November 4, 2017).

[227] Fulton, Joe B., The Reconstruction of Mark Twain: How a Confederate Bushwacker Became the Lincoln of Our Literature. © 2010 LSU Press. pp. 7-8

[228] IBID, pp. 8-10

[229] IBID, pp. 10-11

[230] IBID, p. 11

[231] Mark Twain, The Autobiography of Mark Twain, Edited by Charles Neider.©. 1959 Charles Neider. Pub. First Harper Perennial Edition, 1990. Harper Collins, NY. Pg. 102

[232] IBID, Pg. 162

[233] Fulton, Joe B., The Reconstruction of Mark Twain: How a Confederate Bushwacker Became the Lincoln of Our Literature. © 2010 LSU Press. pp. 96-97

[234] Mark Twain, The Autobiography of Mark Twain, Edited by Charles Neider. © 1959 Charles Neider. Pub. First Harper Perennial Edition, 1990. Harper Collins, NY. Pg. 139

[235] Fulton, Joe B., The Reconstruction of Mark Twain: How a Confederate Bushwacker Became the Lincoln of Our Literature. © 2010 LSU Press. p. 99

[236] IBID

[237] Mark Twain, The Autobiography of Mark Twain, Edited by Charles Neider. © 1959 Charles Neider. Pub. First Harper Perennial Edition, 1990. Harper Collins, NY. Pg. 103

[238] Shelley Fisher Fishkin, 'Lighting Out for the Territory: Reflections on Mark Twain and American Culture'; © 1998, Oxford University Press, p.73

[239] IBID, pp.72-73

240 IBID, p.73
241 IBID, p.75
242 Powers, Ron, Mark Twain: A Life; © 2005 Ron Powers. Pub. Free Press, EBook edition. Simon and Schuster, New York, Publisher.
243 Mark Twain's Letters, Volume 4: 1870–1871. C. 1995 University of California Press. pp. 182-183
244 Samuel L. Clemens, Letter to Josephus N. Larned, 7 August, 1870; Elmira, N.Y. http://www.marktwainproject.org/xtf/view?docId=letters/UCCL11729.xml;query=Frederick%20Douglass;searchAll=;sectionType1=;sectionType2=;sectionType3=;sectionType4=;sectionType5=;style=letter;brand=mtp#1
245 Anna Dickinson to Mary E. Dickinson, 30 March, 1872. Anna E. Dickinson Papers, DLC. Reprinted in Mark Twain's Letters, Volume 5: 1872-1873, C.1997 University of California Press, CA. pp. 67-68
246 Frederick Douglass, My Bondage and My Freedom: Part I- Life as a Slave, Part II- Life as a Freeman, with an introduction by James M'Cune Smith. New York and Auburn: Miller, Orton & Mulligan (1855); ed. John Stauffer, Random House (2003) p. 373
247 Jones, Dr. E. Michael, "Ethnic Cleansing, Philadelphia Style," © 1997 Cultural Wars magazine. https://culturewarsmagazine.com/CultureWars/Archives/cw_recent/ethniccleansing.html. Accessed 4/29/2020
248 Altman, Howard, Brighter Shades of Grays. © March 20-27, 1997. Philadelphia City Paper. https://mycitypaper.com/articles/032097/article027.shtml Accessed 4/29/2020
249 Frederick Douglass, What, to the Slave, is the Fourth of July? (Rochester 1852) © 2005-2017 BlackPast.org, http://www.blackpast.org/1852-frederick-douglass-what-slave-fourth-july Accessed 11/13/2017
250 Hare, Jim, Elmira History: Frederick Douglass visited city many times Star/Gazette, Feb. 4, 2016. http://www.stargazette.com/story/news/local/twin-tiers-roots/2016/02/04/elmira-history-frederick-douglass-visited-city-many-times/79749492/ 11/14/2017
251 IBID
252 Mark Twain, Letter to James A. Garfield, 12 Jan, 1881. Mark Twain Papers | California Digital Library. Copyright © 2007–16 The Regents of the University of California.
253 Langdon, Jr., Jervis Mark Twain Among His Antislavery In-Laws; March 15, 1985 The New York Times: Letters to the Editor; © 2017 The New York Times Company http://www.nytimes.com/1985/04/07/opinion/l-mark-twain-among-his-antislavery-in-laws-146048.html Accessed 08/05/2017
254 McDowell, Edwin, From Twain, A Letter On Debt to Blacks. March 14, 1985 The New York Times: © 2017 The New York Times Company http://www.nytimes.com/1985/03/14/books/from-twain-a-letter-on-debt-to-blacks.html Accessed 08/05/2017
255 IBID
256 IBID
257 IBID
258 Black Baltimore 1870-1920 Warner T. McGuinn: Obituaries; Reprint of Baltimore Sun, July 11, 1937, Washington Afro-American, July 17, 1937. http://msa.maryland.gov/msa/stagser/s1259/121/6050/html/26163000.html. Accessed 08/05/2017
259 IBID
260 Beckwith, Ryan Teague Read President Obama's Commencement Address to Howard University; May 9, 2016 Time © 2017 Time Inc. http://time.com/4322789/barack-obama-commencement-howard-university/ Accessed 08/10/2017
261 McDowell, Edwin, From Twain, A Letter On Debt to Blacks. March 14, 1985 The New York Times: © 2017 The New York Times Company http://www.nytimes.com/1985/03/14/books/from-twain-a-letter-on-debt-to-blacks.html Accessed 08/05/2017
262 IBID
263 IBID
264 Trounson, Rebecca, Her New Take on Twain, November 17, 2005. The Los Angeles Times. © 2018 Los Angeles Times http://articles.latimes.com/2005/nov/17/local/me-twain17 Accessed 6/03/2017
265 Skandera-Trombley, Laura E. Mark Twain in the Company of Women: 1994 University of Pennsylvania Press, Philadelphia, p xxi-xxii
266 IBID p 20
267 IBID, p 7

[268] IBID, p 4

[269] Reprinted from Mark Twain's Letters, 1867-1868, vol. 2: 286-87; Skandera-Trombley, Laura E. Mark Twain in the Company of Women: 1994 University of Pennsylvania Press, Philadelphia, p 45

[270] Skandera-Trombley, Laura E. Mark Twain in the Company of Women: 1994 University of Pennsylvania Press, Philadelphia, p 45

[271] IBID, p 48

[272] SLC to Olivia L. Langdon, 12 Jan 1869, El Paso, Ill. (UCCL 00227). In "Mark Twain's Letters, 1869." Edited by Victor Fischer, Michael B. Frank, and Dahlia Armon. Mark Twain Project Online. Berkeley, Los Angeles, London: University of California Press. 1992, 2007. <http://www.marktwainproject.org/xtf/view?docId=letters/UCCL00227.xml;style=let ter;brand=mtp>, accessed 2017-11-24.

[273] Skandera-Trombley, Laura E. Mark Twain in the Company of Women: 1994 University of Pennsylvania Press, Philadelphia, p 27

[274] IBID, p 30

[275] Twain, Mark Life on the Mississippi; 1917 P.F. Collier & Son Corporation, New York, p 409

[276] IBID, p 19

[277] IBID, p 411

[278] Twain, Mark What is Man, © 1917 The Mark Twain Company. Harper and Brothers, NY. page 5

[279] Meltzer, Milton, Mark Twain Himself. ©1960 Bonanza Publishing, New York. p. 257

[280] Twain, Mark Plymouth Rock and the Pilgrims' as included in the volume "Mark Twain's Speeches," ©1923 by Mark Twain Company, Harper and Brothers, New York, p 90.

[281] Franz, Richard Truth In Jest; Tomorrow's World October 21. 2014. © 2017 Tomorrow's World https://www.tomorrowsworld.org/commentary/truth-in-jest

[282] Mark Twain, John S. Tuckey (1972). "Mark Twain's Fables of Man", p.189, Univ of California Press

[283] Wikipedia contributors, "A Stop at Willoughby," Wikipedia, The Free Encyclopedia, https://en.wikipedia.org/w/index.php?title=A_Stop_at_Willoughby&oldid=836363265. Accessed August 28, 2017.

[284] Redding Planning Commission, Redding, Connecticut Town Plan of Conservation and Development, 2008. http://townofreddingct.org/wp-content/uploads/2014/03/Redding_Town_Plan_2008.pdf Accessed 09/15/2017

[285] Twain, Mark From the last paragraph of The Adventures of Huckleberry Finn

[286] Colley, Brent M. Mark Twain's Redding, Connecticut Home: Stormfield; History of Redding (website); http://historyofredding.net/HRtwainstormfield.htm Accessed 08/30/2017

[287] IBID

[288] Powers, Ron; Mark Twain: A Life, © 2005 Ron Powers. First Free Press trade paperback edition 2006. Simon and Schuster, New York, Publisher. p 623

[289] IBID, p 599-600.

[290] IBID, p 603.

[291] IBID. p 601.

[292] IBIDp 607.

[293] IBIDp. 610-611.

[294] IBID p. 615.

[295] IBID p 616.

[296] Twain, Mark Autobiography of Mark Twain. Edited by Charles Neider. © 1959 by Charles Neider. First Harper Perennial edition, 1990. p 344-345.

[297] Powers, Ron; Mark Twain: A Life, © 2005 Ron Powers. First Free Press trade paperback edition 2006. Simon and Schuster, New York, Publisher. p. 617.

[298] Zaccara, Jennifer; Mark Twain, Isabel Lyon and the "Talking Cure" as featured in Constructing Mark Twain: New Directions in Scholarship, edited by Laura E. Skandera Trombley and Michael Kiskis; p 111

[299] IBID p 112

[300] Skandera-Trombley, Laura, Mark Twain in the Company of Women, © 1994 The University of Pennsylvania Press p 13

[301] IBID, p 16

302 Shelden, Michael, Mark Twain: Man in White, The Grand adventure of his final years. © 2010 Michael Shelden. Published by Random House, NY. p 33.

303 IBID, p 34

304 IBID, p 90

305 IBID,. p 89

306 IBID, p 90

307 Allen, Nick, Mark Twain memoir and the 'filthy-minded' secretary, The Telegraph, UK. ©. June 11, 2010. https://telegraph.co.uk/news/worldnews/northamerica/usa/7821046/Mark-Twain0memoir-and-the-filthy-minded-secretary.html Accessed 4/8/2108

308 Skandera-Trombley, Laura Mark Twain in the Company of Women. © 1994 The University of Pennsylvania Press, p. 176

309 Shelden, Michael, Mark Twain: Man in White, The Grand adventure of his final years. © 2010 Michael Shelden. Published by Random House, NY. p110

310 IBID

311 IBID,. p 152

312 IBID,. p 176.

313 IBID, p 274

314 IBID

315 IBID,. p 276

316 IBID, p 282

317 IBID,. p 292-293

318 IBID,. p 295-296

319 IBID. p 284

320 IBID. p 330-331

321 IBID

322 Skandera-Trombley, Laura Mark Twain in the Company of Women, ©1994 The University of Pennsylvania Press, p. 177.

323 IBID

324 Shelden, Michael, Mark Twain: Man in White, The Grand adventure of his final years. © 2010 Michael Shelden. Published by Random House, NY. p 337

325 IBID,. p 345

326 The New York Times, July 15, 1909; Wants Mark Twain To Explain To Her Mrs. Ashcroft Hurries Back from Her Honeymoon Abroad to Find Out About $4,000 Suit. Formerly His Secretary She Thinks the Attachment on the Humorist's Gift House is the Work of His Daughter. Source: http://www.twainquotes.com/19090715.html. Accessed 4/8/2018.

327 Twain, Mark "The Ashcroft-Lyon Manuscript: Paragraph 25," in Autobiography of Mark Twain, Volume 3. 2015 Mark Twain Papers, © 2007-16 The Regents of the University of California <http://www.marktwainproject.org/xtf/view?docId=works/MTDP10364.xml;style=work;brand=mtp;chunk.id=dv0094#pa2431> Accessed 4/8/18

328 IBID

329 IBID

330 IBID

331 IBID

332 IBID, Paragraphs 49 - 1056

333 Twain, Mark "Closing Words of My Autobiography: Paragraph 37," in Autobiography of Mark Twain, Volume 3. 2015 Mark Twain Papers, © 2007-16 The Regents of the University of California, <http://www.marktwainproject.org/xtf/view?docId=works/MTDP10364.xml;style=work;brand=mtp;chunk.id=dv0093#pa2338> Accessed 3/15/2018

334 Kaplan, Justin (1966). Mr. Clemens and Mark Twain. New York: Simon & Shuster. p. 181.

335 Stone-Lombardi, Kate, Greeley Statue Has People Heading in All Directions, © 1994 The New York Times. Published June 4, 1994, p WC14. https://www.nytimes.com/1994/06/05/nyregion/greeley-statue-has-people-heading-in-all-directions.html Accessed 04/16/2018

[336] SLC (Samuel Langhorne Clemens). 1905. "John Hay and the Ballads." Harper's Weekly 49 (21 October): pp. 5-6; "Editorial narrative following 3 December 1870 to James Redpath" Mark Twain's Letters, A Publication of the Mark Twain Project of The Bancroft Library, General Editor, Robert H. Hirst; Editors: Edgar Marquess Branch, Michael B. Frank, Kenneth M. Sanderson

[337] Quirk, Thomas V. Mark Twain Encyclopedia Britannica, Encyclopedia Britannica, Inc. Published April 14, 2018 https://www.britannica.com/biography.Mark-Twain. Accessed 04/15/2018

[338] Wikipedia contributors. "Tom Sawyer (1930 film)." Wikipedia, The Free Encyclopedia. Wikipedia, The Free Encyclopedia, 27 Jul. 2018. Web. 19 Sep. 2018.

[339] Wikipedia contributors. "Huckleberry Finn (1931 film)." Wikipedia, The Free Encyclopedia. Wikipedia, The Free Encyclopedia, 13 Nov. 2017. Web. 19 Sep. 2018.

[340] Jefferson Evening News, January 25th, 1932 https://newspaperarchive.com/jeffersonville-evening-news-jan-25-1932-p-1/ Accessed 9/25/2018. Newsreel footage may be seen at https://dissolve.com/video/1930s-newsreel-clip-Universal-Newspapers-features-royalty-free-stock-video-footage/001-D378-42-917

[341] Eli Siegel, Book Reviews, Scribner's Magazine, November 1932
https://aestheticrealism.net/reviews/Scribners_DeVoto_1932.htm. Accessed 9/26/2018

[342] The Mark Twain Encyclopedia, © 1993 Garland Publishing, Inc. Editors; LeMaster, Wilson, Hamric. https://books.google.com/books (Accessed 9/26/2018)

[343] Evening Star, Washington, D.C., 1854-1972, February 11, 1934. Page A-13, image 13. Chronicling America, Library of Congress. https://chroniclingamerica.loc.gov (Accessed 11/6/2018)

[344] https://www.whig.com/20180707/mark-twain-left-lasting-impact-on-hannibal-his-boyhood-hometown# Accessed 9/18/2018

[345] Roberta Hagood, The Mark Twain Centennial of 1935 (originally published 1979) © 2009-2018 Gatehouse Media LLC. http://www.hannibal.net/article/20090820/NEWS/308209918

[346] The Hartford Times, May 24, 1934. "$500,000 Twain Memorial Proposed for Hartford". Archive copy furnished graciously by Tracy Brindle, Beatrice Fox Auerbach Chief Curator, The Mark Twain House & Museum, Hartford, CT.

[347] IBID

[348] IBID

[349] IBID

[350] IBID

[351] Hannibal Courier-Post, April 25, 1935. Reprinted in The Fence Painter: Bulletin of The Mark twain Boyhood Home Associates, Vol. V, No. 2, Hannibal, Missouri, Summer, 1985, "Walter Russell's 1935 Works." Copy graciously furnished by Mr. Henry Sweets, Executive Director, The Mark Twain Boyhood Home & Museum, Hannibal, MO.

[352] Roberta Hagood, "Walter Russell: Sculptor, Author, Artist, Scientist and Philosopher." © 1982, The Mark Twain Museum. Copy graciously furnished by Mr. Henry Sweets, Executive Director, The Mark Twain Boyhood Home & Museum, Hannibal, MO.

[353] Copy graciously furnished by Mr. Henry Sweets, Executive Director, The Mark Twain Boyhood Home & Museum, Hannibal, MO.

[354] The New York Herald, Nov. 14, 19?? (The copy I received had a hand-written date with the year 1930, which I believe is inaccurate, based on other available documentation from the time.) Archive copy furnished graciously by Tracy Brindle, Beatrice Fox Auerbach Chief Curator, The Mark Twain House & Museum, Hartford, CT.

[355] IBID

[356] https://pastdaily.com/2014/11/16/mark-twain-100th-birthday-dinner-1935-past-daily-weekend-gallimaufry/ Accessed 9/18/2018

[357] Transcribed from the Gordon Skene Sound Collection, "Mark Twain 100th Birthday Dinner – November 19, 1935."The Past Daily, at pastdaily.com. © Past Daily and Gordon Skene. Accessed 9/18/2018

[358] IBID

[359] https://www.thebeatles.com/feature/our-world-global-satellite-broadcast. Accessed 9/18/2018

[360] US National Archives, Records of the Office of Education. https://www.archives.gov/research/guide-fed-records/groups/012.html#12.5.4. Accessed 9/27/2018

The Elephant on the Raft · 457

³⁶¹ Hagood, J. Hurley and Roberta Roland, Hannibal, Too: Historical sketches of Hannibal and its neighbors. © 1986. Walsworth Publishing Co., Marceline, MO. Copy graciously furnished by Mr. Henry Sweets, Executive Director, The Mark Twain Boyhood Home & Museum, Hannibal, MO.

³⁶² Associated Press, Roosevelt's Speech at Twain Bridge, The New York Times, September 5, 1936. http://www.twainquotes.com/19360905.html (Accessed 9/18/2018)

³⁶³ The Prince and the Pauper, Chapter IV: The Prince's Troubles Begin. http://www.gutenberg.org/files/1837/1837-h/1837-h.htm (Accessed 10/29/2018)

³⁶⁴ IBID, Chapter V: Tom as a Patrician.

³⁶⁵ IBID, Conclusion: Justice and Retribution. (Accessed 10/27/2018)

³⁶⁶ IBID

³⁶⁷ Wikipedia contributors. "The Prince and the Pauper (1937 film)." Wikipedia, The Free Encyclopedia. Wikipedia, The Free Encyclopedia, 24 Sep. 2018. Web. 14 Feb. 2019.

³⁶⁸ IBID

³⁶⁹ Time, May 3, 1937, Cinema: Mauch Twins and Mark Twain, p. 25.© 1937 Time, Inc.

³⁷⁰ Catholic News Service – Newsfeeds 12 April 1937 – Catholic Research Resources Alliance. https://thecatholicnewsarchive.org/?a=d&d=cns19370412-01.1.72&srpos=10&e=-------en-20--1--txt-txIN-The+Prince+and+The+Pauper------ (Accessed 10/31/2018)

³⁷¹ Evening Star. Washington, D.C. 1854-1972, November 22, 1937. Page A-16, image 16, Chronicling America, Library of Congress. https://chroniclingamerica.loc.gov/lccn/sn83045462/1937-11-22/ed-1/seq-16/#date1=1930&index=0&rows=20&words=MARK+Mark+Twain+TWAIN&searchType=basic&sequence=0&state=&date2=1939&proxtext=Mark+Twain&y=6&x=13&dateFilterType=yearRange&page=1 (Accessed 11/6/2018)

³⁷² IBID

³⁷³ IBID

³⁷⁴ Catholic Transcript 10 June 1937 — Catholic Research Resources Alliance. https://thecatholicnewsarchive.orgAccessed 5/23/2019

³⁷⁵ Catholic News Service - Newsfeeds 7 June 1937 — Catholic Research Resources Alliance. https://thecatholicnewsarchive.org. Accessed 5/23/2019.

³⁷⁶ Catholic Transcript 24 February 1938 — Catholic Research Resources Alliance. https://thecatholicnewsarchive.org. Accessed 5/23/2019.

³⁷⁷ "Musical 'Tom Sawyer' Not Bad" by James J. Arnold. Catholic Transcript, Volume LXVI, Number 14, 27 July 1973. Catholic Resource Alliance. https://thecatholicnewsarchive.org. Accessed 5/23/2019.

³⁷⁸ "IBID

³⁷⁹ Wikipedia contributors. "The Adventures of Huckleberry Finn (1939 film)." Wikipedia, The Free Encyclopedia. Wikipedia, The Free Encyclopedia, 28 Aug. 2018. Web. 22 Sep. 2018.

³⁸⁰Proclamation 2362.https://www.fs.usda.gov/Internet/FSE_DOCUMENTS/stelprd3822716.pdf (Accessed 10/31/2018)

³⁸¹ U.S. Dept. of the Interior, National Park Service, National Register of Historic Places. "The Historic and Architectural Resources of The Mark Twain National Forest. https://dnr.mo.gov/shpo/nps-nr/64500853.pdf (Accessed 10/31/2018)

³⁸² https://archive.org/stream/boxofficejulsep137unse/boxofficejulsep137unse_djvu.txt Accessed 4/6/2019

³⁸³https://www.thomaslarson.com/publications/san-diego-reader/116-i-am-your-loving-daughter.html Accessed 4/6/2019

³⁸⁴ http://www.tcm.com/this-month/article/60075|0/The-Adventures-of-Mark-Twain.html

³⁸⁵ Wikipedia contributors. "A Connecticut Yankee in King Arthur's Court (1949 film)." Wikipedia, The Free Encyclopedia. Wikipedia, The Free Encyclopedia, 21 Aug. 2018. Web. 22 Sep. 2018.

³⁸⁶Mark Twain: Television Star, David Bianculli, https://marktwainstudies.com/mark-twain-television-star/

³⁸⁷ Twain, Mark Turning point of my life, Chapter II. http://www.online-literature.com/twain/1324/ p. 132-137 (Accessed 4/15/2018

³⁸⁸ Twain, Mark Turning point of my life, Chapter II. http://www.online-literature.com/twain/1324/ p. 136-137 (Accessed 4/15/2018)

³⁸⁹ IBID, p 132

³⁹⁰ Twain, Mark, The Innocents Abroad, or, The New Pilgrim's Progress, Chapter LIII. Source: Project

Gutenberg's The Innocents Abroad, by Mark Twain (Samuel Clemens) Release Date: August 16, 2006 [EBook #3176] https://www.gutenberg.org/files/3176/3176-h/3176-h.htm (Accessed 4/18/2018)

[391] Twain, Mark, The Death of Jean, From What is Man? (and other essays) 1917 Harper and Brothers, NY. p 110-111

[392] IBID, p113

[393] IBID, p114.

[394] IBID, p 117

[395] IBID, p 125

[396] Referring to the author's first book - "Masters Among Us: An exploration of Supernal Encounters and Miraculous Phenomena" by Thomas Curley, © 2020 Wilder Street Press. Available in ebook and paperback.

[397] Twain, Mark, The Adventures of Huckleberry Finn, Airmont Classic edition, 1962, Airmont Publishing Co., Inc. p. 39-40

[398] IBID

[399] Mark Twain's letters 1886-1900 by Mark Twain. Project Gutenberg Online. http://www.gutenberg.org/files/3196/3196-h/3196-h.htm. Accessed April 2, 2018 at 10:00am

[400] Pond, Major J. B. Eccentricities of Genius 1900 G.W. Dillingham Company, NY. http://twain.lib.virginia.edu/onstage/pondecc.html Accessed 3/07/2018

[401] Associated Press, PBS Airing Film on Mark Twain's Trip Aboard 1st Cruise Ship. Published October 15, 2017. © 2017 Associated Press, NY.

402 Fisher Fishkin, Shelley, Lighting Out for the Territory: Reflections on Mark Twain and American Culture. © 1996 Shelley Fisher Fishkin. Published 1997 by Oxford University Press, New York. p. 186-187

[403] Mark Twain's letters 1886-1900 by Mark Twain. Project Gutenberg Online. http://www.gutenberg.org/files/3196/3196-h/3196-h.htm. Accessed April 2, 2018 at 10:00am.

[404] Tesla, Nikola, My Inventions: Nikola Tesla's Autobiograph y by Nikola Tesla. Edited by Dr. DukeSavage. © 2014 Freedom Fiction. Published by Lulu Press, Inc. 2016. Originally published in 1919 in Electrical Experimenter Magazine

[405] McCullough David, from the introduction to 'The National Archives of The United States' by Herman J. Viola. ©. 1986 Harry Abrams, Inc., NY, publishers. p 13-14.

[406] To the uninitiated, "Thundergod" is the affectionate nickname Def Leppard fans use to refer to Rick Allen

[407] Powers, Ron Mark Twain: A Life. C. 2005 by Ron Powers. First Free Press Trade Paperback edition 2006. Simon and Schuster, NY. p. 200.

[408] Paine, Albert B., Mark Twain: A Biography: The Personal and Literary Life of Samuel Langhorne Clemens, C. 1912, Harper and Brothers, NY. Volume 1, Chapter LIX, p. 322.

[409] Kerouac, Jack. On the Road. https://www.goodreads.com/quotes/3831-the-only-people-for-me-are-the-mad-ones-the. Accessed 7/7/18

[410] Twain, Mark, The Innocents Abroad, or, The New Pilgrim's Progress, 1967 Airmont Publishing Company, Inc. NY, NY. Ch. 3, p. 23.

[411] IBID, p. 441-444

HISTORICAL DOCUMENTS, PHOTOGRAPHS, ETC.

Thank you to the following additional resources of public domain images, documents, photos:

- U.S. National Archives and Records Administration, Public Domain, https://commons.wikimedia.org/w/index.php?curid=73784067
- The New York Public Library Digital Collections, Public Domain Picks, https://digitalcollections.nypl.org/collections/lane/public-domain-picks
- Wikimedia Commons, https://commons.wikimedia.org/wiki/Main_Page
- Library of Congress
- The Center for Mark Twain Studies, Elmira, NY
- The Mark Twain Project, Berkeley, CA
- Papers of Mark Twain, Clifton Waller Barrett Library, Special Collections, University of Virginia, Charlottesville, VA. http://ead.lib.virginia.edu/vivaxtf/view?docId=uva-sc/viu0005.xml